D0914494

STRATEGIC MARKETING MANAGEMENT

THEORY AND PRACTICE

ALEXANDER CHERNEV

Kellogg School of Management
Northwestern University

No part of this publication may be recorded, stored in a retrieval system, or transmitted in any form or by any means electronic, mechanical, photocopying, recording, scanning, or otherwise, without the prior written permission of the author.

While the publisher and the author have used their best efforts in preparing this book, they make no representations or warranties with respect to the accuracy or completeness of the contents of this book and specifically disclaim any implied warranties of merchantability or fitness for a particular purpose. The advice and strategies contained herein may not be suitable for your situation. Neither the publisher nor the author shall be liable for any loss of profit or any other commercial damages, including but not limited to special, incidental, consequential, or other damages.

Strategic Marketing Management | Theory and Practice

ISBN: 978-1-936572-58-8

January 2019

Author website: Chernev.com

Supplemental materials: MarketingToolbox.com

Published by Cerebellum Press | Chicago, IL | USA

ORGANIZATION OF THE BOOK

MAIN TOPICS

CHAPTERS

1 THE FRAMEWORK FOR MARKETING MANAGEMENT

1. Marketing as a business discipline
2. Marketing strategy and tactics
3. Marketing planning and management

2 UNDERSTANDING THE MARKET

4. Understanding customers
5. Gathering market insights

3 DEVELOPING A MARKETING STRATEGY

6. Identifying target customers
7. Developing a customer value proposition
8. Creating company value

4 DESIGNING VALUE

9. Managing products
10. Managing services
11. Managing brands
12. Managing price
13. Managing incentives

5 COMMUNICATING VALUE

14. Managing communication
15. Personal selling

6 DELIVERING VALUE

16. Managing distribution channels
17. Retail management

7 MANAGING GROWTH

18. Gaining and defending market position
19. Developing new market offerings
20. Customer relationship management

8 MARKETING TOOLBOX

A. Segmentation and targeting workbook
B. The business model workbook
C. Sample marketing plans

TABLE OF CONTENTS

About the Author

Alexander Chernev is a professor of marketing at the Kellogg School of Management, Northwestern University. He holds a PhD in psychology and a second PhD in business administration from Duke University.

Dr. Chernev has written numerous articles focused on business strategy, brand management, consumer behavior, and market planning. His research has been published in the leading marketing journals and has been frequently quoted in the business and popular press, including *The Wall Street Journal, Financial Times, The New York Times, The Washington Post, Harvard Business Review, Scientific American, Associated Press, Forbes,* and *Business Week*. He was ranked among the top ten most prolific scholars in the leading marketing journals by the *Journal of Marketing* and among the top five marketing faculty in the area of consumer behavior by a global survey of marketing faculty published by the *Journal of Marketing Education*.

Dr. Chernev's books — *Strategic Marketing Management, Strategic Brand Management, The Marketing Plan Handbook,* and *The Business Model: How to Develop New Products, Create Market Value, and Make the Competition Irrelevant* — have been translated into multiple languages and are used in top business schools around the world. He has served as an area editor for the *Journal of Marketing* and on the editorial boards of leading research journals, including the *Journal of Marketing Research, Journal of Consumer Research, Journal of Consumer Psychology, International Journal of Research in Marketing, Journal of the Academy of Marketing Science,* and *Journal of Marketing Behavior*.

Dr. Chernev teaches marketing strategy, brand management, and behavioral decision theory in MBA, PhD, and executive education programs at the Kellogg School of Management. He has also taught in executive programs at INSEAD in France and Singapore, at the Institute for Management Development (IMD) in Switzerland, and at Hong Kong University of Science and Technology. He has received numerous teaching awards, including the Core Course Teaching Award, Kellogg Faculty Impact Award, and the Top Professor Award from the Kellogg Executive MBA Program, which he has received eleven times.

In addition to research and teaching, Dr. Chernev is an Academic Trustee of the *Marketing Science Institute* and advises companies around the world on issues of marketing strategy, brand management, consumer behavior, pricing, strategic planning, and new product development. He has worked with Fortune 500 companies on ways to reinvent their business models, develop new products, and gain competitive advantage. He has helped multiple startups uncover market opportunities, craft their business models, and implement their market strategies.

Acknowledgments

This book has benefited from the wisdom of many of my current and former colleagues at the Kellogg School of Management at Northwestern University: Nidhi Agrawal, Eric Anderson, Jim Anderson, Robert Blattberg, Ulf Böckenholt, Miguel Brendl, Bobby Calder, Tim Calkins, Gregory Carpenter, Moran Cerf, Yuxin Chen, Anne Coughlan, Patrick Duparcq, David Gal, Kelly Goldsmith, Kent Grayson, Karsten Hansen, Julie Hennessy, Dawn Iacobucci, Dipak Jain, Sachin Gupta, Ata Jami, Robert Kozinets, Aparna Labroo, Lakshman Krishnamurthi, Eric Leininger, Angela Lee, Sidney Levy, Michal Maimaran, Eyal Maoz, Blake McShane, Kevin McTigue, Vikas Mittal, Vincent Nijs, Mary Pearlman, Neal Roese, Derek Rucker, Mohan Sawhney, John Sherry, Jr., Louis Stern, Brian Sternthal, Rima Touré-Tillery, Anna Tuchman, Alice Tybout, Rick Wilson, Song Yao, Philip Zerrillo, Florian Zettelmeyer, and Andris Zoltners.

I owe a considerable debt of gratitude to Philip Kotler, one of the leading thinkers in the field of marketing, who through his insightful writings sparked my interest in marketing. I would also like to thank Andrea Bonezzi (New York University), Aaron Brough (Utah State University), Pierre Chandon (INSEAD), Akif Irfan (Goldman Sachs), Mathew Isaac (Seattle University), Ryan Hamilton (Emory University), Kevin Keller (Dartmouth University), Alexander Moore (University of Chicago), and Jaya Sah (Goldman Sachs) for their valuable comments. I am also grateful to Joanne Freeman for editing this book with a very keen and helpful eye.

PREFACE

Marketing is both an art and a science. It is an art because intuition and creativity can play a major role in the development of a successful marketing campaign. Many brilliant marketers such as McDonald's founder Ray Kroc, Starbucks founder Howard Shultz, Microsoft founder Bill Gates, and Apple founder Steve Jobs did not have formal marketing training. Rather, they used their creativity and gut feel to build successful billion-dollar enterprises.

Marketing is also a science because it captures the generalized knowledge that reflects the experiences of multiple companies across a diverse set of industries. This knowledge complements managers' intuition and enhances their ability to design successful offerings that create market value. The scientific aspect of marketing that reflects the logic underlying the processes of creating and managing value is captured in the principles, theories, and frameworks outlined in this book.

This book offers a systematic overview of the fundamentals of marketing theory, defines the key principles of marketing management, and presents a value-based framework for developing viable market offerings. The theory presented stems from the view of marketing as a value-creation process that is central to any business enterprise. The discussion of marketing theory is complemented by a set of practical tools that enable managers to apply the knowledge contained in the generalized frameworks to specific business problems and market opportunities.

The information on marketing theory and practice contained in this book is organized into eight major parts. The first part defines the essence of marketing as a business discipline and outlines an overarching framework for marketing management that serves as the organizing principle for the information presented in the rest of the book. Specifically, we discuss the role of marketing management as a value-creation process, the essentials of marketing strategy and tactics as the key components of a company's business model, and the process of developing an actionable marketing plan.

Part Two focuses on understanding the market in which a company operates. Specifically, we examine how consumers make choices and outline the main steps in the customer decision journey that lead to the purchase of a company's offerings. We further discuss the ways in which companies conduct market research to gather market insights in order to make informed decisions and develop viable courses of action.

Part Three covers issues pertaining to the development of a marketing strategy that will guide the company's tactical activities. Here we focus on three fundamental aspects of a company's marketing strategy: the identification of target customers, the development of a customer value proposition, and the development of a value proposition for the company and its collaborators. The discussion of the strategic aspects of marketing management includes an in-depth analysis of the key principles of creating market value in a competitive context.

The next three parts of the book focus on the marketing tactics, viewed as a process of designing, communicating, and delivering value. Part Four describes how companies design their offerings and, specifically, how they develop key aspects of their products, services, brands, prices, and incentives. In Part Five, we address the ways in which companies manage their marketing communication and the role of personal selling as a means of persuading customers to choose, purchase, and use a company's offerings. Part Six explores the role of distribution channels in delivering the company's offerings to target customers by examining the value-delivery process both from a manufacturer's and a retailer's point of view.

The seventh part of the book focuses on the ways in which companies manage growth. Specifically, we discuss strategies used by companies to gain and defend market position and, in this context, address the issues of pioneering advantage, managing sales growth, and managing product lines. We further address the process of developing new market offerings and the ways in which companies manage the relationship with their customers.

The final part of this book presents a set of tools that illustrate the practical application of marketing theory. Specifically, Part Eight delineates two workbooks: a workbook for segmenting the market and identifying target customers and a workbook for developing the strategic and tactical components of a company's business model. This part also contains examples of two marketing plans—one dealing with the launch of a new offering and the other focused on managing an existing offering.

The marketing theory outlined in this book applies to a wide range of companies—startups and established enterprises, consumer packaged goods companies and business-to-business enterprises, high-tech and low-tech ventures, online and brick-and-mortar entities, product manufacturers and value-added service providers, nonprofit organizations and profit-driven companies. This book combines theoretical rigor with practical relevance to strengthen the marketing skills of a wide array of business professionals—from those creating novel market offerings to those improving on existing ones, from entrepreneurs launching a new business to managers working in established corporations, and from product managers to senior executives.

PART ONE

THE FRAMEWORK FOR
MARKETING MANAGEMENT

INTRODUCTION

It is possible to fail in many ways,
while to succeed is possible only in one way.
— Aristotle, Greek philosopher

The rapid growth of technological innovation, ever-increasing globalization, and the emergence of new business models have made today's markets more dynamic, unpredictable, and interdependent than ever. This increasingly complex environment in which companies operate underscores the importance of taking a systematic approach to marketing management. Such a systematic approach can be achieved by using frameworks.

Marketing frameworks vary in their generality. Some address broad strategic issues, such as identifying target customers and developing a value proposition for these customers, whereas others confront more specific tactical issues, such as product development, branding, pricing, promotion, and distribution. Despite the plenitude of frameworks, the link between strategy and tactics is often lost, depriving a company of a clear path to achieving its goals. Marketing can benefit from a framework that articulates the key aspects of a company's strategy and then translates this strategy into a set of specific tactics that guide a company's actions.

The following chapters present an overarching framework that incorporates both strategic and tactical aspects of marketing management. By offering an integrative view of the key marketing concepts and frameworks, these chapters present a systematic and streamlined approach to marketing analysis, planning, and management. Specifically, the chapters included in this section address the following topics: *marketing as a business discipline, marketing strategy and tactics,* and *marketing planning and management.*

- Understanding the role of **marketing as a business discipline** is the stepping stone for the development of a sound marketing program. Marketing is not just a set of tactical activities such as sales, advertising, and promotion; it also involves strategic analysis and planning, which are the foundation of the company's market success. The essence of marketing as a business discipline and its role as the growth engine of an organization are discussed in Chapter 1.

- **Marketing strategy and tactics** are the two building blocks of a company's business model. Strategy identifies the market in which the company operates and outlines the ways in which an offering will create value for the relevant market participants. Tactics, on the other hand, define the activities employed to execute a given strategy by designing, communicating, and delivering specific market offerings. The key aspects of developing an offering's strategy and designing its tactics are delineated in Chapter 2.

- **Marketing planning and management** delineates a course of action to translate an offering's strategy and tactics into a market reality. The development of an actionable marketing plan is guided by the G-STIC (Goal-Strategy-Tactics-Implementation-Control) framework, which articulates the company's goal and delineates a course of action to reach this goal. The process of market planning and developing a viable marketing plan is discussed in Chapter 3.

The concepts, principles, and frameworks outlined in these three chapters serve as the foundation for the discussion of strategic marketing management presented in this book. They are the foundation on which a company's marketing programs and activities are built. To achieve market success, a company must have a solid understanding of the marketing function and its role within an organization, create a viable business model that defines the company's strategy and tactics, and develop an actionable marketing plan that translates its business model into a market reality.

Chapter One

Marketing as a Business Discipline

Good companies fulfill needs;
great companies create new markets.

—Philip Kotler, founder of modern marketing theory

Marketing is both art and science. It is an intuitive skill and a set of principles soundly grounded in logic and academic scholarship. It reflects the individual experiences of companies across different industries, as well as a set of common principles that stem from these individual experiences and span companies and industries. Building on this view of marketing, this chapter addresses the essence of marketing as a business discipline, focusing on its role as a value-creator and the growth engine of an organization. Specifically, this chapter addresses the following topics:

- *The Essence of Marketing*
- *Marketing as a Value-Creation Process*
- *The Scope of Marketing*
- *Marketing as the Central Function of an Organization*
- *Key Marketing Trends*

The discussion of marketing as a business discipline is complemented by an in-depth overview of three additional topics: The historic role of the marketing function in business management, the marketing myopia phenomenon, and the role of frameworks in marketing management.

The Essence of Marketing

There are many ways to define marketing, each reflecting a different understanding of the role of marketing as a business discipline. Marketing has been defined as a functional area—similar to finance, accounting, and operations—that captures a unique aspect of a company's business activities. Some view marketing as a customer-centric business philosophy. Others see it as a process of moving products and services from concept to customers. Still others view marketing as a specific set of activities that typically involve a particular marketing function such as product development, pricing, promotion, and distribution. And for some, marketing is yet another department in the company's organizational grid.

These diverse views of marketing stem from marketing's numerous functions. Marketing is indeed everything that the above definitions imply: a business discipline, a functional area, a philosophy of thinking, a business process that encompasses a set of specific activities, and a distinct unit of an organization. Diverse as these views of marketing are, they are related conceptually. As a business discipline, marketing embraces a philosophy that gives rise to a set of processes and activities coordinated by the marketing department. Therefore, the key to defining marketing is delineating its core business function, which informs the specific processes and activities involved in marketing management.

Companies vary in the way they view the core function of marketing and its role within the organization. In particular, there are several commonly held, albeit erroneous, views of marketing that stem from the more general misunderstanding of marketing as a business discipline. One popular view is that marketing is a tactical activity tantamount to facilitating sales. This view is particularly common in organizations whose primary activity is selling large inventories of warehoused products and who see the goal of marketing as "selling more things to more people for more money, more efficiently." This view appeals to many managers because it is intuitive, clear, and succinct. The problem with this view is that it does not describe marketing. Rather, it describes sales, an activity related to—but distinct from—marketing. Given the popularity of the view of marketing as primarily sales, it is important to define the boundaries between the two activities.

Marketing is *not* equivalent to selling; it is much broader. Unlike selling, which usually begins once the company has a product to sell, marketing starts long before the product becomes a reality. Moreover, marketing does not stop with the sale of the product; it continues after the customer has made a purchase and involves managing the customer's entire experience with the product—including using, servicing, disposing of, and repurchasing the product. Marketing incorporates all aspects involved in developing the offering that is to be sold. As such, the product is the outcome of a company's marketing activities, not vice versa. The goal of marketing is to create a product that sells, not to sell a product.

The view of marketing as an overarching business discipline that guides a number of specific functions, including sales, is well articulated by the founder of modern management science, Peter Drucker, who writes:

> Marketing is not only much broader than selling, it is not a specialized activity at all. It encompasses the entire business. The aim of marketing is to make selling superfluous. The aim of marketing is to know and understand the customer so well that the product or service fits him and sells itself. Ideally, marketing should result in a customer who is ready to buy.[1]

The idea that marketing can replace sales may sound extreme, but what Drucker points out is that marketing and sales work in concert. A product that is poorly designed because of a lack of marketing insight will require tremendous selling effort, whereas a product that is designed to address an important unmet customer need is likely to generate much greater customer demand and, hence, will require relatively little sales effort. A company can have the best salesforce in the world and still fail in the marketplace if its offerings do not create customer value. On the other hand, a well-designed product requires much less sales effort and can almost sell itself. When Tesla offered its Model 3 electric car, the orders poured in—nearly 200,000 orders within the first 24 hours—because it had crafted a viable product that created customer value by addressing an unmet need.

Another common misconception is viewing marketing as a set of communication activities—advertising, public relations, and social networking—designed to promote the company's offering. The popularity of this view springs from the fact that communication, and especially advertising, is the most visible aspect of the company's marketing activities. Companies that subscribe to this view consider marketing as a means to inform their target customers about the offerings developed by the company's engineers and product designers and to persuade them to buy these products. The problem with this view is that communication, although important, is only one aspect of marketing. Marketing takes place long before the communication campaign is conceived: It guides the development of the offering that will later be communicated to target customers.

Marketing is also misconstrued when it is equated with sales promotions—including price discounts, coupons, rebates, and bonus offerings. The popularity of this view of marketing lies in the fact that sales promotions are a tool that a company can readily use to enhance the value of its offerings by temporarily decreasing their monetary cost. Because they can help the company bring attention to the product in a given market and facilitate adoption by target customers, sales promotions are often equated with marketing. Yet, nudging customers to purchase a company's products reflects only one facet of marketing. This view of marketing as an activity that helps bring products to market and entices customers to buy these products is oblivious to marketing's role in creating the very products that are being promoted.

Equating marketing with sales, advertising, and sales promotions, and thus, viewing it as a tactical activity is a common misperception. This myopic view limits the role of marketing to creating awareness, incentivizing customers to make a purchase, and facilitating sales and precludes a company from mobilizing marketing's full potential to develop a viable business strategy. The view of marketing only as a tactical activity fails to offer a clear understanding of how sales, advertising, and promotions align with and relate to the other tactical aspects of the marketing process, including product development, pricing, and distribution. Furthermore, viewing marketing as a tactical tool fails to take into account the need for an overarching logic that guides and melds the individual marketing activities in a way that creates value for customers, the company, and its collaborators.

Marketing is far more than tactics. It also involves the development of a strategic vision that determines the success of the tactical elements. Marketing encompasses all activities — tactical and strategic — that enable the company to create value in a given market. Marketing as a business discipline is about creating new markets and managing existing ones. Market success, in turn, is defined by the value exchanged by the different market participants: the company, its customers, and its collaborators. Consequently, the primary purpose of marketing is strategic rather than tactical: It is the creation of market value.

As a business discipline, marketing is first and foremost about creating value

Because the ability to create value defines a company's market success, marketing is strategic in nature. Marketing defines the market in which the company operates and the customer needs the company aims to fulfill with its offerings. The various tactical activities — such as sales, advertising, and promotion — are the means used to turn the company's strategy into reality, driven by the ultimate goal of creating market value. Focusing on value recognizes marketing as a pivotal function that pervades all areas of an enterprise. This view of marketing as an integral business discipline forms the basis of the marketing theory outlined in this book.

Marketing as a Value-Creation Process

The focus of marketing is the exchange of goods, services, and ideas that takes place in consumer and business markets. Because the driving force behind an exchange is the creation of value for participants, the concept of value is central to marketing. Accordingly, the discipline of marketing can be defined as follows:

Marketing is the art and science of creating value
by designing and managing viable market offerings

Marketing is an *art* that frequently relies on a manager's creativity and imagination. Brilliant marketers such as King Gillette, Ray Kroc, and Henri Nestlé relied not on formal schooling but on an innate ability to identify unmet customer needs and develop products to meet those needs.

Marketing is also a *science* that has produced a body of generalized knowledge about the process of creating market value. Based on investigation of the successes and failures of numerous companies over the years, this knowledge has allowed marketing science to articulate a set of general principles that distill the experiences of individual companies to capture the essence of the marketing processes. The scientific aspect of marketing that reflects the logic underlying the processes of creating and managing value underlies the principles, theories, and frameworks outlined in this book.

Because the main function of the market exchange is to create *value*, the concept of value is central to marketing. Value is a strategic concept that defines the benefits and costs that participants receive from the market exchange. Therefore, optimizing value for target customers, collaborators, and the company is the key principle that steers managerial decision making and is the foundation for all marketing activities.

The purpose of marketing is not limited to maximizing monetary outcomes such as net income and return on investment. Instead, marketing must be defined using the broader term *success*, which extends beyond monetary outcomes to include all forms of value created in the market. Thus, success is not always expressed in monetary terms such as net income, return on investment, and market share. Many organizations define success in nonmonetary terms that include technological vision, customer satisfaction, and social welfare. Therefore, the goal of marketing is to create value exchanges—whether or not their success is defined in monetary terms—that enable exchange participants to reach their goals.

> *Marketing aims to create superior value for target customers in a way that enables the company and its collaborators to achieve their goals*

As a value-creation process, marketing can be viewed as comprising four key aspects: (1) *identifying value*, which involves uncovering an unmet customer need that the company can fulfill better than the competition while creating value for itself and for its collaborators; (2) *designing value*, which involves developing the actual product or service, defining the brand, setting the price, and deciding on the sales promotions; (3) *communicating value*, which involves informing the relevant marketing entities—target customers, collaborators, and the company employees and stakeholders—about the offering; and (4) *delivering value*, which involves bringing the offering to target customers through a set of distribution channels. These four aspects of creating market value form the backbone of this book.

The Scope of Marketing

Marketing is not limited to products and services: It can also involve events, places, people, real estate, organizations, and even ideas. Anything that can be exchanged can be marketed. In this context, the scope of marketing as a business discipline is very broad, covering the value relationships among different business entities operating across diverse markets.

The market in which a company aims to create value is a central marketing concept. Companies often define their markets through the products they manufacture or the industry in which they operate. Despite its popularity, this is a myopic view of a company's market. Products, as well as entire industries, inevitably become obsolete. After enjoying periods of rapid growth, mainframe computers, VCR tapes, and DVDs faded into oblivion because they were replaced with alternative means—often coming from a different industry—that offered a superior solution for satisfying the same underlying customer need. A product-based definition of the market can also prevent a company from taking advantage of emerging market trends, making it fall behind the competition. Coca-Cola's rather narrow focus on its product—carbonated sodas—rather than on the underlying customer need for hydration and self-expression, made it overlook beverage trends toward fruit-flavored drinks such as Snapple, energy drinks such as Gatorade, and designer water brands such as Vitaminwater.

Customers and the needs that they aim to fulfill, rather than a company's products or the industry in which it operates, are the true defining aspects of a market. Products and industries are a consequence of customer needs; they provide the means of fulfilling customer needs using currently available technologies. Even as the demand for a specific product begins to decline in the face of a superior offering featuring a new technology, the underlying customer need addressed by these offerings persists. As a result, companies that define their markets in terms of products rather than customer needs are destined to decline along with the industries they represent (see the discussion of marketing myopia at the end of this chapter).

Depending on the entities participating in the value exchange, there are three main types of markets: *business-to-consumer*, *business-to-business*, and *consumer-to-consumer*.

- **Business-to-Consumer (B2C)** markets involve offerings aimed at individuals who are typically the end users of these offerings. B2C markets are common for consumer packaged goods companies such as Procter & Gamble, Unilever, and Nestlé, as well as for consumer-focused service companies such as retail banks, hotels, and airlines.

- **Business-to-Business (B2B)** markets are similar to B2C markets, with the key difference that customers are business entities rather than consumers. For example, GE and

Rolls-Royce supply engines to aircraft manufacturers Boeing and Airbus; Intel and Qualcomm supply computer chips to computer and smartphone manufacturers; and Robert Bosch, Johnson Controls, and Continental supply parts for companies in the automotive industry, including Ford, General Motors, and Mercedes-Benz.

- **Consumer-to-Consumer (C2C)** markets are those in which a company facilitates interactions between individual customers. These interactions can involve communications (Facebook, LinkedIn, Instagram, Twitter), monetary transactions (eBay, PayPal, Square), and services (Uber, Airbnb, Freelancer). The C2C market can also involve a B2C market in which the company and its collaborators create value for their customers by providing a platform that enables customer-to-customer interactions.

The B2B market can be further divided into two types of markets. The first type includes the pure B2B markets in which a company creates products and services to fulfill the needs of other businesses that typically are the end users of these products and services. For example, Caterpillar makes excavation equipment for use by construction companies, Canon makes high-volume copy machines for office use, and Applied Materials makes equipment used by companies like Intel to manufacture computer chips. The second type of B2B market includes those in which a company delivers its offerings to another business entity, which, in turn, delivers them to individual users. For example, Boeing, Airbus, and Embraer build planes for different airlines that, in turn, use them to create value for their passengers. This type of market—also referred to as a business-to-business-to-consumer (B2B2C) market—combines B2B and B2C markets and depicts a scenario in which a company, working with its collaborators, creates an offering for consumers. The B2B2C market is common for manufacturers and service providers distributing their offerings through intermediaries (such as dealers, wholesalers, retailers) as well as businesses (such as Intel and NutraSweet) that produce ingredients for offerings created by other companies.

The distinction between the pure B2B and the B2B2C markets is important, although often overlooked. In pure B2B markets, the company's customer is another business. In contrast, in B2B2C markets, the company's customer is the end consumer; the other business is in fact a collaborator that works with the company to create value for the end consumer. Thus, the B2B2C market comprises a B2B market and a B2C market that are inextricably linked for the purpose of creating market value. Consider the manufacturer–retailer–consumer triad. The manufacturer's primary concern is to develop offerings that can fulfill consumer needs better than the competition. In the absence of such offerings, neither the manufacturer nor the retailer will be able to receive value from the market exchange. To this end, the manufacturer and the retailer work together to create value for their customers. In fact, many markets that are traditionally viewed as B2B are in reality B2B2C, meaning that to ensure market success, a company must look beyond its immediate business partner and also strive to create value for the end user of its offerings.

Marketing as the Central Function of an Organization

Because growth is at the heart of every business, a primary function of an organization is successfully managing growth. Without a growth strategy, a company is in danger of losing market position and being outmaneuvered by the competition. To ensure its long-term market success, an enterprise must grow its current markets and develop new markets. The guiding discipline behind an organization's growth strategy is marketing.

Marketing fosters growth by exploring new opportunities, identifying new markets, and uncovering new customer needs. The role of marketing as a central business discipline defining the other business functions is captured in the words of Peter Drucker:

Because the purpose of business is to create a customer, the business enterprise has two—and only two—basic functions: marketing and innovation. Marketing and innovation produce results; all the rest are costs. Marketing is the distinguishing, unique function of the business.[2]

Marketing and innovation foster growth through their symbiotic relationship. Innovation enables marketing by identifying novel means to address customer needs in a way that creates market value. Marketing empowers innovation by shaping new technologies and inventions and aligning them with market needs. Together, marketing and innovation spark growth.

In addition to empowering innovation, marketing facilitates the development of strategies that enable a company to take full advantage of emerging opportunities, capture uncontested markets, and discover the best means to fulfill unmet customer needs. Thus, marketing helps sustain and enhance a company's business position by focusing on new ways in which the company can create value for its customers, collaborators, and stakeholders.

The view of marketing as a central business function has important implications for the role of marketing in the organization. With its primary purpose of creating and sustaining value for customers, the company, and its collaborators, marketing should play a central role in any organization. Business success is only possible when all departments work together to create market value: Engineering designs the right products, finance furnishes the right amount of funding, purchasing buys the right materials, production makes the right products in the right time horizon, and accounting measures profitability in a meaningful way. This type of harmony can only coalesce around a unified interdepartmental focus on creating value—an outcome possible only in organizations where marketing plays a central rather than peripheral role.

The central role of marketing in business management implies that it is not just an activity managed by a single department; it spans all departments. To build a strong organization, managers across all departments must understand the fundamental marketing principles and align their activities in order to develop offerings that create market value. David Packard, cofounder of Hewlett-Packard, observed:

> Marketing is far too important to leave to the marketing department. In a truly great marketing organization, you can't tell who's in the marketing department. Everyone in the organization has to make decisions based on the impact on the customer.

The broad role marketing plays in an organization does not make marketing departments superfluous. On the contrary, marketing departments are the organizational units that guide the development and implementation of the marketing strategy and tactics. At the same time, because the scope of value creation encompasses broad aspects of a company's operations, the marketing department should work with other organizational units within a company to provide strategic direction for carrying out the marketing function. Delegating the marketing function solely to the marketing department is counterproductive and reflects a short-sighted view of the role of marketing in an organization. To succeed, a company must ensure that the marketing focus permeates all of its organizational units, such that all departments think in terms of creating market value.

Key Marketing Trends

The past few decades have been marked by a number of significant technological, economic, regulatory, and social changes that have had a profound impact on the way companies do business. These changes have resulted in a dramatic shift in how companies develop and implement their marketing strategies. This shift is represented by several marketing trends that reflect the fundamental changes in today's marketing environment. Ten such fundamental marketing trends are outlined in more detail below.

- **From customer-centric to customer-driven marketing.** The notion of customer centricity, prominent in the writings of Peter Drucker, was the marketing mantra of the '80s and '90s. The basic premise of customer centricity is that instead of focusing only on technologies and products, companies should focus on identifying and fulfilling customer needs. The importance of focusing on customer needs has not changed and remains a fundamental marketing principle. What has changed, however, is the increased role of customers in defining a company's marketing strategies. Rather than being passive observers of marketing activities, consumers are now empowered to voice their opinions, thereby taking over some aspects of marketing. For instance, brand building—an activity that until recently was controlled almost exclusively by the company—is increasingly shared by companies and their customers, whose collective voice can significantly strengthen or undermine the desired positioning of these companies' brands. In today's networked world, customers have become co-creators of market value.

- **From mass marketing to one-on-one marketing.** With the development of the Internet, the shift from mass marketing to developing customer-specific offerings has been one of the predominant marketing trends. The unprecedented growth of online communications in the past years not only has accelerated this trend but also has markedly enhanced a company's ability to identify its target customers. This fundamental change in part stems from the ability of search engines like Google, social networking sites like Facebook, and retailers like Amazon to provide insights into customer needs and to link these needs with the profile of a particular customer. The ability to directly reach customers is revolutionizing the way companies identify their customers, enabling them to customize their marketing strategies to meet the needs of individual customers.

- **From separate transactions to managing customer journeys.** An increasing number of individuals are always online with their smartphones, tablets, or computers, enabling companies to gain a better understanding of consumers' preferences, choices, and behaviors. Using geolocation and predictive analytics, companies have the ability to reach their target customers with customized messages and offers based on their current needs and physical location. The ability to gain deeper insight into customers' minds and to reach these customers at different points in their decision process have enabled marketers to look beyond individual interactions with customers to managing customers' entire experience with the company's offerings. This runs the gamut from creating awareness of the company's offering, to creating a preference, facilitating purchase, promoting usage, and encouraging customers to repurchase the offering. Understanding and managing customer journeys has become the new mantra of creating customer value.

- **From single offerings to consumer ecosystems.** As technology permeates all aspects of our lives, compatibility has become a primary concern for consumers and businesses alike. As a result, the focus has shifted from developing individual products designed to meet customer needs to developing product platforms that function as customer ecosystems, ensuring seamless functionality between diverse sets of offerings. Consider Apple's ecosystem, which offers unique compatibility across a portfolio of offerings that not only enhances product functionality but also keeps competitors from making inroads into Apple's customers. In fact, Apple has been strategically proactive in building its ecosystem. Following the introduction of the iPhone, it opened its software platform to enable independent software developers to create a variety of applications that enhance the iPhone's functionality, thus creating switching costs for customers considering leaving its ecosystem. Marketing is moving beyond thinking about individual products to thinking about creating sustainable product ecosystems.

- **From static thinking to dynamic strategies.** Marketing has evolved not only in substance but also in the speed with which companies are able to react to changes in the environment. The era of static designs and prices is over, giving way to dynamic models in which products and prices are constantly evolving based on up-to-the-minute supply and demand. Taking advantage of the latest technological innovations, product development cycles have been dramatically compressed, leading to new production, promotion, and distribution models. For instance, the Spanish fashion chain Zara grew into the world's largest fashion retailer by streamlining design, production, and distribution in a way that requires just two weeks (compared to the six-month industry average) to develop a new product and get it to stores. Business agility has become a crucial aspect of a company's marketing activities and an essential ingredient in its future success.

- **From company-centered models to collaborator networks.** The focus of marketing has evolved from maximizing the value of each individual transaction to optimizing the entire value-delivery process. Companies introduce new business models in which the traditional roles of companies and customers are often reversed. For example, realizing that consumers are unlikely to pay to search for information, Google revolutionized the search business model by deriving revenues from the entity being searched rather than the one doing the searching. By doing so, Google has created a value network in which its collaborators rather than customers are the key source of revenues and profits. The increasing complexity of the marketplace and the closer integration of different players in the value-delivery chain have encouraged the proliferation of such value-sharing models. Value-driven collaborator networks are becoming the modus operandi of forward-looking, market-savvy companies.

- **From national to global markets.** The popular metaphor advanced by Thomas Friedman's book *The World Is Flat* accurately captures the dramatic changes globalization brings to the ways in which companies do business. The global marketplace is rapidly becoming a level playing field in which both domestic and international competitors have equal access to markets, and historical and geographic divisions are becoming increasingly less relevant. In a global industry, competitors' strategic positions in major geographic or national markets are influenced by their overall global positions. A global firm that operates and coordinates business activities in more than one country can gain research and development, production, logistical, marketing, and financial advantages not available to purely domestic competitors.

- **From "gut feel" to data-driven marketing.** Today's marketing is data intensive. Companies have access to endless amounts of data about their current and potential customers. They also have an ever-increasing arsenal of tools at their disposal to analyze the available data, and can take advantage of the sophisticated techniques developed to measure the effectiveness of their marketing campaigns. As a result, managers not only need to know marketing theory but also need to be able to identify, procure, and analyze the relevant data. This need has made data analytics an integral part of marketing. Data guide key business decisions and offer metrics for tracking the success of the company's marketing activities. Data-driven decision making can facilitate a more accurate measurement of the effectiveness and cost efficiency of the company's marketing actions, providing ever higher levels of transparency and accountability to marketing actions. This increased level of transparency helps shift the conventional view of considering marketing expenses as a cost to considering them as an investment in the company's future.

- **From manager-driven decisions to artificial–intelligence-based decisions.** As artificial intelligence helps process vast amounts of customer data in real time, it can also anticipate customers' future behaviors along with changes in the marketing environment in which the company operates. As a result, many of the tactical functions that used to be performed by marketing managers—such as designing different versions of an advertising campaign for different markets, purchasing the media, and allocating the ads across different media channels to ensure that they target the right audience—are typically done using sophisticated algorithms that are faster, more effective, and more cost efficient than the managers they are replacing. In this context, while the role of marketing managers is becoming increasingly strategic, focusing on fundamental questions such as identifying target markets and developing value propositions for these markets, it also requires a working knowledge of the capabilities of artificial intelligence and machine learning to ensure the seamless implementation of the selected strategy.

- **From profit-only focus to socially responsible business models.** As customers become concerned about societal issues, an increasing number of organizations blend social responsibility initiatives with their profit-focused activities. Many of the most admired—and most successful—companies in the world abide by high standards of business and marketing conduct that dictate serving the interests of society in addition to their bottom line. Corporate social responsibility is becoming a central principle guiding all business activities, including the ways in which a company sources, produces, and distributes its products, as well as ways in which it interacts with its customers, collaborators, employees, and stakeholders.

The marketing trends outlined above are substantive in nature and have a profound impact on companies' marketing actions. Never before have there been so many fundamental changes in the market environment, business models, and marketing strategies in such a short period of time. These rapid developments are forcing many managers to play catch-up with the technological, social, and regulatory changes and the rapidly evolving competition.

Along with changes come opportunities. Managers who are able to correctly identify the key business trends and develop strategies that take advantage of them will enjoy market success. Those who develop their strategies by looking in the rearview mirror and relying on decades-old business strategies in the belief that their company is immune to the ongoing global changes will slowly but surely fade into oblivion. To paraphrase a popular saying: *When it comes to the future, there are three kinds of people: those who make it happen, those who let it happen, and those who wonder what happened.* Understanding the key marketing trends that have emerged from recent changes in the business environment is the first step toward building a successful and sustainable business and making the future happen.

SUMMARY

As a business discipline, marketing is the art and science of creating value by designing and managing viable market offerings.

Marketing is often equated with tactical activities such as sales, advertising, and sales promotions. Yet, marketing is much broader than sales: It incorporates all aspects involved in developing the offering that is to be sold. The goal of marketing is to create a product that sells, not to sell a product. Marketing is also broader than the company's communication—advertising, public relations, and social networking—designed to promote the company's offering. Marketing takes place long before the communication campaign is conceived: It guides the development of the offering that will later be communicated to target customers.

Marketing is far more than tactics. It also involves the development of a strategic vision that is foundational to the success of the tactical elements. It encompasses all activities—both tactical and strategic—that enable the company to create value in a given market.

Marketing is not limited to products and services; it can also involve events, places, people, real estate, organizations, and even ideas. Depending on the entities participating in the value exchange, there are three main types of markets: business-to-consumer, business-to-business, and consumer-to-consumer.

As the growth engine of the organization, marketing empowers innovation by aligning new technologies and inventions with the current market needs. Marketing helps sustain and enhance a company's business position by focusing on new ways in which the company can create value for its customers, collaborators, and stakeholders.

The way companies develop and implement their marketing programs is influenced by the profound technological, economic, regulatory, and social changes that have shaped the current business environment. These changes have led to a major shift in the way companies create market value—specifically, a shift from customer-centric to customer-driven marketing, from segment-based targeting to one-on-one targeting, from separate transactions to managing customer journeys, from single offerings to consumer ecosystems, from static thinking to dynamic strategies, from company-centered models to value networks, from national to global markets, from "gut feel" to data-driven marketing, from manager-driven decisions to artificial–intelligence-based decisions, and from a profit-only focus to socially responsible business models.

MARKETING INSIGHT: THE MARKETING FUNCTION IN BUSINESS MANAGEMENT

The role of marketing as a business discipline has evolved as a function of an organization's overall business focus. Historically, five business management models have emerged—*production model, product model, selling model, marketing model,* and *market value model* — characterized by the increased role of marketing over time. These five models are outlined below.

- The *production model* reflects an organization's focus on manufacturing goods and services, with relatively little attention placed on understanding customer needs and developing products that fulfill these needs. The production model is based on the notion that the supply of low-cost products will by itself generate the demand for these products and, therefore, that a firm should focus on optimizing manufacturing efficiency. The production model is exemplified by Henry Ford's introduction of the assembly line and the primary focus on lowering production costs without recognizing the need for developing products to match the diverse needs of target customers. Henry Ford's view that "Customers can have any color they want as long as it is black" reflects the mindset of production-oriented companies that are focused on the process of manufacturing rather than on the development of products that fulfill customer needs. Consequently, the role of marketing in production-focused organizations is often limited to estimating the demand for the products that the company plans to manufacture.

- The *product model* goes beyond optimizing the cost efficiency of the production process to focus on product development and innovation. The product model naturally evolves from the production model, whereby a company that has already reached sufficient levels of operational excellence focuses on developing new technologies and products. The product model is illustrated by General Motors' focus on product development and variety in the 1930s, captured in the vision of its president Alfred Sloan: "A car for every purpose and purse." Marketing plays a somewhat greater role in the product model, with an increased focus on the diversity of customer needs. At the same time, product development is still driven by technological innovation rather than by a systematic analysis of unmet customer needs.

- The *sales model* reflects a company's focus on selling to achieve its objectives. The focus on selling is typically a result of mass production and product proliferation that has flooded the market with products and dramatically reduced the unfulfilled demand. As a result, the role of the sales department and the salesforce in the organization increases dramatically, and numerous sales and promotional techniques are developed. Marketing, which primarily involves selling, advertising, and price promotions, is typically considered only after the products are manufactured.

- The *marketing model* reflects the idea that in order to ensure a product's success in the marketplace, customer needs should be examined *before* developing the product, and that the entire product development process should be organized in a way that reflects these needs. The marketing model is marked by the creation of a separate marketing department tasked with identifying customer needs and ensuring that the company's products can satisfy these needs better than the competition. Viewing marketing as a precursor to sales also results in centralizing the marketing planning function within an organization. Despite its increased importance, however, marketing is still considered by many companies as a separate activity focused on uncovering customer needs and designing offerings to fill these needs, and not as an integral component of the overall business planning and management process.

- The *market value model* reflects the idea that marketing should go beyond focusing solely on creating products that fulfill customer needs and instead focus on creating value for the relevant market participants: target customers, the company, and its collaborators. Unlike the marketing model of business management, which tends to be more tactical in nature, the market value model is decisively strategic and is focused on the way the company creates value for all relevant market participants. The market value model views marketing as a central function of the enterprise charged with growing the business in a way that enables the enterprise to reach its goals.

The different roles that marketing has played in business management reflect the evolution of marketing as a business discipline. The focus of marketing has shifted from optimizing the production process and improving a company's products to understanding the needs of the target customer and developing offerings that create value for all relevant market participants: target customers, the company, and its collaborators. This value-based approach has defined marketing as a fundamental business discipline that is essential to the company's market success. The role of marketing as a central concept in business management is underscored by Peter Drucker, who wrote: *Marketing is the unique, central function of the business enterprise... Any organization in which marketing is either absent or incidental is not a business and should never be run as if it were one.*[3]

MARKETING INSIGHT: MARKETING MYOPIA

"Marketing Myopia" is one of the most influential articles in the field of marketing. It was written over a half a century ago by Harvard professor Theodore Levitt, who argued that most companies commit the cardinal sin of defining their business in terms of the industry in which they compete and the products which they produce rather than the customer needs they aim to fulfill. This short-sighted view of marketing stifles the company's growth opportunities and destines them to fail. Using archetypes from a variety of industries—including railroads, the movie industry, the oil and gas industry, the chemical industry, and retail—Levitt documents how the advancement of technology led to the decline of the companies in these industries because they defined their businesses too narrowly. Levitt writes:

> The railroads did not stop growing because the need for passenger and freight transportation declined. That grew. The railroads are in trouble today not because the need was filled by others (cars, trucks, airplanes, even telephones) but because it was not filled by the railroads themselves. They let others take customers away from them because they assumed themselves to be in the railroad business rather than in the transportation business. The reason they defined their industry incorrectly was that they were railroad-oriented instead of transportation-oriented; they were product-oriented instead of customer-oriented.

> Hollywood barely escaped being totally ravished by television. Actually, all the established film companies went through drastic reorganizations. Some simply disappeared. All of them got into trouble not because of TV's inroads but because of their own myopia. As with the railroads, Hollywood defined its business incorrectly. It thought it was in the movie business when it was actually in the entertainment business. "Movies" implied a specific, limited product. This produced a fatuous contentment which from the beginning led producers to view TV as a threat. Hollywood scorned and rejected TV when it should have welcomed it as an opportunity—an opportunity to expand the entertainment business. [...] What ultimately saved Hollywood and accounted for its resurgence was the wave of new young writers, producers, and directors whose previous successes in television had decimated the old movie companies and toppled the big movie moguls.[4]

Levitt further argues that, in the long run, "there is no such thing as a growth industry." Instead there are growth opportunities that a company must choose to embrace and capitalize on. Yet, more often than not, companies erroneously believe that because the industry in which they operate happens to be growing at a particular point in time, it will continue to do so in perpetuity.

There are four main factors that contribute to this myopic view of the future: (1) the belief that growth is assured merely by market expansion and reaching more affluent markets; (2) the belief that there is no competitive substitute for the industry's main product; (3) overemphasis on the importance of mass production and the benefits of economies of scale; and (4) preoccupation with a product rather than the customer need that this product aims to fulfill.

To avoid obsolescence, an organization must become customer centric rather than product centric. This means that managers must think of themselves not as creating products but as creating value by providing solutions to customer problems. Of course, constantly striving to improve the company's products is not problematic per se. The problem is that the product is often defined in the narrowest possible terms, such as railroads rather than transportation or movies rather than entertainment. This problem is exacerbated when the company's efforts are focused on improving product features and production efficiency instead of improving the company's ability to fulfill customer needs. Because there is no guarantee against product obsolescence, long-term market success depends on the company's ability to understand the underlying customer needs that its products aim to fulfill and constantly seek alternative solutions—rather than marginally improve its current products—to address these needs.

MARKETING INSIGHT: THE ROLE OF FRAMEWORKS IN MARKETING MANAGEMENT

Frameworks facilitate decisions in several ways. They help identify alternative approaches to thinking about the decision task, thus providing managers with a better understanding of the problem they are trying to solve. In addition to helping formulate the problem, frameworks provide a generalized approach to identifying alternative solutions. Frameworks further enhance decision making by providing a shared vocabulary with which to discuss the issues, thus streamlining communication among the entities involved in the marketing process.

Because of their level of generality, frameworks are not intended to answer specific marketing questions. Instead, they provide a general approach that enables managers to identify the optimal solution to a particular problem. Using a framework calls for abstracting the problem at hand to a more general scenario for which the framework offers a predefined solution and then applying this solution to solve the specific problem. By relying on the abstract knowledge captured in frameworks, a manager can effectively sidestep the trial-and-error-based learning process (Figure 1).

Figure 1. Making Decisions Using a Framework

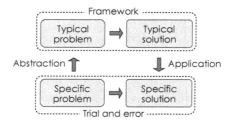

The role of marketing frameworks in business management can be illustrated with the following example. Imagine a consultant who has been asked by a cereal manufacturer for advice on how to price a new cereal. After analyzing the industry dynamics, the consultant identifies five key factors that need to be considered when deciding on the price of the cereal: customer willingness to pay for the cereal; the availability and pricing of competitive offerings; the cost structure and profit goals of the company; the margins that suppliers and distributors charge; as well as more general context factors such as the current economic environment, consumption (health and diet) trends, and legal regulations concerning pricing strategies and tactics.

A month later the consultant receives an assignment from a different client, a gas pipeline manufacturer, asking for help with setting the price for a new pressure valve. The consultant diligently analyzes the industry and ends up suggesting the same five factors: customer willingness to pay, competitive pricing, company costs and goals, collaborator (supplier and distributor) margins, and the current context.

The following month the consultant receives another assignment from a telecommunications company, asking for advice on pricing its new mobile phone. By this time the consultant has realized that the three recent price-setting requests are conceptually similar. Moreover, the consultant realizes that the three tasks entail analyzing the same five factors: customer willingness to pay, competitor prices, company goals and cost structure, collaborator prices and margins, and the overall economic/regulatory/technological context in which the company operates. (These five factors comprise the 5-C framework, which is discussed in the following chapter.)

As the above example illustrates, the effective use of marketing frameworks as a managerial problem-solving tool involves three key steps. First, a manager needs to generalize the specific problem at hand (e.g., how to price a new mobile phone) to a more abstract problem that can be addressed by a particular framework (e.g., how to price a new product). Second, the manager needs to identify a framework that will help answer the specific problem (e.g., the 5-C framework) and use it to derive a general solution. Third, the manager needs to apply the generalized solution prescribed by the framework to the specific problem. The reliance on generalized knowledge captured in frameworks can help managers circumvent the trial-and-error approach to solving business problems.

Marketing frameworks build on already existing generalized knowledge to facilitate future company-specific decisions. In fact, many of the business problems companies face on a daily basis can be generalized into a framework that can be applied to solving future problems. The role of frameworks as a problem-solving tool is captured in the words of French philosopher René Descartes: *Each problem that I solved became a rule which served afterwards to solve other problems.*

CHAPTER TWO

MARKETING STRATEGY AND TACTICS

Strategy without tactics is the slowest route to victory.
Tactics without strategy is the noise before defeat.

—Sun Tzu, Chinese military strategist

The success of an offering is defined by the company's ability to design, communicate, and deliver market value. The particular way in which an offering creates value is determined by the company's business model and its two building blocks: strategy and tactics. The key aspects of developing an offering's strategy, designing its tactics, and crafting a market value map are the focus of this chapter. Specifically, we address the following topics:

- *Marketing Strategy and Tactics*
- *Marketing Strategy: The Target Market* ‖ Target Customers | Competitors | Collaborators | Company | Context
- *Marketing Strategy: The Value Proposition* ‖ Defining the value exchange | The market value principle
- *Marketing Tactics: The Market Offering* ‖ The seven attributes defining the market offering | Marketing tactics as a process of designing, communicating, and delivering value
- *The Market Value Map*

The discussion of marketing strategy and tactics is complemented by an in-depth overview of two additional topics: the 3-C, 4-P, and 5-Forces frameworks and the key aspects of analyzing the market context.

Marketing Strategy and Tactics

A company's success is determined by the ability of its business model to create value in its chosen market. To create value, a company must clearly identify the target market in which it will compete; develop a meaningful set of benefits for its target customers, collaborators, and the company stakeholders; and design an offering that will deliver these benefits to the target market. These activities define the two key components of a company's business model: *strategy* and *tactics*.

- The term **strategy** comes from the Greek *stratēgía*—meaning "generalship"—used in reference to maneuvering troops into position before a battle. In marketing, strategy outlines a company's choice of the market in which it will compete and the value it intends to create in this market. Consequently, marketing strategy involves two key components: the *target market* in which it will compete and the *value proposition* for the relevant market entities—the company, its target customers, and its collaborators. The choice of the target market and the value proposition is the foundation of the company's business model and serves as the guiding principle for making the tactical decisions that define the company's offering.

- The term **tactics** comes from the Greek *τακτική*—meaning "arrangement"—used in reference to the deployment of troops during battle from their initial strategic position. In marketing, tactics refer to a set of specific activities, also known as the marketing mix, employed to execute a given strategy. The market tactics define the key aspects of the offering that the company introduces and manages in a given market, from the benefits this offering creates and how much it costs to how customers will hear about and buy it. The tactics logically follow from the company's strategy and reflect the way the company will make this strategy a market reality. The tactics define the attributes of the market offering, namely, the product, service, brand, price, incentives, communication, and distribution.

A company's strategy and tactics are intricately related. Whereas the strategy defines the target market and the value the company aims to create in this market, the tactics define the attributes of the actual offering that creates value in the chosen market. Because the strategy defines the value that the company aims to create with its offering, deciding on the specific aspects of the offering — be it product features, brand image, pricing, sales promotions, communication activities, or distribution channels — is impossible without knowing whose needs the offering aims to fulfill, what those needs are, and what the competing options are for fulfilling these needs.

Despite the importance of having a strategy, on many occasions managers are tempted to focus on the tactical aspects of the offering without clearly articulating the overarching value-creation strategy. "We just need to decide how to promote our product to increase sales. We don't have time for strategy," might argue the manager charged with running sales promotions. The problem with this line of reasoning is that sales promotions are merely a tool that can be used in many ways to achieve a diverse set of goals set forth by the company's strategy. Without a clearly defined strategy to guide a company's actions, even the best tool might prove counterproductive.

Another common mistake stemming from not understanding the difference between strategy and tactics is substituting tactics for strategy. "Our strategy is to have social media presence," is how one senior manager of a large multinational company articulated his vision for the company's communication efforts. Being on Facebook, Twitter, or Instagram is not a strategy; it is merely one aspect of the company's communication tactics. Tactics do not exist in a vacuum; they aim to implement a particular strategy. Without a clearly articulated strategy, most tactical decisions are destined to fail.

The overview of the strategy and tactics outlined in this chapter focuses on the process of creating value for a particular customer segment with relatively uniform preferences. The process of dividing the market into uniform segments and identifying target customers is discussed in Chapter 7. The key aspects of an offering's strategy and tactics are discussed in more detail in the following sections.

Marketing Strategy: The Target Market

The target market is the market in which a company aims to create and capture value. The choice of the target market is a crucial decision that can determine the viability of the company's market strategy. Indeed, because one of the main goals of a company is to create customer value, the choice of target customers for whom to create value is a key driver of the company's market success.

The target market is defined by five factors: *customers* whose needs the company aims to fulfill, *competitors* that aim to fulfill the same needs of the same target customers, *collaborators* that work with the company to fulfill customers' needs, the *company* managing the offering, and the *context* in which the company operates.

The five market factors are often referred to as the *Five Cs*, and the resulting framework is referred to as the *5-C framework*. This framework offers a simple yet very powerful tool for market analysis to guide the company's decisions and actions. The 5-C framework can be visually represented by a set of concentric ellipses, with target customers in the center; collaborators, competitors, and the company in the middle; and the context on the outside (Figure 1). The central placement of target customers reflects their defining role in the market; the other three entities — the company, its collaborators, and its competitors — aim to create value for these customers. The context is the outer layer because it defines the environment in which customers, the company, its collaborators, and its competitors operate.

Figure 1. Identifying the Target Market: The 5-C Framework

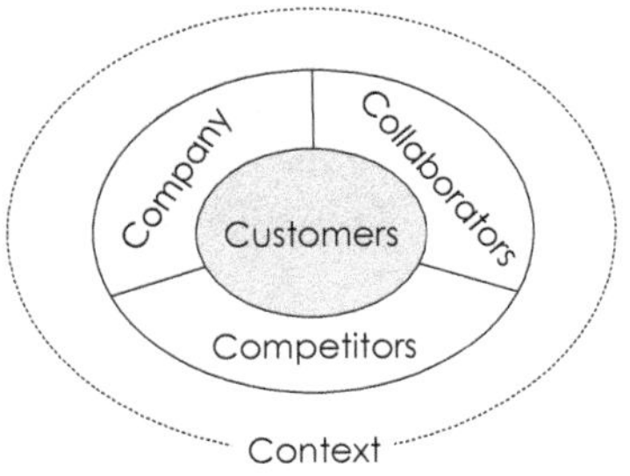

The Five Cs and the relationships among them are discussed in more detail in the following sections.

Target Customers

Target customers are the entities (individuals or organizations) whose needs the company aims to fulfill. Because a key goal of a company's offerings is to create customer value, identifying the right customers is essential for market success. In business-to-consumer markets, target customers are the individuals who are typically the end users of the company's offerings. In business-to-business markets, target customers are other businesses that use the company's offerings. Target customers are defined by two factors: *needs* and *profile*.

- **Customer needs** reflect the specific problem(s) faced by customers that the company aims to address. They determine the benefits that customers expect to receive from the company's offering. Although of critical importance to the company's ability to create customer value, customer needs are not readily observable and are often inferred from customers' demographics and behavior.

- **Customer profile** reflects customers' observable characteristics: *demographics* such as age, gender, income, occupation, education, religion, ethnicity, nationality, employment, social class, household size, and family life cycle; *geolocation* such as customers' permanent residence and their current location at a particular point in time; *psychographics* such as customers' personality, including moral values, attitudes, interests, and lifestyles; and *behavior* such as shopping habits, purchase frequency, purchase quantity, price sensitivity, sensitivity to promotional activities, loyalty, and social and leisure activities.

Both factors—needs and profile—are important in defining target customers. Customer needs determine the value the company must create for these customers, and the customer profile identifies effective and cost-efficient ways in which the company can reach customers with these needs to communicate and deliver its offering. To illustrate, consider the following examples:

iPhone fulfills customers' need for an all-in-one, always-on device that enables them to work, have fun, socialize, and even show off. Customers with this need have diverse profiles: Their ages range from teenagers to adults; they span social classes, income groups, and geographic locations; and they vary in occupation, hobbies, and lifestyles.

Starbucks fulfills customers' need for a place between home and work where they can relax, socialize, and enjoy indulgent coffee drinks handcrafted to their personal taste. Customers with these needs have different profiles: Most are adult urbanites aged 25 to 40 with relatively high incomes, professional careers, and a sense of social responsibility; the second-largest customer segment is young adults aged 16 to 24, many of whom are college students or young professionals.

The choice of target customers is determined by two key principles: The target customers should be able to create value for the company and its collaborators; and, vice versa, the company and its collaborators must be able to create superior value for these target customers relative to the competition. The selection of target customers determines all other aspects of the market: the scope of the competition, potential collaborators, company resources necessary to fulfill customer needs, and the context in which the company will create market value. A change in target customers typically leads to a change in competitors and collaborators, requires different company resources, and is influenced by different context factors. Because of its strategic importance, choosing the right target customers is the key to building a successful business model. The process of identifying target customers is discussed in more detail in Chapter 7.

Competitors

Competitors are entities that aim to fulfill the same need of the same customers as the company. Because the success of a company's offering hinges on its ability to create *superior* customer value, identifying the competitive offerings that customers will also consider when making a choice is essential to a company's ability to gain and defend its market position. Without knowing who the competitors are and what benefits they offer to target customers, it is difficult for a company to design an offering that will successfully provide superior value.

When defining their rivals, companies often fall prey to the myopic view of competition by defining it in traditional category and industry terms. For example, Blockbuster — the once ubiquitous chain of video rental stores — focused on competing with other movie rental businesses and missed the emerging competition from video streaming services such as Netflix and Hulu. In the same vein, Barnes & Noble and Borders booksellers focused exclusively on competing with other brick-and-mortar bookstores and overlooked the emerging online competition from Amazon.

Many companies do not realize that competitors are defined relative to customer needs, rather than the industry within which they operate. For example, digital camera manufacturers do not only compete with one another; they also compete with the manufacturers of smartphones because both digital cameras and smartphones can fulfill the same customer need of capturing a moment in time. By defining competitors based on the customer needs they aim to satisfy rather than a particular category, a company can gain a better understanding of who their current and future competitors are likely to be. To illustrate, consider some of the key iPhone and Starbucks competitors:

iPhone competes with smartphones from other manufacturers, including Samsung, HTC, Huawei, LG, and Xiaomi. It also competes with cameras from Canon, Fuji, Nikon, and Sony; portable music players from Sony, Pioneer, SanDisk, and Apple (iPod); and navigation services and devices from Garmin, Google, Magellan, and TomTom. It even competes with portable game consoles by enabling consumers to play games on their phones.

Starbucks competes with other chain stores offering drip and espresso-based coffee drinks, including Dunkin' Donuts, McDonald's, Costa Coffee, and Peet's Coffee. It also competes with boutique coffee shops offering handcrafted coffee drinks. In addition, Starbucks competes with offerings from the likes of Nespresso and Keurig, whose capsule-based technology enables consumers to easily make drip and espresso coffee drinks at home. Finally, Starbucks competes with traditional coffee producers including Folgers, Maxwell House, and Eight O'Clock Coffee.

Because competition is customer specific, companies that compete in one market can collaborate in another. For example, Apple competes with Microsoft in the market for personal computers and tablets while also collaborating with Microsoft to develop productivity software, including word processing and spreadsheet programs. Likewise, Samsung manufactures many iPhone components even though its Galaxy phones compete directly with the iPhone. Furthermore, because the competition is defined based on the ability of an offering to fulfill a particular customer need, different offerings in a company's product line can compete with one another. For example, different generations of Gillette's razors such as Sensor Excel, Mach3, and Fusion compete with one another to be the preferred shaving device for men.

Collaborators

Collaborators are entities that work with the company to create value for target customers. Because few, if any, companies possess all the resources necessary to create customer value, selecting the right collaborators is paramount for the company to compete in the chosen market. Value creation through collaboration represents a fundamental shift away from the conventional business paradigm in which value is created by the company and then delivered to the customer to a new paradigm in which the value is created jointly by the company and its collaborators. This value co-creation approach calls for involving collaborators in the very process of designing, communicating, and delivering value to target customers.

The choice of collaborators is driven by the complementarity of the resources needed to fulfill customer needs. Collaboration involves outsourcing the resources that the company lacks and that are required to fulfill the needs of target customers. Thus, instead of going through the risky and time-consuming task of building or acquiring resources that are lacking, a company can "borrow" them by partnering with entities that have these resources and can benefit from sharing them. Consider the collaborator networks of Apple and Starbucks:

iPhone benefits from Apple's collaboration with wireless service providers such as AT&T, Verizon, T-Mobile, and Sprint that ensure compatibility of the iPhone across different wireless networks. Apple also collaborates with numerous suppliers such as 3M, Corning, Intel, Foxconn, LG, Samsung, and Qualcomm. In addition, Apple collaborates with various retailers such as Walmart, Target, and Best Buy that make the iPhone available to the public.

Starbucks collaborates with numerous coffee growers around the globe to provide high-quality coffee beans. Starbucks also partners with suppliers that provide various non-coffee items such as water, pastries, snacks, and branded merchandise. In addition, Starbucks collaborates with a variety of retail outlets including grocery chains; mass-merchandisers; warehouse clubs; and convenience stores that sell coffee beans, instant coffee, and snacks.

Common types of collaborators include suppliers, manufacturers, distributors (dealers, wholesalers, and retailers), research-and-development entities, service providers, external salesforce, advertising agencies, and marketing research companies. For example, Procter & Gamble collaborates with the design firm IDEO to develop some of its products, with Diamond Packaging to provide packaging, and with retail giant Walmart for distribution. Walmart collaborates with Procter & Gamble to procure many of its products, with software solutions provider Oracle to streamline its logistics, and with shipping conglomerate Moller-Maersk to transport its goods.

Company

The company is the entity that develops and manages a given market offering. Understanding the goals the company aims to achieve and the resources it has to achieve these goals is important for determining the company's ability to successfully compete in the chosen market.

The company can be a manufacturer that produces the actual goods being sold (Procter & Gamble), a service provider (American Express), an entity engaged in brand building (Lacoste), a media company (Facebook), or a retailer (Walmart). The company is not limited to a single role; it can perform multiple functions. For example, a retailer might have its own production facility, engage in building its own brand, and offer a variety of value-added services.

In the case of enterprises with diverse strategic competencies and market offerings, the term *company* refers to the particular business unit (also called the *strategic business unit*) of the organization managing the specific offering. To illustrate, Apple comprises multiple strategic business units, including iPhone, iPod, iPad, Apple Watch, iTunes, and Apple TV, among others. In the same vein, GE, Alphabet (Google's parent company), and Facebook have multiple business units, each of which can be viewed as a separate company requiring its own business model.

A company's motivation and ability to create market value can be defined by two main factors: *goals* and *resources*.

- **Goals** reflect the end result that the company aims to achieve with a particular offering. Company goals can be monetary, such as maximizing profits, and strategic, such as establishing synergies with other company offerings and creating value for society at large.

- **Resources** reflect the company's characteristics, including the resources that determine its ability to create market value and a sustainable competitive advantage. A company's resources include its assets and competencies such as business facilities; suppliers; employees; know-how; existing products, services, and brands; communication and distribution channels; and access to capital.

To illustrate, consider the goals and resources of Apple and Starbucks.

Apple's (iPhone) resources are characterized by its production facilities; its relationships with suppliers, manufacturers, and distributors; its technology-savvy employees; its intellectual property including know-how, patents, and trademarks; its strong brand; its existing product and service ecosystem; its loyal customer base; and its vast cash reserves. Apple's goals are for the iPhone to be its key revenue and profit driver (monetary goal) and a cornerstone of the company's ecosystem of products and services (strategic goal).

Starbucks' resources are defined by its numerous retail locations, its relationships with coffee growers and distributors, its professionally trained employees, its intellectual property, its strong brand, its loyal customer base, and its access to capital markets. Starbucks' monetary goal—to generate revenues and profits for its shareholders—is complemented by its strategic goal to benefit society and promote social responsibility.

Context

Context describes the environment in which the company operates. Understanding the context is important because even small changes in the market environment can have major implications for the company's business model. The context is defined by five factors:

- **Sociocultural context** includes social and demographic trends, value systems, religion, language, lifestyles, attitudes, and beliefs.
- **Technological context** includes new techniques, skills, methods, and processes for designing, manufacturing, communicating, and delivering market offerings.
- **Regulatory context** includes taxes; import tariffs; embargoes; product specification, pricing, and communication regulations; and intellectual property laws.
- **Economic context** includes factors such as the overall economic activity, money supply, inflation, and interest rates.
- **Physical context** includes natural resources, climate, geographic location, topography, and health trends.

To illustrate, the context in which iPhone and Starbucks operate can be described as follows:

iPhone's context is characterized by people's mounting desire for mobile connectivity that enables them to search, share, and shop on the go; by rapid technological developments, including the availability and speed of wireless connectivity, improved battery life and processing speed, and enhanced image processing; by intellectual property laws enabling the company to protect its patents and trademarks; and by the overall economic conditions that determine customers' disposable income.

Starbucks' context is characterized by the growing popularity of crafted coffee drinks and the desire to socialize in person, as well as by the growing popularity of online communications; by the technological developments that enable the company to better understand its customers, track their buying behavior, and communicate with them on a one-on-one basis; by the favorable trade agreements that influence import tariffs on coffee; by various economic factors, including the state of the local economy and the global commodity prices for coffee; and by the climate and weather patterns across different geographic locations.

Unlike the other four Cs—customers, competitors, collaborators, and company—which describe the different market players in the value-exchange process, the context depicts the environment in which the value exchange takes place. Consequently, changes in the context can influence all the market participants and the ways in which they create and capture market value. In fact, changes in the context, whether they are new technological developments or changes in the regulatory environment, are often the impetus behind disruptive innovations that give birth to new markets and industries. Without thoroughly understanding the intricacies of the context in which a company operates, it is impossible to create a viable business model that will endure the test of time. A more detailed discussion of the market context is offered at the end of this chapter.

Marketing Strategy: The Value Proposition

The value proposition defines the value that an offering aims to create in a given market. A meaningful value proposition allows a company to craft an offering that creates value for all relevant parties in the market exchange—target customers, collaborators, and the company. The primary aspects of developing a value proposition are discussed below.

Defining the Value Exchange

The value proposition defines the value that an offering aims to create for market participants. Designing a meaningful value proposition calls for understanding the *value exchange* among the relevant market entities—customers, the company, its collaborators, and its competitors—that operate in a given context (Figure 2). Accordingly, the value exchange defines how different entities create and capture value in a given market.

Figure 2. Defining the Value Exchange

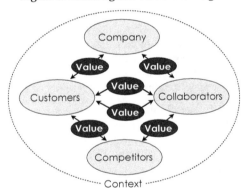

Each of the relationships defining the value exchange is a process of giving (creating) and receiving (capturing) value. Thus, the relationship between the company and its customers is defined by the value the company creates for its customers as well as by the value created by these customers that is captured by the company. In the same vein, the relationship between the company and its collaborators is defined by the value the company creates for these collaborators as well as by the value generated by these collaborators that is captured by the company. The relationship between the company's customers and its collaborators is defined by the value these collaborators create for target customers as well as by the value generated by the target customers that is captured by collaborators.

To illustrate, consider the relationship between a manufacturer, a retailer, and their customers. The manufacturer (the company) partners with a retailer (the collaborator) to deliver an offering to target customers. *Customers* receive value from the product (created by the manufacturer) they purchase as well as from the service (delivered by the retailer) involved in the buying process, for which they offer monetary compensation that is shared by both the manufacturer and the retailer. The *retailer* receives value from customers in the form of margins (the differential between the buying and selling price) as well as value from the manufacturer in the form of various trade promotions. The *manufacturer* receives value from customers in the form of the price they pay for its products (excluding the retailer markup) as well as from the retailer in the form of various services the retailer performs on the manufacturer's behalf.

The three value relationships between the company, its customers, and its collaborators reflect only the company side of the value exchange. No market exists without competitors that aim to create value for the same target customers. The competitive aspect of the value exchange mirrors the company side of the value exchange. Specifically, it consists of three types of value relationships: those between the company's target customers and its competitors, those between the company's target customers and competitors' collaborators (some or all of whom could also be the company's collaborators), and those between the competitors and their collaborators.

To succeed in a competitive environment, a company's offerings must beat the competition and create superior value for all three entities—customers, collaborators, and the company. This is the essence of the market value principle discussed in the following section.

The Market Value Principle

Creating value for all relevant entities involved in the market exchange—target customers, collaborators, and the company—is the overarching principle that guides all company actions. This is the market value principle that encapsulates the company's value proposition:

The offering must create superior value for its target customers and collaborators in a way that enables the company to achieve its goals

The market value principle implies that when developing market offerings, a company needs to consider all three types of value: *customer value, collaborator value,* and *company value.*

- **Customer value** is the worth of an offering to its customers; it is customers' assessment of the degree to which an offering fulfills their needs. The value an offering creates for its customers is determined by three main factors: (1) the *needs* of these customers, (2) the benefits and costs of the company's offering, and (3) the benefits and costs of the alternative means (competitive offerings) target customers can use to fulfill their needs. Simply put, the customer value proposition answers the question: *Why would target customers choose the company's offering instead of the available alternatives?*

- **Collaborator value** is the worth of an offering to the company's collaborators; it is the sum of all benefits and costs that an offering creates for collaborators. The collaborator value reflects an offering's ability to help collaborators achieve their goals better than the alternative offerings. Simply put, the collaborator value proposition answers the question: *Why would collaborators choose the company's offering instead of the competitive offerings?*

- **Company value** is the worth of the offering to the company; it is the sum of all benefits and costs associated with an offering. The value of an offering is defined relative to the company's goal and the value of other opportunities that are available to the company, such as the value of other offerings that could be launched by the company. The company value proposition answers the question: *Why would the company choose this offering instead of the alternative options?*

Because the market value principle underscores the importance of creating value for the three key entities—target customers, the company, and collaborators—it is also referred to as the *3-V principle.* The market value principle implies that the viability of a business model is defined by the answers to three sets of questions related to the value of an offering for customers, collaborators, and the company:

- *What value does the offering create for its target customers? Why would target customers choose this offering? What makes this offering better than the alternative options?*

- *What value does the offering create for the company's collaborators? Why would the entities identified as collaborators (suppliers, distributors, and co-developers) partner with the company?*

- *What value does the offering create for the company? Why should the company invest resources in this offering rather than in an alternative offering?*

The need to manage value for three different entities raises the question of whose value to prioritize. Surprisingly, many companies find it difficult to reach a consensus because of the divergent priorities of the different stakeholders, often represented by different departments within the company. Marketing departments focus on creating customer value; finance departments and senior management focus on creating company (shareholder) value; and the salesforce focuses on creating value for collaborators, such as dealers, wholesalers, and retailers.

The "right" answer is that the company needs to balance the value among its stakeholders, customers, and collaborators to create an optimal value proposition. Here, the term *optimal value* means that the value of the offering is balanced across the three entities, such that it creates value for target customers and collaborators in a way that enables the company to achieve its strategic goals. Optimizing customer, company, and collaborator value is inherent in the market value principle, which is the cornerstone of market success (Figure 3).

Figure 3. The 3-V Market Value Principle

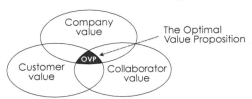

An offering that satisfies the market value principle is said to have an *optimal value proposition* (OVP). Failure to create superior value for any of the three market entities inevitably leads to an unsustainable business model and failure of the business venture. The root cause of virtually all business failures can be traced to the inability of the company's offering to deliver superior value to target customers, collaborators, and/or the company. Therefore, developing a value proposition that can fulfill the needs of all relevant participants in the value exchange is the overarching principle of any marketing activity.

The market value principle and the concept of the optimal value proposition can be illustrated with the following examples:

iPhone. Customers receive value through the functionality and prestige of the iPhone, for which they offer Apple and its collaborators monetary compensation. Collaborators (wireless service providers) receive the strategic benefit of associating their service with a product that is in high demand and likely to promote greater usage of their services. In return, these collaborators invest resources in making their services compatible with iPhone's functionality. Another set of collaborators (retailers) receives monetary benefit (profits) from selling the iPhone as well as the strategic benefit of carrying a traffic-generating product. Retailers, in turn, invest monetary and strategic resources (shelf space, inventory management, and salesforce) to deliver the iPhone to its customers. In return for developing, advertising, and distributing the iPhone, the company (Apple) receives monetary compensation from consumers purchasing the iPhone as well as the strategic benefit of strengthening its brand and its ecosystem of compatible Apple products.

Starbucks. Customers receive value through the functional benefit of a variety of coffee beverages as well as the psychological benefit of expressing certain aspects of their personality through the choice of a customized beverage, for which they deliver monetary compensation. Starbucks collaborators (coffee growers) receive monetary payments for the coffee beans they provide and the strategic benefit of having a consistent demand for their product, in return for which they invest resources in growing coffee beans that conform to Starbucks' standards. By investing resources in developing and offering its products and services to consumers, the company (Starbucks) derives monetary benefit (revenues and profits) and the strategic benefits of building a brand and enhancing its market footprint.

The value proposition reflects the company's expectation of the value that the offering will create for the three key market entities. The value proposition is not a tangible offering in and of itself. Rather, value is created by specific offering(s) the company and its collaborators design, communicate, and deliver to target customers. The key aspects of developing offering(s) that create market value are discussed in the following section.

Marketing Tactics: The Market Offering

Marketing tactics define the company's offering by delineating the specific attributes describing the actual good that the company deploys to fulfill a particular customer need. Whereas a company's strategy determines its target market and the value it seeks to provide to relevant market participants, tactics determine the specific offering that will deliver the value outlined in the strategy. The key attributes defining a company's offering and the way they come together as a process of designing, communicating, and delivering value are outlined in the following sections.

The Seven Attributes Defining the Market Offering

A company's offering is defined by seven attributes: product, service, brand, price, incentives, communication, and distribution. These seven attributes are also referred to as the *marketing mix*—the combination of specific activities employed to execute the offering's strategy. These seven tactics defining the offering are the tools that managers have at their disposal to create market value (Figure 4).

Figure 4. Marketing Tactics: The Seven Attributes Defining the Market Offering

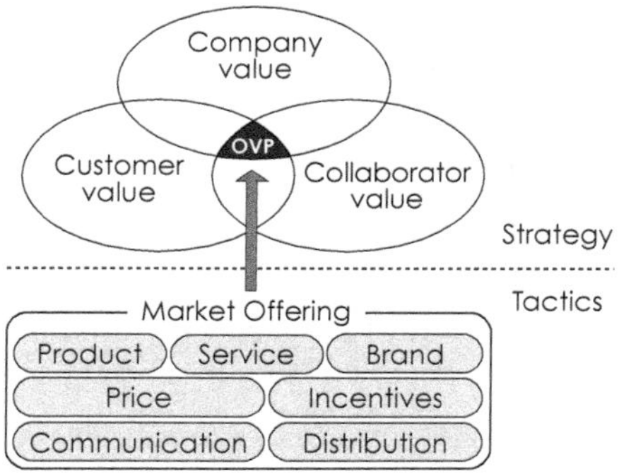

The seven attributes that delineate the market offering are defined as follows:

- The **product** aspect of an offering reflects the benefits of the good with which the company aims to create market value. Products can be both tangible (e.g., food, apparel, and automobiles) and intangible (e.g., software, music, and video). Products typically entitle customers to permanent rights to the acquired good. For example, a customer purchasing a car or a software program takes ownership of the acquired product.

- The **service** aspect of an offering reflects the benefits of the good with which the company aims to create value for its customers without entitling them to permanent ownership of this good (e.g., movie rental, appliance repairs, medical procedures, and tax preparation). The service aspect of the offering is closely related to its product aspect such that some offerings might be positioned as either a product or a service. For example, a software can be offered as a product, with customers purchasing the rights to a copy of the program, or as a service, with customers renting the program to temporarily receive its benefits. Many offerings involve both product and service components. For example, a mobile phone offering includes a product component—the physical device that customers acquire—as well as a service component that includes wireless connectivity and device repairs.

- The **brand** is a marketing tool that aims to inform customers about the source of the products and services associated with the brand. The brand helps identify the company's products and services, differentiate them from those of the competition, and create unique value beyond the product and service aspects of the offering. For example, the Harley-Davidson brand identifies its motorcycles; differentiates these motorcycles from those made by Honda, Suzuki, Kawasaki, and Yamaha; and elicits a distinct emotional reaction from its customers, who use Harley-Davidson's brand to express their individuality.

- The **price** is the amount of money the company charges its customers and collaborators for the benefits provided by the offering.

- **Incentives** are tools that enhance the value of the offering by reducing its costs and/or by increasing its benefits. Common incentives include volume discounts, price reductions, coupons, rebates, premiums, bonus offerings, contests, and rewards. Incentives can be offered to individual customers, the company's collaborators (e.g., incentives given to channel partners), and the company's employees.

- **Communication** informs the relevant market entities — target customers, collaborators, and the company's employees and stakeholders — about the specifics of the offering.

- **Distribution** defines the channel(s) used to deliver the offering to target customers and the company's collaborators.

The seven attributes defining the offering are illustrated by the following examples:

iPhone. The *product* is the actual phone, defined by its physical characteristics and functionality. The *service* is the wireless connectivity provided by the telecommunications companies as well as the assistance offered by Apple in using and repairing the phone. The *brand* is the iPhone identity marks (e.g., its name and logo) and the associations that it evokes in people's minds. The *price* is the amount of money Apple charges for the iPhone. *Incentives* are the promotional tools such as temporary price reductions that provide additional value for iPhone customers. *Communication* is the information conveyed by press conferences, media coverage, and advertisements that inform the public about the iPhone. *Distribution* encompasses the channels — Apple's own stores and authorized resellers — that make the iPhone available to the public.

Starbucks. The *product* is the variety of coffee and other beverages, as well as food items available. The *service* is the assistance offered to customers prior to, during, and after purchase. The *brand* is Starbucks' name, logo, and the associations it evokes in customers' minds. The *price* is the monetary amount that Starbucks charges customers for its offerings. *Incentives* are the promotional tools — loyalty programs, coupons, and temporary price reductions — that provide additional benefits for customers. *Communication* is the information disseminated via different media channels — advertising, social media, and public relations — informing the public about Starbucks' offerings. *Distribution* includes the Starbucks-owned stores and Starbucks-licensed retail outlets, through which Starbucks' offerings are delivered to its customers.

Marketing Tactics as a Process of Designing, Communicating, and Delivering Value

The seven marketing tactics — product, service, brand, price, incentives, communication, and distribution — can be viewed as a *process of designing, communicating, and delivering* customer value. The product, service, brand, price, and incentives are the aspects of the offering that define its value; communication is the process of communicating the offering's value; and distribution is the value-delivery aspect of the offering (Figure 5). Customer value is created across all three dimensions, with different attributes playing distinct roles in the value-creation process.

Figure 5. Marketing Tactics as a Process of Designing, Communicating, and Delivering Customer Value

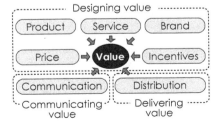

Because they define the key benefits and costs, the product, service, brand, price, and incentives are the *key value drivers* of the offering. Communication and distribution are the *channels* through which the benefits created by the first five attributes are communicated and delivered to target customers. Thus, communication informs customers about the functionality of a product or service, builds the image of its brand, publicizes its price, apprises buyers of sales promotions, and advises them about the availability of the offering. Likewise, distribution delivers a company's products and services, delivers customer payments to the company, and delivers the offering's promotional incentives to customers and collaborators.

The value-creation process can be examined from both the company and customer perspectives. From a company's perspective, value creation is a process of *designing, communicating,* and *delivering* value. From a customer's perspective, however, these three components of the value-creation process correspond to the *attractiveness, awareness,* and *availability* of the offering.[1] Thus, an offering's ability to create customer value is determined by the answers to the following three questions:

- *What makes the offering attractive to target customers?*
- *How will target customers become aware of the offering?*
- *How will target customers acquire the offering?*

The answer to the first question outlines the customer benefits and costs associated with the product, service, brand, price, and incentives aspects of the offering. The answer to the second question outlines the way in which the company will communicate the specifics of the offering to its target customers. The answer to the third question outlines the way in which the company will make the offering available to its target customers. In this context, the customer-centric approach to managing the *attractiveness, awareness,* and *availability* of an offering complements the company-centric approach to managing the process of *designing, communicating,* and *delivering* value to target customers (Figure 6).

Figure 6. Marketing Tactics: Company Actions and Customer Impact

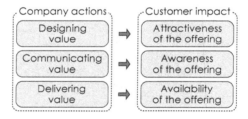

The process of designing, communicating, and delivering value can be illustrated with the following examples:

iPhone. The *value-design* component of this Apple offering involves development of the actual product (the iPhone) and service (Apple's own service and that of the wireless carriers), the creation of the iPhone brand (crafting the iPhone name, designing the logo, and defining the image that Apple wants to be associated with the iPhone in people's minds), setting the price, and deciding on the type of incentives to use to promote customer demand. The *value-communication* component of the iPhone involves communicating the features and benefits of the phone and the related services, communicating the elements of the iPhone brand, as well as informing customers about the iPhone price and incentives. Finally, the *value-delivery* aspect of the iPhone involves physically delivering the phone to buyers, servicing the phone, delivering the brand-related information, collecting payments, and delivering the incentives.

Starbucks. The *value-design* aspect of Starbucks' offerings involves the creation of its portfolio of products, ranging from espresso drinks to various food items and even wine; designing the service experience; defining its brand (selecting the brand name, designing the logo, and defining what the Starbucks brand should mean to its customers); setting prices for all possible combinations of its various drinks and sizes; and deciding what, when, and how many sales promotions to offer (such as discounts on certain drinks, 2-for-1 promotions, and loyalty programs). The *value-communication* aspect of Starbucks involves informing and educating customers about different drinks and food items available, communicating Starbucks' service policies (such as the promise that a customer's drink will be perfect every time), promoting the meaning of the Starbucks' brand, communicating its prices, and informing customers about relevant incentives. Finally, the *value-delivery* aspect of Starbucks involves delivering its products and services to customers, delivering the brand-related information, collecting consumer payments, and delivering incentives to target customers using appropriate channels (e.g., newspaper inserts, online banner advertisements, and proximity-based mobile promotions).

The Market Value Map

For practical purposes, the strategy and tactics delineating a company's business model can be represented as a value map that outlines the ways in which an offering creates value for its target customers, collaborators, and the company. The market value map is a schematic presentation of the business model, enabling managers to clearly articulate the key aspects of the company's strategy and tactics. Thus, the primary purpose of the value map is to visually outline the key aspects of the business model and serve as a guide that lays out the company's strategy and tactics.

The market value map follows the structure of the business model and comprises the three key components — *the target market, the value proposition*, and *the market offering* — that define the offering's strategy and tactics. Accordingly, the market value map is visually represented as a matrix: The left side outlines the key elements of the company's strategy — the target market (customers, collaborators, company, competitors, and context) and the value proposition (customer value, collaborator value, and company value) — and the right side outlines the market offering defined by its seven key attributes (product, service, brand, price, incentives, communication, and distribution). The components of the market value map and the key questions defining each component are shown in Figure 7.

Figure 7. The Market Value Map

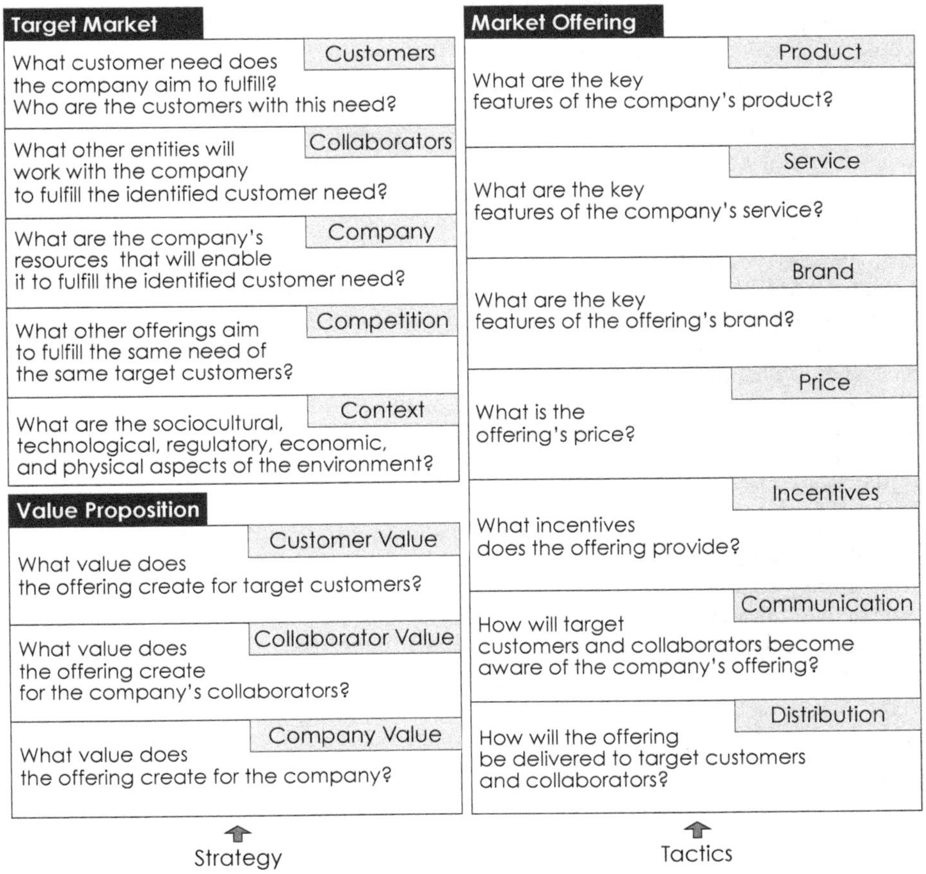

Target Market

Customers
What customer need does the company aim to fulfill?
Who are the customers with this need?

Collaborators
What other entities will work with the company to fulfill the identified customer need?

Company
What are the company's resources that will enable it to fulfill the identified customer need?

Competition
What other offerings aim to fulfill the same need of the same target customers?

Context
What are the sociocultural, technological, regulatory, economic, and physical aspects of the environment?

Value Proposition

Customer Value
What value does the offering create for target customers?

Collaborator Value
What value does the offering create for the company's collaborators?

Company Value
What value does the offering create for the company?

Market Offering

Product
What are the key features of the company's product?

Service
What are the key features of the company's service?

Brand
What are the key features of the offering's brand?

Price
What is the offering's price?

Incentives
What incentives does the offering provide?

Communication
How will target customers and collaborators become aware of the company's offering?

Distribution
How will the offering be delivered to target customers and collaborators?

Strategy   Tactics

The market value map outlines the ways in which an offering creates value for the three relevant market entities—customers, collaborators, and the company. Because each of these entities requires its own value proposition and employs different tools to create value, the market value map can be divided into three, more detailed maps: a customer value map that reflects the way an offering creates value for target customers, a collaborator value map that reflects the way an offering creates value for the company's collaborators, and a company value map that reflects the way an offering creates value for the company. Examples of these three types of value maps are shown in Appendix B at the end of this book.

SUMMARY

A company's success is defined by its ability to create value in the chosen market. To create value, a company must clearly identify the target market in which it will compete, develop a meaningful value proposition that enables it to create and capture value in this market, and design a viable market offering. These key activities form the two building blocks of a company's business model: *strategy* and *tactics*.

Strategy identifies the market in which the company competes and the value the company intends to create in this market. Marketing strategy involves two components: the target market and the value proposition.

The *target market* is defined by five factors that form the 5-C framework: *customers* whose needs the company aims to fulfill, *competitors* that aim to fulfill the same needs of the same target customers, *collaborators* that work with the company to fulfill customers' needs, the *company* managing the offering, and the *context* in which the company operates. The choice of target customers determines all other aspects of the target market: the scope of the competition, potential collaborators, company resources necessary to fulfill customer needs, and the context in which the company will create market value.

The *value proposition* defines the value that an offering aims to create for target customers, collaborators, and the company. An offering's value proposition must provide a clear answer to three questions: Why would target customers choose the company's offering instead of the available alternatives? Why would collaborators choose the company's offering instead of the alternative options? Why would the company choose this offering instead of the alternative options? Creating value for target customers, the company, and its collaborators is the overarching principle that guides all company actions. This principle, known as the *market value principle*, states that to succeed in a given market the company must create superior value for its target customers and collaborators in a way that enables it to achieve its goals.

Tactics are the specific activities employed to execute the offering's strategy; they are the means that managers have at their disposal to create market value. Tactics outline the seven key attributes of the offering (also referred to as the *marketing mix*) that the company deploys in the target market: product, service, brand, price, incentives, communication, and distribution. Tactics can be viewed as a process of *designing, communicating,* and *delivering* value, where product, service, brand, price, and incentives compose the value-design aspect of the offering that defines its *attractiveness* for target customers; communication captures the value-communication aspect that aims to create *awareness* of the offering among target customers; and distribution reflects the value-delivery aspect of the offering that ensures the *availability* of the offering to target customers.

The value-based approach to developing a business model and crafting the strategy and tactics of a market offering guides the development of a *market value map* that outlines the specific ways in which an offering creates value for its target customers, collaborators, and the company. The market value map follows the structure of the business model and comprises three key components—the target market, the value proposition, and the market offering—that outline the offering's strategy and tactics.

MARKETING INSIGHT: 3-C, 4-P, AND 5-FORCES FRAMEWORKS

The Market Value framework outlined in this chapter is not the only business model framework in existence. There are a number of frameworks that address different aspects of business models, including the *3-C framework, 4-P framework,* and *5-Forces framework.* The key aspects of these frameworks are outlined below.

The 3-C Framework

The 3-C framework advanced by Kenichi Ohmae suggests that to achieve a sustainable competitive advantage a strategist should focus on three key factors: the corporation, the customer, and the competition.[2] By understanding these three factors and integrating them into a strategic framework (or, to use Ohmae's terminology, a strategic triangle), the company can achieve a sustainable competitive advantage. The corporation's goal is to deliver superior value to its customers, relative to the competition, which, according to Ohmae, results from the corporation's competitive cost advantage.

Applied to marketing, the 3-C framework suggests that managers need to evaluate the marketing environment in which they operate: the strengths and weaknesses of their own company, the needs of their customers, and the strengths and weaknesses of their competitors. The 3-C framework is simple, intuitive, and easy to understand and use—factors that have contributed to its popularity.

Despite its popularity, the 3-C framework has important limitations that hinder its applicability to marketing analysis. A key limitation of the 3-C framework is that it overlooks the company's collaborators and the context in which the company operates. The importance of collaborators in today's networked environment can hardly be overstated; virtually all business activities involve some form of collaboration to create an offering, communicate its benefits, and deliver it to customers. In the same vein, the economic, technological, sociocultural, regulatory, and physical context in which the company operates plays a significant role in formulating its business model and can determine the ultimate success or failure of the company's offerings.

Many of the shortcomings of the 3-C framework are overcome by the 5-C framework (discussed earlier in this chapter), which extends the 3-C framework to add collaborators and context as key strategic factors in analyzing the market structure. The inclusion of collaborators is a reflection of the important role a company's collaborators (e.g., suppliers and distributors) play in the process of creating, communicating, and delivering value to target customers. In fact, many successful offerings such as the Linux operating system, Mozilla Firefox Internet browser, and Wikipedia, the user-contributed online encyclopedia, are based entirely on collaboration. In the same vein, including the context as a key market factor reflects the importance of the variety of economic, regulatory, technological, and political factors that could influence the value of the offering for target customers. Another important advantage of the 5-C framework is that it reflects the relationships between the key market factors and, specifically, the central role the choice of target customers plays in defining the other market factors.

The 4-P Framework

The 4-P framework, introduced by Jerome McCarthy in the 1960s, offers a tool for planning and analyzing the implementation of a given marketing strategy.[3] This framework identifies four key decisions that managers must make with respect to a given offering: (1) what features to include in the *product*, (2) how to *price* the product, (3) how to *promote* the product, and (4) in which retail outlets to *place* the product. These four decisions, often referred to as the marketing mix, are captured by the four Ps: product, price, promotion, and place (Figure 8).

Figure 8. The 4-P Framework

The 4-P framework is simple, intuitive, and easy to remember—factors that have contributed to its popularity. Despite its simplicity, the 4-P framework has a number of limitations that significantly limit its relevance in the contemporary business environment. One such limitation is that it does not distinguish between the product and service aspects of the offering. The fact that the 4-P framework does not explicitly account for the *service* element of the offering is a key drawback in today's service-oriented business environment, in which a growing number of companies are switching from a product-based to a service-based business model.

Another important limitation of the 4-P framework is that the *brand* is not defined as a separate factor and instead is viewed as part of the product. The product and brand are different aspects of the offering and can exist independently of each other. An increasing number of companies such as Lacoste, Prada, and Disney outsource their product manufacturing in order to focus their efforts on building and managing their brands.

The 4-P framework also comes up short in defining the term *promotion*. Promotion is a broad concept that includes two distinct types of activities: *incentives*, such as price promotions, coupons, and trade promotions; and *communication*, such as advertising, public relations, social media, and personal selling. Each of these two activities has a distinct role in the value-creation process. Incentives enhance the offering's value, whereas communication informs customers about the offering without necessarily enhancing its value. Using a single term to refer to these distinct activities muddles the unique role that they play in creating market value.

The limitations of the 4-P framework can be overcome by defining the market offering in terms of seven, rather than four, factors—product, service, brand, price, incentives, communication, and distribution—as outlined by the marketing tactics framework discussed earlier in this chapter. The four Ps can be easily mapped onto the seven attributes defining the market offering, whereby the first P comprises product, service, and brand; price is the second P; incentives and communication are the third P; and distribution is the fourth P (Figure 9). Thus, the marketing mix framework outlined earlier in this chapter presents a more refined version of the 4-P framework that offers a more accurate and actionable approach to designing a company's offering.

Figure 9. The Four Ps and the Marketing Mix

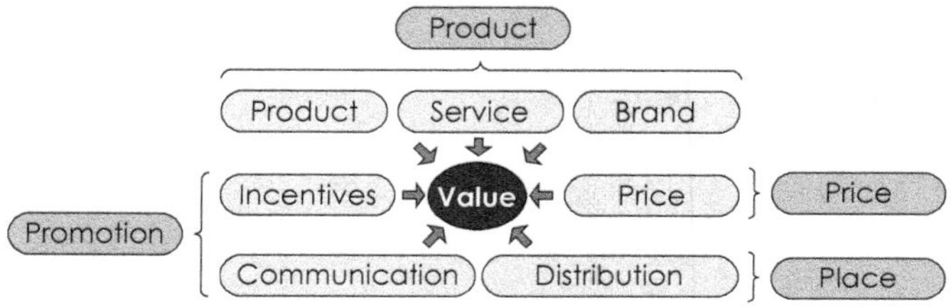

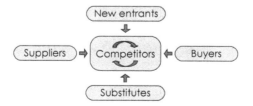

The Five Forces Framework

The Five Forces framework, advanced by Michael Porter, offers an industry-based analysis of the competition and is often used for strategic industry-level decisions such as evaluating the viability of entering (or exiting) a particular industry.[4] According to this framework, competitiveness within an industry is determined by five factors: the bargaining power of suppliers, the bargaining power of buyers, the threat of new entrants, the threat of substitutes, and rivalry among extant competitors (Figure 10). The joint impact of these five factors defines the competitive environment in which a firm operates. The greater the bargaining power of suppliers and buyers, the threat of new market entrants and substitute products, and the rivalry among existing competitors, the greater the competition within the industry.

Figure 10. The Five Forces of Competition

The Five Forces framework shares a number of similarities with the 5-C framework, as both frameworks aim to facilitate analysis of the market in which a company operates. At the same time, these frameworks differ in the way they define the market. The Five Forces framework takes an industry perspective to analyze the competition in the market. In contrast, the 5-C framework is customer-centric rather than industry-focused, meaning that it defines the market based on customer needs rather than the industry in which the company competes. As a result of its customer centricity, the 5-C framework defines competitors based on their ability to fulfill customer needs and create market value, and is not concerned with whether the company and its competitors operate within the bounds of the same industry. Accordingly, the concept of substitutes is super-fluous in the context of the 5-C framework because from a customer's point of view, substitutes are merely cross-category competitors that aim to fulfill a particular customer need.

The industry focus of the Five Forces framework makes it particularly relevant to analyzing the competitive structure within a given industry. At the same time, when it comes to analyzing an offering's ability to create market value, the Five Forces approach has much lower explanatory power. In such scenarios, the 5-C framework is typically a better fit because of its customer focus and its view of the market as defined by customer needs rather than in terms of a particular industry.

MARKETING INSIGHT: ANALYZING MARKET CONTEXT

To succeed, a company must understand the environment in which it operates. This environment—also referred to as the marketing context—comprises a number of factors that are likely to influence the marketing exchange among the company, its customers, collaborators, and competitors. Specifically, there are five key context factors: *economic* (e.g., economic growth, money supply, inflation, and interest rates); *technological* (e.g., the diffusion of existing technologies and the development of new ones); *sociocultural* (e.g., demographic trends, value systems, and market-specific beliefs and behavior); *regulatory* (e.g., import/export tariffs, taxes, product specifications, pricing and advertising policies, and patent and trademark protection); and *physical* (e.g., natural resources, climate, and health conditions). These five context factors are illustrated in Figure 11, which is a more nuanced representation of the 5-C framework discussed earlier in this chapter.

Figure 11. Context Analysis

Analyzing the marketing context is important when developing a new course of action, as well as when monitoring the company's progress toward implementing an already existing plan. It enables a company to better understand the environment in which it operates and tailor its actions to take advantage of the intricacies of this environment. The key aspects of the marketing context—economic, technological, sociocultural, regulatory, and physical—are discussed in the following sections.

Economic Context

A company's ability to create value for target customers, collaborators, and shareholders is a function of the overall economic environment in which it operates. The economic environment in any given market can be characterized by a variety of factors, including the gross domestic product (GDP), economic growth, government spending, international trade, unemployment rate, level of savings and debt, commodity prices, exchange rates, inflation, interest rates, money supply, taxation, stock prices, and housing prices.

Adapting a company's business model to the overall economic condition is a prerequisite for ensuring sustainable market growth. A business model that has proven successful in times of rapid economic growth may fail during a recession. Limited money supply and credit availability may not only curb a company's expansion plans but also threaten the company's very existence. For example, the deteriorating economic conditions and limited money supply during the 2007-2008 financial crisis resulted in a record number of bankruptcies in the United States.

In addition to the overall state of the economy, specific economic factors can further influence a company's market performance. Thus, fluctuations in exchange rates can have a significant impact on net income of companies with global exposure. For example, the depreciation of the U.S. currency against the euro had a positive impact on the dollar-denominated sales revenues of many U.S.-based companies that sell their products in Europe but had a negative impact on the euro-denominated revenues of many European companies that sell their products in the United States. The lower cost of borrowing money, reflected in declining interest rates, can further stimulate business, providing companies with growth opportunities and lowering the entry barriers for potential competitors. Stock market prices may influence a company's ability to expand via mergers and acquisitions, and housing prices can create a wealth effect, influencing consumers' spending behavior.

A company's performance can also be influenced by long-term economic trends. Globalization and the rapid changes in the economic environment underscore the importance of understanding environmental implications for a company's business activities. Companies that are able to foresee changes in the economic environment and manage to adjust their business models accordingly are more likely to succeed than those who fail to recognize changes and adapt to them.

Technological Context

The technological environment may influence the way companies operate in two ways: by producing *sustaining technologies* that lead to improvements in a company's operations within the boundaries of its current business model and *disruptive technologies*, which facilitate the creation of entirely new business models.

The impact of *sustaining technologies* can influence a company's performance in two ways: by improving the effectiveness of the value-creation processes and by improving their cost efficiency. Thus, improvement in the *effectiveness* of a company's ability to create viable market offerings is associated with the development of new technologies that enable the creation of better performing products and services. In addition to helping constantly improve a company's products and services, technological developments have facilitated the ability of companies to effectively interact with their customers by uncovering new means of communication and improving the effectiveness of existing ones. Furthermore, technological developments have improved existing distribution systems by enhancing their availability, speed, and accuracy.

Along with improving the effectiveness of the company's operations, technological developments have contributed to improving the *cost efficiency* of these operations by streamlining various aspects of a company's distribution channels such as packaging, transportation, and inventory management. The cost savings stemming from lower manufacturing, communication, and distribution costs have helped many companies improve their bottom line as well as enhance the customer and collaborator value created by their offerings.

In addition to optimizing a company's existing products and services, technology influences a company's market success by breaking the standard industry operating mold and creating new market offerings and a novel business model. Such *disruptive technologies* have fundamentally changed many industries. For example, the development of the Internet revolutionized retailing (Amazon), auctions (eBay), communication (Twitter), social networking (Facebook), information search (Google), transportation (Uber), hospitality (Airbnb), and entertainment (Netflix).

The current technological environment is characterized by the rapid emergence of new technologies in virtually all industries including energy, pharmaceuticals, healthcare, communications, manufacturing, and education. Not only are new technologies being developed at an increasing rate but the cycle from invention to business application has been significantly shortened. This rapid adoption of new technologies is facilitated by increasing rates of global collaboration and transfer of technologies stemming from the global expansion of production, marketing, and research activities. These factors contribute to the ever-increasing impact of the technological context on a company's business activities.

Sociocultural Context

The sociocultural environment is important to a company's success in both domestic and global markets. The key aspects of the sociocultural environment include factors such as language, education, beliefs, attitudes, values, customs, habits, lifestyle, views of aesthetics, fashion, style, religion, spirituality, social organization, and stratification. The sociocultural environment is further influenced by a number of demographic factors such as population size and growth, age dispersion, geographic dispersion, ethnic background, mobility, education, employment, and household composition.

An aspect of the sociocultural context that is particularly relevant for a company's marketing activities involves the market-specific beliefs, values, and behaviors held by consumers. These factors can influence a consumer's reaction to different facets of a company's offering and determine its ultimate market success. For example, country of origin plays a less important role in the United States than it does in many countries around the world, where the same product can be sold at different prices depending on where it is manufactured. In fact, in some countries, buying behavior is determined to a larger degree by the country of origin than by the offering's brand name.

To account for the cross-cultural differences across different markets, many global companies have modified their product development, branding, pricing, incentives, communication, and distribution strategies to optimally adapt their offerings to the cultural specifics of each individual market in which they compete. For example, the iconic Marlboro symbol — the lone cowboy — is typically shown as a part of a group in many Asian countries with a collectivist culture where riding alone is associated with being an outcast rather than serving as an expression of freedom. Not taking into account the sociocultural context can undermine an offering's value proposition. For example, following its global positioning strategy, Gerber featured a cute baby on the label of its packaged baby food in Africa, creating customer confusion in countries like Ethiopia, where a large segment of the population is illiterate and labels typically feature the contents of the package.[5]

A company's market success depends not only on understanding the specifics of the sociocultural environment in which it operates but also on a company's ability to predict the likely changes in this environment. Understanding and acting on key sociocultural trends enables a company to develop a successful long-term marketing strategy. Among the important sociocultural trends is changing demographics in many countries, reflected in factors such as population growth, average age, ethnic composition, and social stratification. For example, a key sociocultural trend of global consequence is the emergence of a middle class in many newly industrialized countries, including China, India, and Brazil.

Regulatory Context

The regulatory context is defined by two types of factors: factors influencing a company's overall *strategy* (target customers, the company, and its collaborators and competitors) and factors influencing its *tactics* (product, service, brand, price, incentives, communication, and distribution). These factors are discussed in more detail below.

Regulations concerning a company's overall *strategy* fall into one of the following four key domains: (1) customer-related regulations, such as age restrictions for certain activities (e.g., driving, drinking, and smoking), place restrictions (e.g., smoking in public places), and possession restrictions (e.g., drugs, firearms); (2) company-related regulations, which include factors pertaining to relationships between the company management and its shareholders; (3) collaborator-related regulations, which seek to define the relationships among collaborating entities and protect them from potential abuse of power; and (4) competitive regulations, which seek to define the relationships among competing entities in a way that protects weaker competitors from abuse of power on the part of the stronger ones (e.g., anti-monopoly legislation) while at the same time protecting consumer interests (e.g., anti-collusion legislation).

Marketing-tactics regulations concern the company's activities with respect to the seven marketing mix decisions: product, service, brand, price, incentives, communication, and distribution. For example, these regulations may involve product and service specifications, brand protection (e.g., trademark laws), regulations pertaining to pricing and price incentives (e.g., predatory pricing and price fixing), communication-specific regulations (e.g., comparative advertising), as well as regulations concerning distribution channels (e.g., laws designed to protect trade from unlawful restrictions and monopolization).

Because regulations play a pivotal role in all aspects of marketing management, a company needs to master the regulatory aspect of its business activities and understand its dynamics to effectively function in a given market. Regulatory context is market specific and is constantly evolving in response to changes in the economic, technological, sociocultural, and physical aspects of the marketing environment.

Physical Context

A company's market success is also a function of the surrounding physical context, which includes topography, natural resources, climate, weather, and the overall health conditions. These factors can influence all aspects of the process of creating market value, including designing the company's offerings, communicating their benefits, and delivering these offerings to target customers.

The *topography* of the region where the company operates can have a significant impact on its ability to effectively design, communicate, and deliver its offerings. For example, the availability of natural resources — including energy, metals, and water — is likely to influence the technologies used by companies as well as the manufacturing and distribution costs. Topography also influences the routing of goods and the choice of transportation mode as well as distribution costs, delivery schedules, and inventory management.

Climate exerts important influence on a company's business activities. Because climate factors such as temperature, humidity, and rainfall tend to influence product functionality, companies often optimize their products for a particular climate. For example, motor oils are formulated to have different levels of viscosity (thickness) to ensure consistent performance in different temperatures. Special packaging is developed to safeguard products that are adversely affected by extremes in temperatures or large changes in humidity.

A company's business activities are influenced not only by the regional climate conditions but also by changes in these conditions. For example, an increase in the average annual temperature (global warming) can lead to lower yields of fruits and vegetables that thrive in cooler temperatures and higher yields of warm-climate plants. As the cold season shortens, winter sports are likely to suffer, whereas warm-weather activities are likely to grow. In addition to climate changes, which reflect the more stable weather patterns, daily weather conditions can also influence a company's business. For instance, ice cream consumption is likely to increase when it is hot and decline as the weather cools down. Abnormal weather conditions can disrupt the production and delivery of a company's products.

Health conditions can influence the business activities of companies directly involved in health management (e.g., pharmaceutical companies, biotechnology companies, and health-management organizations) as well as those not directly related to health care. For instance, the demand for a cold medicine is likely to be affected by the overall health conditions in a given market. A pandemic, such as avian influenza and swine flu, can have a profound effect on all areas of business including food, tourism, hospitality, and transportation.

The physical environment not only influences a company's business model but can also shape other context factors. Understanding the relationships among the individual economic, technological, sociocultural, and regulatory context factors is an important aspect of evaluating a company's environment.

CHAPTER THREE

MARKETING PLANNING AND MANAGEMENT

A man who does not think and plan long ahead
will find trouble right at his door.
—Confucius, Chinese philosopher

To achieve market success, a company needs to develop a sound marketing plan and create an organizational structure and a set of processes to manage its activities. The key aspects of the process of marketing planning and management are the focus of this chapter. Specifically, we address the following topics:

- *Company Planning and Management* || Defining the company culture and values | Defining the company mission and vision | Assessing a company's market position

- *Planning and Managing Market Offerings* || The G-STIC framework for marketing management | Setting a goal | Developing the strategy and tactics | Defining the implementation | Identifying controls

- *Developing a Marketing Plan* || The purpose of the marketing plan | The key principles of developing a marketing plan | The structure of the marketing plan | Updating the marketing plan | Conducting a marketing audit

The discussion of marketing planning and management is complemented by an in-depth overview of three additional topics: developing a marketing plan, conducting a marketing audit, and the key product-management frameworks.

Company Planning and Management

Marketing planning and management can occur on two different levels. First, these activities can focus on analyzing, planning, and managing the entire company or a particular operating unit of the company. Alternatively, they can focus on analyzing, planning, and managing one or more of the company's offerings. This section addresses the key issues involved in analyzing, planning, and managing a company or distinct company units. The remainder of the chapter addresses the process of analyzing, planning, and managing a company's offerings.

Defining the Company Culture and Values

Company *culture* is commonly defined in terms of the shared values, beliefs, norms, and experiences that guide the actions of an organization and define its character. The company culture permeates all aspects of the business—the look and feel of the company's offices, the way employees dress, and the way they interact with one another. Because it involves all aspects of a company's business activities, defining and managing the organizational culture is of utmost importance to achieving market success.

The company culture in many organizations is not expressly defined. Instead, it is often an implied code of behavior that has organically developed over time based on the values held by the company management and employees. As researchers Frei and Morriss put it, "Culture guides discretionary behavior and it picks up where the employee handbook leaves off. Culture tells us how to respond to an unprecedented service request. It tells us whether to risk telling our bosses about our new ideas, and whether to surface or hide problems. Culture tells us what to do when the CEO isn't in the room, which is of course most of the time."[1]

A company's culture is a reflection of the *core values* that the company has embraced. Core values are the deeply ingrained moral principles that guide all company actions; they are the essential and enduring tenets of an organization. The values must stand the test of time and are largely independent of the current economic environment, competitive landscape, or the company's market offerings. There is no universal set of core values that applies to all companies; each company has its own idiosyncratic set of core values that define what the company stands for.[2]

Most companies tend to have only a few core values, typically between two and five. For example, Southwest Airlines defines its core values on two main dimensions: "Live the Southwest way," meaning "warrior spirit, servant's heart, and fun-LUVing[3] attitude"; and "Work the Southwest way," meaning "safety and reliability, friendly customer service, and low costs."[4] McDonald's defines its value system on three key dimensions: responsible leadership—commitment to using its scale for good, including good for people, for the industry, and for the planet; inclusiveness—commitment to being one of the world's most universal, democratic brands and welcoming customers of every culture, age, and background; and progressiveness—commitment to relentless innovation and always moving forward.[5]

A company's culture and its core values are interrelated such that the culture reflects the core values and vice versa. Consider Google, a company known for its unique collaborative culture. It provides its employees, referred to as "Googlers," with innumerable perks that include free gourmet food and snacks, complimentary massages, on-site daycare, and free fitness classes and gym memberships. More important, the company culture encourages collaboration with its peer-to-peer learning program where courses—which include a variety of topics from management, data visualization, and public speaking to yoga, kickboxing, and parenting—are initiated and designed by employees. To empower creativity and innovation, all employees are encouraged to spend 20% of their time working on what they think will most benefit Google.

What makes Google's culture unique, however, is not so much the employee benefits as the company's mission and value system that ultimately defines how Googlers feel about the company, how team members treat one another, and how the management treats employees. Google's core values are spelled out for all employees, defining what the company believes and stands for.[6] True to its vision and core values, Google's hiring strategy is based as much on the applicant's value system and the degree to which it fits that of the company as on his or her specific skill set. Co-founder Larry Page succinctly captured Google's key value when he stated, "It's important that the company be a family, that people feel that they're part of the company, and that the company is like a family to them."[7]

Defining the Company Mission and Vision

A *mission* is a clear, concise, and enduring statement of the reasons for an organization's existence. Often referred to as its *core purpose*, a company's mission is a long-term goal that provides company employees and management with a shared sense of purpose, direction, and opportunity. Thus, after Sony's co-founder Akio Morita set the ambitious goal to make music on the go available to everyone, his company invented the Walkman, the first portable cassette player. In the same vein, the founder of FedEx, Fred Smith, set the audacious goal to deliver mail anywhere in the United States the very next morning.

Defining a company's mission and vision can be greatly facilitated by addressing the five vital questions suggested by Peter Drucker: *What is our business? Who is the customer? What is of value to the customer? What will our business be? What should our business be?*[8] A company must continuously ask and answer these questions to ensure that its mission reflects the new market realities. When Amazon launched in 1995, it had the vision "to be Earth's most customer-centric company, where customers can find and discover anything they might want to buy online, and endeavors to offer its customers the lowest possible prices." Amazon continues to pursue this goal today, but its customers are now worldwide and have grown to include consumers, sellers, content creators, developers, and enterprises.[9]

Unlike the company's culture, which is often implicit, a company's mission is often explicitly articulated in a mission statement that defines the purpose of an organization. The mission statement can be thought of as a positioning statement of an organization. Peter Drucker succinctly describes the essence of a company's mission statement as follows:

> The effective mission statement is short and sharply focused. It should fit on a T-shirt. The mission says why you do what you do, not the means by which you do it. The mission is broad, even eternal, yet directs you to the right things now and into the future so that everyone in the organization can say: "What I am doing contributes to the goal."

A company's mission statement captures the soul of the company and delineates its reason for being. A well-crafted mission statement is defined by four key characteristics. A mission statement should be:

- **Meaningful.** The mission statement must clearly articulate the main goal(s) the company aims to achieve. For example, Google defines its mission as "To organize the world's information and make it universally accessible and useful."[10]

- **Value-driven.** The mission statement must reflect the company's values. It should inspire employees, provide them with a sense of purpose, and help build and sustain the company culture. For example, Patagonia defines its mission as "Build the best product, cause no unnecessary harm, use business to inspire and implement solutions to the environmental crisis."[11]

- **Enduring.** The mission statement takes a long-term view. Unlike a company's goals and objectives, which tend to be updated as the company achieves certain benchmarks, the mission statement should persist over time and be changed only when it ceases to be relevant. For example, Nike defines its mission as "Bring inspiration and innovation to every athlete in the world."[12]

- **Succinct.** The mission statement should be short and memorable. Long-winded multipart mission statements that attempt to capture all possible nuances of a company's ambitions tend to be less effective than short and to-the-point statements that the company employees can readily understand, remember, and internalize. For example, IKEA defines its mission as "To create a better everyday life for the many people."[13]

A concept closely related to the company's mission is its *vision*, which defines what the company will look like in the future. Unlike the company mission, which focuses on what the company is aiming to achieve, the vision describes what the company will become as it fulfills its mission. Thus, by creating a mental image of the future, a company's vision serves as a source of aspiration for the employees and stakeholders.

For example, Starbucks' mission is "To inspire and nurture the human spirit – one person, one cup, and one neighborhood at a time,"[14] whereas its vision is "To establish Starbucks as the premier purveyor of the finest coffee in the world while maintaining our uncompromising principles as we grow."[15] McDonald's mission is "To delight each customer with unmatched quality, service, cleanliness and value every time,"[16] whereas its vision is "To be our customers' favorite place and way to eat and drink."[17] Southwest Airlines' mission is "To connect people to what's important in their lives through friendly, reliable, and low-cost air travel," and its vision is "To become the world's most loved, most flown, and most profitable airline."[18]

A company's mission and vision can be related to the notion of "Big, Hairy, Audacious Goals" (BHAG), which reflect ambitious goals that are nearly impossible to achieve. BHAGs typically aim to reinvigorate the entire company by providing a long-term vision of what the company wants to become and what it ultimately aims to achieve. For example, in the 1950s,

Sony set as its long-term goal to "become the company most known for changing the world-wide poor-quality image of Japanese products."[19] Thus, when broadly defined and ambitious, a company's long-term goals reflect its vision for the future.

Note that even though the mission and vision reflect different aspects of what a company aims to achieve and how it sees itself, these two concepts are closely related and often prove difficult for company employees and stakeholders to distinguish. Because the concepts of mission and vision are similar, for practical purposes many companies use them interchangeably and employ only one of the two concepts.

Assessing the Company's Market Position

Along with defining the company's culture, mission, and vision, strategic planning also involves assessing the company's market position and articulating strategies for strengthening the company's ability to create market value. Assessing the company's market position typically involves assessing its strengths, weaknesses, opportunities, and threats. This analysis is captured by the SWOT framework, which presents a straightforward approach for evaluating a company's overall business condition.

As implied by its name, the SWOT framework entails four factors: the company's *strengths* and *weaknesses*, and the *opportunities* and *threats* presented to the company by the environment in which it operates. The four factors are organized in a 2×2 matrix based on whether they are internal or external to the company, and whether they are favorable or unfavorable from the company's standpoint (Figure 1).

Figure 1. The SWOT Framework for Assessing a Company's Market Position

To illustrate, factors such as loyal customers, strong brand name(s), patents and trademarks, know-how, skilled employees, and access to scarce resources are typically classified as strengths, whereas factors such as disloyal customers, weak brand name(s), and lack of technological expertise are viewed as weaknesses. Similarly, factors such as the emergence of a new, underserved customer segment and a favorable economic environment are considered opportunities, whereas a new competitive entry, increased product commoditization, and increased buyer and supplier power are considered threats.

When evaluating the company strengths, one must consider the importance of each factor deemed a strength, the extent to which the company possesses this factor, and the degree to which the company can sustain this strength over time. Likewise, the assessment of company weaknesses must take into account the importance of each factor identified as a weakness, the extent to which it is relevant for the company, and the degree to which it is likely to persist over time.

In the same vein, when evaluating a potential opportunity, a company must consider two factors: the desirability of the outcome that ideally can be achieved by taking advantage of the opportunity and the likelihood that the company will succeed in achieving this outcome. Likewise, when evaluating a potential threat, a company must consider the potential impact of the threat should it become a reality as well as the likelihood that this threat will actually materialize.

The SWOT framework can also be thought of as a reorganization of the 5-C framework (customers, collaborators, company, competitors, and context) discussed in Chapter 2, in which the Five Cs are partitioned into favorable or unfavorable factors. Thus, the analysis of strengths and weaknesses focuses on the company, and the analysis of opportunities and threats focuses on the other four Cs describing the market in which the company operates, defined by customers, collaborators, competitors, and context.

Following the assessment of the company's market position is the development of actionable strategies to strengthen this position. SWOT analysis logically suggests four approaches that a company might adopt to ensure market success: enhance its strengths, overcome its weaknesses, take advantage of emerging opportunities, and neutralize impending threats. The ultimate goals of these four strategies is to enable the company to design, communicate, and deliver offerings that create superior market value. The processes by which a company develops successful market offerings are discussed in the following section.

The G-STIC Framework for Marketing Management

A company's future hinges on its ability to develop successful market offerings that create superior value for target customers, the company, and its collaborators. Market success is rarely an accident; it is typically a result of diligent market analysis, planning, and management. To succeed in the market, a company must have a viable business model and an action plan to make this model a reality. The process of developing such an action plan is captured in the G-STIC framework discussed in the following sections.

The G-STIC Approach to Action Planning

The backbone of market planning is the action plan, which articulates the company's goal and delineates a course of action to reach this goal. The development of an action plan is guided by five key activities: setting a *goal*, developing a *strategy*, designing the *tactics*, defining an *implementation* plan, and identifying a set of *control* metrics to measure the success of the proposed action. These five activities comprise the G-STIC (Goal-Strategy-Tactics-Implementation-Control) framework, which is the cornerstone of marketing planning and analysis (Figure 2). The core of the action plan is the business model comprising the offering's strategy and tactics.

Figure 2. The G-STIC Framework for Marketing Management

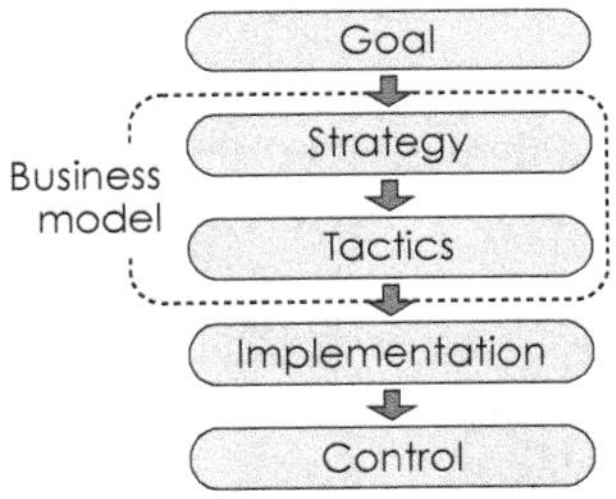

The individual components of the G-STIC framework are outlined in more detail below.

- The **goal** identifies the ultimate criterion for success; it is the end result that the company aims to achieve. The goal has two components: the *focus*, which defines the metric reflecting the desired outcome of the company's actions (e.g., net income), and the performance *benchmarks* quantifying the goal and defining the time frame for it to be accomplished.

- The **strategy** defines the company's *target market* and its *value proposition* in this market. The strategy is the backbone of the company's business model.

- **Tactics** define the key attributes of the company's offering: *product, service, brand, price, incentives, communication*, and *distribution*. These seven tactics are the tools that the company uses to create value in the chosen market.

- **Implementation** defines the processes involved in creating the market offering. Implementation includes *developing* the offering and *deploying* the offering in the target market.

- **Control** evaluates the success of the company's activities over time by evaluating the company's *performance* and monitoring the changes in the market *environment* in which the company operates.

The key components of the marketing plan and the key factors describing each component are outlined in Figure 3.

Figure 3. The G-STIC Action-Planning Flowchart

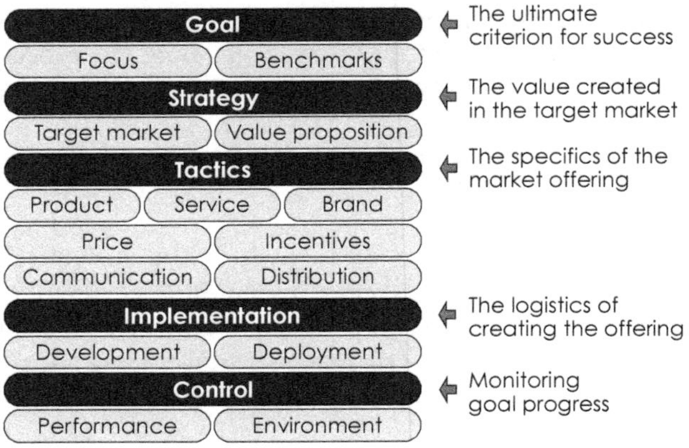

The G-STIC framework offers an intuitive approach to streamlining a company's activities into a logical sequence that aims to produce the desired market outcome. Note that even though the G-STIC framework implies a particular sequence, starting with the definition of the company's goal and concluding with identifying controls for measuring performance, marketing planning is an iterative process. Thus, even though the development of a marketing plan often starts with the identification of an unmet customer need that the company can fulfill better than the competition, it can also start with a technological invention that enables the company to create market value. In this context, the G-STIC framework describes the key elements of the iterative process of marketing planning (Goal, Strategy, Tactics, Implementation, and Control) and outlines a logical sequence of organizing these elements without prescribing the order in which these elements are developed.

The key aspects of the action plan are examined in more detail in the following sections. Because the offering's strategy and tactics were discussed in depth in the previous chapter, the focus here is on the remaining three aspects: goal, implementation, and control.

Setting a Goal

The marketing plan starts with defining the goal that the company aims to achieve. This goal then becomes the beacon that guides all company activities. Without a well-defined goal, a company cannot design a meaningful course of action and evaluate its success. The importance of having a clear goal is captured in the words of the English mathematician and author of *Alice's Adventures in Wonderland*, Lewis Carroll: *If you don't know where you're going, any road will get you there.* This insight applies to business as well: Without a set goal, a company is like a ship without a rudder.

Setting a goal involves two decisions: identifying the *focus* of the company's actions and defining the performance *benchmarks* to be achieved. These two aspects of setting the goal are discussed in more detail below.

Defining the Goal Focus

The focus identifies the key criterion for a company's success; it is the metric defining the desired outcome of the company's activities. Based on their focus, goals can be monetary or strategic:

- **Monetary goals** involve monetary outcomes such as net income, profit margins, earnings per share, and return on investment. Monetary goals are the primary performance metric for for-profit enterprises.

- **Strategic goals** involve nonmonetary outcomes that are of strategic importance to the company. Common strategic goals include growing sales volume, creating brand awareness, increasing social welfare, enhancing the corporate culture, and facilitating employee recruitment and retention. Strategic goals are the main performance metric for nonprofit enterprises as well as for offerings of for-profit companies that have the primary function of supporting other, profit-generating offerings. For example, Amazon might break even (or even operate at a loss) in making, promoting, and distributing some of its Kindle devices and yet view them as a strategically important platform for its retail business.

Monetary goals and strategic goals are not mutually exclusive: A company might aim to achieve certain strategic goals with an otherwise profitable offering, and a strategically important offering might contribute to the company's bottom line. In fact, long-term financial planning must always include a strategic component in addition to setting monetary goals. In the same vein, long-term strategic planning must always include a financial component that articulates how achieving a particular strategic goal will translate into financial benefits.

Companies are increasingly looking beyond sales revenue and profit to consider the legal, ethical, social, and environmental effects of marketing activities and programs. For example, when Ben Cohen and Jerry Greenfield founded Ben & Jerry's, they divided the traditional financial bottom line into a "double bottom line" that also measured the environmental impact of their products and processes. That later expanded into a "triple bottom line" — people, planet, and profits — to reflect the societal impact of the firm's entire range of business activities.

Defining Performance Benchmarks

Performance benchmarks outline the quantitative and temporal criteria for reaching the goal. Consequently, there are two types of performance benchmarks that work in concert to define the company goal:

- **Quantitative benchmarks** define the specific milestones to be achieved by the company with respect to its focal goal. For example, goals such as "increase market share by 2%," "increase retention rates by 12%," and "improve the effectiveness of marketing expenditures by 15%" articulate benchmarks that quantify the set goal. Quantitative benchmarks can be expressed in either relative terms (e.g., increase market share by 20%) or absolute terms (e.g., achieve annual sales of one million units).

- **Temporal benchmarks** identify the time frame for achieving a particular milestone. Setting a timeline for achieving a goal is a key decision because the strategy adopted to implement these goals is often contingent on the time horizon. The goal of maximizing next quarter's profits will likely require a different strategy and tactics than the goal of maximizing long-term profitability.

Overall, the company goal must address three main questions: *what* is to be achieved (goal focus), *how much* should be achieved (quantitative benchmark), and *when* should it be achieved (temporal benchmark). To illustrate, a company might set the goal of generating net income (goal focus) of $50 million (quantitative benchmark) in one year (temporal benchmark). Answers to these questions capture the essence of the company's goal and serve as a beacon that guides the company's strategy and tactics.

Setting Market Objectives

Based on their focus, goals vary in their level of generality. Some goals reflect outcomes that are more fundamental than others. Therefore, a company's goals can be represented as a hierarchy headed by a company's ultimate goal, which is implemented through a set of more specific goals referred to as market objectives.

Unlike the ultimate goal, which is typically defined in terms of a company-focused outcome, *market objectives* delineate specific changes in the behavior of the relevant market factors — customers, the company, collaborators, competitors, and context — that will enable the company to achieve its ultimate goal. The different types of market objectives are illustrated in Figure 4 and outlined below.

Figure 4. Market Goals and Objectives

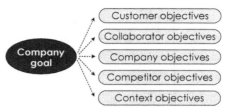

- **Customer objectives** aim to change the behavior of target customers (e.g., increasing purchase frequency, switching from a competitive product, or making a first-time purchase in a product category) in a way that will enable the company to achieve its ultimate goal. To illustrate, the company goal of increasing net revenues can be associated with the more specific customer objective of increasing the frequency with which customers repurchase the offering. Because the customers are the principal source of a company's revenues and profits, a company's ultimate goal typically involves a customer-focused objective.

- **Collaborator objectives** aim to elicit changes in the behavior of the company's collaborators, such as providing greater promotional support, better pricing terms, greater systems integration, and extended distribution coverage. To illustrate, the company goal of increasing net revenues can be associated with the more specific collaborator objective of increasing the shelf space available for the offering in distribution channels.

- **Company (internal) objectives** aim to elicit changes in the company's own actions, such as improving product and service quality, reducing the cost of goods sold, improving the effectiveness of the company's marketing actions, and streamlining research-and-development costs. For example, the company goal of increasing net revenues can be associated with the more specific internal objective of increasing the effectiveness and cost efficiency of its communication.

- **Competitive objectives** aim to change the behavior of the company's competitors. Such actions might involve creating barriers to entry, securing proprietary access to scarce resources, and circumventing a price war. For example, the company goal of increasing net revenues can be associated with limiting competitors' access to target customers by creating exclusive distribution agreements with retailers serving these markets.

- **Context objectives** are less common and usually implemented by larger companies that have the resources to influence the economic, business, technological, sociocultural, regulatory, and/or physical context in which the company operates. For example, a company might lobby the government to adopt regulations that will favorably affect the company by offering tax benefits and subsidies, and impose import duties on competitors' products.

Defining market objectives is important because without a change in the behavior of the relevant market entities, the company's ultimate goal is unlikely to be achieved. Indeed, if there is no change in any of the five market factors (the Five Cs), the company is unlikely to make progress toward its goals. To illustrate, a company's ultimate goal of increasing net income by $100 million by the end of the fourth quarter can involve different objectives. A customer-specific objective might be to increase market share by 10% by the end of the fourth quarter. A collaborator-related objective might involve securing 45% of the distribution outlets by the end of the fourth quarter. And a company's internal objective might call for lowering the cost of goods sold by 25% by the end of the fourth quarter.

Defining marketing objectives involves prioritizing different alternatives in order to determine the activities most likely to help the company achieve its ultimate goal. Prioritizing objectives is important because it enables the company to better manage resources by bringing into focus the activities that are most likely to accelerate the company's progress toward its ultimate goal. Prioritizing objectives also helps align potentially conflicting activities associated with these objectives. Indeed, while some objectives tend to complement one another (e.g., increasing market share and increasing the number of distribution channels), others might involve activities with conflicting outcomes. For example, increasing market share while decreasing marketing expenses could be challenging because increasing market share typically involves greater investment in various promotional activities.[20] In this context, prioritizing alternative objectives and honing in on the most important ones can help the company articulate the best course of action to achieve its ultimate goal.

Developing the Strategy and Tactics

The strategy and the tactics define the business model of an offering. The processes of developing the market strategy and designing the tactics were discussed in detail in Chapter 2. Consequently, this section offers only a brief outline of these two concepts.

Developing the Strategy

The strategy delineates the value created by the company in a particular market. It is defined by the company's *target market* and its *value proposition* for this market.

- The **target market** defines the market in which the company aims to create value. It is defined by five factors: *customers* whose needs the company aims to fulfill, *competitors* that aim to fulfill the same needs of the same target customers, *collaborators* that work with the company to fulfill the needs of customers, the *company* managing the offering, and the *context* in which the company operates.

- The **value proposition** reflects the benefits and costs of the company's offering that define the value the company aims to create in the target market. The value proposition has three components—*customer value*, *collaborator value*, and *company value*—which reflect the value created by the company for these market entities. The development of a value proposition is often complemented with the development of a *positioning* that defines the key benefit(s) of the company's offering in a competitive context.

Designing the Tactics

Tactics—also referred to as the *marketing mix*—define the actual offering that the company introduces in the target market. The tactics logically follow from the company's strategy and reflect the way the company will make this strategy a market reality. The tactics delineate the seven attributes that define the company's offering: *product, service, brand, price, incentives, communication,* and *distribution*. Working in concert, these attributes define the value that the company's offering creates in the target market.

Defining the Implementation

Marketing implementation is the process that turns a company's strategy and tactics into actions and ensures they accomplish the plan's stated goals and objectives. A brilliant marketing plan counts for little if not implemented properly. As the French writer Antoine de Saint-Exupéry succinctly put it: *A goal without a plan is just a wish.*

Implementation directly follows from the company's strategy and tactics, such that each strategic decision is translated into a set of tactics, which are then translated into an implementation plan. In this context, implementation defines the activities that aim to make the business model a reality. Implementation involves three key components: *developing the company resources, developing the offering,* and *commercial deployment of the offering.*

Developing the Company Resources

Resource development aims to secure the competencies and assets necessary to implement the company's offering. Resource development can involve developing *business facilities* such as manufacturing, service, and technology infrastructure; ensuring the availability of reliable *suppliers*; recruiting, training, and retaining *skilled employees*; developing relevant *products, services,* and *brands* that can serve as a platform for the new offering; acquiring the *know-how* needed to develop, produce, and manage the offering; developing *communication* and *distribution* channels to inform target customers about the company's offering and deliver the offering to them; and securing the *capital* necessary to develop these resources. The resources necessary to succeed in the chosen market are discussed in more detail in Chapter 6.

Developing the Market Offering

Offering development involves the processes that transform the company's strategy and tactics into an actual good that is communicated and delivered to the company's target customers. Offering development involves managing the flow of information, materials, labor, and money in order to create the offering that the company will deploy in the market. Thus, offering development involves designing the *product* (procurement, inbound logistics, and production) and *service* (installation, support, and repair activities); building the *brand*; setting retail and wholesale *prices* and *incentives* (coupons, rebates, and price discounts); designing the means of *communication* (message, media, and creative execution); and setting the channels of *distribution* (warehousing, order fulfillment, and transportation).

Commercial Deployment

Commercial deployment includes activities such as setting the timing of the offering's market launch, defining the resources involved in the launch, and determining the scale of the launch. It logically follows the process of developing an offering by delineating the process of bringing the offering to market. Commercial deployment can be selective, initially focusing on specific markets in order to assess the market reaction to the offering, or it can involve a large-scale rollout across all target markets. In cases of selective commercial deployment, the marketing plan defines the primary market in which the offering will first be introduced and outlines the key activities associated with the launch of the offering. The marketing plan further identifies the timing and the processes involved in expanding the offering beyond the primary market so that it can reach all target customers and achieve its full market potential.

Identifying Controls

The constantly changing business environment requires companies to be agile and continuously realign their actions with market realities. Most companies strive to make their marketing operations more effective and cost efficient and to better assess the return on their marketing investment in order to ensure that they are on the right track to achieve their goals. Controls help a company ensure that its actions are aligned with its strategy and tactics in a way that will enable the company to achieve its ultimate goal.

The primary function of controls is to inform the company whether to proceed with its current course of action, reevaluate its actions and realign the underlying strategy and tactics, or abandon its current course of action and develop a different offering that better reflects the current market realities. Controls involve two key components: *evaluating the company's performance* and *monitoring the market environment*.

Evaluating Performance

Evaluating performance involves tracking the company's progress toward its goal, as defined by its focus and benchmarks. Evaluating a company's monetary performance can involve assessing the top line by comparing the desired and actual sales revenue outcomes, as well as assessing the bottom line and identifying inefficiencies in its operations.

Performance evaluation can reveal one of two outcomes: adequate goal progress or a discrepancy (performance gap) between the desired and the actual performance. When the progress is adequate, the company can stay the course with its current action plan. In contrast, when performance evaluation reveals a gap whereby a company's performance lags behind the benchmarks set, the company's action plan must be modified to put the company back on track toward achieving its goal.

Monitoring the Environment

Monitoring the environment aims to identify market opportunities and threats. It enables the company to take advantage of new opportunities such as favorable government regulations, a decrease in competition, or an increase in consumer demand. It also alerts a company of impending threats such as unfavorable government regulations, an increase in competition, or a decline in customer demand.

Once the key opportunities and threats have been identified, the current action plan can be modified to take advantage of the opportunities and counteract the impact of threats. Because it aims to align a company's actions with the changes in the market in which it operates, monitoring the environment in which the company operates is a prerequisite for business agility and a necessary condition for sustainability of the company's value-creation model.

The Marketing Plan

The marketing plan is the central instrument for directing and coordinating a company's marketing efforts. It is a tangible outcome of a company's strategic planning process, outlining the company's ultimate goal and the ways in which it aims to achieve this goal. The function of the marketing plan, its key principles, structure, and updating process are outlined in the following sections.

The Purpose of the Marketing Plan

The ultimate purpose of the marketing plan is to guide a company's actions. To this end, the marketing plan must effectively communicate the company goal and proposed course of action to relevant stakeholders: company employees, collaborators, shareholders, and investors.

Because marketing covers only one aspect of a company's business activities, the marketing plan is narrower in scope than the business plan. In addition to focusing on the marketing aspect of the company's activities, the business plan addresses financial, operations, human resources, and technological aspects of the company's offerings. The marketing plan may include a brief overview of other aspects of the business plan, but only to the extent they are related to the marketing strategy and tactics.

The marketing plan serves three main functions: (1) delineate the company's goal and proposed course of action, (2) inform the relevant stakeholders about this goal and course of action, and (3) persuade the relevant decision makers of the viability of the goal and the proposed course of action. These functions are covered in more detail below.

- **Delineate the company goal and proposed course of action.** Because marketing plans are written documents, they often force managers to be specific in their analysis and articulate in greater detail different aspects of the proposed action. This greater level of detail enables the marketing plan to serve as a guide for tactical decisions such as product development, service management, branding, pricing, sales promotions, communication, and distribution. In addition to articulating the proposed course of action, the marketing plan can identify the composition of the team managing the offering and the allocation of responsibilities among individual team members.

- **Inform relevant stakeholders of the goal and proposed course of action.** By providing uniform information to all stakeholders, the marketing plan helps ensure that all relevant parties have an accurate understanding of the specifics of the offering. Because most offerings are developed, promoted, and distributed in collaboration with external entities, having a common understanding of the primary goal and the proposed course of action to achieve that goal is essential for an offering's success.

- **"Sell" the proposed goal and course of action.** An important and often overlooked function of the marketing plan is to persuade the relevant stakeholders of the viability of the set goal and the identified course of action. The marketing plan can be the key factor in senior management's decision to proceed with the proposed course of action and the primary driver of collaborators' decision to support the company's offering.

The overarching goal of the marketing plan is to inform relevant stakeholders about the company's action plan and ensure that their actions are consistent with the company's ultimate goal.

The Key Principles of Developing a Marketing Plan

Most marketing plans suffer from a common problem. Rather than fulfilling their vital mission of steering a company's actions to attain a stated goal, they are frequently written merely to fulfill the requirement of having a document filed in the company archives. As a result, instead of outlining a meaningful course of action, marketing plans often comprise exhaustive analyses of marginally relevant issues and laundry lists of activities without delineating whether and how these activities will benefit the company. This lack of internal logic and cohesiveness often leads to haphazard actions that fall far short of helping the company achieve its ultimate goal.

To be effective, the marketing plan must outline a sound goal, propose a viable action plan to achieve this goal, and communicate this goal and action plan to the target audience. To this end, the marketing plan must be *actionable, relevant, clear,* and *succinct.*

- **Actionable.** The marketing plan should be specific enough to guide the company's activities. It must delineate the proposed changes in the product, service, brand, price, incentives, communication, and distribution aspects of the company's offering. In addition, it also must present the specific time frame for implementing these changes and specify the entities responsible for implementing them.

- **Relevant.** The marketing plan should clearly articulate the company goal and specific objectives and delineate a course of action aimed at achieving the stated goal and objectives. To this end, the marketing plan must link each proposed activity with an objective and clearly articulate how this activity will benefit the company. Without relating the company actions to its goal and objectives, a marketing plan can become a list of unrelated activities that add little or no value to the company's ability to achieve its goal and can even end up being counterproductive by diverting resources from more meaningful activities.

- **Clear.** The marketing plan aims to inform the relevant stakeholders about a company's action plan and convince them of the viability of the proposed action. Therefore, the marketing plan should clearly articulate the goal the company aims to achieve and delineate the essence of the proposed action. Because the marketing plan contains information concerning different aspects of the proposed action—its goal, strategy, tactics, implementation, and metrics for evaluating its performance—this information must be presented in a systematic manner that underscores the logic of the proposed course of action. The clarity of a manager's thought process is reflected in the organization of the marketing plan: Streamlined marketing plans indicate streamlined business thinking.

- **Succinct.** Most marketing plans suffer from a common problem: They are unnecessarily long and filled with marginally relevant information. Managers developing such plans are often driven by the misguided notion that the length of the plan reflects the depth of thinking about the proposed course of action and, hence, that longer marketing plans are inherently more viable than shorter ones. While it is true that the length of the marketing plan is sometimes used as an indicator of broader analysis and deeper thinking, shorter plans are often more useful than longer ones. Indeed, in an environment where managers are overwhelmed with a plethora of company-specific and market-related information, streamlined marketing plans help focus managers' attention on what really matters by underscoring the key aspects of the proposed course of action. When it comes to writing marketing plans, it is often the case that *less is more.*

Following the above four principles—actionability, relevance, clarity, and conciseness—can help the company ensure that its marketing plan will effectively guide its market actions and enable the company to reach its strategic goals.

The Structure of the Marketing Plan

Most marketing plans share a common structure: They start with an executive summary, followed by a situation overview; they then set a goal, formulate a value-creation strategy, delineate the tactical aspects of the offering, articulate a plan to implement the offering's tactics, define a set of control measures to monitor the offering's progress toward its goals, and conclude with a set of relevant exhibits. The key components of the marketing plan and the main decisions underlying each individual component are illustrated in Figure 5 and summarized below.

Figure 5. The Marketing Plan

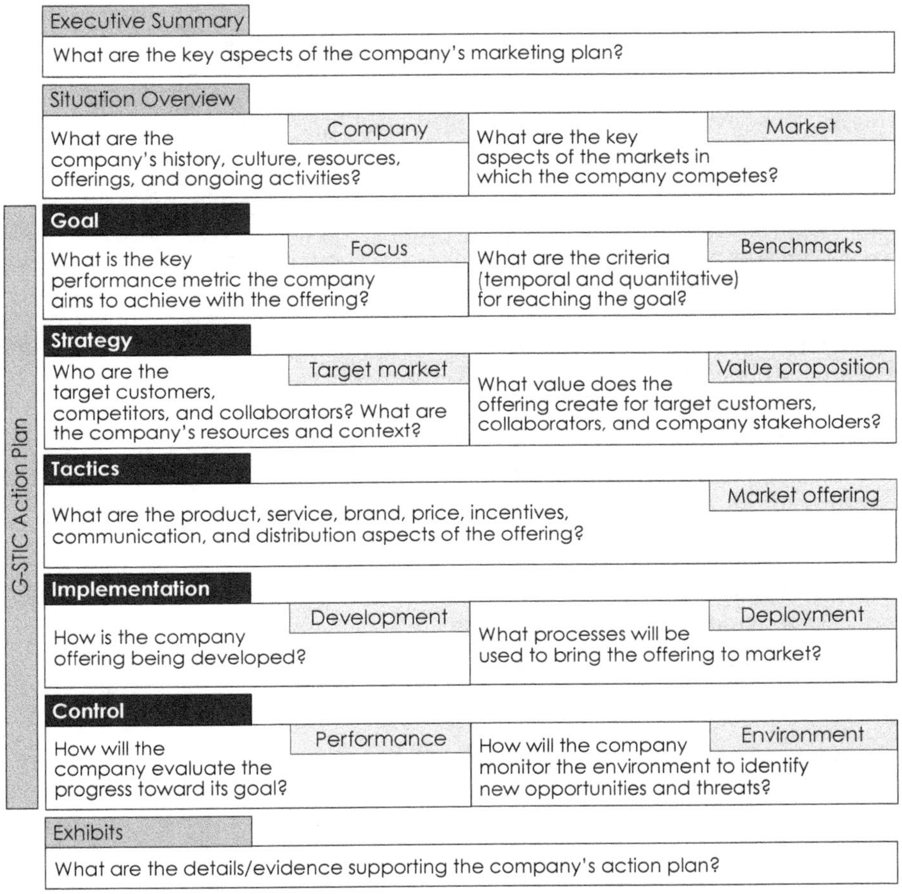

- The **executive summary** is the "elevator pitch" for the marketing plan—a streamlined and succinct overview of the company's goal and the proposed course of action. The typical executive summary is one or two pages long, outlining the key issue faced by the company (an opportunity, a threat, or a performance gap) and the proposed action plan.

- The **situation overview** section of the marketing plan provides an overall evaluation of the company and the environment in which it operates, and identifies the markets in which it competes and/or will compete. Accordingly, the situation overview involves two sections: (1) the *company overview*, which outlines the company's history, culture, resources (competencies and assets), and its portfolio of offerings, and (2) the *market overview*, which outlines the markets in which the company operates and/or could potentially target.

- The **G-STIC** section is the core of the marketing plan. It identifies (1) the *goal* the company aims to achieve; (2) the offering's *strategy*, which defines its target market and value proposition; (3) the offering's *tactics*, which define the product, service, brand, price, incentives, communication, and distribution aspects of the offering; (4) the *implementation* aspects of executing an offering's strategy and tactics; and (5) *control* procedures that evaluate the company's performance and analyze the environment in which it operates.

- **Exhibits** help streamline the logic of the marketing plan by separating the less important and/or more technical aspects of the plan into a distinct section in the form of tables, charts, and appendices.

The ultimate goal of the marketing plan is to guide a company's actions. Accordingly, the core of the marketing plan is defined by the key elements of the G-STIC framework delineating the company's goal and the proposed course of action. The other elements of the marketing plan—the executive summary, situation overview, and exhibits—aim to facilitate an understanding of the logic underlying the plan and provide specifics of the proposed course of action. An outline of the key components of a marketing plan following the G-STIC framework is given at the end of this chapter and detailed marketing plan examples are outlined in Appendix C at the end of this book.

In addition to developing an overall marketing plan, companies often develop more specialized plans that can include a product development plan, service management plan, brand management plan, sales plan, promotion plan, and communication plan. Some of these plans can, in turn, encompass even more specific plans. For example, the communication plan often comprises a series of activity-specific plans such as an advertising plan, public relations plan, and social media plan. The ultimate success of each of these individual plans depends on the degree to which they are aligned with the company's overall marketing plan.

Updating the Marketing Plan

Once developed, marketing plans need updating in order to remain relevant. Marketing management is an iterative process in which the company executes its strategy and tactics while simultaneously monitoring the outcome and modifying the process accordingly. Continual monitoring and adjustment enable the company to assess its progress toward the set goals as well as take into account the changes in the market in which it operates. The dynamic nature of marketing management is ingrained in the G-STIC framework, where the control aspect of planning (the "C" in the G-STIC framework) is explicitly designed to provide the company with feedback on the effectiveness of its actions and the relevant changes in the target market.

Updating a marketing plan involves modifying the company's current course of action and can include the need to reevaluate the current goal, redesign the existing strategy (identify new target markets, and modify the overall value proposition of the offering for customers, collaborators, and the company), change the tactics (improve the product, enhance the service, reposition the brand, modify the price, introduce new incentives, streamline communication, and introduce new channels of distribution), streamline the implementation, and develop alternative controls.

There are two main reasons for updating the marketing plan: to *close performance gaps* and to *respond to changes in the target market*. These two reasons are discussed in more detail below.

Closing Performance Gaps

Performance gaps involve a discrepancy between a company's desired and actual performance on a key metric defined by the company's goal, such as net income, profit margins, and sales revenues. Performance gaps typically stem from three main sources: *incomplete information* about the target market, *logic flaws* in the marketing plan, and *implementation errors* that involve poor execution of a viable marketing plan.

- **Incomplete information.** When developing the marketing plan, managers rarely have all the necessary information at their fingertips. It is often the case that, despite the voluminous amount of information accumulated by the company, certain strategically important pieces of information—competitive intelligence, technological developments, and future government regulations—are not readily available. As a result, managers must fill in the information gaps by making assumptions. Updating the plan to reduce the uncertainty contained in such assumptions and increasing the accuracy of the information that serves as the basis for the company's marketing plan can bolster the plan's effectiveness.

- **Logic flaws.** Another common source of performance gaps is the presence of logic flaws in the design of the marketing plan. For example, the proposed strategy might be inconsistent with the set goal, which means an otherwise viable strategy might not produce desired results. In the same vein, the offering's tactics might be inconsistent with the desired strategy, whereby product attributes might not create value for target customers, the price might be too high, and/or communication and distribution channels might be inadequate. The presence of logic flaws in the marketing plan necessitates revising the plan to eliminate any inconsistencies in the ways the company aims to create market value.

- **Implementation errors.** Performance gaps can also stem from implementation errors involving poor execution of an otherwise viable marketing plan. This type of error occurs because managers do not adhere to the actions prescribed by the marketing plan (e.g., because they are unfamiliar with the plan), because their (erroneous) intuition based on prior experience contradicts the proposed course of action, or because of lack of discipline (often imbued in a company's culture) to systematically implement the agreed-on marketing plan. The presence of implementation errors calls for revising the process of managing the offering and reevaluating the relevant personnel.

Responding to Market Changes

Market changes involve changes in one or more of the Five Cs: (1) changes in target customers' demographics, buying power, needs, and preferences; (2) changes in the competitive environment, such as a new competitive entry, price cuts, launch of an aggressive advertising campaign, and expanded distribution; (3) changes in the collaborator environment, such as a threat of backward integration from the distribution channel, increased trade margins, and consolidation among retailers; (4) changes in the company, such as the loss of strategic assets and competencies; and (5) changes in the market context, such as an economic recession, the development of a new technology, and the introduction of new regulations.

To illustrate, in response to the change in the needs and preferences of its *customers*, many fast-food restaurants, including McDonald's, redefined their offerings to include healthier options. To respond to the new type of *competition* from online retailers, many traditional brick-and-mortar retailers—such as Walmart, Macy's, Barnes & Noble, and Best Buy—redefined their business models and became multichannel retailers. In the same vein, many manufacturers redefined their product lines to include lower tier offerings in response to their *collaborators'* (retailers) widespread adoption of private labels. The development or acquisition of *company* assets, such as patents and proprietary technologies, can call for redefining the underlying business models in virtually any industry. Finally, changes in *context*, such as the ubiquity of mobile communication, e-commerce, and social media, have disrupted extant value-creation processes, forcing companies to redefine their business models.

To succeed, the ways in which a company creates market value must evolve with the changes in the market in which it operates. A number of formerly successful business models have been made obsolete by the changing environment. Companies that fail to adapt their business models and market plans to reflect the new market reality tend to fade away, their businesses engulfed by companies with superior business models better equipped to create market value. The key to market success is not only generating a viable market plan but also honing the ability to adapt this plan to changes in the market.

Conducting a Marketing Audit

A marketing audit is an in-depth examination of the marketing aspect of an offering or the entire company in order to identify overlooked opportunities and problem areas and propose a course of action to strengthen the company's performance. An effective marketing audit is defined by four key characteristics: It must be *systematic, comprehensive, periodic,* and *unbiased.*

- **Systematic.** The marketing audit is a methodical examination of the environment in which the organization operates, its marketing objectives and strategies, and its specific activities. To this end, the marketing audit follows the G-STIC approach and analyzes the soundness of the company's goals, strategy, tactics, implementation, and controls. Accordingly, the marketing audit can identify problems and opportunities at each step of the design and implementation of the marketing plan and incorporate them into a meaningful action plan.

- **Comprehensive.** The marketing audit involves all key marketing activities of a business rather than being focused on a particular marketing activity such as pricing, communication, and distribution. Although audits examining specific aspects of a company's offering are useful, they might not be able to accurately capture the cause-and-effect relationships that drive the company's performance. For example, low sales volume could stem from a variety of factors including inferior company products, inadequate pricing, and limited distribution. A comprehensive audit can help locate the actual source of problems and recommend effective solutions for addressing these problems.

- **Periodic.** Many firms begin marketing audits only when confronted with a problem, often defined in terms of the company's inability to reach its goals. This approach has two main drawbacks. First, focusing only on existing problems fails to identify the potential issues early. Instead, problems are detected only when they have had a negative impact large enough to be noticed. Second, and more important, focusing only on problems might make the company overlook promising opportunities that could represent future areas for growth.

- **Unbiased.** Marketing audits tend to be more beneficial when conducted by an external entity since self-audits, in which managers rate their own operations, can be overly subjective and might fail to identify problems that would be readily apparent to an impartial observer. Even when managers strive to be impartial, internal assessments might end up being biased, reflecting managers' own views, theories, and motives. In this context, third-party auditors can bring the necessary objectivity, as well as cross-category and cross-industry experience, without being distracted by day-to-day management tasks.

The organization of the marketing audit in many ways resembles the organization of the marketing plan. The key difference is that while the marketing plan is directed forward and charts a course of action that the company should undertake, the marketing audit is directed at the company's past, present, and future. It examines the company's current and past performance in order to ensure the right course for the future. Because it follows the organization of the marketing plan, the marketing audit follows the G-STIC framework and comprises five key components: *goal audit, strategy audit, tactics audit, implementation audit,* and *controls audit.* An outline of the key components of a marketing audit based on the G-STIC framework is given at the end of this chapter.

SUMMARY

Marketing planning and management can occur on two levels. They can focus on analyzing, planning, and managing the company (or a specific business unit within the company) or, alternatively, they can focus on analyzing, planning, and managing one or more of the company's offerings.

A key aspect of company planning and management involves defining the company culture, values, mission, and vision. Company *culture* reflects the shared values, beliefs, norms, and experiences that guide the actions of an organization and define its character. A company's *core values* are the deeply ingrained moral principles that guide all its actions. A company's *mission* is a clear, concise, and enduring goal that provides company employees and management with a shared sense of purpose, direction, and opportunity. Finally, a company's *vision* defines what the company will look like in the future.

Company planning and management also involve assessing the company's market position (e.g., using SWOT analysis), and, ultimately, developing a strategy to strengthen each business unit's ability to create market value.

From the point of view of designing a particular offering, marketing planning is a process defined by five main steps: setting a *goal*, developing the *strategy*, designing the *tactics*, defining the *implementation* plan, and identifying the *control* metrics to measure progress toward the set goal. These five steps comprise the G-STIC framework, which is the backbone of market planning.

The *goal* identifies the ultimate criterion for success that guides all company marketing activities. Setting a goal involves identifying the *focus* of the company's actions and defining the specific quantitative and temporal performance *benchmarks* to be achieved. A company's ultimate goal is translated into a series of specific market objectives that stipulate the market changes that must occur in order for the company to achieve its ultimate goal.

The *strategy* delineates the value created by the company in a particular market, and is defined by the company's target market and its value proposition for this market. The *target market* defines the offering's target customers, collaborators, company, competitors, and context (the Five Cs). The *value proposition* specifies the value that an offering aims to create for the relevant market entities—target customers, the company, and its collaborators.

The *tactics* outline a set of specific activities employed to execute a given strategy. The tactics define the key attributes of the company's offering: product, service, brand, price, incentives, communication, and distribution. These seven tactics are the means that managers have at their disposal to execute a company's strategy.

The *implementation* outlines the logistics of executing the company's strategy and tactics, and involves developing the resources necessary to implement the company's offering, developing the actual offering that will be introduced in the market, and deploying the offering in the target market.

The *control* delineates the criteria for evaluating the company's goal progress and articulates a process for analyzing the changes in the environment in which the company operates in order to align the action plan with market realities.

The *marketing plan* can be formalized as a written document that communicates the proposed course of action to relevant entities: company employees, stakeholders, and collaborators. The core of a company's marketing plan is the G-STIC framework, which is complemented by an executive summary, a situation overview, and a set of relevant exhibits. To be effective, the marketing plan must be actionable, relevant, clear, and succinct. Once developed, marketing plans must be updated to remain relevant. To ensure that its plan is adequately implemented, a company must periodically conduct marketing audits to identify overlooked opportunities and problem areas and recommend a plan of action to improve the company's marketing performance.

MARKETING INSIGHT: DEVELOPING A MARKETING PLAN

There are two types of marketing plans: plans for launching a new offering and plans for managing an existing offering. Because these two types of plans share a similar structure, the template shown here applies to both cases. The main text reflects an outline of a marketing plan for launching a new offering, and the text in square brackets indicates the additional information that needs to be included when developing a plan for managing an existing offering. Detailed examples of marketing plans using this template are given in Appendix C at the end of this book.

Executive Summary

Provide a brief overview of the situation, the company's goal, and the proposed course of action.

Situation Overview

Provide an overview of the situation—current/potential customers, collaborators, competitors, and context—in which the company operates and identify relevant opportunities and threats. [Provide an overview of the company's progress toward its current goals. Highlight the recent changes in the market, such as changes in buyer preferences, a new competitive entry, and a change in the regulatory environment.]

Goal

Identify the company's primary goal and market-specific objectives.

- *Primary Goal.* Identify the company's ultimate goal by defining its focus and key performance benchmarks. [State the company's current progress toward this goal.]
- *Market Objectives.* Identify the relevant customer, collaborator, company, competitive, and context objectives that will facilitate achieving the primary goal. Define the focus and key benchmarks for each objective. [State the company's current progress toward each objective.]

Strategy: Target Market

Identify the target market in which the company will launch its new offering. [Underscore the key changes in the target market.]

- *Customers.* Define the need(s) to be fulfilled by the offering and identify the profile of customers with such needs. [Identify any recent changes in customer needs/profile.]
- *Collaborators.* Identify the key collaborators (suppliers, channel members, and communication partners) and their strategic goals. [Identify any recent changes in collaborators.]
- *Company.* Define the business unit responsible for the offering, the relevant personnel, and key stakeholders. Outline the company's core competencies and strategic assets, its current product line, and market position. [Identify any recent changes in the company's core competencies and strategic assets, its current product line, and market position.]
- *Competitors.* Identify the competitive offerings that provide similar benefits to target customers and collaborators. [Underscore any recent changes in the competitive environment.]
- *Context.* Evaluate the relevant economic, technological, sociocultural, regulatory, and physical context. [Identify any recent changes in the context.]

Strategy: Value Proposition

Define the offering's value proposition for target customers, collaborators, and the company.

- *Customer value proposition.* Define the offering's value proposition, positioning strategy, and positioning statement for target customers. [Highlight the proposed changes in the customer value proposition.]
- *Collaborator value proposition.* Define the offering's value proposition, positioning strategy, and positioning statement for collaborators. [Highlight the proposed changes in the collaborator value proposition.]
- *Company value proposition.* Outline the offering's value proposition, positioning strategy, and positioning statement for company stakeholders and personnel. [Highlight the proposed changes in the company value proposition.]

Tactics

Outline the key attributes of the market offering. [Highlight the proposed changes in tactics.]

- *Product.* Define relevant product attributes. [Highlight the proposed product changes.]
- *Service.* Identify relevant service attributes. [Highlight the proposed service changes.]
- *Brand.* Determine the key brand attributes. [Highlight the proposed changes to the brand.]
- *Price.* Identify the price(s) at which the offering is provided to customers and collaborators. [Highlight the proposed price changes.]
- *Incentives.* Define the incentives offered to customers, collaborators, and company employees. [Highlight the proposed changes to incentives.]
- *Communication.* Identify the manner in which the key aspects of the offering are communicated to target customers, collaborators, and company employees and stakeholders. [Highlight the proposed changes to communication.]
- *Distribution.* Describe the manner in which the offering is delivered to target customers and collaborators. [Highlight the proposed changes to the distribution.]

Implementation

Define the specifics of implementing the company's offering. [Highlight the proposed implementation changes.]

- *Resource development.* Identify the key resources needed to implement the marketing plan and outline a process for developing/acquiring deficient resources. [Highlight the proposed changes in the current resource-development approach.]

- *Offering development.* Outline the processes for developing the market offering. [Highlight the proposed changes to the current process of developing the offering.]

- *Commercial deployment.* Delineate the process for bringing the offering to target customers. [Highlight the proposed changes in the current market-deployment approach.]

Control

Identify the metrics used to measure the offering's performance and monitor the environment in which the company operates. [Highlight the proposed changes in the controls.]

- *Performance evaluation.* Define the criteria for evaluating the offering's performance and progress toward the set goals. [Highlight the proposed changes in the metrics used to evaluate performance.]

- *Analysis of the environment.* Identify metrics for evaluating the environment in which the company operates and outline the processes for modifying the plan to accommodate changes in the environment. [Highlight the proposed changes in the metrics used to evaluate the environment and modify the action plan.]

Exhibits

Provide additional information to support specific aspects of the marketing plan. This information may include target market data (e.g., industry overview, company overview, and customer trend analyses); financial calculations (e.g., break-even analysis, best/worst case scenario analysis, and customer value analysis); details pertaining to the marketing mix (e.g., product specifications, communication plan, and distribution structure); implementation (e.g., an overview of the processes of developing and deploying the offering); and control (e.g., performance metrics and analysis of the environment).

MARKETING INSIGHT: CONDUCTING A MARKETING AUDIT

A marketing audit is an in-depth examination of a company's marketing activities in order to identify overlooked opportunities and problem areas and recommend a plan of action to improve the company's marketing performance. The marketing audit follows the G-STIC framework and comprises five key components: *goal audit, strategy audit, tactics audit, implementation audit,* and *controls audit.* These components of the marketing audit are outlined below.

Goal Audit

- *Goal focus.* Does the company have clearly defined performance metrics it aims to achieve? Are these metrics adequate?

- *Performance benchmarks.* Is the company goal defined by a set of quantitative and temporal benchmarks? Are these benchmarks adequate given the company's resources and market conditions?

Strategy Audit: Target Market

- *Customers.* Who are the company's target customers? Do they vary in their needs and behaviors? What are the opportunities and threats associated with these customers? Should the company continue to serve these customers?

- *Collaborators.* Who are the company's collaborators? What are the opportunities and threats associated with these collaborators? Should the company continue to partner with these entities?

- *Competitors.* Who are the company's competitors? What are the threats that these competitors pose to the company? Are there any competitive opportunities that the company could take advantage of?

- *Company.* What resources must the company have in order to create superior value for its target customers? Does the company have these resources? Can the lacking resources (if any) be built/acquired within the time frame defined by the company's goal?

- *Context.* What are the sociocultural, technological, economic, regulatory, and physical aspects of the environment in which the company operates? What are the opportunities and threats associated with each of these contexts?

Strategy Audit: Value Proposition

- *Customer value.* What value does the offering create for target customers? Does it create superior value relative to the competition? How would the likely changes in the target market influence customer value in the short and long run?

- *Collaborator value.* What value does the offering create for collaborators? Does it create superior value relative to the competition? How would the likely changes in the target market influence collaborator value in the short and long run?

- *Company value.* What value does the offering create for company stakeholders? Does it create superior value relative to the alternative offerings the company could develop? How would the likely changes in the target market influence company value in the short and long run?

Tactics Audit

- *Product.* What are the key product attributes of the offering? What value does the product create for target customers, collaborators, and the company? Is this product competitive?

- *Service.* What are the key service attributes of the offering? What value does the service create for target customers, collaborators, and the company? Is this service competitive?

- *Brand.* What are the key brand attributes of the offering? What value does the brand create for target customers, collaborators, and the company? Is this brand viable?

- *Price.* What is the offering's price? What value does it create for target customers, collaborators, and the company? Is this price competitive?

- *Incentives.* What incentives—monetary and nonmonetary—are associated with the offering? What value do they create for target customers, collaborators, and the company? Are these incentives competitive?

- *Communication.* How are target customers, collaborators, and company employees/stakeholders made aware of the offering? What is the communication message, media, and creative execution? Are they adequate given the company's goal, strategy, and tactics?

- *Distribution.* How do target customers and collaborators acquire the offering? What distribution does the company use to deliver the offering to its customers and collaborators? Are these distribution channels adequate given the company's goal, strategy, and tactics?

Implementation Audit

- *Resource development.* What resources—business facilities, suppliers, skilled employees, product/service/brand platforms, know-how, communication/distribution channels, and capital—does the company rely on to implement the offering? Are these resources optimal given the company's goal, strategy, and tactics?

- *Offering development.* What processes does the company use to manage the flow of information, materials, labor, and money to create its offering? Are these processes optimal given the company's goal, strategy, and tactics?

- *Commercial deployment.* How does the company bring its offering to market and how does it manage the offering's performance in the short and long run?

Control Audit

- *Performance evaluation.* What processes and metrics does the company use to measure progress toward its goals? How frequently is the company's performance on these metrics assessed? Are these processes, metrics, and the frequency of their assessment adequate?

- *Monitoring the environment.* What processes and tools does the company use to evaluate the environment in which it operates to identify growth opportunities and threats? How frequently does the company analyze the environment for changes? Are these processes, tools, and the frequency of assessing the environment adequate?

MARKETING INSIGHT: KEY PRODUCT-MANAGEMENT FRAMEWORKS

An important aspect of implementing the marketing plan involves determining the optimal sequence of specific activities prescribed by the marketing plan and the timetable for accomplishing these actions. To this end, managers can benefit from utilizing established approaches to sequencing a company's activities, determining an implementation timeline, and assigning the responsibilities for implementing these activities. Three popular approaches that can facilitate the implementation of the marketing plan are outlined below.

Critical Path Method

The Critical Path Method (CPM) is a mathematically derived algorithm for scheduling project activities. CPM is based on the notion that the implementation of a project is controlled by a relatively small set of activities whose path takes the most time to move through the activity network (i.e., the sequence of activities that adds up to the longest overall duration). The goal of CPM, therefore, is to identify these "critical" activities and use them as the backbone (often referred to as the critical path) of the project schedule. To this end, the CPM calculates the longest path of planned activities from the beginning to the end of the project, as well as the earliest and latest that each activity can begin and end while keeping the project on schedule. This allows other less crucial activities to be planned around the activities composing the critical path.

The process of identifying the critical path is illustrated in Figure 6. Here, specific outcomes are depicted by circles and individual activities are depicted by arrows; the numbers associated with each arrow indicate the duration (e.g., in weeks) of the corresponding activity. Analysis of the relationship among the different outcomes indicates that Outcomes C and D need to be completed prior to achieving the desired Outcome E, Outcomes A and B need to be achieved prior to achieving Outcome C, and Outcome A needs to be achieved prior to achieving Outcome D. Analysis of the time necessary to complete each individual activity further indicates that the longest path through the network is A-C-E (12 weeks). Hence, A-C-E is the critical path that should be used as the backbone for scheduling the remaining activities.

Figure 6. The Critical Path Method

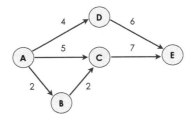

A potential limitation of the CPM model is its reliance on a manager's ability to estimate the interdependence and the relative completion time of the individual activities necessary for completing the project. This limitation of the CPM model is addressed in an alternative approach commonly referred to as the Project Evaluation and Review Technique (PERT), which allows a range of durations to be specified for each activity. Thus, PERT is very similar to CPM in that both models employ the notion of a critical path and involve the same six implementation steps. The key distinction between the two is the manner in which the duration of a given activity is estimated. Unlike CPM, which relies on a single duration estimate, PERT involves calculating a weighted average of three different estimates of the expected completion time (optimistic, most likely, and pessimistic).

Responsibility Assignment Matrix

The Responsibility Assignment Matrix (RAM) is a commonly used approach for linking business processes to the company's organizational infrastructure and assigning project-related activities to specific entities within the organization. RAM outlines the key components of a project and designates the functional role (e.g., project manager, product engineer, salesforce manager) and/or the specific entity responsible for the implementation of each task. The matrix typically lists the key business tasks on the vertical axis and lists the corresponding roles on the horizontal axis (Figure 7). Each role can be performed either by an individual or a team, and each individual/team can play multiple roles.

Figure 7. The Responsibility Assignment Matrix

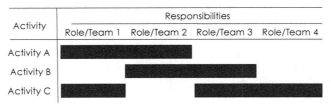

The Responsibility Assignment Matrix is sometimes referred to as RACI, an acronym for the key roles involved in action planning: responsible, accountable, consulted, and informed. Here, *responsible* refers to the entity responsible for completing the task (e.g., product engineer); *accountable* refers to the entity accountable for the accurate and timely completion of the task (e.g., project manager); *consulted* refers to entities that are provided with information about the project and engage in two-way communication (e.g., functional experts such as accounting, legal, and IT departments); and *informed* refers to entities that are kept informed about progress only through one-way communication (e.g., cross-functional teams affected by the project outcome).

Gantt Matrix

The Gantt matrix maps the individual tasks and their timeline in a format that enables a manager to easily identify the optimal sequence and duration of these tasks in the context of the entire project. A popular method of representing the implementation plan, the Gantt matrix uses bars to visually represent the timeline and duration of each individual task. Named after Henry Gantt—an American mechanical engineer and management consultant—this chart typically indicates the start and the finish dates of the key project tasks (Figure 8).

Figure 8. Gantt Matrix

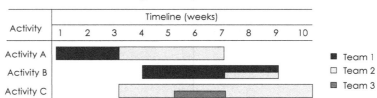

The typical Gantt matrix lists on the vertical axis all the tasks to be performed and lists on the horizontal axis a description of each task (e.g., task specifics, skill level needed to perform the task, and the individual/team assigned to the task); horizontal bars represent the starting time and duration of each task.

PART TWO

UNDERSTANDING THE MARKET

INTRODUCTION

Before you build a better mousetrap,
it helps to know if there are any mice out there.

—Yogi Berra, American professional
baseball player, manager, and coach

Understanding the market in which a company aims to create value is essential for the development of a viable business model and a sound marketing plan. The process of creating market value starts by identifying an unmet customer need and determining the ways in which the company can fulfill this need better than the competition. To develop an offering that creates market value, a manager must conduct research to gather insights into the market in which the company competes.

The following chapters outline the key issues involved in analyzing the market in which the company aims to create value. These issues include understanding how customers derive value from a company's offerings and the ways in which they make purchase decisions as well as defining the processes for gaining market insights. Specifically, the chapters included in this section address two topics: *understanding customers* and *gathering market insights*.

- **Understanding customers** is the starting point for identifying market opportunities and formulating a meaningful marketing strategy. Without understanding the needs customers want to fulfill, the ways in which they evaluate the available alternatives that can fulfill these needs, and the decision process buyers use to choose among these alternatives, a company will find it challenging to develop a successful market offering. The key issues pertaining to understanding customers are discussed in Chapter 4.

- **Gathering market insights** is the key to developing both a viable strategy and a desirable market offering. Marketing research facilitates decision making by providing managers with the relevant information needed to select target markets, design viable offerings that create value in these markets, and implement marketing programs in the most effective and cost-efficient manner. Gathering insights about the market in which the company competes replaces gut-feel choices with evidence-based decisions in which managers supplement their own judgment with market data. The process of gathering market insights is discussed in Chapter 5.

Understanding the market in which the company competes and, specifically, the value drivers that determine the way in which customers make decisions is essential for developing viable market offerings. Market knowledge enables the company to design products and services that deliver customer value in a way that benefits the company as well as its collaborators. It can give the company a leg up on its competitors by enabling it to better align its marketing activities with customer needs and develop an optimal value proposition that benefits all relevant market entities—the company, its customers, and its collaborators.

CHAPTER FOUR

UNDERSTANDING CUSTOMERS

*Human behavior flows from three main
sources: desire, emotion, and knowledge.*

— Plato, Greek philosopher

U nderstanding customer decisions and behavior is the starting point for identifying market opportunities and formulating a company's marketing strategy. Without understanding the needs customers aim to fulfill, the ways in which they evaluate the available alternatives that can fulfill these needs, and the decision processes they use to choose among these alternatives, a company is unlikely to succeed in developing an offering that will be embraced by its target customers. Because we focus on decision processes used by individuals, throughout this chapter we use the terms *customer* and *consumer* interchangeably. In this context, we address the following topics:

- *The Customer Decision Journey* ‖ The decision journey as a process | The decision journey as a social interaction

- *Need Activation* ‖ Understanding customer needs | Customer need states | The dynamics of customer needs

- *Information Search* ‖ Gathering information from external sources | Retrieving information from memory | Levels of involvement in information processing

- *Evaluating Market Offerings* ‖ Understanding the value function | Reference-point dependence | Loss aversion | Diminishing marginal value

- *Choice* ‖ The rational model of choice | The psychology of choice

- *Purchase, Usage, and Repurchase* ‖ From choice to purchase | Usage and satisfaction | The path to repurchase

The discussion of understanding the customer is complemented by an in-depth overview of three additional topics: Maslow's theory of human needs, the process of joint decision making, and decision heuristics and biases.

The Customer Decision Journey

The term *customer decision journey* is used to describe different aspects of customer decisions and behaviors—from initially considering a product or service to purchasing and using it.[1] The intuition behind the decision journey is that people's behavior can be better understood if viewed not as an isolated act but as a sequence of events driven by individuals' desire to fulfill an active need. The customer journey approach takes the perspective of an individual customer to examine how this customer adopts and uses a company's offering. It reflects all customers' experiences in fulfilling a given need.

Understanding the decision journey allows a company to drive growth by aligning its activities with customer needs. This alignment comes from gaining a holistic view of a customer's interactions with an offering and identifying the specific stages and decisions a customer goes through when fulfilling a particular need. Analyzing these stages of the decision process is important because each stage is typically associated with different company goals, involves different company actions, and is measured with different outcome metrics. Only by understanding the customer decision journey can a company optimize a customer's overall experience of the company's offering and successfully manage sales growth.

The Decision Journey as a Process

A customer's decision journey can be defined by six main experiences: *need activation, search, evaluation, choice, purchase, and usage*. The different stages of customer decision processes are illustrated in the *decision journey map* depicted in Figure 1 and outlined in more detail below.

Figure 1. The Decision Journey Map

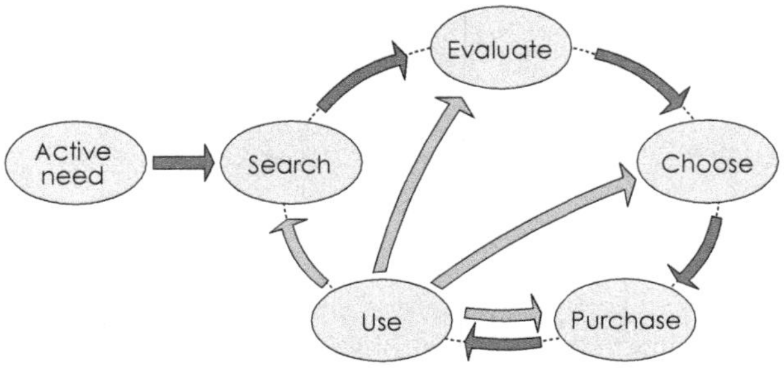

- **Need activation.** People do not aim to fulfill all their needs at all times; rather, at any given moment, they focus on active needs. A need becomes active when individuals are confronted with a gap between the desired and actual state of affairs involving an important aspect of their well-being. Need activation can be triggered by a variety of internal and external factors. For example, a consumer's need for a new car may be activated because a pay raise at work increased this consumer's desire for a more prestigious car. Alternatively, the need might be activated by witnessing a car accident and realizing the importance of a car's safety features. Events leading to the activation of a given need are often referred to as need triggers.

- **Information search.** Once a need has been activated, the consumer often seeks information that is pertinent to deciding how to fulfill that need. This process includes searching for information about the important dimensions (offering attributes) that must be considered, the relative importance of these dimensions, the available options, and the performance of these options on the key dimensions. For example, a consumer who is considering the purchase of a car might seek to identify the key attributes to consider, such as power, safety, fuel efficiency, and style; decide on the relative importance of these attributes; identify the different cars that could potentially fit his needs; and gather information about these cars' performance on the key attributes.

- **Evaluation of the alternatives.** Because in most cases there are multiple options available to choose from, decision makers often evaluate a relatively small subset of options in more detail. This subset, often referred to as a *consideration set*, contains options that decision makers believe best fit their needs. In this context, the consideration stage of the customer decision journey involves two related processes: selection of the more attractive options and rejection of options perceived to be inferior. The size of the consideration set varies depending on the importance of the decision to be made, the number and complexity of the available options, as well as the consumer's own decision-making abilities. The size of the consideration set tends to decrease over time; the initial choice set is often reduced to a subset of two or three options. For example, a consumer seeking to buy a car might reduce his consideration set to five brands, which upon further consideration might be further reduced to two options.

- **Choosing an option.** Following the formation of a consideration set, decision makers single out the option(s) that best meet their needs. When the consideration set does not contain an option that is superior on most dimensions, decision makers must trade off benefits and costs of the different options, meaning that they have to give up the benefits of one attribute in order to gain the benefits of another. For example, when choosing a fuel-efficient car over a more powerful car, a consumer must make a tradeoff and sacrifice performance for better fuel efficiency.

- **Making a purchase.** Customers might not instantly buy offerings they have chosen. Indeed, even though purchases frequently occur soon after a choice is made, choice and purchase can also be temporally distant from one another. For example, a consumer who has chosen a particular car might not immediately purchase it because the need it aims to fulfill is not imminent, because of budgetary constraints, or because the car is not available in the dealerships accessible to this consumer.

- **Using the offering.** Purchase is typically followed by customers using the offering, which involves the actual consumption of the product or service, solving the problems that occur during consumption, and disposing of or ending use of the offering. For example, after purchasing a car, a consumer will drive the car, replace a flat tire, and ultimately, trade in the car for a new one. A customer purchasing a company's offering does not guarantee that the offering will be used in the manner expected by the company. For example, a consumer might be unfamiliar with the features of a newly purchased vehicle and either ignore or misuse some of them.

- **Repurchasing the offering.** Because customers have recurring needs, their interaction with the company's offering is often an iterative process that involves multiple consumer journeys. Based on a customer's prior experience with selecting, buying, and using the offering, this customer might simply repurchase the offering without considering other options or, alternatively, restart the journey by forming a new consideration set, and ultimately making a different purchase decision. For example, a customer leasing a car might replace his current car with a newer model without considering other options or decide to make a fresh start by considering several alternative options available on the market.

The consumer journey does not always occur as a series of sequential steps, as shown in Figure 1. Instead, it is often an iterative process in which individuals go back to update and revise earlier steps. For example, an active need can become less prominent, the search process can be modified and the initial consideration set extended to include options not initially considered, and the criteria used by consumers to evaluate the considered options might evolve. Furthermore, the decision rules for choosing among options might change, the ultimately purchased option might not be the one initially chosen, and the usage experience might force the consumer to return the item and restart the decision process.

It is also important to note that the different stages of the decision process are not always as clearly separated as depicted in Figure 1. For example, the processes of searching for information, evaluating the available options, and choosing the most attractive alternative are often intertwined; selection of a choice strategy might influence the formation of the consideration set and the ways in which different options are evaluated. In the same vein, the choice of an option and the act of purchasing that option might occur simultaneously, as in the case of impulsive purchases.

The sequence in which individuals go through the different stages of the decision process may also vary. For example, even though on most occasions customers have to purchase the offering prior to using it, in some cases, such as with free trials, customers might have the option to experience the offering prior to making a purchase. In such cases, pre-purchase consumption is likely to influence option evaluation and choice. In this context, the decision journey map should be viewed as a generalized representation of the key steps in the decision process rather than as an exact depiction of a specific sequence of steps taken by individuals to reach a decision.

The Decision Journey as a Social Interaction

People do not make decisions in a vacuum. They are influenced by their social environment while simultaneously shaping this environment by sharing their opinions with others. Thus, each stage of a customer's decision journey might be influenced by others, and at each stage customers might influence other customers by sharing their beliefs and experiences. This peer-to-peer communication can inform potential buyers about the offering and its value proposition more effectively than the company's own communication.

Customers share their decision journey for a variety of reasons. Some use their market experience as a context for connecting with others, enabling them to maintain and expand their social connections. Customer communications might also be driven by the desire to dissipate negative emotions associated with a particular product, service, or company, as well as to share the emotions associated with positive experiences. Information sharing can also be driven by the desire to impact the market by rewarding companies that excel in creating superior customer value and punish those who do not. Finally, sharing information relevant to their self-identity can serve as a means of self-expression, allowing customers to declare their preferences and value systems.

People can share their experiences throughout the entire decision journey. For example, consumers might share a problem they are facing in search of recommendations for how to approach the issue at hand. As they shop, consumers might describe their search process, share their consideration set and their evaluations of the considered alternatives, reveal their most preferred option, articulate the criteria for its choice, and inform others about the purchase process. Once they have made a purchase, consumers may continue to share their usage experience and (dis)satisfaction with the offering and share whether/how they intend to repurchase the offering in the future.

In addition to sharing information, customers are also influenced by the information they receive from others. For example, after hearing of a friend's experience on a trip to the Caribbean, a consumer might actively consider taking his own Caribbean vacation. This consumer might then proceed to search for suitable vacation options by asking friends about the best sources for gathering relevant information. While evaluating potential resorts and choosing among them, the consumer might also be influenced by online reviews posted by people who have visited these resorts. Finally, this consumer's actual experience at the resort might be influenced by the expectations derived from the online reviews and personal stories from friends and family.

Need Activation

Most decisions are driven by a particular need (or needs) that individuals aim to fulfill at a given point in time. Without understanding the underlying needs that drive behavior, it is impossible to design offerings that meet these needs and create customer value. The role of needs as the impetus for customer behavior, the different need states, and the dynamics of customer needs are discussed in more detail below.

Understanding Customer Needs

A need can be defined as a physiological or psychological requirement for the well-being of an organism. When needs are unmet, they motivate people to take actions to fulfill them. Unmet needs can be defined by two main factors: their *strength*, which reflects the magnitude of the tension created by the state of deficiency and the urgency a consumer feels to reduce it, and their *direction*, which reflects the desired end state and serves as a goal that guides consumer decisions and actions.

Needs vary in their importance, such that some needs are prioritized over others. One of the most popular theories of this prioritization of needs was developed by American psychologist Abraham Maslow. His theory delineates a hierarchy of five basic human needs: biological and physiological needs, safety needs, love and belongingness needs, esteem needs, and a need for reaching one's potential, referred to as self-actualization needs. These five needs are often depicted as levels within a pyramid, with the need for self-actualization as the pinnacle (Maslow's theory is discussed in more detail at the end of this chapter).

The need for self-actualization is closely related to the need to define and express one's identity. Self-expression allows people to distinguish themselves from others; to define their own values, beliefs, and needs; and to validate their own self-identity. The backbone of a consumer's identity is the value system that reflects the principles, standards, or qualities that a consumer holds in high regard. The value system is the mechanism that regulates the behavior of individual consumers, companies, and society as a whole. Because of its fundamental role in regulating an individual's behavior, the need to self-actualize and express one's identity plays a crucial role in defining consumer preferences.

Needs are closely related to *wants* but differ in their level of generality: Needs are a general requirement for an individual's well-being, whereas wants are specific manifestations of a given need. In this context, wants are often associated with a particular category or even a specific product or service that could satisfy a need. For example, hydration, transportation, and entertainment are needs; the desire to have a carbonated beverage, to drive an electric car, and to watch movies on demand are specific wants.

Preferences are also closely related to needs and refer to the specific benefits that individuals expect to receive from a given product, service, or brand. Preferences are often expressed in terms of comparisons with other relevant offerings. In this context, preferences can be thought of as the best available means for fulfilling a given want. For example, consumers might prefer Pepsi to Coke as a carbonated beverage, prefer Tesla Model S to a Chevrolet Volt as an electric car, and prefer Netflix to Amazon Prime Video as a means of watching movies on demand.

Because needs are an innate aspect of human beings, they cannot be created. In this context, marketers do not "create" needs; instead they activate and shape extant consumer needs to create specific wants and preferences. For example, marketers do not create a "need" for Pepsi; instead they promote the idea that Pepsi satisfies the pre-existing consumer need for hydration, stimulation, and self-expression. Because the concepts of needs, wants, and preferences are intricately related, throughout this book we use the term "needs" in a more general sense to also include specific consumer wants and preferences.

Customer Need States

Even though people have a variety of needs they aim to fulfill, they do not pursue all these needs at all times. Instead, individuals focus on the needs that are active and prioritize these needs depending on their relative importance. In this context, a need state reflects the extent to which a particular need is active. Based on the degree to which a given need is active, the assessment of this need can be classified into one of three need states: *problem, indifference,* or *delight.*

- **Problem.** Customers perceive an important need as a problem when they are *unsatisfied* with the existing means to fulfill it. These customers recognize that they have a problem (an unmet need), are unhappy with the status quo (doing nothing), and actively seek a solution to fulfill their unmet need. For example, the iPhone addressed a problem faced by many consumers who had to carry multiple devices such as a phone, an organizer, a music player, and a camera. Likewise, Dollar Shave Club addressed consumers' problem of having to pay more than $5 for a single shaving cartridge.

- **Indifference.** Customers are indifferent when they are *reasonably satisfied* with the current options and are willing to continue their current behavior. Even though their needs might not be perfectly met and better alternatives might be available, indifferent customers do not consider this as a problem and are not actively seeking better options. For example, although Google's Nest learning thermostat can benefit consumers by automatically monitoring energy usage, many consumers are satisfied with less sophisticated thermostats that do a reasonably good job of regulating the temperature in their residences. Likewise, even though ultra-high-definition TVs can lead to a better viewing experience, most consumers are reasonably satisfied with their high-definition TVs.

- **Delight.** Customers are delighted when they are *extremely satisfied* with the current means of fulfilling a given need, believe that this need has been fully addressed, and tend to ignore alternative solutions. For example, Amazon's goal of meeting or exceeding expectations aims to delight its customers in order to deter them from exploring other options and to create barriers for competitors considering entering its markets. In the same vein, The Ritz-Carlton, Nordstrom, and Zappos (owned by Amazon) aim to earn customer loyalty by offering a level of service that delights their customers.

People vary in the degree to which they aim to fulfill a particular need, such that certain need states are more likely to motivate individuals to seek means to fulfill this need. Specifically, people are more likely to be proactive in seeking to address important unmet needs that they perceive to be a problem (a pain point) than to address needs that have been largely met and are not perceived to be an important problem. This difference in the urgency with which people are likely to act stems from the fact that the value customers expect to receive from addressing a pain point tends to be greater than the value they expect to receive from enhancing an already satisfactory experience (Figure 2).

Figure 2. Customer Need States

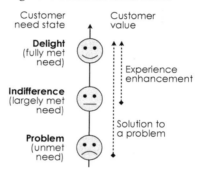

Active needs become goals that individuals aim to fulfill. The intensity with which individuals pursue a given goal is often determined by their need state. Thus, need states viewed as problems are likely to lead to goals that individuals prioritize. Consequently, individuals are likely to allocate more resources to pursue problem-solving goals and set a shorter time frame for achieving them. In contrast, need states reflecting a person's indifference are likely to lead to low-priority goals characterized by the allocation of fewer resources for their pursuit and a longer time horizon in which to accomplish them. As a result, problem-solving (also referred to as irritant-removing) offerings that aim to fulfill an active need tend to be adopted much faster than experience-enhancing offerings that necessitate activation of the relevant need in order to be considered.

The Dynamics of Customer Needs

Needs vary in the degree to which they are active in a customer's mind. People can have different levels of awareness of a need, different degrees of urgency to fulfill the need, and different magnitudes of obstacles they are willing to overcome to satisfy the need. The more active a need is, the more likely it is to be associated with high levels of awareness, urgency, and willingness to overcome obstacles. The different levels of need activation are determined by the importance of a given need and the magnitude of the gap between the current and the desired need state.

Once activated, a need creates a state of tension that drives the individual to reduce or eliminate it. This process of reducing tension—also referred to as need fulfillment—begins when a dormant need is activated. The realization of a deficiency can stem from an internal signal, as in the case of hunger, or from external factors, such as the availability of an offering that promises higher levels of need fulfillment. As a result of realizing the deficiency between the current and the desired state of affairs, consumers begin to seek a means to close this need gap and formulate a goal that will guide their need-fulfillment decisions and behaviors.

Once an active need is fulfilled, its prominence in an individual's mind tends to decrease, and the need becomes dormant until it is activated again. This pattern of need fulfillment is driven by a process of satiation, whereby the value derived from the consumption experience tends to decrease as consumption increases. For example, in food consumption, satiation refers to the end of the desire to eat after a meal. In most cases, satiety is a temporary state that tends to dissipate over time. In the case of food consumption, satiety declines as the consumed nutrients are processed and the state of hunger returns.

The relationship between the activation and satiation processes in need fulfillment is illustrated in Figure 3. Here, the horizontal axis reflects the consumption starting with a need activation. This point represents a state where the consumer has realized a problem in fulfilling a particular need, defined as a discrepancy between the current and the desired means available to fulfill this need. The location of the horizontal axis and, specifically, the point at which it crosses the vertical axis reflects the desired benefits a customer aims to achieve that will ultimately lead to satisfying the active need. In this context, need activation alerts the individual of the presence of an unmet need and sets a goal toward which individuals direct their decisions and actions.

Figure 3. The Dynamics of Customer Needs

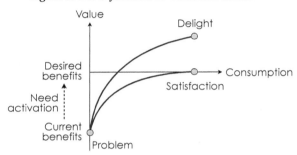

As individuals take active steps toward fulfilling the activated need, the gap between the current and the desired benefits decreases, accompanied by a corresponding increase in the level of satisfaction. The utility delivered by an offering is not bound by the level of benefits desired by the customers: In some cases, it can exceed customer expectations and offer an experience that delights the customer. Note that the concave shape of the curve depicting need satiation is used for illustration purposes only. The shape of the need-satiation curve can vary widely depending on the type of need and the means used to fulfill this need.

Information Search

To identify the available means to fulfill an active need, consumers gather relevant information from two types of sources: external and internal. Consumers might search for information across a variety of external sources by reading product reviews, talking to friends, visiting the company website, and talking to sales associates at the retail outlets where the company's offerings are sold. Alternatively, consumers might rely on retrieving information from internal sources such as accumulated memories of past experiences. The key aspects of these two types of information search are outlined in more detail below.

Gathering Information from External Sources

Customers can gather information from external sources in either an active or passive manner. In some cases, customers gather information actively by engaging in activities like reading product reviews, talking to friends, and talking to sales representatives. Alternatively, customers might gather information passively simply by paying attention to the relevant information that they encounter during their daily routine, such as advertisements embedded in magazines, websites, and television programming. In general, the more important the active need, the greater the likelihood that the customer will actively seek the information needed to make a decision.

Attention is, by definition, selective, meaning that people consciously or subconsciously choose which information to process and which to ignore. In general, people are more likely to notice and pay attention to information that is related to a current need, while screening out unrelated information. For example, a person seeking to buy a car is likely to pay more attention to car-related information such as car advertisements, car financing offers, and car-related discussions on social media.

People are also more likely to pay attention to objects that are unusual and stand out from the surrounding environment. Because we receive most information through our eyes, visual properties of the objects play an important role in determining the amount of attention an object is likely to draw. For example, warm colors such as red, yellow, or orange are more likely to draw attention than cool colors such as blue and green.

Retrieving Information from Memory

In addition to gathering information from their environment, people also rely on the information stored in their memory. Psychologists distinguish between three types of memory: *sensory memory, short-term memory,* and *long-term memory.* When people receive information, they perceive this information on a sensory level, briefly store parts of this information in their short-term memory in order to evaluate its relevance, and, subsequently, either discard it or store it in their long-term memory. The three types of memory are discussed in more detail below.

Sensory Memory

The sensory memory is the shortest term component of memory, enabling individuals to retain impressions of sensory information. The sensory memory is a repository for information received through the five senses of sight, hearing, smell, taste, and touch. Sensory memory does not require any conscious attention and operates on a subconscious level. Information is stored in the sensory memory for a very short period of time—typically less than a second—before it is either dismissed or passed on to the short-term memory.

Short-Term Memory

The short-term memory, also referred to as *working memory*, has limited capacity and serves as a temporary repository of information that is being processed at any point in time. For example, when listening to an advertisement, consumers hold the beginning of the message in short-term memory while attending to the rest of the message.

Research in cognitive psychology has suggested that the working memory has limited capacity, holding only a small amount of information (typically around seven units of information such as words, numbers, or letters) in an active, ready-to-process state. The length of time that the information stored in the short-term memory is retained depends on the relevance of this information and typically ranges from 10 to 15 seconds. Unless consumers retain this information, it will dissipate and will no longer be accessible. The transfer of information from short-term to long-term memory can be facilitated by rehearsal, which involves mental repetition of the information and relating it to other previously acquired knowledge.

Long-Term Memory

Unlike the short-term memory, the long-term memory acts as a more permanent storage of information and has exponentially greater capacity. Long-term memory involves two core processes: encoding and retrieval. Memory encoding describes how and where information is stored into memory. In general, the more attention we pay to the meaning of information during encoding, the stronger the resulting associations in memory will be. Memory retrieval, on the other hand, is the way information is evoked from memory. The link between encoding and retrieval is not perfect: Information might be available in the long-term memory but not be accessible for recall at a particular point in time. Information that is easily retrieved is often referred to as top-of-mind information.

Long-term memory is often represented as an associative network comprising a set of nodes, representing units of information, that are interconnected by links. In this context, encoding (memorizing) and retrieving (recalling) information can be viewed as an activation process that spreads from node to node; when an activated node is encoding external information or retrieving internal information stored in long-term memory, other nodes are also activated if they're associated strongly enough with the initially activated node. The ability to memorize and recall information in any given situation is determined by the information captured by different nodes as well as by the strength and organization of the associations among these nodes.

Levels of Involvement in Information Processing

Because consumers are constantly bombarded with myriad bits of information, they process it in a selective fashion. Thus, individuals pay attention only to a small part of the information available to them, encoding only a subset of this information in memory in a way that makes it readily available for retrieval. Because people consciously process only the information that they have paid attention to and can recall from memory, information processing can be represented as a funnel in which only a small part of the available information is considered when making purchase decisions (Figure 4). The extent to which the available information is screened out is determined to a large degree by an individual's level of involvement, such that greater levels of involvement typically lead to greater levels of attention, higher recall, and more deliberate information processing.

Figure 4. The Information Processing Funnel

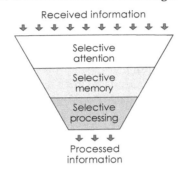

Research in psychology and behavioral economics argues that, based on their level of involvement, people engage in two types of information processing. Sometimes people engage in controlled, deep, systematic, and/or effortful evaluation of the available information, and at other times the evaluation is automatic, shallow, heuristic, and/or mindless.[2] These two types of information processing are referred to as System 1 and System 2 processing, respectively, and are most prominently articulated by recipient of the Nobel Prize in Economic Sciences, Daniel Kahneman.[3]

These two modes of processing represent different ways of taking in information and making decisions. System 1 operates automatically and quickly, with little or no effort; in contrast, System 2 is subject to conscious judgments, is slower, and requires much greater mental effort. Furthermore, System 1 is nonverbal, is characterized by reduced vigilance, and is focused on recognition rather than comparison. In contrast, System 2 is intricately linked to language, is vigilant, and is focused on analysis and comparison rather than recognition. System 1 is associative, heuristic-based, and relatively independent of an individual's working memory, whereas System 2 is analytic, rule-based, and limited by working memory capacity.

The distinction between System 1 and System 2 processing has significant implications for consumer decision making. Consumers with a low level of involvement are more likely to rely on System 1 when evaluating the available information and, consequently, are more likely to employ *associative thinking*, relying on recognition and pattern matching and focusing on the similarities of the available options. In contrast, consumers who display a high degree of care are more likely to rely on System 2 when evaluating the available information and, consequently, are more likely to employ *analytical thinking*, systematically comparing and contrasting the available options and focusing on both the similarities and differences of these options.

The determination of which of the two systems an individual will use when evaluating the available information is a function of several factors including decision importance, individuals' prior preferences, purchase frequency, time available to make the decision, and the complexity of the decision task. In general, decisions that are relatively less important, involve habitually purchased items, are made under time pressure, and involve relatively simple choices (e.g., a small number of options described by a limited number of attributes) tend to be associated with lower levels of involvement and rely on System 1 processing. Thus, most low-cost, frequently purchased products are characterized by low-involvement decision making that relies primarily on System 1, whereas most important, non-trivial decisions tend to rely on System 2 processing.

Evaluating Market Offerings

The concept of customer value is central to defining any market. Without understanding what motivates consumers and how they construe value, a company can neither develop a meaningful strategy nor design an offering that will appeal to its target customers. The formulation of a viable market strategy and tactics begins with understanding customer needs and the ways in which target customers evaluate market offerings.

Understanding the Value Function

Value reflects the worth of an item; it is an individual's assessment of an offering with respect to this offering's ability to fulfill certain needs. Value is not an attribute of the company's offering; it is created when a customer interacts with the company's offering. To create customer value, the company must ensure that the key attributes of its offering are aligned with consumer needs. This alignment requires that managers understand the value customers place on different attributes of the company's offering.

The company creates customer value by designing and modifying the seven attributes defining its offering—product, service, brand, price, incentives, communication, and distribution. The question then is how changes in the attributes of the offering translate to customer value. For example, if a company doubles the performance of its offering on a given attribute (e.g., display resolution of a mobile phone), would this double the value customers derive from this attribute? Or, more general, what is the relationship between the performance of the company's offering on a given attribute and corresponding customer value? The answer to these questions is given by the value function, which reflects the relationship between the attributes of an offering and the value it creates for target customers.

Customers do not evaluate market offerings based on their objective attribute characteristics; rather, their evaluations are based on the subjective value they derive from these attributes. The *value function* reflects the way in which individuals translate the attributes of the offering into subjective benefits and costs. Determining the way in which customers evaluate the performance of a company's offering on different attributes and how they combine these valuations to form an overall assessment of this offering enables the company to identify and prioritize improvements to attributes that are likely to create customer value.

Research in psychology and behavioral economics suggest that the value function can be represented by an S-shaped curve where the horizontal axis represents the actual performance and the vertical axis represents the value derived from that performance (Figure 5).[4] The origin of the two axes defines the buyer's reference point and is also the point on the value curve that separates gains from losses (on the vertical axis) and offering improvements from detractions (on the horizontal axis).

Figure 5. The Value Function

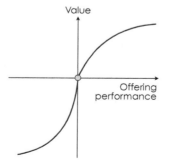

The value function is characterized by three key properties: *reference-point dependence*, meaning that individuals use a reference point to evaluate the available offerings; *loss aversion*, which means that people consider losses more important than corresponding gains; and *diminishing marginal value*, meaning that improving an offering's performance produces marginally diminishing increases in the value created by this offering. The three properties of the value function are discussed in more detail below.

Reference-Point Dependence

Reference-point dependence reflects the fact that people often do not have well-articulated preferences and, consequently, base their evaluations of market offerings on the context in which they consider these offerings. Specifically, reference-point dependence implies that the value of an offering is determined in terms of deviation from a reference point; disadvantages of an offering are framed as losses and advantages as gains (Figure 6). To illustrate, when considering the processing power of a computer, consumers are likely to use the power of their current computer as a reference point. As a result, the same computer is likely to be evaluated as an improvement (gain) by consumers used to a less powerful computer and as a downgrade (loss) by consumers used to a more powerful computer.

Figure 6. Reference-Point Dependence

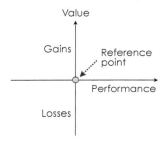

The principle of reference-point dependence is frequently used in pricing, whereby buyers are given two prices — the "regular" price that aims to serve as a reference point and the "sale" price that reflects a discount from the regular price. This practice tends to be more effective when consumers do not have sufficient expertise to objectively assess the value of the offering and when actual product quality is not readily observable. In such cases, buyers tend to focus their attention on the difference between the "regular" and the "sale" price and rely on this difference — rather than on the actual benefits provided by the offering — to make a choice. The reference-point dependence principle is an important aspect of the pricing model of many retailers, including JCPenney, JoS. A. Bank, and Kohl's. Likewise, the "new and improved" product development strategy builds on the principle of reference-point dependence to focus buyers' attention on the marginal improvement of the offering vis-à-vis its predecessor.

Loss Aversion

Loss aversion builds on the principle of reference-point dependence to assert that people value positive (gains) and negative (losses) deviations from the reference point asymmetrically, placing more weight on losses than gains. This asymmetry implies that the subjective experience of losses is exaggerated relative to that of corresponding gains. This valuation pattern is reflected by the value function's steeper slope for losses than gains (Figure 7).

The effect of loss aversion can readily be seen if one compares the differences in the subjective valuation of a change in the performance of the offering (reflected on the horizontal axis in Figure 7) that is of the same magnitude in terms of its absolute value but occurs in opposite directions — an improvement in one case and a detraction in the other. The subjective experience and evaluation of this change vary depending on the nature of the change (advancement or detraction), such that losses loom larger than gains of the same magnitude. Thus, the loss-aversion principle implies that people place higher value on something they need to give up compared with something of equivalent value they stand to gain.

Figure 7. Loss Aversion

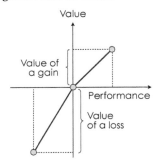

Consider, for example, investors' reactions to fluctuations in the stock market: A loss of $1,000 hurts proportionally more than the satisfaction derived from a gain of $1,000. In the same vein, consumers are likely to vary in their reactions to adding and deleting product features, such that the disutility from removing a feature tends to be greater than the utility of adding that same feature.

Loss aversion is also one of the principles upon which the no-questions-asked return policy of many retailers is built. Once customers take possession of the offering their reference point changes, and the status quo of having the offering becomes the reference point for the subsequent decision regarding the disposition of this offering. As a result, returning the offering is no longer considered as a non-gain but as a loss, which creates disutility and decreases the likelihood that the buyer will return the offering. Thus, the shift in the reference point following the purchase process, combined with customers' tendency to overweight losses relative to gains, leads to a decrease in the initial probability of a purchase resulting in a return.

Diminishing Marginal Value

The principle of diminishing marginal value states that the benefits from improving an offering's performance on a particular dimension does not increase in a linear fashion, and that after a certain point improving the offering's performance will produce marginally diminishing increases in the benefits created by this offering. Diminishing marginal value implies that increasing an offering's performance does not produce an equivalent increase in consumer utility. Rather, the value function is concave, such that improving the offering's performance will have greater impact on its subjective value at a lower level of performance; as the offering's overall performance improves, further improvements will have progressively decreasing impact (Figure 8).

Figure 8. Diminishing Marginal Value

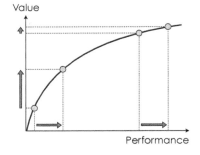

The effect of diminishing marginal value can readily be seen if one compares the differences in the subjective valuations of the same changes in the offering's performance (depicted on the horizontal axis in Figure 8) that occur at different levels of performance. The diminishing marginal value principle implies that an increase in an offering's performance on a given attribute will yield greater value when the initial level of this attribute's performance is low rather than when it is high. Once an offering reaches a certain level of performance on a given attribute, further improvements in performance on this attribute tend to be perceived as relatively less valuable. In lay terms, the more customers have of something, the less an improvement means to them.

Consider, for example, the effect of improving the processing power of a computer on the value a buyer derives from this improvement: When the computer's processing power is relatively low, even small increases in processing power have a relatively large impact. As the processing power becomes relatively high, the same increase in power that used to produce a large increase in perceived performance now has much less impact. A similar effect can be observed with other products, such as the number of blades in a razor: The increase from one to two blades was perceived as a great enhancement, but as the overall number of blades increased from two to three, four, then five, the marginal increase in the perceived value from adding another blade was not as large as it was with the second blade.

Choice

The three properties of the value function—reference-point dependence, loss aversion, and diminishing marginal value—describe how people assess the value of the individual attributes of an offering. They do not, however, explicitly address how individuals combine these attributes to form an overall valuation of the choice alternatives and decide among them. To fully understand customer decision processes a manager must be cognizant of the different strategies people use to decide among the available alternatives.

The Rational Model of Choice

The rational model of choice assumes that people carefully and deliberately assess the available offerings and then choose the one that has the highest value. Specifically, the rational choice model assumes that people have clear and consistent preferences among the available alternatives that allow them to readily identify the most attractive option. In this context, the value an individual derives from evaluating market offerings is determined by three key factors: (1) the *attributes* defining these offerings, (2) the relative *importance* of these attributes for the consumer, and (3) the offering's *performance* on these attributes. An offering's ratings on these three factors is combined to create an overall valuation, and the offering with the highest valuation is ultimately selected by the consumer.

For example, when choosing a mobile phone, a consumer might consider several attributes including battery life, operating system, brand reputation, phone size, camera resolution, and price. These different attributes might vary in importance for this consumer, such that battery life, operating system, and brand reputation are of utmost importance and price of least importance. In the process of choosing a mobile phone, this consumer is likely to assess how well the available offerings perform on each of the above attributes. Combining the different aspects of the valuation process will yield this consumer's assessment of the value of each of the available decision alternatives. Finally, the consumer will select the phone with the highest overall valuation.

The valuation process implied by the rational model of choice can be represented with the following equation:

$$V_A = f(w_i, a_i)$$

Here V_A is the value of offering A, i is an index that specifies the particular attribute being evaluated, w_i is the importance of that attribute, and a_i is the offering's performance on that attribute. The index i ranges from 1 to the total number of attributes describing a given offering (n). The symbol f means that the value depends on attribute importance (w_i) and offering performance (a_i), without implying a specific relationship between these factors. To choose among multiple offerings, consumers typically compare their valuations of each of the available options (e.g., V_A versus V_B versus V_C) and select the one with the highest value.

For simplicity, the value function (f) is commonly assumed to be the sum of the offering's performance on individual attributes (a_i), weighted (multiplied) by the importance of these attributes (w_i). Because the valuation of an offering is represented as a sum of weighted attribute-level evaluations of an offering's performance, this value function is commonly referred to as the *weighted-additive model* of consumer choice. Assuming such a relationship between the different aspects of the offering, the value function can be represented as follows:

$$V_A = w_1 \cdot a_1 + w_2 \cdot a_2 + w_3 \cdot a_3 + \ldots + w_n \cdot a_n$$

Suppose that the consumer in the above example is using a 10-point scale to evaluate the importance of each attribute of a mobile phone, rating battery life, operating system, and brand reputation as 9; the phone size and camera resolution as 5; and price as 1. Furthermore, let's say that this consumer is using a 10-point scale to evaluate the performance of each phone on each attribute, rating the battery life of the first phone (A) as 4, the operating system as 8, the brand reputation as 6, the phone size as 5, the camera resolution as 7, and the price as 9. Accordingly, the valuation of camera A can be calculated as: $V_A = 9*4+9*8+9*6+5*5+5*7+1*9 = 231$. Following the same logic, the consumer can evaluate the other options (e.g., V_B and V_C) and choose the one with the highest value.

Despite its popularity, the rational model of choice, in general, and the weighted-additive model, in particular, have an important limitation: They assume that individuals evaluate the available information in a systematic fashion. Specifically, the rational model implies that when choosing products, people systematically assess each option's performance on all attributes and then combine these assessments to choose the option with the highest score. In reality, however, this is often not the case, and people frequently make choices that are different from those prescribed by the weighted-additive model. These differences concern both how people evaluate individual options and how they choose among the available options. The alternative ways in which people evaluate a company's offerings and how they choose among the available options are discussed in more detail in the following sections.

The Psychology of Choice

Buyers rarely sort through offerings in the diligent and unbiased fashion formalized by the rational choice model. Instead, buyers use decision shortcuts, referred to as heuristics, for less important choices, and rely on a more effortful level of reasoning for more deliberative decisions. These two types of decision processes are described in more detail below.

Choice Based on Heuristics

When considering the available choice alternatives, buyers pursue two conflicting goals: On one hand, they are trying to make an accurate decision by choosing the option that best fits their needs and, on the other hand, they are trying to minimize the mental effort involved in the decision. As a result, the decision-making process is not entirely "rational" in the sense that consumers do not always engage in the thorough decision process prescribed by the rational choice model. Instead they are guided by the principle of *bounded rationality*, whereby the accuracy of their decision process is bound by the limited amount of mental effort they are willing to allocate to a particular decision task.

The tradeoff between accuracy and effort is a key principle guiding the decision process. Buyers often sacrifice accuracy to minimize the time and effort involved in making less important decisions so that they can be more diligent when it comes to more important decisions. To minimize decision effort when making mundane decisions, buyers often employ shortcuts, or *heuristics*, that aim to circumvent cognitive effort, often at the expense of choice accuracy.

One common approach to minimize decision effort involves reliance on the *satisficing heuristic* (a combination of the terms *satisfy* and *suffice*). Individuals using a satisficing heuristic evaluate the available options only until an acceptable option is found, at which point they select this option and terminate further evaluation even if this decision means potentially forgoing a better option. Thus, rather than considering all available options, individuals relying on this heuristic choose the first option that meets their decision criteria. This limited and nonsystematic consideration of options might lead consumers using the satisficing heuristic to choose different options depending on the order in which they evaluate the available alternatives. Because it does not involve evaluating all available options and uses a relatively low benchmark for identifying an acceptable option, the satisficing heuristic is often used by individuals who are not very engaged in the decision and are more likely to rely on System 1 rather than System 2 processing.[5]

Another way in which buyers can simplify their decisions is by focusing only on the most important attribute describing the choice options and selecting the option with the highest value on that attribute without considering the other attributes. For example, when choosing a mobile phone, consumers might focus only on price and select the cheapest option without considering the attributes of the other available options. Similar to the satisficing approach, this heuristic (also referred to as *lexicographic heuristic*) can save decision makers time and effort but at the same time can impair the accuracy of their choices.

To minimize cognitive effort, buyers might also set a threshold that must be met in order for an option to be considered. Thus, some buyers would not seriously consider a mobile phone that does not have a headphone jack, regardless of its price. This heuristic, commonly referred to as *elimination-by-aspects*, involves gradually reducing the number of alternatives in a choice set, evaluating one attribute at a time, and eliminating all options that do not meet the predefined criteria. For example, a consumer may first compare a number of mobile phones on the basis of brand, then battery life, and finally price, until only one option remains. The elimination-by-aspects heuristic implies a *non-compensatory decision process*, meaning that high levels on one dimension of an offering cannot offset low levels on another—for example, low performance of a mobile phone on battery life cannot be offset by high brand reputation.

Choice Based on Reasons

An important assumption of the "rational" choice model is that individuals associate a numerical value with each alternative. People, however, do not always deliberate about choices in this way. Instead of quantifying the attractiveness of different choice options, people might form qualitative judgments (reasons) for and against each option and then choose the option that is supported by the strongest reasons. This reason-based view of choice implies that when considering decision alternatives, people formulate reasons to choose some options and reject others.

The reason-based view of decision making is often a better reflection of the way people deliberate about choices than the rational choice model. Indeed, when facing a decision problem, people rarely attempt to estimate the overall values of the available alternatives. Instead, they try to come up with reasons for and against each option. When decision makers have good reasons for and against each option or conflicting reasons for competing options, they are faced with a quandary that cannot be resolved by simply comparing the numeric values of these options. Instead they must reconcile conflicting reasons and develop a convincing rationale for the decision that they can use to justify the choice to themselves and others.

Reason-based choice can lead to outcomes that differ from those predicted by rational choice models. For example, consider the impact of adding product features or promotional premiums (such as bonus offerings) that are valued by some consumers but have little or no value for others. The rational choice model would predict that adding such features could only increase (but never decrease) the desirability of the company's offering. Yet, adding unneeded features or promotional premiums might decrease rather than increase the attractiveness of the offering for consumers even though the added features or premiums do not reduce the actual value of the product in any way.[6] This pattern of evaluations is consistent with the notion that decision makers evaluate the available options in terms of reasons and are less likely to select the augmented option because the unneeded feature provides them with a reason *not* to choose that option.

Purchase, Usage, and Repurchase

Choice is typically followed by a purchase of the selected offering, consumption of the purchased product or service, and, frequently, a repurchase of the offering. The key considerations underlying these decisions are discussed in the following sections.

From Choice to Purchase

Once buyers make up their minds about which option to buy, the next logical step is to purchase that option. In many cases, the decision to buy a product or service and the actual purchase can occur almost simultaneously. Impulsive purchases, like items bought at the cash register while waiting in line, are one of many examples of contemporaneous choice and purchase decisions. On many occasions, however, the choice decision and the actual purchase are temporally separated. For example, a consumer might not rush out to the store to buy a mobile phone after deciding to upgrade. This delay between choice and purchase might be due to lack of time, limited financial resources, or merely because there is no urgent need to upgrade.

The temporal gap between choice and purchase might range from a few minutes to years or, in some cases, decades. Consider, for example, the decision journey that leads to the purchase of Porsche's flagship sports car, the 911 Carrera. According to Porsche, the typical 911 buyer in the United States is 46 to 65, with an average age of 52. Most of these buyers, however, did not develop an affinity for this car just prior to making the purchase. Instead, many current Porsche buyers made the decision to buy the car when they were teenagers but were unable to do so due to budgetary constraints and family considerations.

There are many reasons why the purchase of an already selected offering might be delayed. One set of reasons involves various constraints: limited time to complete the purchase, lack of sufficient financial resources, product unavailability, and a variety of situational factors such as not having a payment method (e.g., cash or credit card) or the physical means to place an order at the moment (e.g., not being near a store and/or not having a mobile device handy). For example, a consumer might decide to buy Apple's newest iPhone but delay the actual purchase due to the high price of the device as well as the limited availability of the phone immediately after its release.

Buyers may also delay purchasing if there is not an urgent need for the benefits afforded by the company's offering. When buyers are reasonably satisfied with the status quo, they might not want to rush to make the purchase because the immediate benefit of the offering is unclear. In such cases, buyers might wait for an opportune moment to make the purchase (such as when they are already in the store or on the store's website), or delay purchase in anticipation of a price decrease or eventual sales promotions. Thus, a consumer who has decided to upgrade to the new iPhone might not immediately purchase it because the current iPhone meets this consumer's needs reasonably well and there is no urgency to replace it.

Distinguishing the choice decision from the act of purchase is important because a buyer who has selected an option with the intention to buy will not necessarily end up purchasing that option. Multiple factors might sway buyers' behavior away from the initially chosen option. These factors can be broadly grouped into two types: *external* and *internal*. Thus, after buyers have selected the option they intend to buy, they might come across external factors like additional information about a competitive option that offers superior performance at a lower price. Likewise, buyers might discover new information concerning the performance, price, or availability of their most preferred option that will make this option less attractive and will make them reconsider their initial selection.

In addition to being influenced by external factors, buyers might reconsider their choices even in the absence of new information about the available options. This change of heart is often driven by a phenomenon called *cognitive dissonance*, a state of unease caused by simultaneously holding two or more contradictory thoughts. For buyers who have made a choice, this unease stems from the tradeoffs that have been made to reach a decision. Indeed, rarely do buyers face a situation in which one option is clearly the best choice. Most options have both pros and cons. Once buyers make a choice, they have to accept the disadvantages of that choice and forgo the advantages of other options. Realization of these consequences creates post-decisional dissonance whereby buyers try to reconcile the fact that the chosen option has certain drawbacks and the rejected options have certain advantages. This dissonance might lead to a state of uncertainty and post-decision regret that causes buyers to worry that they might not have made the best choice. This regret, in turn, might lead buyers to return to the evaluation (or even search) stage, reevaluate their decision process, and make a different choice.

Usage and Satisfaction

Early models of buyer behavior considered the purchase of an offering as the endpoint of the decision journey. This is a rather narrow view of the ways in which customers experience market offerings, as it fails to consider the profound impact that using the purchased offering and satisfaction with this offering can have on decision processes and behavior.

The ways in which people use products and services define their consumption experience. In the case of physical goods, the experience often starts with the delivery of the offering, includes unpacking and setting up the offering, actual use of the product or service, solving usage problems and managing malfunctions, and disposing of the product. Customers' experience at each of these stages contributes to their overall consumption experience and satisfaction with the offering.

Customer satisfaction reflects how products and services offered by a company match a customer's needs and expectations. The degree to which customers are satisfied or dissatisfied with an offering depends on three key factors: *needs, expectations about the offering's performance*, and *actual experience with the offering*.

- **Needs** are the core driver of behavior, a key criterion for evaluating offering attractiveness, and a principal determinant of customer satisfaction. Thus, the ultimate goal of an offering is to fulfill a particular customer need(s). The more important a need is and the greater the urgency of fulfilling that need, the greater the level of satisfaction (or dissatisfaction) that a customer is likely to derive from experiencing the company's offering.

- **Expectations** stem from a variety of factors that include customers' needs and preferences; their prior experience with the same or a similar offering; the brand image and reputation of the company associated with the offering; and the relevant company, collaborator, and peer-to-peer communications. For example, a consumer seeking to upgrade his phone might set high expectations for a company's new offering because of positive experience with his current phone, the reputation of the company, company advertisements, the recommendation of the salesperson, the positive product ratings and comments online, and recommendations from friends.

- **Consumption experience** reflects the way in which a particular customer experiences the company's offering. Consumption experience is not merely a description of the features of a company's product or service; it is a customer's subjective perception of this product or service. The consumption experience can vary across customers, usage occasions, and offering attributes. For example, after upgrading to the new phone, a consumer might discover that some of the features of his current phone (such as a dedicated headphone jack) are no longer available on the new model. At the same time, the data transfer from the old to the new phone occurred flawlessly and with minimal effort, in part due to the salesperson's assistance at the time of purchase.

When evaluating an offering, buyers' needs and expectations typically serve as a reference point. In this context, buyers evaluate an offering's functional, psychological, and monetary dimensions by considering whether the offering meets their needs and expectations on each dimension. For example, a consumer might determine that although a phone's functionality does not meet his expectations, the phone's brand delivers as expected in terms of psychological value by conveying status and prestige, and the monetary value is greater than initially expected due to an in-store sales promotion that lowered the phone's price.

The comparison of needs and expectations with the actual experience can yield one of three possible outcomes. First, buyers can be *satisfied* when their needs are fulfilled and expectations are confirmed. This satisfaction implies that the buyers' actual experience matches needs and expectations. Second, buyers can be *dissatisfied* when their needs are not met and the actual experience is inferior to expectations. Finally, buyers are *delighted* when their needs are met and (positive) expectations are confirmed. For delighted customers, the actual experience fulfills their needs and exceeds their expectations.

Both needs and expectations must be met for a customer to be satisfied. Thus, an offering that is otherwise capable of fulfilling customer needs might leave the customer dissatisfied if it fails to meet this customer's expectations. In the same vein, when customers have negative expectations (for example, when forced to choose among unattractive alternatives), an offering that meets these expectations would not lead to high levels of satisfaction because it fails to fulfill the underlying customer need. In general, the comparison of needs and expectations with the actual experience tends to have an asymmetric effect on satisfaction, such that the negative effect of failing to meet expectations is much stronger than the positive effect of exceeding expectations.

The Path to Repurchase

Because customers have recurring needs, their interaction with the company's offering is often an iterative process that involves multiple customer decision journeys. In this context, there are several basic ways in which customers' journeys might evolve as they look to repurchase an offering.

First, a customer might repeat the entire journey by seeking new information about the available options, forming a new consideration set, and making a new choice that might or might not include the previously purchased option. Alternatively, a customer might revise the consideration set without actively seeking new information. For example, a customer might expand the consideration set by including initially discarded options or shrink the initial consideration set by excluding some of the previously considered options. A customer might also select a different option from the same consideration set used to make the initial decision. Finally, a customer might simply go back and repurchase the offering without considering other options.

Clearly, the latter scenario—straight rebuy—is the most desired option for the company whose products or services was initially chosen by the customer. The degree to which this behavior is likely to occur depends on a variety of factors, including the "stickiness" of the particular product category, the degree to which the company's offering can create customer value, the company's customer retention activities, and competitors' actions. For example, in many service industries—including insurance, financial services, and media subscription services—straight rebuy rates can be very high, with up to 80% of consumers renewing their service without engaging in a deliberative decision process. In addition, the repurchase decision can be driven by brand loyalty as customers continue to buy the same brand without considering other options. For example, in the ketchup category, many consumers have established preferences, with Heinz and Hunt's customers staying with their preferred brand without giving this decision a second thought.

Repurchasing behavior is not always a deliberative decision process. In many cases it is driven by habit. Habits are repetitive behaviors that involve routinized decision making with no or limited information seeking and evaluation of alternative options. Habits stem from routine purchases of offerings whose performance the customer has been satisfied with over time. The choice of many staple consumer products such as milk, bread, orange juice, and peanut butter is driven by habitual decision making.

Purchasing by habit provides two important benefits to customers. First, habitual purchases minimize decision effort—an important benefit given that people make myriads of decisions daily. Habitual buying eliminates the need to search for new information, evaluate the alternative options, and engage in deliberate decision making for every purchase. By relying on prior experience and simply repurchasing some relatively less important items, customers can free up cognitive resources for decisions they consider more important. In addition to minimizing decision effort, habitual buying minimizes the risks associated with the purchase. Purchasing an offering that a customer has been satisfied with minimizes the risk that the offering will not match this customer's preferences and will fail to fulfill the relevant customer need.

Once formed, habits do not exist in perpetuity. Satisfaction with the previously purchased option is essential for a habit to be sustained. If buyers are dissatisfied with the experience of using a product or a service, they might switch from routine decision making to a more deliberative decision process that involves considering multiple options and making a new choice. Dissatisfaction with the routinely purchased offering is not the only reason why customers might choose to break their purchasing habit. Customers might change their routine due to boredom and engage in a more complex decision process to discover and experience something new. Customers might also break from a habit for fear that by using the same offering over and over they might be missing out on better options available in the market.

Another factor that might force buyers to break an established habit are changes in the availability, quality, or price of the market offerings. For example, the product consumers usually buy might be out of stock or the product might have changed — its price might have increased, its quality might have deteriorated, or its functionality might have been modified. Or, consumers might have become aware of an alternative and potentially superior option. In these cases, consumers are likely to break their habit and engage in more thoughtful decision making before making a choice.

SUMMARY

Understanding customer decisions and behavior is the starting point for identifying market opportunities and formulating a company's marketing strategy. The key aspects of buyers' decisions and behaviors are often described in the context of a decision journey that takes the perspective of an individual customer to examine how this customer adopts and uses a company's offering. A customer's decision journey can be defined by six main experiences: *need activation, search, evaluation, choice, purchase, and usage*.

Need fulfillment is a basic requirement for an individual's well-being. People do not pursue all their needs at all times. Instead, they focus on the needs that are active and prioritize these needs depending on their relative importance. Based on the degree to which a given need is active, it can be classified into one of three need states: *problem, indifference,* or *delight*. Active needs create a state of tension that drive the individual to reduce or eliminate them. Once an active need is fulfilled, its prominence in an individual's mind tends to decrease, and the need becomes dormant until it is activated again.

To identify the best means to fulfill their needs, people *search* for information from two types of sources: external and internal. Individuals process information in a selective fashion; they pay attention only to a small part of the information available to them, encode only a subset of this information in memory, and then use only a portion of this information to make a decision.

The *evaluation* of the available offerings is a function of a consumer's assessment of their benefits and costs. Customers evaluate market offerings based not on their objective attribute characteristics but on the subjective value customers derive from these attributes. The *value function* reflects the way that individuals translate the attributes of the offering into subjective benefits and costs. The value function has three key properties: reference-point dependence, loss aversion, and diminishing marginal value.

The rational model of *choice* assumes that buyers have already articulated preferences for the available options, that they carefully and deliberately evaluate the pros and cons of these options, and that they ultimately choose the option that offers the highest value. In reality, however, buyers rarely sort through offerings in the diligent and unbiased fashion formalized by the rational choice model. Instead, buyers use decision shortcuts, or heuristics, for less important choices, and rely on a more effortful level of reasoning for more deliberative decisions. Furthermore, in addition to calculating the utility of the different options, buyers often rely on qualitative judgments, or reasons, to choose some options and reject others.

The choice of a product or service and the actual *purchase* can occur almost simultaneously, as in the case of impulsive purchases, or they can be temporally separated because of factors such as lack of time, limited financial resources, and lack of an urgent need for the benefits provided by the offering. In cases when choice and purchase do not take place at the same time, customer preference might be swayed from the initially chosen option by a variety of factors such as encountering a more attractive option, uncovering negative information about the chosen option, or simply a change of mind about a selection.

The ways in which people *use* products and services defines their consumption experience and satisfaction. The degree to which customers are satisfied or dissatisfied with an offering depends on three key factors: customer needs, customer expectations about the offering's performance, and customers' actual experience with the offering. Because customers have recurring needs, their interaction with the company's offering can include multiple decision journeys that may involve repeating the entire journey starting with seeking new information about the available options or circumventing some of the steps and repeating only a subset of the entire journey.

MARKETING INSIGHT: MASLOW'S THEORY OF HUMAN NEEDS

Maslow's Hierarchy of Needs is a theory of human needs introduced by American psychologist Abraham Maslow. This theory organizes the drivers of human motivation into a series of increasingly unsatisfied needs, the higher of which emerge only as the lower ones are satisfied. The basic premise of Maslow's theory is that motivations arise from unfulfilled needs, which might be physiological, like the need for food, or psychological, like the need for love, friendship, or respect. Specifically, Maslow identifies five basic types of needs that are arranged in a hierarchy, such that lower needs tend to subside as they are increasingly satisfied and are replaced by newly emerging higher needs (Figure 9).

Figure 9. Maslow's Hierarchy of Needs

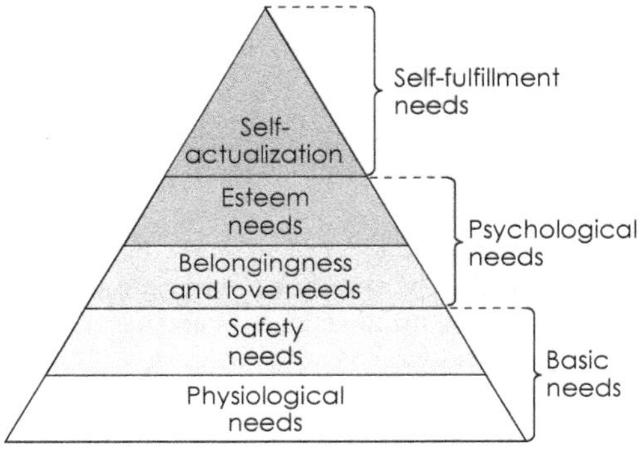

- *Physiological needs.* The lowest needs in the hierarchy are physiological and must be satisfied for human survival. The need for food, water, sleep, and rest are all examples of physiological needs. When these needs are not met, fulfilling them becomes a prime motivator.

- *Safety needs.* Once physiological needs are largely met, a person's motivations tend to be driven by a need for safety. The desire for freedom from dangerous situations and violence is a tangible example of this need. Even in times of relative safety, this need can manifest itself in preferences for less risk or more familiar settings. As with physiological needs, individuals whose need for safety is not sufficiently met will be motivated primarily by this need and will organize their behaviors around it.

- *Belonginess, love, and esteem needs.* In a smoothly functioning society, both the physiological and safety needs of a person are largely satisfied, resulting in the emergence of social needs. The lower of these social needs in the hierarchy is the need for love, affection, and belonging. Once the need for love, affection, and belonging begins to be satisfied, the need for esteem emerges. This need is centered around people's desire for respect and appreciation from themselves and from others.

- *Self-actualization.* Once physiological, safety, and esteem needs are basically satisfied, people focus on the need for self-actualization, the pinnacle of the hierarchy of needs. This need can be described broadly as a need for self-fulfillment which stems from converting one's potential into reality. The need for self-actualization manifests differently from person to person. In some, it might be expressed as a desire for creation through art, writing, or invention. In others, it can take the form of athletic or academic excellence.

Introduced over half a century ago, Maslow's theory remains highly influential today. At the same time, it has a number of important limitations. Thus, even though people tend to move up the hierarchy from physiological needs to the need for self-actualization, it is possible that for some people higher needs can dominate motivation even while lower needs remain unsatisfied. For example, a starving artist who wants to continue expressing herself through painting even at the expense of proper nourishment prioritizes a higher level need over a lower level one. Likewise, a person might be willing to sacrifice more basic needs like affection and safety for the sake of a cause. Furthermore, the view of needs as being satisfied at a certain absolute level does not always realistically portray the nature of motivation. Thus, it is possible that as needs are increasingly satisfied people become more motivated by expectations of future satisfaction. For example, some people might never be satisfied at any level of pay. Instead, as their pay increases year after year, the joy at getting a pay raise is replaced by an expectation that their pay will increase further. In this context, Maslow's theory is often viewed as a framework for understanding people's needs rather than as an ironclad law.

MARKETING INSIGHT: MAKING JOINT DECISIONS

Marketers often think of customers as individuals whose behavior is determined almost exclusively by their own preferences. In reality, however, many purchase decisions are formed with input by multiple entities that directly or indirectly influence customer behavior. For example, the decision to purchase high-ticket items such as a house and a car is often made jointly by all members of the household. In the same vein, decisions concerning children—including the choice of food, apparel, toys, medical treatments, and educational institutions—are often determined jointly by both parents with input from their kids.

The different entities participating in joint decisions often play different roles depending on the nature of their involvement in the decision process. In particular, joint decision making can involve entities playing six different roles: *initiator, influencer, gatekeeper, decision maker, buyer,* and *end user.*

- The *initiator* activates a particular need and initiates the decision process. For example, a spouse might notice that a refrigerator is not working properly, or a child might want a new toy for an upcoming birthday.

- *Influencers* are the entities that shape consumer preferences by expressing relevant views and recommendations. For example, a salesperson might offer advice and recommend a particular brand of refrigerator, and a child's choice of a toy might be influenced by the preferences of his friends.

- *Gatekeepers* influence the decision process by imposing restrictions on the offerings being considered—such as performance, brand, cost, and the time frame for making the decision. For example, a spouse might "veto" the purchase of a refrigerator that exceeds a certain price point, and a bank might not approve a loan for a house that exceeds the consumers' purchasing power.

- The *decider* is the entity that makes the ultimate selection of what, why, and when to buy. The decider might or might not have initiated the decision process. For example, the spouse who has noticed the refrigerator malfunction might end up ultimately choosing the new refrigerator, and a parent might end up deciding which toy to buy for the child who desires a new toy.

- The *buyer* is the entity that makes the actual purchase. Even though on many occasions, the decider and the buyer are the same entity, in some cases these two different roles can be fulfilled by different individuals. One spouse might delegate to the other the task of purchasing the decided-upon item. For example, following the decision about which refrigerator to buy, one of the spouses might delegate the actual purchase task to the other one.

- The *end user* is the individual who will ultimately use the offering. The end user might be an individual or, in the case of shared-usage offerings, a group of individuals. For example, a refrigerator is likely to be used by all members of the household, whereas a toy might be used by one person.

Because many decisions involve multiple entities that play diverse roles in the decision process, identifying these entities (the decision-making unit) and understanding how decisions are being made (the decision-making process) is an important prerequisite to designing market offerings that create customer value. The process of making purchase decisions that involve multiple parties and the development of selling strategies that appeal to the different members of the decision-making unit are discussed in more detail in Chapter 15.

MARKETING INSIGHT: DECISION HEURISTICS AND BIASES

Heuristics are simple decision rules (or mental shortcuts) that people use to save time and minimize cognitive effort when forming judgments and making decisions. Rather than considering all relevant aspects of the decision task at hand, heuristics tend to focus only on the most relevant aspect(s) of the problem while paying little or no attention to others. This simplification (and sometimes oversimplification) often leads to decisions characterized by lower accuracy and systematic deviations from optimal outcomes. These systematic deviations, also referred to as cognitive biases, are particularly likely to occur when people have to make complex decisions with limited information while facing time constraints. Some of the most common decision biases are outlined below.

- *Base-rate neglect* is a decision bias in which people fail to take into account the likelihood of an event occurring in the category represented by this event. Consider a new defect-identification device that always detects the presence of a defect but also reports false positives (a working device erroneously diagnosed as defective) 5% of the time. On average, one in a thousand products is defective. Suppose that the device indicates a particular product is defective. What is the probability that this device is really defective? The correct probability is about 2%, although those who do not take into account the low proportion (base rate) of defective products would answer that the probability is as high as 95%.[7]

- *The status quo bias* reflects people's tendency to stick with the status quo—that is, doing nothing or maintaining one's current or previous decision.[8] One explanation relates the status quo bias to loss aversion, whereby the potential loss from moving away from the reference point outweighs the corresponding gain (because the value function is steeper in the loss domain). One of the most prominent examples of the status quo bias involves the impact of the default option on organ donation: across European countries, the "opt out" countries (where the default option is to become a donor unless a customer opts out) have drastically higher proportions of the population in the potential organ donor pool—a difference of at least 60 percentage points—compared to "opt in" countries (where the default option is not to become a donor).[9]

- The *confirmation bias* reflects people's tendency to look for information that supports their existing beliefs, interpret ambiguous data as supporting those beliefs, and reject data that go against those beliefs. For example, imagine that a manager holds a belief that running sales promotions around major holidays is a good idea because every time a promotion is put in place the sales volume goes up. This bias stems from the fact that the manager gathers only confirmatory evidence supporting his belief without gathering disconfirming evidence (e.g., testing whether not running a promotion would lead to lower sales volume).

- *The attraction effect* reflects people's tendency to evaluate options based on their relative advantage (rather than on their inherent value), whereby adding an option that is inferior to one of the other options in the set tends to increase the choice share of the (relatively) superior option. Consider the case of Williams-Sonoma, which used to offer one home bread maker priced at $275. Later, it extended its product line by adding a second home bread maker that had similar features, was slightly larger, and was priced more than 50% higher than the original bread maker. This relatively inferior (significantly more expensive but only slightly better) addition to the available choice set did not sell well; however, the sales of the less expensive bread maker nearly doubled.[10]

- *The compromise effect* reflects people's tendency to avoid options with extreme values in favor of the options with moderate values on all attributes.[11] For example, when presented with a choice set comprising a high-price/high quality option, a low price/low quality option, and an option that has average price and quality, consumers might choose the latter option because it offers a compromise between options with extreme values on price and quality. Thus, consumers end up choosing an alternative that appears to be a compromise in the particular choice set under consideration, even though it is not the best alternative on any one dimension.

CHAPTER FIVE

GATHERING MARKET INSIGHTS

*Some people use statistics as a drunk man uses
lamp-posts — for support rather than for illumination.*
— Andrew Lang, Scottish poet, novelist, and anthropologist

M arket research provides managers with insights that help them create and capture value. It facilitates effective decision making by furnishing managers with the relevant information needed to assess tradeoffs inherent in solving business problems. Market research aims to replace gut-feel choices with evidence-based decisions in which managers supplement their own judgment with data to solve business problems. This chapter addresses the following market research topics:

- *Market Research as a Process* || Market research as a business function | Problem-driven market research
- *Defining the Business Problem and Formulating the Research Question* || Defining the business problem | Formulating the research question
- *Selecting the Research Method* || Exploratory research | Descriptive research | Experimental research
- *Gathering and Analyzing the Data* || Gathering primary data | Gathering secondary data | Analyzing the data
- *Interpreting the Results* || Assessing the validity of the data | Managing decision errors
- *Solving the Business Problem* || Evidence-based decision making | Selecting a course of action

The discussion of gathering market insights is complemented by an in-depth overview of two additional topics: the key principles in establishing causality and popular research methods.

Market Research as a Process

The primary purpose of market research is to guide managerial decision making. Effective business decisions require that managers understand the market in which the company competes. This understanding is achieved through market research, a process designed to generate insights that aid decision making. The role of market research as a business function and the problem-driven nature of gathering market insights are outlined in the following sections.

Market Research as a Business Function

Market research provides managers with relevant data to inform their decisions. The insights generated through market research help managers create value by providing them with an understanding of the environment in which they compete. This information helps managers shape strategies to enter new markets and protect their positions in existing markets. Market research also provides managers with an opportunity to test potential decisions before expending significant resources to implement them. By breaking down a business problem into a series of research questions and testable hypotheses, market research provides managers with an opportunity to rigorously validate and improve their ideas.

Market research promotes rigorous analytical thinking about business problems. Its process of asking concrete, testable, and relevant questions forces managers to elucidate business problems clearly and provides a systematic and detailed framework for thinking through complex problems and their solutions. This added clarity can, in turn, lead to a better understanding of the assumptions underlying potential solutions to business problems.

Conducting market research is a collaborative process in which a research team finds solutions to business problems based on market insights. Research teams include managers to oversee the project and practitioners who conduct the day-to-day work of gathering and analyzing data. Conducting market research typically involves four different entities: business managers, research project managers, market insights teams, and data analytics teams.

- **Business managers** set the direction of a market research project, evaluate the strategic and tactical implications of the research findings, and use these findings to make business decisions.

- **Research project managers** oversee the day-to-day progress of a project. They work in close collaboration with market insights and data analytics teams to ensure that a research project achieves its goals and they communicate the findings to business managers.

- **Market insights researchers** gather and analyze the relevant data as defined by the scope of the research project. These teams are composed of experts in gathering data through experiments, surveys, interviews, and focus groups.

- **Data analytics researchers** organize and analyze data gathered in the course of the company's regular business activities as well as the data collected by the market insights teams. Data analytics teams are highly skilled in working with large amounts of data (often referred to as "big data") in order to understand the relationships between events and predict market outcomes.

Coordinating the research activities across these different entities is essential for gathering meaningful market insights. Thus, business managers must have a basic knowledge of market research in order to formulate an actionable research question. Research project managers need to be provided with the relevant context to accurately understand the research problem and address it in a meaningful way. Market insights and data analytics researchers need to be skilled in gathering and analyzing market data in order to carry out a project efficiently. Working together, these four different entities inform managerial decision making by furnishing relevant market data.

Problem-Driven Market Research

The ultimate goal of market research is to facilitate the process of identifying, analyzing, and solving business problems. In this context, market research can be viewed as a multi-stage process that begins with the identification of the business problem that needs to be addressed and concludes with a proposed solution to resolve the identified problem. This view of market research as a problem-solving process is depicted in Figure 1.

Figure 1. The Problem-Driven Market Research Process

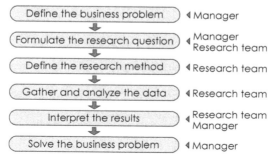

The first step in the market research process is to define the business problem that the company aims to address. Defining the business problem is typically accomplished by company managers, with the market research team playing little, if any, role in the process. Business problems addressed by market research can include a broad range of issues, from finding target customers and developing new offerings to understanding factors leading to poorly performing products and determining the best allocation of marketing resources.

Once the business problem is defined, the market research team collaborates with managers to create a set of concrete questions that will be used to generate insights. To this end, managers work closely with the market research team to translate the business problem into well-defined research questions that can be answered using existing research methodologies. Following the formulation of research questions, the research team defines the specific research method(s) that will be employed to address these questions and gather and analyze the relevant data. Determining the best means of gathering and analyzing the data is typically conducted with little, if any, participation from the company's managers.

In the final stages of the project, managers step in to generate insights and solve the business problem. After the data are collected and analyzed, research project managers, working closely with analytics teams, interpret the results to relate the findings to the initial research question asked and rule out alternative explanations. Finally, informed by the data, marketing managers must make a decision that will address the business problem. The key steps in this problem-driven approach to market research are discussed in more detail in the following sections.

Defining the Business Problem and Formulating the Research Question

The research process starts with defining the business problem the company needs to solve, followed by formulating the specific research question(s) that needs to be addressed in order to solve the business problem. The business problem is defined by the company's managers and requires a thorough understanding of the company's strategic goals and business model. The research question, on the other hand, is formulated jointly by company managers and the market research team, who determine the specific information that needs to be gathered in order to address the identified business problem. The key aspects of these two processes are discussed in the following sections.

Defining the Business Problem

Most business problems fall into one of two categories: problems that require analyzing the market in which the company operates and problems that involve developing a course of action that enhances the company's ability to create value in this market. *Market-analysis problems* involve evaluating market opportunities, assessing changes in the market, understanding competitors' offerings, and investigating the gap between the company's desired and actual performance. *Action-planning problems*, on the other hand, involve the development of a new offering and the modification of an existing offering (Figure 2).

Figure 2. Key Types of Business Problems

The two types of business problems often represent different phases in the development and modification of offerings. Most market-analysis problems are strategic in nature, focusing on understanding the target market and the value proposition. In contrast, most action-planning problems are tactical in nature, focusing on developing a market offering that best implements the company's strategy. The types of business problems faced by a company are discussed in more detail below.

Market-Analysis Problems

Market-analysis problems call for gaining a better understanding of a market in order to generate or modify a viable value-creation strategy. The most common market-analysis problems include *market-opportunity problems*, *market-change problems*, and *performance-gap problems*.

- **Market-opportunity problems** call for evaluating the viability of introducing a new offering to take advantage of the identified opportunity. Market-opportunity problems involve identifying an unmet customer need and assessing the company's ability to fulfill this need better than the competition.

- **Market-change problems** call for evaluating the impact of a change in the environment in which the company operates. Market changes can involve changes in target customers (e.g., changes in customer needs and preferences), changes in the competitive environment (e.g., a new competitive entry), changes in the company's collaborators (e.g., increased pressure to provide more favorable terms to retailers), and changes in the context in which the company operates (e.g., economic recession, the development of a new technology, and the introduction of new regulations).

- **Performance-gap problems** address a discrepancy between a company's desired and actual performance on a key metric such as net income, profit margins, revenues, and market share. Performance-gap problems call for assessing the magnitude of the problem and identifying its antecedents (e.g., its primary cause) and consequences.

Market-analysis problems tend to be rather strategic in nature and are closely linked with the identification of a target market in which the company will compete, the development of a meaningful value proposition, and improvement of the company's market performance. Research projects focused on market-analysis problems are often followed by projects that explore alternative solutions to address the identified problems.

Action-Planning Problems

Action-planning problems involve the development of an action plan to take advantage of an identified market opportunity, respond to a market change, or close a performance gap. Common action-planning problems involve the *development of a new offering* and the *optimization of an existing offering*.

- **Offering-design problems** involve defining the key attributes of the company's offering. This type of problem typically entails designing the product, service, and brand aspects of the offering, determining the offering's price and incentives, developing a meaningful communication campaign, and developing an effective distribution system.

- **Offering-optimization problems** involve modifying an already existing offering in order to improve its market performance. This type of problem typically includes altering the aspects of the offering that are suboptimal with respect to their ability to create market value. Thus, offering-optimization problems aim to align the design, communication, and distribution aspects of the offering with the current market realities.

Because they result in a specific course of action aimed at improving an offering's market position, action-planning problems typically arise from solutions offered to market-analysis problems. In this context, addressing action-planning problems usually involves the tactical aspects of the offering and focuses on the ways in which these tactics can be implemented to become a market reality.

Formulating the Research Question

To address the business problem, a manager needs to formulate a meaningful research question that identifies the relevant information needed to solve the problem at hand. As a result, the research question is almost always narrower in scope than the business problem it aims to solve. Thus, the research question does not reflect all the intricacies of the underlying business problem but rather is focused on uncovering the information that is pertinent to making a well-informed business decision. Most research questions fall into one of two types: *market-analysis questions* and *market-planning questions*.

Formulating Market-Analysis Research Questions

Market-analysis research questions aim to offer insights into the specifics of the market in which the company operates. Because they focus on the issues pertaining to the target market and the value that the company creates and captures in this market, market-analysis questions are typically strategic in nature. Thus, they concentrate on the key aspects of the market in which the company operates and the ways in which the company creates value for target customers, collaborators, and company stakeholders. There are four types of market-analysis research questions:

- **Market-demand questions** identify market needs that are not fully addressed by the company and its competitors. This type of question aims to identify an unmet customer need that the company can fulfill better than the competition.

- **Targeting questions** identify the customers that the company will prioritize when considering its offerings. These questions also involve identifying the customer profile—demographics, geolocation, psychographics, and behaviors—as well as assessing the size and growth potential of target markets.

- **Segmentation questions** aim to group customers into segments such that the members of each segment are similar to one another and different from members of other segments in terms of the value they seek and can offer. Segmentation questions often precede targeting questions by helping define the focal unit of the company's targeting decisions.

- **Marketing-context questions** focus on the changes in the context in which the company operates. This type of question might address changes in customer needs, collaborator goals, and competitor offerings, as well as track larger sociocultural, technological, regulatory, economic, and environmental trends.

Market-analysis questions are often interrelated, such that market-demand and marketing-context questions are typically followed by segmentation and targeting questions. For example, when reevaluating a company's market strategy, a manager might start by asking questions that identify unmet customer needs and determine the overall size of the market and then proceed with questions aiming to segment the market and select target customers.

Formulating Action-Planning Research Questions

Action-planning research questions offer insight into the specifics of the offering with which the company aims to create and capture market value. The goal of action-planning questions is to address specific issues pertaining to the design, communication, and delivery of the company offering. Accordingly, common action-planning research questions fall into the following categories:

- **Offering-design questions** involve the product, service, brand, price, and incentives aspects of the offering. These questions aim to facilitate the design of new offerings, explore market reaction to the company's existing offerings, and make recommendations on how to improve the market value created by these offerings.

- **Communication questions** examine the ways in which the company informs the relevant market entities about the specifics of its offering. Communication questions involve issues such as defining the target audience, identifying the optimal communication channels, streamlining the communicated message, and assessing communication effectiveness.

- **Distribution questions** examine the ways in which the company offering is delivered to target customers and collaborators. Distribution questions involve issues such as identifying the optimal distribution channels, defining the distribution logistics, as well as examining the effectiveness of the existing means of distribution.

Because they focus on specific aspects of managing a company's offering, action-planning questions are typically related to and often stem from the findings of market-analysis questions. Thus, unlike market-analysis questions that typically focus on strategic issues such as identifying the target market and the value that the company can create in this market, action-planning questions focus on the ways in which a company can develop an offering that will create value in this market.

Key Principles in Formulating Research Questions

Formulating meaningful questions is essential to attaining consequential information that will facilitate managerial decision making. Unless it is guided by clearly defined and relevant research questions, market research is unlikely to deliver any useful information. In the words of American inventor Charles Kettering, "A problem well stated is a problem half solved." In the context of market research, well-stated questions have four properties: They are *relevant*, *actionable*, *concrete*, and *simple*.

- **Relevant** questions aim to provide information that is directly related to solving the focal business problem. Relevance is particularly important given the tendency of many managers to generate questions that are only tangentially related to the problem at hand. While at first glance it might seem that more information is always better, it is important to realize that each additional question involves the extra cost of gathering, processing, and interpreting the related information. As a result of this added complexity, generating too many questions can water down the resources available for conducting market research. More important, gathering and analyzing information that is irrelevant or only tangentially related to the issue at hand can distract managers from addressing the focal business problem.

- **Actionable** questions are directly related to the different courses of action a company can take to address an impending problem or take advantage of a market opportunity. A popular approach to generating actionable market research is to first lay out the alternative actions the company might take after the research study is complete and then outline the specific information the company needs to receive in order to decide how to act. To this end, a manager might generate scenarios of potential outcomes and link them to the identified courses of action. Developing the research questions from the viewpoint of the particular decisions the company must make can help ensure that the gathered data will be actionable, will benefit managerial decision making, and will be obtained in a cost-efficient manner.

- **Concrete** questions are clearly articulated and specific. They should allow for empirical testing, meaning that it should be relatively easy to envision how these questions can be addressed through market research. General questions such as "understand the customer" and "analyze the industry" can take many directions and are likely to produce answers that are very broad and not very informative with respect to the specific business problem that the company needs to address. The more specific the research question, the more precise the answer furnished by market research is likely to be.

- **Simple** questions address a single issue and are articulated in a straightforward fashion that leaves no place for ambiguity. Simplicity is important because of the tendency of many managers to formulate questions that are overly complicated, which, in turn, leads to unfocused market research and output that does not inform the business

problem at hand. A workable remedy for dealing with problems that appear to require complex questions is to break down the compound questions into several simpler questions that can be readily addressed.

Formulating research questions that are simple, actionable, concrete, and relevant greatly
increases the chances that market research will produce informative results. Because it requires knowledge of both the business problem and the research tools available to address
this problem, formulating the research questions is best accomplished by marketing managers in collaboration with the leader of the market research team. Such collaboration can go a
long way to ensure that the research output can help improve managerial decision making
and enhance the company's ability to create market value.

Selecting the Research Method

Once the research question has been formulated, the next step is to select the research method
that will be used to collect market data. Based on the approach used to gather market insights, there are three basic types of research methods: *exploratory*, *descriptive*, and *experimental*.

Exploratory Research

Exploratory research helps managers in the early stages of a market research project attain a
general understanding of the business problem, generate new ideas, and formulate hypotheses. This type of research often leads to insights that can be used as a starting point for
setting the direction of a project and generating more specific research questions. Thus, this
type of research is not focused on quantifying the obtained insights or establishing causal
relationships. Common exploratory methods include *observation*, *personal interviews*, *focus
group interviews*, *activity-based tasks*, and *exploratory data mining*.

Observation

Observation examines people's behavior in their natural environment to gain insights into
their needs and the ways in which they address these needs. Many observational methods
are derived from ethnography, a branch of anthropology that examines the sociocultural aspect of people's lives.

Observation can involve monitoring people's physical behavior, including the way they
go about evaluating, buying, and consuming products and services in order to fulfill their
needs. For example, researchers might visit consumers in their homes or offices to observe
their behavior in their natural environment to gain insight into their needs, daily rituals, and
product usage. A less intrusive method of observation involves remotely monitoring the behavior of consumers who have consented to participate in the study by using video cameras
embedded in their homes, offices, and even cars. Observation can also include tracking people's online behavior, including the websites they visit, the content they focus on, and the
information they share online.

A key advantage of observation is that it captures individuals' behavior in their natural
environment. Furthermore, observation typically does not require researchers to have preliminary hypotheses about specific relationships that might exist in the market. On the downside, however, observation often provides qualitative data that might be difficult to quantify
to test its empirical validity (with the notable exception of using "big data" to observe individuals' online behavior). In addition, in the vast majority of cases, observation cannot be
used to establish causality.

Personal Interviews

Personal interviews explore in depth people's views, experiences, beliefs, and motivations to
uncover their unmet needs, understand how they make decisions, and identify factors that
influence their behavior. Interviews can be conducted in person or indirectly, using questionnaires administered by mail or online. Based on the way they are conducted, interviews
can be structured, unstructured, or semi-structured.

Structured interviews ask participants predefined questions without allowing for any follow-up questions or conversation. They can be thought of as questionnaires administered either in person, online, or by mail. *Unstructured interviews* do not follow a predetermined agenda and resemble a conversation in which respondents' answers determine the course of the interview. Finally, *semi-structured interviews* combine features of both structured and unstructured interviews: They contain predefined questions but also allow follow-up questions and interaction when responses warrant further elaboration.

In addition to the way they are conducted, personal interviews can vary in their depth. Some interviews are relatively straightforward and focus on issues such as individuals' preferences, shopping behavior, and demographic information. In contrast, in-depth interviews aim to uncover the deeper motives that drive individuals' behavior. These interviews often use projective techniques emanating from psychology—such as word association, sentence completion, and picture interpretation—to gain a better understanding of the deeper motivations that drive consumer behavior.

The main advantage of personal interviews is that they can provide a wealth of information on specific topics that are of interest to researchers. In addition, the interactivity of the interviews provides researchers with greater flexibility in adapting the questions based on individuals' responses. On the downside, however, interviews can be a costly way to gather information, especially when they are conducted in person. Another potential drawback of interviews is the so-called desirability bias (also referred to as the demand effect), whereby respondents tailor their answers in a way that they believe will please the interviewer. For example, when asked whether they like a company's product, respondents tend to overstate the degree to which they find this product attractive as well as the likelihood of purchasing the product.

Focus Groups

Focus groups are interviews conducted with groups rather than individuals. They involve engaging carefully selected participants in a free-flowing discussion aimed at revealing their collective opinions on a given topic. Participants in these groups usually are the company's target customers, whose views, insights, and ideas the company aims to explore in an interactive social context.

Focus groups are typically moderated by a professional facilitator whose role is to keep the discussion on point, explore potentially interesting ideas suggested by participants, and ensure that all participants have the opportunity to share their thoughts. The facilitator can also offer a meaningful interpretation of the discussion and relate it to the business problem the company aims to address. Focus-group interviews can be conducted in person or in online settings, with online focus-group interviews growing in popularity because of the lower costs and the greater ease of execution.

A key advantage of focus groups over one-on-one interviews is that they offer a broader range of insights, ideas, and opinions that stem from the socially interactive nature of the group discussion. Focus groups shed light on social dynamics, indicating how an individual's ideas are likely to be received by others. Focus groups are also faster and more cost efficient than individual interviews. On the downside, the interactions among the focus group participants have the potential to influence the discussion in a way that overemphasizes some ideas and overlooks others.

Activity-Based Studies

Activity-based studies probe people's thoughts by asking them to perform specific tasks such as drawing a picture, role-playing a situation, or arranging a series of images to create a narrative. These methods are rooted in the idea that people's beliefs, feelings, and motivations are better captured by actions rather than words. For example, study participants might be asked to collect pictures representing their thoughts and feelings related to an aspect of their lives. These pictures are then used as the basis for in-depth interviews to gain better insight into their individual beliefs, needs, and preferences. Alternatively, respondents might be asked to draw cartoons of typical users of a brand, write an obituary for a brand, or compare a brand to an animal, a car, or a magazine. Because they offer an alternative approach to understanding target customers, activity-based studies are often used to complement observational studies, personal interviews, and focus groups.

Exploratory Data Mining

Exploratory data mining uses existing data to find patterns that can help managers formulate research questions. Exploratory data mining often involves analyzing consumers' social media communication and search behavior. It includes analyses that look for changes in consumer preferences, needs, or attitudes; maps the growth of product categories; and examines general macroeconomic or demographic trends that influence consumer behavior. In addition to providing insights into consumers' behavior, exploratory data analysis can involve examining the behavior of the other market entities, including the company's competitors and collaborators. A company can also use exploratory data analysis to gain a better understanding of its own operations, assess the performance of different business units, and examine the market impact of its offerings.

Descriptive Research

Descriptive research is similar to exploratory research in that it helps the company gain information about the market in which it aims to create value. However, unlike exploratory research, which is primarily qualitative in nature, descriptive research gathers *quantitative* information. Thus, descriptive research can provide information about the size of a given market, the demographic characteristics of the company's target customers, the market position of competitive offerings, and the sales volume attainable by the company. Descriptive research aims to answer four key questions: *Who? What? Where?* and *When?* It does not address the question *Why?*

Common types of descriptive research include customer research, competitive research, and company research.

Customer research helps companies assess business opportunities by estimating the size and the potential of a given market. This assessment can then help a company determine whether a particular market is sufficiently attractive to justify market entry as well as grow and defend a company's market position. Customer research can also facilitate the identification of different types of buyers by dividing the market into segments based on customers' likely response to the company's offering. The resulting segmentation helps companies decide which segments to target and which to ignore, as well as optimize their offerings for the chosen segments.

Competitive research informs the company about the market position of its competitors, focusing on factors such as competitor size, market share, promotional activities, and distribution network. Gaining competitive insight enables the company to better understand the strengths and weaknesses of its competitors, assess the degree to which they present a viable threat to the company's offerings, and ultimately develop a course of action to counteract competitive threats and strengthen its market position.

Company research informs the company about the market performance of its own offerings. For example, research can inform the company about key performance metrics such as the market share of its products and services, the strength of its brand, and the availability of its offerings across different distribution channels. Company research might also investigate the cost efficiency of the company's internal operations, the allocation and productivity of its salesforce, and the capacity utilization of its production facilities.

Descriptive research can also examine broader trends in a particular product category or the economy in general to gain a better understanding of whether and how these trends might influence the company's business model. In this context, descriptive research might help identify the key factors defining the environment in which the company operates as well as quantify their likely impact on the company's products, services, and brands.

Experimental Research

Experimental studies allow managers to understand cause-and-effect relationships in the market. They typically involve changing one factor (e.g., product design) to establish whether it has a causal impact on another factor (e.g., offering desirability). This level of control distinguishes experimental research from exploratory and descriptive studies in which an observer passively gathers information. The causal relationships established through experimental research can provide a more thorough understanding of customers and their behaviors than other forms of research. The terms *causal research* and *experimental research* are often used interchangeably because experiments are the main method used to establish causality.

The key benefit of experimentation is its ability to establish causal relationships in which a change in one factor necessarily leads to a change in another factor. For example, an experiment can determine whether an increase in sales is caused by a company's new advertising campaign and not by another factor like a general improvement in the economy. Only experimentation can prove causality in this way by controlling for other variables that could influence the relationship between the factors of interest. Other forms of research can only reveal correlations that may suggest, but cannot prove, a causal relationship.

By altering a particular attribute in a controlled environment, experiments can examine the impact of a company's action on customer mindset (what customers think) and customer behavior (what customers do). Customer *mindset* can be measured by examining their awareness of the offering, their beliefs about the offering's features, their preference for the offering, their intent to purchase the offering, and their intent to recommend this offering to other customers. Examining customer *behavior* typically involves assessing whether customers will actually purchase the offering, how customers use the offering, and whether they will advocate the offering to other customers (Figure 3).

Figure 3. Experimentation as a Tool for Gathering Market Insight

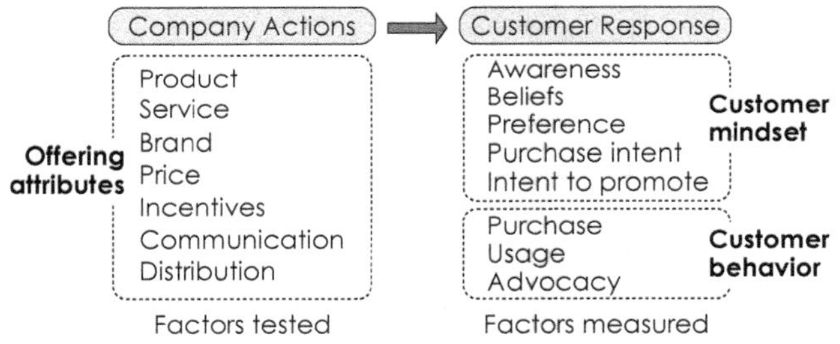

The factors that are seen as possible causes of an outcome of interest are commonly referred to as *independent variables*, whereas factors that change as a result of a change in the independent variables are referred to as *dependent variables*. In this context, experimental research aims to establish a link between independent and dependent variables, focusing on the degree to which changes in different independent variables can predict (or explain) changes in the dependent variables.

The simplest version of an experiment, referred to as *A/B testing*, involves two conditions: an experimental condition used to measure the impact of the factor of interest (e.g., product design, brand name, or price) and a control condition used as a basis of comparison. Depending on whether the experimental and control conditions are designed by the researcher or have naturally occurred in the market, there are two types of experiments: controlled experiments and natural experiments.

Controlled experiments intentionally expose consumers to different experimental conditions to observe their responses. Controlled experiments can be conducted in an artificial setting, as in the case of lab studies, or in a real market environment, as in the case of field studies. For example, to examine the impact of price on sales volume, a researcher might invite respondents to a research facility and ask them to indicate the likelihood of their purchasing the products of interest at different price points. Alternatively, a researcher might set up a field experiment in which a retailer varies the prices at which the products of interest are sold to different customers in order to observe their reactions.

Rather than assigning respondents to different experimental conditions, *natural experiments* take advantage of differences that already exist in the market and use these differences to draw inferences about the relationships of interest. For example, to understand the impact of changes in price on sales volume, a manager might examine the changes in sales of products (the dependent variable) as a function of the historic fluctuation of their prices (the independent variable).

Because they rely on extant data and do not require a special setup, natural experiments are typically less costly and easier to conduct. At the same time, because managers do not have direct control over the event being studied, the observed pattern of behavior might not be caused by the factor of interest (e.g., a product's price) but might stem from a different factor (e.g., a change in the price of the competitive products) that happen to coincide with the factor of interest. As a result, natural experiments are generally less likely to detect causal relationships than are controlled experiments.

Gathering and Analyzing Market Data

Based on the way it is gathered, market data can be primary or secondary. *Primary data* involve original information collected by the company to address the specific question of interest to the company. In contrast, *secondary data* involve already existing information that has been collected by the company or a third party for purposes unrelated to the specific question of interest to the company.

Gathering Primary Data

Primary data consist of information collected to answer specific research questions. Gathering primary data offers several benefits. First, primary data can provide a high level of detail on topics that are particular to a company and its offerings (unlike secondary data, which have not been collected for the company and are typically more general in nature). Furthermore, primary data can provide information that is current (unlike secondary data, which often is dated and might not adequately represent the current state of affairs). Finally, primary data can remain proprietary to the company and, therefore, is not available to competitors. On the downside, however, gathering primary data tends to be relatively expensive and time consuming.

Two issues merit attention when gathering primary data: determining the sample size and selecting study participants. These two issues are discussed in more detail below.

Determining the Sample Size

The key tradeoff when considering sample size is between accuracy, complexity, and cost, such that increasing the sample size tends to increase the accuracy of the study while also increasing its costs and vice versa. In this context, the sample size should be large enough to answer research questions with sufficient accuracy while keeping research costs at bay.

Everything else being equal, larger sample sizes tend to better represent the underlying population and allow for the detection of smaller effects. At the same time, using larger samples tends to increase the cost and complexity of the study as larger amounts of data must be acquired and analyzed. Small samples, on the other hand, are more manageable and less costly—features that make them desirable from a cost-efficiency perspective. At the same, small samples have several drawbacks. First, by virtue of their size, smaller samples are less likely to be representative of the entire population. Furthermore, small samples tend to decrease the ability of the study to detect the effects of interest. Thus, even if an effect exists in reality, a study using a small sample might not distinguish it from the random noise that is inherent in the data.

Selecting an optimal sample size is central to gathering accurate data while keeping costs under control. To this end, companies often use statistical methods to determine the right sample size that has sufficient power to detect the effects of interest and yet enable the company to keep research costs low. The ability to collect data online has dramatically reduced the cost of research, enabling companies with access to online data like Amazon, Facebook, Google, and Tencent to run thousands of studies using large samples.

Selecting Study Participants

Having the right sample size, albeit important, is not enough. The chosen sample must also adequately reflect the characteristics of the population it aims to represent. In this context, an important challenge in selecting study participants is controlling for *selection bias* to ensure that the sample adequately represents the target population. For example, out of convenience a manager might test the desirability of a new product only in a single city even though this product targets a much broader market.

In order for the study results to be generalizable to the entire market, the research sample must reflect the characteristics of the population from which it is drawn. For example, a manager trying to understand a particular market should make sure that the research sample reflects the characteristics of that market on all key dimensions—including age, gender, income, occupation, level of education, religion, ethnicity, employment status, geographic location, population density, social class, household size, and stage in the life cycle. A research sample that reflects the characteristics of the population under consideration is referred to as *representative*. The closer to representative a sample is, the more likely that insights gathered from a study will translate to the broader population.

A common problem in selecting study participants is the *self-selection bias*, whereby individuals who respond to the survey share a common characteristic, thus producing a sample that is not representative of the target market. For example, a customer satisfaction survey is more likely to elicit responses from those who are extremely dissatisfied with the company's offering, resulting in a biased assessment of the overall level of satisfaction among all customers. A common approach to minimizing the self-selection bias involves randomly assigning respondents to different study conditions and ensuring that selected respondents actually end up participating in the study.

The case of the *Literary Digest* poll serves as a cautionary tale about the danger of selecting a biased research sample. In an effort to predict the outcome of the 1936 U.S. presidential election between incumbent Franklin D. Roosevelt and challenger Alfred Landon, *Literary Digest* sent out 10 million mock ballots to people across the country. The list of names was acquired by scouring sources like telephone books, magazine subscriptions, and club memberships. Almost 2.5 million people returned the mock ballots and the magazine confidently predicted that Landon would win with 57% of the vote. It turned out, however, that Roosevelt won the election with 62% of the vote, almost opposite of what the *Digest* had predicted. The *Digest's* faulty predictions were a result of poor sampling. By sampling respondents from telephone books and magazine memberships, it had inadvertently sent out ballots to a disproportionately large percentage of middle- and upper-class people. Indeed, in the 1930s telephones were a luxury; as a result, lower income voters were not well represented in telephone books and, hence, among the poll participants.

Gathering Secondary Data

Unlike primary data, which involve original information collected to address a specific question of interest to the company, secondary data involve already existing information that has been collected for a different purpose. The main advantage of secondary data is that they are readily available and in most cases less costly than primary data. On the downside, however, because they have already been collected for a different purpose, secondary data might neither be current nor directly relevant to the current research project. As a result, many companies tend to use secondary data to augment the problem-specific primary data.

A company can obtain secondary data from external sources or, alternatively, it can gather these data internally. Common external and internal sources of secondary data are delineated in more detail below.

Obtaining Secondary Data from External Sources

There are numerous organizations devoted to collecting and disseminating data that can be useful for market research projects. These sources are most useful when it is impractical for a company to collect the data needed for a research project. Common external data sources include *government agencies*, *academic institutions* and *think tanks*, and *market research companies*.

Government agencies, especially in developed economies, regularly publish data covering economic and demographic issues and can serve as a cost-efficient and reliable way of gathering market insights. Some governments even have several branches that specialize in collecting information, like the U.S. Census Bureau and Eurostat in the EU. Because in many cases these data have been collected for decades, they can be particularly valuable for tracking trends over time.

Academic institutions and *think tanks* also regularly collect data that are readily available to the public. Unlike government institutions, which focus primarily on economic and demographic data, academic and think tank research centers tend to cover a broader range of topics. For example, organizations like the Pew Research Center and NORC have been publishing data for decades on a wide array of public attitudes on issues ranging from cultural mores and technology to the economy.

Market research companies specialize in collecting and distributing data. The data gathered by market research companies are broader in scope than those collected by government agencies, academic institutions, and think tanks. For example, companies like Mintel provide a wealth of reports on consumer trends affecting various categories. Other companies like Nielsen gather data on shopper behavior collected from paid consumer panels. Yet other companies like Experian aggregate large amounts of data on tens of millions of consumers from multiple disparate sources. Unlike the other external sources of secondary data, the data gathered by most market research companies are not freely available and can be costly to acquire.

Obtaining Secondary Data from Internal Sources

In addition to gathering data from a third party, a company might obtain secondary data from internal sources. Indeed, most companies readily possess significant amounts of data that can be used to address research questions. For example, a company might have collected data reflecting visits to the company website, the information search patterns of online shoppers, and the buying behavior of its customers.

Within the company, secondary data are typically provided by the market research department, which can gather and analyze the relevant information. Internal secondary data can involve information pertaining to the company's customers, its collaborators, as well as the company's own operations. For example, customer data might include information on customer sign-ups, website search data, purchase data, loyalty program data, customer satisfaction data, information on customer complaints, as well as qualitative descriptions of the company's interactions with customers. In the same vein, collaborator data might involve information about the company's suppliers and distribution channels on issues such as sales volume, pricing, and sales promotions.

In addition to gathering secondary data about the other market entities, a company can gather data about its own operations. For example, a company can gather information about the market performance of its offerings on metrics such as sales revenues, sales volume, market share, and profitability. Internal company data can also inform managers about more complex issues such as the market response to the company's promotional activities, the relationship between a company's advertising and sales volume, and the impact of salesforce compensation on productivity.

Analyzing the Data

Data collection is followed by analysis of the data, which aims to establish significant patterns and trends that can shed light on the research question at hand. The specifics of data analysis are to a large degree a function of the nature of the data. In this context, two types of approaches to data analysis can be distinguished: analysis of structured data and analysis of unstructured and semi-structured data.

Analyzing Structured Data

Structured data are information that is organized in a highly ordered fashion. Structured data typically involve text or numerals organized in rows and columns. Examples of structured data include responses to closed-ended survey questions, lists of names and addresses, and company financial information. Because of its high degree of organization, structured data are the easiest type of data to analyze. The analysis of structured data typically involves organizing, summarizing, and modeling the data.

Organizing the data involves streamlining the available information by collapsing it into a smaller number of relevant metrics. A common approach to organizing data is segmentation, which encompasses a set of techniques that separate the data into mutually exclusive groups. Segmentation can be as simple as dividing data by the values of a specific variable. A more complex segmentation technique is clustering, which combines multiple variables to create groups that most differ from one another.

Summarizing the data involves generating descriptive statistics that abstract the available information. One of the simplest methods for summarizing involves assessing averages. Comparing averages is often used to find differences between groups in conjunction with statistical tests like the t-test. Averages can also be used as a simple way of finding trends in longitudinal data—for example, by inspecting average sales revenues over time. Another popular approach involves examining the distribution of the individual data points. For example, the data could be summarized in the form of a frequency table that counts the number of times a particular event (e.g., sales promotion) appears in the data.

Data modeling involves analyzing the relational properties of the data to examine the link between the variables of interest. One of the most common modeling methods is regression analysis, which aims to uncover the relationship between factors that the company can control (dependent variables) and the desirable outcomes (independent variables). For example, regression analysis might examine the relationship between price, advertising, and sales promotions on the one hand and sales volume on the other. Another common method involves time-series analysis, which examines the changes in a particular factor over time, often in order to forecast its future performance. For example, a company might examine the sales of a particular product since its market launch and use these data to forecast future sales.

Analyzing Unstructured and Semi-Structured Data

Unstructured data involve information that does not involve text or numerals and is not organized in a matrix format featuring rows and columns. Most of the data that people encounter on a daily basis are unstructured. Examples of unstructured data include images, sounds, videos, books, and social media posts. *Semi-structured data* involve information that has some structure but is not fully organized and contains some unstructured components. Examples of semi-structured data include freeform text from consumer surveys, databases of entries from social media, and databases containing audio-visual information.

Analyzing unstructured and semi-structured data starts with applying structure to the dataset and then analyzing it using methods similar to those used in analyzing structured data. For example, analyzing social media posts often starts with first imposing a certain type of structure such as a matrix showing the frequency of occurrence for words of interest. As a result, analyzing unstructured data typically requires substantially more effort than analyzing structured data. Two commonly used techniques for analyzing unstructured and semi-structured data are natural language processing and metadata analysis.

Natural language processing involves analyzing natural streams of recorded or written text. For example, a company might analyze freeform text to understand the sentiment of the communicator—a technique commonly referred to as sentiment analysis and used to gauge popular sentiment on social media that is associated with the company's products, services, and brands.

Metadata analysis involves examining the information linked to the gathered data. Unstructured data, particularly when collected online, are often associated with a set of automatically collected metadata. For example, social media posts are often associated with information such as the time that the comment was left, the person's name and location, and how this person arrived at the website. By analyzing these metadata in combination with other unstructured-data techniques such as natural language processing, a company can gain additional customer insights.

Interpreting the Results

Following data analysis, researchers must relate the empirical findings to the business problem that the company aims to solve to ensure that the research findings can, in fact, help solve this problem. Accordingly, at this stage researchers go beyond analyzing the gathered data to include the business context in which the specific research question is being asked. Interpreting the research data involves two key issues: *assessing the validity of the data* and *managing decision errors*.

Assessing the Validity of the Data

Data validity reflects whether the reported results are methodologically sound. There are two commonly distinguished types of validity: *internal validity*, reflecting how well a study is designed, and *external validity*, reflecting how well the results of a study can be generalized beyond the experimental setup to the market the study aims to examine.

Internal Validity

Internal validity reflects whether the study actually measures what it purports to measure. In other words, internal validity is a measure of the degree to which the findings of the study are logically sound and cannot be accounted for by factors other than those explicitly manipulated or measured. Common threats to internal validity include experimental design errors and analysis errors.

Experimental design errors occur when a study does not accurately measure the factors of interest. For example, vaguely worded or leading questions are likely to result in answers that do not accurately address the issue the study aims to investigate. Another common error is the use of experimental designs that lend themselves to the social desirability bias, thus enabling respondents to guess the purpose of the experiment and answer accordingly. The social desirability bias often stems from a respondent's desire to reciprocate being rewarded for participating in a study and can overshadow the impact of the factors that the experiment aims to investigate.

Analysis errors refer to inaccuracies in the assessment of the data. These errors can include data entry errors, miscalculations when processing the available data, and applying statistical analysis methods inappropriately. For example, a common type of error involves deciding how to analyze the data *after* looking at the data. The problem here is that researchers might selectively focus only on those aspects of the data that are most likely to produce significant (and desired) results, which, in turn, will lead to inaccurate conclusions about the market. Planning out analyses before engaging with the data can help prevent these types of analysis errors.

External Validity

External validity concerns the extent to which the results of a study can be generalized. In other words, the question here is whether the same findings would hold in other cases — for example, for different people, places, or times. A finding with high levels of external validity is more likely to carry over into real-world situations. External validity is threatened when research is conducted in a way that fails to approximate the real-world scenario it aims to explain. When a study is conducted with populations and methodologies that differ too widely from the actual situations they are trying to explain, the findings are less likely to be externally valid.

In the case of experimental research, a study that lacks external validity might take place in highly artificial environments or subject research participants to overly simplified or abstract situations. In the case of descriptive research, studies lacking external validity might use data derived from situations that are too different from the situation under consideration, which means that information found in the confines of the study will fail to materialize in the real world. Another factor that undermines external validity involves using participants who are not representative of the entire market the study aims to investigate. In this context, a common threat to external validity is the self-selection bias, whereby respondents who agreed to participate in the study are not representative of the entire population.

Managing Decision Errors

When drawing conclusions from market research, some errors are inevitable. Many of these errors go beyond erroneous calculations, poor sampling, or faulty assumptions. Rather, they are the unavoidable consequence of using samples to infer the properties of a broader population. Even the most carefully designed research and conscientiously conducted analysis has some likelihood of suggesting a conclusion that turns out to be incorrect.

There are two types of decision errors: *false positives* (also referred to as *Type I* errors) and *false negatives* (also referred to as *Type II* errors). A false-positive error is a result that indicates a particular factor is present when in reality it is not. Conversely, a false-negative error is a result that indicates the absence of a particular factor when in reality it is present (Figure 4).

Figure 4. Managing Decision Errors

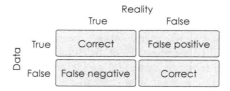

Consider an online retailer that conducts a study to determine whether a specific change to its website will increase sales. The retailer devises an A/B test with a subset of its customers, in which some are shown the original website and others are shown the new website. Here, the study outcome is positive if the new website has a high probability of increasing sales, and negative if the new website does not increase sales. In this scenario, a false positive would mean the test indicates that the new website increases sales when in reality it does not. A false negative would mean the test indicates that the new website does not increase sales when in reality it does.

Because using research samples (instead of examining the entire population) involves probability estimates rather than certain outcomes, all studies using samples tend to be associated with a certain degree of error. Moreover, the two types of error are directly related, such that reducing false positives leads to an increase in false negatives and vice versa. In this context, when evaluating the data, it is necessary to decide what type of error is more (less) desirable. The likelihood of making each type of error depends on the decision criteria set by the researcher. The more stringent the criteria for avoiding false-positive errors, the greater the likelihood of making a false-negative error.

In determining the right balance between false-positive and false-negative errors, managers will often weigh the probability of making a mistake and the consequences of that mistake against its likely benefits. In the example above, a manager might decide to implement the website change as long as the result shows less than a 10% chance of a false positive because the change in the website is relatively minor and the consequences of a false positive are immaterial. Conversely, when there are significant negative consequences for being mistaken, the manager might err on the side of caution and decide to accept the result only if it shows less than a 1% chance of a false positive. Thus, understanding the likelihood and consequences of potential errors is essential to control risk and make informed decisions based on market research.

Solving the Business Problem

Once the relevant market insights have been gathered, a manager needs to solve the business problem. All prior steps in the market research process are conducted to help managers make an informed decision that will address the problem facing the company. The two key aspects of managerial decision making at this point involve *relating the research findings to the business problem* and *selecting the best course of action.*

Evidence-Based Decision Making

Strictly speaking, solving the business problem is not part of the processes of gathering market insights but rather is the ultimate goal of gathering and analyzing market data. Indeed, the focus of market research is to gather relevant market insights, which involves acquiring relevant data, analyzing these data to identify significant patterns and trends, and ultimately, answering the research question at hand.

Once the data have been gathered, the research process shifts from the research team back to the manager who, using the research insights, must make a decision and take a course of action to address the problem facing the company. A manager's decision process at this point is guided by the company's ultimate goal — to create value for target customers, the company, and its collaborators (Figure 5).

Figure 5. Evidence-Based Decision Making

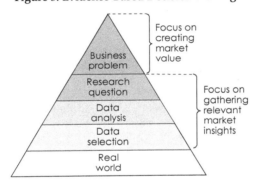

One of the key drivers of market success is the meaningful use of market insights to inform managerial decision making. The notion that managers should rely on the market research data to make business decisions might sound trivial at first glance. However, in reality many managers tend to ignore the data and make decisions based on their intuition either because they do not trust the data or because they are unsure how to relate the data to the problem at hand. The problem with this approach is that managers' gut feel, regardless of their experience, is never a substitute for up-to-date, relevant, and valid market insights. Thus, while individual experience and intuition are important, evidence-based decision making is the foundation of consistent market success.

Despite the conventional wisdom that more data are always better, large amounts of marginally relevant data have the potential to confuse managers and obscure relevant insights. Therefore, a manager must carefully screen the research findings and discard the data that are not directly relevant to the problem under consideration. This screening involves looking at each research finding, determining the degree to which it informs a solution to the business problem, and bringing to the forefront the findings relevant to the decision at hand. When screening out the irrelevant data, managers should pay attention to the findings that are supported by multiple data sources — a convergence implying greater reliability of the findings. The greater the consistency of the data obtained using different methods and from different sources, the more dependable the data.

Another important aspect in relating the research data to the business problem involves understanding the limitations of the findings. Indeed, because market data are typically voluminous and multi-faceted, it is often the case that when reviewing the research findings managers will discover ambiguous or conflicting information. They may further realize that important data are missing or not valid. While the analysis can proceed even after such discrepancies have been discovered, it is important to identify these limitations and be mindful of them when making business decisions. Understanding the shortcomings of the data can help safeguard against overreliance and overgeneralization of the research findings, leading to a more sound business decision.

Selecting a Course of Action

The ultimate goal of gathering market insights is to enable the manager to select the best course of action that will enable the company to achieve its goals. In this context, market research aims to identify the key decision options and delineate the pros and cons associated with each alternative. At this point it is up to the manager to weigh the pros and cons of the different options and determine the optimal course of action. Market research, no matter how accurate and timely, can only suggest — not decide on — the specific actions that the company should take (Figure 6).

Figure 6. Making Necessary Tradeoffs

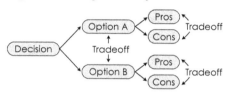

Because most options available to the manager tend to be imperfect and involve different pros and cons, solving business problems involves making tradeoffs to select the alternative that is best aligned with the company goals. Making tradeoffs is inherently difficult because it requires managers to give up performance on one dimension in order to gain performance on another. In such situations, managers are often tempted to collect more data or conduct additional analyses, hoping that the new data will clearly favor one of the decision options, thus eliminating the need for a tradeoff. While in some scenarios gathering additional data can be clearly beneficial, in other cases it can waste time and resources, ultimately increasing rather than decreasing the ambiguity associated with the decision.

The difficulty associated with making tradeoffs often leads to so-called "analysis paralysis," whereby managers, reluctant to make a decision, constantly seek additional information, hoping that it will relieve them of the burden of having to commit to a particular course of action. This situation is well captured in the words of famed German philosopher Johann Wolfgang von Goethe, who noted, *The first sign we don't know what we are doing is an obsession with numbers*. One approach to avoiding such decision stalemates is acknowledging that gathering additional data carries the cost of missed opportunities stemming from a manager's indecision. Putting off a decision by stalling for additional data is de facto a decision to stay the course and maintain the status quo.

A decision error opposite to analysis paralysis stems from overconfidence, whereby managers are unrealistically convinced that the chosen course of action is correct and do not even consider the possibility that they might be wrong. Overconfidence often leads to overestimating the chances of success of a given action, leading managers to take action without carefully considering the drawbacks of the chosen alternative and the benefits of alternative courses of action. Overconfident managers also tend to succumb to the *confirmation bias*, which involves selectively focusing on information that is consistent with their preferred course of action and ignoring information that is inconsistent with their preferences. A common form of overconfidence is the tendency to overestimate the likelihood of events that involve highly desirable outcomes. This type of overconfidence (also known as the wishful-thinking bias) can result in managers significantly discounting or even ignoring the likelihood of adverse consequences stemming from the proposed action.

A practical way to curb overconfidence and identify the potential drawbacks of the proposed course of action is to imagine that the decision has turned out to be a disaster a year later and to think about the factors that have contributed to this outcome. This approach is grounded in the so-called hindsight bias (also called the "I-knew-it-all-along" effect), which refers to people's tendency to see an event that has already occurred as easily predictable, even in the case of events that are unforeseeable and could not have been reliably predicted. Thus, imagining that the decision at hand has already been implemented and looking back to identify the reasons for its failure can help managers be more realistic in assessing the drawbacks of the different courses of action.

SUMMARY

Market research facilitates effective decision making by providing the relevant information needed to assess tradeoffs inherent in solving business problems, while at the same time offering managers an opportunity to rigorously validate and improve their ideas.

The market research process starts with *defining the business problem* the company needs to solve. Most business problems fall into one of two categories. *Market-analysis problems* call for gaining a better understanding of a market in order to generate or optimize a viable value-creation strategy. Common market-analysis problems include market-opportunity problems, market-change problems, and performance-gap problems. *Action-planning problems*, on the other hand, involve the development of an action plan to take advantage of an identified market opportunity, respond to a market change, or close a performance gap. Common action-planning problems include the development of a new offering and the optimization of an existing offering.

Problem definition is followed by *formulating the research question*—a process that determines the specific information that needs to be gathered in order to address the identified problem. The research question is typically narrower than the business problem it aims to solve and is focused solely on uncovering the information that is pertinent to making a well-informed business decision. Most research questions fall into one of two types: *market-analysis questions* (e.g., marketing-demand, targeting, segmentation, and context questions) and *market-planning questions* (e.g., offering-design, communication, and distribution questions). To be meaningful, research questions must be relevant, actionable, concrete, and simple.

Once the research question has been formulated, the next step is to *define the research method* used to collect market data. There are three basic types of research methods. *Exploratory research* helps the company attain a general understanding of the business problem, generate new ideas, and formulate hypotheses. Common exploratory methods include observation, personal interviews, focus group interviews, activity-based tasks, and exploratory data mining. *Descriptive research* aims to gather quantitative information about the target market. Common types of descriptive research include customer, competitor, and company research. *Experimental research* aims to establish cause-and-effect relationships in the market. There are two types of experimental research: controlled experiments that are designed by researchers and natural experiments that take advantage of naturally occurring changes in the market.

Gathering market data involves collecting information pertaining to the research question. *Primary data* involve original information collected by the company to address the specific question of interest to the company. The key issues in gathering primary data are determining the sample size and selecting study participants. *Secondary data* involve already existing information that has been collected by the company or a third party for purposes unrelated to the specific question of interest to the company. Secondary data can be obtained from external sources such as government agencies, academic institutions and think tanks, and market research companies, or, alternatively, they can be gathered from internal sources such as customer databases containing browsing, buying, and usage information.

Data collection is followed by *analysis of the data*, which aims to establish significant patterns and trends that can shed light on the research question at hand. There are two types of data analysis: analysis of structured data that includes text or numerals organized in a matrix format featuring rows and columns, and analysis of unstructured and semi-structured data such as images, sounds, videos, books, and social media posts.

Following data analysis, researchers must *interpret the data* by relating the empirical findings to the business problem at hand. This involves two key issues: *assessing the validity of the data* and *managing decision errors*. Data validity reflects whether the reported results are methodologically sound. There are two types of validity: *internal validity*, reflecting how well a study is designed, and *external validity*, reflecting how well the results of a study can be generalized beyond the experimental setup to the market the study aims to examine. When drawing conclusions from market research, some error is inevitable. There are two types of decision errors: *false positives*, which suggest that a particular factor is present when in reality it is not, and *false negatives* that indicate the absence of a particular factor when in reality it is present.

Solving the business problem, although not part of the research process, is its direct consequence. Once the data have been gathered, the research process shifts from the research team back to the manager who, using the research insights, must make a decision and take a course of action to address the problem facing the company. Market research, no matter how accurate and timely, can only suggest—not decide on—the specific actions that the company might take.

MARKETING INSIGHT: KEY PRINCIPLES IN ESTABLISHING CAUSALITY

Because the primary purpose of experimentation is to establish causal relationships between factors of interest, understanding the key principles of causality is essential to designing meaningful experiments. To establish causality, the relationship between the factors of interest should meet three criteria: *covariance*, *precedence*, and *absence of rival explanations*.

- *Covariance* reflects a relationship between two factors, whereby changes in one of the factors are associated with changes in the other. For example, an increase in advertising expenditures might be associated with an increase in sales volume. Covariance is a necessary but not sufficient condition to establish causality. Thus, two factors can display the same pattern without being causally related. For example, examining the relationship between spurious factors such as the per capita consumption of cheese and the total revenue generated by golf courses shows that they are highly correlated even though there is no logical connection between them. Covariance, by itself, is not sufficient to infer a causal relationship.

- *Precedence* of one factor in relation to another means that this factor (the cause) is expected to come before the other (the effect). Indeed, logic dictates that in order for one factor to cause another, it must occur first in time. For example, if advertising indeed causes an increase in the sales volume, one would expect to observe the increase in advertising activity *prior* to observing a change in sales volume. Establishing precedence is important because two factors might co-occur without having a causal relationship. For example, while better company performance is often associated with more charismatic CEOs, bringing a charismatic CEO into an organization does not improve its subsequent performance. On the contrary, it has been shown that it is the improvement in a company's performance that causes the public to evaluate its CEO as charismatic.[1]

- *Absence of rival explanations* means that the proposed causal relationship between two events might depend on a third, unobserved, factor. Thus, even though two factors co-occur, it is possible that a third factor is causing both of the first two factors. For example, a researcher observing that an increase in the sales of ice cream is correlated with an increase in crime might incorrectly conclude that ice cream sales are causing crime. This association, however, might be caused by a third factor, such as hot weather, that increases both crime and ice cream consumption. In the same vein, an increase in sales following an advertising campaign in reality might have been caused by a drop in price that coincided with the company's advertising.

To ensure that all three prerequisites of causality are met, experiments typically involve a control condition that is identical to the experimental condition in all aspects except for the factor of interest. To this end, the experiment should involve respondents with similar profiles who are presented in the same manner with versions of the offering that vary only on the factor being tested. Consequently, any difference in the response between the experimental and the control conditions can be uniquely attributed to the factor of interest rather than to the difference in the profiles of the respondents participating in the study.

Because there are multiple factors that can influence an offering's success, managers are often tempted to simultaneously vary several attributes of the offering to more expediently and cost efficiently understand their impact. The problem with this approach is that simultaneously testing multiple factors makes it difficult to untangle the unique impact of the individual factors. For example, an increase in customer demand following simultaneous improvement of the offering's performance and a reduction in its price makes it difficult to determine which factor—performance or price—is responsible for the increase in customer demand. Because a company's offering is defined by several attributes that, in concert, drive customer demand, the effectiveness of different aspects of the offering can be best understood by testing the market impact of each attribute, both individually and in combination with the other attributes describing the offering.

MARKETING INSIGHT: POPULAR MARKET RESEARCH METHODS

Market research utilizes a wide array of techniques to help managers answer research questions. By familiarizing themselves with some of the most common market research methods, managers can gain a better understanding of the possibilities that market research affords. Some of the most popular methods in market research include *conjoint analysis*, the *top-box score*, and the *net promoter score*.

Conjoint Analysis

Conjoint analysis is a method for assessing the value that people attach to different attributes of the company's offering. It is commonly used to ascertain the relative importance of product attributes and to help determine the optimum level of these attributes. It is particularly useful for choosing among different combinations of attributes when designing or modifying a company's offering. A typical conjoint study involves showing respondents a series of pairs of options that represent different combinations of attribute values and asking them to select their preferred option from each pair. By examining the dispersion of respondents' preferences as a function of the options' attribute values, conjoint analysis can help identify the relative importance of the different attributes describing the company's offering as well as the offering's "ideal" values on these attributes.

Conjoint analysis is based on the premise that directly asking individuals to identify the relative importance of the attributes describing a company's offering is not very informative because individuals' "true" preferences are better revealed when they make a choice and have to give up better performance on one attribute in order to gain performance on another. Thus, by designing a series of choices in which respondents have to trade off the pros and cons of the available options, conjoint analysis can help uncover the utility created by different levels of performance across attributes describing the company's offering.

Consider a cereal company deciding between two different flavors, three different brand names, and four different prices. This yields 24 different offering concepts (2 x 3 x 4) that are presented in pairs to respondents, who are asked to indicate their preferred option in each pair. Analysis of the pattern of individuals' responses enables researchers to determine the ideal attribute combination of flavor, brand name, and price and the value that respondents place on each attribute describing the company's offering. Moreover, conjoint analysis enables identification of the attribute tradeoff rates — that is, the performance that an individual is willing to give up on one attribute in order to gain advantage on another (e.g., the premium individuals are willing to pay for their preferred option).

The Top-Box Score

The top-box score is a method for measuring customers' intent to acquire a given product or service, usually within a certain time frame (month, quarter, year). This popular approach to estimating purchase intent involves a five-point scale with responses ranging from "definitely would buy" to "definitely would not buy."

- ☐ Definitely would buy
- ☐ Probably would buy
- ☐ Might or might not buy
- ☐ Probably would not buy
- ☐ Definitely would not buy

The popularity of this approach to measuring purchase intent stems from its simplicity, which makes it easy to execute and interpret. Despite its popularity, and in part because of its simplicity, this approach has several drawbacks. An important shortcoming of asking individuals to directly express the likelihood of their purchasing a given offering is that people have a tendency to overstate the actual probability that they will buy the offering. To account for people's tendency to overestimate the probability of actually purchasing the offering, the stated purchase responses are typically corrected.

A common methodology for correcting the overestimation bias involves using adjustment coefficients derived from comparing predicted and actual purchase rates within the specific industry. To illustrate, for consumer packaged goods, respondents' answers are adjusted as follows: "Definitely would buy" responses are reduced by 20% (which implies that only 80% of those stating that they will definitely buy the product will end up buying it); "probably would buy" responses are reduced by 70% (which implies that only 30% of those stating that they will probably buy the product will end up buying it); and responses falling into the three remaining categories are considered to be no-purchase responses. Because analysis of the responses is focused on the first two answers, this method is often referred to as the top-box approach.

To illustrate, consider a scenario in which 10% of respondents indicated that they would definitely buy the offering, 33% indicated that they would probably buy it, 31% were indifferent, 21% indicated that they would most likely not buy it, and 5% indicated that they would definitely not buy it. Provided that the 80/30 adjustment holds for this industry, the top-box score is 10%*80% + 33%*30% = 18%, meaning that in reality only 18% of potential customers are likely to purchase the offering.

The Net Promoter Score

The net promoter score stems from the idea that people's true preference for a given offering is reflected in the likelihood that they will recommend this offering to others. Accordingly, the net promoter score is a metric designed to measure the likelihood that customers will spread positive word of mouth about a company, its products, and/or its brands.[2]

The net promoter score is calculated by asking the company's customers to indicate the likelihood that they will recommend the company, its offerings, and/or its brands to another person (*How likely is it that you will recommend this product to a friend or colleague?*). Responses are typically scored on a 0–10 scale, with 0 meaning extremely unlikely and 10 meaning extremely likely.

Based on their responses, customers are divided into one of three categories: *promoters* (those with ratings of 9 or 10), *passives* (those with ratings of 7 or 8), and *detractors* (those with ratings of 6 or lower). The net promoter score is then calculated as the difference between the percentage of a company's promoters and detractors. For example, if 40% of a company's customers are classified as promoters and 25% are classified as detractors, the company's net promoter score is 15%.

The net promoter score has gained popularity among managers because of the intuitive appeal of its underlying assumption that a person willing to recommend an offering must find it attractive. Another contributor to the popularity of this method is its simplicity: It involves a single straightforward question.

Despite its popularity, the net promoter score, like most other market research methods, is not universally applicable. For example, people might be unwilling to recommend an offering to others if they think that the value created by the offering is idiosyncratic, such that people with different needs and preferences might not appreciate the benefits of the offering. As a result, the net promoter score is best used in combination with other research methods to gain a better understanding of the market in which the company operates.

PART THREE

DEVELOPING A MARKETING STRATEGY

INTRODUCTION

All men can see the tactics whereby I conquer,
but what none can see is the strategy out of which victory is evolved.

—Sun Tzu, Chinese military strategist

Marketing strategy articulates the logic of the value-creation process. Specifically, strategy identifies the market in which the company operates and outlines the ways in which it creates market value. Because a company's target market, including its competitors and collaborators, is largely determined by the customer need(s) the company aims to fulfill, the choice of target customers is central to defining the market in which the company aims to create value.

The following chapters outline the key aspects of developing an offering's strategy: identifying target customers whose needs the company aims to fulfill with its offering, developing a value proposition for these customers that can fulfill their needs better than competitive options, and creating value for the company that can enable it to achieve its strategic goals. Specifically, the chapters included in this section address the following topics: *identifying target customers, developing a customer value proposition*, and *creating company value*.

- **Identifying target customers** is the stepping stone for developing an effective marketing strategy. The identification of target customers involves grouping potential buyers into segments, selecting which segments to target, and determining actionable strategies to reach the selected customers. Because the ultimate goal of identifying target customers is to create market value for customers, collaborators, and the company, the basic principles of segmentation and targeting hold for both consumer and business markets. The key aspects of identifying target customers are discussed in Chapter 6.

- **Developing a customer value proposition** articulates the benefits and costs of the company's offering for target customers. Specifically, the value proposition delineates all relevant benefits and costs that reflect the value customers are likely to receive from the company's offering. The value proposition is augmented by formulating a positioning that underscores the offering's most important benefit(s). The process of developing a value proposition and positioning is discussed in Chapter 7.

- **Creating company value** delineates the ways in which an offering will benefit the company and enable it to achieve its goals. To build a successful offering, a manager must understand not only how to develop an offering desired by target customers but also how to design it in a way that enables the company to capture value for its stakeholders. The ways in which a company creates value for its stakeholders are discussed in Chapter 8.

These three aspects of a company's strategy—identifying the target market, developing a customer value proposition, and creating company value—stem from the key marketing principle: The success of an offering is determined by its ability to create superior value for its target customers in a way that benefits the company and its collaborators. Hence, the following chapters delineate the processes by which the company identifies customers whose needs it can fulfill better than the competition and develops an optimal value proposition to meet these needs and create company value.

IDENTIFYING TARGET CUSTOMERS

Where your talents and the needs of
the world cross, there lies your calling.
— Aristotle, Greek philosopher

The cornerstone of developing a viable marketing strategy is deciding which customers to target and how to reach these customers in an effective and cost-efficient manner. Failure to identify the right target customers is one of the most common and at the same time most dangerous marketing mistakes. Indeed, it is virtually impossible to develop a meaningful value proposition without clearly identifying customers whose needs the company aims to fulfill with its offering. The concept of targeting and the process of identifying the right target customers are the focus of this chapter. Specifically, we address the following topics:

- *Targeting as a Marketing Concept* || The logic of targeting | Strategic and tactical targeting
- *Strategic Targeting* || Target compatibility | Target attractiveness | Targeting as a means of creating a competitive advantage
- *Tactical Targeting* || Defining the customer profile | Aligning customer value and customer profile
- *Targeting Multiple Customer Segments* || Single-segment and multi-segment targeting | The value-alignment principle in targeting multiple segments
- *Segmenting the Market* || Segmentation as a marketing concept | Strategic and tactical segmentation | Defining the optimal segmentation depth | Key segmentation principles

The discussion of the key targeting concepts is complemented by an in-depth overview of three targeting concepts: occasion-based versus user-based targeting, data-driven targeting, and the long tail phenomenon.

Targeting as a Marketing Concept

Targeting is the process of identifying customers for whom the company will optimize its offering. Simply put, targeting reflects the company's choice of which customers it will prioritize and which customers it will ignore when designing, communicating, and delivering its offering. The logic of identifying target customers and the strategic and tactical aspects of this process are discussed in more detail below.

The Logic of Targeting

Imagine a company operating in a market in which there are two customers with different needs. Which of these customers should the company serve? The intuitive answer is—both. Indeed, all else being equal, the greater the customer base, the greater the company's profit potential. Should the company choose to target both customers, it has two options for developing an offering. One approach is to develop the same offering for both customers (one-for-all strategy), and the other is to develop different offerings based on the needs of each customer (one-for-each strategy).

The *one-for-all strategy* of developing a single offering for the entire market is not very effective for satisfying customers with different needs because the offering will not create value for at least one of the customers (and perhaps even both). For example, if the customers vary in terms of their price sensitivity, developing either a high-quality, high-priced offering or a low-priced, low-quality offering will inevitably fail to fulfill the needs of one of these customers because one will find the offering too expensive and the other will deem it of insufficient quality. Furthermore, developing a mid-priced, mid-quality offering will likely fail to fulfill the needs of both because the offering will still be too expensive for one of the customers and of insufficient quality for the other.

The *one-for-each* strategy of developing a separate offering for each customer might not be effective because the company might not have the resources to develop offerings that meet the needs of both customers. For example, the company might not have the scale of operations to develop a low-priced offering for the price-sensitive customer and lack the technological know-how to develop a high-performance offering for the quality-focused customer. Furthermore, even if the company has the resources to develop separate offerings, both customers might not be able to create value for the company. For example, the customer for the high-quality product might not have the financial resources to afford the company's offering or might have needs that the company cannot fulfill without incurring costs that exceed the benefits received from serving this customer.

The discussion so far has focused on a scenario in which a company operates in a market comprised of two customers. While such markets do exist, especially in a business-to-business context, they are the exception rather than the rule: Most markets comprise thousands and often millions of buyers. This scenario is different not only in the number of customers but also in that some customers are likely to have fairly similar needs that could be fulfilled by the same offering. In such cases, rather than developing individual offerings for each customer, a company might consider developing offerings for groups of customers—commonly referred to as *customer segments*—that share similar characteristics.

The concept of segment-based targeting is illustrated in Figure 1. Here, individual customers are represented by varying shapes and colors based on the differences in their underlying needs. For example, circles might represent quality-focused customers, triangles might represent price-sensitive customers, and squares might represent customers who are looking for a compromise between price and quality. In this context, Figure 1 depicts a scenario in which a company targets quality-oriented customers for whom it will develop high-end offerings, while ignoring the other two customer segments.

Figure 1. Segment-Based Targeting

All potential customers (entire market) → Targeting → Customers whose needs the company aims to fulfill (target market)

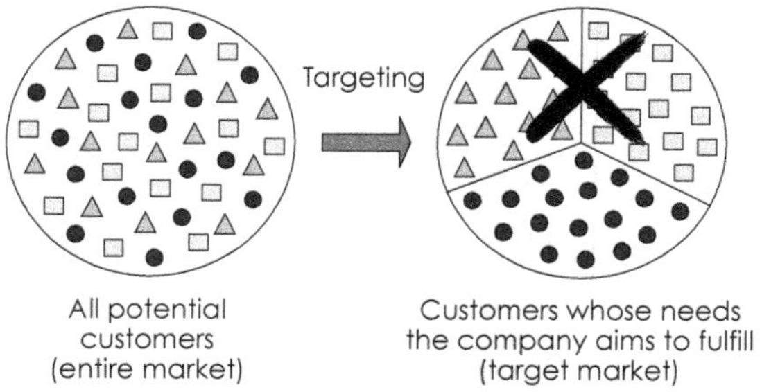

Grouping customers into segments enables a company to improve the cost efficiency of its marketing activities by not having to customize the offering for individual customers, usually with minimal sacrifice to the effectiveness of the offering. From a conceptual standpoint, the process of identifying target customers is virtually the same whether it involves individual customers or customer segments. The key difference is that in addition to identifying the needs of the target customers, segment-based targeting involves grouping customers with similar needs into segments—a process commonly referred to as *segmentation*. The logic of the segmentation process and the key segmentation principles are outlined in more detail later in this chapter.

Strategic and Tactical Targeting

Based on the criteria used to identify customers, targeting can be strategic or tactical. *Strategic targeting* identifies customers whose needs the company aims to fulfill by tailoring its offerings to fit these needs. In contrast, *tactical targeting* aims to identify the ways in which the company will reach strategically important customers. These two types of targeting are not mutually exclusive but rather are two inseparable components of the process of identifying target customers.

Strategic and tactical targeting vary in their goals. Strategic targeting involves trading off market size for a better fit between the offering's benefits and customers' needs. Instead of trying to reach the entire market with an offering that attempts to appeal to a wide variety of customers with diverse needs, strategic targeting calls for a conscious decision to ignore some potential customers in order to better serve others by tailoring the offering to their specific needs. Tactical targeting, on the other hand, does not aim to exclude any potential customers. Instead, it aims to reach *all* strategically important customers in a way that is both effective and cost efficient for the company.

Because they have different goals, strategic and tactical targeting prioritize different factors. Strategic targeting focuses on the *value* that the company can create for and capture from target customers. In contrast, tactical targeting focuses on the *means* by which the company can reach these customers. Working in concert, strategic and tactical targeting aim to answer two questions: *Who* are the customers with whom the company can establish a mutually beneficial relationship? *How* can these customers be reached in the most effective and cost-efficient manner? Here, the first question focuses on the offering's strategy, and the second question addresses the offering's tactics.

Given its focus on creating and capturing value, strategic targeting is concerned with customer needs and preferences (which define the value the company needs to create for these customers) and their resources (which define the value these customers can create for the company). Tactical targeting, on the other hand, is concerned with the customer profile, which reflects customers' readily observable characteristics such as age, gender, income, social status, geographic location, and buying behavior.

Focusing on value is the starting point of the targeting process because value creation is the ultimate goal of any business activity. The drawback of focusing on value is that value is unobservable, which makes it difficult for the company to reach its target customers in order to communicate and deliver the company's offering to them. Focusing on the customer profile, on the other hand, can be beneficial because it is observable, which enables the company to make customers aware of the offering and deliver the offering to them in an effective and cost-efficient manner. The downside of focusing on the profile is that it provides little or no insight into customer needs and preferences, thus making it difficult for the company to create value for its customers. Because neither of the two customer descriptors—value and profile—is sufficient on its own to ensure an offering's market success, targeting must incorporate both factors, with strategic targeting focusing on customer value and tactical targeting focusing on the customer profile.

The two aspects of targeting, strategic and tactical, are discussed in more detail in the following sections.

Strategic Targeting

The process of identifying target customers is guided by the company's ability to develop an offering that will fulfill the needs of these customers better than the competition, and do so in a way that creates value for the company. In this context, strategic targeting starts with identifying the specific customer need(s) that the company aims to fulfill with its offering.

Strategic targeting involves making tradeoffs: It ignores some customers in order to better serve others. Deciding to deliberately forgo some potential customers is one of the most important and at the same time most difficult decisions a company must make. Many companies have failed because they were unwilling to sacrifice market breadth in order to focus only on those customers for whom their offering could create superior value. The key to meaningful targeting is identifying not only customers that the company aims to serve but also those it chooses deliberately *not* to serve. A viable market strategy is not possible without choosing to ignore some customers in order to offer better service to others.

A key consideration when selecting target customers is determining how large the target segment should be. The tradeoff here is between the breadth of the target market and the strength of the company's competitive positioning in that market. Choosing a relatively narrow target market can help the company establish a strong competitive position but at the same time limits the market potential of the offering. Choosing a very broad market segment, on the other hand, presents greater market potential but limits the company's ability to establish a strong competitive advantage.

> *When identifying target customers, a company must strive to select the largest market segment for which it can establish a meaningful point of difference*

As a general rule, developing a separate offering for each customer segment is beneficial when the incremental value created by customizing the offering outweighs the costs of developing the offering. To illustrate, when the cost of customization is relatively high (as with durable goods such as cars, household appliances, and electronic equipment), companies tend to develop offerings that serve relatively large groups of customers, whereas in industries where the cost of customization is relatively low (as in the case of delivering online information), offerings can be tailored for smaller groups of customers.

Strategic targeting is guided by the company's ability to develop an offering that will fulfill the needs of its customers better than the competition, while benefiting the company and its collaborators. Accordingly, when evaluating the viability of a particular customer segment, a manager must address two key questions:

- *Can the company create superior value for these customers?*
- *Can these customers create superior value for the company?*

The answer to the first question is determined by the degree to which the company's resources are compatible with the needs of target customers, that is, the extent to which the company has the assets and competencies necessary to create customer value. The answer to the second question is determined by the degree to which target customers are attractive to the company in terms of their ability to create company value. These two principles of strategic targeting — *target compatibility* and *target attractiveness* — are illustrated in Figure 2 and discussed in more detail below.

Figure 2. Strategic Targeting: Key Principles

Target Compatibility

Target compatibility reflects the company's ability to fulfill the needs of its customers better than the competition. Simply put, target compatibility is a company's ability to create superior customer value. Target compatibility is a function of the company's resources and the degree to which these resources enable it to create value for target customers. Having relevant resources is important because it enables the company to fulfill customer needs in an effective and cost-efficient manner and create an offering that delivers superior value relative to the competition.

The key resources that are essential for the success of a company's targeting strategy include: *business infrastructure, access to scarce resources, skilled employees, collaborator networks, know-how, strong brands, an established ecosystem,* and *access to capital.*

- **Business infrastructure** involves several types of assets: manufacturing infrastructure that comprises the company's production facilities and equipment; service infrastructure, such as call-center and customer relationship management solutions; supply-chain infrastructure, including procurement infrastructure and processes; and management infrastructure, defined by the company's business management culture.

- **Access to scarce resources** provides the company with a distinct competitive advantage by restricting the strategic options of its competitors. For example, a company can benefit from access to unique natural resources, from securing prime manufacturing and retail locations, as well as from acquiring a memorable web domain.

- **Skilled employees** are the company's human resources with technological, operational, and business expertise. For many companies — such as those involved in research and development, education, and consulting — human capital is a key strategic asset.

- **Collaborator networks** include two types of interactions: vertical networks in which collaborators are located along the company's supply chain (suppliers and distributors) and horizontal networks that collaborate with the company in developing and promoting the offering (research and development, manufacturing, and promotion collaborators).

- **Know-how** is the relevant expertise needed to address a particular customer need, including a company's proprietary processes, technologies, and intellectual property such as patents and trade secrets.

- **Strong brands** create value by identifying the offering and generating meaningful associations that create value above and beyond the value created by the product and service aspects of the offering. Brands are particularly important in commoditized industries where the differences between the competing products and services are relatively minor or nonexistent.

- **Established ecosystem** includes relevant products, services, and brands that can facilitate the adoption of the offering by its target customers. For example, the Windows operating system can be viewed as a strategic asset for Microsoft because it ensures product compatibility, thus facilitating customer adoption of related software offerings.

- **Access to capital** provides the company with access to the financing needed to design, produce, communicate, and deliver offerings to target customers.

A company's resources are target-specific. Resources that enable the company to create value for one segment might not create value for another segment. For example, a brand associated with a casual image is likely to be an asset when targeting customers seeking to convey a casual image and a liability for customers seeking to project a more upscale, exclusive image. In the same vein, a company specialized in manufacturing special-order precision medical equipment might not have the resources necessary to produce low-priced mass-market medical devices. Therefore, when choosing a target market a company needs to evaluate its assets from the viewpoint of the particular target segment to ensure the compatibility of customer needs with its own resources.

A company's ability to create value for target customers is a necessary but not sufficient condition for successful targeting. The second important criterion for identifying target customers is the ability of these customers to create value for the company. Thus, in addition to being compatible with the company's resources, the target must be attractive for the company. The key factors in evaluating target attractiveness are discussed in the following section.

Target Attractiveness

Target attractiveness reflects the ability of a given market segment to create superior value for the company. Thus, when selecting customers for whom to tailor its offering, a company must assess the degree to which different market segments can create value for the company and select the segment(s) that best fit the company's goals. A target customer can create two types of value for a company: *monetary* and *strategic*.

Monetary Value

Monetary value refers to customers' ability to generate profits for the company. Monetary value is a function of the *revenues* generated by a particular customer segment and the *costs* associated with serving this segment.

- **Customer revenues** involve money received from customers for the right to own and/or use a company's offering. Customer revenues are influenced by a number of factors, including the size of the market and its growth rate; customers' buying power, brand loyalty, and price sensitivity; the company's pricing power; competitive intensity; as well as various context factors such as the state of the economy, government regulations, and the physical environment.

- **Costs of serving target customers** involve expenses necessary to tailor the offering's benefits to fit target customers' needs as well as to communicate and deliver the offering to these customers. The cost of serving target customers can also include the expenses incurred in acquiring and retaining these customers such as customer incentives, post-purchase support, and loyalty programs.

When assessing the monetary value of a target audience, the revenues received from providing an offering to these customers must be weighed against the costs involved in providing it. Thus, a segment that brings in less revenue but demands a less costly offering might prove to be of greater monetary value to a company than a segment that generates more revenue but demands an offering that is costly to produce, communicate, and distribute. In general, the greater the revenues derived from a particular customer segment and the lower the costs of serving that segment, the more attractive it is to the company.

Because customer revenues and costs are relatively easy to quantify, many companies tend to focus almost exclusively on the monetary aspect of the value created by a given customer segment, while overlooking the strategic value it can create. This is a rather narrow view because the strategic value can be a significant component of the overall value created by target customers.

Strategic Value

Strategic value refers to customers' ability to create nonmonetary benefits for the company. Based on the nature of the value created by customers, there are three main types of strategic value: *social value*, *scale value*, and *information value*.

- **Social value** reflects customers' ability to impact other potential buyers. Indeed, customers might be attractive not only because of the sales revenues they can generate for the company but also because of their social networks and ability to influence other buyers. For example, a company might target opinion leaders, trendsetters, and mavens because of their ability to promote and endorse the company's offering.

- **Scale value** refers to the benefits received from the scale of the company's operations. For example, a company might target low-margin or even unprofitable customers because of the economics of its business model. This is especially true in the case of companies such as airlines, hotels, and cruise lines, which have large fixed costs and relatively small variable costs. Furthermore, a company in its early stages of growth might target low-margin customers in order to build a product and user ecosystem that will serve as a platform for future growth. The success of Uber, Airbnb, Microsoft, eBay, and Facebook networks illustrates the benefits of building large-scale user networks.

- **Information value** reflects the worth of the information provided by customers. A company might target customers because they furnish the company with data about their needs and profile that can help design, communicate, and deliver value to other customers with similar needs. A company might also target customers whose needs precede those of the mass market and who are likely to be early adopters of the company's offering — commonly referred to as lead users — to benefit from their feedback on how to modify and enhance the offering.

CHAPTER 6 IDENTIFYING TARGET CUSTOMERS   111

A key challenge in assessing the strategic value of different customer segments is that, unlike monetary value, strategic value is often not readily observable and is difficult to quantify. For example, a customer's ability to influence others often cannot be directly observed by the company, and even when it can be observed (for example, by assessing the number of followers on social media), the impact of such influence on other customers' preference for the company's offerings is difficult to assess. In the same vein, the likelihood that a prospective customer might provide the company with relevant information, as well as the value of this information, is often difficult to assess in advance. Despite the difficulty in assessing strategic value, it can play a significant role in choosing target customers, either as a complement to the monetary value of these customers or as the main driver of company value. For example, a company might target highly influential customers who might never generate money for the company directly but may influence broader and more profitable segments of the market to take up the company's offering.

Identifying unmet customer needs that a company can fulfill in a meaningful way is a challenging task. Companies with different strategic goals are likely to vary in the way they evaluate the attractiveness of different segments, such that the same customers might be viewed as desirable by some companies and undesirable by others. For example, executives of large companies are often focused exclusively on segments that are likely to generate revenues and profits that are significant enough to have a material impact on the company's bottom line. As a result, these managers tend to ignore smaller, albeit inherently profitable, segments because they are not aligned with the company's appetite for profits. Yet, many of the customer segments that large companies end up competing for in the future are, in fact, the same segments these companies overlooked in the past when they lacked the scale to match the profit goals of these companies. Therefore, when assessing the attractiveness of a given segment, a company must consider not only this segment's current size but also its growth potential and long-term strategic impact.

Targeting as a Means of Creating a Competitive Advantage

Creating and capturing customer value almost always occurs in a competitive context. As a result, to create market value, a company must assess the compatibility and the attractiveness of a given customer segment vis-à-vis the competitors' ability to effectively and profitably serve this segment. Therefore, a key principle of strategic targeting is that the choice of customers should be driven by the company's ability to create an offering that delivers *superior value* to these customers relative to the competition. A company's ability to create a superior offering stems from its resources and the degree to which its resources are superior to those of the competition. This is the resource advantage principle: *To create superior market value, a company must have superior resources relative to the competition.*

Because serving different customer segments often calls for distinct core competencies and strategic assets, the choice of target customers is crucial in defining a company's resource advantage over the competition. The uniqueness of customer needs determines the degree to which a company requires specialized resources to fulfill these needs, as well as the degree of competition for this customer segment. In general, the more unique the customer needs, the more the company requires specialized resources to serve those customers, and the fewer viable competitors likely to exist in the market. Thus, many niche markets tend to require higher levels of specialization from the companies serving them and typically attract fewer competitors compared to mass markets.

From a competitive perspective, the process of identifying a company's target customers is a function of three key factors: customer needs, company resources, and competitor resources. The relationship among these three factors is illustrated in Figure 3. A company's "ideal" target customers are those whose needs the company can fulfill in a way its competitors cannot. Because of their attractiveness and lack of competition, such markets are often referred to as "blue oceans." In contrast, markets in which the company and its competitors have matching resources are characterized by intense competition and are often referred to as "red oceans" (see the discussion of the Blue Ocean Strategy in Chapter 7).

Figure 3. The Resource Advantage Principle

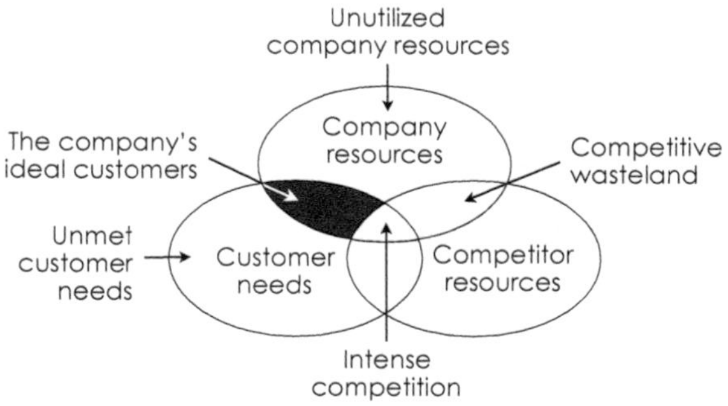

The development of market offerings should always be driven by customer needs. Yet, obsession with the competition often leads companies astray, encouraging them to develop offerings that match those of competitors even in the absence of an underlying customer need. Such a competitor-driven, rather than customer-driven, approach creates a competitive wasteland, squandering company resources by replicating competitors' mistakes while missing real market opportunities. For example, following PepsiCo's launch of Crystal Pepsi, a caffeine-free soda promoted as a "clear alternative" to normal colas, Coca-Cola launched its own clear soda, Tab Clear. Sales were dismal due to lack of customer demand for a clear soda, and both offerings were pulled off the market less than a year after being introduced.

Because a company's resources do not perfectly overlap with customer needs, some of these resources will remain unutilized when serving a particular segment, and some of the customer needs will remain unmet by the company's offering. These unutilized needs and resources can provide the company with directions for future development. Thus, unmet customer needs present the company with an opportunity to develop the necessary resources to create offerings that will fulfill these needs. In the same vein, unutilized company resources call for identifying unmet customer needs and developing offerings to fulfill those needs.

Tactical Targeting

Tactical targeting is similar to strategic targeting in that it involves identifying target customers. However, unlike strategic targeting, which aims to determine which customers to target and which to ignore, tactical targeting aims to identify an effective and cost-efficient approach to communicating and delivering the offering to already selected target customers. The key aspects of tactical targeting are discussed in more detail below.

Defining the Customer Profile

Following the identification of a strategically viable target market, a company must identify the profile of these customers in order to communicate and deliver its offering to them. The challenges in identifying target customers, the essence of profile-based targeting, and its pros and cons are outlined in the following sections.

The Customer Identification Problem

Because strategic targeting reflects a company's ability to create and capture customer value, identifying strategically viable customers is the key to the success of an offering. Identifying target customers based on their needs, however, can be challenging because these needs are not readily observable and therefore cannot be acted upon to communicate and deliver the company's offering.

The challenge of identifying ways to reach customers with a particular need is referred to as the *identification problem*. The issue here is that without being able to identify ways to reach the strategically viable customers whose needs it aims to fulfill with its offering, the company would have to communicate the offering and make it available to *all* customers — an approach that in most cases is neither effective nor cost efficient.

Despite the challenges in identifying target customers, value-based segmentation is almost always the starting point of targeting analysis. This is because the ultimate goal of targeting is to identify customers for whom the company can create superior value relative to the competition, not merely customers whose characteristics the company can readily observe. Only after target customers have been selected based on their potential value to the company would a company seek to find these customers in the broader population. To reach the high-value customer segments in an effective and cost-efficient manner, companies need to identify a set of readily observable characteristics that describe these segments and use these observable characteristics to communicate and deliver its offerings. The process of linking value-based segments to corresponding observable and actionable profiles is the essence of tactical targeting.

Profile-Based Targeting

Tactical targeting identifies effective and cost-efficient ways to communicate and deliver an offering to strategically viable customers by linking the need the company aims to fulfill to observable customer characteristics. These observable factors—referred to as the customer profile—involve four types of descriptors: *demographic, geographic, behavioral,* and *psychographic.*

- **Demographic factors** include customers' descriptive characteristics such as age, gender, income, occupation, level of education, religion, ethnicity, nationality, employment status, population density (urban or rural), social class, household size, and stage in the life cycle. For example, one of the commonly used demographic factors is that of generation, such as Baby Boomers (1946–1964); Generation X (1965–1981); Generation Y, also referred to as Millennials (1982–2000); and Generation Z (2001–present). When target customers are companies rather than individuals, they are identified by factors referred to as firmographics: size, organizational structure, industry, growth, revenues, and profitability.

- **Geographic (geolocation) factors** reflect customers' physical location. Unlike demographic data, which describe *who* the target customer is, geographic data describe *where* this customer is. Some of the geographic indicators—such as a customer's permanent residence, including country, state, city, and neighborhood where the customer lives—are more enduring, whereas others—such as a customer's current location at a particular point in time—are dynamic and frequently change over time. The proliferation of mobile devices that are uniquely tied to individual customers and have the ability to pinpoint their location has dramatically increased the importance of geographic factors in targeting.

- **Behavioral factors** reflect customers' actions. Common behavioral factors include customers' prior experience with the company's offering (e.g., customers new to the category, competitors' customers, current customers, or loyal customers), the frequency with which they purchase the offering, the quantity typically purchased, price sensitivity, sensitivity to the company's promotional activities, loyalty, mode of purchase (online or offline), frequently used retail outlets, role in the decision process (e.g., initiator, influencer, decider, buyer, or user), and the stage in their customer decision journey. Behavioral factors can also include the ways in which customers learn about new products, socialize, and spend their free time.

- **Psychographic factors** reflect facets of an individual's personality, including moral values, attitudes, interests, and lifestyles. Psychographics differ from demographic, geographic, and behavioral factors in that they link observable and unobservable characteristics of target customers. Although values, attitudes, interests, and lifestyles can be ascertained by directly asking individuals about them, psychographics are often not readily observable and instead are inferred from a customer's observable characteristics and actions. For example, a customer's interest in sports (psychographic factor) can be inferred from observing this customer's behaviors, such as subscriptions to sports magazines, viewing sports programming, gym membership, and purchases of sports equipment.

Because they are not readily observable, psychographics are similar to the customer need that the company aims to fulfill. However, unlike the specific customer needs the company aims to fulfill with its offering, psychographics are more general descriptors of an individual's attitudes that in most cases are not directly related to the company's offering. For example, a customer's affinity for sports does not necessarily mean that this customer needs a new tennis racket. Thus, psychographics can be viewed as a bridge between readily observable factors describing target customers (demographics, geolocation, and behavior) and the unobservable customer need that the company's offering aims to fulfill.

The proliferation of online communication and e-commerce has heightened the importance of psychographics by making customer moral values, attitudes, interests, and lifestyles readily accessible to companies. Using their customers' demographic, geographic, and behavioral data, social media companies such as Facebook, Google, and Twitter are able to construct actionable psychographic customer profiles. The same is true for traditional media companies, credit card providers, and online retailers that have data linking individuals' demographic, geographic, and behavioral profiles with their moral values, attitudes, interests, and lifestyle.

The Pros and Cons of Profile-Based Targeting

Because certain demographic, geographic, behavioral, and psychographic characteristics are readily observable, managers often define target customers in terms of their profiles without necessarily focusing on their underlying needs. This approach is based on the notion that customers with similar profiles often share similar needs. For example, customers in the 50+ age group are more likely to use hair replacement and hair coloring aids, skin-tightening creams, and nutritional supplements.

Although intuitively viable, focusing primarily on customer profiles rather than customer needs can lead to misidentifying the target market. The problem with focusing exclusively on customer profiles is that customers with the same demographic, geographic, and behavioral profiles might have different needs, while customers with different profiles might share the same needs. For example, millennials (individuals born between 1982 and 2000) vary in their preferences for soft drinks, with some favoring Pepsi, others preferring Coke, and some opting for non-cola beverages like 7UP and Mountain Dew. At the same time, the profile of loyal Pepsi drinkers extends beyond millennials to include consumers from all generations.

Profile-only targeting can lead not only to misunderstanding customer needs but can also result in misidentifying the company's true competitors. For example, if Pepsi defines its target market as everyone who drinks carbonated soft drinks (behavior-based target), its competitors would be other carbonated soft drink companies. However, if Pepsi targets all individuals who seeks to quench their thirst (need-based target), its competition would include noncarbonated soft drinks, bottled water, fruit juices, tea, and coffee.

Rather than focusing only on the readily observable characteristics of target customers reflected in their profiles, managers should think of profile-based and need-based descriptions of the target market as overlapping sets of identifiers, where the degree of overlap reflects the extent to which a company can use the customer profile as a proxy for the underlying customer need (Figure 4).

Figure 4. Customer Profile and Customer Needs

In cases when the degree of overlap is high, meaning that customers with the same profile are likely to have similar needs, profile-based targeting can be used as a proxy for need-based targeting. For example, age is a good indicator of when men begin shaving, which enables companies like Gillette, Schick, and Harry's to successfully use demographics to target boys in their late teens. In contrast, when the degree of overlap is low, meaning that customers with similar profiles are likely to have different needs, then customer needs, rather than profile, should guide the company's targeting activities. For example, using age as a proxy for the type of car consumers purchase — a sedan, a sports car, or an SUV — is often inappropriate because customers in the same age group might have different needs and, hence, seek different types of cars.

In general, even though profile-based targeting could yield similar results to need-based targeting, such cases are the exception rather than the rule. In most cases, focusing only on customer profile without considering the underlying customer needs can dramatically reduce the accuracy of the company's targeting efforts. The customer need, rather than customer profile, should be the main criterion underlying the company's targeting decision. The process of linking customer needs to customer profiles is discussed in more detail in the following section.

Aligning Customer Value and Customer Profile

An important aspect of tactical targeting involves identifying the profile characteristics of strategically important value-based customer segments. The process of linking value-based and profile-based aspects of target customers, the key factors determining the effectiveness and cost efficiency of the company's targeting activities, and the development of customer personas are discussed in more detail in the following sections.

Identifying Target Customers by Linking Their Value and Profile Characteristics

The relationship between strategic and tactical targeting is illustrated in Figure 5. Strategic targeting is value focused and is a function of the company's ability to create customer value (target compatibility) and customers' ability to create company value (target attractiveness). The focus on value, although crucial for the success of the company's offering, has the important shortcoming that value is unobservable and, hence, cannot readily be acted on to reach target customers. This shortcoming is addressed by tactical targeting, which involves identifying the demographic, geographic, psychographic, and behavioral profile of the strategically selected target customers. Thus, strategic and tactical targeting are two inseparable and complementary aspects of the process of identifying target customers.

Figure 5. Linking Customer Value and Profile

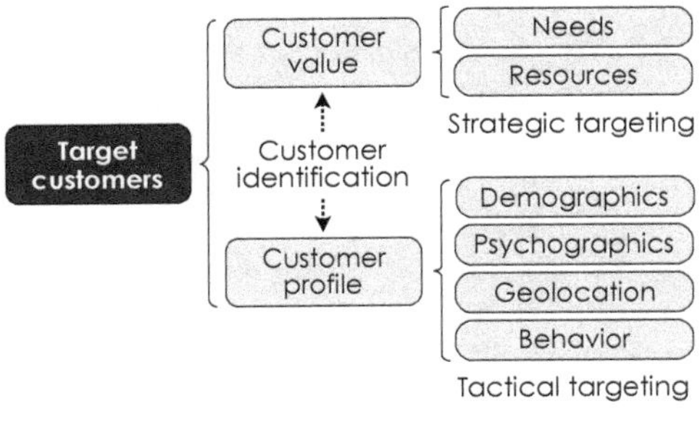

To illustrate, consider a company launching a new credit card featuring a loyalty program that rewards customers with travel benefits, including airline tickets and hotel stays. The strategically important customers include those who need a credit card and would enjoy the travel benefits offered by the card (customer value), use the card frequently, and do not default on the payments (company value). The problem faced by this company is that customer needs are unobservable, meaning that, a priori, it is difficult to know which consumers might enjoy the travel benefits offered by the card. In addition, customers' future use of the credit card and the likelihood of their not defaulting on payments are likewise unobservable. The unobservable nature of the characteristics defining segment attractiveness to the company and segment compatibility with the company's resources makes it difficult for the company to effectively communicate with and deliver the card to target customers.

To solve this problem, the company must link the value-based customer segment with the observable characteristics of customers in this segment. Thus, to identify customers with high card usage and a low likelihood of default, the company might consider customers' credit scores, demographics, geolocation, and purchase behavior, including their buying patterns, items purchased, and credit card usage frequency. Furthermore, to identify customers for whom the company can create value (e.g., those looking for travel rewards), the company might seek out customers who are likely to travel more frequently, read travel magazines and/or watch travel shows, and tend to seek travel-related information. Consequently, to reach these customers, the company might utilize travel-related communication channels to promote its offerings. Thus, by focusing on customers whose profiles are aligned with the value-based target segment, a company can maximize the effectiveness and cost efficiency of its targeting activities.

Reaching target customers in an effective and cost-efficient manner is crucial in order to avoid wasting resources on customers who are either unlikely to benefit from the company's offering or unlikely to create value for the company. Targeting that is too narrow is ineffective because it might overlook strategically important customers. Overly broad targeting, on the other hand, is not cost efficient because it wastes resources on reaching customers that are unlikely to respond favorably to the company's offering. Therefore, when evaluating different tactical targeting options, a manager needs to answer two key questions:

- *Does the company reach all of its target customers to communicate and deliver the offering?*

- *Does the company reach only its target customers to communicate and deliver the offering?*

The above two questions reflect the two main principles of tactical targeting: *effectiveness* (whether the company can reach all target customers) and *cost efficiency* (whether the company's resources are deployed in a way that reaches only its target customers). These two principles are discussed in more detail below.

Targeting Effectiveness

The effectiveness of a company's targeting efforts reflects the degree to which its actions are able to reach *all* of its target customers. Effective targeting must ensure that all strategically viable customers—those whose needs can be fulfilled by the offering in a way that benefits the company and its collaborators—are aware of the company's offering and have access to it.

In an ideal scenario, often referred to as *sniper* targeting, the company communicates and makes its offering available to all strategically viable customers and only to those customers. Such precise targeting, however, rarely happens, especially in markets comprising a large number of individual customers. The two common errors that result in ineffective targeting are choosing profile-based segments that overlap too narrowly with a selected value-based segment or do not overlap with the value-based segment at all (Figure 6). Narrow, or *slice-of-the-pie*, targeting reaches only a subset of target customers that represent a value-based segment, thus missing the opportunity to capture a larger share of the market. Off-base, or *shot-in-the-dark*, targeting occurs when the company tries to communicate and deliver its offering to customers who are not strategically viable and are unlikely to respond favorably to the company's offering.

Figure 6. Tactical Targeting: Effectiveness

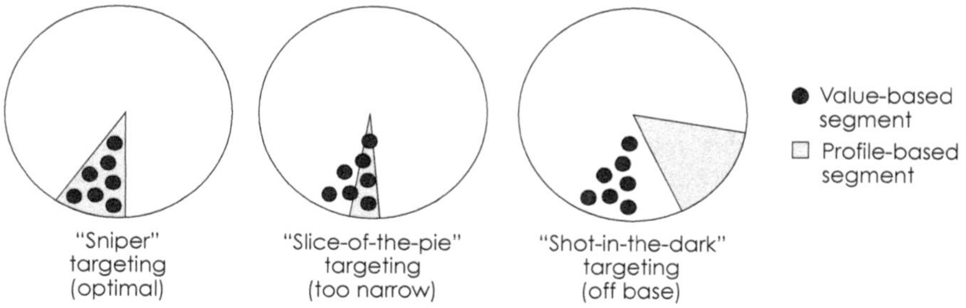

To illustrate, a credit card company targeting a customer demographic that falls in the 18–24 age group might have an overly narrow definition of its target market and could be overlooking buyers who are interested in the company's offering but fall outside of the company-defined age group. Likewise, a company promoting a credit card featuring travel benefits to customers who are not frequent travelers and are not interested in travel benefits exemplifies an off-base targeting approach with little, if any, overlap between customer needs and the offering's benefits.

Targeting Cost Efficiency

The cost-efficiency principle requires that the company's communication and distribution reach *only* its target customers. This principle is focused on managing resources to minimize (and ideally eliminate) expending resources on customers whose needs cannot be effectively addressed by the company's offering or who cannot create value for the company.

The most common error that leads to inefficient targeting involves casting a communication and distribution net that is broader than the desired target customer segment (Figure 7). The problem with this approach, often referred to as *shotgun targeting*, is that it wastes company resources such as time, effort, and money by promoting and distributing offerings to customers who are not interested in the company's offering and/or are unlikely to be able to create value for the company.

Figure 7. Tactical Targeting: Cost Efficiency

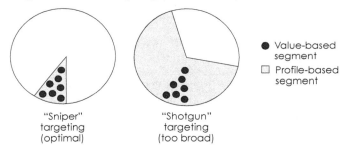

"Sniper" targeting (optimal)   "Shotgun" targeting (too broad)

● Value-based segment
□ Profile-based segment

To illustrate, a company promoting a credit card featuring travel benefits using a variety of mass-media channels targeting diverse customer audiences is likely to cast a very broad net trying to reach customers who will appreciate its unique benefits. Such an approach is effective in the sense that it is likely to reach customers who are the ultimate targets of the company's marketing efforts. Yet, it is cost inefficient because, in addition to target customers, the company bears the cost of reaching customers who are unlikely to be interested in the company's offering.

Creating Customer Personas

Targeting large groups of customers can make it difficult for managers to think of group members as real people whose problems they must solve. Therefore, to facilitate targeting, companies often use fictional representations of their prototypical target customers, referred to as customer personas.

Personas make targeting more concrete by using a vivid representation of the typical target customer that managers can relate to. For example, consider a company developing smart thermostats that help customers save money on their energy bills. The company's target customers are all homeowners interested in lowering their energy bills. A customer persona, on the other hand, is a specific representative of the company's target customers. The customer persona might be an individual named Bob who is interested in saving money on his energy bills (the need that the company aims to fulfill). Bob is in his 40s, married, with a household income of approximately $80,000, has a college degree, lives in an urban area, and owns his own residence (demographic and geographic profile). Bob also prefers to shop online, is technologically savvy, has researched different energy-saving options, and is active on social media (behavioral profile).

Clearly, the customer persona does not represent all target customers. Characterizing the target segment with a representative individual, however, makes it easier to visualize the company's target customers and better understand how likely they are to respond to the company's offering. Because a customer persona is very specific, it might not adequately reflect the needs, demographics, geolocation, psychographics, and behaviors of all target customers. In such cases, a company might use multiple personas to account for the differences among its target customers.

Targeting Multiple Customer Segments

The discussion so far has focused on a scenario in which a firm identifies and targets a single customer segment. Single-segment marketing, however, is the exception rather than the rule. Most offerings exist as part of a product line, with different offerings targeting different customer segments. The concept of targeting multiple segments and the key principles underlying the process of multi-segment targeting are discussed in the following sections.

Single-Segment and Multi-Segment Targeting

As markets become more fragmented, an increasing number of companies develop offerings targeting a greater number of smaller customer segments. Even companies that start with a single offering aimed at a specific target market achieve wider customer adoption over time. As their customer base becomes more diverse, these companies transition from a single offering to a product line with offerings that fit the needs of the diverse customers it serves.

The process of identifying multiple customer segments is similar to identifying a single customer segment, with the main difference that the targeting analysis yields several viable segments. Thus, a direct consequence of the decision to target multiple customer segments is the need to develop unique offerings that satisfy the disparate requirements of each segment (Figure 8). Indeed, because different customer segments vary in their needs and the value they can create for the company, the company must develop a portfolio of offerings that address these distinct needs in a way that benefits the company.

Figure 8. Targeting Multiple Segments

Offering A

Offering B

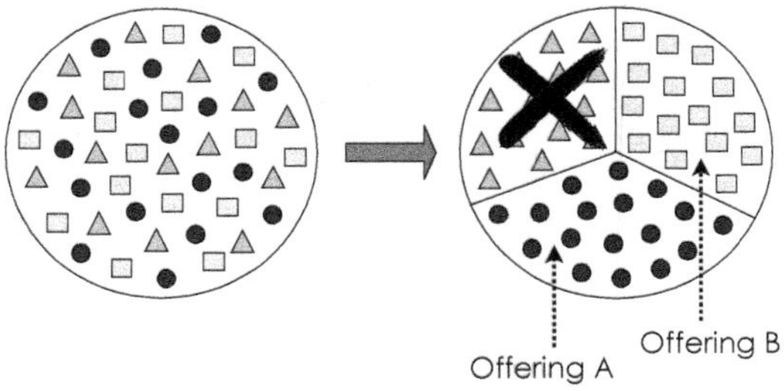

To illustrate, consider a toothpaste manufacturer that has identified four different age-related customer segments—kids, teenagers, adults, and seniors—based on the benefits they are likely to seek in a toothpaste. To successfully target all four customer segments, the company must develop a product line comprising distinct offerings, each targeting a particular customer segment. For kids, who do not see a particular benefit in brushing their teeth, the company might develop toothpaste that offers a fun experience, coloring the toothpaste and designing the packaging in a way that resembles a toy. For teenagers, who tend to be concerned with the social benefits of the toothpaste, a company might emphasize that toothpaste makes them more "kissable" and more attractive to their mates. Adults, on the other hand, might be more interested in the health benefits of the toothpaste, and a company might develop a toothpaste that aims to prevent cavities. Finally, seniors are likely to be concerned with preserving and restoring their teeth, so the company might create toothpaste with corrective benefits such as repairing tooth enamel.

The concept of targeting multiple segments can be better understood when compared with its alternative—one-for-all targeting (also referred to as mass marketing), which describes a scenario in which the same offering is aimed at a diverse set of customers. A classic example of mass marketing is Henry Ford's decision to produce the same car in the same color—the black Model T—for all customers. The alternative strategy, segment-based targeting, involves developing specific offerings for each group of customers with diverse preferences. For example, to compete with Ford's Model T, General Motors offered its customers an extensive array of cars that varied in size, functionality, and color—an approach captured in General Motors President and CEO Alfred Sloan's vision of "a car for every purpose and purse."

The Value-Alignment Principle in Targeting Multiple Segments

The decision to target multiple segments is driven by the same two principles that guide a company's choice of a single segment: (1) The company should be able to create value for customers in this segment and (2) customers in the selected segment should be able to create value for the company. Consequently, targeting multiple segments is a logical choice when a company can identify multiple groups of customers that are both attractive (meaning that they help the company to achieve its goals) and have needs that are compatible with the company's resources.

Because the needs of each customer segment are distinct, a company must develop distinct offerings for each segment it aims to pursue. To this end, the company must evaluate its ability to create value for each segment as well as each segment's ability to create value for the company (strategic targeting) and then identify the means to communicate and deliver the offering to these customers in an effective and cost-efficient manner (tactical targeting). Only when a company can create a viable strategic and tactical targeting approach for each target segment should it consider targeting multiple segments.

Developing distinct offerings for different customer segments does not necessarily mean that the company needs to create an entirely revamped product featuring a different level of service, a distinct brand and price, as well as new incentives, a new communication campaign, and new distribution channels. While scenarios exist in which a company will develop an entirely new offering to address the needs of a new customer segment, more often than not the new offering involves moderate variations on some but not all attributes. For example, to fulfill the needs of different customers, a car manufacturer might develop a new type of vehicle, set a unique price, and develop a unique communication campaign, while offering the same level of service, brand, and incentives, and using the same dealer network.

A company's decision to target multiple segments recognizes the diversity of customer needs and allows a company to design offerings that meet the needs of customers more effectively than a single offering. The downside of targeting multiple segments vis-à-vis a single segment is that creating diverse products often leads to higher development, communication, and distribution costs. Accordingly, targeting multiple segments is warranted only when the company has the resources to develop distinct offerings that can fulfill the needs of each segment better than the competition and in ways that create value for the company.

A common mistake made by companies when targeting multiple customer segments is the lack of clear alignment between the offering's attributes and the value sought by target customers. Thus, rather than developing offerings that address particular customer needs, companies sometimes develop unrelated offerings that stem from their product development and production capabilities. The problem with this approach is that without a clear understanding of how each individual offering will address a particular need of the company's target customers, the resulting offerings might end up competing with one another for the same customer segment while ignoring the needs of another segment. Moreover, the presence of multiple offerings that lack clearly defined target customers might end up confusing customers and hampering their ability to discern among the different offerings. In this context, aligning the attributes of the company's offerings with the benefits sought by each customer segment can go a long way toward ensuring the success of the company's multi-segment targeting strategy.

Segmenting the Market

The process of identifying target customers, which thus far has been the focus of discussion, assumes that customers have already been assigned to distinct segments. In this section, the discussion centers on the key principles that drive the process of dividing potential buyers into market segments.

Segmentation as a Marketing Concept

Segmentation lays the foundation for selecting which customers to target and which to ignore. Dividing customers into distinct groups enables the company to streamline its targeting decisions by combining customers with similar needs and resources into larger segments and consequently dealing with these segments as if they were a single customer. The logic of segmentation as a process and the related concepts of mass marketing and one-to-one marketing are outlined in detail below.

The Logic of Segmentation

Segmentation is a categorization process that groups customers by focusing on those differences that are relevant for targeting and ignoring those differences that are irrelevant. The process of segmentation is based on the notion that the efficiency of a company's marketing activities can be improved by ignoring the nonessential differences among customers and treating customers with similar needs and resources as if they were a single entity. Consequently, segmentation focuses marketing analysis on the important aspects of customer needs, enabling managers to group customers into distinct segments and develop offerings for each segment rather than for each individual customer.

Segmentation involves two opposing processes — differentiation and agglomeration. On one hand, segmentation is a differentiation process that aims to *divide* all buyers in the market into groups by focusing on the differences in their needs and resources with respect to the company's offering. On the other hand, segmentation is an agglomeration process that aims to *group* individual buyers into segments by focusing on the similarities in their needs and resources with respect to the company's offering. Both differentiation and agglomeration aim to produce segments comprising customers with homogeneous preferences, such that customers in each segment are similar to one another and at the same time different from customers in the other segments. Thus, even though differentiation and agglomeration are opposite processes, they aim to achieve the same goal — the creation of distinct segments comprising customers that are likely to respond in the same way to the company's offering.

A common misperception is that the process of identifying target customers starts with dividing customers into segments, and that the decision of which segments to target and which to ignore is made only after market segments have been identified. This is a myopic view of segmentation. There are countless ways to divide potential customers into distinct segments. As a result, without knowing the criteria that are relevant for the purposes of targeting, a company might develop a segmentation that is unrelated to the company's targeting strategy. In this context, segmenting the market without a particular targeting decision in mind is likely to end up an exercise in futility.

Note that although for presentation purposes segmentation typically precedes targeting, from a conceptual standpoint segmentation and targeting are an iterative process of identifying target customers. To be relevant, customer segments must be defined in a way that facilitates targeting. To ensure such relevance, prior to segmenting the market, a manager should have a general idea of who the company's target customers might be and what value the company might be able to create for these customers. Segmentation is targeting-specific, meaning that markets are segmented in a way that facilitates targeting. By the same token, targeting is segment-driven, meaning that a segment must already be defined in order to be selected as a target (Figure 9).

Figure 9. Market Segmentation and Targeting

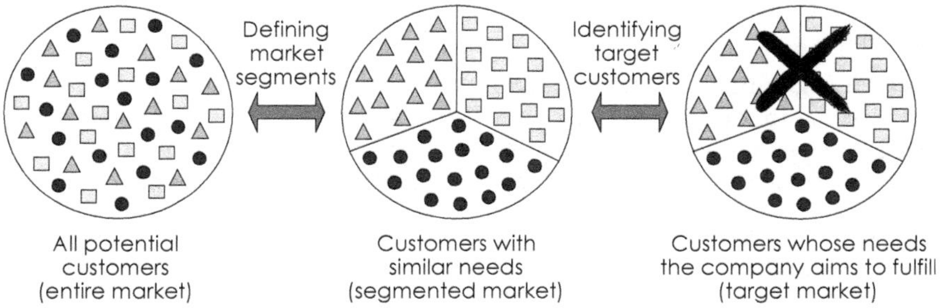

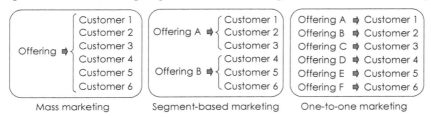

Segmentation, Mass Marketing, and One-to-One Marketing

The concept of segmentation can be better understood when considered in the context of two alternative marketing approaches: mass marketing and one-to-one marketing (Figure 10). Mass marketing refers to a scenario in which the same product or service is offered to all customers. For example, in its early days Coca-Cola Company had a single product that was promoted to all customers. In contrast, in one-to-one marketing, the company's offering is customized for each individual customer. Haute couture—made-to-order, high-end clothing—exemplifies the one-to-one marketing strategy.

Figure 10. Mass Marketing, Segment-Based Marketing, and One-to-One Marketing

Segmentation represents a compromise between the mass-marketing approach and the one-to-one approach. By recognizing the diversity of customer needs, segmentation allows a company to design offerings that meet the needs of customers more effectively than the mass-marketing approach. The downside of segmentation vis-à-vis mass marketing is that developing different offerings for each segment could potentially lead to higher product development, communication, and distribution costs.

Misunderstanding the importance of segmenting the target market is one of the most common marketing mistakes. In the classic article "Marketing Myopia," Theodore Levitt describes this targeting fallacy as "an almost trained incapacity to see that getting 'volume' may require understanding and serving many discrete and sometimes small market segments rather than going after a perhaps mythical batch of big or homogeneous customers."[1] This narrow-minded view of the market as comprising customers with identical preferences naturally leads to the development of a single offering targeting the needs of the "average" customer. Yet, the "average" customer often does not exist. Instead, the market comprises a mix of customers with diverse preferences that remain unaddressed by the company's offering. Even companies that once were able to cover the market with a single offering, over time have found it imperative to extend and reinvent their products, services, and brands to address the distinct needs of different customer segments.

Strategic and Tactical Segmentation

Because segmentation aims to facilitate targeting, it shares many of the same core principles. Based on the choice of criterion used to divide customers into segments, segmentation involves two types of processes: *strategic* and *tactical*.

- **Strategic segmentation** groups customers based on the *value* that the company can create and capture from these customers. Strategic segmentation lays the groundwork for strategic targeting, which involves selecting one (or more) of the identified segments that the company will serve by tailoring its offering to the needs of targeted customers.

- **Tactical segmentation** groups customers into segments based on their *profile* characteristics: demographics and behavior. Tactical segmentation lays the groundwork for tactical targeting, which identifies the specific channels to be used to reach strategically viable customers in order to communicate and deliver the company's offering.

The two types of segmentation and the corresponding targeting decisions are illustrated in Figure 11. The process of identifying target customers is driven by two key decisions: (1) identifying customer needs that the company can fulfill better than the competition can in a way that benefits the company and its collaborators (strategic targeting) and (2) identifying effective and cost-efficient ways to reach these customers to communicate and deliver the company's offering (tactical targeting). Each of these targeting decisions is facilitated by a corresponding segmentation: (1) strategic (value-based) segmentation groups customers based on their needs and the value they can create for the company and (2) tactical (profile-based) segmentation identifies ways (the specific communication and distribution channels) in which the company can reach these customers to communicate and deliver its offering.

Figure 11. Strategic and Tactical Segmentation Facilitates the Process of Identifying Target Customers

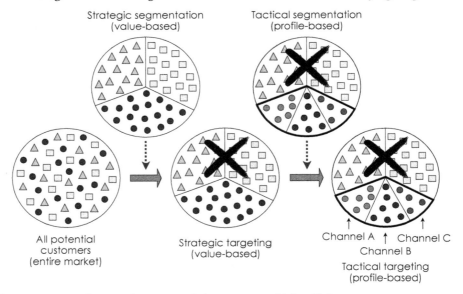

The strategic and tactical aspects of the process of identifying target customers can be described as follows. The first step in identifying target customers involves strategic targeting, which aims to identify a customer need that the company can meet better than the competition in a way that creates value for the company and its collaborators. This strategic targeting is enabled by tactical targeting, which groups customers based on the value they expect to receive and can create for the company. Therefore, once the strategically viable customer segment has been selected, the next step involves tactical targeting, which aims to identify effective and cost-efficient channels to reach this segment. The process of tactical targeting is enabled by a tactical segmentation that aims to identify the demographic, geographic, psychographic, and behavioral profile of customers for whom the company has decided to tailor its offering in order to communicate and deliver the offering to these customers in the most effective manner.

Defining the Optimal Segmentation Depth

An important decision in segmenting a given market is determining the segmentation depth—that is, how many segments to create. The answer to this question is closely linked to the concept of market heterogeneity.

A *heterogeneous market* is composed of customers who vary in the manner in which they are likely to respond to a company's offering. Thus, customers in a heterogeneous market are likely to seek different benefits, have different financial resources, and vary in the ways they can be reached by the company. Because customers in heterogeneous markets have different needs, they cannot be served by the same offering. In contrast, a *homogeneous market* is composed of customers with similar preferences who are likely to behave in a similar manner and, therefore, can be served by the same offering.

By identifying groups of customers with similar preferences, segmentation aims to reduce the heterogeneity of its target customers by forming homogeneous segments that are likely to respond in a similar fashion to the company's offering. Segmentation does not completely eliminate heterogeneity within a segment; customers within each segment still differ on a variety of factors. In well-defined segments, however, these residual differences are less relevant to the company's offering and are unlikely to elicit different responses from customers with respect to the core benefits of the offering. Thus, segmentation focuses on the key factors that determine customer response to the offering and ignores factors that are not directly related to the company's offering.

The decision about how many segments to create when identifying target customers involves balancing the benefits of greater targeting accuracy and greater cost efficiency. Creating a greater number of segments has the benefit of more accurately reflecting the needs of the customers within each segment; however, on the downside, it tends to increase the cost of developing customized offerings for each segment and complicates the management of these offerings. Identifying fewer segments, on the other hand, has the benefit of being more cost efficient but has the downside of producing customer segments with diverse preferences, thus increasing the chance that the company's offering might not appeal to all customers in a given segment.

A practical approach to determine whether a market is homogeneous or needs to be segmented further is to examine the degrees of freedom that the company has when developing its offerings for this market. Generally speaking, the more homogeneous (uniform) a given customer segment is, the fewer degrees of freedom a manager has in addressing the needs of this segment. Conversely, the presence of multiple degrees of freedom during development of an offering indicates that the company's target market is composed of customers with diverse needs and preferences.[2]

For example, when deciding on an offering's price, if an argument can be made for both a low price (so that the offering is affordable for some customers) and a high price (because some customers are not price sensitive), this suggests that the target market is heterogeneous and comprises segments that vary in price sensitivity. Likewise, when faced with a choice in designing a product and an argument can be made in favor of developing both a simple version (for customers who seek basic functionality) and a more complex version (for advanced users), it is likely that the target market contains customers with different needs and preferences that the company is trying to address with a single offering.

In this context, segmentation can be viewed as a process that aims to reduce the degrees of freedom in designing the company's offering. The presence of multiple degrees of freedom is typically an indication that the market consists of customers with diverse needs and preferences and, therefore, can benefit from further segmentation. An optimal segmentation is achieved when there is little or no ambiguity (and, hence, few degrees of freedom) regarding the benefits sought by customers in this segment.

Key Segmentation Principles

To be effective, segmentation should conform to three main principles. It should be *relevant* with respect to the targeting goals; involve segments that are *similar* (homogeneous) with respect to underlying needs; and be *comprehensive*, whereby the segmentation comprises all potential buyers in the market.

- **Relevance.** Because segmentation aims to facilitate targeting, it should group customers based on their likely response to the company's offering. There are countless criteria that could be used to divide customers into segments. Most of these criteria, however, are unrelated to factors that underlie the company's targeting strategy and, as a result, produce market segments that do not facilitate the development of a meaningful strategy and tactics. Accordingly, segmenting markets without a particular targeting purpose in mind is most often a waste of company resources that ends up distracting rather than facilitating managerial decision making.

- **Similarity.** Segmentation aims to group customers so that those within each segment are similar to one another (have homogeneous preferences) in the way they are likely to respond to the company's offering. In general, a larger number of segments leads to greater similarity among the customers within each segment, with the resulting segments more likely to comprise customers with uniform preferences. At the same time, a more granular segmentation calls for the development of a greater number of customized offerings—an approach justified only in cases when the underlying differences between these segments are essential to the company's ability to create customer value. Therefore, to be effective, a segmentation must balance the advantage of creating more homogeneous segments with the disadvantage of creating segments that are not significantly different from one another with respect to the company offering.

- **Comprehensiveness.** Segments should be comprehensive: They should include all potential customers in a given market, with each customer assigned to a segment. Thus, segmentation should produce segments that are collectively exhaustive, meaning that no potential customers are left unassigned to a segment. Not including a particular subset of the market in the segmentation is particularly problematic because it effectively excludes these potential customers from even being considered when identifying potentially viable target customers. In this context, having an exhaustive segmentation that involves all potential customers in a given market is of crucial importance for a meaningful targeting strategy.

Figure 12 illustrates segmentations that violate these three principles. The first scenario (Figure 12A) illustrates a segmentation that uses an irrelevant criterion, such that the resulting segmentation does not capture important differences in customer needs. The second scenario (Figure 12B) illustrates a segmentation that violates the similarity principle, whereby customers in one of the segments have heterogeneous preferences. Finally, the third scenario (Figure 12C) illustrates a non-exhaustive segmentation that fails to include all potential customers.

Figure 12. Common Segmentation Errors

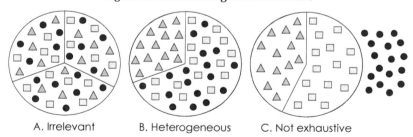

A. Irrelevant   B. Heterogeneous   C. Not exhaustive

To illustrate, consider a credit card company that offers travel-related benefits such as airline miles and hotel points. If this company groups its potential customers based on their affinity to different types of cuisine, in most cases this is likely to produce a segmentation that is irrelevant (it is more likely to be relevant for a restaurant than for a credit card). If this company groups customers based on their income but does not group them based on their affinity for travel, the resulting segments are likely to be heterogeneous (because it includes both people who are interested in travel and those who are not). Finally, if this company focuses solely on certain demographics, such as only those who fall in the 18–55 age group, the resulting segmentation would be non-exhaustive.

A simplified version of the key segmentation principles is the MECE rule, which states that segmentation should yield segments that are both *mutually exclusive* and *collectively exhaustive*. This rule combines two of the three segmentation principles — similarity and comprehensiveness. Thus, the requirement that segments be mutually exclusive means that these segments must be sufficiently different from one another and should not overlap. This requirement can be related to the principle of similarity in segmentation. Indeed, if customers within each segment are similar to one another in the way they are likely to respond to the company's offering, they are also likely to be different from customers in other segments. In the same vein, the requirement that segments be collectively exhaustive means that the segmentation is comprehensive, such that the identified segments include *all* customers in a given market.

Note that the comprehensiveness principle applies to the majority of situations, although not all. Thus, it is possible that a company might deliberately focus on a particular sub-segment in order to segment the market even further based on additional criteria. In such cases, focusing on a particular sub-segment without explicitly considering the other sub-segments is not an issue as long as the company is cognizant of and has considered all sub-segments when selecting target customers.

The development of a sound segmentation is crucial for selecting a viable target market. Segmentation and targeting are two complementary aspects of the process of identifying target customers, such that errors in segmenting the market are likely to lead to a suboptimal choice of target customers. Following the key segmentation principles — relevance, similarity, and comprehensiveness — can help ensure the soundness of the resulting segmentation and its feasibility as a basis for identifying viable target customers.

SUMMARY

Targeting is the process of identifying customers for whom the company will optimize its offering. Targeting involves two decisions: strategic and tactical.

Strategic targeting involves identifying which customers (segments) to serve and which to ignore. Strategic targeting is guided by two key factors: target compatibility and target attractiveness. *Target compatibility* reflects a company's ability to create value for customers; it is a function of a company's resources, including: business infrastructure, scarce resources, skilled employees, collaborator networks, know-how, strong brands, an established ecosystem, and capital. *Target attractiveness* reflects customers' potential to create value for the company; it is a function of monetary factors such as the revenues generated by a particular customer segment and the costs associated with serving this segment, as well as strategic factors such as a segment's social value, scale value, and information value. A key principle of strategic targeting is that the company should be able to create superior value for its customers relative to the competition. To this end, a company must follow the *resource advantage principle* and identify markets in which it has superior resources relative to the competition.

Tactical targeting involves identifying effective and cost-efficient ways to reach strategically viable customers. Tactical targeting links the (typically unobservable) value-based segments to specific observable and actionable characteristics. Such observable characteristics, also referred to as the *customer profile*, include demographic (e.g., age, gender, and income), geographic (e.g., permanent residence and current location), psychographic (e.g., moral values, attitudes, interests, and lifestyle), and behavioral (e.g., purchase frequency, purchase quantity, and price sensitivity) factors. Tactical targeting is guided by two key factors: effectiveness (a company's ability to reach all target customers) and cost efficiency (a company's ability to deploy its resources in a way that reaches only its target customers). To facilitate targeting, managers often use fictional representations of their prototypical target customers, referred to as customer personas.

Segmentation is a categorization process that groups customers by focusing on those differences that are relevant for targeting and ignoring those differences that are irrelevant. Segmentation enables managers to group customers into larger segments and develop offerings for the entire segment rather than for each individual customer.

Segmentation involves two types of processes: *strategic* and *tactical*. Strategic segmentation lays the groundwork for strategic targeting by grouping customers based on the *value* that the company can create and capture from these customers. Tactical segmentation lays the groundwork for tactical targeting by grouping customers into segments based on their *profile* characteristics: demographics, geolocation, psychographics, and behavior.

Segmentation must follow three *principles*: relevance (customers must be grouped on characteristics that are relevant to their likely response to the offering), similarity (segments must comprise customers with similar characteristics), and comprehensiveness (segmentation must include all potential customers).

Marketing Insight: Occasion-Based and User-Based Targeting

Customer needs vary based on the degree to which they evolve over time. Certain needs are relatively stable and do not change much over time, whereas other needs vary such that the same person might have different needs at different points in time. These two types of needs call for different targeting strategies, commonly referred to as *occasion-based targeting* and *user-based targeting*.

Occasion-based targeting groups customers based on purchase and consumption occasions. Occasion-based targeting is particularly relevant when customer needs vary across purchase occasions and the same customer is likely to fall into different usage-based segments at different times. For example, when buying wine, a customer's preference might vary as a function of the occasion (for cooking, for daily consumption, for a special occasion, or for a gift). By focusing on usage occasions rather than on the individual characteristics of the customer, occasion-based targeting accounts for the fact that the same customer is likely to display different needs depending on the occasion. Unlike user-based targeting, which assumes that customer needs do not vary across purchase occasions, occasion-based targeting does not make such an assumption, implying that an individual customer (or segment) can have different needs at different times. Because it accounts for the variability of customer preferences across purchase occasions, occasion-based targeting is the default approach in identifying target customers.

User-based targeting groups customers based on their relatively stable individual characteristics, needs, and behaviors. User-based targeting assumes that the needs of individual customers do not vary across purchase occasions and, hence, that an individual's needs can be fulfilled with a single offering. Accordingly, user-based targeting is appropriate in settings in which customers' needs are relatively stable across purchase occasions and can be used as a reliable predictor of their behavior on any particular purchase occasion. For example, the preference for regular versus light (diet) soft drinks is fairly stable across individuals and can serve as the basis for user-based targeting. Because it is based on the assumption that customer preferences are constant across usage occasions, the user-based targeting strategy can be viewed as a special case of the more general need-based targeting strategy.

Successful companies strive to combine occasion-based and user-based targeting. Consider Hallmark, which offers personal expression products in more than 30 languages and distributes them in more than 100 countries. Hallmark carries 50,000 different products at any one time and sells nearly 5 billion greeting cards every year. The company's success is due in part to combining occasion-based and user-based segmentation of customer needs. To capture different occasions in people's lives, Hallmark has a variety of specialized cards focused on events such as anniversaries, birthdays, graduations, weddings, retirement, and having a baby, as well as on different feelings such as friendship, sympathy, encouragement, and thankfulness. In addition to cards designed to capture different occasions in a person's life, Hallmark has introduced lines targeting market segments based on the more permanent characteristics of their customers. For example, Hallmark's three ethnic lines—Mahogany, Hallmark Sinceramente, and Tree of Life—target African American, Hispanic, and Jewish consumers, respectively. For business customers, Hallmark Business Expressions offers a collection of personalized holiday cards and greeting cards. Tailoring its offering to both usage occasions and the profile of its users has enabled Hallmark to sustain its leading market position for over a century.

Marketing Insight: Data-Driven Targeting

For many decades, marketers have relied on traditional targeting based on demographics, geolocation, psychographics, and behavior to reach new customers. Thus, a manager might set a targeting rule using characteristics that they believe define potential customers. For example, a targeting rule might seek out individuals with a certain income and education level who live in a particular geographic area, have an interest in the benefits provided by the company's offering, and have purchased similar products in the past.

With the advancement of data analytics techniques such as data mining, text analysis, and machine learning, companies are increasingly turning to data-driven methods to more accurately identify target customers. Because of its ability to improve the effectiveness and cost efficiency of traditional targeting methods, data-driven targeting has rapidly gained acceptance as a viable component of a company's targeting efforts.

Data-driven targeting differs from traditional targeting in the way it links the observable characteristics of target customers to their (unobservable) needs. Traditional targeting aims to establish a logical connection between the unobservable customer needs that could be fulfilled by the company's offering and observable customer characteristics (profile). Unlike the traditional top-down approach in which the company seeks to identify the profile of its target customers by developing hypotheses that link customer needs and profile, data-driven targeting examines data patterns in order to identify individuals who match the profile of the company's "ideal" customers. Thus, the bottom-up approach used by data-driven targeting typically relies primarily on the observed relationships between the factors of interest rather than on theory-based arguments and hypotheses.

The backbone of data-driven targeting consists of *data-management platforms* that collect and organize customer data from a variety of online and offline sources. These platforms serve as data warehouses that integrate different types of information, including demographic, geolocation, psychographic, behavioral, transaction, and even biometric data from wearable smart devices. Based on the source of the information, data-management platforms include three types of data. First-party data include information directly collected by the company itself such as website data, mobile app data, and customer relationship management data. Second-party data are typically obtained through a direct relationship with another entity. For example, the keyword data collected by Google's online advertising service Google Ads (formerly AdWords) are second-party data that advertisers receive because of their collaboration with Google. Finally, third-party data include any information collected by an entity that does not have a direct relationship with the company. Unlike first-party and second-party data, which are unique to the company and are not available and/or relevant to other companies, third-party data are aggregated from various sources and are typically bought and sold through data exchanges and are relevant and available to all companies.

Data-driven targeting involves two types of activities: need-based targeting and profile-matching targeting. *Need-based targeting* aims to define the profile of a company's "ideal" customers by linking their offering-specific needs to their observable demographic, geographic, psychographic, and behavioral characteristics. In this context, *data-driven targeting* is similar to traditional targeting, with the key difference that it stems primarily from observed data patterns rather than from hypotheses that link customer needs and profile.

Building on need-based target identification, *profile-matching targeting* taps into large population databases to identify individuals whose profiles are similar to those of a company's "ideal" customers. Unlike need-based targeting, which aims to link customers' needs with their observable profile, profile-matching targeting examines data patterns in order to identify individuals who match the customer profile sought. Using similarity-matching predictive analytics allows companies to identify prospects who display behavior similar to that of already identified "ideal" customers, thus enabling companies to scale up their targeting efforts in an effective and cost-efficient manner.

Consider a company that has identified a small set of "ideal" customers—those who value the benefits provided by the company's offering and are willing to pay for these benefits. Using similarity-matching algorithms, companies like Facebook can scale up the company's initial customer base (often referred to as the "source audience") to create a much larger segment (often referred to as a "lookalike" segment) that is similar to the original target segment on the relevant attributes. To this end, Facebook will sift through its user database to identify individuals whose demographic, geographic, psychographic, and behavioral profiles match the profiles of the company's "ideal" customers. Thus, the essence of Facebook's approach is captured by the old proverb "birds of a feather flock together," which in this context means that consumers with corresponding profiles are likely to behave in a similar fashion.

Profile-matching targeting can be based on a variety of inputs, including segments comprising users who have watched a particular video, segments with profiles similar to users who have completed a specific conversion activity (e.g., click-through advertisement, inquiry form, and sign-up), and segments with profiles similar to those of users who have visited a particular webpage. At the heart of such profile matching is a company's ability to access pooled data, which offers much richer information about its current and potential customers. Virtually all search, media, retail, and credit card companies—including Google, Twitter, YouTube, WeChat, Amazon, Alibaba, Tmall (formerly Taobao Mall), Visa, MasterCard, and American Express—have at their fingertips vast amounts of individual-level data about their users that can be used to predict and potentially influence customers' behavior.

As the amount of individual-level information increases exponentially, companies are not only able to gain much deeper insight into customer needs but also can identify these customers in the population. Thus, by identifying customers most likely to benefit from the company's offering and determining ways to reach them in an effective and cost-efficient manner, data-driven targeting can help close the gap between strategic and tactical targeting.

MARKETING INSIGHT: THE LONG TAIL

The term *long tail* is derived from statistics, in which a long-tailed distribution is characterized by a small number of causes that result in a disproportionately large number of outcomes. In a long-tailed distribution, the bulk of the value in a market comes from the head, while most offerings reside in a long tail and have very little aggregate value. In marketing, *long tail* refers to the part of a market comprising a large number of offerings, each of which produces a relatively small amount of market value.[3] The long tail is the opposite of the "head" of the market, which contains a small number of "hit" offerings, each of which produces a large share of the total market value (Figure 13).

Figure 13. The Long Tail

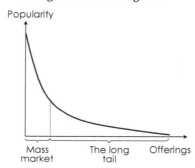

The traditional mass-market approach to marketing focuses on generating "hit" offerings that make up the head of the distribution. With this approach, the low-value long tail, which includes a large number of offerings that serve niche markets, is considered less profitable and receives relatively little attention. However, changes in technology and the emergence of new business models have shifted the focus of many companies from the head of the distribution representing the mass market to the tail of the distribution that comprises niche markets.

The mass-market approach, which views offerings in the head as much more attractive than those in the long tail, reflects the technology of the era in which it emerged. For decades, the world relied on mass media that reached millions of consumers at a time, retail stores that could stock only a limited number of products, and factories geared toward churning out products efficiently at high volumes. These technologies effectively made marketing the large number of niche products in the long tail less valuable to companies. As a result, niche preferences were neglected, and consumer tastes conformed with the small number of hit products in the market. The long tail contributed only a small amount of total market value.

With advancements in technology and the rise of new production, communication, and distribution methods, the factors favoring the mass-market approach have shifted in many industries. Automation and globalization have led to a reduction in the cost of low-volume production. The rapid growth of social media, the increased effectiveness of search engines, and the ubiquity of mobile communications have further allowed consumers to quickly discover niche offerings that cater to their specific tastes. The decline in storage and distribution costs stemming from centralization and automation have enabled companies to store and deliver a larger range of products to consumers at a much lower cost. In this new environment, the long tail of niche offerings holds significantly more value than before. Instead of searching exclusively for hit products, companies now can benefit from satisfying the niche tastes and preferences represented in the long tail.

CHAPTER SEVEN

DEVELOPING A CUSTOMER VALUE PROPOSITION

We would take something old and tired and common — coffee
— and weave a sense of romance and community around it.
— Howard Schultz, founder of Starbucks

The customer value proposition articulates the specific benefits and costs that a company's offering aims to create for its target customers. The customer value proposition guides all tactical decisions involved in designing, communicating, and delivering the company's offering to its customers. The key aspects of developing a customer value proposition are the focus of this chapter. Specifically, we address the following topics:

- *Developing a Value Proposition* || The value proposition as a marketing concept | Identifying the key competitors | Defining the offering's points of difference and the points of parity | Creating a sustainable competitive advantage

- *Positioning the Offering* || Positioning as a strategic decision | Deciding how many benefits to promote | Deciding which benefits to promote | Deciding how to frame relevant benefits

- *Crafting a Positioning Statement* || The positioning statement as a means of communication | Structuring the positioning statement

The discussion of the value proposition and positioning is complemented by an in-depth overview of two additional topics: developing a positioning map and the Blue Ocean strategy.

Developing a Value Proposition

The development of a meaningful value proposition is a central element of a viable marketing strategy. The key issues involved in the development of a value proposition — *understanding the way customers form value judgments, identifying the key competitors, defining the offering's points of difference and points of parity,* and *creating a sustainable competitive advantage* — are discussed in more detail in the following sections.

The Customer Value Proposition as a Marketing Concept

The customer value proposition articulates the value — benefits and costs — a company aims to create for its target customers. The essence of the value proposition and its relation to the process of identifying target customers, the concept of customer value as a reflection of customer needs and offering attributes, the three dimensions of customer value, and a general framework for creating customer value in a competitive context are detailed in the following sections.

Identifying Target Customers and Developing a Value Proposition

Creating customer value is a central component of a company's market strategy, which is built on identifying target markets and developing a value proposition. Crafting a customer value proposition follows the identification of customers that the company will serve with its offering (discussed in more detail in Chapter 6). In this context, an offering's value proposition delineates the value — defined by the specific benefits and costs — that target customers will receive from the offering.

The development of a customer value proposition is intricately related to the identification of target customers. In fact, the processes of identifying target customers and creating a value proposition for these customers are often thought of as a progression. The development of these processes, however, is iterative, such that crafting the value proposition both determines and follows from the choice of target customers. The development of a value proposition determines the identification of target customers because the company's ability to create superior customer value is a key targeting criterion. At the same time, the development of a value proposition follows from the selection of target customers because a meaningful value proposition necessitates focusing on specific customer needs.

For example, a credit card company might identify target customers who like to vacation in different locations and offer these customers reward points redeemable for airline tickets and hotel stays. At the same time, the company's choice of target customers is also driven by its ability to procure travel rewards that are attractive to customers at a cost that will make offering these rewards feasible for the company.

Recognizing the iterative nature of the processes of identifying target customers and the development of a value proposition, the following discussion bases the key aspects of developing a value proposition on the assumption that target customers have already been identified. In this context, the sections below address the concept of the customer value proposition and the role of the competitive context in defining the offering's benefits and costs.

Customer Value as a Function of Customer Needs and Offering Attributes

Customer value reflects the worth of an offering; it is a customer's assessment of the ability of the company's offering to fulfill this customer's needs. The value of an offering is determined by the fit between this offering's attributes and the needs of the target customers: The better the offering's attributes fit the needs of its target customers, the greater the customer value created by this offering (Figure 1).

Figure 1. Value as a Function of Customer Needs and Offering Attributes

Two aspects of value merit attention: Value is intangible and idiosyncratic. Because it is a customer's subjective evaluation of the worth of the company's offering, value is *intangible*; it does not physically exist in the market. Value is not an attribute of a company's offering; it is created when a customer interacts with the company's offering. Only when an offering's attributes are considered by a customer whose needs could be fulfilled by these attributes does the value created by the offering emerge.

Furthermore, because value reflects a customer's assessment of the offering, it is *idiosyncratic*, whereby the same offering can create different value for different customers. Thus, an offering that is appealing to one customer might be of little or no value to another customer. For example, a credit card offering travel benefits can be attractive to a frequent traveler but hold little value for a person who rarely travels or one whose travel expenses are covered by a third party. In the same vein, a lower priced, lower quality offering is likely to be attractive to price-conscious customers and unattractive to those customers seeking high performance and exclusivity.

Understanding customer needs and the benefits customers aim to receive from a company's offering is important because these needs and benefits determine the value proposition of the offering for target customers and guide the key decisions concerning this offering's attributes. Thus, knowing customer needs and the benefits customers seek enables the company to craft a value proposition underscoring the benefits that will fulfill these needs and design an offering to deliver these benefits. Developing an offering without a clearly defined value proposition that articulates the ways in which this offering will create customer value is often a waste of the company's resources. Indeed, without an alignment between the offering's attributes and customer needs, the market success of the offering is more of a gamble than a well-calculated risk.

Dimensions of Customer Value

Depending on the underlying customer needs, an offering can create value across three domains: *functional*, *psychological*, and *monetary*. These three domains of customer value are depicted in Figure 2 and briefly outlined below.

Figure 2. Dimensions of Customer Value

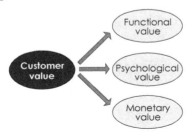

- **Functional value** is defined by the benefits and costs directly related to an offering's performance. Attributes that create functional value include performance, reliability, durability, compatibility, ease of use, customization, form, style, and packaging. For offerings that serve primarily utilitarian functions, such as office and industrial equipment, functionality is often the paramount consideration. The functional value of an offering is gauged by the answer to the question: *What is the functional value of the offering for target customers?*

- **Psychological value** is defined by the psychological benefits and costs associated with the offering. Psychological value goes beyond the functional benefits of the offering to create psychological benefits for target customers. For example, customers might value the emotional benefits provided by a car, such as the joy of driving a high-performance vehicle as well as the social status and lifestyle conveyed by the car. In categories such as luxury and fashion, where customers seek emotional and self-expressive benefits, the psychological value conveyed by the offering is of primary importance. The psychological value of an offering is gauged by the answer to the question: *How do target customers feel about the offering?*

- **Monetary value** is defined by the monetary benefits and costs associated with the offering. Attributes that create monetary value include the offering's price, fees, discounts, and rebates, as well as the various monetary costs associated with using and disposing of the offering. Even though monetary value is typically associated with costs, an offering can also carry monetary benefits such as cash-back offers, monetary bonuses, cash prizes, financial rewards, and low-interest financing. In commoditized categories with undifferentiated offerings, the monetary aspect of the offering is often the dominant criterion for choice. The monetary value of an offering is gauged by the answer to the question: *What are the monetary benefits and costs of the offering for target customers?*

Even though they represent different dimensions of customer value, these domains are not mutually exclusive. For example, the customer value of Apple's iPhone is defined by its performance across all three dimensions. The *functional value* of the iPhone is defined by factors such as its mobile connectivity; its ability to make phone calls, send text messages, and take pictures; and the benefits offered by millions of productivity and entertainment apps. Its *psychological value* stems from factors such as the satisfaction of using an aesthetically pleasing, user-friendly device; from peace of mind that the iPhone will function as described; and from the iPhone's ability to convey one's personality and social status. Finally, the iPhone's *monetary value* is defined by factors such as its price, any available promotional incentives, and its resale value.

In the same vein, Starbucks serves fresh-brewed coffee to millions of customers around the world every week, in the process delivering value across all three domains. Starbucks creates *functional value* for its customers by providing them with energy (caffeine); promoting productivity; and offering them a physical space in which to relax, work, and socialize. Starbucks delivers *psychological value* by becoming part of customers' daily routine, giving them a sense of belonging and a means to express their identity by creating their "own" beverages, in addition to fostering the feeling of moral satisfaction derived from supporting a socially responsible company. Finally, Starbucks' *monetary value* is reflected in its prices and various monetary incentives, including loyalty points, buy-one/get-one offers, and promotional discounts.

The dimensions of consumer value are not universally positive. Because value stems from both benefits and costs, costs might outweigh the benefits on a particular dimension. In most cases, the functional value and psychological value, which reflect the core benefits of the offering, are positive, whereas the monetary value, which involves the price paid by customers for the offering, is negative. For example, a consumer might appreciate the functional benefits of the iPhone and find the Apple brand highly relevant but derive negative value from iPhone's price. Because value is a function of benefits and costs, to create value the benefits across all three dimensions should outweigh the corresponding costs.

Creating Customer Value in a Competitive Context

To create superior market value, it is vital that managers understand the way in which a company's offering creates customer value and how this value compares to the value created by competitors' offerings. The value an offering creates for its customers is determined by three main factors: (1) the needs of these customers, (2) the value created for these customers by the company's offering, and (3) the value created by the alternative means (e.g., competitive offerings) these customers can use to fulfill their needs (Figure 3). Accordingly, the customer value proposition must answer the question: *Why would target customers choose the company's offering instead of the available alternatives?*

Figure 3. The Customer Value Proposition

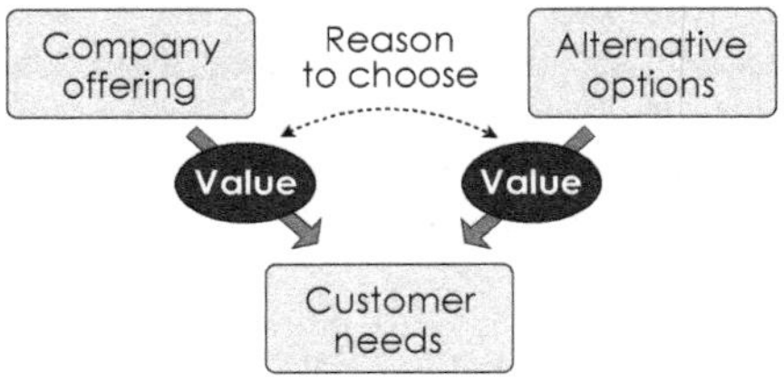

The alternative options are not limited to competitive offerings; they might include a company's own products and services (as is the case when a market leader introduces a new version of its offering that aims to replace the old one) or even makeshift solutions created by customers themselves. Because in most cases the key alternative to a company's offering is an offering developed by another company, the rest of this chapter uses the term competitive offerings in reference to offerings developed by other companies.

To create a meaningful value proposition for its target customers, a company must design an offering that delivers superior benefits relative to the competition. Yet companies often launch products and services without a clear understanding of who their competitors are and why their target customers would choose their offering over competitive offerings. Unfortunately, these companies realize the importance of understanding the competition only after their offering is engulfed by it. Overlooking the competition prevents the company from delivering on one of the key marketing principles: *The success of an offering is defined by its ability to create greater value for target customers than the competition.* Identifying the key competitors and creating a sustainable competitive advantage are key to market success.

Identifying the Key Competitors

Identifying an offering's key competitors is essential to the development of a customer value proposition. Without knowing what other options are available, it is virtually impossible to design an offering that can create superior customer value for target customers. To identify the competitive options, managers should put themselves in the shoes of their customers and ask what alternative means are available to fulfill the need that the company's offering aims to fulfill. A company's competitors include not only the similar offerings that exist within the same industry but all means that can fulfill the same customer need as the company's offering seeks to do.

Depending on whether or not competitive offerings belong to the same industry and product category, competition can be either direct or indirect. *Direct competitors* are offerings that come from the same industry (or product category) and aim to fulfill the same customer need as the company's offering. For example, Coca-Cola competes directly with Pepsi, Canon cameras compete with Nikon, and Marriott competes with Hilton. *Indirect competitors* are those with offerings that compete across different industries (product categories) to fulfill the same customer need. For example, Coca-Cola competes with a variety of non-cola beverages, including juices and water. Canon competes with smartphones like iPhone, Pixel, and Samsung Galaxy. Marriott competes with peer-to-peer online apartment rental platforms such as Airbnb. Thus, indirect competitors include all alternative means outside of the offering's industry that aim to address a particular need.

Because competition is defined relative to the customer need being fulfilled, not industry or product category affiliation, the distinction between direct and indirect competitors is inconsequential. Indeed, customers typically consider offerings that promise to address their needs without regard for industry or category affiliation. Therefore, to ensure market success, a company must look beyond the boundaries of the industry in which it operates and the product category in which it competes and design an offering that creates greater customer value than all alternative means of fulfilling the identified customer need.

A practical approach to identifying a company's key competitors is to evaluate the market through the eyes of target customers, examine the ways in which the company's offering fits into their lives, and pinpoint the alternative means that these customers can use to fulfill the identified need. In particular, there are three key questions that a manager should ask to identify the competition:

- *What means are target customers currently using to fulfill the need addressed by the company's offering?*
- *If the company does not introduce its offering, what would these customers do?*
- *What product, service, or behavior does the company's offering aim to replace?*

The first question aims to identify the competition by examining the *current behavior* of target customers. Specifically, this question aims to uncover the default option against which the company's offering will be evaluated. Identifying customers' current behavior is important because the value of an offering is defined relative to the option(s) that this offering aims to replace.

The second question seeks to identify the competition by examining the *counterfactual behavior* of target customers—their behavior in the absence of the company's offering. The option likely to be chosen if the company's offering were not available is the offering that will end up competing with the company's offering when it is introduced.

The third question aims to identify the competition by examining the *substitution behavior* of the target customers. Because customers often face resource constraints on factors such as time, money, and space, the introduction of a new offering will not necessarily result in an additional purchase; instead the new offering might replace an offering that customers have purchased in the past. Simply put, the introduction of a new offering does not mean that customers will end up buying *more* items but rather that they will buy *different* items. The item(s) customers might forgo by purchasing the company's offering are this offering's competitors.

To illustrate, consider a company launching a new protein snack that offers a nutritious meal on the go for health-conscious consumers. To identify its competitors, a manager can start by examining the *current behavior* of its target customers—what snacks they currently consume. A manager can further examine the *counterfactual behavior* of its target customers and identify the means these customers can use to fulfill their need for on-the-go healthy snacks should the company not introduce its new snack. A manager can also examine the *substitution behavior* that is likely to be displayed by customers: How would their behavior change when the new snack is introduced? What would they take out of (or not put in) their shopping basket if they were to choose the new snack?

The above questions examining customers' current, counterfactual, and substitution behavior represent different ways to identify the competitive offerings. Because these questions examine the same pattern of behavior by target customers, the answers to all three questions should converge on the same set of competitors.

Defining the Offering's Points of Difference and the Points of Parity

In an ideal world, a company's offering would surpass the competitive offerings on all attributes. In reality, however, this is rarely the case. Most offerings have both strengths and weaknesses relative to the competition. Because companies vary in their resources, their offerings differ in the benefits they deliver to target customers. Based on whether an offering's benefits are similar to or different from those of its competitors, the value proposition can be defined on three dimensions: *points of dominance*, *points of parity*, and *points of compromise*.

- **Points of dominance** (PoD) are the dimensions on which a company's offering is superior to the competition. The points of dominance define a company's *competitive advantage*. For example, an offering might have higher reliability, greater comfort, and better performance than the competition.

- **Points of parity** (PoP) are the dimensions on which a company's offering is equal to the competition; these are the attributes on which the company's offering is at *competitive parity* with the competition. For example, an offering's durability might be identical to that of its competitors. Note that the competitive offerings need not be literally identical in their performance to be at parity; the key is that the customers perceive them to offer benefits that are not meaningfully different.

- **Points of compromise** (PoC) are the dimensions on which a company's offering is inferior to the competition. The points of compromise define a company's *competitive disadvantage*. These are the attributes on which customers must compromise in order to receive the unique benefits afforded by the offering. For example, customers might compromise on price in order to gain the higher levels of reliability, comfort, and performance provided by the company's offering.

Each of the above dimensions—points of dominance, points of parity, and points of compromise—reflects the way customers *perceive* the market offerings rather than the actual performance of these offerings. As such, minor differences in market offerings that are not noticed by customers or deemed to be irrelevant do not constitute a competitive advantage. For example, if customers cannot tell the difference in the performance of a 250- and a 260-horsepower car engine or if they find this difference meaningless, these offerings are at competitive parity. By the same logic, an offering might be viewed as having a competitive advantage even when its actual performance is identical to that of competitive offerings, as long as this offering is perceived to be superior by customers. For example, a product associated with a strong brand might be perceived as having superior performance compared to a functionally identical generic product, thus creating a point of dominance.

Creating a competitive advantage is not just about differentiation: It is about differentiation that is meaningful to customers. Because competitive advantage is determined by an offering's ability to create superior customer value, only attributes that are relevant to customer needs can create a competitive advantage. Differentiating on attributes that do not add value for customers does not lead to a competitive advantage. Moreover, differentiation on irrelevant attributes might even decrease the perceived value of the offering if customers believe that the irrelevant attributes come at the expense of other, more important benefits.

The advantages and disadvantages of an offering relative to the competition can be illustrated using a *competitive value map*, which identifies the key attributes that are important to target customers and highlights the competitive advantage, parity, and disadvantage of the company's offering on these attributes (Figure 4). The horizontal axis of the competitive value map identifies the key offering attributes, ordered in terms of their importance to target customers. The vertical axis indicates customers' valuation of the benefits of the available offerings on these attributes. Attributes on which the company's offering can create superior customer value relative to competitive offerings define its competitive advantage, attributes on which it is inferior define its competitive disadvantage, and attributes on which offerings are equivalent define the points of competitive parity.

Figure 4. Competitive Value Map

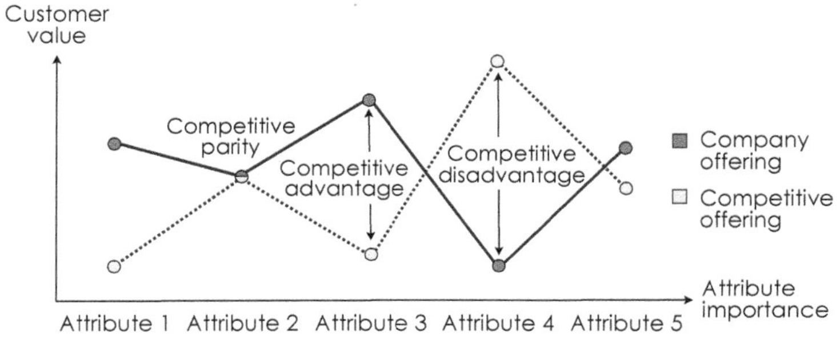

Creating a Sustainable Competitive Advantage

The competitive advantage of an offering reflects its ability to fulfill a particular customer need better than the alternative means of satisfying the same need. An offering's competitive advantage gives customers a reason to choose this offering instead of the other available options. In this context, there are three core strategies to design a value proposition that stand out from the competition: *differentiate on an existing attribute*, *introduce a new attribute*, and *build a strong brand*.

Differentiate on an Existing Attribute

This is the quintessential strategy for creating a competitive advantage. For example, Gillette sets itself apart from its competitors on the quality of its shave. Dollar Shave Club—an online shaving supplies retailer—has established price as its competitive advantage over premium brands such as Gillette. Online shoe retailer Zappos has differentiated itself from its competitors based on the level of customer service it provides. BMW differentiates itself from the competition by the driving experience its vehicles deliver, Volvo differentiates itself by focusing on safety, and Rolls-Royce sets itself apart by emphasizing luxury.

Although differentiating on an important attribute is the most intuitive way to create a competitive advantage, it is often difficult to achieve because as the overall performance of all offerings improves they become more similar. For example, with advancements in the overall quality of television sets, the differences among the available options have become less pronounced, making them more similar to one another in customers' eyes.

Introduce a New Attribute

Instead of enhancing an offering's performance on one of the existing attributes, a company might create a competitive advantage by introducing a new attribute that differentiates its offering. For example, PepsiCo has differentiated its lemon-lime soft drink Sierra Mist by using only all-natural ingredients. Dollar Shave Club introduced subscription-based, direct-to-consumer shipping of shaving supplies. TOMS introduced a "buy one, give one" social responsibility program as an important dimension that differentiates it from traditional shoe manufacturers. Uber introduced cash-free ride payment to streamline the monetary transaction between customers and drivers. The Nest thermostat introduced machine learning as an alternative approach to controlling the temperature in one's home.

Note that differentiating through the introduction of a new attribute does not necessarily mean inventing a completely new attribute. It can also involve focusing on an existing attribute that has been neglected by all competitors and making it a point of difference. For example, household cleaning products manufacturer Method Products has differentiated its offerings by designing aesthetically pleasing packaging, thus introducing a new dimension of competitive differentiation in a category where packaging was viewed as a purely functional attribute. In the same vein, with its egg-shaped, multi-colored iMac enclosed in a translucent plastic case, Apple introduced design as a key point of difference in the personal computer category.

The introduction of a new attribute can offer a powerful, albeit rarely sustainable, advantage. Indeed, a new attribute that is valued by customers is likely to be copied by competitors, which greatly diminishes the competitive advantage of the company pioneering this attribute. Therefore, to create a sustainable competitive advantage and stay ahead of the competition, a company must constantly seek new means of creating customer value.

Build a Strong Brand

A powerful brand can be a source of sustainable competitive advantage and provide customers with a reason to choose the company's offering. As the old saying goes, nobody ever got fired for buying IBM because the IBM brand signified quality, reliability, and compatibility. Likewise, Harley-Davidson owes its success not only to the design of its motorcycles but to a large degree to the strength of its brand. What separates Coca-Cola from the other cola drinks is not just its taste but its image, which has transcended national borders and cultural barriers to reach almost everyone on the planet.

The power of a brand as a source of differentiation is particularly prominent in commoditized product categories such as cereal, soft drinks, and alcoholic beverages. To illustrate, Grey Goose has successfully positioned its product as the World's Best Tasting Vodka, allowing the company to charge significantly higher prices compared to many of its competitors. Grey Goose's example is particularly telling because the underlying product (vodka) is effectively a commodity, defined as "neutral spirits so distilled as to be without distinctive character, aroma, taste, or color."[1] Thus, for most customers who cannot tell the difference in the taste of different premium vodkas, the Grey Goose brand is the main purchase driver.

Although the brand can be viewed as an attribute of the company's offering, it also plays a special role in creating a competitive advantage: It influences customers' perceptions of the offering on dimensions that are not readily visible, such as quality, reliability, and durability. Brands can infuse the company's offering with a unique meaning that goes beyond the actual characteristics of the company's product and service and creates value for its customers. Thus, customers are buying not just Harley-Davidson, Coca-Cola, and Warby Parker products; they are buying the meaning of these brands.

In addition to influencing customer beliefs about the offering, a strong brand can drive customer behavior merely by becoming the first option that comes to a customer's mind as a means of fulfilling a given need. For example, Budweiser consistently promotes its flagship product so that when its customers think of beer, the first brand that comes to mind is "Bud." In the same vein, GEICO spends tens of millions of dollars every year to ensure that when drivers think about car insurance, they consider GEICO first. Likewise, McDonald's aims to be the first fast-food restaurant that comes to mind, ahead of its competitors Burger King, Wendy's, and Taco Bell. Among the non-prescription pain medicines, Tylenol, Advil, and Aleve have gained top-of-mind awareness, helping these brands to sustain their market leadership in a product category filled with functionally identical low-priced generics.

Having top-of-mind brand awareness creates a competitive advantage because the brand that is considered first often becomes the default option against which the other brands are evaluated. This is an important benefit since in the absence of a strong reason to choose an alternative option, buyers are likely to select the default option.

Managing Competitive Differentiation

The above three strategies enable a company to create and enhance its competitive advantage. Despite their common goal, these strategies vary in the ways they elicit competitive differentiation. The first two strategies—*differentiating on an important attribute* and *introduc-*

ing a new attribute—involve modifying the actual product or service that the company deploys in a given market. In contrast, the third strategy—*building a strong brand*—changes the ways customers think about the company's products and services without necessarily changing the actual offering.

The three strategies are not mutually exclusive. They can be employed simultaneously to solidify an offering's competitive advantage. When deciding which strategies to pursue and how to prioritize them, a manager must choose the strategy that creates the greatest value for target customers, the company, and its collaborators. To create a meaningful advantage and make the competition irrelevant, a manager must develop an offering that creates market value in a way that cannot be readily copied by the competition.

Positioning the Offering

Positioning builds on the offering's value proposition to define the key reason(s) for customers to choose the offering. Unlike the value proposition, which identifies all of the benefits and costs of an offering, positioning focuses only on its primary benefit(s). The essence of positioning and the process of developing a positioning strategy are outlined in the following sections.

Positioning as a Strategic Decision

Positioning is a process of designing a company's offering so that it occupies a distinct place in the minds of its target customers; it is the process of creating a meaningful and distinct image of the company's offering in customers' minds.[2] For example, BMW positions its cars as delivering the ultimate driving experience, Volvo emphasizes safety, Toyota focuses on reliability, Ferrari prioritizes speed, and Rolls-Royce underscores luxury. In this context, positioning is akin to the process of developing a value proposition with the key difference that the value proposition reflects *all* benefits and costs of the offering while positioning focuses on the *most important* benefit(s) that tend to drive consumer choice.

In addition to describing the process of defining a distinct image in a customer's mind, the term positioning is also used in reference to the mental representation of the offering that the company aims to create in customers' minds. In this context, positioning reflects the way a company would like its target customers to think about its offering and identifies the primary benefit(s) of the offering that will serve as the main reason for customers to choose it.

The concept of positioning can be better understood when related to the concept of the value proposition. Unlike the value proposition, which reflects *all* aspects of an offering, positioning focuses customers' attention only on the *most important* aspect(s) of the offering. Furthermore, unlike the value proposition, which captures both the benefits and the costs of the offering, positioning focuses only on the benefits in order to accentuate the advantages of the company's offering in a way that provides customers with a compelling reason to choose this offering (Figure 5).

Figure 5. Customer Value Proposition and Positioning

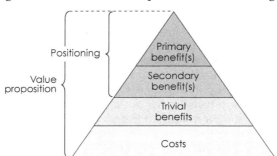

The need to "position" a company's offering in the minds of its customers stems from the fact that most individuals cannot process and remember all the benefits of a company's offering. Rather than presenting its customers with information about all aspects of its offering, a company can make a conscious decision not to promote some of the offering's benefits in order to focus only on the most important ones. Thus, a company might hone in on one or more primary benefits that are of utmost importance to its target customers, while placing relatively less emphasis on benefits that are of secondary importance.

Positioning is a strategic concept that steers the company's tactical decisions, including product and service design, brand building, pricing, development of incentives, and communication and delivery of the offering to target customers. A key component of an offering's strategy, positioning is an internal concept that is not directly shared with the company's customers. Rather, positioning is reflected through the choice of the offering's tactics and, most prominently, in its communication. For example, Domino's' focus on speed led to the tagline *Fresh, hot pizza delivered in 30 minutes or less, guaranteed*. Papa John's Pizza's focus on quality resulted in the tagline *Better Ingredients. Better Pizza*. Tide's focus on cleaning power generated the tagline *If it's got to be clean...it's got to be Tide*. Avis's focus on service resulted in the tagline *We try harder*. Visa's focus on worldwide acceptance spawned the tagline *It's everywhere you want to be*.

The development of a positioning strategy involves three key decisions: *how many benefits to promote*, *which benefits to promote*, and *how to frame these benefits*. These three decisions are discussed in more detail below.

Deciding How Many Benefits to Promote

Positioning is a process of prioritizing the benefits of an offering and selecting the one(s) that a company desires to be most prominently engraved in a customer's mind. Because customers often make decisions relying only on the key benefits of the offering, positioning involves tradeoffs — deciding not to promote certain benefits in order to bring others into focus. Specifically, positioning involves two types of decisions: (1) identifying all benefits that target customers view as important (rather than trivial) and (2) identifying the benefit(s) that target customers view as having primary importance. The process of establishing the hierarchy of benefits based on their impact on target customers is often referred to as *benefit laddering*.

The decision of how many and which benefits to promote is driven by two key factors: the degree to which a given benefit is important to target customers and the degree to which this benefit can be uniquely created by the company's offering. Important benefits that are unique to the company's offering are the points of dominance (PoD) and are typically underscored as primary benefits. On the other hand, important benefits on which the offering is at parity with the competition (PoP) as well as the points of dominance on relatively less important attributes can be featured as secondary benefits in the offering's positioning.

Based on the number of benefits promoted and the nature of these benefits, there are three common positioning strategies: *single-benefit positioning*, *multi-benefit positioning*, and *holistic positioning*.

- **Single-benefit positioning** emphasizes an attribute the company believes will most likely provide customers with a compelling reason to choose its offering. Single-attribute positioning does not imply that the offering is inferior on its secondary attributes; it simply highlights the importance of a single attribute in order to establish a distinct message in the minds of customers. Typically, the primary benefit reflects the most important point of dominance, with the other points of dominance and points of parity the secondary benefits (Figure 6). For example, despite offering multiple benefits that include performance, prestige, luxury, comfort, and safety, the BMW brand underscores a single benefit: performance. In the same vein, GEICO emphasizes the low price of its insurance products, Swatch emphasizes the self-expressive fashion of its watches, and Visa emphasizes the worldwide acceptance of its credit cards.

Figure 6. Single-Benefit Positioning

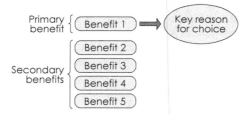

- **Multi-benefit positioning** emphasizes two (or more) attributes of the offering (Figure 7). For example, even though Bayer's Aleve offers multiple benefits—including fast, longer lasting, effective, and safe pain relief—its positioning focuses on its strength and long-lasting effect, captured in the motto *Aleve. All day strong. All day long.* In the same vein, Apple promoted the iPad as a *Magical and Revolutionary Device at an Unbelievable Price,* and Walmart's motto *Save Money. Live Better* highlights the quality and low price of its offerings.

Figure 7. Multi-Benefit Positioning

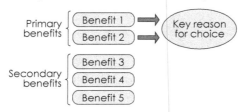

- **Holistic positioning** emphasizes an offering's overall performance without highlighting individual benefits, thus enticing customers to choose the offering based on its performance as a whole rather than on particular benefits (Figure 8). For example, Gillette's positioning as *The best a man can get* aims to create a perception of superior overall performance. Colgate Total, as implied by its name, claims to offer the best overall package of category benefits. Similarly, Amoco's positioning as *America's number one premium gasoline,* Tylenol's positioning as *The brand most hospitals trust,* and Hertz's positioning as the *#1 car rental company in the world* emphasize market leadership to signal superior overall performance.

Figure 8. Holistic Positioning

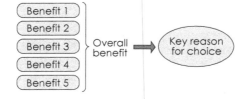

Single-benefit positioning is perhaps the most common strategy. The logic behind single-benefit positioning is threefold. First, focusing on a single benefit can help the company's message break through the media clutter and create a meaningful impression in customers' minds. This is because people tend to form simplified judgments to deal with information overload and focus only on the distinctive aspects of the offering. Another reason favoring single-benefit positioning is that choosing the offering that excels on an important attribute is often considered a valid reason for choice, helping buyers justify their choices to others as well as to themselves. Finally, people tend to believe that a specialized offering that does only one thing must do it very well, whereas an offering that does many things is unlikely to excel in any of them.[3]

Despite its popularity, single-benefit positioning has important drawbacks. The most apparent downside of single-benefit positioning is that it fails to convey the wealth of benefits that create additional value for target customers. Furthermore, the consequences of misidentifying the most important aspect of the offering (i.e., focusing on a single benefit that customers do not care much about) are much greater in this case compared to multi-benefit or holistic positioning. In this context, it is important to keep in mind that single-benefit positioning is not a universal positioning strategy and in many cases alternative approaches, such as multi-benefit and holistic positioning, might be more appropriate.

Deciding Which Benefits to Promote

In addition to choosing how many benefits to promote, a company must also decide which benefits to feature in its positioning. As a general principle, the choice of the benefits to promote is driven by two key considerations: (1) relevance to customer needs, meaning that these benefits should have primary importance for customers, and (2) compatibility with the company's resources, meaning that the company's offering should be able to deliver superior performance on these attributes.

To decide which benefits to promote, a company must first identify the extent to which it can create value for its target customers in each of the three domains—functional, psychological, and monetary—and then assess the degree to which positioning in these domains is sustainable over time. These two aspects of developing a positioning strategy are outlined in more detail below.

Positioning on Functional, Psychological, and Monetary Benefits

Based on the domain of the focal benefits—functional, psychological, or monetary—a company can follow three distinct positioning strategies:

- **Positioning on functional benefits** aims to create customer value by emphasizing the functionality of the company's offering. For example, Energizer emphasizes the longevity of its batteries, Tide emphasizes the cleaning power of its detergents, and BMW emphasizes the driving experience. Functional benefits vary in their scope, such that certain benefits are more specific than other, higher level benefits. For example, in its campaign *Go Tagless*, Hanes underscores the fact that its T-shirts feature a tag that is imprinted directly on the shirt rather than sewn on. Likewise, Arm & Hammer underscores the fact that its toothpaste contains baking soda, and Coca-Cola promotes the natural sweetener stevia as a key ingredient in some of its low-calorie sodas. These specific benefits, in turn, can be related to higher level functional benefits: an imprinted rather than sewn-on tag (specific benefit) implies comfort (general benefit), the presence of baking soda (specific benefit) implies cleaning power (general benefit), and stevia (specific benefit) is associated with managing weight gain (general benefit).

- **Positioning on psychological benefits** emphasizes the psychological value associated with the offering. For instance, offerings such as Montblanc, Rolls-Royce, and Dom Pérignon are positioned to instill feelings of luxury, exclusivity, and prestige. An offering's positioning may also be influenced by the company's positioning as a leader in product innovation, as in the case of Apple, Google, and Samsung, or by its image as a socially responsible organization, as in the case of Ben & Jerry's, Newman's Own, and Ecolab. An offering may also be positioned by emphasizing its risk-minimizing benefits, such as reducing uncertainty and providing peace of mind—a strategy exemplified by Allstate Insurance's tagline, *You're in good hands with Allstate.*

- **Positioning on monetary benefits** emphasizes the monetary value associated with the offering. To illustrate, Aldi, Walmart, and Priceline.com emphasize low cost as a key aspect of their value proposition, and Discover credit card emphasizes its monetary value as *America's number one cash rewards program*. Positioning on monetary benefits is sustainable only when the company has the low-cost structure to ensure the competitiveness of its offering on price.

Companies might position their offerings on the same dimension or, rather than competing head to head, might opt for competing on different types of benefits. For example, in the wet shaving category, shave quality is the functional benefit, having an emotional connection with the offering's brand is a psychological benefit, and low shaving cost is a monetary benefit. Gillette—consistent with its motto, *Gillette, the best a man can get*—focuses on performance; Harry's focuses on psychological benefits, anthropomorphizing its brand and giving human names—Truman and Winston—to its razors; and Dollar Shave Club highlights the monetary benefits of its offering.

The above three positioning strategies are not always mutually exclusive. In some cases, it is possible to develop a positioning that bridges different strategies. For example, Volkswagen has positioned its cars as being both reliable (functional benefit) and economical (monetary benefit). In the same vein, Starbucks is positioned as a purveyor of high-quality coffee (functional benefit) as well as a place where customers can feel at home (psychological benefit). Likewise, Walmart's motto *Save Money. Live Better* reflects its strategy of offering low prices (monetary benefit) and making shoppers feel good about savings they can use to enhance other aspects of their lives (psychological benefit).

Developing a Sustainable Positioning Strategy

An important aspect of deciding how to position an offering is ensuring that it is unique and cannot easily be copied by competitors. In this context, positioning strategies can be ordered in terms of their ability to create a sustainable competitive advantage, with price-based positioning often the easiest to replicate and positioning based on psychological benefits the most difficult to imitate (Figure 9).

**Figure 9. Positioning Strategies Based on their Ability
to Create a Sustainable Competitive Advantage**

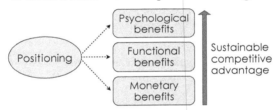

Because customers typically buy products and services based on their functional value, positioning on functional benefits is perhaps the most common type of positioning. The degree to which positioning on functional benefits offers a sustainable competitive advantage depends on the type of featured benefit. In general, positioning on specific features tends to offer a competitive advantage that is more difficult to sustain than the advantage stemming from positioning on higher level benefits. For example, a competitor can readily replace sewn-on tags with imprinted ones, add baking soda to toothpaste, and use stevia as a low-calorie sweetener. As a result, many companies choose to position their offerings on more general benefits in order to make it more difficult for competitors to imitate them. For example, rather than focusing on specific features such as engine performance, anticorrosion technology, and extended warranty, Toyota's positioning is focused on the more general benefit of reliability. In the same vein, rather than focusing on specific features such as crash resistance, automatic emergency braking, and number of airbags, Volvo's positioning reflects the more general benefit of safety.

Functional-benefit positioning has an important limitation with respect to its ability to differentiate a company's offerings from the competition. As an increasing number of products and services reach relatively high performance levels, customers are becoming more indifferent to the variations among competitive offerings because all of them deliver benefits that are satisfactory to most customers. For example, Toyota's long-standing positioning on reliability and Volvo's positioning on safety have been weakened by the fact that at present most cars have satisfactory performance on these two dimensions.

Unable to create a sustainable competitive advantage on monetary and functional benefits, many companies are turning to differentiating on psychological benefits, such as enabling customers to self-express through their brands (e.g., Harley-Davidson, Abercrombie &

Fitch, and Porsche), appealing to their sense of social responsibility (Starbucks, Product Red, and Google), or building an emotional connection (Disney, Hallmark, and Dove). Rather than relying on monetary and functional benefits to convince customers to *buy the company's offering*, positioning on psychological benefits aims to convince customers to *buy into the company's brand*. Because it reflects customers' personality and self-identity, and is therefore the most difficult to imitate, positioning on psychological benefits is a key factor in creating a sustainable competitive advantage. The role of brands as a means of differentiation is discussed in more detail in Chapter 11.

Deciding How to Frame Relevant Benefits

Value judgments do not occur in a vacuum: Value is defined relative to a reference point used to assess the benefits and costs of an offering. The same offering can be viewed as attractive when compared to an inferior offering and as unattractive when compared to a superior offering. Therefore, along with highlighting the benefits of an offering, positioning also includes a frame of reference — the benchmark against which customers will evaluate the benefits of the offering.

The choice of a reference point is of utmost importance when developing an offering's positioning. Because the reference point helps define the benefits of the offering, the same offering can be framed in different ways depending on the specific benefit that the company aims to highlight. Consider Glacéau Vitaminwater — nutrient-enhanced water marketed by the Coca-Cola Company. Vitaminwater has several potential benefits, each requiring a different frame of reference. Thus, as a source of hydration, Vitaminwater can be compared to regular water; as a source of nutrients, it can be compared to vitamins; as a source of energy, it can be compared to energy drinks such as Red Bull and Monster Energy; and to promote its thirst-quenching benefits, it can be compared to other thirst-quenching drinks such as Gatorade and Powerade.

Based on the choice of reference point, five frames of reference can be distinguished: *need-based*, *category-based*, *user-based*, *competitive*, and *product-line framing*.

- **Need-based framing** directly links the benefits of the offering to a particular customer need. For example, Coca-Cola's (1929) positioning as *The pause that refreshes* appealed directly to customers' need for a refreshment. In the same vein, Disneyland's (1955) positioning as *The Happiest Place on Earth*, Miller Lite's *Great Taste . . . Less Filling!* positioning, and Walmart's *Save Money. Live Better* positioning relate the benefits of the offerings to particular customer needs.

- **Category-based framing** defines the offering by relating it to an already established product category. For example, Coca-Cola's (1906) positioning as *The great national temperance beverage* defined Coke through its category membership and BMW's positioning as *The ultimate driving machine* defines its offerings relative to the automobile category. In addition to directly relating an offering to a product category, a company might seek to convey category membership by associating its offering to other offerings that are prototypical for the product category. For example, Chevrolet might relate its hybrid car Volt to Toyota's Prius, which pioneered the hybrid car category, Mercedes might associate its super luxury Maybach with Rolls-Royce, and Tesla might associate its cars with Ferrari to convey membership in the race car category. Note that the association in this case is not driven by the desire to compete for the same customers (as in the case of competitive framing) but rather to use an exemplar to establish category membership.

- **User-based framing** defines the offering by linking it to a particular type of user. For example, Pepsi's classic campaign *Choice of a New Generation* featuring mega-stars like Michael Jackson and Tina Turner aimed at positioning Pepsi as the soft drink for people who saw the "young view of things." In the same vein, Harley-Davidson positions itself as the motorcycle manufacturer for "macho guys (and 'macho wannabes'), mostly in the United States, who want to join a gang of cowboys, in an era of decreasing personal freedom."[4] Luxury brands like Rolls-Royce, Louis Vuitton, and Patek

Philippe are often associated with the upper social class and are often used to convey the image of high status and exclusivity.

- **Competitive framing** defines the offering's value proposition by explicitly contrasting it to competitors' offerings and highlighting those aspects of the offering that differentiate it from the competition. For example, Dollar Shave Club positioned itself directly against Gillette, Apple defined the benefits of its Mac computers relative to Microsoft, and Microsoft positioned its search engine Bing against Google. In the same vein, Truvía positioned itself as a natural sweetener against Splenda, Equal, and Sweet'N Low; and Monster Energy positioned itself against Red Bull by introducing an innovative 16-ounce can and a wide variety of energy drinks. Rather than a particular competitor, the frame of reference can also be a competitive category, as in the case of DiGiorno's *It's not delivery. It's DiGiorno positioning*, 7UP's positioning as the *Un-cola, and* T-Mobile's positioning as the *Un-carrier*.

- **Product-line framing** defines the offering by comparing it to other offerings in the company's product line. Product-line framing highlights the differences between generations of the same offering and typically involves contrasting the benefits of the newly released product with those of the product it aims to replace. For example, Procter & Gamble used the tagline *Five Is Better than Three* to differentiate its five-blade Gillette Fusion razor from its three-blade predecessor, Mach3. Product-line framing is particularly common among market leaders operating in rapidly evolving product categories where technology innovations force companies to constantly upgrade their offerings.

The above five frames of reference can be grouped into the more general categories of noncomparative and comparative frames. *Noncomparative framing* directly relates the value of the offering to the reference point without explicitly contrasting it to other offerings. Need-based, category-based, and user-based frames of reference tend to be noncomparative. In contrast, *comparative framing* defines the offering by contrasting it to other offerings instead of (or in addition to) relating it to particular needs. Competitive framing and product-line framing typically involve comparative frames of reference.

As a general rule, comparative positioning is employed by lesser known offerings trying to gain share from the market leader. Comparative positioning is rarely used by the market leader because by comparing its offering with a lesser known offering with a smaller share, the market leader often ends up implicitly promoting the referent offering. For example, Google's positioning does not involve a comparison with other search engines because it stands to gain relatively little from such comparisons. In contrast, Microsoft introduced its Bing search engine by (favorably) comparing itself to the market leader, Google, aiming to attract some of Google's customers.

Crafting a Positioning Statement

The desired positioning of a company's offering is typically captured in an internal document commonly referred to as a positioning statement. The primary purpose of this document is to share the key aspects of an offering's strategy with the relevant stakeholders involved in the development and management of the offering. The key principles of developing a positioning statement are outlined in the following sections.

The Positioning Statement as a Means of Communication

The positioning statement is a succinct document — usually consisting of a single sentence — that delineates the key components of an offering's strategy. The positioning statement is broader than the offering's positioning in that, along with delineating the offering's positioning, it also identifies its target customers. The primary purpose of the positioning statement is to guide tactical decisions related to the product, service, brand, price, incentives, communication, and distribution aspects of the offering. As such, the positioning statement seeks to communicate the essence of the offering's strategy to all stakeholders in order to ensure that their activities are aligned with the company's goals.

The positioning statement plays an important role because different managers within the company might not have an accurate understanding of the offering's strategy: who the offering's target customers are, why they would choose this offering over a competitor's, and how this offering benefits the company. Accordingly, the positioning statement aims to foster a shared view of the offering's strategy to all relevant entities in the company.

In addition to informing different company entities about the offering's strategy, the positioning statement has an important role in ensuring that the company's external collaborators—including research and development and product design partners, advertising and public relations agencies, channel partners, and external salesforce—correctly understand this strategy. Communicating the offering's strategy to the company's collaborators is particularly important because these entities are typically less familiar with the company's goals and strategic initiatives.

The positioning statement is often confused with an offering's positioning. Although directly related, these concepts reflect different aspects of an offering's strategy. Positioning is narrower in scope, focusing on the key aspect of the offering's value proposition. In contrast, the positioning statement has a broader scope and includes not only the offering's positioning but also a description of how the offering creates value for target customers, the company, and its collaborators.

The positioning statement is also confused with the brand motto and communication tagline. This is because all three capture certain aspects of the offering's strategy. Despite their similarities, however, the positioning statement, the brand motto, and the communication tagline have different functions and are written for different audiences. The positioning statement is an internal company document aimed at company employees and collaborators, and is not intended to be seen by customers. In contrast, the brand motto and the communication tagline are explicitly written for the company's customers. Consequently, the brand motto and communication tagline use catchy, memorable phrases designed to capture customers' attention, whereas the positioning statement is written in a straightforward manner with a focus on the logic rather than on the form of expression.

To illustrate, Gillette's positioning promises the best shaving performance. Its positioning statement can be written as: *For all men who shave, Gillette provides the best shaving experience because it uses the most innovative shaving technology.* Gillette's brand motto is much more succinct and memorable: *Gillette. The Best a Man Can Get.* Finally, one of Gillette's communication taglines for its Fusion ProGlide razor highlights a particular aspect of its razor: *Less Tug and Pull.* In the same vein, BMW's positioning promises a superior driving experience. Its positioning statement can be articulated as: *BMW is the best vehicle for drivers who care about performance because it is designed to be the ultimate driving machine.* BMW's brand motto is: *The Ultimate Driving Machine.* A recent advertising tagline is: *BMW. We Make Only One Thing: The Ultimate Driving Machine.*[5]

Structuring the Positioning Statement

A typical positioning statement involves three components: *target customers, frame of reference,* and *primary benefit(s).* These three aspects of the positioning statement are outlined below.

- **Target customers** are buyers for whom the company will tailor its offerings. These customers are defined by their needs, the key benefit(s) they seek to receive from the offering, as well as by their demographic and/or behavioral profile. The selection of target customers is discussed in more detail in Chapter 4.

- The **frame of reference** identifies the reference point used to define the offering. The frame of reference can be either noncomparative or comparative. *Noncomparative* framing relates the value of the offering to the customer need it aims to fulfill without explicitly comparing it to other offerings; in contrast, *comparative* framing defines the offering by contrasting it to other offerings.

- The **primary benefit** identifies the primary reason why customers will consider, buy, and use the offering. The primary benefit typically highlights the key value driver(s) defining the worth of the offering for target customers. The primary benefit could also involve a *justification* (reason to believe) for why the offering can claim this benefit. Common benefit justifications involve the presence of desirable ingredients (e.g., the presence of hyaluronic acid as a moisturizing ingredient in beauty care products), exceptional performance on a key attribute (e.g., the fastest speed and best coverage among wireless service providers), and brand reputation (e.g., having the best consumer rankings in a given product category).

The customer-focused positioning statement is a blueprint of the way(s) in which the company will create customer value. Accordingly, the core question that the customer-focused positioning statement must answer is: *Who are the offering's target customers and why would they buy and use the company's offering?* The organization and the key components of a customer-focused positioning statement can be illustrated with the following examples.

Example A (Noncomparative Positioning): For [target customers][offering] offers [frame of reference] that is [primary benefit] because [justification of the benefit].

For the tradesman who uses power tools to make a living, DeWalt offers dependable professional tools that are engineered to be tough and are backed by a guarantee of repair or replacement within 48 hours.

Example A (Comparative Positioning): For [target customers][offering] offers [frame of reference] that is more [primary benefit] than [competition] because [justification of the benefit].

For the tradesman who uses power tools to make a living, DeWalt offers professional tools that are more dependable than any other brand because they are engineered to be tough and are backed by a guarantee of repair or replacement within 48 hours.

Example B (Noncomparative Positioning): For [target customers][offering] is the [frame of reference] that provides the best [primary benefit] because [justification of the benefit].

For all men who shave, Gillette Fusion is the razor that provides the best shaving experience because it uses the most innovative shaving technology.

Example B (Comparative Positioning): For [target customers][offering] is the [frame of reference] that provides a better [primary benefit] than [competition] because [justification of the benefit].

For all men who shave, Gillette Fusion is the razor that provides a better shaving experience than Mach 3 because it has the latest shaving technology.

SUMMARY

The value proposition reflects all benefits and costs associated with an offering. Because value is a function of customers' needs, an offering's ability to create value is customer-specific: An offering that creates value for some customers might fail to do so for others.

An offering's *value proposition* is determined relative to the competitive offerings. The value proposition can be defined on three dimensions: points of dominance (dimensions on which a company's offering is superior to the competition), points of parity (dimensions on which a company's offering is equal to the competition), and points of compromise (dimensions on which a company's offering is inferior to the competition). There are three core strategies for designing an offering that dominates the competition: differentiate on an existing attribute, introduce a new attribute, and build a strong brand.

Positioning is the process of creating a meaningful and distinct image of the company's offering in target customers' minds. The development of a positioning strategy involves three key decisions: how many benefits to promote, which benefits to promote, and how to frame these benefits. Based on the *number of benefits*, there are three common positioning strategies: single-benefit positioning, multi-benefit positioning, and holistic positioning. Based on the domain of the *primary benefit*, positioning can highlight functional benefits, psychological benefits, and monetary benefits. Based on the choice of a reference point, positioning can involve need-based framing, which directly links the benefits of the offering to a particular customer need; category-based framing, which defines the offering by relating it to an already established product category; user-based framing, which associates the offering with a particular type of customer; competitive framing, which defines the offering by explicitly contrasting it with competitors' offerings; and product-line framing, which defines the offering by comparing it with other company offerings.

The *positioning statement* is an internal company document that outlines an offering's strategy to guide tactical decisions. A typical positioning statement involves three components: target customers, frame of reference, and primary benefit(s).

MARKETING INSIGHT: DEVELOPING A POSITIONING MAP

Positioning maps reflect customers' perception of the company's offering relative to other available options. Positioning maps typically involve two dimensions, each representing an important attribute of the company's offering. Competing offerings are then placed on the map based on customers' perceptions of their performance on these attributes (Figure 10). Offerings that are closer to one another on the map are likely to be perceived similarly by customers and, hence, are more likely to compete directly. Because they are based on customers' perception of the offerings' performance, positioning maps are also referred to as perceptual maps.

Figure 10. Positioning Map

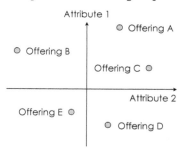

To illustrate, in the case of household appliances, a positioning map can reflect the performance of different offerings on attributes such as durability and price, with higher priced, more durable options placed in the upper right corner and less durable, lower priced options in the lower left corner. In the same vein, a positioning map for headache remedies can illustrate their relative performance on attributes such as effectiveness and duration, with the most effective and longest lasting drugs occupying the upper right corner of the chart and the least effective and shortest duration drugs occupying the lower left corner.

In addition to reflecting the relative performance of market offerings, positioning maps might also reflect the ideal points (ideal combinations of attribute levels) of different customer segments. This is particularly helpful in cases when customer preferences are not uniform, such that higher levels of performance are more desirable (as in the case of attributes such as quality, reliability, durability, and price) but are rather nominally distributed without a consistent preference ordering across different customer segments (as in the case of attributes such as design, color, and taste). By overlaying customer preferences with brand perceptions, a company can reveal customer needs that are unmet by the competition and position its offerings in a way that addresses these needs.

Note that because they reflect customers' perceptions of the offering rather than its actual performance, positioning maps are customer-specific; thus, an offering's position on the value map might vary across customers with different needs and preferences. In the case of attributes for which customer preferences are homogeneous, with higher levels of performance uniformly preferred by all customers (e.g., quality and [low] price), the "ideal" competitive position is in the upper right quadrant of the map. In contrast, when customer preferences are heterogeneous and customers have different valuations of the attributes defining the positioning map (e.g., those reflecting personal taste), perceptual maps can involve multiple "ideal" competitive positions. In such cases, multiple positioning maps can be developed, each reflecting the tastes of a particular customer segment.

Positioning maps are often derived by asking target customers to rate the performance of different offerings on the two most important attributes (identified with the help of focus groups, online discussions, or alternative research techniques). Attributes commonly used as the key positioning dimensions include price, overall quality, and performance on specific attributes such as power, speed, compatibility, reliability, and durability. Customers' ratings are then used as coordinates and plotted onto a two-dimensional map representing their relative positions. In cases when three or more attributes play a key role in customers' decisions, multiple positioning maps are created, each reflecting the offering's performance on two of these attributes.

The two-attribute plots (such as the one shown in Figure 10), although popular, are not the only way to develop perceptual maps. Instead of asking customers to rate different offerings on pre-defined attributes, positioning maps can be derived based on people's ratings of the similarities among the available offerings. In this case the underlying dimensions used to plot the offerings are statistically derived based on individuals' responses. The advantage of this approach is that managers do not have to identify which attributes matter the most to customers. At the same time, because similarity-based positioning maps are statistically derived, the resulting dimensions defining these maps are often difficult to interpret and act on.

In addition to comparing customers' subjective evaluations of the offering's performance relative to the competition, positioning maps can also compare the offering's actual performance with its perceived performance. The purpose of this analysis is to identify areas in which there is a discrepancy between an offering's objective performance and customers' subjective assessment of its benefits. Identifying such discrepancies is essential in order for the company to develop the appropriate strategy to improve customer evaluations of its offerings. Thus, if customers' belief that an offering is inferior stems from the fact that this offering actually underperforms the competition, the company should invest resources to improve the offering. On the other hand, if the problem is customers' perception of the offering's performance rather than its actual performance, the company should focus its efforts on better communicating the benefits of its offering.

MARKETING INSIGHT: THE BLUE OCEAN STRATEGY

The Blue Ocean Strategy is a popular concept advanced by business theorists Kim and Mauborgne that focuses on the development of successful market-innovation strategies.[6] It argues that mature markets are overcrowded, highly competitive red oceans that should be avoided and that priority should be given to the blue oceans—new markets that a company can shape and in which it can be the dominant player. Thus, the Blue Ocean Strategy posits that rather than competing in product categories in which the company faces rivals, a company should uncover an unmet customer need and define an entirely new category in which direct competitors are absent (Figure 11).

Figure 11. The Blue Ocean Strategy

Red Ocean Strategy	Blue Ocean Strategy
Compete in existing markets	Create uncontested markets
Fulfill existing demand	Create new demand
Beat the competition	Make the competition irrelevant
Improve the value-cost tradeoff	Redefine the value-cost tradeoff
Focus on differentiation or low cost	Achieve differentiation at low cost

The Blue Ocean Strategy further asserts that even though technological innovation is an important component of discovering uncontested markets, it is most often not the key driver. Instead, it is the company's ability to find an innovative way of creating value for target customers whose needs are currently unmet that determines success in discovering blue oceans. In addition to providing a strategic direction for growth, the Blue Ocean Strategy includes a set of specific methods for its implementation, which can help managers design and modify the attributes defining the company's offering to maximize its market value. Finding innovative ways to create customer value can be achieved via four basic actions:

- *Eliminate* product attributes that the industry takes for granted but are not important to customers and are costly for the company to implement.

- *Reduce* performance on attributes that are marginally important to customers and are costly to implement. The offering's performance on these attributes can be significantly decreased without having a great impact on the customer value created by the offering.

- *Raise* the offering's performance on attributes that customers care about so that it is well above the industry's standard.

- *Create* new attributes that deliver customer value and have never before been offered by the competition.

Consider, for example, the iMac G3, introduced in 1998 as the first consumer product launched by Apple under the recently returned CEO Steve Jobs. The iMac defied industry tradition by *eliminating* the display as a free-standing item and integrating it with the body of the computer as well as by abandoning then-current technological standards like the floppy drive. The iMac also *reduced* the performance of the iMac compared to the high-end Power Macintosh in terms of both processor speed and built-in memory. In addition, Apple *raised* the performance of the new iMac by enhancing the out-of-box experience and ease of setup—the iMac was designed to be an internet computer and came with a built-in modem at a time when most computers included modems only as optional extras. Finally, Apple *created* an entirely new dimension—aesthetic appeal—on which to differentiate the iMac by crafting an innovative, teardrop-shaped enclosure using translucent, brightly colored plastics. These four actions—eliminate, reduce, raise, and create—enabled the iMac to define a new market whose needs were not adequately served by the extant utilitarian, performance-focused computers.

An important aspect of the Blue Ocean Strategy is the notion that market value can be created not only by adding new functionality and improving product performance but also by intentionally reducing functionality and decreasing product performance. Thus, even though enhancing existing product attributes and adding new ones can increase the attractiveness of the product, removing some of the product's attributes and decreasing its performance on others can lower costs. A company can pass on these savings to customers by reducing the offering's price or, alternatively, reinvest them to enhance product performance on attributes that are highly valued by customers.

The focus on creating value in uncontested markets has the potential to generate high profit margins and rapid growth. Such market success, however, is unlikely to remain unnoticed by the competition and will almost inevitably attract new market entrants. Therefore, to sustain its market success, a company must constantly seek to uncover new customer needs and continue innovating its offerings—not only to stay ahead of the competition but also to make its competitors irrelevant.

CHAPTER EIGHT

CREATING COMPANY VALUE

You can't have a healthy society unless you have healthy companies that are making a profit, that are employing people, and that are growing.
— Michael Porter, professor at the Harvard Business School

arkets comprise companies and customers that interact with one another to create a mutually beneficial value exchange. To build a successful market strategy, a manager must understand not only how to design an offering that is desired by target customers but also that enables the company to create value for its stakeholders. The ways in which a manager can develop offerings that create company value are the focus of this chapter. Specifically, we address the following topics:

- *Dimensions of Company Value*
- *Managing Monetary Value* ‖ The key profit drivers | Managing profits by increasing sales revenues | Managing profits by lowering costs
- *Managing Strategic Value* ‖ Designing strategic value | Communicating strategic value
- *Creating Market Value Through Collaboration* ‖ The essence of collaboration | Types of collaboration | Levels of collaboration | The pros and cons of collaboration
- *Crafting Company and Collaborator Positioning Statements* ‖ Developing a collaborator positioning statement | Developing a company positioning statement

The discussion of the company is complemented by an in-depth overview of two additional topics: quantifying market performance and break-even analysis.

Dimensions of Company Value

Companies are entities established for the purpose of creating value for their stakeholders. To this end, companies develop market offerings that create value for their target customers and at the same time capture value from these customers to create value for their stakeholders and collaborators. Because creating and capturing value is the central function of the company, understanding the ways in which a company can create value for its stakeholders is paramount for the development of a sound business strategy.

A company creates market value by designing, communicating, and delivering offerings in the markets it decides to serve. The value that these offerings generate for the company can be divided into two categories: *monetary* and *strategic*. These two types of value are illustrated in Figure 1 and outlined in more detail below.

Figure 1. Dimensions of Company Value

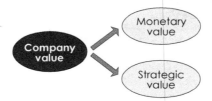

- **Monetary value** involves the monetary benefits of the offering. It is directly linked to a company's desired financial performance and typically includes factors such as net income, profit margins, sales revenue, and return on investment. For example, an offering can create a stream of revenues that, in turn, can increase a company's bottom line. Monetary value is the most common type of value sought from offerings used by for-profit companies.

- **Strategic value** involves nonmonetary benefits that are strategically important to the company. An offering can create strategic value by facilitating the demand for other offerings in the company's portfolio, by strengthening the company's reputation, and by providing the company with information about its target customers. For example, a free software can create value for the company by providing it with a technological platform for developing high-margin offerings, by promoting the company's brand, and by gaining information about customers' preferences and behavior. Offerings that demonstrate market leadership can create value for the company by helping to attract valuable employees and promote brand loyalty. Socially responsible actions that preserve the environment and support important social causes can create company value by strengthening the corporate brand and culture.

Consider the ways in which the iPhone generates value for Apple. The company receives monetary benefits from selling the iPhone. The iPhone also delivers the strategic benefit of creating a strong consumer brand, strengthening Apple's other brands, and expanding Apple's ecosystem of compatible products and services. In the same vein, Starbucks derives monetary benefit from selling its products and services to its customers. Starbucks also receives the strategic benefit of creating a strong consumer brand, enhancing its market footprint, and broadening its portfolio of offerings.

The two dimensions of company value correspond to the two types of company goals — monetary and strategic — whereby the monetary value is reflected in an offering's ability to meet the company's financial goals and strategic value reflects an offering's ability to fulfill a company's strategic goals. The two dimensions of company value are discussed in more detail in the following sections.

Managing Monetary Value

Because creating monetary value is the primary goal for the vast majority of companies, most offerings must either directly or indirectly be linked to profitability. The key profit drivers and strategies to grow profits are discussed in more detail below.

The Key Profit Drivers

To maximize profits, a manager must understand the key drivers of a company's bottom line, prioritize their impact, and focus on changes that will have the greatest impact on profits. The key profit drivers can be presented in the form of a tree-like diagram that delineates the individual factors contributing to the company's bottom line. These profit drivers are outlined in Figure 2 and discussed in more detail below.

Figure 2. The Key Profit Drivers

On the most general level, a company's profit is defined as the difference in revenues and costs. Revenues are a function of the sales volume and the unit price. Costs involve *fixed costs*, which are expenses that do not fluctuate with the number of units produced (e.g., the cost of research and development, equipment, advertising, rent, and salaries), and *variable costs*, which are expenses that fluctuate in direct proportion to the number of units produced and sold (e.g., the cost of raw materials, incentives, and sales commissions). Because some of the fixed costs (e.g., research and development and equipment) are amortized over a long period of time, they are prorated based on the proportion of relevant resources used during the time frame in which profit is being assessed. Accordingly, a company's profit formula can be summarized by the following equation:

$$\text{Profit} = \text{Sales volume} \cdot \text{Unit price} - \text{Variable costs} - \text{Prorated fixed costs}$$

Even though both increasing sales revenues and decreasing costs can have a significant impact on profits, growing revenues rather than cutting costs is more likely to produce sustainable profit growth. Indeed, for most offerings, there are fewer limits on continuously increasing revenues than on continuously reducing costs. Similarly, even though price optimization can have a significant impact on profits, increasing sales volume rather than modifying price is usually the key source of sustainable profitability. This is because in most cases there are greater limits to a company's ability to increase or lower prices compared to its ability to increase its customer base. In this context, growing sales volume is often viewed as the main source of profit growth, subject to optimizing the offering's price and the costs.

The most effective strategy to grow profits depends on a company's goals, resources, and the specific market conditions. In some cases, profitability can best be achieved by increasing sales volume — by attracting new customers or generating incremental volume from current customers. In other scenarios, profit growth might also involve lowering costs — for example, by streamlining operations or reducing marketing expenses. Finally, in some cases profit growth can also be achieved by optimizing (raising or lowering) prices in order to increase profit margins or grow customer demand. Different strategies for achieving profit growth are outlined in more detail in the following sections.

Managing Profits by Increasing Sales Revenues

Increasing sales revenues is the prevalent approach to achieving long-term profitability. Sales growth can be achieved using internal resources — an approach referred to as "organic" growth — or by acquiring or merging with another company. The focus of this section is on organic growth, which is arguably the most common sales growth strategy. In this context, there are two main approaches for increasing sales revenues: *growing sales volume* and *optimizing price*. These two strategies are discussed in more detail in the following sections.

Increasing Sales Revenues by Growing Sales Volume

There are two general strategies to grow sales volume: A company can focus on its current customers by increasing the quantity and frequency of their purchases, or it can focus on acquiring customers that it does not currently serve. Both strategies can play an important role in growing sales volume. Increasing sales to current customers is often considered the path of least resistance to maximize revenues from company customers. Customer acquisition, on the other hand, is essential for driving long-term profitability because of the inevitable attrition that erodes the company's current customer base.

Growing sales volume through customer acquisition can follow two paths: growing the size of the entire market by attracting customers who are new to the product category (market-growth strategy) and attracting customers who already buy similar offerings from competitors (steal-share strategy). Growing sales volume from current customers (market-penetration strategy), on the other hand, aims to increase usage of the company's offerings. These three basic strategies for increasing sales volume — market growth, steal share, and market penetration — are illustrated in Figure 3 and discussed in more detail below.

Figure 3. Strategies for Growing Sales Volume

- The **market-growth strategy** (also referred to as primary-demand strategy) involves increasing sales volume by attracting new-to-the-category customers who currently are not using either the company's or competitors' offerings. Growing the entire market is particularly beneficial for companies that are most likely to gain from the influx of new customers to the market — typically companies with a dominant market share and those who have offerings with a distinct benefit that is highly valued by target customers. The market-growth strategy also tends to be more effective in the early stages of a given category when sales growth is fueled by new customers entering the category, the competition is less intense, and the need to attract competitors' customers is less pronounced. For example, when Red Bull was first introduced to the United States in 1997, much of its strategy involved growing the relatively undeveloped energy drink market.

- The **steal-share strategy** involves growing sales volume by attracting customers who are already category users that buy competitors' offerings. The steal-share strategy is often employed by direct competitors aiming to gain share at the expense of their counterparts. The steal-share strategy is common in mature categories where few new customers are entering the market and the competition for existing customers is relatively intense. The decades-long competition between Pepsi and Coca-Cola is an example of competitors in a mature market engaging in a steal-share strategy.

- The **market-penetration strategy** involves increasing sales volume by increasing the quantity purchased by the company's own customers rather than explicitly trying to "steal" competitors' customers or attract new buyers to the product category. Market penetration can be achieved by increasing the frequency with which customers use and repurchase the company's offering, as well as by encouraging (upselling) customers to purchase the company's other offerings. Because the market-penetration strategy implies that a company already has solidified its market position, this strategy is more appropriate for established enterprises with a loyal customer base than for companies that do not have a strong market presence. For example, Campbell's attempt to increase the consumption of its soups during the summer is an attempt at increasing sales volume from existing customers.

The effectiveness of the market-growth, steal-share, and market-penetration strategies depends on the strategic goals and resources of the company and the specifics of the market in which it competes. In general, the market-growth strategy tends to be more effective in the early stages of the product life cycle, whereas the steal-share and market-penetration strategies are more common in mature markets when market growth has slowed down and companies are seeking alternative strategies to grow their market position. These three strategies are discussed in more detail in Chapter 18.

Increasing Sales Revenues by Optimizing Price

Setting prices is a vital component of managing sales revenues. The impact of pricing on sales revenues depends on the way customers react to changes in price. On the one hand, raising prices increases profit margins, which has a positive impact on sales revenues. On the other hand, raising prices tends to decrease sales volume because of the lower customer value associated with a higher price. Thus, sales revenues can be increased by raising prices in cases when the positive impact of increasing prices is greater than the negative impact of the corresponding decrease in sales volume. Alternatively, sales revenues can be increased by lowering prices in cases when the positive impact of the increase in sales volume is greater than the negative impact of the decrease in price.

The impact of price on sales volume is a function of customers' price elasticity, which reflects the degree to which a change in price leads to a change in quantity sold. The lower the price elasticity, the less sensitive consumers are to price increases, and the more likely it is that raising the price can increase sales revenues (see Chapter 12 for more details). Consequently, in cases where price elasticity is low and the decrease in sales volume caused by a higher price can be offset by an increase in revenues attributed to the higher price, raising prices can lead to greater sales revenues. Alternatively, when price elasticity is high and lost revenues from a price cut can be offset by an increase in sales volume, lowering price can lead to higher sales revenues.

Two issues in managing price merit attention. First, the term *price* is used fairly broadly to reflect not only the list price of an offering but also various monetary incentives that typically accompany the list price. These incentives include price reductions, coupons, rebates, and trade discounts such as volume discounts and trade allowances. Consequently, managing sales revenues requires optimizing not only an offering's price but also the price incentives associated with it. A more detailed discussion of managing price and incentives is offered in Chapters 12 and 13.

Second, because a manufacturer's offerings are in most cases sold by a third party (wholesalers, retailers, distributors, and dealers), its sales revenues are determined not so much by the retail price that customers pay as by the (wholesale) price the company charges its channel partners. Therefore, managing price involves managing not just the final customer price but also managing the prices throughout the retail channel. A more detailed discussion of the company's relationship with its channel partners and the different distribution strategies available is offered in Chapters 16 and 17.

Managing Profits by Lowering Costs

An alternative strategy to growing profits involves lowering costs rather than increasing sales revenues. Based on the type of expense, costs can be grouped into four categories: cost of goods sold, research-and-development costs, marketing costs, and other costs such as general and administrative expenses and the cost of capital. The four types of costs are illustrated in Figure 4, and the corresponding strategies for lowering costs are discussed in more detail below.

Figure 4. Managing Profits by Lowering Costs

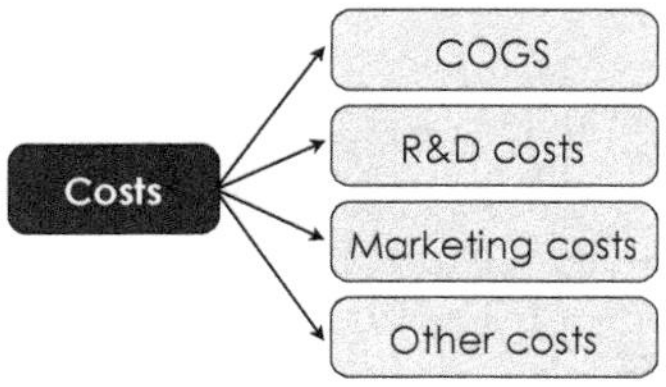

- **Lowering the cost of goods sold.** The term *cost of goods sold* (COGS) describes expenses directly related to creating the goods or services being sold and can have both a variable component (e.g., the cost of raw materials and the cost of turning raw materials into goods) and a fixed component (e.g., the depreciation of equipment). There are two basic ways to lower the cost of goods sold. The first is to *lower the costs of inputs*—such as raw materials, labor, and inbound logistics—used to develop the company's offering. Lowering the costs of inputs can be achieved by outsourcing, switching suppliers, and adopting alternative technologies that use more cost-effective inputs. For example, reducing the costs of ball bearings used as an input by an automaker helps create monetary value. The second approach to managing the cost of goods sold is to *lower the costs of the processes* that transform the inputs into the end product, such as optimizing operations and adopting alternative technologies that use more cost-effective processes. For example, an industrial robot manufacturer might create monetary value for an automaker through the introduction of a new machine that uses less electricity per operation.

- **Lowering research-and-development costs.** Research and development typically involves fixed costs necessary for designing the company's offering, and in many industries accounts for a significant portion of the overall costs. Strategies for decreasing research-and-development costs include adopting technologies that shorten the product development cycle, minimizing equipment costs, and reducing labor costs. For example, the adoption of a novel technology that can significantly abbreviate the time and lower the costs involved in testing the effectiveness of new drugs can be the source of monetary value for a pharmaceutical company.

- **Lowering marketing costs.** Depending on the company's business model, marketing costs can account for a significant portion of the overall costs associated with the offering. Marketing costs involve several types of expenses. The *cost of incentives* includes consumer-focused promotions such as price reductions, coupons, rebates, contests, sweepstakes, and premiums. *Communication costs* comprise advertising, public relations, and salesforce expenditures. *Distribution costs* reflect the margins received by distributors; cost of the salesforce;[1] and trade incentives such as trade allowances, volume discounts, and co-op advertising allowances. *Miscellaneous marketing costs* reflect the costs of factors such as marketing research and marketing overhead. Thus, a company might lower its marketing costs by improving the effectiveness and cost efficiency of its sales promotion, communication, distribution, and market research activities.

- **Lowering miscellaneous other costs.** In addition to decreasing the cost of goods sold, research and development expenditures, and marketing expenses, overall costs can be lowered by decreasing all other costs such as administrative costs, legal costs, and cost of capital. For example, a company might be able to reduce administrative costs by implementing enterprise resource planning software, consolidating its administrative offices, and streamlining its management structure.

The above four types of costs vary in their impact on a company's profit. Cost of goods sold typically is a variable cost, whereas research and development and many of the other costs tend to be fixed (meaning that they are not a direct function of the quantity produced and sold). Marketing costs fall into either the variable or fixed category depending on their type, with most advertising expenses being fixed costs and most incentives (discounts, rebates, and trade promotions) being variable costs.

Managing Strategic Value

Not all offerings are designed to generate profits: Some aim to create brand awareness, promote other offerings in the company's product line, enhance the corporate culture, and facilitate talent recruitment and retention. The ways in which offerings can create strategic value for the company and strategies for showcasing the financial benefits of strategic offerings are discussed in the following sections.

Designing Strategic Value

Although they do not directly generate profits, strategic offerings contribute to the overall profitability of the company through synergies with other profit-generating offerings. Thus, even though a particular offering does not yield profits, it still can be an important component in creating company value by increasing the desirability of the other offerings in the company's product line (Figure 5).

Figure 5. The Profit Impact of Strategic Offerings

Consider, for example, an offering that is part of a two-tier product line in which the basic version of the product or service is offered for free while giving the customer an option to upgrade to a fully functional paid version. Here, the free version of the offering considered by itself generates a loss for the company, since it brings no revenues but incurs development, support, and sales costs. Yet, this offering creates strategic value for the company by promoting the paid version of the offering, which it enables consumers to experience at no cost. For example, Dropbox, Hulu, and Pandora make available both a free basic version of their offerings as well as a paid, fully functional (unrestricted) version.

Another type of strategic offering that delivers product line synergies is the loss-leader strategy employed by many retailers. This strategy entails setting a low price for an offering (often at or below cost) in an attempt to increase the sales of other products and services. For example, a retailer might set a low price for a popular item in an attempt to build store traffic, thus increasing the sales of other, more profitable items. In addition to generating traffic, the loss-leader strategy might have the secondary benefit of strengthening customers' perceptions of the retailer as having low prices.

There are two main approaches to assessing the monetary impact of strategic offerings. The first approach is to estimate the implied monetary value of the synergies created by the offering. For example, if a free offering aims to create awareness of another revenue-generating offering (as in the case of freemium offerings), the financial contribution of the free offering can be assessed in terms of the monetary value of the awareness it creates. An alternative approach to assessing the profit impact of strategic offerings is to consider the strategic and profit-generating offerings together and assess the monetary impact of the company's entire product portfolio. In this case, the financial impact of the complementing offerings—strategic and profit-generating—is treated as if they were a single offering. Either approach can be effective depending on the situation. The key is that, regardless of the chosen approach, a company must clearly articulate how its strategic offerings create value for the company.

Communicating Strategic Value

The issue of relating strategic value to monetary outcomes is particularly important for companies that offer functionally superior offerings at a higher price than their low-price, low-quality competitors. Because buying decisions are often made by purchasing managers whose primary focus is on monetary benefits, many of these managers tend to overlook some of the benefits that do not directly create monetary value.

To better communicate the value of its offerings to financially minded managers, a company might consider expressing the strategic benefits of the offering in monetary terms—a process commonly referred to as *economic value analysis*. The economic value analysis is predicated on the idea that the strategic benefits of an offering can be quantified and monetized based on the long-term financial impact of these benefits on the company (Figure 6).

Figure 6. Economic Value Analysis

Economic value analysis is frequently used by companies selling high-value, high-price offerings to justify their premium prices. Consider the following example: A manufacturer is selling a commercial grade 3-D printer priced at $180,000, which is $25,000 higher than similar offerings from its competitors. At first glance, the company's printer appears overpriced, and the company is considering lowering its price so that it can effectively compete with low-price rivals. Despite its intuitive appeal, this approach often results in foregone revenues and profits for the manufacturer. An alternative approach involves assessing all the benefits and costs associated with the company's offering, monetizing the value of the strategic benefits, and comparing the overall value of the company's offering to that of the competition.

In the above example, the value analysis reveals that four key attributes of strategic importance to buyers include durability, reliability, warranty, and the speed of service. Furthermore, competitive benchmarking shows that on all these attributes the company's offering is superior to the competition. Specifically, the company's offering has greater durability, which translates to two additional years of product usage; greater reliability, which translates to two fewer breakdowns per year; two additional years of warranty; and, on average, speedier repairs thanks to response times for service calls four hours faster than the competition.

Monetizing these benefits suggests that the value of two extra years of printer usage is $6,000; the value of the two fewer breakdowns over the 10-year life of the printer is $14,000; the value of the two years of extra warranty covering service calls and the replacement parts is $9,500; and the value of not having four hours of downtime while waiting for the printer to be serviced during its 10-year life is $11,500. This economic value analysis in this case can be illustrated as shown in Figure 7.

Figure 7. Analyzing the Value of a Company's Offering in a Competitive Context

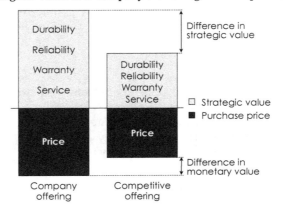

The above analysis indicates that the customer value of the functional benefits delivered by the company's offering is $41,000, which is significantly greater than the $25,000 price difference between the offerings. Specifically, this analysis shows that rather than being overpriced by $25,000, the company's offering is actually *underpriced* by $16,000 relative to the competition. Instead of lowering the price, the company might consider clearly documenting the value of the offering to its customers to shift their focus from factors readily expressed in monetary terms to the overall value of the offering, which includes the monetary (economic) value of the strategic benefits.

Because it estimates the long-term monetary impact of strategic benefits, economic value analysis is related to the notion of the total cost of ownership. Similar to economic value analysis, the total cost of ownership monetizes the nonmonetary aspects of the offering. Unlike economic value analysis, however, the total cost of ownership focuses mostly on the cost side of the value created by the offering. In this context, the concept of total cost of ownership is somewhat narrower in scope compared to the economic value analysis, which examines both the cost savings and revenue increases associated with the functional benefits of the offering.

Creating Market Value Through Collaboration

Collaboration involves entering into a relationship with another entity and delegating to it a subset of the company's activities for the purpose of creating superior market value. The key aspects of managing collaborator relationships are discussed in the following sections.

The Essence of Collaboration

Value creation through collaboration reflects a fundamental shift away from a business paradigm in which a company alone creates customer value to a new paradigm in which the value is jointly created by the company and its collaborators. The shift toward collaborative business enterprises stems from the belief that greater effectiveness and cost efficiency can be achieved from greater expertise and a broader scale of operations achieved through collaboration. Accordingly, collaboration brings together different entities—suppliers, manufacturers, distributors (dealers, wholesalers, and retailers), research-and-development companies, service providers, external salesforce, advertising agencies, and market research companies—to create an effective and cost-efficient value exchange.

Because it involves relationships between business entities, collaboration is often viewed strictly as a business-to-business process unrelated to the company's consumer-focused activities. This view reflects the differences between business and consumer markets on a number of dimensions, including the type of customers served, the type of products and services offered, the selling process, and the nature of the relationship between the buyer and the seller. Yet, despite their differences, a company's business-focused and consumer-focused activities are closely related. They both represent different aspects of an overarching value-creation process that determines the ultimate success of both business-to-business and business-to-consumer activities.

The key marketing principle—creating superior value for target customers in a way that benefits the company and its collaborators—is also the key principle that guides all aspects of collaboration. Therefore, the relationship between a company and its collaborators should always be considered in the context of creating value for target customers. In fact, there are few, if any, "pure" business-to-business relationships that can be considered independently from their ability to create customer value. Most business-focused relationships are business-to-business-to-consumer collaborations, meaning that the business-to-business component can meaningfully exist only as part of the broader customer-focused process of creating market value (Figure 8).

Figure 8. Creating Market Value through Collaboration

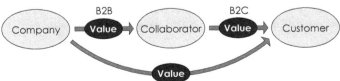

To illustrate, consider the collaboration between a manufacturer and a retailer. The success of this collaboration is determined to a large degree by the ability of the manufacturer to create value not only for the retailer but also for the end customer. If the manufacturer's offerings fail to create value for the customer, the retailer, in turn, will find it difficult to sell the company's offerings to these customers, which ultimately will hinder its collaboration with the manufacturer.

To succeed as a business-to-business enterprise, the manufacturer must envision the entire value-creation chain and design its offering to create value for both its collaborators and end customers. As a result, the sustainability of collaboration depends on the degree to which actions of the companies involved create value for target customers. Failure to create customer value will threaten the viability of the entire collaboration.

Types of Collaboration

Because collaboration centers on creating value, it spans the processes of understanding, designing, communicating, and delivering value to target customers. Accordingly, collaboration can typically occur in four domains:

- **Market-insight collaboration** involves entities that work with the company to better understand the company's customers, collaborators, competitors, and the overall context in which the company operates. For example, consumer packaged goods manufacturers SC Johnson, Kellogg, and Kraft Heinz collaborate with marketing research companies such as Nielsen, Kantar, and IRI in areas involving the analysis of retail data and test marketing of new products.

- **Value-design collaboration** involves entities that partner on product and service development, brand building, price setting, and incentive design. For example, Nike, Samsung, and PepsiCo collaborate with the design company IDEO to develop innovative consumer products. AT&T, Verizon, and Sprint routinely outsource their customer support service to call centers in regions in which these services are more cost efficient. Citibank, MasterCard, and American Airlines combine their branding efforts to create a co-branded credit card. Hotels, airlines, and rental car companies often join in special pricing collaborations offering shared price discounts.

- **Value-communication collaboration** involves partnerships in areas such as advertising, public relations, and social media. For example, to promote their offerings and build strong brands, many Fortune 500 companies partner with media conglomerates WPP, Omnicom, Publicis, Interpublic, Dentsu, and Havas for assistance with promoting their offerings, building strong brands, and managing company reputation.

- **Value-delivery collaboration** involves partnerships with suppliers and distribution channels to provide materials to the company and facilitate the delivery of its offerings to target customers. For example, consumer packaged goods manufacturers such as Nestlé, Unilever, and Kraft Heinz make their offerings available to customers by relying on retail partners such as Walmart, Carrefour, and Tesco.

Note that even though they can serve different functions in the value-creation process, collaborating entities can be involved in all four aspects of understanding, designing, communicating, and delivering value. For example, in addition to delivering the company's offerings to target customers, distribution channels can play an important role in identifying customer needs and preferences, customizing the product, augmenting the service, setting the price, and managing incentives, as well as communicating the offering's benefits by means of in-store advertisements, displays, and direct mail. In the same vein, along with communicating the value of an offering, advertising agencies can gather market insights, facilitate its branding, optimize its pricing, and design and distribute targeted incentives.

Levels of Collaboration

A company's relationship with its collaborators can vary in the extent to which it is formalized. Based on the nature of the relationships among collaborating entities, collaboration can be either *explicit* or *implicit*.

- **Explicit collaboration** involves contractual relationships, such as long-term contractual agreements, joint ventures, and franchise agreements. For example, Microsoft formally collaborates with Apple to develop Office apps for the iOS platform used by the iPhone and iPad. The key advantage of explicit collaboration is that it fosters a formal relationship among collaborating entities that ultimately leads to greater effectiveness and cost efficiency. At the same time, explicit collaboration has certain drawbacks, including lower flexibility, greater switching costs, and the strategic risk of creating a potential competitor by sharing proprietary information.

- **Implicit collaboration** typically does not involve contractual relationships. For example, tens of thousands of software developers indirectly collaborate with Apple to develop iPhone and iPad apps. Implicit collaboration is much more flexible than explicit collaboration. This flexibility, however, comes at the cost of inability to predict the behavior of collaborating entities. Another shortcoming of implicit collaboration is the lower level of commitment, often resulting in collaborators' unwillingness to invest resources to improve the value-creation process. As a result, implicit collaboration is likely to lead to lower cost efficiency compared to explicit collaboration because of a lower degree of coordination.

Because implicit collaboration does not regulate the relationship between the relevant entities, successful collaboration tends to evolve into an explicit agreement between the partnering entities. More formal relationships allow for better coordination of activities between collaborators through the sharing of information, know-how, and other relevant resources.

The Pros and Cons of Collaboration

Despite a company's efforts to optimize the value of its offerings for collaborators, the goals of the company and collaborators often are not perfectly aligned. As a result, collaborator relationships can spawn tensions resulting from the different goal-optimization strategies pursued by the collaborating entities. Such tensions are often facilitated by the power imbalance of the collaborators and frequently lead to explicit conflicts.

Like most business relationships, collaboration has its advantages and drawbacks. Specifically, collaboration offers several important *benefits* for participating entities:

- **Effectiveness.** Collaboration enables companies to specialize in a particular aspect of the value-delivery process such as research and development, manufacturing, communication, and distribution. Because collaboration enables each party to take advantage of the other's expertise, it can provide both entities with a competitive advantage stemming from greater specialization.

- **Cost efficiency.** In addition to facilitating the effectiveness of the value-creation process, collaboration can also increase its cost efficiency because each collaborator can achieve greater economies of scale and experience by specializing in a given function. Specialization might also encourage a company to invest in new technologies that it would not invest in if it lacked a larger scale of operations.

- **Flexibility.** Relative to developing the necessary in-house expertise, collaboration requires a lesser commitment of resources, thus offering much greater flexibility in terms of switching technologies, entering new markets, and exiting existing ones. For example, the development of a new distribution channel requires substantial resources and calls for a long-term commitment, whereas partnering with an already existing distribution channel requires fewer resources and offers much greater flexibility.

- **Speed.** Collaboration enables a company to achieve the desired results much faster than building in-house expertise. For example, a manufacturer can gain access to target markets virtually overnight using an existing distribution chain, whereas launching its own distribution channel would take considerably longer.

Despite its numerous benefits, collaborating with other entities has several important *drawbacks*:

- **Loss of control.** Delegating certain aspects of a company's activities to an external entity often leads to loss of control over the value-creation process. For example, outsourcing manufacturing operations frequently hinders a company's ability to monitor production processes and product quality. Outsourcing also diminishes the company's ability to monitor the financial aspects of the value-creation process.

- **Loss of competencies.** Outsourcing key activities tends to weaken a company's core competencies. For example, outsourcing research-and-development activities over time tends to diminish a company's ability to drive innovation. In the same vein, outsourcing logistics and manufacturing activities can diminish a company's competency in supply-chain management.

- **Empowering the competition.** Outsourcing key activities also might enable collaborating entities to develop a set of strategic competencies, thus becoming a company's future competitor. For example, a collaborator assembling medical devices on behalf of the company might develop its own line of medical devices that will compete with the devices it assembles for the company.

As with most business decisions, entering into a collaborative relationship involves weighing the relevant benefits and costs. When the benefits from the collaboration outweigh the corresponding costs for both the company and its collaborators, the collaboration tends to be sustainable. In contrast, when the collaboration fails to create superior value for either party, the collaboration might be dissolved as the partners pursue alternative options such as finding new collaborators or insourcing.

Crafting Company and Collaborator Positioning Statements

To ensure market success, a company must develop a viable positioning for its collaborators and stakeholders. Thus, similar to the way in which managers develop a customer positioning statement, they must also develop a positioning statement geared toward the company's collaborators and its senior management and stakeholders. The key aspects of collaborator and company positioning statements are discussed in more detail in the following sections.

Developing a Collaborator Positioning Statement

To succeed, an offering has to create value not only for its target customers but also for the company's collaborators. Accordingly, in addition to developing a customer-focused positioning statement, managers need to develop a positioning statement outlining the offering's value for its collaborators.

The collaborator-focused positioning statement is similar to the customer-focused positioning statement (discussed in Chapter 7), with the main difference that instead of identifying target customers and the key aspects of the offering's value proposition for these customers, it identifies the company's key collaborators and delineates the key aspects of the offering's value proposition for these collaborators. The key question that the collaborator-focused positioning statement must answer is: *Who are the offering's key collaborators and why would they work with the company to support its offering?*

The typical collaborator-focused positioning statement consists of three key components: *collaborators, the frame of reference,* and *the primary benefit(s).* The overall structure of the collaborator-focused positioning statement is similar to the structure of the customer-focused statement. Examples of collaborator-focused positioning statements are shown below.

Example A (Noncomparative Positioning): [Offering][frame of reference] is an excellent choice for [collaborators] because [primary benefit].

DeWalt power tools are a great choice for retailers because they are profitable.

Example A (Comparative Positioning): [Offering][frame of reference] is a better choice for [collaborators] than [competition] because [primary benefit].

DeWalt power tools are a better choice for retailers than Makita because they offer price protection from discount retailers.

Example B (Noncomparative Positioning): For [collaborators] who seek [primary benefit], [offering] is an excellent [product category] because [justification of the benefit].

For mass-market retailers who seek to grow profits, Gillette Fusion offers a consumer staple that will generate high profit margins.

Example B (Comparative Positioning): For [collaborators] who seek [primary benefit], [offering] is a better [frame of reference] than [competition] because [justification of the benefit].

For mass-market retailers who seek to grow sales revenues and market share, Gillette Fusion offers a consumer staple that will generate higher profit margins than Gillette Mach3.

Developing a Company Positioning Statement

The company-focused positioning statement identifies the company's business unit managing the offering and outlines its key value proposition for the business unit and the company. The company-focused positioning statement aims to justify the viability of the offering to the senior management and key stakeholders (e.g., company directors) by articulating how the offering will help the company achieve its goals. The key question that this positioning statement must answer is: *Why should the business unit and the company invest in this offering?*

A typical company-focused positioning statement consists of three key components: *the company, the frame of reference,* and *the primary benefit(s).* The overall structure of the company-focused positioning statement is similar to the structure of the customer-focused statement. Examples of company-focused positioning statements are shown below.

Example A (Noncomparative Positioning): [Offering] is an excellent [frame of reference] for [company] because [the primary benefit derived from the offering].

DeWalt power tools are an excellent choice for Black & Decker because they offer high profit margins.

Example A (Comparative Positioning): [Offering] is a better [frame of reference] for [company] than [alternative options] because [primary benefit].

DeWalt power tools are a better strategic option for Black & Decker than Black & Decker Professional power tools because they have a larger margin and generate greater sales volume.

Example B (Noncomparative Positioning): [Offering] is an excellent choice for [company] because [the primary benefit derived from the offering].

Fusion is an excellent option for Gillette because it will assert Gillette's position as the leader in the wet-shaving market and will ensure high profit margins.

Example B (Comparative Positioning): [Offering] is the [frame of reference] that gives [company] greater [primary benefit] than [alternative options] because [justification of the benefit].

Fusion is the wet-shaving system that gives Gillette greater market share than Mach3 because it has higher profit margins.

SUMMARY

The company is an entity established for the purpose of creating value for its stakeholders. To this end, the company develops market offerings that fulfill the needs of target customers and collaborators while at the same time capturing value for its stakeholders. An offering can create two types of value for the company: *monetary* and *strategic.* The monetary value corresponds to the company's financial goals, and the strategic value reflects the offering's ability to fulfill a company's strategic goals.

Achieving sustainable profit growth is the ultimate goal for most companies. Profit growth is achieved by increasing sales revenues and reducing costs. Increasing *sales revenues* is the prevalent approach to achieving long-term profitability. Increasing sales revenues can be achieved through two basic strategies: growing sales volume and optimizing price.

Strategies for growing *sales volume* include the market-growth strategy, which aims to attract customers who are new to the particular product category; the steal-share strategy, which aims to attract customers who are currently buying similar offerings from competitors; and the market-penetration strategy, which aims to increase consumption by the company's current customers.

The impact of *varying the price* on sales revenues depends on the way customers react to changes in price. Sales revenues can be increased by raising (lowering) prices in cases when the positive impact of increasing revenues (sales volume) is greater than the negative impact of the corresponding decrease in sales volume (revenues).

Profit growth can also be achieved by *lowering costs*, including the cost of goods sold, research-and-development costs, marketing costs, and miscellaneous other costs such as general and administrative costs and cost of capital.

The profit impact of *strategic offerings* is measured by assessing the monetary value they create through synergies with other profit-generating offerings. To better communicate the value of its offerings, companies often express the strategic benefits of the offering in monetary terms—a process referred to as economic value analysis.

To succeed in the market, most companies collaborate with other entities to understand, design, communicate, and deliver value to target customers. Accordingly, collaboration can typically occur in four domains: *market insight, value design, value communication,* and *value delivery.* The relationship between a company and its collaborators should always be considered in the context of creating value for their ultimate customers. Furthermore, based on the extent to which the relationships among collaborating entities are formalized, collaboration can be either *explicit,* involving contractual agreements, or *implicit,* based on informal relationships between the companies.

To ensure market success, a company must develop a viable positioning for its collaborators and stakeholders. Thus, similar to the way in which managers develop a customer positioning statement, they must also develop a *collaborator-focused positioning statement,* which articulates the key aspects of the offering's value proposition for the company's collaborators and a *company-focused positioning statement,* which articulates the offering's value proposition for the company stakeholders. Most collaborator-focused and company-focused positioning statements comprise three main components: the target audience (collaborators or stakeholders), the frame of reference, and the offering's primary benefit.

MARKETING INSIGHT: QUANTIFYING MARKET PERFORMANCE

To effectively manage their companies, managers must identify the key performance dimensions and quantify their companies' performance on these dimensions. Quantifying market performance is relevant not only for for-profit companies but also for nonprofit organizations that seek to have an impact on individual consumers, the markets in which these consumers interact with one another and the company, and society as a whole. Specifically, quantifying market performance involves analyses in four areas: *assessing key performance metrics, developing an income statement, conducting a margin analysis,* and *break-even analysis.*

Key Performance Metrics

Market Share: An offering's share of the total sales of all offerings within the product category in which the company's offering competes. Market share is determined by dividing an offering's sales volume by the total category sales volume. Sales can be defined in terms of revenues or on a unit basis (e.g., number of items sold or number of customers served).

$$\text{Market share} = \frac{\text{An offering's sales in a given market}}{\text{Total sales in a given market}}$$

Net Income: Gross revenue minus all costs and expenses (cost of goods sold, operating expenses, depreciation, interest, and taxes) during a given period of time. Net income is also referred to as net earnings.

$$\text{Net income} = \text{Gross revenue} - \text{Total costs}$$

Return on Investment (ROI): Net income as a percentage of the investment required for generating this income.

$$\text{ROI} = \frac{\text{Gain from an investment} - \text{Cost of investment}}{\text{Cost of investment}}$$

Return on Marketing Investment (ROMI): A measure of the efficiency of a company's marketing expenditures, typically calculated in terms of incremental net income, sales revenues, market share, or contribution margin. ROMI can also be calculated with respect to the overall marketing expenditures or to a specific marketing mix variable (e.g., branding, incentives, or communication).

$$\text{ROMI} = \frac{\text{Incremental net income generated by the marketing investment}}{\text{Cost of the marketing investment}}$$

Return on Sales (ROS): Net income as a percentage of sales revenues.

$$\text{ROS} = \frac{\text{Net income}}{\text{Sales revenues}}$$

The Income (Profit and Loss) Statement

The income statement (also referred to as the *profit and loss statement*) is a financial document enumerating a company's income and expenses during a given period. It typically identifies revenues, costs, operating expenses, operating income, and earnings (Figure 9).

Figure 9. The Income (Profit and Loss) Statement

Gross Revenues	
Sales revenues	$ 18,000
Returns and allowances	(3,000)
Total (Gross) Revenues	15,000
Cost of Goods Sold	
Product costs	(4,500)
Services costs	(1,500)
Total Cost of Goods Sold	(6,000)
Gross Profit	9,000
Gross Margin	60%
Operating Expenses	
Sales and marketing	5,000
General and administrative	1,000
Research and development	1,500
Total Operating Expenses	7,500
Operating Income	1,500
Operating Margin	10%
Other Revenues (Expenses)	
Interest expense	(250)
Depreciation and amortization	(100)
Income tax expense	(400)
Total Other Revenues (Expenses)	(750)
Net Income (Earnings)	750
Net (Profit) Margin	5%

Gross (Profit) Margin: The ratio of gross (total) profit to gross (total) revenue. Gross margin analysis is a useful tool because it implicitly includes unit selling prices of products and services, unit costs, and unit volume. Gross margin is different than contribution margin (discussed later): Contribution margin includes all variable costs, whereas gross margin includes some—but often not all—variable costs, a number of which can be part of the operating margin.

$$\text{Gross margin} = \frac{\text{Gross profit}}{\text{Gross revenue}} = \frac{\text{Gross revenue} - \text{Cost of goods sold}}{\text{Gross revenue}}$$

Gross Profit: The difference between gross (total) revenue and total cost of goods sold. Gross profit can also be calculated on a per-unit basis as the difference between unit selling price and unit cost of goods sold. For example, if a company sells 100 units, each priced at $1 and each costing the company $.30 to manufacture, then the unit gross profit is $.70, the total gross profit is $70, and the unit and total gross margins are 70%.

$$\text{Gross profit}_{\text{Total}} = \text{Revenue}_{\text{Total}} - \text{Cost of goods sold}_{\text{Total}}$$

$$\text{Gross profit}_{\text{Unit}} = \text{Price}_{\text{Unit}} - \text{Cost of goods sold}_{\text{Unit}}$$

Gross Revenue: Total receipts from a company's business activities.

Net Margin: The ratio of net income to gross (total) revenue.

$$\text{Net margin} = \frac{\text{Net income}}{\text{Gross revenue}}$$

Operating Expenses: The costs, other than cost of goods sold, incurred to generate revenues (e.g., sales, marketing, research and development, and general and administrative expenses).

Operating Income: Gross profit minus operating expenses. Operating income reflects the firm's profitability from current operations without regard to the interest charges accruing from the firm's capital structure.

$$\text{Operating income} = \text{Gross profit} - \text{Operating expenses}$$

Operating Margin: The ratio of operating income to gross (total) revenue.

$$\text{Operating margin} = \frac{\text{Operating income}}{\text{Gross revenue}}$$

Margin Analysis

Contribution Margin ($): When expressed in monetary terms ($), contribution margin typically refers to the difference between total revenue and total variable costs. The contribution margin can also be calculated on a per-unit basis as the difference between the unit selling price and the unit variable cost. The per-unit margin, expressed in monetary terms ($), is also referred to as the contribution (i.e., the dollar amount that each unit sold "contributes" to the payment of fixed costs).

$$\text{Contribution margin (\$)}_{\text{Total}} = \text{Revenue}_{\text{Total}} - \text{Variable costs}_{\text{Total}}$$

$$\text{Contribution margin (\$)}_{\text{Unit}} = \text{Price}_{\text{Unit}} - \text{Variable costs}_{\text{Unit}}$$

Contribution Margin (%): When expressed as a percentage (%), contribution margin typically refers to the ratio of the difference between total revenue and total variable costs to total revenue. The contribution margin can also be expressed as the ratio of unit contribution to unit selling price.

$$\text{Contribution margin (\%)} = \frac{\text{Revenue}_{\text{Total}} - \text{Variable costs}_{\text{Total}}}{\text{Revenue}_{\text{Total}}}$$

$$\text{Contribution margin (\%)} = \frac{\text{Price}_{\text{Unit}} - \text{Variable costs}_{\text{Unit}}}{\text{Price}_{\text{Unit}}}$$

Marginal Cost: The cost of producing one additional unit.

Trade Margin: The difference between unit selling price and unit cost at each level of a distribution channel. Trade margins can be expressed in monetary terms or as a percentage (Figure 10). Margins are typically calculated based on sales revenue (sales price) rather than based on cost (purchase price).

Figure 10. Calculating Trade Margins

MARKETING INSIGHT: BREAK-EVEN ANALYSIS

Break-even analysis aims to identify the point at which the benefits and costs associated with a particular action are equal, and beyond which profit occurs. The most common types of break-even analyses include break-even of a fixed-cost investment, break-even of a price cut, and break-even of a variable-cost increase.

Break-even analysis of a fixed-cost investment identifies the unit or dollar sales volume at which the company is able to recoup a particular investment, such as research-and-development expenses, product improvement costs, and the costs of an advertising campaign. The break-even volume (BEV) of a fixed-cost investment is the ratio of the size of the fixed-cost investment to the unit margin.

$$\text{BEV}_{\text{Fixed-cost investment}} = \frac{\text{Fixed-cost investment}}{\text{Unit margin}} = \frac{\text{Fixed-cost investment}}{\text{Unit selling price} - \text{Unit variable cost}}$$

The break-even analysis of a fixed-cost investment can be illustrated as shown in Figure 11. Here the break-even point indicates the sales volume beyond which the offering starts generating profits.

Figure 11: Break-Even of a Fixed-Cost Investment

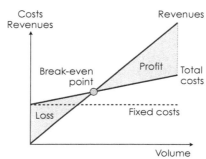

For example, consider an offering priced at $100 with variable costs of $50 and fixed costs of $50M. In this case, BEV = $50M/($100 – $50) = 1,000,000. Thus, for a $50M fixed-cost investment to break even, sales volume should reach 1,000,000 items.

In addition to the break-even analysis of a fixed-cost investment associated with launching a new offering, a company may need to calculate the break-even volume of a change (most often an increase) in its current fixed-cost investment. Typical problems to which this type of analysis can be applied are estimating the incremental increase in sales necessary to cover the costs of a research-and-development project, the costs of an advertising campaign, and even the costs of an increase in the compensation package of senior executives.

To illustrate, consider the impact of an increase in fixed costs from $50M to $60M for a product priced at $100 with variable costs of $50. In this case, BEV = ($60M - $50M)/($100 – $50) = 200,000. Thus, for the $10M fixed-cost investment to break even, sales volume should increase by 200,000 items.

Break-even analysis of a price cut estimates the increase in sales volume needed for a price cut to have a neutral impact on company profits. To break even, lost profits resulting from a lower margin after a price cut must be equal to the additional profits generated by the incremental sales volume from the lower price.[2] BEV Price cut is expressed

$$\text{BEV}_{\text{Price cut}} = \frac{\text{Margin}_{\text{Old price}}}{\text{Margin}_{\text{New price}}}$$

To illustrate, consider the impact of a price cut from $100 to $75 for a product with a variable cost of $50. In this case, Margin $_{\text{Old price}}$ = $100 – $50 = $50 and Margin $_{\text{New price}}$ = $75 – $50 = $25. Therefore, BEV $_{\text{Price cut}}$ = $50/$25 = 2. Thus, for the price cut to break even, sales volume should double at the lower price.

Break-even analysis of a variable-cost increase identifies the sales volume at which a company neither makes a profit nor incurs a loss after increasing variable costs. Typical problems to which this type of analysis can be applied are estimating the incremental increase in sales necessary to cover an increase in the cost of goods sold, estimating the costs associated with increasing an item-specific level of service, and estimating the costs associated with running item-specific incentives (e.g., premiums). The basic principle of calculating the break-even point of an increase in an offering's variable costs is similar to that of estimating the break-even point of a price cut. The difference is that a decrease in the margin generated by the new offering stems from an increase in the offering's costs rather than a decrease in revenues.

$$BEV_{\text{Variable cost increase}} = \frac{\text{Margin}_{\text{Old variable cost}}}{\text{Margin}_{\text{New variable cost}}}$$

To illustrate, consider the impact of an increase in variable costs from \$50 to \$60 for a product priced at \$100. In this case, $\text{Margin}_{\text{Old variable cost}} = \$100 - \$50 = \$50$ and $\text{Margin}_{\text{New variable cost}} = \$100 - \$60 = \$40$. Therefore, the break-even volume of a variable cost increase can be calculated as $BEV_{\text{Variable cost increase}} = \$50/\$40 = 1.25$. Thus, for the variable-cost increase to break even, the ratio of the new to old sales should be 1.25, meaning that sales volume should increase by a factor of .25, or by 25%.

PART FOUR

DESIGNING VALUE

INTRODUCTION

Everything should be made as simple
as possible, but not simpler.
— Albert Einstein, theoretical physicist

Marketing tactics translate a company's strategy into a set of actionable decisions that define the offering the company will deploy in the target market. In this context, marketing tactics refer to a set of specific activities, also known as the marketing mix, employed to execute a given strategy. The marketing tactics reflect all attributes of a specific offering, from the benefits it creates and how much it costs to how customers will hear about it and buy it. The tactics logically follow from the offering's strategy and reflect the way the company will make this strategy a market reality.

Marketing tactics can be viewed as a process of designing, communicating, and delivering value. The value-design aspect of the offering defines the core value the offering aims to create for its target customers and is defined by five key attributes: product, service, brand, price, and incentives. The value-communication aspect of the offering outlines the ways in which target customers will learn about the company's offering, and the value-delivery aspect delineates how the offering will be distributed to customers. The value-design elements of the offering are outlined in Chapters 9–13, whereas the communication and distribution aspects of the offering are outlined in Chapters 14–17.

The chapters included in this section focus on the value-design aspect of the offering and address issues pertaining to managing *products, services, brands, prices,* and *incentives.*

- **Managing products** involves crafting the product-related aspects of the company's offering. The key issues involved in managing a company's products are discussed in Chapter 9.

- **Managing services** involves crafting the service-related aspects of the company's offering. The key issues involved in managing a company's services are discussed in Chapter 10.

- **Managing brands** involves crafting and managing the brand image associated with the company's offering(s). The key branding decisions involved in managing a company's offering(s) are the focus of Chapter 11.

- **Managing price** involves setting and managing the monetary aspect of the offering; it defines the amount of money the company charges for the offering. The key pricing decisions are outlined in Chapter 12.

- **Managing incentives** involves a variety of tools, typically short term, aimed at enhancing the value of the offering by providing additional benefits and/or reducing costs. The key decisions involved in managing incentives are discussed in Chapter 13.

The key to designing a successful offering is to ensure that it can deliver superior value to the relevant market entities—target customers, the company, and its collaborators. To this end, the different aspects of the offering should be aligned in a way that optimizes the value delivered to these three entities. A systematic approach to developing and managing the value-design elements of a company's offering is outlined in the following chapters.

CHAPTER NINE

MANAGING PRODUCTS

A market is never saturated with a good product,
but it is very quickly saturated with a bad one.
—Henry Ford, founder of Ford Motor Company

A company's products—along with its services and brands—are a key source of customer value and one of the primary reasons why customers buy and use a company's offering. In this context, product management aims to optimize the value that a company's products deliver to target customers and do so in a way that benefits the company and its collaborators. The key product-management decisions are the focus of this chapter. Specifically, we address the following topics:

- *Product Management as a Value-Creation Process* ‖ The product as a tool for creating market value | Product attributes and customer benefits
- *Key Product Decisions* ‖ Defining product functionality | Designing the product's physical attributes | Delineating product guarantees and warranties
- *Product Packaging as a Tool for Creating Market Value* ‖ The role of packaging in product design | Designing the packaging | Modifying the packaging
- *Designing Product Lines and Product Platforms* ‖ Designing product lines | Designing product platforms
- *Managing the Product Life Cycle* ‖ The dynamics of the product life cycle | Extending the product life cycle | Managing product obsolescence

The discussion of product management is complemented by an in-depth overview of three additional topics: design thinking, benefit visibility in product design, and product patents.

Product Management as a Value-Creation Process

A key consideration in product management is creating superior customer value. To this end, a manager must understand the role of products as a means of creating market value, the relationship between product attributes and customer benefits, and the role of benefit visibility in product design. These three aspects of product management are discussed in the following sections.

The Product as a Tool for Creating Market Value

The product is a good designed to create value in a particular market. It is one of the seven attributes defining the company's offerings. Working together with the other marketing tactics defining the offering—service, brand, price, incentives, communication, and distribution—the product aims to create value for the relevant market entities: the company, its customers, and its collaborators (Figure 1). In this context, a manager's ultimate goal is to design products that create superior value for target customers in a way that benefits the company and its collaborators.

Figure 1. Product Management as a Value-Creation Process

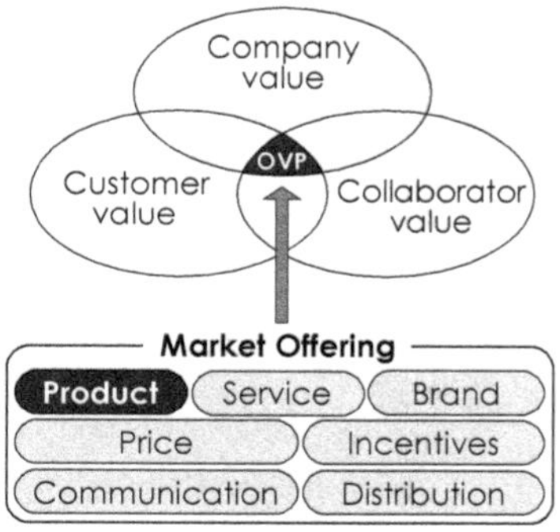

To ensure a product's success, a manager must address three key questions:

- *Does the product create superior value for target customers relative to the competition?*
- *Does the product create superior value for the company's collaborators relative to the other options these collaborators might pursue?*
- *Does the product create superior value for the company relative to the other alternatives available to the company?*

An affirmative answer to these questions implies that the product has an optimal value proposition (OVP) that creates value for target customers, the company, and its collaborators. The development of a meaningful optimal value proposition is the overarching principle guiding all product decisions. To this end, a company must identify the benefits that customers seek to receive from the company's offering and then translate these benefits into specific product features and experiences in a way that enables the company and its collaborators to achieve their goals.

Product Attributes and Customer Benefits

Products are defined by a combination of attributes that deliver particular customer benefits. *Attributes* are objective characteristics of a product, such as certain levels of performance, reliability, and durability. In contrast, *benefits* reflect the subjective value customers derive from using the product. Product attributes can be related to specific benefits, although this relationship is not unidimensional: A particular attribute might be associated with one or more benefits, and a given benefit might stem from multiple attributes (Figure 2).

Figure 2. Product Attributes and Customer Benefits

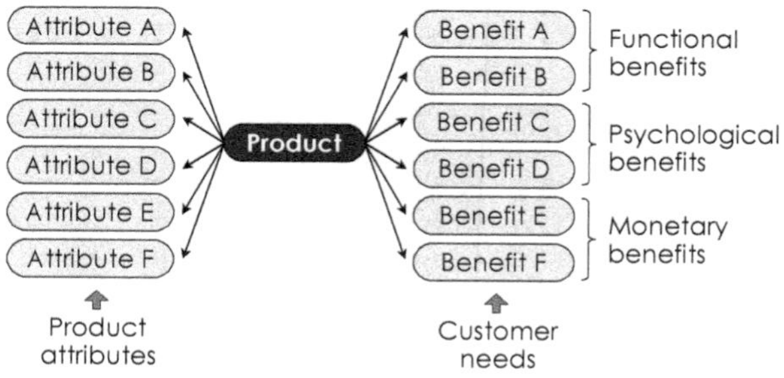

Depending on the underlying customer needs, product benefits can be classified into one of three types: functional benefits that are directly related to a product's performance, psychological benefits that reflect the emotional and self-expressive impact of the product, and monetary benefits that reflect the financial implications of using the product. Accordingly, when developing a new product or modifying an existing one, managers must ask three key questions: *How does the product's functional performance benefit customers? How do customers feel about different product attributes?* and *What is the monetary impact of the different aspects of the product on customers?* Providing meaningful answers to these questions and incorporating them into the product design can help ensure the product's market success.

The relationship between product attributes and customer benefits is better understood in the context of product design and consumption. Product attributes are defined by engineers who are in charge of designing and manufacturing the product. Once customers acquire the product, they experience the benefits stemming from the product's attributes. Thus, while engineers tend to think in terms of product attributes, customers tend to think in terms of the benefits delivered by the product. In this context, a manager's task is to ensure that the product designed by the engineers performs in a way that creates value for target customers—in other words, that product attributes are aligned with the benefits customers expect to receive from the offering.

The way that product attributes are translated into customer benefits is captured by the *value function*, which reflects how changes in the attributes of the company's product influence the value customers receive from this product. Understanding how customers evaluate product performance on different product attributes and how they combine these valuations to form an overall assessment of a company's product enables managers to identify the attributes that must be added, improved, simplified, or removed (see Chapter 4 for a discussion of the properties of the value function and Chapter 7 for a discussion of different approaches to enhance an offering's value).

Key Product Decisions

On the most general level, product development involves four key decisions: defining product functionality, designing the physical appearance of the product, delineating product guarantees and warranties, and creating the product packaging. The first three product decisions are outlined in more detail below and the decisions concerning product packaging are discussed in the following section.

Defining Product Functionality

Defining product functionality involves a series of decisions concerning attributes such as *performance, consistency, reliability, durability, compatibility, ease of use,* and *degree of customization*. These factors are discussed in more detail below.

- **Performance** reflects the key functional attributes of the offering. Products vary in their performance on different attributes. For example, cars vary in engine power, acceleration, comfort, safety, and fuel efficiency; computers vary in processing power, battery life, display size, and connectivity; and snacks vary in taste, nutritional value, and calorie content. In general, higher levels of performance are associated with greater customer benefits, although in some cases the performance on one attribute comes at the expense of the performance on another (e.g., taste and healthiness of a snack).

- **Consistency** reflects the degree to which in-kind products are identical and offer consistent performance. Simply put, consistency means that the same type of product (same SKU) manufactured at different points in time and in different facilities should deliver the same benefits. A popular approach to managing product consistency is the *Six Sigma* methodology of optimizing business processes, which builds on the idea that for an offering to be consistent with specifications, the difference between the actual and desired outcomes should not exceed six standard deviations (a level of consistency that implies that there should be fewer than 3.4 defective items per million outcomes).[1]

- **Reliability** refers to the extent to which a product fulfills its function each and every time it is used over a period of time. Specifically, reliability reflects the probability that the product will operate according to its specifications for the duration of its projected life cycle. Product reliability depends on a variety of factors that include its technical design, the quality of its materials and components, and the degree of care with which it is made and assembled. In general, higher levels of reliability are associated with greater customer benefits, although reliability typically involves greater costs from a company's perspective.

- **Durability** reflects the expected length of the offering's life cycle. Because durability is often an important consideration in a buyer's decision process, products that are more durable tend to be preferred by customers. At the same time, while durable products help companies attract new customers and build loyalty among existing customers, durability tends to have a negative impact on the frequency of repeat purchases because users are often reluctant to replace fully functioning products with new ones. As a result, when designing new offerings, manufacturers have to determine the optimal product durability that will create superior customer value and at the same time leave room for the company to offer meaningful upgrades in the future. This process of designing new products in a way that makes prior generations inferior is often referred to as planned obsolescence and is discussed later in this chapter.

- **Compatibility** refers to the degree to which a product is consistent with certain already existing standards and complementary offerings. Compatibility can be used strategically by companies to create barriers to entry by ensuring that offerings are uniquely compatible with customers' existing systems and processes. Compatibility is also important in networked environments that force users to adhere to a certain standard. To illustrate, the popularity of Microsoft products is to a great degree a function of the need for compatibility when sharing information. Compatibility is also a key consideration in multipart products, where different components must be compatible with one another (e.g., razors and blades).

- **Ease of use** reflects the amount of effort—cognitive, emotional, and physical—involved in using the product. A common misconception is that greater functionality, such as a greater number of features, inevitably leads to greater satisfaction. In reality, however, this is not the case: Adding functionality, especially when customers lack the knowledge necessary to utilize it, can backfire. To illustrate, in an attempt to incorporate the latest technology in its redesigned 7-series sedan, BMW introduced iDrive, an over-engineered computer system used to control most secondary functions of a car, including the audio system, climate, and navigation. Designed to manage more than 700 functions with a single knob, the iDrive had a steep learning curve and quickly became the most controversial feature of the car.

- **Degree of customization** reflects the extent to which the company's products are personalized to fit the needs of individual customers. At one extreme, a company might decide to pursue a mass-production strategy, offering the same products to all customers. At the other extreme, the company might pursue a one-to-one customization in which the company's products are customized for each individual customer. A compromise between the mass-production approach and the one-to-one customization approach is segment-based customization. By developing offerings for groups of customers with similar needs, segment-based customization allows companies to develop fewer offerings while ensuring that these offerings fit well with customer needs. To illustrate, Porsche offers nearly 1,000 customization options for its flagship 911 Carrera, and Nike offers more than 10,000 different design and color sport-shoe customization options through its website nikeid.com. The Coca-Cola Freestyle soda machine can dispense over 100 sparkling and still beverages that customers can mix to match their own taste.

Designing the Product's Physical Attributes

Product design typically involves decisions concerning the physical appearance of the offering, such as its size, shape, and structure. Design plays an important role in manufacturing, transporting, storing, inventorying, and consuming the product. Because customers vary in their preferences and the amounts they consume, packaged goods are often available in a variety of sizes and shapes. For example, Johnson & Johnson's pain relief medicine Tylenol is available in more than fifty different SKU[2] forms—regular, extra strength, and children's dosages; normal and extended relief; tablets, caplets, gelcaps, geltabs, and liquid—all in a variety of sizes.

The look and feel of an offering are particularly important for products that have a primarily aesthetic and self-expressive function, such as luxury cars, designer furniture, and fashion apparel, but are relatively less pertinent for functional products such as manufacturing equipment. Because product styling can create value above and beyond the functional characteristics of the product, it is particularly important in commoditized product categories. For example, Apple revolutionized the personal computer industry by designing computers that were not only powerful and fast but also aesthetically pleasing. Method Products, a home and personal cleaning products company, has managed to successfully differentiate its products through the innovative, futuristic styling of its containers. Tesla managed to build a striking electric car that people *want* to drive, instead of a mediocre car that environmentally conscious consumers feel that they *have* to drive. By using innovative product design, Apple, Method, and Tesla have been able to develop products that stand out in a crowded marketplace in which multiple products are fighting for a share of buyers' attention and buyers' wallets.

In addition to delivering functional benefits, attracting buyers' attention, and creating an emotional connection, product design can also influence consumption. For example, while developing a packaging that would successfully challenge Coca-Cola's iconic 6.5-oz. "swirl" bottle, Pepsi discovered that the design of the bottle influences not only whether buyers will pick it up from the store shelf but also how much they'll drink once they bring it home. The larger the bottle, the greater the rate of consumption. The observation that larger bottles lead to a greater rate of consumption resulted in the development of the two-liter bottle, which has since become one of the most popular containers in the non-alcoholic carbonated beverage category.

Delineating Product Guarantees and Warranties

In addition to creating customer value via the benefits offered by the product, a company can also create value by offering customers reassurance that the product will perform as described and promising some form of reparation should the product fail to meet expectations. Such reassurance can be conveyed by product guarantees and warranties.

A *guarantee* is an assurance that if a product does not function as promised by the company and/or expected by customers, some form of compensation will be provided by the company. Guarantees create value for customers by reducing the functional and monetary risk associated with using the product, by adding credibility to the company's claims, and by delineating the process of addressing eventual product failures. In addition to minimizing customer risk, guarantees can convey product quality by signaling the company's willingness to stand by its products. Guarantees can also benefit the company by sharpening its focus on the customer experience, establishing accountability, facilitating the development of performance standards, and offering guidelines for recovering from failures.

Guarantees can be *overall satisfaction* guarantees that apply to any aspect of the overall product experience regardless of whether it stems from the actual quality of the product or customers' assessment of the product quality, and *specific attribute* guarantees that apply to a particular aspect of the product such as performance, reliability, and durability. In addition, guarantees can be valid for a specific period of time, such as one year, or they can be stipulated for a variable time frame such as for the duration of product ownership by the original buyer.

To be effective, product guarantees must be *relevant, easy to understand,* and *easy to invoke.* The relevance aspect of the guarantee means that the guaranteed feature of the product should be important to customers. Guarantees applied to features that are not important to customers or that are believed by customers to never malfunction generally create little or no customer value. The easy-to-understand aspect of the guarantee means that the company's promise and customers' potential recourse in the case of failure are straightforward and easy to understand. Finally, to be effective, a guarantee must be easy to invoke. This means that the guarantee should have a limited number of exclusions and limitations (which also makes it easier to communicate), so that should the promise stipulated by the guarantee be broken, recourse can be easily obtained with minimal time and effort on the part of the customer.

Warranties are similar to guarantees in terms of the benefits they provide to customers and the company. At the same time, they differ on at least two dimensions. First, warranties are usually associated with a repair or a replacement of the purchased item, whereas guarantees can also involve returning the product for a refund. In addition, guarantees are always free and do not require an added payment. In contrast, warranties that extend the product's existing free warranty can be purchased either when the product is bought or at a later date.

Although guarantees and warranties are tactical in nature, they can play a strategic role in defining the market value created by a company's products. Because they signal product quality in addition to minimizing product risk, guarantees and warranties are often an integral component of the offering's overall value proposition. For example, to build a reputation of quality, reliability, and durability, Hyundai introduced a powertrain warranty on its vehicles that covers up to 10 years or 100,000 miles—much longer than many of its competitors' warranties. In the same vein, Ginkgo, a manufacturer of stainless flatware and tableware accessories, offers a lifetime warranty on its knives to signal their quality and durability.

While enhancing customer value, guarantees and warranties come at a cost to the company. In general, the more generous the guarantees and warranties, the higher the company cost of offering these benefits to customers. Therefore, when designing product guarantees and warranties, a company must carefully consider their pros and cons and their overall impact on the offering's ability to create market value.

Product Packaging as a Tool for Creating Market Value

Packaging refers to the process of enclosing products for distribution, storage, sale, and use. The importance of the packaging stems from the fact that it is a buyer's first encounter with the product, which can determine this buyer's interest in the product and shape the subsequent product evaluation and purchase decision. Because of its ability to influence customer choice, many companies strategically use packaging to create distinct customer value and differentiate their products from the competition.

The Role of Packaging in Product Design

Packaging serves several key functions: *protecting* the product during transportation and storage; physically *containing* liquid, powder, and granular goods; *agglomerating* small items into larger packages; *preventing* tampering, counterfeiting, and theft; providing *convenience* during transportation, handling, storage, display, sale, and consumption; offering *information* on how to transport, store, use, and dispose of the product; *differentiating* the company's product from the competition; and *promoting* the product to potential buyers by providing them with reasons to choose it.

In addition to facilitating the distribution, storage, sale, and use of products, packaging can also be used to create value above and beyond the value created by the product itself. To illustrate, Tiffany's signature blue box highlights the exclusivity of the offering, strengthens the company's brand image, and helps differentiate it from the competition. The role of packaging as an aspect of the offering's brand is further discussed in Chapter 11.

An important aspect of packaging is the *label*, which refers to any written, electronic, or graphic communication placed directly on the package or otherwise associated with the product (e.g., an information tag attached to the product). The primary functions of the label are to communicate information to buyers, channel members, and the company to facilitate identification of the offering; delineate the key attributes of the product; highlight product benefits; provide information about the use, storage, and disposal of the product; increase the product's aesthetic appeal; as well as build and leverage the brand associated with the product.

Because of its role as a means of communication informing buyers about the features and benefits of the product, packaging is subject to a number of legal regulations and restrictions. The Federal Trade Commission Act of 1914 asserted that false, misleading, or deceptive packaging and labels are a form of unfair competition. The Fair Packaging and Labeling Act (1967) set mandatory labeling requirements and enabled the creation of industry-specific packaging regulations. For example, the Food and Drug Administration (FDA) has developed a set of guidelines for the type of information—such as calorie content, fat, carbohydrates, and protein—that food producers must include in labeling their products.

Packaging involves two key decisions: designing the packaging for a new offering and deciding whether and how to modify the packaging of an existing offering. These two decisions are discussed in more detail below.

Designing the Packaging

The development of effective packaging follows a set of core principles that determine the product's ultimate success in the market. These principles are *visibility, differentiation, value transparency*, and *consumption impact*.

- **Visibility.** Shoppers are frequently overwhelmed with information from companies trying to promote their offerings. This information overload often forces customers to tune out and ignore much of the information they deem irrelevant and that does not help them with the decision process. Therefore, effective packaging must stand out in order to break through the clutter, grab shoppers' attention, and persuade them to favorably consider and ultimately purchase the offering.

- **Differentiation.** In addition to attracting shoppers' attention, packaging can help differentiate the company's offering from the competition. Thus, when confronted with multiple options, customers who are pressed for time often use packaging as a key source of information about the offering. Shoppers' reliance on packaging as a key input in their buying decision is further driven by the fact that many companies use packaging as a branding tool, which, in turn, makes it easy for shoppers to identify the brands they are looking for by merely looking at the packaging.

- **Value transparency.** Packaging's visibility and ability to differentiate the company's offering from the competition, although important, do not address another important function of packaging—namely, its ability to clearly communicate the value of the offering to its target customers. Because shoppers typically interact with the packaging at the time of purchase, effective packaging must make transparent the offering's value proposition to shoppers and give them a reason to buy the offering.

- **Consumption impact.** The role of packaging is not limited to influencing shoppers' buying decisions: Packaging can also influence the ways in which customers use the offering. In this context, packaging can have an impact on usage frequency—how often customers use the company's offerings—and usage quantity—how much they consume on each usage occasion. For example, Coca-Cola was able to increase consumption by introducing refrigerator-friendly fridge packs that stack 12 cans in a longer and narrower space and allow individual cans to be dispensed. Heinz boosted consumption of ketchup by introducing a series of packaging design innovations that made it easier to get ketchup out of its container. To this end, Heinz switched from glass bottles to squeezable plastic containers, put the mouth of the container at its base, and widened the opening used to dispense ketchup.

A number of the functions performed by packaging are similar to those performed by advertising. Indeed, both serve as means of communication, informing buyers about the company's offering. Despite their similarities, packaging and advertising vary in the ways in which they convey information as well as in the type of information they aim to convey. Advertising typically strives to create memorable impressions that buyers will act upon in the future. In contrast, because buyers often observe the packaging at the point of purchase, packaging can have almost an instant impact on customers, influencing their purchase decision. Furthermore, in the case of low-priced, familiar products, customers usually spend little time evaluating the available options and often rely on the visual properties of products and their packaging to make a choice. As a result, packaging is often designed to have a more direct, visual impact on the buyer.

Modifying the Packaging

Packaging often evolves over time. One of the most common reasons for modifying packaging is managers' belief that the current packaging has run its course and is no longer able to effectively perform its functions of identifying the offering, differentiating it from the competition, conveying its benefits, and promoting consumption.

A key issue in package redesign is the degree of change to be made — that is, the extent to which the new packaging should be similar or different from the current one. Thus, when redesigning the packaging, managers must balance two considerations. On the one hand, there is the desire to introduce a number of changes in order to convey the new features of the company's product, to advance the brand's new positioning, and to better differentiate the company's offering from the competition. On the other hand, there is the need for continuity, meaning that the package redesign should be sufficiently subtle so that it does not disrupt the sales to current customers. The problem is that in their zeal to differentiate their offerings from the competition and "refresh" the package, managers often overlook the importance of continuity in package redesign.

Continuity is important because most successful offerings derive their revenues and profits from their current customers. Consequently, any gains generated by new customers drawn to the redesigned package must exceed the loss of revenues from loyal customers who find the new package less attractive or confusing. The importance of continuity is underscored by the fact that shoppers are often faced with an overwhelming number of options and, as a result, are unwilling to expend extra effort to examine each option in detail, especially in the case of frequently purchased items.

Because customers usually do not spend much time thinking about the products they habitually buy, they tend to evaluate the available information on a visceral level, focusing on the readily available visual cues without engaging in an in-depth evaluation of the available information. When shoppers are confronted with a radically different packaging of a familiar offering, they are often confused, unable to relate the look and feel of the product they usually buy to the newly redesigned packaging. Such confusion is likely to occur when the company simultaneously changes multiple aspects of the package such as shape, color, logo, messaging, and imagery. Confused shoppers are, in turn, likely to wonder whether the redesigned packaging is associated with the product that they trusted and used to purchase.

In addition to confusing loyal customers, radical package redesign can change the way loyal customers make their purchase decisions. Indeed, in the case of frequently purchased products, especially those that are relatively inexpensive and not overly complex, shoppers tend to engage in low-involvement decision making, focusing on the visual properties of the available options. By dramatically changing the look and feel of the offering, radical package changes are likely to disrupt the habitual repurchase process, forcing customers to engage in a more deliberate evaluation of the available options in order to find the product they are seeking to purchase. As a result, rather than simply and somewhat mindlessly repurchasing the company's offering without even thinking about the other options, shoppers might end up considering and even buying competitors' offerings.

For example, PepsiCo's decision to modify the packaging of its flagship Tropicana Pure Premium orange juice was driven by the noble goal to "reinforce the brand and product attributes, rejuvenate the category and help consumers rediscover the health benefits they get from drinking America's iconic orange juice brand." The new design dramatically changed the color scheme of the package, removed the familiar image of a straw piercing an orange, changed the logo, and moved the key product descriptors such as "No Pulp" to the top of the packaging, where they were less prominent.[3] Following a sharp drop in sales and consumer backlash, PepsiCo reverted to its original package design. In this case, what the company viewed as an improvement in product packaging designed to better communicate product benefits and strengthen its brand ended up being an unnecessary and undesirable change that confused shoppers and obfuscated the meaning of the brand.

The downside of radical changes in product packaging raises the question: Why do companies engage in "revolutionary" packaging redesigns? Sometimes package redesign has less to do with the needs of the market and more to do with the needs of product managers, advertising agencies, and design studios who use innovative package designs as an opportunity to make a name for themselves. Indeed, the conventional wisdom is that there is not much glory in staying the course. Radical changes that lead to successful outcomes, on the other hand, hold the potential to propel managers to the top of the company and reward advertising agencies with creative accolades.

Successful package redesign should start by identifying the information shoppers are looking for and the visual cues—shape, color, logo, messaging, and imagery—they use to discern among the competing offerings. Next, the company should prioritize these elements based on their relevance to the customer and gradually modify them in a way that does not drastically change multiple key elements at once. Unless the company aims to entirely reposition its offering, packaging redesigns must be implemented in a way that takes into account how customers, and especially those who habitually buy the product, will react to the new packaging.

Designing Product Lines and Product Platforms

Most companies manage portfolios that include multiple products. Even companies that start with a single product over time develop additional products targeting customers that seek different benefits and vary in their willingness to pay. In this context, an important aspect of product management involves aligning the individual products with the needs of target customers in a way that maximizes customer value while enabling the company and its collaborators to achieve their goals. The two key aspects of managing product portfolios—*designing product lines* and *designing product platforms*—are outlined in more detail below.

Designing Product Lines

Product lines comprise products that aim to address similar customer needs, typically in the context of the same category. A company can have a single product line or multiple product lines, each containing a group of related products. For example, the Volvo product line targeting the consumer market consists of four types of automobiles—sedan, cross-country, hatchback (station wagon), and SUV/crossover—each of which includes different product variants.

Product lines that target different customer needs using distinct technologies are grouped into *product portfolios*, which include all products and product lines within the company. For example, in addition to its line of consumer vehicles, Volvo's product portfolio includes a line of commercial trucks utilizing both gasoline and natural gas. The relationship between individual products, product lines, and product portfolios is illustrated in Figure 3.

Figure 3. Product Portfolio and Product Lines

When designing their product lines, companies often designate one of their products as the flagship offering. The flagship product typically is the most widely known, best-selling, and/or highly admired offering that represents the quality of the company's product line. For example, Tide is the flagship product for Procter & Gamble's line of laundry detergents, Coke is the flagship product for Coca-Cola, and Mercedes S-Class is the flagship car for Daimler. Because of the strategic importance of flagship products, companies tend to invest heavily in their development and are very diligent when it comes to modifying these products. For example, while introducing a variety of new vehicles — including an SUV (Cayenne and Macan), an affordable sports car (Boxster), and a sedan (Panamera) — Porsche strived to preserve the distinct design and performance of its flagship high-end sports car, the 911 Carrera.

Product-line design aims to ensure that each individual product within the product line targets a particular customer segment and has a unique value proposition that aims to fulfill the needs of this segment. Thus, in addition to designing each product to create superior customer value relative to the competition, product-line design aims to ensure that the different offerings in the company's product line are distinct from one another and do not target the same needs of the same customers.

A key challenge in designing product lines is maintaining the balance between introducing sufficient product variety to address the needs of different customer segments without the potential side effect of confusing customers or encouraging cannibalization. Indeed, if customers are confused when presented with multiple options and cannot determine which product best matches their needs, they might decide to postpone making the purchase or, alternatively, choose a competitors' offering. In the same vein, product lines comprising offerings that are similar in functionality but vary in price are likely to lead to sales of the low-priced offerings cannibalizing the sales of the high-priced ones.

The key principle in designing product lines is that each product should be developed to address the needs of a particular customer segment and that different products should not compete for the same customer segments.[4] Designing (as well as extending and trimming) product lines without a clear understanding of the underlying customer needs each individual product aims to fulfill and without considering the consequences of product cannibalization and customer confusion can be detrimental to the company's market position and bottom line.

To better differentiate their product lines and avoid confusion, companies often associate different product lines with unique brands, each having a different identity and meaning in customers' minds. For example, General Motors distinguishes its product lines by associating them with distinct brands such as Chevrolet, Buick, and Cadillac; Microsoft brands its product lines as Windows, Office, and Xbox; and Unilever's product lines are delineated by brands such as Dove, Axe, Lipton, Knorr, and Surf.

Once designed, product lines do not remain static: They evolve over time. The dynamic aspects of managing product lines — adding new products and deleting existing ones, managing product-line cannibalization, and using product lines to gain and defend market position — are discussed in more detail in Chapter 18.

Designing Product Platforms

Product platforms provide the common architecture on which products are built. Platforms encompass the shared components, designs, technologies, and processes that enable a company to create a set of distinct products that can fulfill the needs of different target customers. A product platform can lead to a range of products based on the same core architecture but with varying features. Unlike product lines, which are typically organized around the different customer benefits created by the company's offerings, product platforms reflect the internal processes involved in developing, manufacturing, promoting, and distributing the products defining a company's product line (Figure 4).

Figure 4. Product Platforms and Product Lines

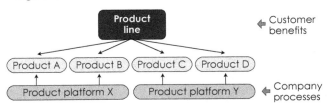

The schematic representation of the relationship between product platforms and product lines shown in Figure 4 is somewhat oversimplified. In reality, most products encompass different components or modules, each sharing a platform with a similar component of another product. As a result, each product in a company's product line can stem from multiple platforms. For example, an automobile can share multiple modules—the power system, chassis, wheels, suspension, and electronic control units—with other automobiles in the company's product line. To illustrate, Volkswagen uses a common platform across a variety of individual car models promoted under four brands: Audi, Škoda, Seat, and Volkswagen. Likewise, General Motors uses common automotive architectures—labeled using the English names of letters of the Greek alphabet such as alpha, epsilon, and gamma—across many of its cars manufactured under the Chevrolet, Buick, Cadillac, and Holden brands. Procter & Gamble uses the same set of ingredients in Tide, Ariel, and Cheer for the U.S., European, and Japanese markets, respectively. Black & Decker uses the same universal motor in more than 100 different consumer power tools.

Product platforms have a different strategic focus than individual products. In platform development, the focus is on streamlining the processes to achieve scale and scope and optimize the use of company resources. In this context, the use of platforms enables companies to achieve a higher degree of standardization across the individual offerings in their product lines, which, in turn, leads to less complex production processes, more efficient use of resources, higher levels of productivity, and lower production costs. In contrast, in developing individual products, the focus is on customization and differentiation in order to create a distinct offering that can create superior value for target customers. By developing a set of common elements that are shared among different products, platform-based design addresses the fundamental tradeoff between customers' desire for distinct products that fulfill their idiosyncratic needs and companies' desire to manufacture standardized products in the most cost-efficient manner.

The ubiquity of product platforms stems from the multiple advantages they offer to manufacturers. One of these advantages is the reduced development and production costs associated with the use of product platforms. Indeed, because they are composed of modules shared across multiple types of products, product platforms can lead to significant economies of scale and scope in designing and producing these modules. Furthermore, reliance on already developed modules, processes, and technologies can dramatically speed up the process of developing new products and bringing them to market. In addition, by enabling the company to pool resources across different products and develop a set of common modules, product platforms can lead to technological breakthroughs that are less likely to occur when resources are dedicated to a single product.

The benefits of using product platforms come with several potential drawbacks. One such drawback is that product platforms, almost by definition, impose constraints on the ways in which products are designed, produced, and managed, which, in turn, can curb radical innovation and lead to less innovative products. Furthermore, because they involve shared components, technologies, and designs, product platforms can encourage the development of products that are very similar in their functionality and appearance, which can lead to customer confusion as well as dilution of the brands associated with these products. Finally, because product platforms become the backbone of the development and manufacture of multiple product lines, they can be very difficult and costly to update or switch out of once they become obsolete.

The discussion so far has focused on internal product platforms that are developed to streamline the design, manufacture, promotion, and distribution of the company's own products. In addition to traditional product platforms, *network platforms* designed to be shared across different companies (Figure 5), have seen rapid growth in the past two decades. For example, Amazon has developed Amazon Marketplace as a platform that can be used by external vendors, Apple developed iTunes as a platform for distributing digital content, and Google developed Google Ads (formerly AdWords) and AdSense as digital advertising platforms. As the complexity of designing, manufacturing, promoting, and distributing individual products increases, companies tend to shift to external platforms that specialize in a particular process and allow them to benefit from economies of scale and scope.

Figure 5. Network Product Platforms

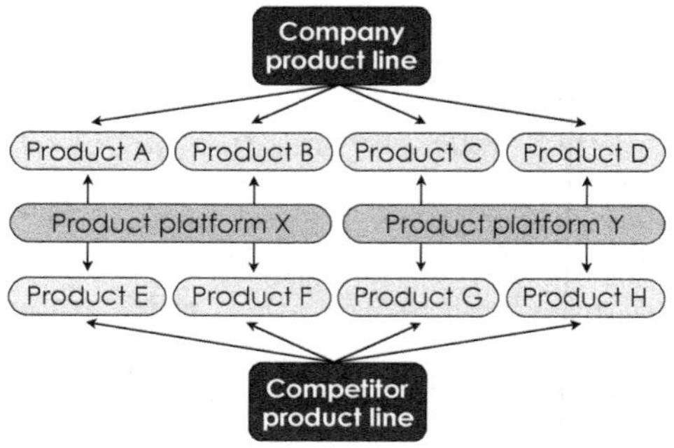

By providing access to resources that might otherwise be out of reach for smaller companies, network platforms effectively lower the barriers to market entry while simultaneously spurring new product development. As a result, platform-based innovators can develop new products and enter new markets much faster, more effectively, and at a lower cost. By providing access to resources needed to develop and launch new products, platforms effectively reduce the scale that individual manufacturers must achieve to be viable, which, in turn, can increase the assortment of custom-tailored products available in the market.

The advancement of networked platforms presents a competitive challenge to companies with their own proprietary platforms. Indeed, outsourcing some of the company's core activities to an external platform might lead to a fundamental change in the design, production, promotion, and distribution processes, as well as the company's entire business model. Switching to a network-platform-based model also implies that a company might have to abandon its current production facilities and equipment, reduce its workforce, as well as share proprietary information with third parties and relinquish control over product development, promotion, and distribution. As a result, despite the multiple benefits of networked product platforms, some companies choose to develop and manage their products using internal product platforms rather than rely on a third-party platform.

Managing the Product Life Cycle

Once introduced in the market, products do not stay static; instead, products have a life cycle where they evolve along with the changes in customer demand, competition, and the overall market conditions. The key issues involved in managing products over their life span involve *understanding the dynamics of the product life cycle, extending the product life cycle,* and *managing product obsolescence.*

The Dynamics of the Product Life Cycle

The concept of a product life cycle is based on the idea that products and product categories have a finite life in which they go through four distinct stages: introduction, growth, maturity, and decline.[5] These stages vary on several dimensions, including the number of product offerings in the market, the nature of communication, the size of the market and its growth rate, the competitive intensity of the market, as well as the revenues and profits generated at each stage. The overall pattern of a product's financial performance across the four stages is illustrated in Figure 6 and outlined in more detail below.

Figure 6. Managing the Product Life Cycle[6]

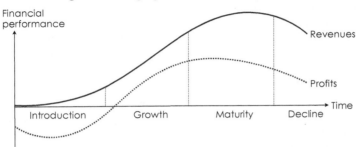

- **Introduction.** At the introduction (also referred to as market development) stage, companies typically offer a single product targeted to the most likely adopters. At this early stage, communication aims primarily to create awareness of the offering among early adopters. The overall size of the market is rather small and growing at a relatively slow pace. Because the market viability of the product is uncertain, there are relatively few competitors entering the market. Given the small but growing market, the revenues are relatively small, albeit showing an upward trend. Because new product development typically involves substantial costs, the profits at this stage are usually negative, meaning that the company is operating at a loss.

- **Growth.** As the product enters the growth stage, the number of customer adoptions increases, and so does the diversity of customers' needs. To address the diverse needs of its target customers, companies begin to introduce product variants designed to better meet the needs of different customer segments. As product sales take off during the growth stage, the number of competitors entering the market increases as more companies recognize the market potential. The size of the market continues to increase and its growth rate accelerates dramatically. Despite the growing number of competitors, the competitive intensity of the market is relatively tame, in part because the market growth leads companies to focus their efforts on attracting new customers to the market instead of trying to steal share from one another. The rapidly growing market and limited competition contribute to the largest rate of revenue and profit growth among all four life-cycle stages. At this stage profits tend to turn positive and the rate of profit growth reaches its peak—the inflection point at which the profit curve turns from convex to concave and the rate of profit growth starts to decline.

- **Maturity.** During the maturity stage, the number of product variants typically peaks as the company develops offerings that appeal to diverse market segments. Because the majority of customers are already aware of the product benefits and many have had a chance to experience the product, communication shifts from building primary demand to differentiating the company's offering by highlighting its benefits vis-à-vis the competition. The market size reaches its peak, but its growth rate starts to decelerate. As the inflow of new customers into the product category slows down, the competition intensifies and companies start competing directly with one another to steal customers and grow market share. Furthermore, as the number of products and competitors tends to peak, the market becomes saturated, and the intensified competition leads to a plateauing and decline in market revenues and profits.

- **Decline.** This stage is characterized by a shrinking market and falling demand for the product. The number of product variants starts decreasing as the product enters the decline stage, profit margins shrink, and companies focus on their best-selling products, phasing out product variants with insufficient volume to meet their profit goals. As the category enters its decline stage, communication continues to emphasize differentiation; however, at this point overall communication expenditures tend to diminish. Competition can become less intense due to fewer competitors because of consolidation and market exit. The overall market growth is negative, and both revenues and profits continue to decline.

Note that the above discussion examines the product life cycle from a product category standpoint rather than from the perspective of a particular company. This distinction is important because a company might not be the first entrant in a given product category and, instead, might enter the market at a later stage of the product life cycle. Regardless of the timing of market entry, the company's performance is likely to be influenced by the dynamics of the market defined by the particular life-cycle stage of the product category.

Extending the Product Life Cycle

As products reach the end of their life cycle, they are often replaced by a new generation of products that take advantage of changes in target markets, including changes in customer preferences, alterations in the competitive landscape, advances in technology, and changes in the regulatory environment. The finite nature of the product life cycle raises the question of whether and how a company can manage its products to prolong their market life. In this context, an important aspect of product management involves actively managing the evolution of the company's offerings over time. Rather than passively waiting for its products to follow their life course and ultimately decline and disappear, a company might choose to plan ahead and develop the next generation of products that will inevitably replace its current offerings.

There are two core approaches to extend the product life cycle: market expansion and product innovation. Market expansion can involve increasing the frequency of usage among the current users of the product, promoting new uses for the product among current users, and discovering new markets for the product. Even though market expansion can help the company extend the life of its products, it does not involve substantive changes in the actual product, leaving it vulnerable to obsolescence caused by the emergence of new technologies. In this context, product innovation, rather than market expansion, is often viewed as a more effective approach to ensure the longevity of a company's products.

The key to successful product innovation is to identify customer needs that are not being met by the current products and develop alternative products that can address these needs. This approach involves applying the product's core technology to new generations of the current product that are better, simpler, more convenient, and/or cheaper. Using such product innovations, a company can create a series of sequential generations of products that extend the product life cycle far beyond the decline stage of the original product (Figure 7). To illustrate, consider Gillette's product development strategy leading to the introduction of Fusion, its eighth-generation wet-shaving razor. Gillette's original razor, introduced in 1903, was replaced by the second-generation Trac II razor (1971), followed by the Sensor (1990), Sensor Excel (1995), Mach3 (1998), Mach3 Turbo (2002), M3Power (2004), Fusion (2006), Fusion ProGlide (2010), and Fusion FlexBall (2014).

Figure 7. Extending the Product Life Cycle Through Innovation[7]

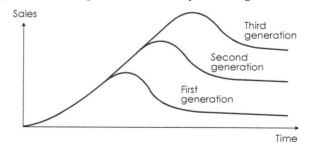

There is a common misconception that succeeding product generations should be more complex and offer more features than the ones they are replacing. This is not always correct. Even though enhancing already existing product attributes and adding new ones can increase the attractiveness of the product for customers, simplifying the product and removing some of its attributes to lower its price can also create customer value. The true criterion for the success of new products is their ability to create greater customer, collaborator, and company value than the current offerings.

Managing Product Obsolescence

Product obsolescence refers to a decrease in the availability of and/or the demand for the product, although its functionality has not decreased. Obsolescence often results in a company limiting or discontinuing the production, promotion, distribution, and support of the product. Based on how the product obsolescence came about, it can be either *involuntary* or *planned*.

Involuntary Obsolescence

Involuntary obsolescence happens when a particular product can no longer perform its core functions in a way that creates market value. Product obsolescence often stems from *technological advancements* that result in a better performing version of the same product. For example, the rapid development of microprocessor technologies and the continued increases in microprocessor capacity are constantly rendering prior generations of microprocessors completely obsolete. Other products that have become victims of technology developments include dot-matrix printers (replaced by ink-jet and laser printers), tape-based answering machines (replaced by digital answering machines), analog phones (replaced by digital phones), rotary phones (replaced by touch-tone phones), cassette tapes (replaced by CDs), and VCRs (replaced by DVDs).

Apart from these evolutionary changes in technology, product obsolescence can be caused by entirely new technologies that replace old ones. For example, the traditional cameras using photographic film, which were the dominant form of photography until the early 21st century, have been made obsolete by the emergence of digital cameras and by the advancements in image-processing software. Other products that have been rendered obsolete by the emergence of revolutionary technologies include the rolodex (replaced by personal digital assistants [PDAs] that were in turn replaced by smartphones), typewriters (replaced by computers), fax machines (replaced by a combination of smartphones and printers), dedicated MP3 players (replaced by smartphones and wearable multi-function devices), pagers (replaced by smartphones), dial-up modems (replaced by broadband routers), and printed phone directories (replaced by search engines and online phone directories).

Obsolescence can also occur when a product is no longer desirable because its design is outdated or its *style* is out of fashion. This type of obsolescence is particularly important in the fashion industry where tastes, styles, and designs can change virtually overnight, and fashion apparel and accessories often have a single-season life span. In this case, obsolescence is caused by consumers' desire to have a more current version of the product even though the new product is functionally equivalent to the older version. A particular feature of obsolescence in fashion is that it is rarely permanent; rather, it follows "fashion cycles" in which stylistically outdated products eventually regain popularity and cease to be obsolete. Examples of such in-and-out obsolete products include fedora hats, saggy and skinny jeans, cargo and harem pants, neon-colored accessories, and furs.

In addition to technological advancements and changes in customer preferences, obsolescence can be caused by changes in the *market context*. For example, increases in labor costs, scarcity and the high cost of raw materials and product ingredients, and high distribution costs can render some products obsolete because they are no longer profitable for their manufacturers. In the same vein, health and environmental regulations can lead to the obsolescence of certain products. For example, products containing the widely used insecticide DDT became obsolete after its worldwide ban for agricultural purposes. Likewise, air conditioners using a particular type of refrigerant (R-22) became obsolete after the Environmental Protection Agency prohibited the manufacture and installation of new appliances containing this ingredient.

Planned Obsolescence

Planned obsolescence occurs when a company intentionally shortens the longevity of its products. Planned obsolescence is particularly common in industries where technological advances have made it possible to design reliable and durable products with a life span that does not necessitate frequent replacement. There are three common types of planned obsolescence: *generation obsolescence*, *product obsolescence*, and *component obsolescence*.

- **Generation obsolescence** aims to make the earlier generation of products obsolete by reducing their functionality in order to transition users to the new generation. Generation obsolescence often involves designing new products in a way that makes prior generations inferior on key dimensions such as functionality, compatibility, and style. For example, to facilitate user migration to later versions of their software, companies systematically terminate support for earlier versions. In addition, the added functionality of the new generation of software often limits its backward compatibility; as a result, once the new software has been adopted by a critical mass of users, the earlier versions become obsolete because of their incompatibility.

- **Product obsolescence**, also referred to as built-in obsolescence, involves designing products so that they wear out or become obsolete at a particular point in time. Product obsolescence can also involve designs that artificially shorten the product's life span in order to force users to repurchase the product even when the new product has the same functional benefits. For example, a kitchen appliance manufacturer can design a refrigerator to last five years even when the cost of doubling its lifetime is relatively small. As a result, customers are likely to repurchase the prematurely obsolete products more frequently, thus increasing the manufacturer's revenues and profits.

- **Component obsolescence**, also referred to as value engineering, is another form of planned obsolescence that involves optimizing the performance of the individual components of the product for its expected lifetime. For example, from a cost perspective, it might not be feasible for a product to include a component that lasts much longer than the average life span of its other components. As a result, a company expecting its product to be obsolete within a given time frame might optimize costs by designing the durability of its components according to the expected product lifetime.

Companies use a variety of strategies to manage different types of obsolescence. *Generation obsolescence* is often driven by the emergence of new technologies that bring greater customer benefits and/or are more cost efficient and strategically important for the company. For example, Gillette's introduction of three-bladed (and later five-bladed) razors, which were designed to provide a superior shaving experience, contributed to the declining popularity of its two-bladed razors. *Product obsolescence*, on the other hand, reflects a company's efforts to design products that reflect customers' willingness to pay for durability and at the same time allow the company to achieve its monetary and strategic goals. For example, if customers are willing to pay only a fraction extra for a dishwasher that is expected to last twice as long as the industry average and yet costs twice as much to produce, a company might decide to forgo durability and design a dishwasher with a relatively short life span. Finally, *component obsolescence* is particularly relevant for products comprising multiple components, as it helps reduce costs by not overspending on components that would significantly outlast the life of the entire product. For example, a car manufacturer might deliberately shorten the life cycle of a vehicle's transmission to be in line with the life cycle of the car's frame, body, and engine.

SUMMARY

Product management aims to optimize the value that a company's products deliver to target customers and do so in a way that benefits the company and its collaborators. To this end, a company must identify the benefits that customers seek to receive from the company's offering and then translate these benefits into specific features and experiences that define the company's products.

Product development involves four key decisions: defining product functionality, designing the physical appearance of the product, delineating product guarantees and warranties, and creating the product packaging.

Defining *product functionality* involves a series of decisions concerning attributes such as performance, consistency, reliability, durability, compatibility, ease of use, and degree of customization. *Product design* typically involves decisions concerning the physical appearance of the offering, such as its size, shape, and structure. *Product guarantees and warranties* offer customers reassurance that the product will perform as described and promise some form of reparation should the product fail to meet expectations.

Packaging serves multiple functions that range from protecting the product during transportation and storage and offering product information to differentiating the company's product from that of the competition and promoting the product to potential buyers. The development of effective packaging follows four key principles: visibility, differentiation, value transparency, and consumption impact. When redesigning the packaging, managers must balance the desire to "refresh" the offering by dramatically modifying the packaging with the need for continuity, such that the package redesign does not disrupt sales to current customers.

Product lines comprise products that aim to address similar customer needs, typically in the context of the same category. Product lines that target different customer needs using distinct technologies are grouped into product portfolios. *Product platforms* provide the common architecture on which a group of products is built; they comprise a set of shared components, designs, technologies, and processes that can lead to a range of products based on the same core architecture but with varying features.

Managing the *product life cycle* involves optimizing the products as they progress through different stages in the marketplace: introduction, growth, maturity, and decline. Because the stages in the product life cycle are characterized by different market conditions, different stages require different marketing strategies. The two core approaches to extend the product life cycle are market expansion and product innovation. Market expansion can include increasing the frequency of usage among the current users of the product, promoting new uses for the product among current users, and discovering new markets for the product. Product innovation aims to identify customer needs that are not being fully met by the current products and develop alternative products to address these needs.

Product obsolescence refers to a purposeful decrease in the availability of and the demand for the product. Obsolescence often results in a company limiting or discontinuing the production, promotion, distribution, and support of the product. Based on how the product obsolescence came about, it can be either involuntary obsolescence, which occurs when a particular product can no longer perform its core functions in a way that creates market value, or planned obsolescence, which occurs when a company intentionally shortens the longevity of its products.

MARKETING INSIGHT: DESIGN THINKING

Traditionally, design has been viewed as a downstream aspect of the product development process, with the role of designers confined to enhancing an already developed idea or product to make it more attractive to customers. In contrast, design thinking gives designers a central role not only in optimizing an existing idea or product but also in the creation of ideas and products.

Design thinking articulates a set of principles fundamental to creating market value and achieving business success. These principles include a focus on understanding the functional and psychological aspects of customer needs, reliance on prototyping as a key means of product development, and the ability to transform early failures into opportunities for improvement and innovation. The pioneers of design thinking, David Kelley and Tim Brown of global design powerhouse IDEO, define design thinking as "a human-centered approach to innovation that draws from the designer's toolkit to integrate the needs of people, the possibilities of technology, and the requirements for business success."[8]

Design thinking broadens the view of functional product performance to encompass the overall customer experience. It bases product innovation on a thorough understanding of what types of products consumers want and need and what they like and dislike about the way products are made, packaged, marketed, sold, and supported. Thus, design thinking is not about brilliant people spontaneously generating new ideas but about finding hidden assumptions and ignored processes that can change the way a company does business.

Initially confined to product design, the concept of design thinking is now considered an integral part of customer-centric product development. Design thinking goes beyond aesthetics, seamlessly blending idea generation and product development to pair customers' needs with technologically feasible solutions. In this broader sense, the goal of design thinking is to identify a customer need that can serve as the basis for creating benefits for the customer and value for the company.

Design thinking can be thought of as a system that involves three overlapping processes: inspiration, ideation, and implementation. *Inspiration* involves defining the problem or uncovering the opportunity that motivates the search for solutions. *Ideation* is the process of generating, developing, and testing alternative ideas to solve the identified problem and take advantage of the market opportunity. Finally, *implementation* is the path that leads from the project stage to making the initial ideas a market reality.

From a strategic perspective, design thinking merges what is desirable from a customer's point of view with what is both technologically feasible and viable in terms of its ability to create company value. Thus, the concepts of desirability (creating customer value), feasibility (creating an actual offering), and viability (creating company value) are central to the concept of design thinking. The application of the concepts of desirability, feasibility, and viability in designing new offerings is discussed in more detail in Chapter 19.

MARKETING INSIGHT: BENEFIT VISIBILITY IN PRODUCT DESIGN

Not all aspects of the offering can be readily observed by customers. Some attributes are associated with greater levels of uncertainty and, as a result, their benefits are more difficult to evaluate than those of other attributes characterized by a greater level of transparency. Thus, based on the level of uncertainty associated with their performance, product attributes can be classified into one of three categories: *search*, *experience*, and *credence*.[9] These attributes are illustrated in Figure 8 and outlined in more detail below.

Figure 8. Benefit Visibility in Product Design

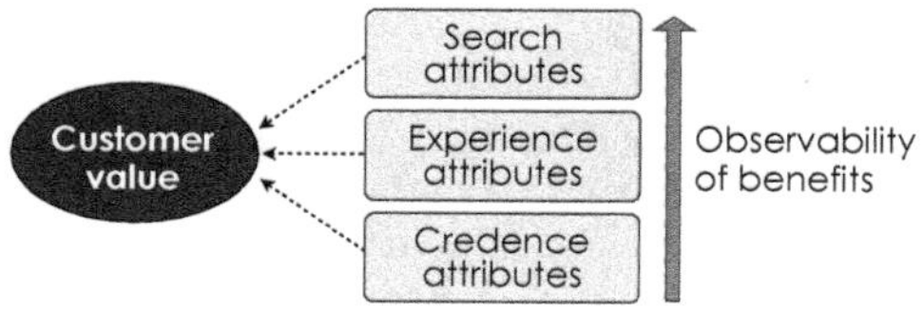

- *Search* attributes are associated with the least amount of uncertainty and are typically identifiable through inspection before purchase. For example, the size and shape of a toothpaste tube, the color of a car, and the type of cuisine offered by a restaurant are search attributes.

- *Experience* attributes carry greater uncertainty and are revealed only through consumption. For example, the flavor of a toothpaste, the comfort of a car, and the taste of a meal in a restaurant are experience attributes because their performance cannot be assessed by merely observing the offering.

- *Credence* attributes have the greatest amount of uncertainty, and their actual performance is not truly revealed even after consumption. For example, the cavity prevention benefits of a toothpaste, the safety of a car, and the calorie count of a restaurant meal are credence attributes because even after experiencing the offerings customers are unable to evaluate their performance.

In general, search attributes are more common for tangible offerings, whereas credence attributes are more typical for intangible offerings. Because services have more intangible properties relative to products, they are heavy on experience and credence attributes; in contrast, search attributes are more typical for products than services. Yet, in most cases both products and services are likely to be defined by attributes that have search, experience, and credence properties.

The distinction between search, experience, and credence attributes is important because it determines the way the product and service aspects of the offering should be communicated to potential buyers. Communicating search attributes is relatively straightforward and merely involves informing target customers about the properties of the company's products and services. Communicating experience attributes is more complex because simply informing buyers about the benefits of the offering is not enough; to fully understand the benefits of the offering buyers must experience it. As a result, products and services that are rich in experience attributes can benefit from product samples and free trials that allow consumers to appreciate the features of the offering. Finally, communicating credence attributes calls for ensuring that customers trust the company's promises. Such trust can be achieved by building a reputable brand that can support the company's claims about the unobservable performance of its products and services.

MARKETING INSIGHT: UNDERSTANDING PRODUCT PATENTS

A product patent for an invention grants an inventor "the right to exclude others from making, using, offering for sale, or selling"[10] this product. Technically speaking, a patent does not grant the patent owner the right to make, use, offer for sale, sell, or import, but the right to exclude others from doing so.

There are three basic types of patents: *utility patents* protect a new and useful method, machine, article of manufacture, or composition of matter, or any new and useful improvement thereof; *design patents* protect a new, original, and ornamental design for an item; and *plant patents* protect any distinct and new variety of an asexually reproduced plant.

A *utility patent* protects (1) methods, including business processes, computer software, and engineering methods; (2) machines, including anything that performs a function; (3) products, including anything manufactured; and (4) compositions of matter, including pharmaceuticals, chemical compounds, and artificial genetic creations. A utility patent cannot be obtained based on a mere idea: It is granted for an example of a new invention and not on the idea of the new invention. To receive a utility patent, an invention must be *useful*, *novel*, *non-obvious*, and *fully described*.

Utility patents require that an invention be actually *useful* or at least have a sound theoretical basis for being useful. The utility of the invention must be immediately apparent to a person of ordinary skill in the art. An invention totally incapable of achieving a useful result cannot receive a utility patent. Furthermore, the invention must be credible, meaning that it must be plausible in view of contemporary knowledge or it must be scientifically documented. For example, to be awarded a utility patent, the effectiveness of a drug must be scientifically documented.

Utility patents require that the invention be *novel*. An invention that has already been patented, described in a printed publication, in public use, on sale, or otherwise available to the public (e.g., an oral presentation at a scientific meeting, a demonstration at a trade show, a lecture or speech, a website, online video, or other online material) cannot be patented. Thus, publishing a detailed description of a new invention without patenting it can prevent others from being able to patent the invention (a practice referred to as defensive publication).[11]

Utility patents require that the invention be *non-obvious*. An invention is considered non-obvious if it appears sufficiently different from other inventions described in the past to a person having ordinary skill in the area related to the invention. For example, inventions that differ merely in color or size from inventions described in the past are ordinarily not patentable.

Utility patents require that the invention be *fully described*, such that it enables people of ordinary skill in the relevant field to understand what the invention is, to reproduce it, and to use it without engaging in further experimentation. The full disclosure requirement is a "quid pro quo" that gives the public detailed information in exchange for being excluded from making or selling the invention for the duration of the patent.

A *design patent* involves the ornamental or aesthetic aspect of an article of manufacture. A design patent may include three-dimensional features such as the shape of the product, or two-dimensional features such as patterns, lines, or color. To be legally protected, the design should not be purely functional, and its ornamental/aesthetic features should not be imposed by the technical functions of the product. Unlike a utility patent, a design patent is primarily aesthetic in nature; it protects only the product's appearance and does not protect any technical aspects of the product to which it is applied (which, in turn, can be protected by a utility patent).

Patents are granted for a fixed time period. In the United States, the term for utility patents is 20 years from the earliest filing date of the application on which the patent was granted. For design patents the term is 14 years from the issue date. In the United States, patent application is made exclusively to the United States Patent and Trademark Office, a federal agency in Washington, DC.

Chapter Ten

Managing Services

There is no such thing as service industries. There are only industries whose service components are greater or less than those of other industries. Everybody is in service.
— Theodore Levitt, marketing educator

Service management aims to optimize the value that a company's services deliver to target customers and do so in a way that enables the company and its collaborators to achieve their goals. Managing services—in concert with managing products and brands—aims to define the value the company's offering will create for target customers. The key service decisions are the focus of this chapter. Specifically, we address the following topics:

- *Service Management as a Value-Creation Process* ‖ Service as a tool for creating market value | The service aspects of an offering
- *Key Service Decisions* ‖ Defining service functionality | Delineating service guarantees and warranties | Designing the physical context of service delivery
- *Delivering Superior Services* ‖ Creating market value through superior service | Managing employee performance | Building a service-oriented company culture
- *Managing Service Recovery* ‖ Identifying service failures | Addressing service failures

The discussion of service management is complemented by an in-depth overview of two additional topics: the gap model of service quality and a systematic approach to managing dissatisfied customers.

Service Management as a Value-Creation Process

Service is an important aspect of a company's offerings. The role of services as a key source of customer value has increased in recent years as many companies including Adobe, Apple, and Microsoft have transitioned from predominantly product-based to more service-oriented offerings. Rather than selling its software outright, these companies have begun renting their software to customers using the software-as-a-service strategy. This shift toward services is, in part, driven by companies' desire to enhance the value customers derive from their offerings as well as to better connect with customers and ensure a superior user experience, greater satisfaction, and deeper loyalty.

Service as a Tool for Creating Market Value

Similar to products, services are goods designed to create value in the marketplace. Service is one of the seven attributes defining the company's offerings. Working together with the other marketing tactics defining the offering—product, brand, price, incentives, communication, and distribution—the service aims to create value for the relevant market entities: the company, its customers, and its collaborators (Figure 1). In this context, a manager's ultimate goal is to design services that create superior value for target customers in a way that benefits the company and its collaborators.

Figure 1. Service Management as a Value-Creation Process

To ensure that the service aspect of the offering creates market value, a manager must address three key questions:

- *Does the service create superior value for target customers relative to the competition?*

- *Does the service create superior value for the company's collaborators relative to the other options these collaborators might pursue?*

- *Does the service create superior value for the company relative to the other alternatives available to the company?*

An affirmative answer to these questions implies that the service has an optimal value proposition (OVP) that creates value for target customers, the company, and its collaborators. The development of a meaningful optimal value proposition is the overarching principle guiding all service decisions. To this end, a company must identify the benefits that customers seek to receive from the company's offering and then translate these benefits into specific service features and experiences in a way that enables the company and its collaborators to achieve their goals.

The Service Aspects of an Offering

Products and services are closely related and share a number of commonalities, which sometimes makes it difficult to draw a clear distinction between them. At the same time, there are several distinctive characteristics that separate products from services. The three main differences are: *ownership, separability,* and *variability.*

- **Ownership.** Unlike products, which typically change ownership (from the seller to the buyer) during purchase, services do not usually involve a change in ownership; instead, the customer acquires the right to use the offering and receive its benefits within a given time frame. For example, travel, hospitality, and professional services deliver their benefits to target customers without providing permanent legal entitlement to the underlying goods.

- **Separability.** Unlike products, which can be physically separated from the manufacturer and distributed by a third party, services are usually delivered and consumed at the same time. Inseparability makes services difficult to inventory—an important consideration in industries such as airlines, hotels, and call centers, where companies with a fixed service capacity face fluctuating customer demand. In such industries, yield management—optimizing the balance of supply and demand—is of utmost importance to ensure customer satisfaction and enable service providers to achieve their goals. For example, an airline can raise prices at times of peak demand and offer sales promotions to stimulate demand in off-peak times.

- **Variability.** Services are characterized by greater variability in performance than products, meaning that service delivery is more likely to vary across different occasions. Indeed, the human element in service delivery makes it difficult to standardize. As a result, service quality varies across service occasions depending on the type of customer, the particular service provider, and the interaction between the service provider and the customer. To illustrate, different customers might receive varying levels of service from the same service provider, and the same service provider might have different interactions with different customers depending on their specific needs and behavior.

Many offerings comprise a combination of products and services. For example, even mundane products such as toothpaste, soap, and milk are accompanied by a service provided by retailers carrying these products, including sales support and returns. More complex products such as cars, consumer electronics, and household appliances are augmented with technical support, delivery, and repair services. At the same time, many services include product components. For example, airlines offer meals, snacks, and drinks; hotels offer toiletries; and car rental companies provide customers with temporary use of automobiles.

Key Service Decisions

Designing the service component of a company's offerings involves three types of decisions: Defining the functional aspects of the service, delineating service guarantees and warranties, and defining the physical context of service delivery. These three aspects of service design are outlined in the following sections.

Defining Service Functionality

The attributes defining service functionality are similar to those defining the functional aspects of the company's products. Thus, creating and managing services involves a series of decisions concerning factors such as *performance, consistency, reliability, compatibility, ease of use*, and *degree of customization*.

- **Performance** reflects the key functional aspects of the service. Key performance dimensions include service quality—that is, the degree to which the service can fulfill the core needs of its target customers—and service speed, which reflects the temporal dimension of the service delivery. For example, in the case of professional services, performance can be defined in terms of the quality of the service (legal advice, tax preparation, medical treatment) and the expediency with which the service was delivered.

- **Consistency** reflects the degree to which a company can deliver the same quality of service over time. Because variability is a key characteristic of service, consistency is of vital importance in service delivery and one of the main contributors to the success of companies such as McDonald's, Starbucks, and Ritz-Carlton. Because consistent performance makes future service outcomes more predictable, consistency is a key prerequisite for building a strong service brand.

- **Reliability** refers to the degree to which a service is likely to be delivered according to its specifications. Reliability is often used as a differentiating point to create a unique positioning for a company's services. For example, FedEx promises "absolutely, positively overnight" delivery service, discount brokerage TD Ameritrade guarantees that certain trades will be executed within five seconds, and Verizon claims to be the most reliable wireless network in the United States, with a call-completion rate of more than 99.9%.

- **Compatibility** refers to the degree to which a service is consistent with already existing standards and complementary offerings. Compatibility is particularly important in networked environments incorporating multiple services from different providers that must interact with one another to deliver a seamless user experience. Compatibility is also important in the case of technology-enabled services that are associated with frequent service modifications and updates that require a smooth transition between the current and the new version of the service. For example, a video streaming service must be compatible with the hardware and software of the device on which it is displayed. In the same vein, different apps must be compatible with the software platform on which they will operate.

- **Ease of use** reflects the amount of cognitive, emotional, and physical effort involved in using a particular service. Easy-to-use services tend to enjoy faster adoption and a more loyal user base because customers might be unwilling to invest the extra effort to switch to competitors offering a more complex service. As in the case of products, a greater number of service options does not always lead to greater customer satisfaction, especially in cases when customers lack the knowledge necessary to utilize these options. For example, Quicken Loans, the largest retail lender in the United States, promotes its Rocket Mortgage services as the easiest and the fastest in the industry. In the same vein, GEICO, one of the largest U.S. auto insurers, emphasizes the ease of receiving an insurance quote.

- **Degree of customization** reflects the degree to which a company's services are personalized to address the needs of each individual customer. Service customization can be contrasted to a scenario in which customers are offered the same type and level of service regardless of their needs and preferences. Customization can be achieved by creating a service that perfectly fits a customer's needs as well as by providing a menu of options to enable customers to tailor the service to their own needs. For example, a news provider might use customers' behavior to infer their preferences and offer news programming that fits those preferences or, alternatively, it might let customers self-select the news they would like to receive. Overall, customization tends to increase perceived service quality, customer satisfaction, and ultimately customer loyalty to the service provider.

Delineating Service Guarantees and Warranties

Service guarantees reflect an assurance that a service will be delivered as promised by the company and expected by customers and that the company will offer some form of compensation in the event the service is found lacking. Guarantees create value for customers by reducing the functional and monetary risk associated with using the service. Guarantees further create customer value by adding credibility to the company's claims and delineating the process of addressing eventual service failures. In addition to creating customer value, guarantees can benefit the company by sharpening its focus on the customer experience, establishing accountability and facilitating the development of performance standards, and offering guidelines for recovering from service failures.

As in the case of products, service guarantees can involve customers' overall satisfaction or satisfaction with a specific attribute of the service. Overall satisfaction guarantees apply to any aspect of the service experience, regardless of whether it stems from the actual quality of the service or customer assessment of the service quality. For example, hotels such as Radisson Blu, Hampton Inn, and Fairfield Inn offer a 100% satisfaction guarantee that their guests will be pleased with their stay. In the same vein, many retailers such as Amazon, Nordstrom, and Neiman Marcus guarantee customer satisfaction with the shopping experience and offer a "no questions asked" return policy on most of their items. Service guarantees might also concern a specific attribute of the service such as speed, duration, functional performance, and monetary gain. For example, for many years Domino's Pizza offered its "30 minutes or it's free" guarantee (which was later replaced with an overall satisfaction guarantee to alleviate the concerns that the half-hour guarantee promoted reckless driving on the part of the delivery drivers).

Service warranties differ from guarantees in two basic ways: They are usually associated with a correction or replacement of the purchased service (rather than a refund) and may involve additional payments (unlike guarantees, which are always free). Accordingly, service warranties are particularly relevant in cases when the delivered service can be rectified (rather than refunded). For example, services involving repair and maintenance of purchased items often offer warranties promising to address defects in materials and workmanship after the original manufacturer's warranty has expired. Service warranties may also cover loss or damage not covered under the original manufacturer's warranty.

Designing the Physical Context of Service Delivery

Unlike products, which in most cases have physical properties, services are largely intangible and do not have physical attributes. In this context, one might assume that packaging as a marketing concept does not apply to services. This is not the case. Although services are intangible, the process of service delivery involves tangible components, sometimes referred to as *servicescape*. For example, FedEx uses airplanes and trucks to deliver packages, Marriott offers hospitality services through its hotels, and 7-Eleven retails convenience products in its vast network of franchisee-operated stores. In the same vein, theme parks are the physical environments in which Disney delivers its magic and creates memorable experiences.

The packaging of services typically refers to the physical environment in which services are delivered as well as the ancillary tangible components of the service delivery. For example, the building of a financial services company, a doctor's office, and a movie theater can be viewed as the package in which the service is being delivered. Following this line of reasoning, the U.S. Supreme Court ruled that the décor of a chain of Mexican restaurants, described as "a festive eating atmosphere having interior dining and patio areas decorated with artifacts, bright colors, paintings and murals" de facto plays the role of service packaging and should be treated as such when it comes to trademark issues.[1]

The fact that services are largely intangible, variable, and experiential in nature (meaning that they are difficult to observe prior to being consumed) makes it more challenging for companies to describe and differentiate their services. Indeed, for many physical products, buyers can draw quality and performance inferences based on their readily observable attributes. In contrast, in the case of services, buyers are often faced with a much greater level of uncertainty because of the scarcity of physical cues from which to draw inferences. As a result, companies must seek ways to offer physical evidence that will inform buyers about the key aspects of their services. This physical evidence is often provided by the tangible elements of the service delivery.

The physical aspect of the service delivery can play a key role in creating market value. Augmenting the service with tangible attributes can benefit the company by enhancing buyers' confidence in the offering. For example, financial institutions aim to convey strength by embedding their services in a physical environment—including the exterior of the building, design of the lobby and reception area, the furnishings, and employee uniforms—that projects stability and permanence. In addition, some companies use symbols that aim to "tangibilize" the intangible aspects of their offerings. To illustrate, Prudential's logo features the Rock of Gibraltar to symbolize financial stability, ING's logo features a lion to signal strength, and Expedia's logo substantiates its services by featuring an airplane flying around the globe.

Delivering Superior Services

Delivering stellar service is at the heart of any customer-centric organization. Service quality is a powerful differentiator that can meaningfully distinguish the company's offerings from the competition and create superior value for customers and the company.

Because services are characterized by great variability stemming from their delivery by employees with varying levels of motivation and expertise, service outcomes are difficult to standardize in a way that ensures superior service quality across all customers and occasions. As a result, understanding and streamlining the processes by which a company can consistently deliver excellent customer service is crucial to a company's ability to generate value for its customers, collaborators, and stakeholders.

The ways in which a company can create market value through superior service, the core principles of managing employee performance, and the process of building and enhancing the company culture are discussed in the following sections.

Creating Market Value Through Superior Service

The key to designing a service-focused organization is understanding that delivering superior service creates value not only for the company's customers but that it is also a key driver of the company's own success. "A business absolutely devoted to service will have only one worry about profits," advocated Henry Ford. "They will be embarrassingly large." To succeed in today's competitive market, a company must harness the power of customer service as a source of creating market value and a tool for competitive differentiation. Customer focus and the ability to deliver superior customer service must become a core competency for any company that aims to achieve market success.

A well-designed service strategy can lead to a virtuous cycle that serves as an engine to create value. This cycle begins with selecting the right employees, providing these employees with adequate training, and motivating them to deliver excellent customer service. Trained, motivated employees are competent at doing their jobs and are content and satisfied with their work and being a part of the company. Competent employees that enjoy their work are, in turn, likely to deliver high-quality service that creates customer value by meeting and exceeding customer needs and expectations.

Customers who are satisfied and delighted with the company's service tend to stay loyal to the company and shift more of their business to the company. Greater customer loyalty means that the company receives greater revenues from its customers while having to spend much less than usual on customer retention, which translates into greater company profitability. As a result of this cycle, the company is able to reinvest some of the profits into hiring, training, and retaining skilled employees, enabling it to continue delivering superior customer value and sustain customer loyalty (Figure 2).

Figure 2. Creating Market Value Through Superior Customer Service

Managing employees—from selecting the right people to ensuring that they deliver superior service—is at the heart of creating customer value and company profits. "If you take care of your employees, your employees will take care of your customers, and your customers will take care of your shareholders," maintains the founder of Virgin Group, Richard Branson. The key role that company employees play in creating market value underscores the importance of building a customer-focused employee culture and developing actionable strategies for managing employee performance. These issues are addressed in more detail in the following sections.

Managing Employee Performance

Superior customer service is the result of deliberate design of the service-delivery process and the painstaking implementation that translates this design into reality. A crucial component of this process is managing the performance of employees whose job is to ensure that the company delivers the service it has promised its customers.

Managing employee performance starts with *recruiting* the right employees, followed by a process of *training* these employees, providing them with the *information* they need to address customers' needs, offering a meaningful incentive structure to *motivate* employees to deliver quality service, *empowering* employees by delegating decision-making responsibilities to them, *monitoring* their performance to ensure consistent service quality, and ultimately developing a company *culture* that helps create and reinforce a customer-centric attitude as a norm of behavior among employees. The key components of managing employee performance are illustrated in Figure 3 and discussed in more detail below.

Figure 3. Managing Employee Performance

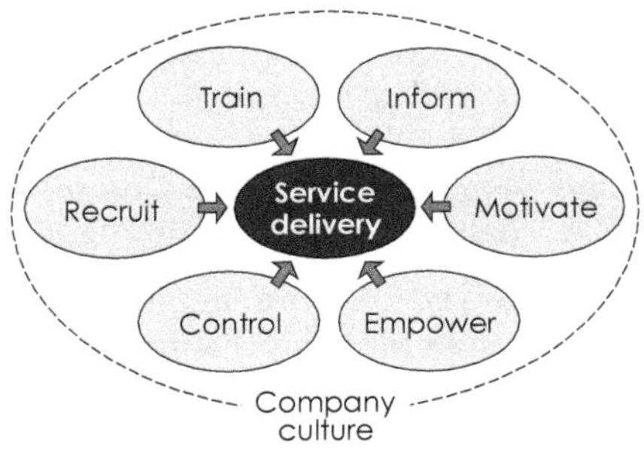

Recruiting Employees

Because services typically involve direct interaction between the company employees and customers, the process of delivering superior customer service begins with the selection of employees who are both capable and motivated to delight the company's customers. Given the importance of front-line employees in shaping a customer's experience, service companies often use a structured process to evaluate candidates and identify the best people for the job. In this context, the criteria on which potential employees are typically evaluated can be classified into three categories: *core skills*, *company fit*, and *relevant experience*.

- **Core skills** are those abilities needed to deliver superior customer service. This skill set includes multiple competencies. *Creativity* refers to a person's ability to come up with an original approach that offers a simple solution to a complex problem. *Teamwork* reflects a person's ability to collaborate with others, both within a team and across the entire company. *Communication skills* reflect a person's ability to express ideas clearly, accurately, and succinctly and to effectively share information. *Analytical skills* reflect an individual's ability to use logical reasoning and common sense. *Capacity to learn* reflects a person's ability to improve performance and acquire new skills. *Drive* includes a person's motivation to achieve, energy level, and perseverance; it reflects a willingness to overcome barriers and go outside one's comfort zone to achieve the set goals. *Management skills* reflect a person's professional poise, as well as the ability to meet deadlines, manage multiple tasks, coordinate different projects, and perform under pressure. *Leadership* reflects a person's ability to seize opportunity and take action, build a team and encourage a shared vision, keep a clear focus on the ultimate goals, and show a willingness to take a personal risk to achieve these goals. Different service roles typically require a different mix of core skills that reflect the primary responsibilities of company employees.

- **Company fit** reflects the degree to which an employee's individual characteristics fit the company profile. *Personality fit* refers to the degree to which an employee's personality fits the company's culture and makes this person enjoyable to work with. *Commitment to the company* reflects the degree to which the prospective employee is really interested in the company. Finally, *interest in the functional area* refers to an employee's interest in a particular service domain such as sales assistance, problem resolution, and technical support. The greater the fit between an individual's interests and the job requirements, the better the chance that this individual will make a valuable contribution to the company.

- **Relevant experience** reflects the degree to which perspective employees already have service-delivery training either in the same or a related industry. Companies operating in a global context might also look for specific characteristics such as language skills and knowledge of the local culture, traditions, and behaviors. Although important, the relevant experience can also be acquired on the job, especially if employees have an innate capacity to learn. Thus, compared to the other two criteria—core skills and company fit—having relevant experience might not be the primary factor in hiring new service employees.

After it has found the right employees, a company must persuade them to join its ranks—a task that can be challenging in cases of experienced and highly skilled candidates. In general, a company's ability to recruit competent employees depends on three factors: *financial compensation*, including base salary and performance bonuses; *nonmonetary benefits* such as working conditions, availability of flexible work schedules, vacation time, and health insurance; and *self-fulfillment benefits* such as moral satisfaction from creating societal value and gaining a sense of achievement, personal growth, and professional development.

Company culture and reputation can play an important role in the hiring and retaining of skilled employees. Employees often place a premium on working for companies whose brands resonate with their own needs, preferences, and value system. As a result, companies with strong reputations find it easier to attract talented employees and keep these employees from leaving. In fact, employees are sometimes ready to accept a lower salary to work for a company with a culture consistent with their own value system.

Training Employees

Even though companies aim to recruit qualified personnel, in most cases new employees need to be informed about the specifics of their job requirements, familiarized with the workflow within their team and the company, and immersed in the company culture. In addition to introducing new employees to their responsibilities within the company, training programs can also promote personal growth by helping employees overcome deficiencies in their skill set and enhance their strengths. Specifically, professional training programs might focus on four distinct sets of skills: *technical, communication, teamwork,* and *management and leadership*.

- **Technical training** focuses on building skills that enable employees to successfully perform their day-to-day responsibilities. For example, a salesperson must be familiar with the merchandise they are offering, know how to implement financial transactions, and be aware of the company's customer service policies. A front desk employee at a hotel must be aware of the room inventory, know how to use reservation and payment systems, be able to manage customer requests, and be familiar with the hotel's general rules and procedures.

- **Communication training** involves strengthening an employee's ability to interact with customers as well as with the other members of their team. This training might focus on the employee's ability to listen to customers and read between the lines to understand their underlying motivation, needs, and wants. In addition, it should develop and enhance their ability to read customers' verbal intonation and body language. An increasingly important component of communication training is developing employees' *emotional intelligence*—their ability to recognize customers' feelings and use this information to guide their own thinking and behavior. This skill often entails the need for employees to harness and manage their own emotions in order to deliver superior customer service.

- **Teamwork training** focuses on enhancing employees' ability to collaborate with others, both within their team and across the entire company. Teamwork training starts with impressing upon employees the importance of working as a team and the benefits of collaboration. Thus, to promote teamwork and foster a spirit of cooperation rather than competition, companies often underscore that the ultimate goal of the organization is to deliver superior customer service and that this goal can be best achieved by the coordinated efforts of all employees working as a team. It is also important for employees to understand that teamwork not only helps coordinate individual efforts to achieve greater effectiveness and efficiency, but that it also can serve as a support network to facilitate the solving of logistical problems and help alleviate the stress and frustration that often arise in service jobs.

- **Management and leadership training** involves strengthening employees' ability to multitask, meet deadlines, and perform under pressure, while fostering their aptitude to take initiative, build a team, and guide that team toward a common goal. To this end, a company might initiate management and leadership training programs designed not only to build and enhance these skills among its employees but also to identify and prepare the next layer of service managers. Indeed, many companies prefer to develop their own service management cadre that is already familiar with the company and its personnel rather than hire external service managers who first need to be trained and whose fit with the company and its culture is much less certain.

Professional training can be carried out using different formats. Formal training programs provide employees with relevant information organized in a structured format and presented in a way that makes it easy to understand and internalize. In addition to formal training programs, both formal and informal mentoring programs play an important role in employee training by providing guidance on how to behave in specific situations, some of which might not be covered in the training programs. In this context, providing an environment that is conducive to on-the-job training, apprenticeship, and mentoring is a key ingredient in building a service-oriented organization.

Informing Employees

To effectively deliver superior customer service, employees must have at their fingertips the data necessary to inform them about customers' needs and preferences, the nature of the problem they are currently facing and the remedies at the company's disposal to address this problem, as well as the value that the customer brings to the company. Providing front-line employees with timely and relevant information is essential to their ability to satisfy and delight customers.

The difficulty with this approach lies in its implementation. In many companies, customer data reside in different departments. As a result, accessing it in a timely fashion presents both a logistical and organizational challenge. From a logistical standpoint, integrating legacy databases and creating a streamlined, user-friendly interface can be very costly and time consuming, and pose both technological risks and organizational challenges. At the same time, companies are often reluctant to give rank-and-file employees access to the company's databases in order to protect customer information for reasons of privacy and competitive advantage. In addition, some managers might feel that sharing their data with other departments might reduce their area of influence within the company.

Informing employees can involve three main types of information: (1) information about customers' needs and preferences to help employees deliver better service to these customers, (2) information about customers' touch points with the company to help ensure consistency of the delivered service, and (3) information about the lifetime value of individual customers to help prioritize customers based on their value to the company. To gather this information and furnish it in a timely manner to customer service representatives, companies use market research and data analytics to develop customer relationship management programs designed to provide up-to-date, customer-specific data that can facilitate the service-delivery process. The development of customer relationship management systems is discussed in greater detail in Chapter 20.

Empowering Employees

Empowering employees means shifting the decision-making power from management to front-line personnel. Depending on the nature of the company and the industry in which it operates, employee empowerment can be implemented in a variety of ways. For example, The Ritz-Carlton has instituted a policy that the first employee who encounters a customer's problem "owns" the problem until it is resolved. To this end, The Ritz-Carlton sees to it that everyone—not just the senior management—has $2,000 per day per guest to fix or improve a guest's experience. As one senior account executive at The Ritz-Carlton explains, "Employee empowerment means being able to use my natural ability to create a lasting memory for guests or resolve a guest issue and have the confidence that my company supports me 100% in my effort."[2]

Empowering employees can enhance service quality in multiple ways. First, it can lead to a faster resolution of customer problems since empowered employees can make a decision on the spot without involving a higher level of management. Empowerment can also lead to a more effective resolution of a customer's problem. Indeed, the problems faced by customers can often be addressed by a variety of possible solutions that customers might be unaware of or might be reluctant to use. In this context, being able to directly interact with customers enables empowered employees to identify the outcome that is likely to be optimal from customers' point of view.

Empowering employees can further increase the efficiency of the organization by cutting down on intra-office communication and shortening the approval-granting process. Another benefit of empowerment is that it delegates responsibility to employees, which can make them feel more engaged, motivate them to perform their jobs more effectively, and increase their overall satisfaction at working for the company. Finally, a company's ability to quickly identify and solve a customer's problem not only can lead to greater customer satisfaction and loyalty but can also become a reputation-builder for the company as customers share their experience with others.

The multiple benefits of employee empowerment come at a cost. Shifting the responsibility for resolving customer problems from managers to front-line employees requires that these employees be diligently selected, trained, and motivated. Indeed, as much as instant resolution of a problem can delight customers, mishandling a problem can escalate customer dissatisfaction with the company and negatively affect the company's image and reputation. Employee empowerment can also lead to greater service variability as different employees might use different standards to assess the nature of a customer's problem and vary in their ability to identify the optimal solution.

Another important consideration in empowering employees is the potential misalignment of employee incentives and the company value involved in deciding how to address a customer's problem. Problems can arise when employees seek to ingratiate themselves with customers by being overly generous when resolving the customer's problem. As a result, the employees' solutions might turn out to be very costly for the company—a problem that can be exacerbated if some customers try to take advantage of the company's employee empowerment policy.

Given the pros and cons of employee empowerment, there is no simple formula for deciding whether, when, and to what extent to delegate problem-solving responsibilities to front-line employees. Developing clear guidelines for handling customer issues, providing examples of effective ways to prevent and handle customer crises, and building a customer-centric culture that encourages employees to see themselves as stakeholders in the company can help alleviate the potential drawbacks of employee empowerment and increase the effectiveness with which an organization is able to deliver superior customer service.

Motivating Employees

Informing and empowering employees is a necessary but often insufficient condition for allowing a company to deliver superior customer service. Indeed, even though some employees might be intrinsically motivated to do their best, not all employees will feel the same way. To motivate all employees and ensure that they are fully engaged in trying to delight customers, companies often implement incentive systems designed to reward employees who take to heart the company's customer service policies.

A company can reward its employees using three basic types of incentives: financial payments such as pay raises and bonuses, nonmonetary benefits such as days off and paid vacations, and psychological rewards such as recognition of accomplishments and achievement awards. In addition to offering rewards, a company can motivate its employees by building a customer-centric culture that makes the drive to delight customers the norm rather than the exception. Employee motivation can also be enhanced by having resources—cash payments, vouchers, free services, and bonus products—at their disposal to address a customer's problem. The availability of such resources is another way in which a company can signal to front-line employees the importance of their role as touch points between the company and its customers.

Developing a policy for motivating and rewarding employees requires companies to carefully balance the desire for excellence in teamwork and exemplary individual performance. Certain reward systems may encourage individual excellence but lead to competition among employees, which may cause some to concentrate on maximizing their own rewards without concern for other employees or the company. Other means of motivation encourage teamwork but give space for free riding, where less motivated employees benefit from the hard work of others. One approach to prevent self-serving behavior on the part of employees is to include them in the company vision. This can be accomplished by clearly articulating the company's aspirations and the goals it aims to achieve, delineating the role of each individual employee in achieving this goal, and treating all employees with respect and dignity.

Another important challenge in developing an effective set of policies that motivate employees to deliver superior customer service is identifying and implementing measurable performance benchmarks that adequately reflect employees' efforts to deliver customer satisfaction and build customer loyalty. Indeed, if the metrics that the company uses to assess employee performance are not well calibrated, they might have no impact on the value the company creates for its customers or, even worse, might end up being counterproductive, decreasing rather than increasing customer satisfaction.

To illustrate, consider the case of a high-end retailer that introduced a compensation policy to reward salespeople based on the sales volume they generated. The new system aimed to increase sales revenues by stimulating productivity and motivating employees to offer a greater level of service to their customers. Several months into the program, however, the retailer discovered that customer satisfaction had not increased but that the opposite had occurred: The satisfaction ratings showed a significant decline. What happened was that instead of helping customers find the merchandise they were interested in, many salespeople were now inclined to stay near the cash register because the new system rewarded the individual who recorded the sale rather than those helping customers make their selection.

Controlling Employees

Monitoring employee performance is important to ensure consistent delivery of superior customer service and identify and correct service breakdowns in a timely fashion. Service breakdowns can stem from a variety of factors such as the lack of employee engagement with the service, insufficient or inadequate training, as well as from misalignment of the employee and company incentives. Consider a customer service representative trying to appease an angry customer who calls to complain about the poor service she received from another employee. As soon as the service representative realizes that he is unlikely to be able to resolve the problem and might instead become the lightning rod for this customer's dissatisfaction, he might be tempted to hang up the phone and move on to the next call.

Monitoring employees' behavior can help a company achieve multiple goals such as assessing the service delivery, identifying skills gaps, providing training to overcome deficiencies, and rewarding outstanding performance. At the same time, enforcing accountability can help ensure that front-line employees follow the customer service guidelines prescribed by the company. In addition to ensuring a superior customer experience, employee monitoring also can help with loss prevention—an issue particularly relevant for employees dealing with money and high-value items.

To effectively monitor the service delivered by its employees, a company must develop internal service quality standards, policies, and guidelines that can be used as a benchmark for evaluating employee performance. To this end, a company can develop a service-quality dashboard that comprises the key performance indicators of successful service delivery and can serve as the basis for an internal service-quality audit.

To assess the quality of the service delivered by its employees, a company can gather data in various ways. A common service quality audit practice involves monitoring employee interactions with customers by routinely recording physical interactions, phone communications, online chats, and email correspondence. The use of data analytic tools such as natural language processing and sentiment analysis enables companies to readily identify potential issues that call for a more detailed analysis by the senior management.

Another popular approach involves the use of *mystery shoppers* — individuals hired by the company or an independent research firm to act as customers and provide detailed reports or feedback about their experience. The identities of "mystery shoppers" are not disclosed to front-line employees so that these shoppers can obtain a more objective picture of the service delivered to customers. Mystery shopping is common in service-oriented industries such as retail, hospitality, and financial services. Mystery shoppers are usually individuals with no affiliation to the company who are paid to report their interaction with company employees. However, it is not uncommon for top management to act as mystery shoppers to gain better insight into the customer service provided by their organization. For example, the founder of IKEA, Ingvar Kamprad, reportedly paid anonymous visits to different store locations around the world to ensure that they delivered a superior customer experience.

The customer service audit can also benefit by actively soliciting feedback from customers who have used the company's services as well as by developing direct channels that enable customers to spontaneously comment on the level of service they have received. Such direct feedback can help identify value-delivery gaps and suggest ways in which a company can improve its services. Customer feedback can also facilitate the development of more accurate performance measurement benchmarks by aligning the company's internal service-quality standards with customers' assessment of the actual service they received.

Building a Service-Oriented Company Culture

Selecting, training, informing, motivating, empowering, and controlling employees does not occur in a vacuum; it is influenced by the company culture that defines the environment in which the employees work. The culture captures the personality of the company and serves as a moral compass guiding the discretionary behavior of its employees. It sets the tone for employee behavior in nontrivial situations where the prescribed norms of behavior do not apply.

A service-oriented culture results from a concerted effort of both company management and employees. Building a meaningful company culture is guided by several factors. It starts with the beliefs held by the management about the company values and the types of behavior endorsed by the company. These management beliefs are then reflected in the company's service policy and used to guide the process of recruiting the right employees, defining the norms of employee behavior, and promoting teamwork. The key components of building a service-oriented company culture are outlined in Figure 4 and discussed in more detail below.

Figure 4. Building a Service-Oriented Company Culture

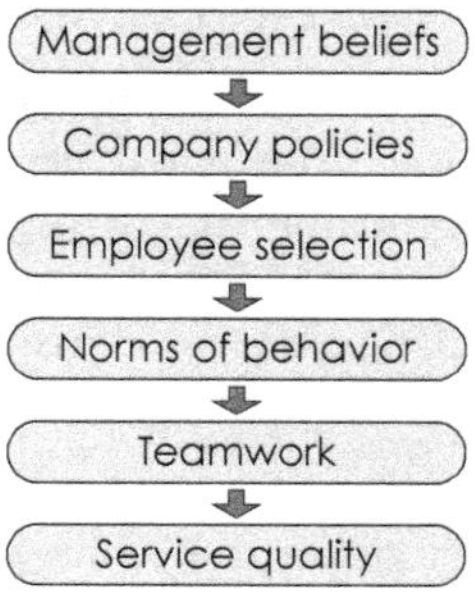

- **Management beliefs** define the set of values that guide the company; these values indicate the type of actions that are encouraged by the company and those that are discouraged. Management beliefs set the tone of the company culture and have a major impact on the way employees interact with customers. Managers that understand the importance of delivering superior service are likely to instill a customer-centric culture in their companies. For example, Amazon founder Jeff Bezos describes his view of the role of customer service in the company's business model as follows: "We see our customers as invited guests to a party, and we are the hosts. It's our job every day to make every important aspect of the customer experience a little bit better." This view has fostered a customer-focused culture that permeates all aspects of Amazon's business activities.

- **Company policies.** To be effective and have a lasting impact, management beliefs are formalized into a set of policies that outline the core values and principles that should guide the service-delivery process. In addition to outlining the overarching company beliefs, policies delineate how these beliefs apply in specific situations and how company employees are expected to behave when interacting with customers and with one another. Service policies address a variety of aspects of employee behavior, from the language used to refer to customers to the remedial actions needed in the case of service recovery. Because they are designed to direct employee behavior, effective policies should be: *comprehensive*, meaning that they should address all areas of employee interactions; *clear*, meaning that they should leave no ambiguity in their interpretation; and *actionable*, meaning that they should inform employees how to act in different situations.

- **Employee selection.** Because the culture resides with the company employees, employee selection can make or break the company culture. Accordingly, when making hiring decisions, service-oriented companies like Zappos, Southwest Airlines, and REI place utmost importance on the degree to which an employee's motivation, personality, and value system fit the company's culture. To this end, having a service-oriented culture — reflected in the company's value system, attitude toward customers and customer service, and its expectations of employee behavior — can greatly facilitate a company's ability to identify individuals that not only will fit the company's culture but will also help reinforce and elevate it.

- **Norms of behavior.** Even the best laid policies are useless unless they are internalized and followed by the company employees. Indeed, some companies have well-articulated policies designed to impart a service-oriented culture that exist only on paper and are largely ignored by employees. As new employees join the company, in addition to reading the company's written policies, they also observe the actual company culture as it is reflected in the norms of behavior that are deemed acceptable in the company's day-to-day activities. In this context, the unwritten norms of behavior that guide how employees act in situations not explicitly addressed by company policies are essential components in helping to shape the company culture.

- **Teamwork.** A company's culture is a shared experience that involves individual employees subscribing to a set of common values and norms of behavior. Because of its shared nature, a strong service culture almost by definition involves employee interaction and seamless teamwork. As an integral component of the company culture, teamwork benefits both customers and employees. Customers benefit from employees coming together to resolve customer problems and provide a better service experience. For employees, teamwork facilitates professional growth while offering an environment in which to enjoy social interactions, develop personal connections, and gain emotional support.

Consider Zappos, an online apparel retailer owned by Amazon and known for its outstanding customer service. Zappos prioritizes cultural fit when hiring new employees, and the cultural fit interview often carries half the weight in the hiring decision. Newly recruited employees spend their first month manning phones in the company's call center, learning how to interact with customers. Upon completion of their time in the call center, Zappos employees are offered $3,000 to leave the company — a strategy used to ensure that employees are committed to the company culture. To provide consistent customer service, Zappos does not hire temporary employees, so all employees are expected to sign up for shifts in the call center during the busy seasons. Call center employees are fully empowered to serve customers and do not have to ask for a manager's approval to address a customer's request. To build such a customer-centric culture, Zappos allocates a portion of its budget to team building. Managers at Zappos play a key role in fostering the company culture and are expected to spend up to 20 percent of their time on employee team-building activities.[3] Zappos' actions aim to ensure that every aspect of service delivery — from articulating management beliefs and setting service policies to recruiting employees, defining the norms of behavior, and fostering teamwork—are aligned with its strategic goal of delivering superior customer experience.

Managing Service Recovery

Service recovery refers to the actions taken by the company to address a service failure. Because variability is an inherent property of the service-delivery process, occasional failure is unavoidable. Thus, a company must have a well-articulated action plan to handle such lapses and minimize the chance of their reoccurring in the future. We address these issues in the following sections, where we focus on identifying and addressing service failures.

Identifying Service Failures

Service failure refers to a service-delivery process that substantially deviates from the company's standards of service in a way that fails to create customer value and leads to customer dissatisfaction. The term *service failure* is typically used in reference to occasional and atypical negative outcomes of the service provided by a company that aims to deliver superior customer service rather than to a consistent pattern of delivering inferior service by a company that lacks a customer service orientation.

Customer Reaction to Service Failures

Service failures and the way in which a company responds to such failures can have a profound impact on customer satisfaction, loyalty, and word of mouth. Service failures initially lead to a variety of negative emotions such as dissatisfaction, disappointment, discontent, anxiety, regret, and even anger. Depending on the way the company approaches the situation and the actions it takes (or does not take) to resolve the problem, customers' emotions can evolve, either turning more positive or becoming even more negative. Consistent with their emotional reaction, customers' behavior might vary from remaining loyal customers and even endorsing the company to leaving the company and discouraging others from using the company's services (Figure 5).

Figure 5. Customer Reaction to Service Failures

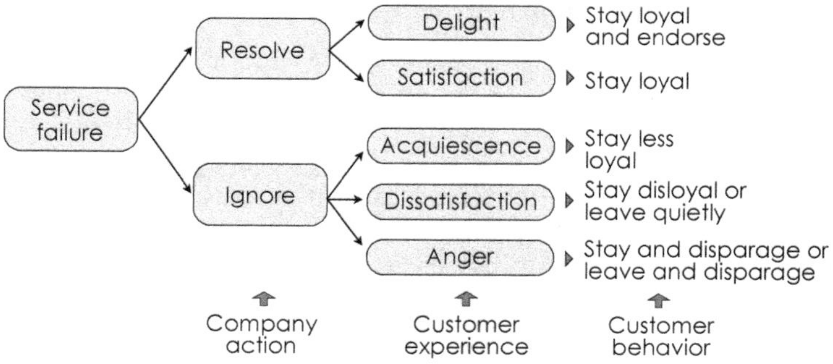

Customers who have complained about their service experience and have received a satisfactory resolution from the company are likely to remain loyal to the company. Some of them, especially those whose expectations were exceeded by the company's service recovery actions, not only stay loyal but also become company advocates, endorsing the company and promoting its services to others. In this case, successful service recovery is able to convert the negative emotions associated with the service failure into a positive assessment of the company's service recovery actions and an overall positive attitude toward the company.

Customers who have voiced their concerns but did not receive a satisfactory resolution from the company have two options: They can leave the company, or they can choose to stay despite the negative service experience. Those who decide to leave might do so shortly after the service failure or, alternatively, might have made up their mind to leave the company at an opportune moment (e.g., a competitive sales promotion). Those who stay might do so for a variety of reasons including inertia, high switching costs, and the lack of feasible alternatives. The fact that they stay with the company, however, does not mean that their attitude and behavior have changed. Many have become less loyal to the company and some might become vocal adversaries, actively pursuing opportunities to openly disparage the company. These customers are usually motivated by their resentment of the company's actions and its unwillingness or inability to address the service failure.

Finally, customers who have experienced service failure but have not complained are also likely to negatively respond to the service experience. They are likely to become less loyal, quietly leave the company, and perhaps even disparage the company in addition to no longer using its services. Among the common reasons why dissatisfied customers do not complain are the lack of time to file a complaint, the amount of effort required to file a complaint, and the lack of information about how to submit a complaint. Perhaps the most important reason for dissatisfied customers not voicing their concerns, however, is that many customers are conditioned to think that companies do not care about their feedback and, hence, they do not believe that their complaint will make a difference.

The fact that customers have not complained to the company does not mean that they will not complain about the company to friends, family, and acquaintances. Indeed, studies show that unhappy customers are much more likely to share their negative service experiences with others than customers who have been delighted by the company's service. The power of social media has made it much easier for customers to share their experiences while dramatically increasing their reach. The potential snowball effect of customer complaints has forced many companies to closely monitor customers' experience to address potential issues before they reach the public domain and to ensure consistent delivery of superior customer service.

Addressing Service Failures

Dealing with service failures involves two types of actions: managing customer dissatisfaction stemming from a service failure that has already occurred and modifying the company's customer management processes and policies to prevent the occurrence of service failures in the future. These two types of actions and the ways in which a company can use service failures to build customer loyalty are outlined in more detail below.

Managing Customer Dissatisfaction

Given that service failures are inevitable, managing dissatisfied customers is an unavoidable component of the service-delivery process. Because service-delivery outcomes stem from the interaction between customers with different needs and expectations and company employees with different skills and training, each service failure is likely to have a unique nuance and require a somewhat customized corrective approach. At the same time, there is a set of general service recovery principles that tend to apply across different industries, companies, and customers. These principles include *understanding the source of customer dissatisfaction, developing an effective course of action, quickly resolving the problem, informing customers about the service recovery process, accepting responsibility for the service failure,* and *fairly adjudicating the situation.*

- **Understand the source of customer dissatisfaction.** Customer dissatisfaction derives from the mismatch between the expected and delivered value during a service encounter. Accordingly, the source of customer dissatisfaction can be traced back to a company's inability to deliver on at least one of the three types of customer value: functional, monetary, and psychological. For example, customers might be frustrated because of the *functional* aspects of the service: the type of hotel room they are given, the delay of their flight, or the quality of a repair service they receive. Customers might also be displeased with the *monetary* aspects of the service, such as the overall cost, unexpected fees and surcharges, or the ways in which the payments have been processed. Finally, customers might be upset by the *psychological* aspects of the service, such as rude, ignorant, and unapologetic behavior from front-line employees;

unfair prioritization of some customers over others; and indifference of the management to customer issues. Understanding the underlying reason for customer dissatisfaction is crucial to a company's ability to remedy the situation because without knowing the cause of the problem, the solution might inadvertently exacerbate the issue rather than solve it.

- **Develop an effective course of action.** A company can take a variety of actions to address a service failure. These actions might involve functional benefits such as upgrading a hotel room, rebooking a more convenient flight, or replacing the defective product; monetary benefits such as offering free service vouchers, discounts, and cash payments; and psychological remedies such as offering apologies from both front-line employees and the management. The key principle when deciding how to respond to a service failure is that the company action should adequately address the source of a customer's dissatisfaction. It is often the case that managers attempt to address the problem without clearly understanding which aspect of the service failure is most important from a customer's perspective and which solution is most likely to satisfy this customer. For example, some customers who were dissatisfied with the room they were offered in a hotel might prefer a better room, others might prefer monetary compensation, and still others might prioritize an apology from the management that acknowledges the company's error and validates the customers' self-image by recognizing their importance to the company.

- **Quickly resolve the problem.** Developing the right course of action to address service failures is not the only factor influencing customer satisfaction. The speed with which the company responds to service failures can make a big difference in customers' response to the company actions. As a general rule, faster responses are more likely to lead to satisfactory outcomes from a customer's standpoint. The longer it takes a company to respond, the greater the customers' anxiety about the service failure, the higher their expectations about what the company should do to rectify the problem, and the more likely they are to escalate the problem by contacting multiple layers of company management as well as sharing the service failure with friends, acquaintances, and the media.

- **Inform customers about the service recovery process.** Customers dislike the uncertainty associated with a service failure as much as they dislike the service failure itself. For example, customers' dissatisfaction with a flight delay can be greatly reduced by informing them about the reason for the delay as well as the current flight status. Updating customers on the nature of the service failure and the progress of service recovery not only reduces customers' anxiety but also shows customers that the company treats them with respect and recognizes their importance to its business. In this context, transparency can go a long way to reduce customer dissatisfaction and minimize the negative aftermath of a service failure.

- **Accept responsibility for the service failure.** Not all service failures are caused by a company's actions. A number of external factors can contribute to a company's inability to deliver on its promise to customers. For example, hotel guests might have to spend a few hours in the dark because of a city-wide power outage, a flight might be delayed due to weather conditions, and a repaired product might fail because of a manufacturing defect unrelated to the performed service. External factors notwithstanding, service failures are most often caused by internal factors such as improperly balancing supply and demand, not developing streamlined service policies, and employing inexperienced front-line employees. In such cases, a company should consider accepting responsibility for the service failure as this shows respect and courtesy to its customers and increases the company's credibility in future customer interactions.

- **Fairly adjudicate the service failure.** Customers expect fairness in resolving service failures. A key factor that contributes to customers' assessment of outcome fairness is whether the company actions are equitable, meaning that the magnitude of the compensation should correspond to the customer inconvenience caused by the service failure. Although many companies believe that customers focus only on the degree to which they perceive the outcome of a service failure to be fair, this is not always the case. It is also possible for customers to be satisfied with a company's service recovery efforts even when the outcome is suboptimal, as long as they believe that the company followed a fair process to reach that outcome. This procedural fairness involves factors such as whether customers are treated in accordance with the company's policies, whether these policies were well articulated in advance, and whether these policies are customer-centric and have been designed to be equitable from a customer's viewpoint.

The conventional wisdom is that when managing dissatisfied customers, a company should aim to avoid customer attrition and minimize the potential damage to the company's reputation. An alternative, and often more fruitful, approach is to find the silver lining in the service failure and maximize the potential gains rather than focus solely on curtailing the losses. Companies should manage service failures not necessarily as a process of minimizing the threat of losing dissatisfied customers but as an *opportunity* to strengthen the loyalty of its existing customers and acquire new ones. Service recovery should focus on building customer loyalty, not just on reducing attrition.

Anecdotal evidence suggests that customers who experience outstanding service recovery following a service failure can be more satisfied and delighted with the company than if the service failure had not occurred to begin with. In other words, service failure followed by excellent service recovery can *increase* customer satisfaction and loyalty. The reason for this somewhat paradoxical outcome is that many customers understand that in most service situations mistakes are inevitable and will accept a mistake as long as the company is willing to correct it in a timely and fair manner. In this context, accepting responsibility and fixing the error as expediently as possible becomes a positive sign that resolves uncertainty about the company's behavior in the case of future service failure and informs customers that the company will take the necessary steps to ensure that their customers receive the best possible service.

When managing dissatisfied customers, it is important to balance the costs of addressing the source of customer dissatisfaction with the potential company benefits associated with resolving customers' complaints. Because customer experiences are idiosyncratic, it is likely that not every dissatisfied customer has a valid reason to be discontented with the company. Thus, some customers might have unrealistically high and/or different expectations about the service they receive from the company, the way a company should deal with a service failure, and how customers should be compensated for the service failure. Accordingly, a company might be better off "firing" customers whose expectations and demands it is unlikely to be able to fulfill.

Preventing Future Service Failures

In addition to managing dissatisfied customers, another aspect of addressing service failures involves implementing a set of policies and procedures to prevent service failures from happening in the first place. To this end, a company can utilize a number of strategies including *identifying service failures early on, actively soliciting customer feedback, learning from customer defections, anticipating future service failures, developing actionable service-recovery policies,* and *balancing supply and demand.*

- **Identify service failures early on.** Companies often realize that they have a service-delivery crisis when it is too late. One of the reasons is that management takes an action to remedy the problem only after a customer's complaint comes to their attention. The problem with this approach is two-fold. First, by the time the complaint reaches senior management, the service-delivery failure has already escalated. Second, and perhaps more important, many dissatisfied customers end up not complaining at all. Indeed, most customers usually do not complain after receiving unsatisfactory service. Moreover, of those who complain, the vast majority voice their complaints to front-line employees; only a very small percentage of dissatisfied customers make the effort to complain to senior management. As a result, the customer complaints that management is privy to are just the tip of the iceberg of unresolved customer grievances.

One popular approach to identify service failures involves monitoring publicly available customer communications such as social network interactions, blog posts, and website content. Using artificial intelligence, machine learning, and sentiment analysis, a company can process large volumes of relevant data to detect potential issues with its services, identify customers who voice concern about these issues, and reach out to these customers to better understand the problem and propose a solution. Another popular approach involves using mystery shoppers (discussed earlier) whose goal is to observe and report to senior management on the quality of service delivered by front-line employees.

- **Actively solicit customer feedback.** Companies vary in the degree to which they seek customer input. Some actively reach out to customers to find potential service deficiencies and identify areas for improvement. Others are less proactive, often shielding themselves from any form of inbound customer communication. At the heart of the company's decision on whether to solicit customer feedback and how much to solicit lies managers' understanding of the value of customer feedback. Indeed, gathering customer feedback comes at the cost of company resources—time, effort, and money—that have to be allocated to managing inbound customer communication. Companies that choose to actively seek customer feedback often treat the corresponding costs not as an expense but as a long-term investment in understanding customer needs and cultivating customer loyalty. These companies view complaining customers not as a nuisance that has to be dealt with but as an invaluable source of information indicating current and potential problems and often suggesting ways to circumvent these problems.

- **Learn from customer defections.** Even after defecting, customers can create value for the company by offering insights into the reasons that prompted them to stop using the company's services. Collecting this type of data is often challenging because many of these customers might be unwilling to further interact with the company. Yet these customers can offer valuable insights into the reasons for customer attrition as well as the measures that a company can take to decrease customer churn. One approach to gathering such insights involves offering monetary rewards to customers who participate in a survey that can be administered either by the company itself or by a third party that can be more impartial in collecting and analyzing the data.

- **Anticipate service failures.** Individual cases of service failure, almost by definition, are difficult to predict since failure often has unique antecedents and consequences. At the same time, there are situations in which service failures are more likely to occur. These scenarios include periods of unusually high demand, the launch of new services, changes in key service personnel, the introduction of new policies, and the implementation of new customer relationship management software. Although ultimately designed to improve the quality of customer service, these changes often lead to temporary disruptions in the service flow, greater variance in service quality, and a greater likelihood of service failures. Anticipating service disruptions allows a company to act preemptively to minimize customers' dissatisfaction with eventual service failures by informing them about the forthcoming changes, offering incentives during the time when service disruptions are most likely to occur, and training and empowering front-line employees to resolve service failures on the spot.

- **Develop actionable service-recovery policies.** Dissatisfied customers often complain on the spot to front-line employees, giving the company the opportunity to immediately address the issue. To be able to take advantage of this opportunity, however, a company needs to have a clearly defined service-recovery policy that informs employees how to handle service recovery and empowers them to resolve the problem. Without an actionable service-recovery policy, front-line employees are bound to push the problem up the chain of command, which in turn is likely to delay the company's response to the service failure. Moreover, the manager who will ultimately have to resolve the problem is likely to get a second-hand account of the situation and hence might not be familiar with the specific circumstances of the service failure and the source of customer dissatisfaction. As a result, not only is the company's response likely to be delayed; it also might not adequately resolve a customer's concerns.

- **Balance supply and demand.** One of the most common sources of service failures is a company's lack of capacity to fulfill customer demand at peak times. Indeed, because services are usually delivered and consumed at the same time, they cannot be inventoried, thus making it challenging for some companies to optimize the balance of supply and demand. To optimize the utilization of its resources, a company should be able to accurately forecast a variety of factors, such as the number of customers that will ultimately receive the service within the scheduled time frame (e.g., show up for a scheduled flight on time), the available facilities and equipment (e.g., the number of planes that are at a particular airport and have passed the technical inspection), and the number of qualified employees available to serve these customers (e.g., pilots who are at the same airport and have been cleared to fly the plane). Given the complexity of yield management in service delivery, forecasting errors are inevitable. Therefore, a company must make a tradeoff between the two possible types of errors: maximize capacity at the expense of a greater number of service failures or minimize the likelihood of service failures at the cost of lower efficiency of operations. The ways in which a company can resolve this tradeoff depends on its overall strategy: High-margin companies tend to prioritize the customer experience, whereas low-margin companies tend to prioritize operational efficiency.

When developing a strategy to prevent service failures, it is important to consider both the benefits and the costs of such a strategy. Statistically speaking, some percentage of service failures is inevitable. In this context, a company must determine the level of service consistency it aims to maintain and what degree of service failure it can tolerate in order to achieve its overarching goals. Thus, a mass-market company with a high-volume, low-margin profit formula might be set up to provide a lower level of service and, hence, be willing to tolerate a higher level of service failures. In contrast, a company with a low-volume, high-margin business might strive to deliver an impeccable service experience and, hence, be more focused on eliminating service failures altogether. In this context, aligning the service aspect of the company's offering with its overarching goal and value-creation model is paramount for achieving market success.

SUMMARY

Service management aims to optimize the value that a company's services deliver to target customers and do so in a way that benefits the company and its collaborators.

Services are defined by three main characteristics: *ownership, separability,* and *variability*. Unlike products, which typically change ownership (from the seller to the buyer) during purchase, services do not usually involve a change in ownership; instead, the customer acquires the right to use the offering and receive its benefits within a given time frame. Furthermore, unlike products, which can be physically separated from the manufacturer and distributed by a third party, services are usually delivered and consumed at the same time. Finally, services are characterized by greater variability in performance than products, meaning that service delivery is more likely to vary across different occasions.

Designing services involves three types of decisions: defining the functional aspects of the service, delineating service guarantees and warranties, and defining the physical context of service delivery. *Service functionality* defines the core benefits delivered by the service provider on attributes such as performance, consistency, reliability, compatibility, ease of use, and degree of customization. *Service guarantees and warranties* reflect assurance that a service will be delivered as promised by the company and expected by customers and that the company will offer some form of compensation in the event the service is found lacking. The *physical aspect* of the service delivery involves augmenting the service with tangible attributes in order to optimize the service experience and strengthen the offering's brand.

A key aspect of service delivery is managing the performance of a company's employees. *Managing employee performance* starts with *recruiting* the right employees, followed by a process of *training* these employees, providing them with the *information* they need to address customer needs, offering meaningful incentives to *motivate* employees to deliver quality service, *empowering* employees by delegating decision-making responsibilities to them, *monitoring* employee performance to ensure consistent service quality, and ultimately developing a *company culture* that helps create and reinforce a customer-centric attitude as a norm of behavior among employees.

A company's culture is an integral component of the service-delivery process. The culture captures the personality of the company and serves as a moral compass guiding the discretionary behavior of its employees. A *service-oriented culture* results from a concerted effort of both company management and employees. Building a meaningful company culture is guided by several factors: It starts with the beliefs held by the management about the company values and the types of behavior endorsed by the company. These management beliefs are then reflected in the company's service policy and used to guide the process of recruiting the right employees, defining the norms of employee behavior, and fostering teamwork.

Service recovery refers to the actions taken by the company to address a service failure. Dealing with service failures involves managing customer dissatisfaction stemming from a lapse in service that has already occurred and preventing the occurrence of service failures in the future. The key approaches to *managing customer dissatisfaction* include understanding the source of customer dissatisfaction, developing an effective course of action, quickly resolving the problem, informing customers about the service recovery process, accepting responsibility for the service failure, and fairly adjudicating the situation. The key approaches to *preventing service failures* include identifying service failures early on, actively soliciting customer feedback, learning from customer defections, anticipating future service failures, developing actionable service-recovery policies, and balancing supply and demand.

MARKETING INSIGHT: THE GAP MODEL OF SERVICE QUALITY

Designing and managing the service component of a company's offering can be greatly facilitated by identifying and circumventing service-delivery failures. To this end, a popular problem-solving approach to managing services is the gap model of service quality.[4] This model delineates the service-delivery processes, the key types of interactions defining these processes, and the inconsistencies (gaps) in a company's efforts to create customer value.

According to the service-gap model, customers' assessment of a service experience depends on their perceptions of the actual service delivered by the company and their expectations of what the service should be. These expectations are influenced by a variety of factors including the company communication, the word-of-mouth information about the service customers have received from various sources, the specific needs customers aim to fulfill with the service, as well as customers' prior experience with the company's service. The actual service delivered by the company, on the other hand, is determined by the way the company has designed its service-delivery process, which reflects the beliefs held by management about the level of service the company should deliver to its customers. The key components of the gap model of service delivery are illustrated in Figure 6.

Figure 6. The Gap Model of Service Quality[5]

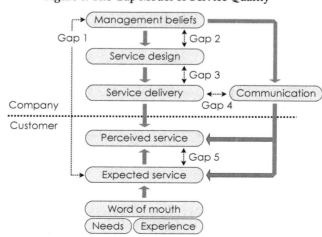

A key premise of the service-gap model is that there are five areas in which service-delivery failures, referred to as service gaps, are most likely to occur. Identifying and preventing these service breakdowns provide the foundation for developing a sound service-delivery process. The five commonly encountered service gaps are outlined in more detail below.

- *The market-insight gap* (Gap 1) reflects a discrepancy between customer expectations and management perceptions of what constitutes good service. To illustrate, the management of a fast-food chain might believe that customers prioritize the number of items on a menu, whereas in reality customers might be most concerned with the speed of service. Market-insight gaps often stem from poorly executed customer research, management's misinterpretation of the research findings, and a poor market strategy that targets customers with diverse (heterogeneous) needs and expectations.

- *The service-design gap* (Gap 2) reflects a discrepancy between management's perception of customer needs and the way these needs are translated into actionable service specifications. To illustrate, managers might know that speed of service is the most important factor for customers but have failed to establish clear policies to guide the behavior of front-line employees. Service-design gaps often stem from the inability of a company's management to translate market insights articulating specific customer needs and expectations into a set of standardized and actionable customer service policies. Service-design gaps can also result from a company's inability to balance supply and demand, such that it lacks the internal resources to meet customer demand while providing an adequate level of service.

- *The service-delivery gap* (Gap 3) reflects a discrepancy between the service-quality specifications and the actual service delivered. For example, despite the presence of well-articulated customer service guidelines and policies, employees might be unwilling or unable to perform to the level of service detailed by management. Service-delivery gaps often stem from deficiencies in recruiting, training, informing, and motivating employees. Furthermore, because service delivery is an interactive process, it also depends on customers' reaction to the service. Thus, service quality can be jeopardized by customers who fail to provide accurate information about themselves and their needs and preferences, refuse to follow the conventional norms of communication, or otherwise disrupt the service-delivery process.

- *The service-communication gap* (Gap 4) reflects a discrepancy between the communicated and the delivered service. This gap is created when the company's communications (advertising, public relations, and personal selling) misrepresent the service that customers will receive. For example, a fast-food chain might promise quick and friendly customer service without being able to deliver on its promise. Service-communication gaps often stem from a mismatch between the company's desire to promote its services to generate customer demand and its ability to actually deliver superior customer service. Communication gaps can range from relatively minor overpromising, with the company mildly exaggerating the benefits of its service, to a relatively dramatic (and potentially illegal) misrepresentation of its services, with little overlap between the promised and delivered service.

- *The service-expectation gap* (Gap 5) reflects a discrepancy between the expected and the perceived service. Because customer expectations influence their service experience, customers with different service expectations are likely to form different perceptions of the same service episode. Customers' service expectations are influenced by a variety of factors including their needs and preferences; their prior experience with the company and its services; communication from third-party sources including friends and family, media, and the company's competitors and collaborators; as well as the company's own communication.

Because it maps out the key aspects of the service-delivery process, the gap model is often used to perform service quality audits within the organization. To this end, a company would start by identifying the key steps in its service-delivery process, identify the areas in which service-delivery discrepancies might occur, test for the presence of actual service gaps, and, if needed, develop an action plan to close service gaps and streamline the service-delivery process. In this context, the service-gap model can be related to the customer decision journey map (discussed in Chapter 4), which also aims to identify the key steps in creating customer value. The key difference between these two approaches is that the customer decision journey map offers an overarching view of the value-creation process from a customer's perspective, whereas the service-gap model focuses on one aspect—service—of the value-creation process and does so from both the company and the customer perspectives. In this context, these two approaches complement each other to enable the company to better understand and manage the process of creating market value.

MARKETING INSIGHT: MANAGING DISSATISFIED CUSTOMERS

Given the downside of having a dissatisfied customer as well as the potential upside of turning an unhappy customer into a happy one, it is important that a company develop a strategy to manage dissatisfied customers. To do this, a company might follow four key principles—captured by the acronym SAFE—to deal with the dissatisfied customers:

- *Solve.* Address the problem and find a solution that satisfies the customer. The first step to finding a solution is understanding the nature of the problem from the customer's viewpoint. This is important because companies sometimes misunderstand the cause of a customer's dissatisfaction and consequently invest time and effort in solving the wrong problem. Therefore, the starting point for solving a customer's problem is to clearly define the nature of the problem. Moreover, a clearly defined problem often implies a solution (or a set of possible solutions) that the company can undertake to remedy the situation.

- *Acknowledge.* To effectively manage dissatisfied customers, the company must acknowledge its mistake when pertinent and accept responsibility for the situation that has caused the dissatisfaction. Accepting responsibility, although often contrary to the advice a company might receive from its legal team, can play a key role in appeasing dissatisfied customers, for whom admission of guilt on the part of the company is a sign that the company cares and will work to prevent similar errors in the future.

- *Fast.* Quickly responding to failures is a key component in managing dissatisfied customers. It shows customers that the company cares about resolving the problem, whereas a slow response might escalate customers' dissatisfaction and lead to negative word of mouth. The longer the company waits to respond to the situation that has caused customer dissatisfaction, the more company resources (both time and money) it takes to eradicate the dissatisfaction.

- *Effortless.* Companies can benefit from making it easy for customers to voice their concerns. One of the key challenges in managing customer dissatisfaction is identifying the dissatisfied customers. Managers often assume that dissatisfied customers are those who reach out to the company to voice their concerns. Although popular, this assumption is rather myopic. While it is true that complaining customers are typically dissatisfied with the company's offerings, not all dissatisfied customers end up complaining to the company. Rather than complain, some dissatisfied customers simply stop patronizing the company and buying its offerings. Studies show that the vast majority of dissatisfied customers do not complain to the company because they do not know to whom to complain, because communicating their dissatisfaction takes too much time and effort, or because they do not think that the company cares about their opinion.[6] In this context, an important aspect of managing dissatisfied customers is making it easy for them to share their concerns with the company. Thus, rather than burying the company's contact information deep in the company website and in the small print of company messages—a common practice for many companies that view customer communication as a nuisance and an unnecessary expense—making it easy for customers to find this information by featuring it prominently can help the company get a better grasp of the areas in which it fails to deliver customer value and improve its ability to identify and manage customer dissatisfaction.

Because occasional service failures are inevitable even in companies that pride themselves on delivering superior service, managing dissatisfied customers is an important aspect of managing the service aspect of a company's offerings. Following the above four principles—solving the problem, acknowledging the company's role in the problem, quickly addressing the issue, and making the process of rectifying service failures effortless from a customer's standpoint—can help the company mitigate the negative impact of service failures and put the company on the right track to create superior customer value.

CHAPTER ELEVEN

MANAGING BRANDS

If you are not a brand, you are a commodity.
— Philip Kotler, founder of modern marketing theory

Brands are one of the company's most valuable assets. Brands benefit customers by creating value that goes beyond the product and service aspects of the offering. By bolstering customer demand, brands enable the company to capture greater value from its customers while at the same time strengthening the impact of the other marketing tactics, ensuring greater collaborator support, and facilitating the hiring and retaining of skilled employees. The key aspects of creating and managing brands are the focus of this chapter. Specifically, we address the following topics:

- *Branding as a Value-Creation Process* || Brands as a tool for creating market value | Creating a meaningful brand image
- *Brand Strategy* || Brands as a means of creating customer value | Brands as a means of creating company value | Brands as a means of creating collaborator value | Brand positioning and brand mantra
- *Brand Tactics* || Brand identifiers | Brand referents
- *Managing Brand Portfolios* || Single-brand strategy | Multi-brand strategy | Cobranding strategy | Choosing a brand-portfolio strategy
- *Brand Dynamics* || Extending the brand | Repositioning the brand
- *Brand Valuation* || Brand equity as a marketing concept | Measuring brand equity | Brand power as a marketing concept | Measuring brand power | Aligning brand power and brand equity

The discussion of brand management is complemented by an in-depth overview of two additional topics: the role of brands as a means of self-expression and luxury branding.

Branding as a Value-Creation Process

Branding is the process of endowing a company's offerings with a unique identity in order to differentiate them from the competition and create value above and beyond the value delivered by the other aspects of the offering. The role of brands as a tool for creating market value and the ways in which companies create a distinct image in the minds of its target customers are discussed in more detail in the following sections.

Brands as a Tool for Creating Market Value

Brands have a long history as a means of distinguishing the goods of one producer from those of another. Some of the earliest known brands were used to mark the identity of a good's maker or owner. These simplest forms of branding were observed in the ancient civilizations of Egypt, Crete, Etruria, and Greece. During the Roman Empire, more distinctive forms of branding, including the use of word marks in addition to graphics, began to emerge.

The importance of brands dramatically increased by the end of the 19th century when the proliferation of mass-produced, standardized products—a direct consequence of the Industrial Revolution—created the need for unique marks to help consumers distinguish between these products. As manufacturers began producing on a larger scale and gained wider distribution, they started engraving their mark into the goods to distinguish themselves from their competition. Along with these changes, the nature of brands was transforming from simply marking the ownership of the product to identifying its maker and serving as a symbol of product quality.

Brands have become ubiquitous in modern society. They are not limited to physical goods such as food products, cars, cosmetics, and pharmaceuticals. Brands are used to identify services (American Express, Netflix, and Uber); companies (Procter & Gamble, Walmart, and Starbucks); nonprofit organizations (UNESCO, FIFA, and American Red Cross); events (Olympic Games, Wimbledon, and Super Bowl); individuals (Lady Gaga, Madonna, and Michael Jordan); groups (music groups, sport teams, and social clubs); administrative units (countries, states, and cities); geographic locations (Champagne, Cognac, and Camembert); and ideas and causes (education, social justice, and health).

Brands are not limited to consumer offerings; they also play an important part in business markets. Business-to-business enterprises have built strong brands that span industries, including consulting (McKinsey & Company, Boston Consulting Group, Accenture, and Prophet); commercial equipment manufacturing (Boeing, DuPont, Caterpillar, and Applied Materials); and software solution services (SAP, Oracle, Akamai, and Alibaba).

Brands are a distinct marketing tool used to identify an offering, differentiate it from similar market offerings, and create market value above and beyond that created by the other attributes of a company's offering. Accordingly, brand management is a process of designing and sustaining a mental image in people's minds that enables the company to identify its products and services, differentiate them from the competition, and create distinct market value.

Brands are one of the seven attributes defining the company's offerings. Together with the other attributes of the offering—product, service, price, incentives, communication, and distribution—brands aim to create an optimal value proposition (OVP) for the company, its customers, and its collaborators (Figure 1). Therefore, a manager's goal is to build brands that create superior value for target customers in a way that benefits the company and its collaborators.

Figure 1. Branding as a Value-Creation Process

Creating value for target customers in a way that benefits the company and its collaborators is the overarching principle guiding all branding decisions. The means by which brands create customer, company, and collaborator value are outlined in more detail in the following sections.

Creating a Meaningful Brand Image

Building strong brands calls for creating a meaningful brand image in customers' minds. The brand image is the network of all brand-related associations that exist in a customer's mind.

It reflects how customers see a particular brand through the lens of their own set of values, beliefs, and experiences.

Brand image can be visually represented as an association map delineating the key concepts linked to the brand name. Figure 2 illustrates streamlined brand association maps representing a customer's (hypothetical) image of the Apple and Starbucks brands. Here, the nodes represent the different concepts related to each of these brands in this customer's mind, and the lines connecting them represent the brand associations. The nodes closer to the brand indicate thoughts that are directly associated with the brand, and the nodes that are farther away indicate the secondary associations that are less prominent in a customer's mind.

Figure 2. Brand Association Maps of Apple and Starbucks

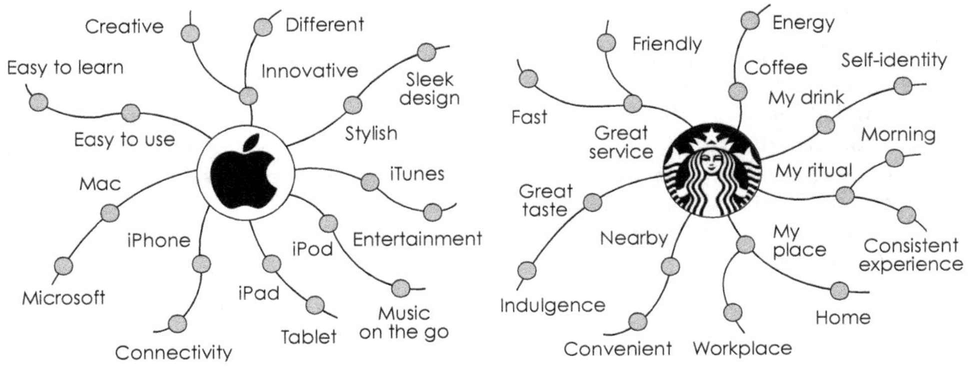

The type of associations brands evoke, as well as the breadth, strength, and attractiveness (positive vs. negative) of these associations, reflect the degree to which a given brand has successfully created a relevant, well-articulated, and positive image in a customer's mind. The stronger the brand, the greater the number of relevant benefits, usage occasions, experiences, concepts, products, and places associated with it—and the stronger and more positive these associations are. In this context, brand management aims to facilitate the formation of a variety of strong, meaningful, and positive brand associations in the minds of its target customers.

Ideally (from a company's standpoint), the brand image that exists in the mind of each of its customers should be consistent with the image the company aims to project. In reality, however, this is not always the case. Because the brand image exists in a customer's mind and stems from this customer's individual needs, values, and knowledge accumulated over time, the same brand might evoke different brand images across customers. For example, some customers might associate the Starbucks brand with handcrafted espresso coffee drinks while for different customers it might represent a part of their daily routine; others might think of Starbucks as a place to meet with friends. In the same vein, different customers might associate the Apple brand with user-friendly technology; with particular products such as the iPhone, iPad, or Apple Watch; with innovation, creativity, and being different; with other technology brands such as Microsoft, Google, and Samsung; and even with the company's own retail stores.

Given the idiosyncratic nature of customers' experiences, a company's ability to create a consistent image of its brand in customers' minds is often limited to identifying and communicating the key concepts that it would like customers to associate with the brand. Because the actual image formed in customers' minds varies based on customers' unique interactions with the brand, having a clearly articulated brand strategy can help the company overcome the diversity of customers' individual experiences and build a brand image that reflects the essence of the company's brand.

Brand Strategy

The process of building strong brands is guided by a clear understanding of the value they create for target customers, the company, and its collaborators. The different ways in which brands create market value are discussed in the following sections.

Brands as a Means of Creating Customer Value

One of the primary goals of brands is to create value for their target customers. To this end, brands create three types of customer value: *functional*, *psychological*, and *monetary*.

Functional Value

Brands can create functional value in two ways: by *identifying* a company offering and by *signaling* specific aspects of the offering's functionality.

- **Identifying the company offerings.** Brands enable customers to identify a company's products and services and distinguish them from those of its competitors. For example, if Tide laundry detergent was not associated with a unique brand, customers would have difficulty locating it and would have to examine the ingredients of many detergents to ensure that the product they purchase is indeed the Tide detergent produced by Procter & Gamble. The identification function of brands is particularly important in the case of commoditized products that are similar in their appearance and performance.

- **Signaling performance.** In addition to identifying the offering, brands can inform customers about the functional performance of the products and services associated with the brand. For example, the Tide brand signals cleaning power, the Crest brand signals effective cavity protection, and the DeWalt brand signals durability. Not only can brands inform customers about the performance of products and services, but in some cases they can also change the way customers experience these products and services. For example, the taste of beer, the scent of perfume, and even the effectiveness of a drug might be influenced by customers' knowledge of their brand names.

Psychological Value

Psychological value is often the key source of the market value created by brands. Indeed, because brands evoke specific associations in a customer's mind, they can convey a wider range of emotions and deeper meaning than the other attributes of the offering. Specifically, the psychological value created by brands stems from three types of benefits: *emotional*, *self-expressive*, and *societal*.

- **Emotional value.** Brands can create emotional value by evoking an affective response from customers that can involve a wide range of positive emotions. For example, Allstate Insurance Company (*You're in good hands with Allstate*) aims to convey peace of mind with its brand, and Hallmark (*When You Care Enough to Send the Very Best*) evokes the feeling of love and affection.

- **Self-expressive value.** In addition to creating emotional benefits, brands can create self-expressive value by enabling individuals to express their identity. For example, brands like Harley-Davidson, Oakley, and Abercrombie & Fitch stand for different lifestyles, enabling consumers to express their unique personality by displaying these brands. In addition to allowing consumers to express their individuality, brands like Rolls-Royce, Louis Vuitton, and Cartier create psychological value by enabling their customers to highlight their wealth and socioeconomic status. The role of brands as a means of self-expression is discussed in more detail at the end of this chapter.

- **Societal value.** Brands can also create societal value by conveying a sense of moral gratification from contributing to society. For example, brands like TOMS, Product Red, UNICEF, Doctors Without Borders, and Habitat for Humanity that represent humanitarian causes create customer value by taking a stand on relevant social issues and implementing a variety of socially responsible programs.

Monetary Value

In addition to creating functional and psychological value, brands can also create monetary value. Specifically, brands can create two types of monetary benefits: *signaling price* and generating *financial value.*

- **Signaling price.** Brands can signal the overall level of prices associated with the company's products and services. For example, the Walmart brand conveys the idea of low prices, fostering the belief that its offerings are priced lower than its competitors. The price image conveyed by a brand is particularly important when buyers are unaware of the competitiveness of the price of a given offering. In such cases, consumers often rely on the brand to infer the attractiveness of an offering's price. Price image is discussed in more detail in Chapter 17.

- **Financial value.** In addition to signaling an offering's monetary value, brands can also carry inherent monetary benefits, which are reflected in the higher price of branded offerings on the secondary market. For example, a Louis Vuitton handbag commands a much higher resale price compared to a functionally equivalent unbranded handbag. In fact, the financial benefit of brands is one of the key factors in valuing alternative investments such as wine, watches, and automobiles.

Not every brand creates all three types of customer value. In fact, some of the positioning strategies implied by the different types of brand value might be mutually exclusive. For example, a brand signaling monetary benefits (e.g., low price) might not be credible in signaling product performance and conveying wealth and social status. In this context, the different types of customer value can serve as a guide to developing a brand's value proposition rather than as a requirement that a brand create value for customers on each of the three dimensions.

Brands as a Means of Creating Company Value

Brands can create company value on two main dimensions: *strategic* and *monetary.* The specific ways in which brands create strategic and monetary value for the company are outlined below.

Strategic Value

The strategic value created by brands reflects the nonmonetary benefits that a company derives from associating its products and services with a given brand. Specifically, brands can *bolster customer demand, amplify the impact of the other marketing tactics, ensure greater collaborator support,* and *facilitate the hiring and retaining of skilled employees.*

- **Bolstering customer demand.** Because brands create customer value, they generate incremental demand for a company's offerings. Thus, a customer who is not interested in an unbranded product might be interested in a branded version of the same product, provided that this customer finds the brand meaningful and relevant. In addition to increasing the attractiveness of the company's offerings, brands might facilitate product/service usage, which often leads to greater repurchase frequency. Offerings associated with an attractive brand are also more likely to encourage customer advocacy, which, in turn, is likely to further promote sales. For example, Zappos, Harley-Davidson, Apple, and Abercrombie & Fitch have a loyal consumer following that helps expand the demand for offerings associated with these brands.

- **Amplifying the impact of other marketing tactics.** In addition to directly bolstering customer demand, brands can increase the effectiveness of the other attributes defining the company's offering. Thus, brands can enhance customer perceptions of product performance by making branded products appear more powerful, reliable, durable, safe, attractive, tasty, or visually appealing than their unbranded counterparts. For example, consumers are likely to think that a drug is more effective if it is associated with a reputable pharmaceutical brand. Furthermore, because brands create incremental customer value, companies tend to charge higher prices for branded products than for unbranded products. For example, Advil-branded ibuprofen is priced significantly higher than the generic version, and Morton-branded salt commands a substantial price premium over the unbranded version. Not only do customers find branded products more attractive and pay extra for them, they are also more willing to search for the branded product across distribution channels and bypass more convenient retailers that do not carry their favorite brand even when a functionally equivalent substitute is readily available. Customers are also likely to react more favorably to incentives and communication from a brand they patronize and ignore those from unbranded products.

- **Ensuring greater collaborator support.** Strong brands can create value for the company by securing greater support from its collaborators. For example, strong brands give manufacturers power over retailers, enabling them to negotiate more advantageous agreements, resulting in a better distribution network and greater promotional support (on-hand inventory, product placement, and sales support). In the same vein, retailers with a strong brand can command greater support and better margins from manufacturers of products that are either unbranded or associated with weak brands.

- **Facilitating the recruiting and retaining of skilled employees.** Employees often place a premium on working for companies whose brands resonate with their own needs, preferences, and value systems. As a result, companies with strong brands find it easier to attract and retain talented employees. Moreover, employees are sometimes ready to sacrifice part of their compensation and accept a lower salary to work for a company with a favorable brand.[1] An additional benefit of brand power is a brand's ability to build, enhance, and sustain the company culture. This is because a brand can create a strong sense of identification among its employees, increase their morale, and bolster their teamwork.

Monetary Value

Along with their strategic benefits, brands can create monetary value for the company by *generating incremental revenues and profits, increasing company valuation,* and *creating a separable company asset.*

- **Generating incremental revenues and profits.** A brand's ability to generate incremental demand and command higher prices naturally leads to higher sales revenues and profits. In addition, customers' affinity for a particular brand can enable the company to negotiate better financial terms with its collaborators (e.g., suppliers and distributors), further increasing the company's profit margins.

- **Increasing the valuation of the company.** Brands' ability to generate incremental net income can, in turn, enhance the monetary value of the company, such that companies with strong brands receive higher market valuations. In this context, the monetary value of the brand (brand equity) is determined by the future value of the cash flow that is likely to be generated by the company's brand.

- **Creating a separable company asset.** In addition to contributing to a company's valuation, brands might generate additional value for the company if they are acquired by another entity. Thus, certain brands might have significantly higher value when acquired by another company with better opportunities to unlock the true value of the brand.

Brands as a Means of Creating Collaborator Value

Similar to the ways in which brands create company value, brands create two types of value for collaborators: *strategic* and *monetary*.

- **Strategic value.** The strategic value created by a given brand reflects the nonmonetary benefits that a company's collaborators derive from associating the brand with their offerings. Specifically, partnering with a strong brand can generate incremental demand for collaborators' products and services. For example, collaborating with established airline, hotel, and retail brands can bolster the demand for a bank's credit cards by attracting customers that are loyal to its branding partners. In addition to bolstering customer demand, partnering with a strong brand can strengthen collaborator brands. Thus, cobranding with a well-established and well-liked brand can have a "halo" (spillover) effect, adding credibility to a collaborator that is less known or less relevant.

- **Monetary value.** In addition to strategic value, brands can create monetary value for collaborators by generating incremental revenues and profits. Greater customer demand for company-branded offerings usually leads to higher sales revenues and profits for the company's collaborators. For example, cobranding with Intel (*Intel Inside* campaign) has enabled computer manufacturers to charge higher prices for their products, thus increasing their profit margins. In the same vein, partnering with fashion brands like Chanel, Prada, and Giorgio Armani enables Luxottica, the world's largest eyewear manufacturer, to sell its designer-designated offerings at a premium compared to products sold under its own brand name.

Brand Positioning and Brand Mantra

The development of a sustainable value proposition and brand image can be facilitated by articulating a streamlined *brand positioning* and *brand mantra* that succinctly convey the essence of the brand. These two aspects of brand building are outlined in more detail below.

Brand Positioning

To create a meaningful value proposition and brand image, a company must identify the strategically important brand associations and make them primary in target customers' minds. Therefore, in addition to defining the functional, psychological, and monetary value that the brand creates for target customers, the company must develop a clear brand positioning strategy that reflects the company's view of how its target customers should think about the brand.

The term *positioning* is used in reference to both the *process* of creating a meaningful and distinct image in customers' minds, and the *outcome* of the positioning process—the mental image that the company aims to create in customers' minds. The latter meaning of brand positioning is akin to *brand image,* with the key difference that brand positioning is the set of brand associations that the company *aims to create* in its customers' minds, whereas the brand image consists of the brand associations that *actually exist* in a customer's mind. Furthermore, unlike brand image, which is an idiosyncratic representation of the brand in a customer's mind, brand positioning reflects a set of common benefits that the brand aims to create for all target customers. In this context, the brand image reflects the ways in which individual customers internalize the brand's positioning.

The general principles that apply to positioning an offering (discussed in Chapter 7) also apply to positioning the offering's brand. Because the brand is one of the attributes of the company's offering, the positioning of the offering's brand at least partially overlaps with the overall positioning of the offering. At the same time, brands that span product categories usually have a broader positioning than the actual products and services that carry the brand name. For example, the positioning of BMW as the ultimate driving machine is defined by a set of higher level, more general benefits compared to the positioning of the company's individual offerings—including its sedans, coupes, roadsters, sport activity vehicles, and sport wagons. Indeed, while consistent with the positioning of the BMW brand as the ultimate driving machine, the specific BMW vehicles offer different sets of benefits, target different customers, and have different competitors.

Brand Mantra

To facilitate the process of developing a consistent and meaningful brand image, a company can benefit from clearly identifying the core meaning of the brand that it aims to imprint in customers' minds. For example, despite offering multiple benefits that include performance, prestige, luxury, comfort, and safety, BMW has identified the superior driving experience as the core meaning of its brand and has focused its efforts on creating a corresponding brand image in customers' minds. This core meaning of the brand, which defines what the brand stands for, is also referred to as the *brand mantra.*

The brand mantra is the brand's promise to its customers — the primary association the company uses to anchor the image of the brand in customers' minds. The brand mantra is usually a short phrase encapsulating the essence of the brand in the clearest and most effective way. For example, Nike's brand mantra is *authentic athletic performance*, Disney's brand mantra is *fun family entertainment*, The Ritz–Carlton's brand mantra is *impeccable hospitality*, BMW's brand mantra is a *superior driving experience*, Harley-Davidson's brand mantra is *personal freedom*, and Walmart's brand mantra is *everyday low prices*. The ultimate goal of the brand mantra is to ensure that company employees and collaborators have an accurate understanding of the image that the brand aims to instill in customers' minds so that they can act in a manner consistent with that image.

The brand mantra typically reflects the core competency of the company. Thus, Nike's brand mantra is a reflection of its core competency in designing athletic apparel and equipment. The Ritz-Carlton's brand mantra is a reflection of its core competency in service excellence. Disney's brand mantra is built on its expertise in developing entertainment products and experiences. BMW's brand mantra reflects its expertise in designing high-end performance vehicles. Walmart's brand mantra is a reflection of its core competency in effective and cost-efficient operations.

In addition to articulating the essence of the brand, the brand mantra provides direction and sets boundaries for managing the brand. Thus, the brand mantra implicitly defines how far the company can "stretch" the brand and identifies the products and services that should and should not be associated with it. For example, because the BMW brand represents the ultimate driving experience, extending it to cars that fail to fulfill this promise or to products unrelated to a superior driving experience should be avoided because it is inconsistent with the essence of the BMW brand. Thus, an important aspect in defining the brand mantra is deciding what the brand is and what it is not.

The brand mantra is an internal concept that guides a company's brand-building activities. As an internal concept, the brand mantra is not directly communicated to the brand's target customers. Instead, the brand mantra is typically captured in the brand motto, which is communicated to customers. For example, Nike's brand mantra is reflected in its motto *Just do it*, Disney's brand mantra is reflected in the brand motto *Where dreams come true*, The Ritz-Carlton's brand mantra is captured by its motto *Ladies and gentlemen serving ladies and gentlemen*, BMW's brand mantra is reflected in its motto *The ultimate driving machine*, and Walmart's brand mantra is captured in the motto *Save money. Live better*.

The concept of *brand mantra* is related to *brand positioning* in that both terms reflect the essence of the brand. The key difference between these two concepts is the perspective they take. The brand mantra defines the essence of the brand in order to streamline the process of brand management and ensure that the brand stays on point. Brand positioning, on the other hand, articulates the way a company wants its brand to be perceived by its customers, including the specific concepts it wants the brand to be associated with. As a result, the brand mantra delineates the "soul" of the brand without referencing its competitors, whereas brand positioning can relate brand benefits to those of competitive brands. Note, however, that despite these differences, a brand's mantra and its positioning are closely related and, in many cases, tend to overlap.

Brand Tactics

Brand tactics are the key characteristics defining the brand; they are the tools that the company uses to position the brand and create the desired brand image in customers' minds. Brand tactics are defined by two types of attributes: brand identifiers and brand referents.

Brand identifiers are brand attributes that are created, managed, and owned by the company for the primary purpose of identifying the brand and differentiating it from the competition. Common brand identifiers include brand name, logo, motto, character, soundmark, product design, and packaging. *Brand referents* are brand attributes whose value the company aims to leverage by associating them with its brand name. Unlike brand identifiers, brand referents typically exist independently of the company; they are not created, managed, and owned by the company. Common brand referents include needs, benefits, experiences, occasions, places, people, concepts, objects, products and services, and other brands. Brand referents help create meaningful associations in customers' minds by relating the brand to things that are meaningful to these customers.

The key brand identifiers and brand referents, and their use as brand design elements, are discussed in more detail in the following sections.

Brand Identifiers

Brand identifiers are the brand elements that are developed, managed, and owned by the company. The primary function of brand identifiers, as the name suggests, is to uniquely identify the company's offering and differentiate it from the competition. For example, the Coca-Cola name, logo, and swirling bottle design help differentiate the company's offerings by enabling its customers to easily locate the company's products, which, in turn, enables The Coca-Cola Company and its distributors to capture the revenues generated by these products. In a legal context, brand identifiers are similar to trademarks.

The key brand identifiers are the *name, logo, motto, character, soundmark, product design*, and *packaging*. The brand name typically serves as the primary identifier of the brand to which the other identifiers are linked. Depending on its strategic goals, a brand can use one or more identifiers. In general, the use of a greater number of identifiers enables a company to better distinguish its brand from the competition. The key brand identifiers are illustrated in Figure 3 and discussed in more detail in the following sections.

Figure 3. Key Brand Identifiers

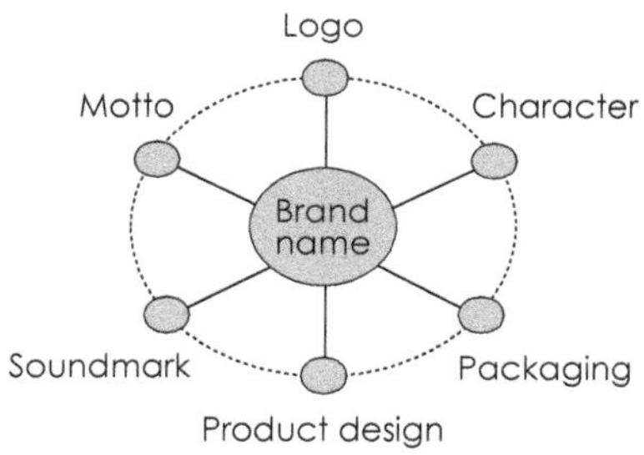

Brand Name

The brand name is the key brand element that links all other brand elements. Based on the degree to which they are afforded trademark protection, there are five categories of brand names. Arrayed in descending order, which roughly reflects their eligibility for trademark status and the degree of protection accorded, these categories consist of *fanciful, arbitrary, suggestive, descriptive*, and *generic* names.[2]

- **Fanciful** (fabricated) names involve words that do not have any particular meaning and have been invented for the sole purpose of serving as a brand name. Examples of fabricated brand names include Google, Kodak, Xerox, Exxon, Diageo, Verizon, Altria, Häagen-Dazs, Pixar, and Accenture.

- **Arbitrary** names involve commonly used words that are unrelated to the company's business and, hence, do not suggest or describe a significant ingredient, quality, or characteristic of the company's products and services. Examples of arbitrary names include Apple for computers, Camel for cigarettes, Virgin for airlines, and Diesel for jeans.

- **Suggestive** names require imagination or thought to determine the nature of the products and services associated with the brand. Examples of suggestive names include Tide for laundry detergent, Greyhound for transportation, Coppertone for sunscreen lotion, Nike for sports gear, DieHard for auto batteries, SnackWell's for snacks, Lean Cuisine for frozen entrées, and 42 Below for vodka (referring to the southern latitude where the vodka is produced on New Zealand's 42nd parallel and to the 42% alcohol content of the product).

- **Descriptive** names depict the product category and/or the key benefit associated with the company's products and services. Examples of descriptive names include Toys"R"Us, Whole Foods, Wonderful Pistachios, Designer Shoe Warehouse, Pizza Hut, Travelocity, Jell-O, PowerBar, Rubbermaid, and Pop-Tarts. Descriptive names can also feature phonetic spelling of a common word such as Zappos (*zapatos* is the Spanish word for shoes), Flickr, Tumblr, Kix, Krispy Kreme, and Rice Krispies.[3]

- **Generic** names are the common names used to refer to associated products and services, such as *salt* when used in reference to sodium chloride. Because a generic name does not distinguish the products or services of the company from those of other entities, it affords no legal protection. Strictly speaking, generic names are not brands because they describe the actual products or services rather than identify and differentiate their producer.

The difference between these types of brand names can be illustrated with the following example. *Soap* in reference to a bar of soap is a generic name, *Lavender Handmade Soap* is a descriptive name, *Ivory Soap* is a suggestive name (the soap is actually white and the implication is that it will help make the skin ivory), *Rainbow* is an arbitrary name, and *Camay* is a fanciful name.

The level of trademark protection afforded to a brand name is a function of its distinctiveness. Fanciful names are considered to be the most distinctive and therefore enjoy the highest degree of legal protection, followed by arbitrary and suggestive names. Descriptive names are the most difficult to protect because they are not inherently distinctive; thus, in order to gain legal protection they must acquire secondary meaning so that the name comes to signify the producer of the goods rather than the goods themselves. For example, Designer Shoe Warehouse signifies a particular shoe retailer rather than just a warehouse selling designer shoes. Finally, generic names are considered public domain and cannot be protected as trademarks.

The choice of a brand name involves a tradeoff between the ease of communicating the essence of the brand and the degree to which a brand is afforded legal protection. Descriptive names readily communicate the type of offerings associated with the brand and, thus, require fewer resources (time, money, and effort) to establish a meaningful brand image in customers' minds. On the downside, however, from a legal standpoint, descriptive names are the most difficult to protect. Fanciful names, on the other hand, benefit from the greatest degree of legal protection. Because fanciful names are devoid of inherent meaning, however, creating a meaningful brand image in this case is associated with the need to expend significantly more resources.

Brand Logo

Brand logo is a sign comprising a unique combination of letters, fonts, shapes, colors, and/or symbols that aim to visually identify the brand. Based on their structure, there are five types of brand logos: wordmark, letterform mark, pictorial mark, abstract mark, and emblem. These different types of logos are described in more detail below.

- **Wordmark.** A company's logo might involve a distinctive text-only typographic representation of the brand name. Examples of wordmark brand logos include Coca-Cola, Visa, CNN, IBM, eBay, Google, FedEx, Subway, AIG, Xerox, Canon, Ray-Ban, Microsoft, Philips, Sony, and PayPal.

- **Letterform mark.** The brand logo might involve only a single letter (usually the first letter of the company) with a unique typographical treatment. Examples of letterform logos include Chanel, LG, Hilton, McDonald's, Facebook, Honda, Westinghouse, Herman Miller, Yahoo, Univision, Beats, and Quiznos.

- **Pictorial.** The brand logo might involve a pictorial representation of the brand. Examples of pictorial logos include Shell's seashell, Twitter's bird, Nestlé's nest, NBC's peacock, Starbucks' siren, Target's concentric circles, and Lacoste's crocodile.

- **Abstract.** The brand might also involve an abstract image that has no inherent meaning. Examples of abstract logos include Mercedes, Nike, Adidas, Chase, Time Warner, Hyatt Place, Audi, and Microsoft.

- **Emblem.** The brand logo might also involve a more complex representation that includes different brand logo components and usually features the name of the brand. Examples of emblem logos include Ferrari, Harley-Davidson, NFL, Heineken, Cadillac, Versace, Burberry, and Prada.

The choice of the logo elements is important because in addition to differentiating the brand they can also help convey a particular meaning. Thus, Coca-Cola's red color might be perceived to be more energetic compared to the more peaceful brown color featured by UPS. Similarly, fonts used by Disney in different movie franchises are more playful, whereas fonts used by FedEx, UPS, and DHL are more serious. In the same vein, the Rock of Gibraltar in Prudential's logo symbolizes financial stability, the lion in ING's logo conveys financial strength, and the crown in the Rolex logo symbolizes prestige and achievement.

Brand Motto

The brand motto is a phrase that identifies the brand by articulating the brand's positioning to its target customers. Based on the nature of the underlying message, brand mottos can be *imperative, descriptive, declarative, superlative, provocative,* and *promise-based.*

- **Imperative** mottos involve a call for action. Examples of imperative mottos include Nike's *Just Do It,* YouTube's *Broadcast Yourself,* Ford's *Go Further,* United Airlines' *Fly the Friendly Skies,* American Express' *Don't Leave Home Without It,* Kodak's *Share Moments. Share Life,* Coca-Cola's *Twist the Cap to Refreshment,* Subway's *Eat Fresh,* eBay's *Buy It. Sell It. Love It,* and Vodafone's *Make the Most of Now.*

- **Descriptive** mottos depict a key benefit of the products and services associated with the brand. For example, Walgreens' motto *The Pharmacy America Trusts* captures the brand's key functional (pharmacy) and psychological (trust) benefits. Other examples of descriptive mottos include M&M's' *Melts in Your Mouth, Not in Your Hands,* Intel's *Intel Inside,* IBM's *Solutions for a Small Planet, Fortune* magazine's *For the Men in Charge of Change,* and Rice Krispies' *Snap, Crackle, Pop.*

- **Declarative** mottos involve a general statement that typically does not contain a specific brand promise. For example, De Beers' *A Diamond Is Forever,* Coca-Cola's *Always Coca-Cola,* LG's *Life's Good,* Calvin Klein's *Between Love and Madness Lies Obsession,* Levi's' *Quality Never Goes Out of Style,* Kay Jewelers' *Every Kiss Begins with Kay,* JCPenney's *When It Fits You Feel It,* and Tag Heuer's *Success. It's a Mind Game* exemplify declarative brand mottos.

- **Superlative** mottos claim category leadership on an important dimension. Budweiser's *King of Beers,* BMW's *The Ultimate Driving Machine,* Porsche's *There Is No Substitute,* Gillette's *The Best a Man Can Get,* John Deere's *Nothing Runs Like a Deere,* and Pizza Hut's *The Best Pizzas Under One Roof* exemplify superlative mottos.

- **Provocative** mottos involve a claim that challenges certain conventions. For example, Apple's *Think Different,* Adidas' *Impossible Is Nothing,* Diesel's *For Successful Living* (can a pair of jeans really make one's life more successful?), Volkswagen's *Drivers Wanted,* Microsoft's *Where Do You Want to Go Today?,* UPS's *What Can Brown Do for You?,* Clairol's *Does She… Or Doesn't She?,* and McDonald's' *Did Somebody Say McDonald's?* exemplify provocative brand mottos.

- **Promise-based** mottos articulate a promise that a brand makes to its customers. Nestlé's *Good Food. Good Life,* Target's *Expect More. Pay Less,* Sears' *Good Life. Great Price,* Walmart's *Save Money. Live Better,* Avis' *We Try Harder,* Smuckers' *With a Name*

Like Smucker's, It Has to Be Good, Burger King's *Have It Your Way*, and State Farm's *Like a Good Neighbor, State Farm Is There* exemplify promise-based brand mottos.

The choice of the brand motto is important because it directly relates the essence of the brand to its customers. To be effective, the motto must articulate the brand mantra for its target customers in a way that identifies the brand, differentiates it from the competition, and creates unique customer value. The choice of the specific motto format — imperative, descriptive, declarative, superlative, provocative, or a promise — is determined by the overall positioning of the brand and the image it aims to establish in customers' minds.

Brand Character

The brand character is a fictional personality that embodies the essence of the brand (Figure 4). Popular brand characters include the Michelin Man (1898), Johnnie Walker (1908), Mr. Peanut (1917), Betty Crocker (1921), Kellogg's Tony the Tiger (1951), Ronald McDonald (1963), Ernie Keebler (1969), the Pillsbury Doughboy (1969), the Nesquik Bunny (1970s), the Energizer Bunny (1989), Aflac's Duck (2000), and Geico's Gecko (2002).

Figure 4. Brand Characters as Brand Identifiers

Michelin Man   Johnnie Walker   Mr. Peanut   Tony the Tiger   Ronald McDonald   Nesquik Bunny

Brand characters are commonly used as brand identifiers for several reasons. First, brand characters are an additional means of identifying the company's brand and differentiating it from the competition — a benefit that is especially important for commoditized products and services where the actual differences between the competitive market offerings are not well pronounced. A character's personality can add a deeper meaning to the brand and succinctly express more complex values, ideas, and emotions than can be communicated by words and graphics. In addition, customers (especially children) often find it easier to establish a meaningful connection with brand characters, especially when the brand characters are anthropomorphized and have a distinct personality. For example, brand characters such as Tony the Tiger, Betty Crocker, and the Nesquik Bunny create value by humanizing the company's offering and establishing an emotional connection between the brand and its target customers. Finally, because they are vivid, rich in imagery, and memorable, characters can help brands break through communication clutter and create a distinct image in customers' minds.

Despite their multiple advantages, the use of characters has several drawbacks. Even though brand characters help differentiate commoditized offerings, in the case of products and services that have inherent distinguishing characteristics, brand characters might not create marginal value and, instead, might distract customers from the unique benefits of the offering. For example, cars rely on product design to express the personality of their brand, making brand characters superfluous. Furthermore, because brand characters tend to be associated with a specific set of values, ideas, and emotions, they might not appeal to all target customers; for some customers, the brand character might end up decreasing rather than increasing the overall value of the brand. Finally, a brand character typically requires a relatively long time horizon to become meaningful brand identifiers.

Brand Soundmark

The brand soundmark uses sound to uniquely identify a particular brand. Soundmarks help increase brand recognition, establish an emotional connection with a brand, enhance the brand meaning, and foster brand engagement. There are three common types of soundmarks: *tune, music,* and *jingle.*

- **Tune** involves a simple and easily remembered melody. Intel's tune, NBC's chime, Microsoft's ding, 20th Century Fox's fanfare, and Samsung's ringtone exemplify various tunes used as brand soundmarks.

- **Music** involves a wordless melody designed to complement a brand's identity. For example, the music used by De Beers in its "Shadows and Light" campaign became part of its brand identity, enhancing the emotional aspect of the brand. Music is commonly used in movies and has helped transform many movie franchises — including Star Wars, James Bond, and Indiana Jones — into multi-billion-dollar licensing businesses.

- **Jingle** involves a melody comprising words and vocalization. This is perhaps the most common form of soundmark used in branding consumer products and services. Popular examples of jingles include *I'm Lovin' It* (McDonald's); *Have you had your break today?* (McDonald's); *Double your pleasure, double your fun* (Doublemint); *Kiss a little longer, stay close a little longer, hold tight a little longer — longer with Big Red!* (Big Red); *Gimme a break, gimme a break, break me off a piece of that Kit Kat bar* (Kit Kat); *I wish I was an Oscar Mayer Wiener* (Oscar Mayer); and *Snap, Crackle, Pop* (Kellogg's Rice Krispies).

Soundmarks can also involve various sounds such as the roaring of MGM's lion, Harley-Davidson's distinctive V-twin engine sound, and modulations of spoken words as in the case of the word *Aflac* repeated by Aflac's duck.

The growing popularity of soundmarks is a function of their ability to enhance a company's capacity to differentiate its brand by bolstering its unique identity. Soundmarks introduce another dimension on which a company can identify its offering(s), differentiate them from the competition, and create distinct market value. The importance of soundmarks in creating a relevant and memorable brand is heightened by the fact that different sensory modalities (e.g., sound and vision) tend to work together to strengthen the overall brand image. In this context, employing sound as another mode of expressing and reinforcing brand identity can also increase the impact of the other brand identifiers.

Packaging

Packaging can serve as a brand identifier by associating an offering with a particular brand. Packaging elements that commonly play the role of brand identifiers include shape, color, graphics, and text. Individual packaging elements need not be unique to serve as brand identifiers; however, the combination of elements (the overall look and feel) must enable customers to identify the brand.

Examples of product packaging that serves as a brand identifier include Coca-Cola's swirl bottle, the Heinz octagonal ketchup bottle, Smucker's' distinctive jar with the gingham lid design, Jif's squeezable lemon-shaped lemon juice bottle, Grey Goose's frosted glass bottle with a silhouette of flying geese, Red Bull's packaging with the words "Red Bull" in a red font placed centrally between the blue and silver trapezoids, and Tiffany's robin's-egg blue box wrapped with a white bow.

The role of packaging as a brand identifier is not limited to products. Packaging can also play an important role in services, where the context in which a service is delivered can perform a brand-identifying function. For example, many fast food establishments, restaurants, and coffeehouse chains including McDonald's, TGI Fridays, Chili's, Starbucks, and Dunkin' Donuts use store design and ambiance to identify and reinforce their brands in the minds of their customers. In the same vein, many mass-merchandisers and specialized retailers including Walmart, Target, Home Depot, IKEA, Best Buy, Apple, and Nike use store design to convey their brands and differentiate them from those of competitors. Likewise, many high-end fashion retailers such as Louis Vuitton, Prada, Hermès, and Dior have engaged the expertise of renowned architects to design their stores in a way that communicates the essence of their brands. Even the brown color of the UPS delivery trucks and driver uniforms can be viewed as an aspect of service packaging that plays a key role as a brand identifier.

Product Design

Product design can serve as a brand identifier when it indicates the source of the product and distinguishes it from products offered by others. Product design elements that commonly play the role of brand identifiers include shape, color, flavor, texture, scent, and sound. As in the case of packaging, individual product design elements need not be unique to serve as brand identifiers; however, the combination of the product design elements (the overall look and feel) must be able to indicate the source of the product and distinguish it from other products.

Examples of product design that serves as a brand identifier include the design of the Hermès Birkin bag, the pink color of Owens Corning fiberglass insulation, the shape of the Volkswagen Beetle, the shape and color of the bright-orange Goldfish crackers by Pepperidge Farm, the pale-blue color and diamond shape of Pfizer's drug Viagra, the taste and texture of Oreo cookies, the fragrance of Chanel N° 5 perfume, and the red soles of Christian Louboutin shoes.

Key Principles in Designing Brand Identifiers

The creation of brand identifiers is guided by several overarching principles. To be effective, brand identifiers must be *memorable, unique, protectable, strategic,* and *communicable.*

- **Memorable.** Because one of the key functions of a brand is to help its target customers locate the branded offering, brand identifiers must be easy to recognize and recall. Compare, for example, the brand names of two 5-star Las Vegas hotels: Venetian and Vdara. The former brand is memorable and meaningful; the latter is much less so.

- **Unique.** An important function of brand identifiers is to differentiate the company's offering from the competition. In order to uniquely identify the company and its offerings, brand identifiers must be unique. Compare, for example, the brand names of the following convenience store chains: *7-Eleven, Maverik, Stop and Shop, Grab and Go,* and *One Stop Shop.* The first two brands stand out and the other three are commonplace.

- **Protectable.** Brand identifiers must be defendable against unauthorized use and legal claims. Protectability is particularly important in cases when a brand name becomes a common term that refers to all products and services that perform the same function (e.g., Xerox for copying, Rollerblade for inline skating, Velcro for a hook and loop fastener), leaving the company at risk of losing its right to the exclusive use of that name (a process referred to as generification or genericide). To illustrate, *escalator* (Otis Company), *zipper* (B.F. Goodrich), *aspirin* (Bayer), *heroin* (Bayer), *thermos* (Thermos GmbH), *laundromat* (Westinghouse), *cellophane* (DuPont), *videotape* (Ampex Corporation), and *dry ice* (Dry Ice Corporation of America) are former trademarked names that lost their protected status because of popular use and have become generic terms referring to a particular type of product.

- **Strategic.** Brand identifiers must be aligned with the overarching brand strategy such that the meaning implied by brand identifiers corresponds with the essence of the brand. For example, Procter & Gamble changed the name of *Oil of Olay* (which originally was derived from the word *lanolin*—its key ingredient) to *Olay* in order to better align it with the value proposition (non-greasy feeling) of many of its products as well as to extend the brand to a broader range of products. In the same vein, Starbucks dropped the word coffee from its logo—a change consistent with its strategy to expand beyond coffee and serve light meals and alcoholic beverages.

- **Communicable.** Brand identifiers must be compatible with different types of media. The advancement of online communication has placed a number of limitations on presenting graphically complex identifiers, including the removal of special punctuation that cannot be readily entered into a web browser, to ensure that the brand logo can be clearly displayed as an app on smart devices. For example, British book retailer Waterstones streamlined its name by dropping the apostrophe to ensure consistent brand identification of its online and brick-and-mortar stores. In the same vein, mail-order flower distributor 1-800-FLOWERS modified its name to 1800FLOWERS.com to ensure brand-name consistency across different media channels.

Brand Referents

Brand referents are the brand elements whose value the company aims to leverage by linking them to its brand name. For example, BMW associates its brand with referents such as performance, driving experience, luxury, precision engineering, adventure, and Germany; Starbucks associates its brand with referents such as coffee, espresso, custom-crafted drinks, great taste, friendly service, and social impact; and Apple associates its brand with innovation, style, creativity, functionality, and ease of use.

Brand referents are similar to brand identifiers in that they aim to create a set of meaningful associations in people's minds. However, unlike brand identifiers, which are owned and managed by the company, brand referents exist independently of the company. Furthermore, unlike brand identifiers whose primary function is to identify the company's offering, brand referents typically do not uniquely identify the company's offerings. For example, although *coffee* is a brand referent for Starbucks, it also is used by other coffee chains such as Peet's Coffee, Seattle's Best Coffee, Tim Hortons, Costa Coffee, and Lavazza. Rather than uniquely identifying a company's products and services, the primary function of brand referents is to enhance the value of the brand by "borrowing" the meaning associated with the referents. Thus, using relevant brand referents enables the company to shape the image of the brand in customers' minds.

Consider two of the brand elements defining Nestlé's Nespresso brand: its logo featuring a white letter N on a black background, and its brand ambassador, George Clooney. Here, Nespresso's logo serves the function of a brand identifier, and George Clooney plays the role of a brand referent. Nespresso's logo is owned by Nestlé, but Nestlé does not own and has little control over George Clooney (other than through his contractual obligations as a celebrity endorser). Nespresso's logo adds value to the brand primarily by establishing the unique identity of Nestlé's offering and differentiating it from the competition. In contrast, George Clooney—the winner of two Oscars and three Golden Globe Awards, and ranked by *Time* magazine as one of the 100 most influential people in the world—creates value for the Nespresso brand by allowing it to leverage his image and reputation. Nestlé describes George Clooney as "the perfect personification of the understated elegance and authenticity that make *Nespresso* what it is today."[4]

Brand referents can be thought of as nodes in the network of associations defining the image of a given brand in customers' minds. To illustrate, in the Starbucks map depicted in Figure 2 earlier in this chapter, *indulgence, energy, convenience,* and *self-identity* illustrate the needs the company seeks to fulfill and the benefits customers expect to receive from the brand; *great service, friendly, fast, consistent experience,* and *perfect taste* describe brand-specific experiences; *morning* and *my ritual* define the usage occasions typically associated with the brand; *nearby* reflects the place where the brand is usually consumed; and *coffee* defines the relevant product category. In the Apple map, *entertainment, music-on-the-go, connectivity, stylish,* and *sleek design* depict the need fulfillment and the benefits customers expect to receive from the brand; *different, innovative,* and *creative* are brand-related concepts representing abstract ideas and general notions; *easy-to-use* and *easy-to-learn* describe the brand-specific experience; *phone* and *tablet* define the product categories associated with the brand; and *Mac, iPhone, iPad, iPod, iTunes,* and *Microsoft* are the brands associated with the Apple brand.

Brand referents vary in the type of associations they aim to create. Despite their variety, there are several common types of referents used by companies to shape and enhance the meaning of their brands. Such common brand referents include *needs, benefits, experiences, occasions, activities, places, people, concepts, objects, products and services,* and (other) *brands.*

- **Needs.** Because brands aim to create customer value, a company might choose to establish a direct association between a particular customer need and its own brand. To accomplish this, a company might promote the link between the customers' need and its brand as a means to fulfill this need. For example, Sprite has associated itself with thirst (*Obey your thirst*), Snickers has focused on hunger (*You're not you when you're hungry*), and Harley-Davidson has focused on the need for self-expression (*Live to ride, ride to live*).

- **Benefits.** Instead of referring to a particular need of its target customers, a company might associate its brands with a particular benefit of the offering as a means of fulfilling this need. For example, Energizer emphasizes durability (*Keeps going and going and going*), Tide focuses on cleaning power (*If it's gotta be clean, it's gotta be Tide*), FedEx emphasizes speed and reliability (*When it absolutely, positively has to be there overnight*), Coca-Cola highlights refreshment (*The pause that refreshes*), Pepsi highlights taste (*The taste of the new generation*), and Walmart and Target highlight low prices (*Always low prices. Always*; *Expect more. Pay less*).

- **Experiences.** A company might also associate its brand(s) with different experiences, including feelings, emotions, and senses. For example, Hallmark associates itself with caring (*When you care enough to send the very best*), Campbell's soup and KFC associate themselves with taste (*M'm! M'm! Good!*; *Finger lickin' good*), Disneyland relates itself to fun and happiness (*The happiest place on earth*), American Red Cross associates itself with compassion (*The greatest tragedy is indifference*), Toyota associates itself with a special driving experience (*Get the feeling*), and American Airlines associates itself with a superior flying experience (*Something special in the air*).

- **Occasions.** Because many purchase and usage decisions are occasion-based, companies often relate their brands to particular events and situations in the lives of their customers. For example, Corona beer is associated with a vacation at a tropical beach, Kodak is associated with special occasions, Kit Kat is associated with taking a break, Korbel California Champagne associates itself with New Year's celebrations, and De Beers associates its brand with engagements and anniversaries.

- **Activities.** Brands might also use as referents specific activities that their target customers typically engage in. For example, Nike is associated with playing sports, Google is associated with online search, Rollerblade is associated with inline skating, Xerox is associated with copying, Procter & Gamble's Mr. Clean is associated with household cleaning, and Facebook is associated with social networking.

- **Places.** Brands can refer to various geographic locations, countries, states, and cities in order to establish their identity. For example, Foster's beer and Yellow Tail wine are associated with Australia (*Foster's — Australian for beer*), Harley-Davidson underscores its American heritage (*American by birth. Rebel by choice*), Rice-A-Roni references San Francisco (*Rice-A-Roni — the San Francisco treat*), The Boston Beer Company associates its brand Samuel Adams with Boston, Saks Fifth Avenue associates itself with New York City's iconic Fifth Avenue, and Visa highlights its omnipresence (*VISA — It's everywhere you want to be*).

- **People.** Because customers can easily relate to other people, companies often associate their brands with individuals. For example, Swiss watchmaker Tag Heuer has associated its brand with a variety of celebrities including Brad Pitt, Tiger Woods, and Uma Thurman. Apple has associated its brand with Albert Einstein, Pablo Picasso, Martin Luther King, Jr., Mahatma Gandhi, and John Lennon. Brands can also be associated with a group of people representing a social class or a lifestyle rather than a particular individual. For example, *Fortune* magazine associates itself with economic and political leaders (*For the men in charge of change*).

- **Concepts.** Brands can also refer to more abstract ideas, concepts, and thoughts. For example, Aston Martin refers to the concepts of *beauty* and *soul*; Calvin Klein refers to the concepts of *love*, *madness*, and *obsession*; Apple refers to the concept of *thinking different*; Volkswagen refers to the concept of *thinking small*; IMAX refers to the concept of *thinking big*; 3M refers to *innovation*; HP refers to *inventing*; Product Red promotes the idea of *battling AIDS in Africa*; Benetton promotes the idea of *diversity*; and Dove promotes the idea of *natural beauty*.

- **Objects.** Brands can be associated with objects that represent a particular aspect of the image it aims to create in customers' minds. For example, IBM uses the planet as a referent (*Solutions for a smart planet*), Chevrolet trucks are associated with a rock (*Like a rock*), and the laundry detergent Ajax uses dirt as a referent (*Stronger than dirt*).

- **Products and services.** A brand can position itself by referencing a particular product or service so that thinking about the brand evokes the product/service and thinking about the product/service evokes the name of the brand. Brands with strong product category associations include Quaker (oatmeal), Chiquita (bananas), Dole (pineapples), Perdue (chicken), De Beers (diamonds), Morton Salt (salt), and FTD (flowers). In the same vein, brands that have strong associations with particular services include Amazon (online retail), eBay (online auctions), FedEx (overnight delivery), and H&R Block (tax preparation).

- **Brands.** Companies use other brands as referents for different reasons. First, companies can associate (cobrand) their brand with another brand (their own or a collaborator's brand) to leverage its value. For example, the iPhone is cobranded with its parent brand, Apple; Courtyard hotels are cobranded with Marriott, their parent brand; Lenovo is cobranded with Intel; and Chase is cobranded with Visa. Alternatively, a company can use a competitor's brand as a referent in order to contrast it with its own brand. For example, to underscore its benefits, T-Mobile compared itself to Verizon, Apple compared itself to Microsoft, and Microsoft's Bing compared itself to Google.

The choice of brand referents is important because they help customers form brand associations by linking the brand name with important mental constructs—needs, benefits, experiences, occasions, activities, places, people, concepts, objects, products and services, and other brands—that are meaningful to target customers. To ingrain their brands in customers' minds and make these brands more relevant, companies use multiple referents, each designed to create a distinct and meaningful brand association. Because brand referents (together with brand identifiers) are the tools a company uses to create a favorable brand image, the individual brand elements must converge in a way that leads to a consistent and meaningful value proposition and positioning.

Managing Brand Portfolios

As companies grow, they expand their offerings to appeal to a broader range of customers. As a result, an important decision facing a company is whether its new offerings should be associated with the same brand or use different brands. There are three core approaches to building brand portfolios: *single-brand strategy*, *multi-brand strategy*, and *cobranding strategy*.

Single-Brand Strategy

Single-brand strategy (also referred to as *umbrella branding* or *branded house*) involves using the same brand across a variety of diverse offerings. For example, BMW, Mercedes, GE, Heinz, and FedEx use a single brand for nearly all their products and services. In this case, the individual offerings are differentiated by generic designators rather than brands. For example, Mercedes uses letters, BMW uses numbers, and GE combines the GE brand with common words such as aviation, healthcare, power, oil and gas, and transportation to reference the individual offerings in their company portfolios. In addition to using the same brand name, a more subtle form of the single-brand strategy involves using names with the same prefix to highlight the commonality across individual brands. For example, Nescafé, Nesquik, Nestea, and Nespresso are used by Nestlé to brand different beverages.

The single-brand strategy has a number of important advantages: It leverages the equity of an existing brand, benefiting from the instant recognition of this brand while avoiding the costs associated with building a new brand. Using a single brand can also strengthen the brand by increasing its visibility across product categories and purchase occasions.

Despite its advantages, the single-brand strategy has several drawbacks. One such drawback is that the single-brand strategy makes it difficult to establish a meaningful brand image across a broad set of product categories and purchase occasions. For example, Bic faced challenges when it tried to use its brand—primarily known for ballpoint pens, cigarette lighters, and disposable razors—in product categories such as perfume and underwear. Using a single brand also carries the risk of a spillover of negative information across brands, whereby poor performance by any product in the brand portfolio can hurt the reputation of the entire brand. Furthermore, using a single brand does not take advantage of the opportunity to build a new brand, thus creating a separable company asset that can increase the value of the company.

Multi-Brand Strategy

Multi-brand strategy (also referred to as a *house of brands*) involves using separate brands for different products and/or product lines. For example, Tide, Ariel, Cheer, Bold, and Era are individual brands of laundry detergent managed by Procter & Gamble, which also owns a variety of brands across different product categories, including Charmin, Braun, Bounty, Old Spice, Pampers, Luvs, Always, Head & Shoulders, Herbal Essences, Gillette, Crest, and Pantene. Unilever's brand portfolio includes Bertolli, Skippy, Jif, Dove, Lipton, Knorr, Axe, and Rexona. Diageo manages dozens of alcoholic beverage brands including Smirnoff, Tanqueray, Johnnie Walker, José Cuervo, Baileys, Hennessy, Guinness, Dom Pérignon, and Moët & Chandon. Yum! Brands owns KFC, Pizza Hut, and Taco Bell.

The multi-brand portfolio strategy has a number of important advantages. Using multiple brands enables a company to establish a unique brand identity for different product categories and purchase occasions—a strategy particularly relevant when targeting diverse customer segments across different product categories. Using multiple brands also limits the possibility of a spillover of negative information about a specific brand to other brands in a company's portfolio. A portfolio of unique brands also has greater market value because each brand represents a distinct company asset that has its own valuation and, if needed, can be divested.

Despite its advantages, the multi-brand strategy has several drawbacks. Because each brand has its own identity and is designed to create unique value for its target customers, creating a portfolio of distinct brands involves substantial financial and managerial resources. Furthermore, the multi-brand strategy does not capitalize on the breadth of the company's portfolio of offerings to enhance brand visibility and impact. Another downside is that for a brand to have a relevant and meaningful image in customers' minds, it must be internalized by customers and related to a particular set of needs, values, and purchase occasions—a process that can take years and even decades.

Cobranding Strategy

Cobranding involves using two (or more) of the company's brands, with one of the brands typically serving as an umbrella brand. Cobranding can involve one of two core strategies: *sub-branding* and *endorsement branding*.

- **Sub-branding** combines an umbrella brand with a lower tier brand in a way that underscores the umbrella brand. Sub-branding is very common among car manufacturers. For example, Jeep Cherokee, Jeep Renegade, and Jeep Wrangler are sub-brands of Jeep, which serves as the anchor brand. In the same vein, Dodge sub-brands—Dodge Charger, Dodge Durango, and Dodge Viper—underscore the parent brand.

- **Endorsement branding** combines an umbrella brand with a lower tier brand in a way that underscores the lower tier brand, with the umbrella brand playing a secondary role. For example, Courtyard by Marriott, Residence Inn by Marriott, and SpringHill Suites by Marriott showcase the individual brands, with the Marriott umbrella brand used to support the focal brand. In the same vein, Kit Kat, Carnation, Toll House, and Coffee-mate are free-standing brands, all of which also feature the Nestlé brand that serves as an endorser.

Cobranding is often viewed as the middle ground between single-brand and multi-brand portfolio strategies. As such, it combines the benefits of these two strategies: single branding's cost efficiency and multi-branding's ability to create a unique brand identity tailored to different needs and purchase occasions.

Despite its advantages, cobranding has several important drawbacks. Compared to the single-brand strategy, cobranding involves building individual brands, which can involve significant financial and managerial resources. Furthermore, associating the same umbrella brand with different brands can make it more difficult for these brands to establish their own unique identity. Cobranding can also facilitate a spillover of negative information across brands, whereby negative information associated with one brand can spread to other brands (although spillover is less likely compared to the single-brand strategy).

Choosing a Brand-Portfolio Strategy

A company's options when designing its brand portfolio can be viewed as a continuum on which different strategies—single-brand, new sub-brand, new endorsed brand, and independent new brand—are arranged based on the degree to which offerings in the company's product portfolio share the same brand (Figure 5).

Figure 5. Single-Brand, Cobranding, and Multi-Brand Portfolio Strategies

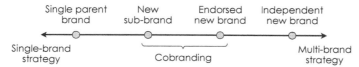

Because each brand-portfolio strategy has its pros and cons, the choice of a specific branding strategy is driven by the overarching goal the company aims to achieve with its products, services, and brands. Thus, the single-brand strategy is more common for companies that operate within a single industry and, hence, are less likely to benefit from having brands with distinct identities and meanings. In contrast, companies with product and service portfolios that span diverse categories are more likely to benefit from having multiple brands, with each brand tailored to specific customer needs.

The single-brand strategy is also more likely to be used by companies whose expertise is in domains other than brand building, such as technology development and product design. In contrast, the multi-brand strategy is more common for companies with brand-building expertise that understand the value created by brands and have the resources to build new brands in an effective and cost-efficient manner. The multi-brand strategy is also more common for consumer companies that cater to diverse customer segments and less common for industrial companies that often use a single brand to differentiate their offerings.

The cobranding strategy offers a compromise between having to invest time, money, and effort to build a new brand from scratch, and the limitation of being constrained by the meaning contained in a single brand. As a result many companies are using cobranding—sub-branding or endorsement branding—as a way to build on the strength of their existing brands, while at the same time enabling these companies to develop unique identifiers and meanings to differentiate their products and services.

Brand Dynamics

Once created, brands don't stay still; they evolve over time as markets change. Thus, changes in customer needs, strategies adopted by competing brands, and goals that the company aims to achieve with its brand serve as the impetus for managers to modify their brands. There are two common ways in which managers can modify their brands: *extending the brand*, which involves broadening the set of offerings associated with the brand, and *repositioning the brand*, which involves changes to the identity and meaning of a company's brand.

Extending the Brand

Extending the brand involves using an existing brand in a different context, such as a different product category or a different price tier. For example, when launching an ice cream product line, Starbucks used its current brand, thus extending the meaning of the brand beyond coffee to include frozen packaged goods sold in traditional grocery stores. Depending on whether the newly added products are substantively different in functionality or price, there are two types of brand extensions: *vertical* and *horizontal*.

Vertical Brand Extensions

Vertical brand extensions stretch the brand to a product or service in a different price tier. Depending on the direction in which the brand is being extended, there are two types of brand extensions: upscale extensions in which the brand is associated with an offering in a higher price tier, and downscale extensions in which the brand is associated with an offering in a lower price tier (Figure 6).

Figure 6. Vertical Brand Extensions

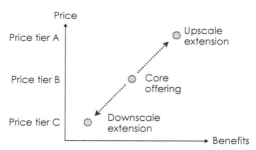

Upscale brand extensions associate an existing brand with offerings in a higher price tier with which the brand is not currently associated. For example, Apple extended its product line with the Apple Watch Edition series featuring 18-karat gold and priced between $10,000 and $17,000. Volkswagen introduced Volkswagen Phaeton, a luxury car with prices starting at around $70,000 and extending as high as $100,000. E. & J. Gallo Winery introduced its Gallo Signature Series collection of premium wines priced significantly higher than its mainstream wines.

Upscale brand extensions are appealing to companies for several reasons. The first and perhaps most obvious reason is that using an existing brand is much easier and more cost effective than building a new brand. Another factor adding to the appeal of upscale brand extensions is that they can help raise the image of the core brand. For example, adding the Watch Edition series underscores Apple's positioning as a self-expressive luxury brand—an important aspect of Apple's brand image in many developing countries. In the same vein, introducing Phaeton helped Volkswagen raise its brand image, and adding the Signature Series wines helped E. & J. Gallo Winery enhance the image of its core Gallo brand.

Despite their benefits, upscale brand extensions have important drawbacks. The key disadvantage of extending a brand upwards is that the existing brand associations tend to hurt rather than help the upscale extension. For example, adding the Gallo brand to a premium wine might make it less attractive to consumers who associate the Gallo brand with more affordable wine. In the same vein, one of the key reasons for Phaeton's commercial failure was that it was branded as a Volkswagen; consumers did not want to pay $80,000 for a car prominently featuring the VW logo and sold in Volkswagen dealerships. Because of these limitations, successful upscale brand extensions are rare.

Downscale brand extensions use an existing brand for offerings in a lower price tier with which the brand is not currently associated. For example, Mercedes-Benz introduced its Mercedes-branded A-Class, which was significantly more affordable than its core product line. In the same vein, BMW extended its product line downscale by introducing the BMW 1-Series, Porsche launched its entry-level Porsche Boxster, and Giorgio Armani introduced a more affordable version of its offerings with Armani Exchange.

Downscale brand extensions offer a number of important benefits. First, they enable a company to leverage an established brand name to new offerings without investing the time and resources needed to build a new brand. In addition, unlike upscale brand extensions, where the core brand often is a liability, for downscale extensions, the core brand is an asset that adds value to the new offering. Downscale extensions further benefit the company by introducing its brand to target customers who currently might not be able to afford the brand's higher end offerings but are likely to be able to do so in the future. For example, high-end retailer Neiman Marcus and upscale fashion designers including Carolina Herrera, Marc Jacobs, and Oscar de la Renta have partnered with Target to develop an entry-level luxury collection to attract younger, less affluent consumers who in the future might become customers of their pricier fashions.

On the downside, downscale brand extensions face several important challenges. Associating an upscale brand with an affordable product can hurt the brand image. For example, Jaguar's brand image was negatively influenced by the launch of its entry-level X-Type sedan, which was built on a Ford platform and used many components from Ford's mainstream vehicles. Another drawback of downscale brand extensions is that they can increase the likelihood of product line cannibalization, whereby the sales of the downscale offering come at the expense of the company's higher priced offerings. For example, instead of buying higher end Mercedes, BMW, or Audi models, customers might purchase their lower end models while still receiving the benefit of being associated with a premium brand. Because the lower end models also tend to have lower profit margins, product line cannibalization associated with downscale brand extensions is usually detrimental to company profitability.

To mitigate the potential drawbacks of downscale brand extensions, companies often introduce new brands that are cobranded with the core brand. For example, *Armani* uses *Armani Jeans, Armani Exchange*, and *Armani Collezioni* to differentiate its lower end offerings from the high-end, ready-to-wear *Giorgio Armani* line and the haute couture line, *Armani Privé*. In general, the greater the disparity between the price tiers involved in the downscale extension, the greater the need to distance the involved brands (and create a new brand rather than use an existing brand) to minimize the chance of diluting the core brand. Because of the drawbacks of downscale brand extensions, some companies choose to develop an entirely new brand rather than extend their existing brands. For example, Dow Corning introduced a new brand Xiameter to differentiate its low-price, no frills silicone products from its namesake-brand premium-quality products.

Horizontal Brand Extensions

Horizontal brand extensions involve using a brand in a product category with which it is not currently associated (Figure 7). For example, Armani extended its brand from clothing to home furnishings, such as bedding and towels, and even to hotels; Timberland extended its brand from boots to outerwear and travel gear; Porsche extended its brand from sports cars to sedans and sport utility vehicles; and Yamaha extended its brand from musical instruments to multiple categories including audio equipment, golf products, and motorcycles.

Figure 7. Horizontal Brand Extensions

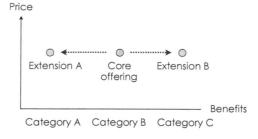

Horizontal brand extensions are typically priced in the same tier as the core brand. For example, many luxury designer brands such as Gucci, Dolce & Gabbana, Louis Vuitton, and Burberry have stretched their brands by introducing fragrances and cosmetics, which, as a product category, are more affordable than apparel and handbags. Despite their lower price point relative to apparel and handbags, the cosmetic products offered by Gucci and other luxury designers maintain their top price-tier position and are priced at a premium relative to most other cosmetic brands.

Horizontal brand extensions offer several important benefits to companies. Similar to vertical extensions, they use an existing brand to launch an offering — an approach that is much more cost efficient and involves less time and effort compared to building a new brand. For example, Crest leveraged its reputation in dental care to extend its brand to teeth whitening with the launch of Crest Whitestrips. Horizontal brand extensions also enable a company to leverage the power of its core brand by adding value to newly launched offerings. Unlike downscale extensions, which enable customers to purchase less expensive offerings carrying the same brand name, horizontal extensions offer different functionality that might complement rather than substitute for the brand's core offerings.

Horizontal brand extensions — such as different beverage flavors — also help fulfill the variety-seeking needs of customers without their having to leave the brand family. Presence in different product categories helps increase a brand's visibility across a variety of usage occasions and attain greater prominence in retail stores. For example, Montblanc, Ralph Lauren, Armani, and Oakley have benefited from cross-category availability because they offer more opportunities for customers to express their identity with their brands.

Despite their advantages, horizontal brand extensions have important drawbacks. A key concern with horizontal brand extensions is brand dilution, which can occur when a brand is extended to diverse product categories. For example, extending the Starbucks brand to non-coffee products that include ice cream, craft beer, wine, and small food plates might detract from its perceived coffee-related expertise. In addition to diluting the image of the core brand, brand extensions might detract from rather than add value to the new offering. For example, Colgate-Palmolive launched ready-to-eat meals branded as *Colgate Kitchen Entrees*, even though the Colgate brand was strongly associated with toothpaste rather than food. Brand extensions also carry the hidden cost of foreclosing the chance for a company to build a new, distinct brand that has its own unique value proposition for a particular customer segment.

Repositioning the Brand

Repositioning a brand involves changing the brand strategy — its target customers and/or its value proposition. For example, Philip Morris' flagship brand, Marlboro, originally introduced in 1924 as a women's cigarette tagged *Mild as May*, in 1954 was repositioned around the rugged cowboy image of the Marlboro Man, which was more relevant to male smokers. Target, which in the '90s was seen as just another discount retailer selling average-quality products at low prices, repositioned its brand to focus on value-priced designer apparel and merchandise, and, in the process, became the second-largest value retailer in the United States, after Walmart. Pabst Blue Ribbon, once considered a working-class beer, repositioned itself to appeal to a new customer segment and become the beer of choice for hipsters, college students, and millennials.

Brand repositioning is distinct from brand extension in that brand extension involves associating the brand with new products and/or services that previously were not associated with it. In contrast, brand repositioning involves a change in the meaning of the brand without necessarily changing its scope by adding new products and/or services. Whereas brand extension typically aims to preserve the meaning of the brand and expand it to a broader range of offerings, brand repositioning aims to change the meaning of the brand.[5]

The most common reason for changing the positioning of a brand is to respond to changes in the market in which this brand operates. The five main reasons to reposition a brand (corresponding to the 5-C framework) are outlined below.

- **Changes in target customers.** A common reason for repositioning a brand is to ensure that it remains relevant to the changing needs of its target customers. For example, to increase its appeal to younger customers, Procter & Gamble repositioned its half-century-old beauty brand, Oil of Olay, by abbreviating the name to Olay (to avoid associations equating oil to "greasy"), streamlining the design of its logo, and replacing the woman's image (which resembled a nun) on the label with that of a younger woman. In the same vein, to reverse the decline in market share and attract new customers, Procter & Gamble repositioned Old Spice from a stale baby boomer brand to a contemporary male grooming brand for younger consumers.

- **Changes in the company's goals.** A company might reposition its brand to reflect a change in its strategic focus. For example, to strengthen its market position, Diesel shifted its image from a middle-of-the-road jeans company to an upscale lifestyle brand. A company also might change its brand name to better align it with a company's global expansion strategy. To illustrate, to increase the global appeal of its brand, the Brazilian mining company Companhia Vale do Rio Doce (Doce River Valley Company) changed its brand name to Vale.

- **Changes in the collaborator network.** A company might reposition its brand to reflect a change in its collaborator and brand partnerships. For example, following acquisition by its collaborator FedEx, the Kinko's chain of copy and print centers was repositioned as FedEx Kinko's (which later became FedEx Office). In the same vein, following acquisition by its collaborator UPS, the Mail Boxes Etc. chain of business service centers was repositioned as The UPS Store.

- **Changes in the competitive environment.** A change in a competitor's positioning often induces the company to reposition its brand to preserve and enhance its competitive advantage. For example, Procter & Gamble's product line, which is branded as Mr. Clean (with minor variations) around the world, is sold in the United Kingdom and Ireland under the brand name Flash (without any references to the Mr. Clean brand name and its brand character) because the name Mr. Clean was already in use by a different company.

- **Changes in the context.** Brand repositioning might also stem from changes in the economic, technological, sociocultural, regulatory, and physical context in which the company operates. For example, in 1991, Kentucky Fried Chicken abbreviated its name to KFC to avoid paying license fees to the State of Kentucky, which trademarked the name in 1990. A decade and a half later, after reaching an agreement with the State of Kentucky in 2006, KFC began to reintroduce its original name, repositioning itself once again as Kentucky Fried Chicken.

Brand repositioning, although common, is not the only option to better align the meaning of the brand with the current market realities. Rather than reposition a brand—a process that involves a major change in its value proposition—a company might choose to make more subtle changes to the brand's value proposition. These changes, dubbed *brand revitalization*, typically involve relatively minor changes in the brand tactics, such as refreshing the brand logo, modifying the brand motto, and replacing the brand spokesperson. Unlike brand repositioning, however, brand revitalization involves changes that concern the peripheral aspects of the brand while leaving its core value proposition intact.

Brand Valuation

There are several reasons why a company can benefit from having an accurate estimate of the value of its brands. Knowing the monetary value of a brand is important in *mergers and acquisitions* to determine the premium over the book value of the company that a buyer should pay. Knowing the monetary value of its brand(s) is also important in order to determine the value of the entire company for *stock valuation* purposes. Brand valuation is also important in *licensing* to determine the price premium that brand owners should receive from licensees for the right to use their brand. Having an accurate estimate of the value of the brand also matters in *litigation* cases involving damages to the brand to determine the appropriate magnitude of monetary compensation. Assessing the value of the brand is also important for evaluating the *effectiveness* of a company's brand-building activities, for cost-benefit analysis to justify brand-building expenditures, as well as to decide on the allocation of resources across brands in a company's portfolio.

For a company to succeed in building strong brands, it must have a clear understanding of how the brand creates market value, as well as the metrics and processes for assessing the value of the brand. The two aspects of brand value—*brand equity* and *brand power*—are outlined in more detail in the following sections.

Brand Equity as a Marketing Concept

Brand equity is the monetary value of the brand. It is the premium that is placed on a company's valuation because of brand ownership. The monetary value of a brand is reflected in the financial returns that the brand will generate over its lifetime. Understanding the concept of brand equity, managing its antecedents and consequences, and developing methodologies to measure brand equity are of utmost importance for ensuring a company's financial well-being.

For years, companies spent millions of dollars on brand building without established accounting procedures to assess the value of the brands they created. The issue of brand valuation came into prominence in the 1980s when the wave of mergers and acquisitions, including the $25 billion buyout of RJR Nabisco, served as a natural catalyst for the increased interest in brand valuation and the development of more accurate brand valuation methodologies. Because the value of the brands owned by a company is not reflected in its books,[6] setting a fair price for brand assets that a firm has built over time is of utmost importance, especially given the fact that the value of a company's brands could exceed its tangible assets.

Brand equity is a part of goodwill, an accounting term referring to the monetary value of all intangible assets of a company. Goodwill is a way to document that—in addition to tangible assets such as property, plants, materials, and investments—a company's assets also include an intangible component comprising brands, patents, copyrights, know-how, licenses, distribution arrangements, company culture, and management practices. Thus, goodwill is much broader than brand equity and includes not only the value of the company's brand, but also the value of the company's other intangible assets.

Goodwill is recorded on a company's books when it acquires another entity and pays a premium over the listed book value of assets. For example, if a company pays $1 billion to acquire another company with book assets of $500 million, the other $500 million would be recorded in the books of the acquirer as goodwill. One of the reasons for the discrepancy between the book value and the market value of a brand is that acquired brands are recognized as assets for tax and accounting purposes, whereas internally generated brands are not.[7] Thus, a company that has built a brand from scratch cannot recognize it as an asset in its financial statements because it developed these brands internally and charged the related costs to expenses. In this context, goodwill is a way to recognize the market value of a brand when it is acquired.

Measuring Brand Equity

Despite the importance of brand equity, there is no single universally agreed-on methodology for its assessment; rather, there are several alternative methods, each emphasizing different aspects of brand equity. Three common approaches to measuring brand equity are the *cost approach*, the *market approach*, and the *financial approach*. All of these approaches view brands as separable and transferable company assets that have the ability to generate a stream of revenue. Where these approaches differ is in conceptualizing the sources of brand equity and the reliance on different methodologies to quantify the value of the brand.

Cost Approach to Measuring Brand Equity

The cost approach involves calculating brand equity based on the costs involved (e.g., marketing research, brand design, communication, management, and legal costs) to develop the brand. The cost method can be based on the historical costs of creating the brand by estimating all relevant expenditures involved in building the brand, or it can be based on the replacement cost—the monetary expense of rebuilding the brand at the time of valuation.

In general, the cost approach is fairly intuitive and is commonly used for evaluating a company's tangible assets. The challenge in applying this approach to assessing brand equity is that estimating the costs a company must incur to build an identical brand is extremely complicated, especially in the case of well-established brands that over the course of many years, and in some cases decades, have carved out a place in customer minds. Because of this limitation, the cost approach is more relevant for assessing the value of freshly minted brands for which the brand replacement costs are easier to identify—although even in this case accuracy is constrained because the cost approach might not take into account a brand's full potential to create market value.

Market Approach to Measuring Brand Equity

The market approach measures brand equity as the difference between the sales revenues of a branded offering vs. the sales revenues of an identical unbranded offering, adjusted for the costs of building the brand. For example, to assess the value of the Morton Salt brand, one would compare the sales revenues generated by the branded product with the sales revenues generated by its generic equivalent—regular salt—and then subtract the cost of building and managing the brand. This approach is summarized by the following equation:

$$\text{Brand equity} = \text{Sales revenues}_{(\text{Brand})} - \text{Sales revenues}_{(\text{Generic})} - \text{Branding costs}$$

In cases when a generic equivalent of the branded product is not readily available in the market, an alternative approach might involve using a test market to estimate the price difference between a single unit of a branded offering and (a prototype of) an identical unbranded offering, adjusted for sales volume and branding costs.

A key advantage of the market approach over the cost-based approach is that it requires fewer assumptions in assessing the value of a brand. At the same time, the market approach has a number of important drawbacks that limit its validity and relevance. One of the largest drawbacks is that this method focuses only on one metric of brand value (the price premium) and does not consider other aspects of value created by the brand, such as more favorable terms for a branded product from a company's collaborators as well as a brand's impact on a company's ability to recruit and retain skilled employees. Furthermore, this approach assumes that the company has fully utilized the value of its brand and, hence, does not take into account the value created by potential product-line extensions, brand extensions, and licensing opportunities.

The market approach also does not include the potential differences in the cost structure associated with branded and unbranded products, whereby the difference in prices could also be attributed to differences in production costs rather than the price premium commanded by the brand. Another important limitation of the market approach is that it does not account for the future risks associated with the brand, which can include the loss of trademarks, changes in the competitive landscape, and changes in customer preferences. In addition, the market approach is not readily applicable to companies using an umbrella-branding strategy, in which a single brand is used across different product lines in diverse product categories.

Financial Approach to Measuring Brand Equity

The financial approach assesses brand equity as the net present value (NPV) of a brand's future earnings. This approach typically involves three key steps: estimating the company's future cash flow, estimating the contribution of the brand to this cash flow, and adjusting this cash flow using a risk factor that reflects the volatility of the earnings attributed to the brand. The financial approach is summarized by the following equation:

$$\text{Brand equity} = \text{NPV of future cash flows} \cdot \text{Brand contribution factor} \cdot \text{Risk factor}$$

By considering a wider range of factors, the financial approach addresses some of the shortcomings of the cost-based and market-based approaches. At the same time, the financial approach is also subject to several important limitations. The first limitation is the difficulty in accurately estimating the future cash flow derived from the branded offerings. This difficulty stems, in part, from the fact that a brand's ability to generate future cash flow is contingent on a number of extraneous factors that are difficult to predict. For example, a brand's reputation can be damaged by a product failure or a catastrophic event such as occurred in the Tylenol poisonings (1982), the Ford–Firestone tire recall (2000), and the BP Gulf of Mexico oil spill (2010). The cash flow generated by a brand can also be influenced by a change in the market in which it operates. To illustrate, the switch to digital technology greatly reduced the size of the existing market for Kodak and Xerox, significantly diminishing the market value of these brands.

Furthermore, it is difficult to separate the cash flow attributable to the brand from the cash flow attributable to non-brand factors like production facilities, patents and know-how, product performance, supplier and distribution networks, and management skills. Consider, for example, two pizza companies, one distributing its pizzas through a delivery service and the other selling its pizzas to cafeterias. Both companies might have similar sales revenues and profits yet vary significantly in terms of their brand equity. For the company that sells its pizzas directly to customers in competition with other pizza-delivery companies such as Domino's, Pizza Hut, and Papa John's, the brand plays an important role in driving company sales and profits. In contrast, for the company that sells its pizzas to cafeterias that offer their customers a single pizza option, the brand is likely to play a relatively small role in driving sales, with product quality, service, and the distribution network being the key revenue drivers. The assessment of brand contribution can be further complicated when a company manufactures both branded and unbranded (e.g., sold to retailers as a private label) versions of the same product.

Another important limitation of the financial approach is the difficulty of accurately estimating the life span of a brand, which is a prerequisite for defining the duration of the future cash flow attributable to the brand. The financial approach also does not take into account the brand value that has not been fully realized in the market, such as the value stemming from future brand extensions and licensing agreements.

The shortcomings of the different valuation methods underscore the importance of developing alternative valuation methods that employ testable assumptions and use diverse methods to measure brand value. Such approaches must take into account the strategic value of brands, including the potential for extending the brand beyond its current target markets and product categories, as well as the brand's power to influence the behavior of different market entities.

Brand Power as a Marketing Concept

Unlike brand equity, which reflects the monetary value of the brand to the company, brand power reflects the brand's ability to influence the behavior of the relevant market entities — target customers, company collaborators, and company employees. Thus, brand power reflects the difference in the ways customers, collaborators, and company employees respond to the brand. For example, if knowledge that an offering is associated with a particular brand does not change consumers' response, the brand is lacking in power and the company's offering is effectively a commodity.

Brand power is the differential impact of brand knowledge on customers' response to a company's marketing efforts.[8] A brand has greater power when customers react more favorably to an offering because they are aware of the brand. Brand power is not always positive; for certain customers, the value of the brand might be negative, making customers less likely to purchase an offering when it is associated with a particular brand. For example, some customers display a strong loyalty to the Harley-Davidson brand and would purchase only a Harley-Davidson motorcycle, whereas for others the Harley-Davidson brand might be a detractor because it conveys unfavorable associations.

Aggregated across all customers, the brand-induced change in customers' behavior generates monetary value for the company, which is reflected in the company's brand equity. The key determinant of brand power is the brand image, which reflects all beliefs, values, emotions, and behaviors customers associate with the brand. Thus, to build a powerful brand, a company must focus its activities on creating a meaningful brand image in customers' minds that can influence their behavior in a way that creates value for the company (Figure 8).

Figure 8. Brand Power and Brand Equity

In addition to influencing customer behavior, brand power benefits the company by influencing the behavior of its collaborators and employees. Thus, brand power benefits the company by increasing the likelihood that target customers will purchase the branded offering, will use it frequently, and will be more likely to endorse this offering. Greater brand power also influences collaborators' behavior by increasing their willingness to work with the company. In addition, brand power helps the company attract a skilled workforce while enhancing employee loyalty and productivity.

Measuring Brand Power

Brand-driven behavior is the impact of the brand on customer actions. Examining brand-driven behavior focuses on the impact of the brand on three types of customer activities: *choice*, *usage*, and *advocacy*.

- **Choice.** Assessing the impact of the brand on choice focuses on the degree to which the presence of the brand influences the sales of branded offerings. A popular approach to examining the impact of the brand on customer choice involves using test markets in which some of the individuals are offered the branded version of the product and others are offered a generic (unbranded) version of the same product. Another popular approach to measure brand power involves a brand-substitution test in which the company brand is replaced with a competitor's brand, and the focal measure is the difference in choice between of the offerings carrying the two brands.

- **Usage.** Assessing the impact of the brand on usage focuses on the extent to which the brand influences the consumption of branded products. The methods for examining the impact of brand on product usage are similar to those employed in examining the impact of the brand on choice. In addition, the impact of the brand on usage can be examined with various exploratory methods (see Chapter 5 for more detail). For example, researchers might interview consumers to gain better insight into how they interact with brands and the role brands play in their overall consumption experience. Brand usage can also be examined using activity-based methods such as creating a picture-based or photo-based narrative depicting a customer's experience with the brand.

- **Advocacy.** Assessing the impact of the brand on advocacy focuses on the degree to which the brand is likely to make customers become brand advocates and try to convince others to adopt and use the offerings associated with the brand. A popular approach to measuring brand advocacy involves analyzing the content of consumers' online communication. The rapidly growing popularity of this approach stems from the fact that a large proportion of brand recommendations occur online and, hence, are readily observable and can be analyzed to single out the drivers of positive brand communication. In addition to analyzing the content of customer communication, which reflects what customers are saying about the brand, brand advocacy can be examined by analyzing the tone (sentiment) of customer communication, which focuses on factors such as emotionally laden words, phrases, and syntax to identify how customers feel about the brand. Another popular approach to measuring brand advocacy is the Net Promoter Score (discussed in Chapter 5) although its applicability to measuring brand power is rather limited due to its inability to discern the impact of the brand from the impact of the other aspects of the offering.

A key challenge in measuring brand power is that the brand is only one of many factors influencing a customer's behavior; other variables such as product/service quality, price, incentives, communication, and availability also can have a significant impact on choice. Therefore, isolating the impact of the brand from that of the other market factors is essential for assessing the true power of a brand.

Aligning Brand Power and Brand Equity

Greater brand power does not automatically lead to greater brand equity. For example, the brand equity of Nissan is estimated to be higher than the brand equity of Porsche even though Porsche is a stronger brand, as reflected in its greater price premium compared to Nissan. Likewise, even though Armani and Moët & Chandon have greater brand power than Gap and McDonald's, the brand equity of the latter is estimated to be higher.[9]

Because brand equity is a function of brand power as well as a company's ability to utilize this power in a given market, brand equity is not always a perfect indicator of brand power. Instead, brand equity reflects the degree to which the company is able to utilize the power of the brand. Brand power, in turn, is determined by the company's strategy and tactics as well as the impact of the various market forces: customer needs; competitor and collaborator actions; and the economic, technological, sociocultural, regulatory, and physical context in which the company operates.

Because brand power and brand equity are not perfectly correlated, it is possible to identify instances in which a brand's power exceeds its monetary value, as well as instances in which a brand's monetary valuation is overstated relative to the brand's power. A brand is undervalued when its brand equity does not take into account the full market potential of the power of this brand. In contrast, a brand is overvalued when its equity overstates the underlying brand power. From a marketing perspective, brands whose brand equity is undervalued, meaning that their brand power is not fully monetized by the company, present brand-building opportunities. From an investment perspective, undervalued brands present acquisition opportunities for companies that can unleash the hidden power of these brands.

SUMMARY

Brand management is a process of designing and sustaining a mental image in people's minds that enables the company to identify its products and services, differentiate them from the competition, and create distinct market value.

Brands create functional, psychological, and monetary *customer value*. Brands create functional value by enabling customers to identify a company's offering and by signaling the offerings' functionality. Brands create psychological value by offering emotional, self-expressive, and societal benefits to its customers. Brands create monetary value by signaling the offerings' monetary cost and enhancing the financial value of the offering.

Brands create strategic and monetary *company and collaborator value*. Brands create strategic value for the company by bolstering customer demand, amplifying the impact of the other marketing tactics, ensuring greater collaborator support, and facilitating the hiring and retaining of skilled employees. Brands create monetary value for the company by generating incremental revenues and profits, increasing the valuation of the company, and creating a separable company asset. In addition, brands create value for the company's collaborators by strengthening collaborators' own brands as well as by generating incremental demand, revenues, and profits.

To ensure that the brand image creates market value, it must be guided by a clear understanding of the meaning of the brand, which is reflected in the brand positioning and the brand mantra. *Brand positioning* is the process of creating a meaningful and distinct image of the brand in target customers' minds. *Brand mantra* defines the essence of the brand and its core promise to its customers. The brand positioning and mantra delineate the specific attributes defining the brand.

Brand attributes are the tools that the company uses to position the brand and create the desired brand image in customers' minds. Brand building involves two types of attributes: *brand identifiers*, which are owned and managed by the company, and *brand referents*, which are not owned by the company but whose value the company aims to leverage by linking them to its brand name. The key brand identifiers are the name, logo, motto, character, soundmark, product design, and packaging. Common brand referents include needs, benefits, experiences, occasions, activities, places, people, concepts, objects, products and services, and other brands.

Building *brand portfolios* involves one of three core strategies. The *single-brand strategy* (also referred to as *umbrella branding* or *branded house*) involves using the same brand across diverse offerings. The *multi-brand strategy* (also referred to as a *house of brands*) involves using separate brands for different products and product lines. *Cobranding* involves using two (or more) of the company's brands, with one of the brands typically serving as an umbrella brand. Cobranding can involve sub-branding, which underscores the umbrella brand, and endorsement branding, in which the umbrella brand plays a secondary role.

Brand extension involves using an existing brand name in a different context, such as a different product category or a different price tier. *Vertical brand extensions* stretch the brand to a product or service in a different price tier. Specifically, upscale extensions associate the brand with an offering in a higher price tier, whereas downscale extensions associate the brand with an offering in a lower price tier. *Horizontal brand extensions* stretch the brand to a product category with which it is not currently associated.

Brand repositioning involves changing the meaning of the brand — without extending the brand to unrelated product categories. The five key reasons to reposition a brand are changes in one or more of the Five Cs: target customers, company goals, the collaborator network, the competitive environment, and the market context.

Brand valuation involves assessing brand equity and brand power. *Brand equity* is the monetary value of the brand: It reflects the financial returns that the brand will generate over its lifetime. Three common approaches to measuring brand equity are the cost approach, the market approach, and the financial approach. Brand equity stems from *brand power*, which is the brand's ability to influence the behavior of the relevant market entities — target customers, collaborators, and company employees. A brand is undervalued when its brand equity does not take into account its full market potential. In contrast, a brand is overvalued when its equity overstates the underlying brand power.

MARKETING INSIGHT: BRANDS AS A MEANS OF SELF-EXPRESSION

Brands create customer value by enabling consumers to express their identity. In this context, brands act as symbols that convey a set of values reflecting an individual's self-image. Based on the type of image they project, self-expressive brands can be defined along three basic dimensions: *status*, *personality*, and *expertise*.

- *Status brands* reflect an individual's membership in a particular socioeconomic class. Status brands are related to the Veblen effect (named after economist and sociologist Thorstein Veblen), which refers to the acquisition of goods mainly for the purpose of displaying social status, income, and wealth. Status brands are particularly popular in a socioeconomic environment characterized by the creation of new wealth and the upward mobility of certain social groups (for example, emergence of an upper and a middle class in developing countries). Because they symbolize wealth, status brands are priced at a premium relative to the other brands in the same product category. Rolls-Royce, Bugatti, Louis Vuitton, Cartier, and Brioni exemplify status brands.

- *Personality brands* express consumers' individual values and preferences. Personality brands are less about asserting individuals' status, wealth, and power than about reflecting their idiosyncratic beliefs, preferences, and values. Unlike status brands, which have a price point that makes them unattainable by the majority of the population, personality brands typically are not differentiated on price and, hence, can be attained by a larger segment of the population. Harley-Davidson, Abercrombie & Fitch, UGG, Quicksilver, and Oakley exemplify personality brands.

- *Professional brands* convey an individual's expertise in a particular area. Professional brands are usually highly specialized in an area in which they have established superior functional performance. For example, the use of DeWalt-branded tools, which is designated for professional-grade equipment, helps enhance construction workers' perceived expertise and credibility. CAT (construction equipment), Montblanc (business management), and Paul Mitchell (hair care) exemplify professional brands.

A brand's value proposition does not need to be constrained to a single dimension; it might involve all three dimensions. For example, even though Bugatti is a status brand (with cars priced at over $1 million), it can also be viewed as a personality brand that expresses certain aspects of its owners' character as well as a professional brand in the context of an auto racing sports event. Likewise, even though Montblanc is positioned foremost as a professional brand, it is also a status and personality brand. In the same vein, although Harley-Davidson is first and foremost a personality brand, its relatively high price point adds a dimension of status.

The self-expressive meaning of brands is context specific and varies across countries, cultures, and social groups. Brands that are personality symbols in some countries can play the role of status symbols in others. For example, Harley-Davidson in the United States is a self-expressive brand signifying personal freedom, whereas in many developing countries it is also perceived as a status symbol due to its exclusivity and high price.

MARKETING INSIGHT: LUXURY BRANDING

In economics, luxury goods are defined based on the relationship between a change in consumer income and the demand for a particular good. In this context, luxury goods are defined as products and services for which demand rises more than proportionately to a change in income—for example, a 10% increase in income might lead to a 20% increase in demand for a luxury product. This view of luxury, however, is not very practical because it does not articulate the key actionable characteristics that define a luxury offering.

From a marketing perspective, luxury goods are defined by five key characteristics (the "Five Es" of luxury). Luxury brands are:

- *Extravagant.* Luxury is indulgent; it is not necessary. This aspect of luxury is definitional: luxury is the opposite of necessity. The primary function of luxury is hedonic; the utilitarian function (if present) is secondary.

- *Exquisite.* Luxury is of the highest quality; it is the best of the best in its category.

- *Exclusive.* Luxury is scarce; it is in limited supply and is not mass produced.

- *Expensive.* Luxury is priced significantly higher than most of the offerings in its category.

- *Expressive.* Luxury enables buyers to showcase their social status and wealth; an increase in one's wealth or social status often leads to conspicuous consumption of luxury goods.

Luxury brands span industries and product categories, including retail (Le Bon Marché, Neiman Marcus, Selfridges, Harvey Nichols, David Jones, and Harrods), hospitality (Burj Al Arab, Four Seasons, Mandarin Oriental, St. Regis, and The Ritz-Carlton), fashion (Louis Vuitton, Gucci, Bottega Veneta, Prada, and Hermès), jewelry (Buccellati, Bulgari, Cartier, Graff, Harry Winston, Piaget, Tiffany, and Van Cleef & Arpels), watches (Audemars Piguet, Blancpain, Breguet, Franck Muller, Parmigiani Fleurier, Patek Philippe, and Vacheron Constantin), cosmetics (Chanel, Guerlain, Helena Rubinstein, Lancôme, Givenchy, and Dior), liquor (Château Petrus, Château Lafite Rothschild, Dom Pérignon, Louis Roederer Cristal, Bollinger, and Goût de Diamants), and automobiles (Rolls-Royce, Bentley, Ferrari, Aston Martin, Lamborghini, and Bugatti).

Classifying individual brands according to luxury is rather subjective. Even though the concept of luxury is universal, the ultimate determination of what constitutes luxury and which brands convey a luxury image varies across markets. As a result, the distinction between luxury and non-luxury brands is not clear-cut. In fact, there is an entire category of brands that bridge the gap between ordinary and luxury products, which are often referred to as accessible (or affordable) luxury. Accessible luxury aims to make luxury available to a wider range of shoppers. In some sense, accessible luxury is an oxymoron: true luxury by definition is exclusive and, hence, not readily accessible. What makes the accessible luxury brands like Michael Kors, Kate Spade, Coach, Tory Burch, and Ralph Lauren viable is the fact that they offer middle-class consumers an opportunity to experience "a touch of luxury" at a price that is not prohibitively high for their income level.

Chapter Twelve

Managing Price

Price is what you pay. Value is what you get.
— Warren Buffett, American investor and philanthropist

Pricing directly influences the monetary value that the offering creates for target customers, the company, and its collaborators. Setting the right price enables the company to capture market value and achieve its monetary and strategic goals. Even though setting the perfect price cannot guarantee success, erroneous pricing can lead to a failure in the marketplace. The key aspects of price management are the focus of this chapter. Specifically, we address the following topics:

- *Pricing as a Value-Creation Process* || Price as a tool for creating market value | Key factors in setting the price
- *Setting the Price to Create Customer Value* || Understanding price elasticity | Price as a targeting tool | Psychological aspects of pricing
- *Setting the Price to Create Company Value* || Determining an offering's cost structure | Defining the company's pricing goals | Managing price dynamics
- *Setting the Price in a Competitive Context* || Competitive price–benefit analysis | Understanding price wars | Circumventing price wars

The discussion of price management is complemented by an overview of the key pricing concepts and price fairness.

Pricing as a Value-Creation Process

Many companies do not think strategically about pricing. Instead, they consider pricing merely as a means to achieve a certain level of profits based on costs incurred in developing, manufacturing, and promoting their offerings, while taking into account the prices of competitive offerings. This approach lacks a clear understanding of pricing as an important attribute of their offering, which, in concert with the other offering attributes, can create superior value for target customers, the company, and its collaborators. The role of price as a tool for creating market value and the key factors that a company must consider when setting a price are discussed in the following sections.

Price as a Tool for Creating Market Value

The price is the amount of money the company charges its customers and collaborators for the benefits provided by the offering. Pricing is an important marketing decision that influences the value created by an offering for its customers, collaborators, and the company. From a customer's perspective, the price is a key factor in defining the offering. In fact, the price–quality tradeoff (giving up product benefits in order to pay less or vice versa) is one of the most important decisions that customers weigh when making a choice. Furthermore, because prices are readily observable, customers often rely on prices to infer the offering's performance on unobservable attributes such as durability, reliability, as well as overall quality.

In addition to playing a key role in influencing customer choice, pricing also plays an important role in creating value for the company. Price is the only attribute defining the company's offering that directly creates revenues for the company; all other offering attributes — product, service, brand, incentives, communication, and distribution — incur costs. Because of their direct impact on a company's bottom line, pricing decisions can make or break the company's financial performance. Finally, an offering's price defines the value of an offering to the company's collaborators by determining the monetary benefits and costs created by this offering.

Because of its direct impact on the monetary value it creates for customers, the company, and collaborators, setting the price is an integral aspect of defining the value of the offering. As one of the seven attributes defining the market offering, price works in tandem with the other marketing tactics to create an optimal value proposition (OVP). In this context, the optimal price complements the offering's product, service, brand, incentives, communication, and distribution aspects to create superior value for target customers in a way that benefits the company and its collaborators (Figure 1).

Figure 1. Pricing as a Value-Creation Process

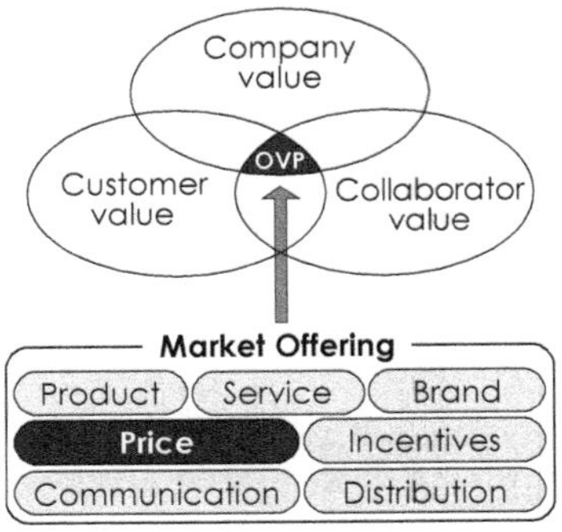

Despite the fundamental role price plays in designing and managing a company's offerings, there is little consensus on what constitutes the optimal pricing strategy. Although pricing approaches vary, successful pricing strategies share an understanding that the pricing decision should not be made in isolation but must be treated as an integral component of the offering's strategy and tactics. Accordingly, setting the optimal price is driven by a variety of considerations, including the company's strategic goals, customers' price elasticity, and the psychological aspects of customers' response to the offering's price. The role of these factors in setting the optimal price is discussed in more detail in the following sections.

Key Factors in Setting the Price

When setting the price, managers must consider two types of factors: *strategic factors* that address the market in which the company's offering aims to create value and *tactical factors* that address the ways in which price interacts with the other marketing tactics — product, service, brand, incentives, communication, and distribution — to create market value. These two types of factors are outlined in more detail below.

Strategic Factors Influencing the Price

The Five Cs — customers, company, collaborators, competitors, and context — are of strategic importance in setting and managing prices. Thus, price is a function of customers' willingness to pay for the offering's benefits, such that greater willingness to pay typically translates into higher prices. Pricing is also a function of the company's goals and cost structure, whereby aggressive sales goals and lower cost structure often result in lower prices. In addition, pricing is influenced by the company's collaborators (e.g., channel partners), such that more powerful channels (e.g., Walmart, Costco, and Carrefour) require lower prices. Because most purchase decisions involve choosing between competing offerings, an offering's price is also influenced by competitors' prices. Moreover, pricing is a function of various economic, technological, sociocultural, regulatory, and physical factors of the environment in which the company operates.

Optimal pricing policies take into account all five of the above factors. Yet, for a variety of reasons—simplicity, lack of relevant data, or mere ignorance of the market forces—some companies use simplified pricing approaches that rely on a single factor. For example, *demand pricing* sets prices based on customers' willingness to pay for the benefits afforded by the company's offering, *cost-plus pricing* and *markup pricing* add a premium to the cost of the product, and *competitive pricing* uses competitors' prices as benchmarks. While each of these methods has merit, taking into account only a subset of factors that could potentially influence the market value created by an offering provides a limited understanding of the market forces and often leads to suboptimal pricing policies.

Tactical Factors Influencing the Price

In addition to being a function of the Five Cs, price is also influenced by the other marketing tactics: product and service characteristics, brand, incentives, communication, and distribution. Thus, attractive and unique products and services command higher prices compared to less differentiated offerings. Price is also a function of the offering's brand, with strong brands commanding substantial price premiums over weaker brands and unbranded offerings, even when the actual quality of the offering is the same.

In addition to the product, service, and brand aspects of a company's offering, pricing depends on the available incentives (e.g., promotional allowances, price discounts, and coupons), which determine the final amount buyers pay for the offering. Price can also be influenced by a company's communication and set in a way that facilitates communication. For example, Subway's pricing was in part driven by its ability to create a memorable advertising campaign promoting $5 footlong sandwiches. An offering's price is also a function of its distribution, such that channels with a lower cost structure are able to offer lower prices.

Setting the Price to Create Customer Value

A key criterion when setting the price is to ensure that the company's offering can create value for its target customers, meaning that the benefits customers receive from the offering correspond to its price. To this end, a manager must know how to assess customers' price elasticity, understand how to use price as a segmentation and targeting tool, and recognize the importance of the psychological aspects of pricing.

Understanding Price Elasticity

To set the optimal price, a manager must understand the relationship between the offering's price and customer demand for that offering. Typically, sales volume is inversely related to price: Lowering the price results in an increase in the sales volume, and vice versa. The degree to which changing the price influences sales volume is referred to as *price elasticity*. Lowering the price in order to increase volume is most effective in cases where demand is elastic, meaning that a small change in price leads to a large change in sales volume. In contrast, in cases where demand is inelastic, profits might often be increased by raising the price because the decrease in sales volume resulting from the change in price is likely to be relatively small.

To illustrate, consider the price–quantity relationship illustrated in Figure 2, which depicts the impact of a price drop on purchase quantity for two products associated with different price elasticity. Even though for both products the change in price is identical—a price drop from $15 to $10—the impact of this price drop on consumer demand is not the same. For the product with inelastic demand, the quantity sold increased from 20 to 25 units, whereas for the product with elastic demand, the quantity sold increased from 20 to 50 units. In this way, elasticity determines the impact that a change in price will have on sales of a product.

Figure 2. The Price Elasticity of Demand

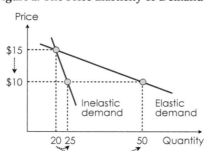

Price elasticity is quantified as the percentage change in quantity sold (ΔQ%) relative to the percentage change in price (ΔP%) for a given product or service. Because in most cases the quantity demanded decreases when the price increases, this ratio is negative; however, for practical purposes, the absolute value of the ratio is used, and price elasticity is often reported as a positive number.

$$E_p = \frac{\Delta Q\%}{\Delta P\%} = \frac{\Delta Q \cdot P}{\Delta P \cdot Q}$$

To illustrate, a price elasticity of 2 means that a 5% price increase will result in a 10% decrease in the quantity sold. In cases where (the absolute value of) price elasticity is greater than 1, demand is said to be elastic, meaning that a percentage change in price causes a larger percentage change in quantity demanded. In contrast, when (the absolute value of) price elasticity is less than 1, demand is said to be inelastic, meaning that a percentage change in price results in a smaller percentage change in quantity demanded. When (the absolute value of) price elasticity is equal to 1, demand is said to be unitary, meaning that a change in price results in an equal change in quantity demanded. In general, the higher the elasticity, the greater the volume increase resulting from a price reduction.

Because price elasticity reflects proportional changes, it does not depend on the units in which the price and quantity are expressed. Furthermore, because price elasticity is a function of the initial values, the same absolute changes in price can lead to different price elasticity values at different price points. For example, the volume decline resulting from lowering the price by five cents might be 5% when the initial price is $1.00 but is only 1% when the initial price is $5.00.

Note that price elasticity can be asymmetric with respect to the direction of the changes in an offering's price, such that increasing and lowering the price by the same amount can have a different impact on purchase quantity. The relative impact of price increases and price cuts depends on a variety of factors such as the level of the offering's current price, the degree to which the offering is differentiated from the competition, and the extent to which the customer has alternative means to fulfill the need addressed by the offering.

For example, for an offering priced at $9.99, a ten-cent price increase is likely to have much greater impact on demand than a ten-cent price decrease (because the price increase brings the offering into the $10+ price tier, whereas the price decrease does not change the offering's current price tier). In the same vein, an offering with a strong brand would be associated with lower price sensitivity to price increases than to price drops, meaning that the offering is likely to lose relatively fewer customers when its price is raised and gain many more customers when its price is lowered. Likewise, when consumers have alternative means of fulfilling their needs, such as aggressively priced competitive offerings, they might react more strongly to a price increase than to a price drop.

In general, buyers tend to be more price sensitive when an offering is perceived to be a commodity and there are many alternative options available. In contrast, buyers tend to be less price sensitive when they pay only a fraction of the total cost (as in the case of medical products and services largely covered by insurance) and when the purchase price is a relatively small component of the total cost of the offering over its lifetime (as in the case of printers, where the cost of cartridges vastly exceeds the price of the device).

Price elasticity has important implications for setting the offering's price. Thus, if demand is elastic, lowering the price (or running sales promotions) might have a positive impact on the company's net income because the decline in profit margins stemming from the price drop might be offset by a corresponding increase in the sales volume. In contrast, when demand is inelastic (meaning that the buyers are relatively insensitive to changes in price), raising the price might be a viable option to increase the company's net income because in this case the loss of volume due to the increase in price might be offset by the corresponding increase in profit margins.

Price as a Targeting Tool

Companies typically do not set a single price for an offering but rather implement a pricing structure that involves different price points based on the specifics of the markets in which they intend to compete. Because buyers' willingness to pay is one of the key market characteristics, companies use pricing as a tool to segment and target different customer segments (Figure 3).

Figure 3. Price Segmentation as a Targeting Tool

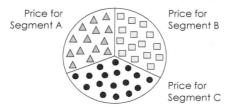

The practice of charging a different price for the same good or service is referred to as price segmentation (in economics literature, price segmentation is commonly referred to as price discrimination). There are three types of price segmentation: first-degree, second-degree, and third-degree.

First-degree price segmentation (also referred to as perfect price segmentation), occurs when a company charges a different price for every offering sold based on each customer's willingness to pay for that offering. For example, Amazon might offer different prices to different customers based on their needs and price sensitivity, inferred from their prior purchase history. Second-degree price segmentation involves setting a different unit price for different quantities, such as charging lower unit prices for larger quantity purchases. For example, a company might offer a price schedule where the price progressively declines with the increase in the purchase quantity. Finally, third-degree price segmentation involves setting different prices for different customer segments. Such segments can be defined based on their buying power (e.g., high-income vs. low-income consumers), timing of the purchase (e.g., advance vs. last-minute purchase of airline tickets), and the type of distribution channel (e.g., convenience store vs. supermarket).

Price segmentation benefits companies by enabling them to customize the value they capture from individual customers. The ability to offer different price levels for their products and services and, specifically, the ability to offer lower prices to certain customers also allows companies to serve different market segments that they might not be able to serve using a universal price policy. In addition, charging different prices at different points in time helps companies better manage the customer flow—an approach commonly referred to as yield pricing. For example, many restaurants offer "happy hour" pricing during off-peak periods to smooth demand as well as to attract more price-sensitive customers that otherwise might not end up patronizing the establishment.

In the ideal scenario, a company would segment customers based on their willingness to pay for the company's offering. In reality, however, customers' willingness to pay is not readily observable and must be inferred from the visible customer characteristics and the purchase occasion. Commonly used characteristics that can serve as a proxy for customers' willingness to pay include customer demographics, geolocation, and behavior.

Customer demographics typically used to segment customers based on price include age, income, occupation, employment status, population density of their location (urban or rural), social class, household size, and stage in the product's life cycle. For example, a company might offer lower prices to children and seniors, large families, and low-income consumers. Customer geolocation can be used to segment customers based on the availability of competitive options. For example, a company might set lower prices to match the competitive offerings available in physical proximity to the customer.

Instead of (or in addition to) setting prices based on customer demographics, a company might also set prices based on customers' buying behavior. In this context, commonly used segmentation criteria involve purchase quantity (e.g., offering lower prices to customers purchasing larger quantities), time of purchase and use (e.g., yield-management pricing including peak-load pricing and early-/late-purchase discounts), and distribution channel (e.g., offering different prices in different retail channels).

A meaningful price-based targeting requires that a company be able to identify different segments that vary in their willingness to pay for the company's offerings. Furthermore, because charging different prices for the same product creates arbitrage opportunities, a company must keep different customer segments apart to ensure that the lower priced items sold to one segment are not resold on a secondary market (such as eBay, Alibaba, and Craigslist) to other segments with a higher willingness to pay. Another important consideration involves managing the perception of price fairness to ensure that buyers perceive the differential pricing as fair based on the sociocultural norms of the market in which the company operates.

Psychological Aspects of Pricing

Buyers do not always evaluate prices in an objective fashion; instead, their reaction to an offering's price depends on a variety of psychological effects. The most common psychological pricing effects include *reference-price effects, price–quality inferences, price–quantity effects, unit-pricing effects,* as well as *price-tier* and *price-ending effects.*

Reference-Price Effects

To assess the attractiveness of the price of an offering, people typically evaluate it relative to other prices, which serve as reference points (see Chapter 4 for a discussion of reference points). These reference prices can be either internal, such as a remembered price from a prior purchase occasion, or external, such as the readily available price of a competitive offering. By strategically using the reference price, a company can frame the price of its offering in a way that makes it more attractive to potential buyers—for example, by comparing it to a more expensive competitive offering or to a higher regular price for the same offering.

There are several types of internal reference-price points that buyers can use when evaluating an offering's price. Thus, reference prices might reflect the typical price at which the offering is sold. Alternatively, buyers might set the reference price as the last price they paid for the offering. The reference price might also be the "fair" price—that is, the price at which buyers think the product or service should be sold. The reference price might be based on buyers' reservation prices—that is, the highest or the lowest price they are willing to pay for the offering. Furthermore, the reference price might also include buyers' expectations of future price increases or decreases based on their market observations and prior experiences.

Buyers' reference prices are also influenced by the prices of the other market offerings. For example, when buyers are uncertain about how much they ought to pay for a particular product or service, they often use competitors' prices for similar offerings as a reference point. Furthermore, the relative prices of other offerings in a company's product line can serve as reference points and, thus, influence customer demand. For example, restaurants often price wine they are trying to dispose of as the second cheapest in its menu assortment because many customers who are not willing to spend much on wine are often embarrassed to select the least expensive one.

Because buyers often lack accurate price knowledge and do not have a well-defined idea of how much they should pay for a given item, companies use reference points to "frame" an item's price. For example, a $250 set of car floor mats might seem exorbitantly expensive if considered as a separate item but might seem more sensible if purchased along with an $80,000 car. In the same vein, a $100 price tag for a pair of jeans might seem excessive; however, it might seem reasonable when buyers are informed that the price is a markdown from the original price of $250. Likewise, a customer might be willing to walk a few blocks to avoid paying double for a $5 item but might be unwilling to do so to save the same $5 on a $100 item. As the above examples show, reference points are important because they shape the way people evaluate prices and make purchase decisions.

Price-Quality Inferences

When evaluating the available options and making purchase decisions, buyers believe they get what they pay for, often employing the dictum "there's no such thing as a free lunch." This heuristic reflects consumers' fundamental belief that price and quality are related, with higher quality implying higher price and, vice versa, that lower priced items are likely to be of lower quality.

Given the prevalence of consumers' belief in the price–quality correlation, some manufacturers have deliberately set their prices to signal exceptional product quality, a pricing policy referred to as image (or prestige) pricing. For example, Screaming Eagle—one of Napa Valley's most expensive wine brands—has priced its flagship wine upwards of $3,000 per bottle—a price that sends a clear signal about the quality of the wine. In the same vein, luxury brands such as Hermès, Louis Vuitton, and Bottega Veneta set premium prices for their products in order to convey an image of quality, exclusivity, and prestige.

The belief that price reflects quality, although popular, is not held by all consumers and across all purchase occasions. Buyers are more likely to use price as a proxy for quality in cases when information about the actual quality of the product or service is not readily available. Furthermore, to draw price-quality inferences, buyers must perceive markets to be efficient, meaning that they believe the prices observed in the market accurately reflect product quality.

Not all purchase occasions are perceived to accurately reflect the price-quality relationship. When buyers have a valid reason to attribute the price to factors other than product quality, they might not infer quality from price. For example, when the low price can be attributed to the retailer rather than the manufacturer, price-quality inferences are less likely to occur. Thus, consumers might not necessarily think that items offered at low prices during a store-closing sale are of low quality and instead frame the low price as a deal stemming from a retailer's misfortune. In the same vein, a consumer who pays $10 for a glass of beer in an upscale restaurant, $4 for a bottle of water in an airport, or $5 for a soda at a movie theater might not necessarily infer that these products are of superior quality but rather consider it a reflection of the pricing policy of the particular retail outlet.

Price-Quantity Effects

People tend to be more sensitive to changes in price than to changes in quantity. To illustrate, the sales volume of a ten-pack of hot dogs priced at $2.49 is likely to decline to a greater extent following a $.50 price increase (a ten-pack for $2.99) than following a two-item reduction in unit volume (an eight-pack for $2.49), even though on a per-item basis, the eight-pack is more expensive than the ten-pack. The same principle applies to reducing the weight and size of a product since customers tend to pay more attention to price than to the actual quantity purchased.

The price-quantity effect does not imply that buyers are indifferent to receiving smaller quantities of the product with no price increase. It simply means that they are less dissatisfied with receiving smaller quantities at the same price than receiving the same quantities at a higher price. Furthermore, the price-quantity effect does not depend on customers failing to perceive changes in quantity. Consumers' preference for receiving a smaller quantity of the offering rather than paying a higher price holds even when these changes are transparent and buyers are fully aware of the reduced quantity.

Increases in commodity, transportation, and energy costs have pressured many manufacturers to consider raising prices to meet their profit goals. However, concern that an outright price increase could lead to a decline in consumption and customer defection to competitors' products has prompted companies to reduce the package size and product quantity while leaving the price essentially unchanged. As a result, the past two decades have seen multiple examples of this product-reduction strategy.

For example, instead of raising the price of its ice cream, Dreyer's Grand Ice Cream reduced the package size to 1.5 quarts from 1.75 quarts. Frito-Lay reduced the quantity of chips in its bags from 12 to 10 ounces. Unilever reduced the size of a jar of Hellmann's mayonnaise from 32 to 30 ounces, shrunk the jar of Skippy peanut butter from 18 to 16.3 ounces, and downsized Shedd's Country Crock spread from 48 to 45 ounces. Kellogg has shrunk boxes of Froot Loops, Cocoa Krispies, Corn Pops, Apple Jacks and Honey Smacks by 2.4 ounces on average. Henkel Corporation downsized bars of its Dial soap from 4.5 to 4 ounces. PepsiCo replaced its 96-ounce jug of Tropicana orange juice with an 89-ounce bottle. Procter & Gamble reduced the number of paper towels in its Bounty brand from 60 to 52.

Unit-Pricing Effects

Unit-pricing effects refer to customers' reaction to two different ways in which price can be presented to customers: unit-based pricing and usage-based pricing. Unit-based pricing involves expressing the price of an offering in terms of its total cost. In contrast, usage-based pricing reflects the cost of the good spread over a particular time frame. Consider, for example, Hästens Vividus—a custom-made bed built by master artisans in Köping, Sweden. The bed contains layers of flax, horsetail hair, and cotton and wool batting, which, according to the company make it "the world's most comfortable bed." To make its $150,000 price tag more palatable, Hästens informs potential buyers that if they keep the bed for 25 years and get eight hours of sleep every night, the cost is $2 per hour.[1]

Usage-based pricing also was one of the key factors contributing to the success of the Dollar Shave Club. Rather than pricing its cartridges on a per-item basis, as most cartridges sold through traditional retail channels do, the online startup priced its shaving products on a monthly basis, charging its customers $1 (plus shipping and handling), $6, or $9 for a monthly supply depending on the number of blades per cartridge. Within only a few years of its launch, Dollar Shave Club was able to gain more than ten percent of the wet-shaving market in the United States, most of which came from Gillette, even though on a per-shave basis, Gillette's razors were actually cheaper. Men unwilling to pay $5 per Gillette cartridge (that they were likely to shave with for about three weeks) were paying $9 per month for cartridges that were likely to be of inferior quality thinking that they were saving money.

From the point of view of economics, buyer preferences should be invariant across different presentations of the same price, meaning that as long as the ultimate price paid by the buyer is the same, item-based and usage-based pricing formats should produce the same outcome. In reality, however, even when the ultimate price of offerings using item-based and usage-based pricing is exactly the same, customer reaction to the price and the likelihood that they will ultimately purchase a company's offering are not.

The difference in buyer response to being presented with the total price of the item and being presented with the item's cost spread over a period of time can be attributed to the different reference points used by the buyer in evaluating the offering's value. For example, $2 per hour for (arguably) the best sleeping experience and $9 for an entire month of shaving present the offering's price in a more favorable light than a $150,000 bed and an 8-pack of cartridges priced at $40. Thus, changing the frame of reference from a relatively large single expense to a series of relatively small, mundane expenses can have a significant impact on buyers' evaluation of an offering's prices and can be an important aspect of a company's pricing policy.

Price-Tier and Price-Ending Effects

Price-tier effects reflect people's tendency to think of individual prices in terms of levels or tiers, rather than as a continuum. While this price categorization helps minimize cognitive effort and simplify the way people evaluate pricing information, it also can lead to biased perceptions of the actual prices because of the ways people encode prices into distinct tiers. For example, an item priced at $1.95 is typically encoded in the "$1+" price tier, whereas an item priced at $2.00 is typically classified in the "$2+" price tier. As a result, paying $1.95 for an item is more likely to be associated with spending $1 rather than $2.

This tiered price encoding leads to the somewhat paradoxical scenario that while the difference between items priced at $1.45 and $1.46 is correctly perceived as one cent, the difference between items priced at $1.49 and $1.50 is perceived as ten cents, and the difference between items priced at $1.99 and $2.00 is perceived as one dollar. The price-tier effect is often attributed to people's tendency to process numbers from left to right and round down the last digits of the price rather than rounding them to the nearest whole number.

Related to price-tier effects are *price-ending effects*, whereby customers' perception of prices is a function of the price endings. Some of the effects of price endings can be readily observed in the case of price-tier effects, whereby people are more sensitive to changes in price endings across different price tiers than within the same price tier. For example, the difference in prices of items that cost $1.45 and $1.48 is perceived to be smaller than the difference in prices of items that cost $1.49 and $1.51, even though the actual price difference is greater in the former case.

In addition to influencing price-tier perceptions, price endings can influence perceived prices by suggesting the presence of a bargain or a discount. For example, prices ending in 9 are often perceived as offering a better deal than prices ending in other digits—a finding commonly attributed to the fact that in many countries consumers have been culturally conditioned to associate prices ending in 9 with discounts and better deals. For example, one study has documented that a clothing item tested at the prices of $34, $39, and $44, sold best at $39, outselling even the cheaper $34 price.[2] Prices with 9-endings are not the only ones that influence price perceptions; for example, because prices ending in 4 or 7 are less frequent, they are likely to stand out and are often interpreted by buyers as an indication that the retailer has seriously considered the price and based it on the actual cost of the item being sold.

Apart from influencing price perceptions, price endings can also influence the perceived quality of the company's offering. For example, while prices ending in 9 might create the perception of a discount, prices ending in 0 and 5 might create the perception of quality. This effect is often attributed to the fact that prices ending with 0 and 5 are easier to remember, retrieve from memory, and evaluate. This ease in processing the pricing information can, in turn, translate into perceptions of quality. In the same vein, rounding the prices without displaying decimal points is more likely to lead to perceptions of quality and prestige than prices displaying decimal points.

Price-tier and price-ending effects are commonly utilized by retailers to attract price-sensitive buyers while at the same time maximizing profit margins. Thus, by making relatively minor changes in price endings, sellers can send a strong signal to price-conscious buyers about an offering's overall price (e.g., whether it is well priced and presents a deal), and convey an offering's overall quality and brand image to quality-conscious shoppers. Understanding the ways in which buyers evaluate pricing information and the impact price perceptions have on their buying and consumption behavior can help companies maximize the market value created by their offerings.

Setting the Price to Create Company Value

Because sales volume and profits are a function of price, setting the right price can be an important driver of a company's ability to achieve its goals. Some of the key issues when setting an offering's price involve determining an offering's cost structure, defining the company's pricing goals, and choosing the pricing format. These issues are discussed in more detail in the following sections.

Determining an Offering's Cost Structure

Market demand and a company's cost structure are two key factors that determine the range of prices that allow an offering to profitably exist in a market. Market demand, driven by customer willingness to pay, sets the ceiling for the price that a company can charge for its offering. In contrast, the company costs involved in developing, promoting, and distributing the offering set the floor for profitable pricing.

The key factors that merit consideration in determining an offering's cost structure include the magnitude of the offering's fixed and variable costs, as well as the ways in which costs vary as a function of the scale and scope of the processes involved in designing, communicating, and delivering the offering.

Fixed and Variable Costs

Not all costs are created equal. Based on whether they depend on the production quantity, the total costs associated with an offering can be divided into two categories: *fixed costs* and *variable costs*.

Fixed costs are expenses that do not fluctuate with output volume within a relevant period. Typical examples of fixed costs include research-and-development expenses, mass-media advertising expenses, rent, interest on debt, insurance, plant-and-equipment expenses, and salary of permanent full-time employees. Even though their absolute size remains unchanged regardless of output volume, average fixed costs per unit become progressively smaller as volume increases. These savings result from spreading the fixed costs over a larger number of output units.

Unlike fixed costs, which do not depend on the produced quantity, **variable costs** are expenses that fluctuate in direct proportion to the output volume of units produced (Figure 4). For example, the cost of raw materials and expenses incurred by consumer incentives such as coupons, price discounts, rebates, and premiums are commonly viewed as variable costs. Other expenses, such as distribution channel incentives and salesforce compensation, can be classified as either fixed or variable costs depending on their structure (e.g., fixed salary vs. performance-based compensation).

Figure 4. The Relationship Between Variable and Fixed Costs

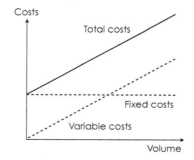

Deciding which costs are fixed and which costs are variable depends on the time horizon. For example, in the short run, the salaries of permanent full-time employees will be considered fixed costs because they do not depend on output volume. In the longer run, however, a company may adjust the number and/or salaries of permanent employees based on the demand for its products or services—a scenario in which these costs would be considered variable rather than fixed. Thus, in the long run, all costs could be considered variable.

An important concept related to that of fixed and variable costs is break-even analysis. Generally speaking, break-even analysis aims to identify the point at which the benefits and costs associated with a particular action are equal and beyond which profit occurs. Common types of break-even analyses include break-even of a fixed-cost investment, which indicates the unit or dollar sales volume at which the company is able to recoup a particular fixed-cost investment; break-even of a price cut, which reflects the increase in sales volume needed for a price cut to have a neutral impact on company profit; and break-even of a variable-cost increase, which identifies the sales volume at which a company neither makes a profit nor incurs a loss after increasing variable costs. The different types of break-even analyses are discussed in more detail in Chapter 8.

An Offering's Cost as a Function of Scale and Scope of Production

The costs of an offering are not set in stone: They often vary as a function of the quantity produced and the synergies among different types of offerings in the company's portfolio. The effects of these two factors are commonly referred to as *economies of scale* and *economies of scope*.

Economies of scale refer to the tendency of greater manufacturing and sales volume to lead to a decrease in per-unit costs. This relationship between production output and unit costs is closely related to the concept of the *experience curve*: The more experience a firm has in producing a particular offering, the lower its costs. A classic example of economies of scale and experience-curve pricing is the Ford Model T, where the goal of creating an affordable car resulted in scaling up production in a way that dramatically reduced the costs of each automobile.

Note that the relationship between costs and production volume is not monotonic: As the output volume increases, marginal costs tend to decrease initially until they reach the point at which they begin to increase, leading to diseconomies of scale. Thus, rather than the company experiencing continued decreasing costs with increasing output, diseconomies of scale can lead to an increase in marginal costs when output is increased. Diseconomies of scale can be caused by a variety of factors that are typically related to managing an increasingly large workforce and complex production logistics.

Economies of scope involve synergies among different offerings in a company's portfolio and are based on the notion that the average total cost of production tends to decrease as the number of different goods produced increases. Economies of scope are conceptually similar to economies of scale in that an increase in size typically leads to lower costs. Unlike economies of scale, however, where cost savings stem from increasing the scale of production for a single offering, economies of scope refer to cost savings resulting from synergies among different offerings in a company's portfolio. For example, Microsoft can develop both a word processing program and a spreadsheet program at a lower average cost than if two different companies were to produce each program separately. This is because both programs (Word and Excel) share a common platform and are promoted and distributed (often as a bundle) using the same channels.

As in the case of economies of scale, economies of scope do not always lead to a cost advantage: In many cases a firm producing a variety of different offerings is less efficient than separate firms that specialize in the production of a single offering. Diseconomies of scope often stem from the relative benefits of specialization, whereby focusing on a single product or service enables a company to achieve scale of production and gain the relevant experience — an advantage that could outweigh the potential benefits associated with synergies among different offerings.

An Offering's Costs as a Function of Price

Common intuition suggests that an offering's price is a function of the costs associated with developing and producing this offering. This, however, is not always the case. In some situations, the price drives costs and not the other way around. In other words, rather than taking an offering's costs as a given and using them to set the offering's price, a manager might start by determining the price at which the offering should be sold and use this price to determine the offering's costs. The view of price as a driver of an offering's costs dates back to Henry Ford, who wrote:

We have never considered any costs as fixed. Therefore we first reduce the price to the point where we believe more sales will result. Then we go ahead and try to make the prices. We do not bother about the costs. The new price forces the costs down. The more usual way is to take the costs and then determine the price; and although that method may be scientific in the narrow sense, it is not scientific in the broad sense, because what earthly use is it to know the cost if it tells you that you cannot manufacture at a price at which the article can be sold? [...] One of the ways of discovering [the cost] is to name a price so low as to force everybody in the place to the highest point of efficiency. We make more discoveries concerning manufacturing and selling under this forced method than by any method of leisurely investigation.[3]

The notion that an offering's price can determine its costs runs counter to the traditional view of pricing, according to which a company sets an offering's price based largely on the offering's costs and desired profit margins. To ensure that the offering achieves the desired level of sales, the company would also stimulate customer demand by running a promotional campaign. An alternative approach involves starting with identifying the price that can help achieve the desired sales volume. The company then would design an offering that delivers the benefits sought by customers — at a cost that allows the offering's selling price to accommodate customers' ability and willingness to pay while enabling the company to reach its profit goals.

Of course, starting with customers' willingness to pay to determine the cost of the offering is not applicable to every situation. At the same time, it is important to think of costs not as a given but rather in relation to the offering's price and customer demand. Examining the price elasticity of demand can help determine the optimal price at which the company can achieve its profit goals, which, in turn, can guide the design of the offering in a way that can make this price a reality.

Defining the Company's Pricing Goals

When setting the price for an offering, a company must first decide on the overall monetary and strategic goals it aims to achieve. In this context, one important consideration is whether the offering should focus on gaining market share while sacrificing some of the profit margin or on maximizing the per-unit profit at the expense of sales volume. The corresponding two pricing strategies — penetration pricing and skim pricing — are illustrated in Figure 5 and outlined in more detail below.

Figure 5. Penetration, Skim, and Loss-Leader Pricing

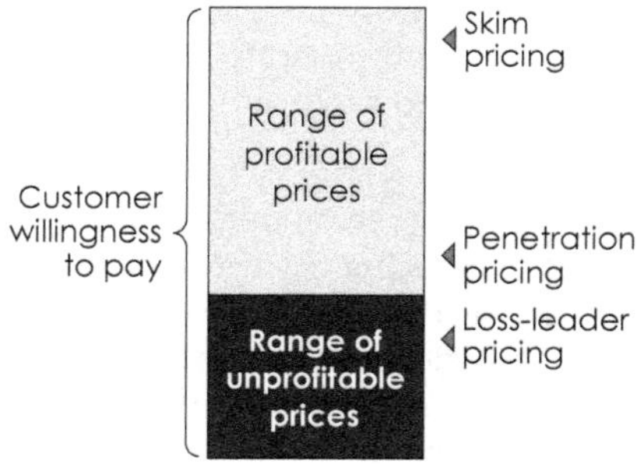

Penetration pricing involves setting relatively low prices in an attempt to gain higher sales volume, albeit at lower profit margins. A classic example of penetration pricing comes from Swedish retailer IKEA, known for its affordable furniture and household items. Although the low prices make each sale less profitable, the high sales volume generated by the low prices more than offsets the low margins. Another example of penetration pricing is Dollar Shave Club, which was able to gain share from the premium-priced market leader Gillette by introducing a low-priced offering featuring a free razor and a monthly supply of cartridges starting at $1.

A particular case of penetration pricing is *loss-leader pricing*, whereby a company sets a low price for an offering (often at or below cost) in an attempt to increase the sales of other offerings. A retailer might set a low price for a popular item in an attempt to build store traffic, thus increasing the sales of other, more profitable items. For example, on Black Friday—one of the busiest shopping days in the United States when many consumers do their Christmas shopping—many retailers drop the prices on a few high-demand items, such as the most popular children's toy, to attract buyers to their stores in the hope of making up loss-leader deficits with profit from other products that customers purchase during their shopping trip.

An extreme version of penetration pricing is *freemium pricing*, whereby a company gives away a restricted (either in terms of functionality or duration) version of the offering for free in an attempt to introduce potential buyers to its offering, gain market share, and ultimately convert some of the buyers to the paid, fully functional version of the offering. Examples of companies using the freemium model include Dropbox, Box, Evernote, Survey Monkey, Slack, Spotify, and Amazon Web Services. Freemium pricing is most often used for offerings with negligible variable costs that make the marginal cost of giving away a free item close to zero, as in the case of purely digital offerings.

In general, penetration pricing is more appropriate in cases where (1) demand is relatively elastic, such that lowering the price is likely to substantially increase sales volume, (2) the target market is increasingly competitive, (3) cost is a function of volume and, as a result, significant cost savings are expected as cumulative volume increases, (4) being the market pioneer can lead to a sustainable competitive advantage, and (5) the company has the resources to mass produce the offering.

Skim pricing involves setting a high price to "skim the cream" off the top of the market. Skim pricing targets customers who actively seek the benefits delivered by the offering and are willing to pay a relatively high price for it. For example, when launching a new generation of mobile phones, manufacturers often introduce a product line that contains a fully featured, high-price offering targeting consumers who seek the most benefits and are willing to pay a premium for these benefits. Thus, by setting high prices, skim pricing maximizes profit margins, usually at the expense of market share.

Skim pricing is also used to attract early adopters willing to pay higher prices at the initial stages of the product life cycle. For example, popular books, videogames, movies, and music albums are initially released at relatively high prices, targeting customers who are willing to pay a premium to be among the first to experience the offering. Skim pricing is also very common, if not universal, in the case of luxury offerings that target the higher end of the market. Indeed, because luxury products and services are by definition expensive and exclusive, skim pricing is the rule rather than the exception.

Skim pricing can be related to image pricing, which involves setting a high price for the purpose of signaling the high quality of an item. Image pricing is commonly used when the quality of an offering is not readily observable and buyers rely on observable cues, such as price, to infer performance (as in the case of the Screaming Eagle, Bottega Veneta, and Louis Vuitton examples discussed earlier). Image pricing can be thought of as a special case of skim pricing that, in addition to targeting high-margin buyers, aims to influence buyers' perceptions of the offering's quality.

In general, skim pricing is more appropriate in cases where (1) demand is relatively inelastic and lowering the price is not likely to substantially increase sales volume, (2) there is little or no competition for the target segment, (3) cost is not a direct function of volume, and significant cost savings are not achieved as cumulative volume increases, (4) being the market pioneer is unlikely to result in a sustainable competitive advantage, and (5) the company lacks the capability to mass produce the offering.

The decision to follow either skim or penetration pricing is not set in stone. Thus, a company might use skim pricing when entering a market in which there is pent-up demand for the company's product and little or no competition. As the competition intensifies and many of the early adopters have already acquired the offering, the company might switch to penetration pricing and increase revenue through greater volume rather than higher margins.

Managing Price Dynamics

Company prices are not immutable. Once set, they often evolve over time based on factors such as supply and demand, competitive offerings, and the overall market environment. Moreover, in some cases, rather than setting the prices at which target customers would buy its offerings, a company might let the prices be set dynamically by the market forces. The key methods that companies use to dynamically manage prices involve *price adjustments*, *auction pricing*, *price negotiation*, and *reverse pricing*.

Price Adjustments

Unlike the traditional approach, in which prices remain relatively stable and demand is stimulated by incentives, an increasing number of companies have adopted *dynamic pricing*, which involves a range of prices that change frequently to adapt to market conditions. Dynamic pricing is a common practice in industries such as hospitality, travel, and energy, where supply is constrained and cannot be varied to accommodate fluctuation in demand.

For example, time-based pricing is commonly used in the hospitality industry, where higher prices are charged during the peak season and other high-demand periods. In the same vein, airlines set prices taking into account factors such as the day of the week, time of day, and the number of seats available. Such dynamic pricing aims to align the available inventory with customer demand in a way that enables the company to maximize revenues by narrowing its focus on customers with the highest willingness to pay.

In addition to being driven by inventory considerations, price dynamics might stem from a company's desire to maximize revenue based on customers' willingness to pay for the company's products and services. For example, a retailer might vary the price of sodas, beer, and ice cream depending on the weather, charging higher prices to skim the market demand or, alternatively, charging lower prices to drive traffic and create a favorable price image.

One common instance of dynamic pricing is *surge pricing*. However, unlike the general case of dynamic pricing, which can involve price fluctuations in both directions (price increases as well as price decreases), surge pricing exclusively involves premium pricing. Surge pricing is often used by electric utilities to raise prices in periods of high demand. Another common example of surge pricing involves Uber, which charges surge rates as a multiplier of the base fare during periods of high demand.

On some occasions companies can also permanently lower their prices to accommodate changes in the market in which they operate. Unlike sales promotions, which typically involve short-term monetary incentives, *price rollbacks* are relatively permanent changes in a company's base prices. For example, Walmart, known for its everyday low pricing, uses lasting price rollbacks rather than temporary price discounts to deliver greater value to its customers.

An important issue in dynamic pricing is managing customers' perceptions of the fairness of the company's prices. Raising prices based solely on customer demand and the availability of alternative options can breed resentment from the public and damage the company's brand image. This is particularly true for products and services that are basic necessities, such as utilities, public transportation, and pharmaceutical products. The issue of price fairness is addressed in more detail at the end of this chapter.

Auction Pricing

An auction is a process in which potential buyers place competitive bids on goods or services, which are then sold to the highest bidder. The auction model is commonly used for unique items such as art, antiquities, and rare artifacts; for items that must be sold within a given time frame; and when sellers are willing to let the market set the price of the items being sold. The three most common types of auctions include English auctions, Dutch auctions, and sealed-bid auctions.

English auctions start with a suggested opening bid reserve or a starting price that is set by the seller. As buyers try to outbid one another, the price of the item is raised progressively until either the auction is closed or no higher bids are received. In *Dutch auctions*, the price of an item is lowered until it gets a bid, and the first bid made is the winning bid. Thus, unlike English auctions, where the price rises as bidders compete, in Dutch auctions the price declines as the auction progresses. Finally, in *sealed-bid auctions*, all bidders simultaneously submit sealed bids to the auctioneer, and the highest bidder usually wins the items. Unlike the English auction, where bidders can submit multiple bids based on previous bids by others, in sealed-bid auctions each bidder submits a single bid and cannot adjust the bid based on competing bids.

The above three types of auctions have pros and cons that determine their usage. Thus, an English auction is typically used in real estate, art, antiques, and vehicles. Companies that use English auctions include fine art auction houses Christie's and Sotheby's and online auctioneers eBay and Taobao. Dutch auctions are often used in financial markets (e.g., the Department of the Treasury uses Dutch auctions to raise funds for the U.S. Government) as well as in certain commodity markets (e.g., Aalsmeer Flower Auction in the Netherlands — the world's largest flower auction — is set up as a Dutch auction). Sealed-bid auctions are often used when soliciting requests for proposals (RFP) for longer term service, development, and manufacturing contracts (when used for procurement purposes, the winning RFP bid is often the lowest rather than the highest).

Sellers use auctions in cases when there is considerable uncertainty about the optimal price of an item, both in terms of the item's objective value as well as how much potential buyers are willing to pay for it. Thus, rather than trying to guess the ideal price of its offerings, a company might let market forces set the price based on buyers' willingness to pay. Auction pricing is also very common in the case of unique items such as art, antiques, and real estate where the seller aims to identify the buyer who has the highest willingness to pay for each item. In addition to helping set the price for unique items, auction pricing is used to set spot prices in commodity industries where the supply and demand constantly fluctuate.

Price Negotiation

Price setting is not always a unidirectional process in which buyers respond to the prices set by the company or compete with one another to obtain the offering. On many occasions, the final price is negotiated by the buyer and seller. For example, prices for many big-ticket consumer goods such as real estate, cars, and custom furniture, as well as commercial products such as aircraft, trucks, and information technology products, are typically determined in a negotiation between the seller and the buyer. Price negotiation is also a very common approach in setting the price for customized services such as consulting, education, and financial management.

Successful price negotiation on the part of the seller hinges on several factors. First, sellers should be able to accurately assess buyers' willingness to pay in order to drive the negotiation to a price that is close to the highest price buyers are willing to pay for the item. Second, sellers should be aware of their own reservation price, that is, the lowest price they are willing to accept for the item. Finally, sellers should be versed in the dynamics of the negotiation process, which involves understanding buyers' negotiation strategies (e.g., knowing when the buyer is bluffing) as well as understanding the limitations of their own negotiation strategies (e.g., complying with the legal regulations concerning price communication and negotiation). To this end, sellers must also take into account the emotional aspects of price negotiations and develop strategies for managing buyers' emotions as well as their own.

The nature of price negotiations varies based on whether these negotiations involve business-to-business or business-to-consumer transactions. Thus, business markets are characterized by a long purchase cycle, a decision-making unit that involves multiple entities, and a fairly complex decision process (see Chapter 15 for a more detailed discussion). Furthermore, because price negotiations are common in business transactions, buyers and sellers are not only well informed about the offering's attributes but also tend to be more experienced negotiators, able to see through each other's negotiation tactics.

Unlike business markets, consumer markets in developed countries offer most products and services at fixed prices, and price negotiation is less common. Nevertheless, some retailers, especially smaller ones and those offering customized products and services, are willing to negotiate prices in order to secure the sale. In addition to a direct negotiation where the sale price is the amount agreed upon by the seller and the buyer, another form of price negotiation in consumer markets involves price-match guarantees, where retailers promise to match other retailers' lowest advertised price (or refund the price difference) for the same item. In this context, price-match guarantees enable customers to request better pricing while at the same time limiting the scale and scope of these requests by using competitors' prices as a reference point.

Sellers rely on negotiation to set prices in cases when they believe that it enables them to better assess customers' willingness to pay for a given offering than alternative pricing methods would. Price negotiation can also create value (often referred to as transaction utility) for buyers by providing them with a sense of satisfaction derived from receiving a concession from the seller. In addition, negotiation can be rooted in the business culture in which buyers and sellers interact, such that in some cultures negotiating prices is very common. On the downside, however, negotiation can be time consuming and require a greater amount of company resources (e.g., trained salesforce or a robust artificial intelligence solution). Furthermore, while negotiating prices has the potential to help the company better identify customers' willingness to pay, it can also backfire if the company mishandles the negotiation and sets a suboptimal price or loses the sale altogether.

Reverse Pricing

Reverse pricing (also referred to as name-your-own pricing) is similar to auction pricing in that buyers have to place a bid for the item they wish to acquire. Unlike auctions, where buyers directly compete with one another, in reverse pricing buyers submit their bids to the company, which then decides how many and which bids to accept. Companies utilizing reverse pricing include Priceline.com, Groupon, and eBay.

A particular form of reverse pricing is *pay-what-you-want pricing*. This pricing format is similar to reverse pricing in that buyers set the purchase price of a given item. The key difference is that in reverse pricing the seller has the ability to reject bids that do not meet certain criteria, such as a minimum purchase price or volume. In contrast, in the pay-what-you-want approach the seller does not control the price set by the buyer. Pay-what-you-want pricing is used primarily when the marginal costs of the offering are low, such as in the case of digital content: information, music, and video. Pay-what-you-want pricing is also used when the average price paid by consumers is likely to be higher than the cost of the offering and thus has the potential to generate additional sales while minimizing the risk of financial loss.

One of the first major cases of customer-determined pricing was the album *In Rainbows* by English rock band Radiohead, self-released in 2007 as a pay-what-you-want download. Another notable example is The Metropolitan Museum of Art, which lets New York residents determine how much they should pay for admission tickets. In the same vein, Panera Bread gives customers freedom to pay whatever they can afford for every item on the menu at its Panera Cares cafes—nonprofit outlets designed to feed those in need and raise awareness of poverty in the United States.

Letting customers set prices has a number of limitations. The most obvious problem is free riding, whereby customers pay less than what they think the product or service is worth. In addition, many customers might not have realistic perceptions of the costs associated with different items and end up paying significantly less than an item's actual cost to the company. As a result, the practical application of pay-what-you-want pricing is rather limited.

Setting the Price in a Competitive Context

Companies do not set prices in isolation: Their prices reflect the competitive environment in which they operate. Indeed, because a company's ultimate goal is to create greater value for its target customers than the value created by its competitors, the pricing policies of competitors have a direct impact on the customer value created by the company. Therefore, to ensure market success, a company must assess the price-to-benefit ratio of its offerings vis-à-vis those of the competition, clearly understand the antecedents and consequences of price wars, and develop a policy on how to respond to a threat of a price war. These issues are discussed in the following sections.

Competitive Price–Benefit Analysis

The price–benefit analysis examines the price–benefit tradeoff across the company's different market offerings. At the heart of the price–benefit analysis is the notion that a company's focus should not be on price alone but also on the offering's value, defined as a function of the perceived benefits and perceived price. The price–benefit relationship is best illustrated using competitive price–benefit maps, which reflect the perceived price–benefit tradeoffs associated with a particular offering in a competitive context (Figure 6).

Figure 6. Competitive Price– Benefit Map

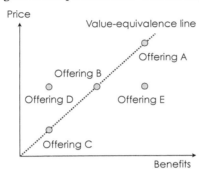

The value-equivalence line in Figure 6 represents offerings for which the ratio of perceived benefits and perceived price is the same: higher benefit, higher priced offerings are positioned toward the upper right (Offering A); lower benefit, lower priced offerings are positioned toward the lower left (Offering C). Offerings A, B, and C deliver equivalent value, with Offering A delivering higher benefits at a premium price and Offering C delivering fewer benefits at a lower price. Offerings below the value-equivalence line (Offering E) deliver superior value relative to the offerings on or above the value-equivalence line, whereas offerings above the value-equivalence line (Offering D) deliver inferior value relative to the offerings on or below the value-equivalence line.

In a truly efficient market, all offerings should lie on the value-equivalence line. In reality, however, offerings might vary in the value they deliver to customers; some offerings (Offering E) deliver superior value (higher benefits at a lower price), whereas others (Offering D) deliver inferior value (lower benefits at a higher price). These value discrepancies are likely to influence the market shares of the offerings, such that value-advantaged options are likely to gain share, whereas value-disadvantaged options are likely to lose share. This implies that, over time, the sales of offerings A and B are likely to shift to Offering E, and the sales of Offering D are likely to shift to offerings B (and ultimately E) and C.

An important aspect of price–benefit analysis is that it reflects perceived rather than actual benefits and prices of the available offerings. This is important because customer perceptions of an offering's price depend on a variety of factors (some of which were discussed earlier in this chapter), such that the perceived price might not adequately reflect an offering's actual price. Moreover, just because an offering has a particular feature does not imply that this feature will translate into a meaningful customer benefit. In other words, customers might not accurately perceive the offering's performance and misconstrue its true benefits. Because customers' behavior reflects their subjective beliefs about the offering's price and benefits, understanding these beliefs and incorporating them in a company's pricing is the key to creating market value.

Understanding Price Wars

Price wars are very common in competitive markets. Price wars can involve price reductions offered directly from manufacturers to end users (price discounts, volume discounts, and coupons). Price wars also might involve price cuts and incentives offered by manufacturers to retailers, which, in turn, might prompt retailers to lower their prices, thus provoking a price war. Price wars can also be initiated by retailers who aggressively compete for the same customers.

Price wars often start when a company is willing to sacrifice margins to gain sales volume. Price cuts, the forerunner of price wars, are popular among managers because they are easy to implement and typically produce fast results, especially when a company's goal is to increase sales volume.

Not every price cut, however, leads to a price war. The likelihood that a price cut will trigger a price war depends on several factors:

- **Offering differentiation.** Price wars are more likely when offerings are undifferentiated and can be easily substituted, such that a price cut is likely to instantly attract competitors' customers.

- **Cost structure.** Companies are more likely to engage in price wars when significant economies of scale can be achieved by increasing volume and both the company and its competitors stand to gain if they increase their output.

- **Market growth.** Price wars are more likely to occur when markets are stagnant, and to grow sales a company has to steal share from its direct competitors.

- **Customer loyalty.** Companies are more likely to engage in price wars in markets in which customers are price sensitive (meaning that they are not brand loyal and are willing to trade off performance for lower price) and their switching costs are low.

Price wars are easy to initiate but costly to win. Winning a price war often comes at the expense of a significant loss of profits, making it more of a Pyrrhic victory than a true success. Price wars are detrimental to a company's profitability for several reasons:

- **Fixed-cost effect.** Price reductions have an exponential impact on profitability. To illustrate, in the absence of an increase in sales volume, reducing the price of an offering with a 10% profit margin by 1% will result in a 10% decrease in operating income.

- **Competitive reaction.** Because in most cases competitors can easily match price cuts, they are rarely sustainable. Firms with similar cost structures can quickly lower their prices in response to a competitor's action.

- **Increased price elasticity.** Price wars often result in a shift in customers' future price expectations, such that the lowered prices become the reference points against which future prices are judged.

- **Brand devaluation.** Emphasis on price tends to erode brand power. This effect is exacerbated by the heavy price-focused communication campaigns that tend to accompany most price wars (because a company needs to promote the low price so that it can generate sufficient incremental volume to offset the lost profits resulting from the decrease in price).

Price wars rarely enable companies to achieve their strategic goals, and in most cases the only beneficiaries of a price war are the company's customers. In general, the best strategy for a company to win a potential price war is to avoid it.

Circumventing Price Wars

Even companies not seeking a price war are often confronted with a scenario in which a competitor initiates a price cut. The gut reaction of most managers in such cases is to respond with a matching price cut. This reaction, however, is often premature and suboptimal. Only after evaluating the antecedents and likely consequences of the price cut can a company identify the optimal response strategy. A relatively simple approach for developing a strategic response to a competitor's price cut is outlined below.

- **Verify the threat of a price war.** Price wars are often caused by miscommunication of pricing information or misinterpretation of a competitor's goals. For example, when competitive prices are not readily available (e.g., in contract bidding), a company might incorrectly believe that a particular competitor has significantly lowered its price. It is also possible that a competitor's price decrease is driven by internal factors, such as clearing inventory (e.g., prior to introducing a new model), rather than by an intention to initiate a price war. Thus, before responding to a competitor's actions, it is imperative to validate whether the threat of a price war is real.

- **Evaluate the likely impact of the competitor's actions.** To determine the best course of action, a company must first identify which of its own current and potential customers are most likely to be affected by competitors' price cuts, assess the likely response of these customers to the price cut, and consider their value to the company. In certain cases, a company might choose to abandon markets that have no strategic importance and in which customer loyalty is low.

- **Develop segment-specific strategies to address the competitive threat.** There are three basic strategies to respond to the threat of a price war: staying the course, repositioning an existing offering by lowering its price and/or increasing its benefits, and adding new offerings. The decision to stay the course and ignore a competitor's price cut reflects a company's belief that the price cut will not have a significant impact on the company's market position, that the price cut is not sustainable and will dissipate by itself, or that serving the customer segment targeted by the price cut is no longer viable for the company. In contrast, repositioning the existing offering reflects a company's view that the market has fundamentally changed and the value of its offering must be realigned with the new market realities. Alternatively, a company might launch a downscale extension (a fighting brand) to attract price-sensitive customers without discounting its premium offering (see Chapter 18 for a discussion of these strategies).

Using a systematic approach to evaluate the threat of a price war and develop an appropriate response is paramount to sustaining the profitability of the market in which a company competes and ensuring the company's long-term success in this market. A visceral reaction to a competitor's price cut can be as detrimental to a company's future as the very action that provoked the company's response.

SUMMARY

Price defines the monetary aspect of the value a company's offering aims to create and capture in the market. When setting the price, managers must consider two types of factors: *strategic factors* that deal with the offering's target market (customers, competitors, collaborators, company, and context), and *tactical factors* that deal with the ways in which price interacts with the other attributes of the offering (product, service, brand, incentives, communication, and distribution).

To set the optimal price, a manager must understand the relationship between the offering's price and customer demand. *Price elasticity* reflects the degree to which changing the price influences sales volume. High price elasticity means that a small change in price leads to a large change in sales volume, whereas low elasticity means that the decrease in sales volume resulting from the change in price is relatively small.

Because buyers' willingness to pay is one of the key market characteristics, companies use pricing as a targeting tool (a practice referred to as price segmentation). Commonly used price-segmentation criteria include purchase quantity, time of purchase or use, and distribution channel.

Because buyers do not always evaluate prices in an objective fashion, companies often use *psychological pricing* that takes advantage of a variety of effects stemming from behavioral economics, such as reference-price effects, price–quality inferences, price–quantity effects, unit-pricing effects, as well as price-tier and price-ending effects.

When setting an offering's price, a company can employ one of two core strategies: skim pricing and penetration pricing. By setting high prices, *skim pricing* maximizes profit margins, usually at the expense of market share. In contrast, *penetration pricing* involves setting relatively low prices in an attempt to gain higher sales volume, albeit at lower margins.

Company prices are not immutable: Once set, they often evolve over time based on factors such as supply and demand, competitive offerings, and the overall market environment. The key methods that companies use to dynamically manage prices involve price adjustments, auction pricing, and price negotiation.

The *price–benefit analysis* examines the price–benefit tradeoff across the different market offerings. At the heart of the price–benefit analysis is the idea that a company's focus should not be solely on price but also on the offering's value, defined as a function of the perceived benefits and perceived price. The price–benefit relationship is illustrated with price–benefit maps, which reflect the perceived price–benefit tradeoffs associated with a particular offering in a competitive context.

Competing on price often results in a *price war*, which typically starts when companies are willing to sacrifice margins to gain market share. Price wars are likely to occur when offerings are undifferentiated, when capacity utilization is low, when significant economies of scale can be achieved by increasing volume, when markets are mature and a company has to steal share from its direct competitors to grow sales, and when customers' price elasticity is high and switching costs are low.

An effective approach for developing a *strategic response to a price cut* calls for verifying the validity of the threat of a price war, prioritizing customers who are most likely to be affected by a competitor's price cut based on their value to the company and price elasticity, and developing segment-specific strategies to address the competitive threat. Price wars rarely enable companies to achieve their strategic goals, and usually the only beneficiaries of a price war are the company's customers. In most cases, the best strategy for a company to win a potential price war is to avoid it.

MARKETING INSIGHT: KEY PRICING CONCEPTS

Captive Pricing: See *complementary pricing.*

Competitive Pricing: Pricing method that uses competitors' prices as benchmarks for price setting. A popular version of this approach, referred to as *competitive-parity pricing*, involves setting the offering's price in a way that puts it at parity with that of competitors.

Complementary Pricing: Pricing method applicable to uniquely compatible, multipart offerings, whereby a company charges a relatively low introductory price for the first component of the offering and higher prices for the other components. Classic examples include razors and blades, printers and cartridges, and cell phones and cell phone service. The unique compatibility of the offering's components is crucial to the success of complementary pricing—for example, only the printer manufacturer should be able to sell cartridges that fit its printers.

Cost-Plus Pricing: Pricing method in which the final price is determined by adding a fixed premium to the cost of the product. Cost-plus pricing is used in industries where profit margins are relatively stable. See also *markup pricing.*

Cross-Price Elasticity: The percentage change in the quantity of a given offering sold caused by a percentage change in the price of another offering.

Deceptive Pricing: The practice of presenting an offering's price to the buyer in a way that is deliberately misleading. Deceptive pricing is illegal in the United States.

Demand Pricing: Pricing method that involves setting prices based on customers' willingness to pay for the benefits afforded by the company's offering.

Experience-Curve Pricing: Pricing method based on an anticipated lower cost structure, resulting from scale economies and experience-curve effects.

Image Pricing: Pricing method that involves setting a high price for the purpose of signaling the high quality of an item. See also *price signaling.*

Loss-Leader Pricing: Pricing method that involves setting a low price for an offering (often at or below cost) in an attempt to increase the sales of other products and services. For example, a retailer might set a low price for a popular item in an attempt to build store traffic, thus increasing the sales of other, more profitable items.

Markup Pricing: Pricing method that involves adding a standard markup to the cost of the offering. Markup pricing is very similar to cost-plus pricing, with the key difference that rather than being calculated as an item-specific dollar amount (as in the case of *cost-plus pricing*), the added premium is calculated as a percentage of an item's cost. Because of its standardized nature, markup pricing is more common among intermediaries (such as wholesalers, dealers, and retailers) that carry large quantities of different items. For example, a wholesaler might add a standard percentage markup to all of the offerings it distributes based on the cost of the goods sold.

Predatory Pricing: Pricing method that involves selling below cost with the intent of driving competitors out of business. Predatory pricing is illegal in the United States.

Prestige Pricing: Pricing method in which the price is set at a relatively high level for the purpose of creating an exclusive image for the offering.

Price Fixing: Pricing method in which companies conspire to set prices for a given product or service. Price fixing is illegal in the United States.

Price Segmentation: Pricing method that involves charging different buyers different prices for goods of equal grade and quality.

Price Signaling: (1) Pricing method that aims to capitalize on price–quality inferences (higher priced products are also likely to be higher quality), primarily used when the actual product benefits are not readily observable (also known as prestige pricing); (2) Indirect communication (direct price collusion is prohibited by law) between companies aimed at indicating their intentions with respect to their pricing strategy.

Product-Line Pricing: Pricing method in which the price of each individual offering is determined as a function of the offering's place in the company's product line.

Second-Market Discounting: Pricing method in which a company charges lower prices in more competitive markets, such as when exporting goods to developing countries.

Two-Part Pricing: See *complementary pricing*.

Yield-Management Pricing: Pricing method in which the price is set to maximize revenue for a fixed capacity within a given time frame (frequently used by airlines, hotels, and cruise ships).

MARKETING INSIGHT: MANAGING PRICE FAIRNESS

When evaluating the prices of market offerings, buyers judge not only whether these prices are inherently attractive and adequately reflect the benefits of the offering; they also evaluate whether or not the prices are fair. These price-fairness judgments are customer-specific, reflecting a buyer's subjective assessment of whether the price is reasonable, acceptable, or justifiable. Because price-fairness judgments are idiosyncratic, they might vary across individual buyers, such that a price seen by some as fair might be perceived as unfair by others.

Price-fairness judgments comprise two components: an assessment of whether the actual price is fair (also referred to as outcome fairness) and an assessment of whether the process and method used to set the price are fair (also referred to as procedural fairness). Thus, *outcome fairness* reflects customers' evaluation of the favorability of the asked price relative to other prices that the seller could have charged for the offering. In other words, outcome fairness reflects customers' assessment of whether an offering's price is a good deal or is overpriced. For example, a customer would likely evaluate a 12-oz. can of Coke sold by a vending machine for $5 as unfair because its regular price is significantly less. In contrast to outcome fairness, *procedural fairness* reflects customers' evaluation of whether the seller adhered to the commonly accepted social norms when setting the price. For example, Coca-Cola's intent to use vending machines that charge higher prices during hot weather has led to a strong public backlash from consumers, who perceived this pricing practice to be unfair.

The key factors that determine whether buyers perceive a price to be fair include price comparison, price knowledge, availability of alternative options, the relationship between the buyer and the seller, and the perceived motivation of the seller.

- *Price comparison.* Price-fairness judgments typically occur when buyers observe price discrepancies in similar transactions. These transactions can involve other buyers purchasing identical or similar items, prices of competitive offerings, and prior purchases made by the same buyer. In general, the greater the similarity between transactions—the purchased items and the context in which they were purchased—the more likely buyers are to make price comparisons and form price-fairness judgments.

- *Price knowledge.* To form price-fairness judgments, buyers must have a certain level of price knowledge to detect the presence of price discrepancies. Thus, buyers must be aware of the regular price of the offering, prices of competitive offerings, and/or how much other buyers have paid for similar or identical offerings. In general, the greater the price knowledge, the greater the likelihood that buyers will detect a price discrepancy and will form price-fairness judgments.

- *Availability of alternative options.* Setting high prices in a scenario in which buyers do not have viable substitutes readily available to them can breed resentment from the public and damage the company's brand image. This is particularly true for products and services that are considered necessities, such as utilities, public transportation, and pharmaceutical products. In one extreme example, after Turing Pharmaceuticals acquired the rights to the 60-year-old Daraprim—the only medication available for treating several rare life-threatening diseases—it increased the price from $13.50 per tablet to $750 per tablet, a 5,000 percent jump. Turing's actions resulted in a public outcry about price-gouging, followed by a congressional inquiry into the company's pricing practices.

- *Relationship between the buyer and seller.* Buyers are likely to interpret price discrepancies and form price-fairness judgments in the context of their prior interactions with the seller. Thus, buyers may assume that minor price discrepancies involving offerings they are loyal to have occurred for legitimate reasons and form more favorable price-fairness judgments of that offering compared to buyers who have not established a relationship with the seller. At the same time, when confronted with a major price increase, loyal buyers may perceive this as a breach of trust in their relationship with the retailer and, consequently, form stronger judgments about the unfairness of the high price than non-loyal customers would.

- *Perceived motivation of the seller.* In addition to observing price discrepancies and evaluating their magnitude, buyers also draw inferences about the motive behind these discrepancies, especially when there are no obvious reasons for them to exist. For example, buyers might attribute the higher prices to an increase in costs, limited supply, or the seller's desire to maximize profits. In general, buyers are less likely to perceive higher prices to be unfair when they are attributed to factors that the company cannot control, such as an increase in costs of the goods sold. Conversely, buyers are more likely to perceive higher prices as unfair when they see them as the result of factors controlled by the company, such as the motivation to increase profits.[4]

Managing customers' perceptions of the fairness of the company's prices is particularly important in dynamic pricing, where prices vary frequently. These fluctuations create situations in which consumers are offered prices that are higher than the prices they paid for the product in the past (or will pay in the future) as well as higher than those paid by other customers. Managing such price fluctuations is important because buyers are more likely to perceive them as unfair, often leading them to behaviors guided by negative emotions. To cope with negative emotions, buyers often engage in actions that aim to hurt the reputation of the seller by spreading negative information about the seller's business practices.

Because companies tend to tailor the prices of their offerings to match customers' needs and willingness to pay, price discrepancies and, hence, the potential for forming price-(un)fairness judgments are inevitable. In this context, a company must develop a strategy to minimize the possibility of customers forming unfavorable price-fairness judgments. One such strategy involves informing customers about the reasons for charging higher prices, particularly when these reasons are external to the company (such as increases in the cost of materials and labor).

In the case of scarce goods, one approach to avoid perception of unfair pricing is to use an allocation method that does not directly involve price. For example, at the launch of the iPad, Apple limited sales to only two iPads per person to ensure more equitable allocation and avoid a secondary market in which iPads would be sold at a premium. In the same vein, because of extremely high demand, tickets for the traditional end-of-year concerts by the Vienna Philharmonic are drawn using a lottery at the beginning of each year—an approach that enables music lovers from around the world to have an equal chance to purchase the highly desired tickets.

CHAPTER THIRTEEN

MANAGING INCENTIVES

But wait, there's more!
— Ron Popeil, inventor
and infomercial salesman

Incentives are inducements that aim to enhance the value of an offering by increasing its benefits or, more frequently, by reducing its costs. The ultimate goal of incentives is to incite action on the part of the company's target customers, collaborators, and employees. Because they typically are used to increase sales volume, incentives are often referred to as sales promotions. The key aspects of designing and managing incentives are the focus of this chapter. Specifically, we address the following topics:

- *Managing Incentives as a Value-Creation Process* || Incentives as a tool for creating market value | Factors contributing to the proliferation of incentives
- *Customer Incentives* || Monetary customer incentives | Nonmonetary customer incentives | The pros and cons of customer incentives
- *Collaborator Incentives* || Monetary collaborator incentives | Nonmonetary collaborator incentives | The pros and cons of collaborator incentives
- *Company Incentives* || Monetary company incentives | Nonmonetary company incentives | The pros and cons of company incentives
- *Managing Incentives in a Competitive Context* || Using incentives as a means of competitive differentiation | Managing push and pull promotions | Communicating incentives

The discussion of managing incentives is complemented by an in-depth overview of sampling as a promotional tool and an outline of the game-theory view of sales promotions.

Managing Incentives as a Value-Creation Process

Companies use incentives for a variety of reasons: to retain their current customers and attract new ones, to ensure collaborator support, as well as to increase the productivity and ensure the loyalty of their employees. To this end, the primary function of incentives is to enhance the value created by an offering for its customers, collaborators, and the company. The role of incentives as a tool for creating market value and the factors contributing to the proliferation of incentives are outlined in more detail in the following sections.

Incentives as a Tool for Creating Market Value

Incentives enhance the value of an offering by providing additional benefits or reducing costs. Most incentives are temporary in nature and are designed to facilitate sales by enabling the company to respond in a timely manner to changes in the market, such as a decline in customer demand, competitive price discounts, time-defined company goals, pressure from channel partners, or a weak economy.

Incentives are one of the seven attributes defining the company's offering. Working with the other offering attributes—product, service, brand, price, communication, and distribution—incentives aim to enhance the offering's value for target customers, collaborators, and the company (Figure 1). Accordingly, a manager's ultimate goal is to design incentives that create optimal value for target customers, collaborators, and the company.

Figure 1. Managing Incentives as a Value-Creation Process

Depending on the entity for which they aim to create value, most incentives fall into one of three categories: incentives given to *customers* (coupons, loyalty programs, sweepstakes, contests, and premiums); incentives given to the company's *collaborators*, most often channel partners (price cuts, volume discounts, allowances, and co-op advertising); and incentives given to the company's *employees* (awards, bonuses, rewards, and contests).

In addition, incentives can be either *monetary* (e.g., volume discounts, price reductions, coupons, and rebates), or *nonmonetary* (e.g., premiums, contests, and rewards). Unlike monetary incentives, which typically aim to reduce an offering's costs, nonmonetary incentives typically aim to enhance the offering's benefits. The most common types of incentives are outlined in Figure 2.

Figure 2. Incentive Types

	Monetary incentives	Nonmonetary incentives
Customer incentives	Coupons, rebates, volume discounts, price reductions	Premiums, rewards, sweepstakes, loyalty programs, prizes, contests
Collaborator (trade) incentives	Slotting, stocking, advertising, display, and market-development allowances; spiffs; volume discounts and rebates; off-invoice incentives; cash discounts; inventory financing	Contests, bonus merchandise, buyback guarantees, sales support and training
Company incentives	Monetary bonuses and rewards	Nonmonetary bonuses and rewards, recognition awards, contests

The key aspects of customer, collaborator, and company incentives are outlined in more detail in the following sections.

Factors Contributing to the Proliferation of Incentives

In the United States alone, companies spend over $500 billion annually on various forms of sales promotions. Incentives represent a significant part of a company's promotional budget, often exceeding two-thirds of the resources allocated for promoting the company's offering, with the remainder spent on advertising and other forms of communication. Of the resources allocated to incentives, the vast majority is usually spent on trade incentives, followed by customer incentives and incentives directed at company employees. In addition, a significant amount of communication resources is directed to informing target customers, collaborators, and company employees about the specifics of the incentives.

The role of incentives in the value-creation process has dramatically increased in the last several decades. The reasons for the increased use of incentives can be traced back to two types of factors: strategic factors related to the market in which the company competes and tactical factors related to the alternative tools that a company can use to design, communicate, and deliver its offering.

Strategic Factors Contributing to the Proliferation of Incentives

The strategic factors that have contributed to the increased importance of incentives reflect changes in the five factors (the Five Cs) defining the market in which a company aims to create value:

- **Customers** have become more attuned to incentives and are more likely to positively respond to a company's promotional activities. Years of ongoing sales promotions have conditioned customers to expect and wait for lower prices and/or nonprice rewards. Moreover, in an environment characterized by increasing product proliferation and commoditization, many customers use the presence of sales promotions as a decision rule that enables them to circumvent the cognitively taxing process of evaluating the available alternatives by simply choosing the option being promoted. As a result, customers' expectations of future sales promotions can make them delay planned purchases until the selected item is on sale, which, in turn, hinders a company's ability to sell its products and services in the absence of sales promotions.

- **Collaborators**, and particularly retailers, have gained significant clout over producers. The main reason for this power shift from manufacturers to retailers is the consolidation of the retail sector, which has resulted in large national and multinational channels such as Walmart, Carrefour, Costco, and Amazon. Large retail chains have gained significant buying power, which enables them to negotiate better deals with manufacturers and demand a variety of trade incentives such as greater volume discounts, promotional allowances, and rebates. Many retailers have leveraged their market position to launch lower priced store brands (private labels) that directly compete with manufacturers' brands—in turn, forcing manufacturers to launch various sales promotions in order to stay competitive.

- **Companies** have become more dependent on sales promotions as a key tool to gain and defend market position. The fact that most incentives are designed to have an immediate impact on sales makes them a popular tool among managers who need to boost sales volume to achieve their sales targets. With ever-increasing pressure from shareholders, companies are tempted to prioritize short-term goals, which in turn leads to over-reliance on incentives to boost short-term performance. In this context, managers whose compensation and reward systems are tied to achievement of quarterly and annual sales goals find incentives a dependable quick fix to generate short-term sales. In addition to the obsession with short-term outcomes, the popularity of incentives also stems from their readily observable effectiveness. Indeed, because most incentives have an immediate impact on sales, managers can easily assess their effectiveness (especially when compared to assessing the effectiveness of alternative forms of promotion such as advertising). The transparent effect of incentives helps increase accountability for marketing expenditures by directly relating the costs of sales promotions to the corresponding increase in sales volume.

- **Competitors** have also increased their sales promotional activities—in part driven by the same short-term goals as the company and in part in response to the company's own promotions that aim to steal share from the competition. Because consumer and trade promotions are easy to initiate, they also can be readily matched by competitors, which often leads to "sales promotion wars" in which competing entities try to outdo one another in luring customers and collaborators with promotional offers. Thus, the most successful promotions that help increase sales are ultimately matched by a competitive promotional activity that aims to defend competitors' market share and stimulate their own sales growth.

- **Context**—specifically, technological developments and changes in sociocultural norms—have further encouraged the proliferation of sales promotions. The ubiquity of mobile devices that are uniquely tied to individual users and can pinpoint their geolocation enables marketers to more precisely design and implement sales promotions. Increased marketer reliance on incentives is also propagated by the growing "always-on" and "fear-of-missing-out" trends that reflect a change in sociocultural norms, whereby individuals are expected to stay online all the time. The ability to better identify and locate always-on consumers increases the effectiveness of sales promotions and enables companies to more efficiently track their results, which serves as yet another factor contributing to the popularity of sales promotions.

Tactical Factors Contributing to the Proliferation of Incentives

In addition to changes in the market in which the company competes, the proliferation of incentives is also caused by the decrease in the effectiveness with which other offering attributes—product, service, brand, price, communication, and distribution—can create market value.

- **Product** and **service** commoditization has made it more difficult for companies to differentiate their offerings on functional benefits, forcing companies to seek alternative means of differentiation, which often involve price discounts, bonus offerings, and other types of sales promotions. The burgeoning number of new product and service introductions has further contributed to the growth of incentives as companies seek effective ways to differentiate these products and induce customers to try them.

- **Brand** proliferation has further contributed to the growth of sales promotions as an ever-increasing number of brands compete for customers' attention and loyalty. Furthermore, customers' ability to readily assess the performance of the company's products and services using other customers' ratings has greatly diminished the role of brands as a signal of quality. Faced with increased brand competition and declining brand power, many companies shift their promotional budgets toward incentives to enhance the value of their offerings.

- **Price** is a relatively inflexible tool for responding to rapidly changing market conditions. Indeed, lowering prices typically involves a long-term, strategic change in the value proposition of a company's offering. In contrast, incentives are short-term tactical activities that can be readily used to align the offering's value proposition with the needs of target customers, collaborators, and the company. Furthermore, because incentives are considered temporary measures, they often require fewer layers of approval to be initiated, which in turn facilitates their usage. As a result, managers frequently rely on incentives to make their offerings more attractive to customers.

- **Communication** has become a much less effective tool for enticing new customers to try the company's products and services as well as for building loyalty among existing customers. As customers are bombarded with hundreds and sometimes thousands of messages on a daily basis, a company's ability to break through the clutter has greatly diminished, forcing companies to "spice up" their messages by introducing incentives.

- **Distribution** channels play an increasingly important role in consumer decisions as more choices are made at the point of purchase. Following this trend, manufacturers allocate a greater share of their promotional budgets to in-store sales promotions to nudge consumers toward buying their offerings. Moreover, many retailers see consumer incentives as an effective tool for building traffic and growing sales and, as a result, are willing to partner with manufacturers to implement and even co-sponsor sales promotions.

Customer Incentives

Customer incentives are inducements that aim to enhance the value of an offering for its target customers. Customer incentives can be offered by the producer as in the case of manufacturer incentives and by channel members as in the case of retailer incentives. Because retailers have direct contact with buyers at the point of purchase, in addition to their own incentives they also implement incentives on behalf of manufacturers (also referred to as pass-through incentives). For example, a manufacturer might engage retailers carrying its products to distribute and redeem coupons, offer a two-for-one promotion, or temporarily lower the price on some of its products.

Based on the nature of the reward involved, customer incentives can be divided into two types: *monetary* and *nonmonetary*.

Monetary Customer Incentives

Monetary incentives aim to increase the value of the offering by reducing its costs, thus providing customers with an inducement to purchase the offering. The most common types of monetary incentives include *coupons*, *rebates*, *volume discounts*, and *temporary price reductions*.

- **Coupons** are certificates that entitle the buyer to receive a price reduction for a given product or service at the time of purchase. Coupons are the oldest and arguably most widely used form of customer incentives. They are often used as a means of price segmentation because they are effective with price-sensitive customers, who are willing to trade off time and effort (by locating the coupon and using it at the point of purchase) in order to save money. In addition to entitling customers to a price reduction, coupons also help create and enhance customers' awareness of the company's offering. Coupons are most often distributed as free-standing inserts (FSI) in newspapers and magazines, online, via direct mail, or at the point of purchase. Coupons can also be affixed to the product (as in the case of coupons offering instant discounts), or they can be placed inside the package or generated at the time of purchase at the checkout counter (as in the case of bounce-back coupons redeemable on the next purchase of the same or a related item).

- **Rebates** are cash refunds given to buyers after they make a purchase. Rebates are less popular than coupons and usually require greater effort from buyers (e.g., filling out the rebate form) as well as the disclosure of certain personal information (e.g., buyer's name and the mailing address to which the rebate will be sent). Most rebates require time to be processed and, as a result, the customer might have to wait weeks or sometimes months to receive the monetary compensation offered by the rebate. An exception to the latter aspect of rebates are instant rebates that are redeemed at the time of purchase. Because customers effectively end up paying a discounted price, instant rebates are functionally similar to temporary price reductions.

- **Volume discounts** are price reduction offers that are conditional on the purchase of multiple items. By incentivizing buyers to purchase larger quantities, volume discounts allow retailers to transfer some of their inventory (and, hence, reduce inventory costs) to the buyer, who now will have to store larger quantities of the purchased items. Volume discounts are popular among retailers who are trying to free up inventory space (e.g., for a higher margin item), in the case of perishable products, as well as for products (e.g., food and beverage offerings) where a larger purchase quantity is likely to increase consumption.

- **Temporary price reductions** involve a straightforward lowering of the offering's price without requiring buyers to take any additional action such as bring a coupon, fill in a rebate form, or buy multiple items. Temporary price reductions are akin to changing an offering's price, with the key difference that the changes are not permanent. (In fact, the short-term nature of temporary price reductions is the reason why they are considered an incentive-related decision rather than a pricing decision). In addition, temporary price reductions are typically framed as a discount off the original price. As a result, the original price now serves as a reference point against which customers assess the attractiveness of the promotional offer.

Nonmonetary Customer Incentives

Nonmonetary incentives typically aim to enhance the value of the offering by increasing its benefits rather than lowering its costs. The most common types of nonmonetary customer incentives are *premiums, prizes, contests, sweepstakes, games,* and *loyalty programs.*

- **Premiums** are bonus products or services offered for free or at deeply discounted prices as an incentive to purchase a particular offering. Premiums can be delivered instantly with the purchase (packaged with the product) or can require the customer to send in a proof of purchase to receive the premium. A popular form of premium is the buy-one-get-one (or two-for-one), where the buyer receives a bonus item identical to the item purchased. Another common type of premium are toys included with the purchase of products consumed by kids, such as cereal and fast-food meals. For example, McDonald's' decision to include toys with its Happy Meals made it de facto the largest toy retailer on a unit basis, distributing close to a billion toys per year.

- **Prizes** offer customers the opportunity to win an award as an incentive for purchasing a particular offering. Unlike premiums, where the reward is given with every purchase, in the case of prizes the actual reward is given to a relatively small number of participants. Prizes can be both monetary and nonmonetary. For example, Pepsi's *Twist and Win* promotion involved specially marked Pepsi products with various instant awards that ranged from cash to free gas, drinks, and movie tickets imprinted under the bottle cap.

- **Contests, sweepstakes, and games** involve prizes that typically require customers to submit some form of entry to participate. Contests typically require a proof of purchase, whereas sweepstakes are usually not contingent on customers purchasing the offering. Winners are selected by a panel of judges (in the case of contests), by a drawing (in the case of sweepstakes), or by an objective criterion such as points collected (in the case of games).

- **Loyalty programs** involve rewards related to the frequency, volume, and type of products and services purchased. Loyalty programs can be both monetary, such as cash rewards, and nonmonetary, such as frequent-flyer airline awards, frequent-stay hotel awards, and loyalty points that can be converted into bonus products and services. Unlike most of the other types of incentives, loyalty programs primarily target a company's existing customers and are designed to ensure their long-term loyalty as well as increase the quantity purchased by these customers. In addition to retaining its current customers, loyalty programs can attract new customers who are assessing the pros and cons of competing brands prior to deciding to patronize a particular company. For example, American Airlines—which in 1981 was one of the first major companies to introduce a loyalty program—launched its frequent-flyer program as a tool to move away from competing purely on price to building a loyal customer base.

The Pros and Cons of Customer Incentives

Customer-focused incentives offer multiple benefits to companies. Incentives are most frequently used to increase the sales of an offering. To this end, companies often use incentives to attract new customers as well as to encourage more frequent and larger purchases by existing customers. In addition, companies use incentives to stimulate demand in product categories where consumption depends on the purchase quantity. For example, customers who have purchased a larger amount of food than usual because of a sales promotion are often likely to end up consuming more food just because it is readily available.

Incentives can also encourage customers to purchase a company's offering within a time frame consistent with the company's goals. For example, a sales promotion run during the last quarter of the accounting year can help a company meet the desired annual sales goal. Furthermore, because sales promotions are easy to initiate and generate a positive (albeit often short-term) customer response, companies find them an increasingly effective tool not only to gain new customers but also to rebuff competitors' efforts to steal their customers.

In addition to helping the company increase sales, incentives enable the company to optimize the value of the offering for different customers by selectively offering incentives to particular customer segments. For example, a company might optimize profits by selectively offering discounts to economically disadvantaged customers, frequent buyers, and high-volume buyers while having less price-sensitive segments pay full price.

Another important benefit of incentives involves the inferences that customers are likely to draw about the performance of the company's products and services, as well as the image of its brand. Thus, if a company offers its products and services at a low price, consumers might draw negative inferences about the quality of the company's offerings. In contrast, when consumers see a company's offerings on sale, they are likely to attribute the low price to the promotional activities of the retailer rather than to the quality of the offering.

Despite their advantages, customer incentives have a number of drawbacks. First, most incentives have a short-term effect, which limits their ability to create a sustainable competitive advantage. Indeed, most sales promotions cause an initial peak in sales followed by a return to pre-promotional sales levels. Furthermore, in many cases the promotional peak is followed by a post-promotional dip below the initial baseline because buyers take advantage of the promotion to purchase larger than usual quantities of the goods on sale and stockpile them for future consumption.

Incentives can also cannibalize regular-price sales from customers who would have purchased the offering without incentives. In this context, a portion of the company's promotional activities are likely to end up subsidizing sales that would have occurred anyway. The larger the company's market share and the less targeted its sales promotions, the more likely it is that such cannibalization will take place. Consequently, the company can end up spending money and effort selling discounted goods to customers who would have purchased them at the regular price.

In addition, frequent use of incentives can "train" customers to anticipate promotions and time their purchases accordingly. As a result, buyers become accustomed to purchase primarily on the basis of a discounted price rather than on the basis of the benefits associated with the product, service, and brand aspects of the offering. Moreover, frequent use of incentives leads to communication that involves advertising sales promotions rather than informing buyers about the nonprice benefits of the company's offering.

Another potential downside of incentives is their cost, which includes not only the cost of the incentive provided to customers but also the costs of implementing that incentive. For example, the expenses associated with implementing a couponing program includes distribution costs, processing costs charged by the retailer redeeming the coupons, as well as the costs of misredemption, which involves erroneous or fraudulent coupon redemptions. Given that coupons have a low redemption rate to begin with, a dollar-off coupon can end up costing the company twice as much (although this number can be much lower in the case of targeted coupons that are digitally distributed and redeemed).

Furthermore, because of incentives' direct and often immediate impact on sales, managers are tempted to rely on incentives as a universal solution to gain market share rather than develop a sustainable value-creation market strategy. Thus, sales promotion expenditures incur an opportunity cost since money spent on incentives is money that is not spent on activities that create long-term market value, such as product development, brand building, and expanding distribution channels.

The complex nature of customer incentives and their multiple advantages and drawbacks call for a careful evaluation of the specific circumstances in which they are used. To this end, a manager must clearly identify the market opportunity that should be addressed (or the problem that should be solved) to ensure that the use of incentives will indeed produce the desired outcome and that incentives are the most effective means (compared to the other marketing tactics) to achieve that outcome.

Collaborator Incentives

Most collaborator incentives are offered to downstream members of a distribution channel, including wholesalers, distributors, dealers, and retailers. These incentives, also referred to as trade incentives, can be used to achieve a variety of goals: to acquire shelf space for new products as in the case of slotting allowances; to encourage distributors to carry higher levels of inventory to avoid stock-outs as in the case of stocking allowances, inventory financing, and volume discounts; and to encourage distributors to promote the company's offerings as in the case of advertising and display allowances. Similar to customer incentives, trade incentives can be either *monetary* or *nonmonetary*.

Monetary Collaborator Incentives

Monetary incentives involve payments or price discounts given by the manufacturer to channel members as encouragement to carry a particular offering or as an inducement to promote an offering to customers. Common monetary incentives include *slotting, stocking, cooperative advertising, display,* and *market-development allowances; spiffs; volume discounts; volume rebates; off-invoice incentives; cash discounts;* and *inventory financing.*

- **Slotting allowances** are incentives paid to a channel member — a wholesaler, dealer, or retailer — to allocate shelf space for a new product. Slotting allowances are designed to offset the costs associated with inventorying the new items, redesigning store shelves, and informing the employees about the new offerings.

- **Stocking allowances** are incentives paid to a distributor to carry extra inventory in anticipation of an increase in demand. Stocking allowances are often used in conjunction with extensive advertising campaigns and consumer incentive programs that are likely to lead to a spike in demand for the promoted offering.

- **Cooperative advertising allowances** are incentives paid by the manufacturer to channel members in return for featuring the manufacturer's offerings in their advertisements. The magnitude of the allowance can be determined as a percentage of the distributor's advertising costs or as a fixed amount per unit.

- **Display allowances** are incentives paid by the manufacturer to channel members in return for prominently displaying the manufacturer's products and services. Display allowances can involve end-of-aisle displays (endcap displays), larger and better shelf space, as well as free-standing displays featuring manufacturers' products.

- **Market-development allowances** are incentives offered to channel members in return for creating demand for the company's products. Market-development allowances are often used by manufacturers to create awareness of their offerings in local markets by leveraging retailers' knowledge and influence in these markets.

- **Spiffs** are incentives such as cash premiums, prizes, or additional commissions given directly to the salesperson (rather than to the retailer) as a reward for selling a particular item. Because they encourage the retailer's sales personnel to "push" the product to customers, spiffs are often referred to as "push money." The term "spiff" stems from the use of the word in the middle of the 19th century in reference to somebody smartly dressed (hence *to spiff up* — to improve the appearance of a place, a product, or a person).

- **Volume discounts** are price reductions offered to channel members based on the volume of a manufacturer's products purchased, with higher volumes typically associated with greater discounts.

- **Volume rebates** are incentives paid by the manufacturer to a distributor as a reward for achieving certain sales-quantity benchmarks. For example, a car manufacturer might offer a volume rebate to dealers only if they have sold a certain number of cars per month.

- **Off-invoice incentives** refer to any temporary price discounts offered by manufacturers to channel members. Off-invoice incentives are offered for a fixed period of time for the purpose of encouraging retailers to purchase larger quantities of the man-ufacturer's products and/or to pass some of the price reduction through to consumers in order to stimulate demand.

- **Cash discounts** are price reductions for payments made instantly or within a prede-fined time frame prior to the invoice due date. For example, a company might offer a two percent discount if an invoice due in 90 days is instead paid in 30 days.

- **Inventory financing** involves loans provided to a distributor for acquiring manufac-turers' goods. Inventory financing can be structured as an inventory-backed revolv-ing line of credit or a short-term loan made to the retailer by the manufacturer. Inven-tory financing is particularly relevant for retailers that must pay manufacturers in a shorter period than it takes them to sell the merchandise and receive payments from their customers.

Most monetary allowances are offered to marketing channel members as a reward for conducting promotional activities on behalf of the manufacturer, and these allowances are typically implemented as a discount from the wholesale price rather than as a separate pro-motional payment. From an accounting standpoint, depending on the way they are struc-tured, trade allowances can be considered as a discount to the channel or as a separate mar-keting expense.

Nonmonetary Collaborator Incentives

Nonmonetary incentives involve rewards given by the manufacturer to channel members as encouragement to carry a particular offering or as an inducement to promote an offering to customers. Common nonmonetary incentives include *buyback guarantees, sales support and training, bonus merchandise,* and *contests.*

- **Buyback guarantees** are agreements that the manufacturer will buy back from chan-nel members product quantities not sold within a certain time frame. The purpose of buyback guarantees is to encourage channel members to carry larger inventory (in order to avoid stock-outs) by minimizing their financial risk.

- **Sales support and training** involve various forms of aid offered to familiarize distrib-utors with the offering and facilitate sales. This form of trade promotion is common in industries with more complex offerings that require sales support staff to be versed in the product specifics and be able to explain them to customers.

- **Bonus merchandise** involves free goods offered as a reward for stocking a particular item or in lieu of a monetary allowance. Thus, rather than giving channel members monetary compensation for carrying a particular good, the manufacturer can provide extra units of its merchandise at no extra cost.

- **Contests** involve performance-based rewards such as vacation trips, cars, and mone-tary compensation given to the best performing individuals or teams among a com-pany's collaborators. Contest winners can be determined based on factors such as the number of units of a particular product sold, the number of new accounts opened, and the number of promotional activities launched.

The Pros and Cons of Collaborator Incentives

Collaborator-focused incentives offer multiple benefits to companies. These incentives can help persuade channel members to carry a company's offerings, making these offerings read-ily available to target customers. Incentives can further persuade channel members to carry larger inventories of their offerings in order to ensure against stock-outs. Trade allowances can induce channel members to promote the company's offerings by securing prime shelf space, placing point-of-purchase product displays, and otherwise promoting the company's offerings. Collaborators can also facilitate the implementation of pass-through promotions by delivering the company's incentives such as coupons, price discounts, and bonus offerings directly to customers. Finally, trade incentives such as spiffs, contests, bonus merchandise, and volume discounts and rebates can help motivate channel members to push the company's offerings.

Despite their advantages, trade incentives have a number of drawbacks. A key drawback are the high costs associated with the design and implementation of trade incentives. Indeed, as consolidated retailers gain power, they are in a stronger position to demand compensation from manufacturers for all activities designed to support their offerings. Retailers, on the other hand, are faced with rapidly evolving buyer preferences, a growing number of new product introductions, and ever-increasing competition, which, in turn, force them to streamline their operations and demand compensation for all incremental activities in order to achieve their profit goals.

In addition to their high costs, trade incentives can lead to channel conflicts stemming from the different goals of manufacturers on the one hand and channel members on the other. For example, incentives such as spiffs that are paid directly to the salesforce can put the interests of the manufacturer at odds with the interests of the retailer: The salesforce is motivated to push the offerings of a particular company that might not fit with the optimal profit-maximization strategy of the retailer. Furthermore, the offering promoted by the company might not be the best option for the retailer's customers, which, in turn, can damage this retailer's reputation among its customers.

Another downside of trade incentives is noncompliance with the promotion rules. Because a manufacturer might have to deal with hundreds and sometimes thousands of retailers, it is often challenging to ensure that retailers have indeed performed the services they have been paid for. For example, retailers might choose not to pass through the price discounts to their customers, fail to ensure that the company's products are always in stock, or fail to promote the company's offerings according to the conditions of the promotional allowance.

Some channel members end up abusing the sales promotion programs. For example, some engage in forward buying—purchasing a greater quantity during the promotional period in order to sell it after the promotion expires. Others go even further by diverting merchandise from regions in which a sales promotion is in effect to stores in regions in which the sales promotion is not currently in effect. Another form of abuse involves erroneous or fraudulent coupon redemptions that can range from genuine errors in coupon processing to more egregious offenses such as counterfeiting, wholesale coupon trading, and the submission of coupons from non-existent retail outlets.

Finally, designing, implementing, and enforcing trade incentive programs can be a very complex endeavor. Indeed, trade promotions involve multiple layers of deals related to different channel members, different products and services, different geographic regions, and different time frames. As a result, managing trade incentives might eat up a substantial amount of managerial time and effort, potentially distracting the company from building a sustainable competitive advantage and from designing offerings that inherently create market value.

To determine whether to provide incentives to each of the company's collaborators, as well as the type and magnitude of these incentives, a manager must carefully examine the value that its offerings create for collaborators and how these incentives are aligned with the company's strategic goals. Indeed, because incentives are easy to implement and often have immediate impact, managers can be tempted to use them as a universal tool to bolster sales volume. In this context, considering both the pros and cons of incentives is essential for the development of a sound market strategy.

Company Incentives

Although often overlooked, company incentives can play an important role in managing a company's offering. Similar to customer and collaborator incentives, company incentives can be divided into two categories: *monetary* and *nonmonetary*.

Monetary Company Incentives

Monetary incentives are often used to supplement the regular compensation received by employees in the form of a salary or commissions. They are similar to commissions in that they depend on employee performance and are typically conditional on achieving a specific performance benchmark such as units sold, sales revenues, and customer satisfaction. The most common forms of employee monetary incentives are cash bonuses and contests.

- **Monetary bonuses** are monetary rewards for employees—managers, customer service representatives, and salesforce—who meet certain performance benchmarks. Monetary bonuses can involve direct cash payments, or they can be tied to the company's performance as in the case of stock options.

- **Monetary contests** are performance-based rewards given to the best performing employees. Unlike monetary bonuses, which are given to all employees that have achieved certain performance outcomes, contests reward only the top performer(s).

Monetary incentives can be an effective means for companies to manage employees' compensation in a way that reflects their overall performance while at the same time introducing a competitive component. Indeed, the use of incentives given only to top performers (as in the case of contests) enables the company to motivate employees by benchmarking their performance based not only on the goal set by the company but also on the levels attained by top achievers.

Nonmonetary Company Incentives

Nonmonetary incentives are a popular form of employee incentives that are used either in combination with or as a replacement for monetary incentives. Unlike monetary incentives, where benefits are expressed using a common currency, nonmonetary incentives vary widely in the type of benefit received by employees. The most common types of nonmonetary incentives include bonuses, contests, and awards.

- **Nonmonetary bonuses** include a variety of incentives such as vacation incentives (e.g., extra vacation days), travel incentives (e.g., business class travel and a company car), and entertainment incentives (e.g., expense account).

- **Nonmonetary contests** involve performance-based nonmonetary rewards such as vacation trips, cars, free merchandise, and other prizes. Similar to monetary contests, nonmonetary contests reward only the best performers.

- **Recognition awards** acknowledge an employee's professional achievements and are an important component in creating and managing a company's culture by underscoring the company's values and the behaviors it aims to encourage. Common recognition awards include certificates of appreciation, employee of the month/quarter/year awards, and leadership and management awards.

The popularity of nonmonetary incentives can be attributed to several factors. First, nonmonetary awards acknowledging employee achievements can be more meaningful than a relatively small amount of cash to employees who would like to make a difference and appreciate the fact that their work is valued by the company. In addition, compared to cash, nonmonetary incentives can be perceived as being of a more personal nature, which, in turn, helps build an emotional bond between the company and its employees. Finally, in some cases, a company can acquire the benefits awarded to the employee at a significantly lower cost than their market value, thus making the nonmonetary awards more cost effective for the company.

The Pros and Cons of Company Incentives

Company-focused incentives can help motivate employees to increase productivity and achieve higher levels of performance, foster teamwork, and stimulate creativity. Incentives are a particularly common tool for motivating the salesforce in order to achieve greater sales effort, foster lead development and conversion to sales, promote new products and services, and stimulate off-season sales. Incentives are also often used to motivate the company's management by recognizing their leadership skills and rewarding them for the company's overall performance.

An important benefit of incentives is their variety, which enables the company to match the nature of the reward with the benefits sought by individual employees. Thus, the company can reward some of its employees with additional monetary compensation, whereas other employees might derive greater benefit from nonmonetary benefits such as extra vacation time, free merchandise, or recognition of their exemplary work ethic. Apart from their functional and monetary benefits, incentives can also deliver important psychological benefits by demonstrating that the company cares about its employees and appreciates their achievements.

In addition to increasing employee productivity, teamwork, and creativity, incentives can play an important role in attracting new employees and retaining a company's current workforce. To this end, companies use a variety of incentives including signing bonuses, moving expenses, and temporary housing in order to increase the likelihood of hiring and retaining excellent employees by "sweetening" their compensation package. Offering short-term incentives rather than a more permanent compensation package can also help the company address the uncertainty involved in hiring new employees and hedge its bets by minimizing long-term commitments.

Company incentives are not without shortcomings. Similar to the way in which customers and channel members get habituated to incentives, employees might become accustomed to receiving incentives, which, in turn, might make these incentives less effective. In addition, competitive incentives such as contests can end up being detrimental to the company's culture, engendering a competitive rather than collaborative environment. In the same vein, rewarding top performers to boost their motivation might end up demotivating those who were not rewarded. Finally, without a diligent performance-monitoring system in place, productivity-based incentives might encourage some employees to adopt unethical (and sometimes illegal) work practices, such as circumventing legal requirements and regulations, delivering inferior product quality, and misrepresenting the company's offering to buyers.

A classic example of counterproductive behavior induced by pay-for-performance incentives is the snake-catching bounty introduced in India during British rule. In order to free Delhi from a plague of snakes, the city's governor introduced a bounty on cobra skins. Because catching cobras is rather challenging, the reward was quite high. This, in turn, created a profitable business of farming snakes and collecting a reward for their skins. As the number of bounty claims increased exponentially, it became clear that the incentive was ineffective, and the governor decided to abandon the snake-catching initiative. Once farming cobras was no longer profitable, the snakes were released into the city streets, aggravating the original problem.[1]

Cases when pay-for-performance incentives backfire, promoting counterproductive actions on the part of the very employees they intend to motivate, abound in more recent history. When Sears introduced a profit-sharing plan in its auto centers whereby mechanics benefited financially from every new component installed, some employees were found to have persuaded customers to authorize unnecessary replacement of car parts.[2] In the same vein, in an attempt to increase the average number of products held by a customer—a commonly used measure of success in retail banking—Wells Fargo created an incentive structure touting its "eight is great" goal, meaning that employees had to get eight Wells Fargo products into the hands of each customer. Struggling to achieve their quotas, employees began to open additional accounts and order credit cards for their current customers—without their knowledge and authorization. The ensuing scandal and negative publicity created long-term damage to the company's reputation. In addition, Wells Fargo agreed to pay $185 million in fines to settle the matter and announced that it would fire over 5,000 employees involved in opening fraudulent accounts.[3]

To ensure that performance-based incentives serve their purpose and will not backfire by promoting unethical or otherwise counterproductive behavior, managers should carefully consider the behavioral implications of the proposed incentives. When used judiciously, and in a way that accounts for employee abuse of the company's reward policies, incentives can have a significant impact on company performance and the value that the company creates and captures in the market. Therefore, designing a meaningful incentives program aimed at attracting, motivating, and rewarding company employees while monitoring their performance can play a key role in enabling the company to achieve market success.

Managing Incentives in a Competitive Context

Compared to the other marketing tactics, incentives are relatively easy to implement and, as a result, many companies rely on incentives to better align the value of their offerings with the current market conditions. The widespread use of incentives as a universal value-management tool underscores the importance of identifying whether and how to use incentives in a way that benefits target customers, the company, and its collaborators. The key aspects of managing incentives to create market value—using incentives as a means of competitive differentiation, managing push and pull promotions, and communicating incentives—are discussed in the following sections.

Using Incentives as a Means of Competitive Differentiation

In the ideal scenario, incentives create market value and generate sales that could not be achieved by the other marketing tactics. While most incentives are able to boost the value of an offering in the short term, this boost in many cases is short-lived, often having adverse consequences on the offering's ability to create market value in a sustainable fashion.

Sales promotions often fail to create long-term value because of the ease with which competitors can match, and thereby negate, the competitive advantage they create. Moreover, by focusing buyers' attention on the monetary aspect of the offering, sales promotions systematically erode the power of the offering's brand by implicitly endorsing the view that the competing offerings are de facto commodities that can only be differentiated by price. Accordingly, sales promotions in general, and price promotions in particular, should be viewed as ancillary means rather than main tools to achieve competitive differentiation.

Not all incentives are detrimental to the company's ability to create a sustainable competitive market position for its offerings. Incentives that are directly related to the benefits of the company's offering and are aligned with the positioning of the company's offering can help strengthen the company's market position and increase the power of its brand. Incentives that can benefit the company's long-term market position include loyalty programs as well as premiums, prizes, contests, and games that are directly related to the benefits delivered by the company's offering. For example, airline, hotel, and credit card loyalty programs enhance the brands of these companies. In the same vein, Coca-Cola's "look under the cap" promotion helps the company maintain top-of-mind awareness by offering consumers the opportunity to win a variety of prizes based on the unique code under the bottle cap.

It is important to keep in mind, however, that incentives are auxiliary tools that in most cases are not designed to be the primary sources of creating customer value and, accordingly, should not be overused. Therefore, when designing a company's incentives, a manager should consider both their short-term and long-term impact to ensure that they are aligned with the company's overall strategy for creating market value.

Managing Push and Pull Promotions

An important aspect of managing a company's promotional activity involves determining the balance between customer-focused and channel-focused promotions. In this context, two core approaches can be identified: push promotions and pull promotions. These two types of promotions differ in the flow of incentives and communications between the company, its channel partners, and target customers (Figure 3). Here the term "promotion" is used in a more general sense to refer both to incentives (sales promotions) and communication.

Figure 3. Push and Pull Promotions

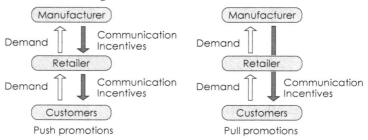

Push promotions   Pull promotions

Push Promotions

Push promotions stimulate demand for a company's offering by incentivizing channel members so that they have a vested interest to push the product downstream to end users. For example, the manufacturer can offer large trade allowances and discounts on its products and services to retailers. These promotions help generate store traffic, giving retailers a vested interest in selling the product. The manufacturer can also educate a retailer's salesforce about the benefits of its offerings and provide the retailer with promotional materials, thus facilitating the sales process.

The advantages of push promotions are that they are easier for the manufacturer to implement, since in this case the promotional activities are outsourced to channel members. In addition, because a large number of consumers make their buying decisions at the point of purchase, store-level promotions can be very effective in influencing their choices. The growing power of retailers demanding competitive trade discounts and allowances makes it even more difficult for manufacturers to ensure that their offerings are readily accessible to their target customers without relying on push promotions.

Despite their multiple benefits, push promotions have several important drawbacks. A key downside of push promotions is that in most cases they do not enable the manufacturer to directly promote its brand and build brand loyalty among its customers. Indeed, because in this case retailers carry out most of the communication and sales promotion, manufacturers do not have direct contact with customers and must rely on channel members to inform customers about the benefits of its offerings. The challenge here is that retailers are not always interested in building strong manufacturer brands because as these brands gain strength their dependence on retailers tends to decline, which in turn erodes retailers' power. This misalignment of the ultimate goals of manufacturers and retailers often leads to retailers not implementing the push promotions as intended by the manufacturer. For example, a retailer might decide not to pass through price discounts as the manufacturer intends and instead leave prices unchanged, keeping the discount for themselves. Another important downside of push promotions is the opportunity cost, whereby excessive spending on trade promotions can drain the company's promotional budget, hindering its ability to build strong brands and create a loyal customer base.

Pull Promotions

Pull promotions create demand for a company's offering by promoting the offering directly to end users, who in turn demand the offering from intermediaries, and ultimately "pull" it through the distribution channel. To illustrate, the manufacturer can extensively advertise its products and services to end users and promote its offerings using means such as coupons, rebates, games, and contests.

The advantage of pull promotions is that they enable the company to interact with its customers without the involvement of an intermediary. Companies can use this direct line of communication to promote the benefits of its offerings and associate these benefits with its brand, thus building a meaningful brand image in the minds of its customers. The ability to build customer loyalty and a strong brand can play a crucial role for manufacturers that are trying to gain power over retailers. Indeed, faced with customer demand for a manufacturer's offerings, retailers are likely to feel pressured to carry these offerings in order to please their customers, which, in turn, gives the manufacturer some leverage over retailers.

One of the main drawbacks of pull promotions is the increasing cost of effectively reaching target customers. Customers are constantly bombarded with a multitude of messages, making it difficult to break through the clutter to communicate the company's message and build a meaningful brand image. And while many companies have managed to create direct lines of communication with their current customers through mobile apps, loyalty programs, and online forums, attracting new customers has become more challenging. Another drawback of pull promotions is the increasing complexity of implementing a successful customer-focused communication and sales promotion program, which requires a certain level of market knowledge and expertise in design and delivery to carry it out in an effective and cost-efficient manner. As a result, companies that lack such expertise often choose to allocate a greater portion of their promotional budget to push promotions and delegate their implementation to channel members.

Communicating Incentives

When developing an incentives program, it is important to inform its recipients about the program's existence and specifics. In this context, it is essential to determine the extent to which a company should advertise its sales promotions. On the one hand, in order to take advantage of the sales promotion, buyers should be aware of it and understand its value. On the other hand, however, there is the concern that extensively advertising sales promotions can lead to cannibalization of regular sales that would have occurred even in the absence of the sales promotion.

The extent to which a company should advertise its incentives depends on the strategic goals it aims to achieve. Thus, if the goal is to use sales promotions as a customer acquisition vehicle, then a company should invest heavily in advertising these promotions. Indeed, without advertising, virtually all sales are likely to be generated from customers who have already decided to purchase the offering and who would have bought it even without the promotion. In this case, the sales promotion effectively subsidizes purchases that would have occurred anyway. Moreover, when encountering an unexpected sale, loyal customers might end up buying larger quantities to take advantage of the promotion. This stockpiling for future consumption can further erode the company's profitability as it ends up selling larger quantities of its offerings to its regular customers at a lower price.

The degree to which a company is likely to be affected by sales promotions cannibalizing its regular sales depends on the company's market share. As a result, market leaders are more likely to end up cannibalizing their current sales by promoting their incentives compared to smaller share companies that stand to gain much more by using incentives to attract competitors' customers. For example, Gillette which has a commanding share in the wet-shaving market, is much more likely to cannibalize its current sales by running a sales promotion compared to smaller share companies like Schick, Dollar Shave Club, or Harry's.

Not all incentives aim to attract new customers. Some are designed to encourage consumption by the company's current customers by stimulating the overall product category usage and/or increasing the company's share of the category at the expense of the competition. In such cases, a targeted communication of sales promotions is often a more sensible approach than widespread advertising. Indeed, because incentives designed to increase consumption by current customers and incentives aiming to attract new customers are likely to offer different benefits, poor targeting can lead to customer confusion and an ineffective use of the company's resources.

SUMMARY

Incentives aim to increase the value of an offering by increasing its benefits or reducing costs. Most incentives are temporary in nature and are designed to enable the company to respond in a timely manner to changes in the market such as a decline in customer demand, competitive price discounts, pressure from channel partners, or a weak economy.

Companies use incentives for a variety of reasons: to retain their current customers and attract new ones, to ensure collaborator support, as well as to increase the productivity and ensure the loyalty of their employees. When developing incentives, a manager's ultimate goal is to enhance the value an offering creates for target customers, the company, and its collaborators.

Incentives represent a significant portion of a company's promotional budget. Of the resources allocated to incentives, the vast majority is usually spent on trade incentives, followed by customer incentives and incentives directed at company employees. The growth of incentives is a function of changes in the target market (the Five Cs) and a decrease in the effectiveness of the other tactics—product, service, brand, price, communication, and distribution—to create market value.

Most incentives fall into one of three categories: customer incentives, collaborator incentives, and company incentives.

Customer incentives can be divided into monetary incentives that typically aim to reduce an offering's costs (coupons, rebates, volume discounts, and temporary price reductions) and nonmonetary incentives that often aim to enhance the offering's benefits (premiums, prizes, contests, sweepstakes, games, and loyalty programs).

Most *collaborator incentives* are offered to members of the distribution channel and involve slotting, stocking, advertising, display, and market-development allowances; spiffs; volume discounts and rebates; off-invoice incentives; cash discounts; and inventory financing. Similar to customer incentives, trade incentives are either monetary (discounts and allowances) or nonmonetary (buy-back guarantees, sales support and training, bonus merchandise, and contests). Trade incentives can have multiple objectives such as gaining distribution coverage, encouraging channel members to stock the offering at certain inventory levels (to avoid stock-outs or to transfer inventory from the manufacturer to distributors), and encouraging channel members to promote the company's offering.

Company incentives commonly involve rewards for employees who meet certain performance benchmarks. These incentives include performance-based awards such as monetary and nonmonetary bonuses, employee recognition awards, and contests.

Managing promotions calls for finding the right balance between customer-focused and channel-focused promotions. *Push promotions* create demand for a company's offering by incentivizing channel members, who in turn push the product downstream to end users. *Pull promotions*, on the other hand, create demand for a company's offering by promoting the offering directly to end users, who in turn demand the offering from intermediaries and ultimately "pull" it through the channel.

MARKETING INSIGHT: SAMPLING AS A PROMOTIONAL TOOL

Sampling involves giving potential buyers the option to experience the company's offering. Sampling is a popular form of new product introduction in the food and beverage, cosmetics, and pharmaceutical industries. Sampling is also very popular in the case of digital products and services such as trial subscriptions for games, news, music, and video services.

A popular form of sampling for digital offerings is freemiums, which involve a two-part offering in which the basic version of the product or service is offered for free while giving the customer an option to upgrade to a fully functional paid version. The freemium model is commonly used to promote a new offering by enabling consumers to experience the offering at no cost. For example, Amazon (Kindle), Dropbox, Hulu, and Pandora make available both a free basic version of their offerings as well as a paid, fully functional (unrestricted) version.

The primary purpose of sampling is to facilitate the introduction of a new product or service to the market by enabling target customers to directly experience a company's offering. For this reason, even though they are traditionally considered as an incentive, samples and free trials are in fact more a form of communication rather than a sales promotion. Indeed, sales promotions *increase the value* of the company's offering by decreasing its costs and/or increasing its benefits. In contrast, samples and free trials have no impact on the value of the company's offering; their main purpose is to *inform* customers about the benefits of the offering. Thus, unlike price discounts, coupons, and rebates, samples rarely create incremental residual value. In most cases, after sampling the offering customers choosing to purchase the offering will do so at the regular price and receive the same benefit as if they had not sampled the offering.

Sampling is a form of communication because it informs target customers about the benefits of an offering. Rather than telling a story about the offering's benefits via a commercial, direct mail, or an online banner, sampling informs customers about the offering by letting them experience these benefits firsthand. In this context, sampling is particularly effective for products and services that are rich in experiential attributes, the value of which cannot be determined by merely observing the offering but can be readily assessed upon consumption. For example, providing a customer with the opportunity to taste a snack as a free sample can be exponentially more effective at convincing a customer to purchase the product than a commercial stating that this snack is indeed delicious.

The success of a company's sampling campaign hinges on three key factors. First, the cost of the sample to the company should be relatively small compared to the sales revenues and profits it is expected to generate. Thus, offerings that best lend themselves to sampling are those that have a high sample-to-purchase conversion rate, a low unit cost, and a high unit profit margin. Second, customers should be able to experience the benefits of the offering during trial. Indeed, whereas using sampling to convey benefits that can be readily experienced—such as the taste of a snack— can inform customers about the offering, using sampling to convey benefits that are not readily observable—for example, the health benefits of a snack—is unlikely to change customers' beliefs about the offering. Finally, there should be a clear path to purchase, meaning that the company should have a mechanism in place to generate sales from customers who found the offering attractive. Because sampling does not incentivize customers to make an immediate purchase, sampling programs often involve a sales promotion such as a price discount, coupon, or instantly redeemable rebate in order to convert sampling to sales.

MARKETING INSIGHT: APPLYING GAME THEORY TO MANAGING SALES PROMOTIONS

The prisoner's dilemma illustrates a decision paradox whereby acting in one's own self-interest, although logically more desirable, leads to a suboptimal outcome for all parties involved. It is typically illustrated with the following scenario. Consider two men suspected of committing a crime being interrogated in separate rooms. Each has the option of confessing or not confessing to the crime. If only one of the two prisoners confesses, he is offered a one-year sentence in exchange for his testimony against the other, who will receive a ten-year sentence. However, if both of them confess, each will get a five-year sentence. Finally, if neither confesses, some of the charges will be difficult to prove, and as a result both will receive a three-year sentence. The outcomes for different confession scenarios are depicted in Figure 4.

Figure 4. The Prisoner's Dilemma

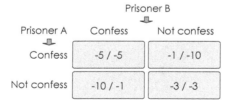

The prisoner's dilemma illustrates an interesting paradox: Even though not confessing leads to the fewest collective years in prison for the two prisoners (six years total), from their individual standpoints, each of them would be better off confessing. Consider, for example, the options of Prisoner A. Regardless of the actions of the other prisoner, it is in the best interest of Prisoner A to confess. Thus, if Prisoner B confesses, Prisoner A is better off confessing since he will receive a five-year sentence rather than a ten-year sentence. Furthermore, if Prisoner B does not confess, Prisoner A is again better off confessing since he will receive only a one-year sentence rather than a three-year sentence. The same holds for Prisoner B, who would be better off confessing regardless of the actions of Prisoner A. As a result, if guided by their own self-interest, both prisoners would spend five years in prison rather than three years, which would have been the case had they been able to collaborate with each other. Thus, the prisoner's dilemma illustrates a counterintuitive scenario in which acting in one's own self-interest does not produce an optimal outcome.

In marketing, the prisoner's dilemma is often used to illustrate how following a logical thought process can result in companies engaging in actions that will leave them in a worse state than if they had stayed the course. Consider a scenario in which two competitors contemplate offering price discounts to boost revenues and profits. The payoff of running sale promotions is such that if both companies discount their offerings, each would generate $10 million in profits (Figure 5). If neither of them discounts its offerings, however, both companies would be better off, with each generating a profit of $15 million. Finally, if only one of them runs an unmatched sales promotion, it would double its profits to $20 million, whereas its competitor would generate only $5 million. Thus, consistent with the logic of the prisoner's dilemma, by acting in their own self-interest, both companies are likely to discount their offerings, even though both would have been better off not offering discounts.

Figure 5. The Prisoner's Dilemma in Sales Promotions

	Company B	
Company A	Discount	Not discount
Discount	$10M / $10M	$20M / $5M
Not discount	$5M / $20M	$15M / $15M

Despite its popularity in illustrating the competitive reaction to a company's promotional activities, the application of the prisoner's dilemma to marketing problems is subject to several important limitations. First, the prisoner's dilemma depicts a one-period game in which each of the parties makes a single decision that determines the ultimate outcome. In reality, this is rarely the case as companies can rapidly respond to a competitor's actions by launching a new promotional campaign or modifying the existing one. In addition, unlike the prisoners in the above scenario who are unable to communicate with one another, a company can signal its intentions through a variety of means such as making statements to the media and launching an aggressive promotional campaign designed to make competitors aware of its resolve to defend its market position. Therefore, even though the general notion that acting in one's own self-interest can lead to a suboptimal market outcome holds in many scenarios, applying the prisoner's dilemma to managing sales promotions must take into account the specific market context in which these decisions are made.

PART FIVE

COMMUNICATING VALUE

Introduction

*The single biggest problem in communication
is the illusion that it has taken place.*

—George Bernard Shaw, playwright,
cofounder of London School of Economics

Communication informs target customers, collaborators, and company employees and stakeholders about the company's offering. Communication, particularly in its most popular form—advertising—is the most visible aspect of a company's marketing activities. Communication is not limited to advertising and includes a variety of ways—such as social media, paid search, and personal selling—in which a company informs the relevant market entities about its offerings.

Communication is a key component of a company's activities aimed at creating market value. It informs the target audience about the product, service, brand, price, and incentives aspects of the offering as well as about the offering's availability. As a result, an offering's communication is closely related to the other marketing tactics, and its content typically reflects the key attributes of the company's offerings: its product, service, brand, price, incentives, and distribution.

Communication can be indirect, as in advertising, whereby the company's message is embedded in a specific media form to reach the target audience. Alternatively, communication can involve a direct interaction between the company and its target audience, as in the case of personal selling. Indirect and direct communication are discussed in the two chapters included in this section. In particular, these chapters address the issues pertaining to *managing communication* and *personal selling*.

- **Managing communication** articulates the ways in which the company informs the relevant market entities—target customers, collaborators, and stakeholders—about its offerings. The key aspects of managing communication—including setting communication goals, identifying the target audience, crafting the communication message, selecting the right media, developing the creative execution, and measuring communication effectiveness—are discussed in Chapter 14.

- **Personal selling** is a specific form of communication that involves direct interaction between the seller and the buyer. The key aspects of personal selling as a value-creation process, managing the salesforce, and the art of personal selling are discussed in Chapter 15.

Communication aims to convey meaningful information about the company's offering to the relevant market entities—target customers, the company, and its collaborators. To achieve this goal, all aspects of the offering's communication, from defining its goal and crafting the communication message to designing the creative solution and measuring the communication effectiveness, should be aligned in a way that maximizes their impact on each of these three entities. A systematic approach to developing such an integrated approach to marketing communication is outlined in the following chapters.

CHAPTER FOURTEEN

MANAGING COMMUNICATION

*A good advertisement is one which sells the
product without drawing attention to itself.*
—David Ogilvy, founder of Ogilvy & Mather

Communication informs target customers, collaborators, and company employees and stakeholders about the benefits of the company's offering. Communication is one aspect of marketing that has undergone dramatic changes in the past decade and is continuing to evolve rapidly. Despite these changes, there are a number of enduring marketing principles that are at the heart of successful communication campaigns. The core principles of marketing communication are outlined in this chapter. Specifically, we address the following topics:

- *Communication as a Value-Creation Process* ‖ Communication as a tool for creating market value | Key trends in communication management | Developing an effective communication campaign

- *Setting Communication Goals* ‖ Defining the focus of the communication campaign | Defining performance benchmarks | Aligning the communication goals with the customer decision journey | Determining the communication budget

- *Designing the Communication Strategy* ‖ Identifying the target audience | Developing the communication message

- *Selecting the Media* ‖ Outbound media | Inbound media

- *Designing the Creative Execution* ‖ Message source | Message appeal | Message complexity

- *Evaluating Communication Effectiveness* ‖ Measuring awareness | Measuring preferences | Measuring behavior

The discussion of communication management is complemented by an overview of the key advertising concepts, the essence of programmatic advertising, and an outline of the process of developing a communication plan.

Communication as a Value-Creation Process

Market success is rarely possible without an effective communication campaign that creates awareness of the company's offering among its target audience. The role of communication as a tool for creating market value, the key trends in communication management, and the process of developing a viable communication campaign are discussed in the following sections.

Communication as a Tool for Creating Market Value

Communication informs the relevant market entities—target customers, collaborators, and the company—about the specifics of the offering. Companies spend billions of dollars each year to advise buyers about the availability of their offerings, explain the benefits of these offerings, spread the word about price cuts, and promote product and corporate brands. In the words of Leo Burnett, founder of the Leo Burnett advertising agency, *Advertising says to people, "Here's what we've got. Here's what it will do for you. Here's how to get it."*

Communication is one of the seven attributes that define a company's offering. Unlike the first five attributes—product, service, brand, price, and incentives—which largely define the value of the offering, communication informs target customers about various aspects of the offering. As a result, communication creates value by informing different market entities—target customers, collaborators, and the company employees and stakeholders—about the offering's optimal value proposition (OVP). Therefore, when developing a communication campaign, a manager's ultimate goal is to inform target customers, collaborators, and company employees and stakeholders about the offering and the ways in which it will create market value (Figure 1).

Figure 1. Communication as a Value-Creation Process

Based on the target audience, there are three types of communication: customer-focused, collaborator-focused, and company-focused (internal). While all three types of communication are important, the one that is the most complex and typically absorbs most of a company's resources is customer-focused communication. Collaborator-focused and internal communication share many commonalities with customer-focused communication but are typically more straightforward to implement. Accordingly, the remainder of this chapter will focus on the communication a company aims at its customers.

Key Trends in Communication Management

Communication has undergone more sweeping changes than any of the other marketing tactics. Over the past decade, several significant developments have dramatically altered the way companies communicate with their current and potential customers. Some of the major developments in marketing communication are outlined below:

- **Micro-targeting.** Communication has evolved from mass-media formats such as television and print to personalized *one-on-one communication*. Companies are now able not only to better identify the needs of their customers but also to target individual customers with customized messages delivered at the right place and time. This micro-targeting calls for automated (programmatic) management of the company's communication, which is guided by algorithms derived from customers' behavior and demographics. The key aspects of programmatic advertising are discussed in more detail at the end of this chapter.

- **Inbound communication.** Another important development is the switch from company-driven communication to customer-initiated interactions, where customers are not merely recipients of company messages but actively search for information about companies and their offerings. This switch from purely outbound communication such as advertising, event sponsorship, and direct marketing to a hybrid format that also incorporates inbound communication using text, video, and audio search has revolutionized the ways companies interact with their customers. As a result, most communication campaigns combine both inbound and outbound activities in order to better promote the company's offerings.

- **Peer-to-peer communication.** Another important development that is changing the communication landscape is the growth of *peer-to-peer communication*, which sometimes eclipses the company's own communication. As an increasing number of customers are informed about the available offerings by other customers through product reviews and social media, a company's ability to shape customer preferences directly is gradually decreasing. This transparency of customer experiences forces companies to invest in developing superior products and services and ensure that their communication is aligned with the value created by their offerings.

- **Geolocation.** The ubiquity of interactive mobile devices such as phones, tablets, and wearable technology that are uniquely tied to a particular user and are almost always "on" has enabled companies to geolocate their customers virtually anywhere anytime. In this context, geolocation plays an increasingly important role in identifying customers based on their active needs — that is, needs that they are currently trying to fulfill. For example, informing a person who is in the vicinity of a restaurant about its menu and ongoing promotions is far more effective than providing this information when the person is ten miles away.

- **Predictive analytics.** To effectively reach their target audience, a growing number of companies are using predictive analytics to better detect customer needs and design a message tailored to these needs. Many of these companies couple predictive analytics with geolocation to forecast customers' location and send targeted offers before customers reach their destination. As a result, companies are becoming more proficient at crafting messages that are tailored to fit customer needs and reaching customers at times and in places when these messages can be most impactful and more likely to elicit the desired customer response.

- **Occasion-based targeting.** A growing trend in managing communication is occasion-based targeting that defines the communication audience in terms of specific usage occasions (see Chapter 6 for a more detailed discussion of occasion-based targeting). Occasion-based targeting is more flexible than targeting individuals based on their demographics because it accounts for the fact that the same person might have different needs depending on the occasion involved. Defining the target audience in terms of specific usage occasions rather than demographics, allows companies to reach their customers at times when their communications are likely to have the most impact. Furthermore, combining demographic and occasion-based information can help a company significantly improve its targeting and dramatically increase the effectiveness and cost efficiency of its communication campaign.

- **Measurability.** The proliferation of online communication coupled with the ubiquity of personal mobile devices offer dramatically improved capabilities for measuring the effectiveness of communication campaigns. The ability to better track how a specific communication impacts individual consumers allows companies to more effectively calibrate their message and creative execution, choose the most effective media channel, and ultimately determine the optimal level of communication expenditures.

Developing an Effective Communication Campaign

The changes in the ways companies interact with their customers add an extra layer of complexity to the task of effectively managing communication campaigns. This complexity highlights the importance of using a systematic approach — such as the G-STIC framework outlined in Chapter 3 — to communicate the company's offering. Consistent with this framework, managing communication can be defined by five key actions: setting the communication *goal*, articulating the communication *strategy*, designing the communication *tactics*, *implementing* the communication campaign, and *controlling* (evaluating) the campaign results. The key aspects of managing communication are outlined in Figure 2 and discussed in more detail in the following sections.

Figure 2. The G-STIC Framework for Managing Communication

A company's communication campaign is guided by its overarching marketing strategy, defined by the choice of target market and the company's value proposition for this market. Building on this marketing strategy, the communication campaign starts with setting a *goal*, defined by its *focus*, which delineates the key criterion for the success of the communication campaign, and performance *benchmarks*, which outline the quantitative and temporal criteria for reaching the communication goal. Following articulation of the goal is the development of a communication *strategy* and, specifically, the identification of the target *audience* and the *message* that will be communicated to this audience. The communication strategy is then translated into *tactics*, which involve determining the specific *media* used to transmit the message and the *creative* execution that aims to express the message in the chosen media format. Next, is the *implementation*, which involves the practical execution—*development* and *deployment*—of the campaign. Finally, *control* measures the *performance* of the campaign while monitoring for changes in the *context* in which communication takes place.

The G-STIC framework offers an intuitive approach to streamlining a company's communication activities into a logical sequence that aims to produce the desired outcome. It is important to note, however, that even though the G-STIC framework implies a particular sequence, starting with the definition of the communication goal and concluding with identifying controls for measuring campaign effectiveness, the development of a communication campaign is an iterative rather than a linear process. Thus, the development of a communication plan often starts with the identification of the target audience that the company aims to reach with its campaign and the message that it aims to convey to this audience. In this context, the G-STIC framework describes the key components of the iterative process of developing a communication campaign and outlines a logical sequence of organizing these components without prescribing the order in which these elements are developed.

The key aspects of developing a communication campaign—setting communication goals, identifying the target audience, developing the message, selecting the media, designing the creative execution, and evaluating communication effectiveness—are outlined in the following sections.

Setting Communication Goals

Communication goals articulate the particular outcomes that a company aims to achieve with its communication campaign in a specific period of time. As in the case of the company's overall goal, setting the communication goal involves two main decisions: identifying the *focus* of the company's actions and defining the performance *benchmarks* to be achieved. These two aspects of setting the communication goal and the factors that influence their selection are discussed in more detail below.

Defining the Focus of the Communication Campaign

The focus identifies the key criterion for the success of the communication campaign. It is the metric defining the desired outcome of the company's communication activities. Based on their focus, there are three types of communication goals: *creating awareness, building preferences*, and *inciting action*.

- **Creating awareness.** A communication campaign might aim to make the target audience aware of a company's offering. For example, a toy manufacturer might want to inform its target customers about a new toy, a retailer might want to communicate its new sales promotions, and a movie studio might want to create awareness of an upcoming movie release. In cases when the company launches a new-to-the-world product or service, the communication might also aim to create awareness of the entire product category. For example, when launching its video streaming service, Netflix had to inform its customers about its offering while in the process explaining the benefits of the entire fixed-fee-based streaming business model. Creating top-of-mind awareness of the entire product category is also a common communication goal for many industry associations tasked with promoting the consumption of a particular good such as cotton, milk, and alternative energy.

- **Building preferences.** A communication campaign might also aim to create and strengthen customer preference for the offering by enhancing the offering's desirability. Preference-building goes beyond generating awareness of the company's offering among the target audience to convey the value it creates. This value can be expressed in terms of its superiority to another offering, as in the case of comparative advertising, or by focusing on the offering's ability to fulfill customers' needs without necessarily comparing it to another offering, as in the case of noncomparative advertising.

- **Inciting action.** A communication campaign might aim to motivate customers to engage with the offering and take an action such as obtaining more information about the company's offering, visiting a retailer that carries it, and ultimately purchasing it. For example, a pharmaceutical company might encourage consumers to contact a doctor to obtain more information about a particular drug, a car manufacturer might encourage buyers to visit its dealerships, and an electronics manufacturer might encourage shoppers to buy its newest device.

These three goals are interdependent, such that some can be viewed as prerequisites for others. Thus, enhancing an offering's attractiveness implies that target customers are already informed about the offering's existence. Similarly, a call for action implies that customers are already informed about the offering and find it desirable. Therefore, when determining the focus of its communication campaign, a company must be cognizant of customers' awareness and beliefs about its offering(s), prioritize the outcomes it aims to achieve, and ensure that these outcomes are aligned with its overall marketing goals.

A company's communication goals can be related to the customer decision journey, which delineates the processes by which buyers fulfill an active need—from initially considering a product or service to purchasing and using it. In this context, the customer decision journey is defined by six main experiences: need activation, search, evaluation, choice, purchase, and usage (see Chapter 4 for a detailed discussion of the customer decision journey).

The stages in the customer decision journey can be associated with different communication goals as shown in Figure 3. *Creating awareness* is crucial during the initial stages of the customer journey when buyers are unaware of their unmet needs and/or are unaware of the availability of a company's offering as a means of fulfilling that need. Once buyers are aware of the company's offering, *preference-building* gains primary importance to generate initial interest in the offering and strengthen existing preferences in order to ensure that customers will end up choosing the company's offering. After buyers have decided on their preferred offering, *inciting an action* typically takes prominence to nudge them to make a purchase, foster usage, and encourage repurchase of the offering without considering other options.

Figure 3. Communication Goals as a Function of the Customer Decision Journey

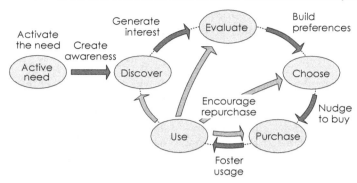

Note that the relationship between communication goals and stages in the decision journey is not clear cut. All three goals—creating awareness, building a preference, and inciting action—can be relevant at multiple stages of the decision journey. For example, a company might create awareness of sales promotions to nudge buyers toward purchasing the offering, suggest new uses for the offering, as well as inform customers about distribution channels in which they can repurchase the offering. Likewise, a company might aim to strengthen buyers' preferences even after they have chosen its offering in order to facilitate usage and repurchase. Finally, inciting action can involve encouraging buyers to seek additional information about the offering (e.g., visit a company's website) and engage in a preference-building activity (e.g., participate in an experiential event organized by the company) long before the buyers have chosen the company's offering.

Defining Performance Benchmarks

Performance benchmarks outline the quantitative and temporal criteria for reaching the communication goal. Consequently, there are two types of performance benchmarks that define the company's communication goal:

- **Quantitative benchmarks** define the specific milestones to be achieved by the company with respect to its focal communication goal. For example, a company might aim to create awareness of a new offering among 50% of its target customers, increase by 20% the number of buyers who prefer its brand to its primary competitors, or increase traffic to the company's website by two million visitors. Quantitative benchmarks can be expressed in either relative terms (e.g., increase awareness by 20%) or absolute terms (e.g., generate two million incremental visits).

- **Temporal benchmarks** identify the time frame for achieving a particular milestone. Setting a timeline for achieving a goal is a key strategic decision because the communication campaign adopted to implement these goals is often contingent on the time horizon. An aggressive communication goal that aims to achieve a particular outcome in a short period of time will likely require a different campaign than the goal of achieving the same outcome over a longer period of time.

To be actionable, the communication goal should clearly articulate the focus of the campaign and its quantitative and temporal benchmarks. To illustrate, consider the following examples of communication goals:

Create top-of-mind awareness (goal focus) of the danger of running out of milk among 50% of adult California residents (quantitative benchmark) in six months (temporal benchmark).

Increase the number of consumers who believe that the company's offering is superior to the competition (goal focus) by 20% (quantitative benchmark) in one year (temporal benchmark).

Generate one million (quantitative benchmark) website visits (goal focus) in the second quarter (temporal benchmark).

The above three goals focus on different outcomes: The first goal focuses on creating awareness, the second goal is focused on strengthening preferences, and the third aims to incite action. In addition, some communication campaigns define the desired outcome in relative terms, whereas others define the goal as an absolute number. The key principle when choosing the focus and benchmarks of the communication campaign is that they must be consistent with the company's overall marketing strategy and enable the company to create superior value for its target customers, collaborators, and stakeholders.

Determining the Communication Budget

An important aspect of developing a communication campaign is determining the optimal level of expenditures required to achieve the set communication goals. Generally speaking, communication costs can be divided into two categories: costs of developing the creative content and media costs that involve securing communication channels, such as the cost of air time, magazine space, and outdoor billboards. For many companies, and especially those with significant resources allocated for communication, media costs far exceed the costs associated with creative development.

Companies vary in how much they spend on communication campaigns. As a percentage of sales, industrial equipment companies tend to spend less on communication than do consumer goods companies such as those in cosmetics, food, and beverages. Top U.S. advertisers such as Procter & Gamble, AT&T, General Motors, Comcast, Verizon, and American Express spend billions of dollars annually to promote their new offerings, persuade consumers about their benefits, and ultimately nudge them to make a purchase.

There is no universal method that works for all companies and in all circumstances. Instead, there are three key factors that a company must consider in order to determine the optimal communication budget: its *communication goals*, the *cost of achieving these goals*, and the *available resources*.

- **Communication goals.** The nature of the company's goals—specifically the degree to which they are ambitious in terms of number of customers to be reached, the time frame for reaching them, and the desired outcome—can have a significant impact on the expenditures needed to achieve these goals.

- **Cost of achieving the communication goals.** The cost of achieving the company's communication goals depends on a variety of factors such as the level of benefits created by the offering, the degree to which the offering is differentiated from the competition, the level of communication expenditures by the competition, the effectiveness of competitive communication, the existing level of awareness and acceptance of the offering among target customers, as well as the company's ability to use resources in an effective and cost-efficient manner.

- **Available resources.** The overall level of communication expenditure depends on the company's resources. A small business with limited access to capital is likely to spend less on communication than an established large enterprise or a well-funded startup.

The above three factors are interrelated, such that communication goals are often set while considering the cost of achieving these goals and the resources that the company can allocate to the communication campaign. Indeed, articulating a communication goal without taking into account whether the company has the resources to achieve this goal can be counterproductive and is likely to cause disruptions when implementing the campaign. Setting the communication budget based solely on the resources allocated to running a communication campaign (e.g., as a percentage of sales revenues) without considering the ultimate goals that the campaign aims to achieve can also lead to either underfunding or overinvesting in the campaign.

Designing the Communication Strategy

The communication strategy comprises two key components: the audience targeted by the company's communication and the message that the company aims to convey to this audience. These two aspects of designing a communication strategy—identifying the target audience and developing the communication message—are discussed in the following sections.

Identifying the Target Audience

Identification of the target audience is a key component of developing a communication strategy that can have a significant impact on the effectiveness and cost efficiency of the communicated message. There are two complementary aspects of identifying the target audience: strategic and tactical. Strategic targeting involves identifying the audience targeted by the company's communication. In contrast, tactical targeting involves identifying the specific ways in which the company can reach strategically important audiences with its message in the most effective and cost-efficient way. The two aspects of the target audience—*strategic* and *tactical*—are outlined in the following sections.

Strategic Target Identification

The target audience is the intended recipient of the company's communication. Because communication is one aspect of an offering's tactics, identification of the target audience follows from the strategic choice of target customers for the company's offering. The target audience for the company's communication might differ from an offering's target customers. Target customers are the users of the offering—the entities for whom the company designs its offering. In contrast, the target audience for the company's communications consists of people that the company aims to inform about its offerings.

Most often, the target audience for a company's communication consists of the same customers targeted by the company's offering. This, however, is not always the case. For example, parents buying food and clothing for their kids are often the target audience for a company's communication campaign although they are not the end users. In the same vein, a company selling business software applications might develop a communication campaign targeting senior executives who will ultimately have to approve the purchase even though these executives might never actually use the software. A company might also develop a communication campaign aimed at the purchasing department of a potential client in order to create awareness of the company's offerings, even though the employees working in the purchasing department typically are not the target customers for the company offerings. Accordingly, the target audience can be broader than the offering's target customers and include initiators, influencers, gatekeepers, decision makers, and purchasers involved in selecting, buying, and using the offering (see Chapters 4 and 15 for a more detailed discussion of the entities involved in the decision-making process).

To correctly identify the target audience, a company must understand how target customers make decisions, identify the entities that are involved in the decision-making and purchasing process, and determine which of these entities can benefit from receiving information about the company's offering. Thus, the target audience for the company communication might fully or partially overlap with the offering's target customers and/or might focus on a different set of individuals who are involved in the decision and purchase of the offering without ever using it.

From a strategic standpoint, identifying the target audience can follow two paths: It can focus on the relatively stable characteristics of individuals that do not change much over time—an approach commonly referred to as user-based targeting; or, alternatively, it can focus on preferences that are context-specific and vary across usage occasions—an approach commonly referred to as occasion-based targeting (see Chapter 7 for a more detailed discussion).

User-based targeting is more appropriate in cases where the needs of the target audience are relatively stable across purchase occasions and can be used as a reliable predictor of behavior on any particular purchase occasion. For example, the preference for non-GMO, organic products is fairly stable across individuals and can serve as the basis for user-based targeting. In contrast, *occasion-based targeting* is more appropriate when the needs of the target audience vary across purchase occasions, and the same individual might display different behaviors depending on the purchase/consumption occasion. For example, the preference for different types of cuisine might vary over time such that the same individual might display different behaviors depending on the purchase/consumption occasion. Because it accounts for the variability of individuals' preferences across purchase occasions, occasion-based targeting can be thought of as the more general targeting approach (whereas user-based targeting makes the assumption that preferences are constant across usage occasions).

Tactical Target Identification

Following identification of the target audience is identification of the ways in which the company can reach these customers. Reaching target audiences can be difficult because needs are not readily observable and, therefore, cannot be acted upon to communicate and deliver the company's offering. To reach the strategically important target audience in an effective and cost-efficient manner, the company needs to identify the observable characteristics associated with the needs of the target audience and use these characteristics to identify the optimal communication channels.

The primary goal of tactical targeting is to ensure effective and cost-efficient delivery of the company's communication. An overly broad targeting that includes audiences unrelated to the company's offering is not cost efficient because it wastes resources on reaching individuals that are unlikely to respond favorably to the company's offering. Targeting that is too narrow, on the other hand, is ineffective because it might overlook audiences that are strategically important for the company. Accordingly, tactical targeting is driven by two key principles: *effectiveness*, which reflects a company's ability to reach *all* desired recipients with its communication, and *cost efficiency*, which reflects the degree to which a company's communication efforts are deployed in a way that reaches *only* its target audience.

To enable the company to reach its target audience in the most effective and cost-efficient manner, tactical targeting must answer three main questions: *whom* to reach and *where* and *when* is the optimal opportunity to reach this audience. To address these questions, a company must identify the observable characteristics (the profile) of the strategically viable audience and identify the ideal touch points to inform this audience about the company's offering.

To determine the optimal opportunity (where and when) to reach the target audience, companies increasingly rely on their ability to track people's behavior, including their physical location and online activity. Examining an individual's online activity can help better understand, and even predict, this individual's current needs. For example, the information that an individual visits a particular website, the day and time of this visit, the pages visited, the amount of time spent on each page, the links clicked on, and the searches made enable companies to gain insight into this individual's specific needs and preferences. Furthermore, combining individuals' past online behavior with their current online activity enables companies to develop and serve content that is most likely to appeal to these individuals at a particular point in time.

Geotargeting enables a company to deliver content to its audience based on customers' current geographic location, determined by their mobile devices. Geotargeting is particularly important because location contains information about a customer's environment at a given time, which, in turn, makes it easier to deliver a relevant message that is aligned with the particular stage in this customer's decision journey. For example, delivering a message featuring a sales promotion to a customer visiting a grocery store can help the company increase the chances that this person will not only pay attention to the advertisement but also be more likely to change his or her behavior in response to the communication content.

Combining online and geolocation data can enable companies to dramatically increase the effectiveness of their advertising campaigns. Together, online and geolocation data can provide insights into individuals' behavior over time and paint a more complete picture of their needs and their stage in the decision journey. This information, in turn, allows the company to more specifically address these needs. For example, knowing that an individual who walks into a Cadillac dealership has done thorough online research, frequently visiting both Cadillac and Mercedes websites and comparing prices across different Cadillac dealers, can help determine this individual's stage in the decision process, which, in turn, can be used to streamline the communication message. Thus, the greater amount of information from diverse sources a company has and the better its ability to meaningfully interpret these data, the greater the chance that this company can deliver the right message at the right time to the right customer.

Developing the Communication Message

Following identification of the target audience, the second component of a company's communication strategy aims to develop the message to be communicated to this audience. Here, a manager must choose the specific aspect(s) of the offering on which to focus the communication campaign. The essence of the communicated message and the decision of which offering attributes to promote are discussed in the following sections.

Determining the Message Content

The message is the information that the company aims to share with the target audience. The specifics of the company's message depend on which aspects of its offering the company aims to promote. Accordingly, the message can involve one or more of the other attributes defining the company's offering: *product*, *service*, *brand*, *price*, *incentives*, and *distribution*.

- **Communicating product and service information** informs the target audience about the specifics of the company's products and services, detailing their key benefits such as performance, reliability, durability, and ease of use.

- **Communicating the brand** informs the audience about the identity and meaning of the company's brand to create a unique, evocative image in customers' minds.

- **Communicating the price** informs the target audience about the monetary cost of the company's offering—its actual price as well as the total cost of ownership, including shipping, setup, maintenance, and disposal costs.

- **Communicating incentives** informs the target audience about the different sales promotions associated with the offering, such as temporary price reductions, volume discounts, rebates, coupons, and premiums.

- **Communicating distribution** informs the target audience about the offering's availability and the ways to obtain the offering.

Depending on its communication goals, a company can choose to promote one or more aspects of its offerings. For example, consider Cadillac, a division of General Motors that builds luxury vehicles worldwide. Based on its communication goals, Cadillac can tailor its message in a way that emphasizes different aspects of the company's offering. Thus, it might focus on the benefits of the *product*, emphasizing the design, performance, and comfort of its vehicles. The company might also communicate different aspects of its *service*, such as its OnStar emergency, security, and connectivity service, as well as its certified auto repair service and its automobile financing service.

Rather than focusing on the specific aspects of its cars and related service, Cadillac might focus its communication campaign on building its *brand*, emphasizing its roots as one of the oldest automobile brands in the world, its reputation of being at the forefront of innovation, and its image of luxury, performance, and prestige. Cadillac might also choose to advertise the *prices* at which its vehicles are sold—for example, to highlight the affordability of some models and the exclusivity of others. Another communication goal that Cadillac might pursue is to inform its target customers about *incentives* such as cash-back offers, price discounts, and special financing. Finally, Cadillac might choose to inform target customers about the *availability* of its offerings by informing them of the location of its dealerships.

Deciding Which Benefits to Promote

Another important aspect of developing the communication message is deciding how many and which benefits of the offering to promote. Here, more is not always better. Even though the notion of promoting all relevant benefits of the offering might sound appealing, cramming a plethora of benefits into a single communication campaign might be counterproductive by making it less likely that these benefits will register in buyers' minds. Therefore, a company must carefully consider the pros and cons of promoting different benefits and focus on those that are most likely to produce the desired impact on buyers' behavior.

The key principle guiding the choice of the message to be communicated is that it must be consistent with the overarching communication goals. This principle follows from the general notion that the strategy of any action must be aligned with the ultimate goal this action aims to achieve. For example, if the company's communication goal is to inform customers about the functional benefits of the offering, the message should focus on its product and service aspects. In contrast, if the goal is to inform customers about an ongoing or future sales promotion, the message should focus on the offering's incentives. Similarly, if a company has introduced a new distribution channel, it might benefit from focusing its communication on informing customers about the availability of its offering.

An important consideration when deciding on the message content is the degree to which the information contained in the message can lead to a change in customers' knowledge, beliefs, and behavior toward the company's offering. To this end, managers must take into account the principle of diminishing returns (discussed in Chapter 4). This principle implies that the marginal impact of improving a company's performance on a given attribute tends to decrease over time as the company invests resources in improving that attribute. In the context of designing the communication message, this principle implies that the market impact of promoting the same benefit will decline over time.

For example, when launching a new offering, a company might benefit from promoting its performance and unique benefits. On the other hand, if target customers are already aware of the benefits of the company's products and services, focusing on other aspects of the offering—such as building the offering's brand and informing customers about the offering's price, incentives, and availability—might prove to be a more effective allocation of the company's resources. Thus, to increase the effectiveness of its communication campaign, a company must identify the areas in which additional information can have the greatest impact on the target audience and design its message accordingly.

Another key consideration when deciding on the communication message involves balancing its short-term and long-term impact. Thus, communicating an offering's functional performance and its brand image tend to have a lasting positive impact that persists even after the company stops transmitting the message. In contrast, promotion-focused communication is able to increase the attractiveness of the offering in the short term but often has a detrimental long-term impact on customers' valuation of the offering. Indeed, once the sales promotion is over, customers who have been conditioned by the company's advertising to value the offering for its low price and monetary incentives are more likely to view the company's offering as a commodity and are less likely to purchase it. To this end, a company must carefully consider the overall impact—both short term and long term—of the offering attributes it chooses to communicate.

Selecting the Media

The media defines the particular means the company uses to convey its message to the target audience. Based on the entity that initiates the communication, media can be divided into two types: *outbound* and *inbound*.

Outbound Media

Outbound media involves channels used for communication that are initiated by the company. Outbound media can be divided into three main types: *paid, owned,* and *earned.*

Paid Media

Paid media involves marketing communication in which a company relays its message using media owned by a third party and absorbs most or all of the media costs (e.g., the cost of air time and print space). The key advantages of paid media are its reach and the fact that the company can largely control the content of its message. For example, a company can reach millions of people with a Super Bowl commercial featuring company-developed content promoting its offerings. The main downside of paid media is that the company must pay to gain access to the audience reached by the media and in most cases does not have exclusive use of the media, giving it little or no control over other messages that appear in close proximity to its own message.

Popular forms of paid media include *media advertising, direct advertising, personal selling, event sponsorship,* and *product placement.*

- **Media advertising** involves the use of third-party paid media to convey the company's message. The most popular forms of advertising media include audiovisual (traditional commercials, online video, and infomercials), radio, print (promotional brochures, embedded advertisements in newspapers and magazines), online, outdoor (posters and billboards), and point-of-sale materials (front-of-the-store, end-of-aisle, and signs displayed in close proximity to the promoted item).

- **Direct advertising** is a form of communication in which the company's message is delivered directly to a particular recipient as a free-standing piece of information rather than embedded in third-party media (as in the case of media advertising). Common means of direct advertising involve catalogs, promotional letters, flyers, and other materials, emails, text messages, and customized online advertisements. Because it often aims to elicit an immediate response, such as a purchase by a recipient of a promotional email, this form of communication is also referred to as direct response advertising.

- **Personal selling** is a form of marketing communication that relies on the interaction between the buyer and the seller to inform customers about the company's offering, persuade them about the offering's benefits, and ultimately, convince them to purchase the offering. Personal selling can play an important role in both business and consumer markets. The key aspects of managing personal selling are discussed in more detail in Chapter 15.

- **Event sponsorship** involves backing events and activities of interest to the offering's target customers. Rather than directly conveying a company-designed message as does advertising, event sponsorship associates the company's brand with the essence of the event, enabling the public to connect with the brand on a more personal level. For example, by sponsoring national Olympic teams, companies aim to associate their brands with the spirit of the games and enrich the meaning of their brands by linking them to memorable experiences. Event sponsorship can also involve supporting events such as concerts, art exhibitions, and drives that aim to secure funds and raise awareness of a particular social cause. In addition to sponsoring events, companies also use their names to sponsor venues—stadiums, arenas, and concert halls—in which popular events take place.

- **Product placement** involves embedding (placing) a company's offering within a particular form of entertainment, such as a sports event, television show, or movie. For example, the James Bond movie franchise has served as a venue for promoting a variety of products such as Aston Martin cars, Omega watches, and Belvedere vodka by embedding them in the movie plot. Similar to event sponsorship, product placement embeds the company's brand in a relevant context, but unlike event sponsorship it also features the use of the company's products. Because the company provides financial support to promote its brand(s) in this way, this communication form is often referred to as branded entertainment.

In addition to identifying the overall format, the media decision also involves determining the specific communication channels within each media type. For example, in the domain of television advertising, the media-channel decision involves selecting particular shows and time slots in which the company's message will be best positioned to reach and influence its target customers. Beer brands often choose to advertise during popular sports events with predominantly male audiences (e.g., the Super Bowl), whereas cosmetic brands choose to advertise during television programming targeting predominantly female audiences.

The choice of the appropriate media and the allocation of resources across different types of media are a function of the effectiveness and cost efficiency with which different media outlets are able to communicate the company message. For example, advertising and personal selling typically present the company's message in a more direct way to an audience that is fully aware of advertisers' efforts to influence their preferences and behavior. In contrast, event sponsorship and product placement tend to influence the target audience in a subtler way, often by leveraging the audience's goodwill toward the organization partnering with the company or the individual using the offering. In addition, compared to event sponsorship and product placement, which tend to be place- and time-specific, advertising is readily scalable across different regions and can be repeated as needed to have the maximum impact.

Owned Media

Owned media involves marketing communications in which a company relays its message using its own media channels. The key advantages of using media owned by the company are that there are no payments to a third party for media rights and the company retains exclusive use and control of the media. The key downside of owned media is its limited reach, which means the company might incur additional expenses to drive traffic to its own media channel.

Popular owned media formats include the *company's physical and virtual space, product packaging, experiential events, direct mail, personal* selling, and *samples.*

- **Physical and virtual space** controlled by the company can serve as an important venue for the company's communication. The ambiance created by a company's physical retail locations, showrooms, and offices as well as by its website is sometimes able to convey the essence of the company's brand better than a commercial or a print advertisement. The physical and virtual space also provides the context in which the company informs the public about the key aspects of its offerings. A company can use its own media for external communication targeting its customers and the general public, as well as for internal communication to its employees and stakeholders.

- **Product packaging**—including labels, signs, and inserts containing offering-related information—is particularly relevant at the point of purchase when buyers are evaluating the product in order to make a purchase decision. Product packaging can also contain usage-related information designed to enable buyers to maximize the value they receive from the company's offering. Packaging might also contain information and promotional materials concerning repurchasing the product.

- **Experiential events** are promotional events organized by the company. Thus, rather than sponsoring an event organized by a third party, a company might organize its own event centered around its products, services, and brands. In this case, because the company is organizing the event, it also owns the media—the context in which it can embed its desired message. As a result, unlike sponsored events, which are not directly focused on the company's offerings, company-organized events are typically designed for the sole purpose of informing the target audience about the company's offerings, strengthening their preferences for these offerings, and ultimately convincing them to buy and use these offerings. For example, Harley-Davidson arranges bike rides for Harley owners, Hershey offers factory tours featuring the chocolate-making process, and German appliance maker Miele organizes cooking events featuring well-known chefs. Experiential events such as auctions, art exhibitions, concerts, galas, and dinners commonly serve as vehicles for nonprofit organizations to secure funds and raise awareness of the issues represented by these organizations.

- **Direct mail** involves sending company-developed materials such as text, email, regular mail, and catalogs directly to the target audience.[1] Direct mail might be used to make the target audience aware of a company's offering, strengthen its preference for this offering, and elicit a behavioral response such as contacting the company for additional information or purchasing the offering. Direct mail is also often used to reach a company's collaborators as well as for internal purposes to share information with company employees and stakeholders.

- **Personal selling** involves direct, typically one-on-one, interaction with a company representative or a salesperson. Personal selling can involve face-to-face interaction as in the case of sales presentations or can be done by phone or online as in the case of telemarketing. The key difference between personal selling and most other types of communication is that there is direct two-way communication between a salesperson and a target customer. Note that personal selling can be considered as owned media when the salespeople are hired by the company; however, when sales representatives work purely on commission for multiple companies, personal selling is akin to paid rather than owned media. A detailed discussion of personal selling as a communication tool is offered in Chapter 15.

- **Samples** include product samples and free service trials that enable buyers to directly experience the company's offering. Product samples and free trials are often used in connection with new product introductions to familiarize customers with the offering and encourage them to adopt it. Samples can be distributed by mail (in the case of consumer packaged goods); online (in the case of digital products such as digital newspapers, music samples, and movie trailers); or at the point of sale or another physical location. Note that even though samples are often referred to as incentives, this description mischaracterizes their function. Indeed, samples do not change the value of the offering by increasing its benefits or reducing its costs (as do incentives) but merely enable target customers to experience the company's offering. Thus, the primary function of samples and free trials is to inform customers about the offering's benefits (see Chapter 13 for a detailed discussion).

As is the case with paid media, the choice of the particular type of company-owned communication channel depends on this channel's effectiveness and cost efficiency. The use of a company's own physical and virtual real estate, product packaging, direct email, and virtual samples (e.g., free digital products and service trials) tends to be the least costly for the company, whereas personal selling, experiential events, and the distribution of physical samples tend to be associated with higher costs. In most cases, the higher costs associated with some of the company's own channels reflect the greater effectiveness of these channels at relating the company's message to the target audience. Note, however, that the effectiveness of the different channels is not always directly related to their cost, meaning that less expensive channels are not always less effective than costlier channels. In this context, a company's goal when choosing the optimal channel mix is to identify the channels that have the highest likelihood of engaging and informing the target audience at minimal cost to the company.

Earned Media

Earned media involve marketing communications in which a company's message is relayed using media owned by a third party at no cost to the company. The three most popular forms of earned media are *press coverage*, *social media*, and *word of mouth*. These three types of media are similar in that neither the media source nor the content of the message is owned or directly controlled by the company. At the same time, they differ in that press coverage typically relies on professionally managed media outlets, whereas social media and word of mouth primarily involve interpersonal communication.

- **Press coverage** encompasses communication activities by professionally managed media outlets such as newspapers, journals, magazines, television, and radio. With press coverage—unlike advertising and other forms of paid media—the company does not pay for the media (e.g., space in a newspaper or air time in a radio show) that carries the message. To gain press coverage, a company might work with other entities (reporters, lobbyists, and opinion leaders) who use their influence to change beliefs, attitudes, and behaviors of the public. Note that even though the company does not pay for the actual media, press coverage can involve substantial costs in securing the desired publicity (e.g., paying for services of a public relations agency tasked with ensuring adequate press coverage of a company's offerings, activities, and events).

- **Social media** is a form of personal communication that uses a variety of digital communication platforms such as Twitter, Facebook, Instagram, LinkedIn, Snapchat, WeChat, Pinterest, and YouTube. Social media can also involve online discussions, blogs, podcasts, reviews and ratings, chat rooms, and emails.[2] Unlike press coverage, which is managed by professional media organizations, social media involves primarily peer-to-peer communications. Over time, a small number of social media outlets, such as those used by celebrities and opinion leaders, accumulate large audiences and become, in effect, de facto professional media outlets.

- **Word of mouth** involves peer-to-peer communication that is conducted in person rather than via digital platforms (as in the case of social media). Word of mouth was the prevalent format of personal communication prior to the emergence of social media. Because it occurs in the physical space, word of mouth can be more personal and impactful than social media, although its ultimate impact is determined by the source and the content of the message. Word-of-mouth communication can influence social media communication and vice versa. For example, after hearing a rumor, an individual might share it online by tweeting about it. This tweet might then spawn an in-person discussion, thus carrying over the message from the online to the physical world.

A key advantage of earned media is that the company does not have to pay for the media as it does for a space in a newspaper, air time on a radio show, or a physical billboard. Another important advantage of earned media is that because the message comes from a third party that typically has no vested interest in the company's offering, it is often viewed as more credible than a message directly sponsored by the company. The key downside of earned media is that because the company does not pay for the media, it does not control the message and, hence, cannot ensure that the conveyed message is consistent with the company's strategic goals.

Inbound Media

Inbound media involves communication initiated by other entities—customers, collaborators, company employees and stakeholders, and the general public—rather than the company. For example, consumers might not just passively view a company's advertisements; they might actively seek out information by conducting an online search, visiting a company's website, or talking to a salesperson. In this case, rather than trying to reach out to target customers to pique their interest and provide them with relevant information, a company's aim is to address inquiries from customers who have already displayed interest in the company and its offerings.

Inbound media formats vary depending on the nature of the communication channel in which they take place. Common types of inbound media include online search, personal interaction, phone, online interactive forums, regular mail, and email.

- **Online search** involves customers actively seeking offering-relevant information across different formats: text, video, and audio. The growth of online search is in part attributable to the effectiveness of popular search platforms such as Google, YouTube, Amazon, Siri, and Alexa, which put relevant product information at customers' fingertips. The popularity of online search has also led to the development of search marketing tools such as search engine optimization (SEO) and search engine marketing (SEM). SEO and SEM are discussed later in this chapter.

- **Personal interaction** is perhaps the oldest form of inbound communication, allowing customers with questions about the company's offerings to interact directly with company representatives. This form of communication is particularly important for establishing and maintaining personal relationships with customers and building and maintaining customer loyalty.

- **Phone communication** enables customers to interact with the company to receive relevant information and address specific issues related to the company and its products. It is similar to personal interaction except that it is not conducted face to face.

- **Online interactive forums**, such as online live chat, enable the company to connect with website visitors, understand their needs and objectives, and provide them with the information they need. The advantage of this type of media is that it gives customers an opportunity to interact instantly with the company without leaving the company website. In addition, from a company's perspective, this type of communication can be very cost efficient because it lends itself to automation (e.g., using artificial intelligence to generate meaningful responses to customer inquiries).

- **Mail** and **email** are alternative forms of inbound media that benefit customers who prefer to communicate by articulating their thoughts more carefully and in a format that preserves the specifics of the interaction for future reference.

During the past decade, the importance of inbound media has increased dramatically, with online search becoming the key inbound media format. Despite the popularity of online search, the other types of inbound media also play an important role in company communication by adding an interactive component to the search process. The key to managing inbound media is understanding the ways customers learn, consider, buy, and use the offering and providing them with a venue to connect with the company to increase the value they derive from the company's offerings.

Designing the Creative Execution

The creative execution defines the specific implementation of the company's message. It translates the company's communication strategy into a message that is tailored to the specific type of media that can best convey information to target customers. The creative aspect of the offering's communication aims to express the offering's value proposition in a way that will resonate with and engage its target customers. Thus, rather than merely enumerate the specific attributes or benefits of the offering, the creative solution must translate the company message into a meaningful and engaging story.

The key to developing an effective creative solution is maintaining the balance between the marketing and the entertainment components of the communication campaign. Because of the ever-growing competition to capture buyers' attention, companies are often tempted to develop overly creative campaigns designed to break through the clutter of competitive messages. While creativity per se is a virtue, in business communication creativity should never be achieved at the expense of the marketing content. *We want consumers to say, 'That's a hell of a product' instead of, 'That's a hell of an ad,'* notes Leo Burnett, whose namesake agency created some of advertising's most well-known characters and campaigns of the 20th century, including Tony the Tiger, the Pillsbury Doughboy, and the Marlboro Man.

The creative solution is media specific. Thus, print advertising involves decisions concerning the copy (wording of the headline and the body text), visual elements (pictures, photos, graphics, and logos), format (size and color scheme), and layout (the arrangement of different parts of the advertisement). Radio advertising involves decisions dealing with the text (wording of the dialogue and narration), audio (music, dialogue, and sound effects), and duration (length). Television advertising involves decisions concerning the visual elements (imagery), text (wording of the dialogue, voice-over narration, and printed text), audio (music, dialogue, and sound effects), and duration (length of the commercial).

Developing the creative solution to convey the communication message involves three basic elements: *message source*, *message appeal*, and *message complexity*.

Message Source

An important aspect of translating the communication strategy into an engaging story is deciding on the source of the company message—that is, who will be telling the story. For example, the source of the message can be the company in general, as in the case of an advertisement merely listing the features and benefits of the company offering. Alternatively, the message can stem from a company employee or stakeholder that represents the company, as in the case of an employee discussing the benefits of the offering or the company's CEO making an announcement in response to an issue concerning a company's offering.

The message does not need to come from the company or its employees. It can come from the public, as when ordinary users share their experiences with the company's offering. It can also stem from independent experts discussing and ultimately endorsing the company's offering, such as medical professionals promoting a particular drug. Finally, the source of the message can be a celebrity—a movie star, supermodel, or socialite with a large social media following—who endorses the company's offering either for monetary compensation (paid endorsers) or because of a real appreciation for the offering (unpaid endorsers).

The influence of the source on the ultimate impact of the message depends on the expertise, likability, and trustworthiness of the source. Thus, the greater the specialized knowledge of the source, the greater the potential impact of the message conveyed by this source. In addition, messages from sources that are likable, physically attractive, engaging, witty, and overall favorably regarded tend to be more influential. Source trustworthiness that reflects the degree to which the source truly believes in the message can further amplify the message and enhance the ultimate impact of company communication.

Message Appeal

Message appeal reflects the approach used to communicate the company's message. Most creative solutions involve one of two types of appeals: information-based and emotion-based.

- **Information-based appeals** typically rely on methods such as factual presentations (straightforward presentations of the relevant information), demonstrations (illustration of the offering's key benefits in a staged environment), problem-solution examples (identifying a problem and showcasing an offering that will eradicate the problem), product comparisons (offering A is better than offering B), slice-of-life stories (illustration of the offering's key benefits in everyday use), and testimonials (endorsements of the offering by ordinary users or celebrities). Information-based appeals assume rational processing on the part of the recipient.

- **Emotion-based appeals** typically play on people's feelings. Broadly speaking, there are two types of emotional appeals: positive appeals that revolve around love, romance, and joy, and negative appeals that evoke fear, guilt, and shame. Positive appeals focus on emotional states that individuals look forward to and try to achieve, whereas negative appeals focus on emotional states that people try to avoid. For example, consumers might be encouraged to buy a particular brand of toothpaste to either make them more attractive to their romantic partners (positive appeal) or to prevent tooth decay (negative appeal). Both types of appeals can be effective depending on the specific market situation, including the type of offering being promoted; consumers' beliefs, needs, and preferences; and the competitive context.

Information-based appeals also tend to be more effective for utilitarian offerings such as home appliances, office equipment, and electronics, where functionality is the primary consideration when making a choice. In contrast, emotion-based appeals tend to be more effective for hedonic offerings such as with beauty products, vacations, and apparel, where customer choices are often driven by emotions.

In addition, information-based appeals tend to be more effective when consumers are likely to be paying more attention to and thinking about the message in order to adequately comprehend its content. Emotion-based appeals, on the other hand, can be effective even when consumers are less involved and are not paying very close attention to the message. In this context, the choice of message appeal calls for careful consideration of recipients' level of involvement when processing the company's communication.

Message Complexity

Communication messages vary in complexity: Some have a relatively straightforward message and others involve multifaceted messages that are more complex. For example, some messages present one-sided arguments touting the benefits of the offering, whereas others involve two-sided messages presenting arguments in favor of and against the offering. In addition, messages can be noncomparative, focusing on the offering's ability to fulfill a particular customer need, or comparative, demonstrating the offering's ability to fulfill a given customer need better than the alternative options.

A key factor in determining the optimal message complexity is the level of involvement of the target audience and, specifically, the degree to which the recipients have the cognitive resources to process the message and elaborate on its content. Thus, a more complex message might not be appropriate for an audience that is relatively uninvolved because these customers do not care about the product, perceive the product to be a commodity with few differences between brands, or are distracted and not paying attention to the message content. For example, many consumers might not care much about learning the differences between different brands of paper tissues and, as a result, process the information contained in the message in a haphazard manner. At the same time, in certain circumstances, such as purchasing professional equipment, providing detailed product specifications can be beneficial for articulating the ways in which the company's offering creates superior customer value.

Ensuring a fit between the complexity of the message and the willingness and ability of the audience to process this message is important because a mismatch can be counterproductive. For example, a comparative ad that aims to demonstrate the contrast between the company's offering and its competitors might create the erroneous impression that the products are similar to each other. This is because processing contrast-based messages requires greater effort on the part of the recipients compared to messages that focus on a single offering. Less involved recipients also might fail to grasp the essence of a comparative message and simply aggregate the stated pros and cons of the offering without considering the arguments for why the advantages of the offering outweigh any disadvantages.

The mismatch between the complexity of the message and the target audience's level of involvement is one of the most common problems in creative execution. This mismatch often stems from the difference in the involvement levels of the marketing managers and the creative team designing the message and the recipients of the message. Bombarded with hundreds of ads and promotional offers every day, consumers increasingly pay less attention to each individual message and, as a result, are less likely to allocate the cognitive resources needed to delve into the complex reasoning embedded in a given message. In contrast, the manager and the creative team that generates the communication are deeply involved with the offering and with developing a memorable message that will also enable the marketing team to showcase its creativity. The disparity between overly involved marketers and uninvolved consumers can lead to counterproductive outcomes when the company message is either ignored by consumers or, even worse, is misconstrued to mean the opposite of what was intended.

Evaluating Communication Effectiveness

Depending on the company's goals, communication might aim to achieve different outcomes. Therefore, a meaningful approach to evaluating communication effectiveness is to link the particular performance metrics to the overarching communication goals. Accordingly, communication effectiveness can be assessed based on its ability to *create awareness*, *build preference*, and *incite action*.

Measuring Awareness

Measuring awareness can involve assessing whether the target audience has been exposed to the offering's message, has understood the message, and can recall the message.

Measuring *exposure* aims to establish whether a company's communication has reached its intended audience. To this end, a company can assess the number of people who view a particular television program, read a newspaper, or visit a website, and use this as a basis to determine the number of people who have been exposed to a company's message. In addition to measuring exposure, communication effectiveness can involve assessing *understanding*, which reflects the degree to which the target audience has comprehended the communication message. For example, a company can conduct a focus group to test whether the target audience has comprehended the intended message of its communication campaign.

Another popular measure of communication effectiveness is assessing *recall*, the degree to which the target audience remembers the company's advertisement and, more important, its message. Two types of recall can be measured: aided and unaided.

Aided recall refers to a person's ability to remember whether they have been exposed to a particular communication and/or the content of the communication message when explicitly asked about it. To assess aided recall, respondents are typically given a list of brand names following the presentation of a series of advertisements and asked to recall whether they have seen any of these brands in a given period of time (e.g., during the past week). In contrast, unaided recall refers to a person's ability to spontaneously recall an advertisement without being directly prompted to do so. To assess unaided recall, respondents are typically asked to recall all brands they have seen advertised in a given period of time.

Measuring Preferences

Measuring preferences involves assessing the degree to which the company's communication was able to form, strengthen, or change customer beliefs about its offering(s). A common approach to measuring preferences is assessing customers' brand-specific beliefs before and after they have been exposed to a company's communication.

Because preferences for established brands (which often are among the largest advertisers) are difficult to change with a single communication, companies often measure the attitude toward the advertisement (rather than the beliefs about the offering) on the premise that if the target audience likes the advertisement, then this attitude will translate into liking the company's offering. While this approach is not without merit, the connection between customers liking the advertisement and their attitude toward the advertised brand has not been validated. Thus, the mere fact that the audience likes the company's communication does not necessarily mean that the company has achieved its strategic goals.

An alternative approach to measuring preferences is asking the target audience to make a *choice* among different offerings before and after being exposed to the company communication. The greater the relative choice share of the offering following the company communication, the more effective this communication is. In addition to asking customers to make a choice, companies often measure customers' behavioral intentions — for example, by asking respondents to indicate the likelihood of purchasing the product within a given time frame (as in the top-box method discussed in Chapter 5).

Preferences can also be captured by monitoring social media activity, including blog entries, social media posts, as well as shared photos and videos. Because in this case preferences are usually embedded in the broader context of the conversation and are often not explicitly stated, companies use a variety of data analysis methods for extracting and interpreting the information relevant to the company's offering to infer individuals' preferences.

Measuring Behavior

Measuring behavior involves assessing customer actions resulting from the company's communication, such as buying the offering; contacting the company to inquire about the offering, visiting a company's stores, showrooms, or website; and clicking on a company's online banners.

Intuitively, it might seem that sales are the best measure of communication effectiveness. This, however, is not always the case. The problem with relying on sales as a measure of effectiveness is that most often the impact of communication is not immediate (especially in cases of brand-building communication). As a result, the impact of communication is typically confounded with a variety of unrelated factors such as changes in price, incentives, competitive actions, and purchase cycle, which makes it difficult, if not impossible, to disentangle the unique contribution of communication from the observed changes in sales volume.

Furthermore, evaluating the behavioral impact of a communication campaign depends on the type of message conveyed. Thus, communicating incentives such as price discounts tends to have an immediate impact on sales, whereas brand-building communication takes much longer to produce visible results. This differential impact implies that using sales as a benchmark of effectiveness is likely to underestimate the impact of brand-building communication and overestimate the role of incentive-focused communication.

Measuring the effectiveness of a communication campaign also depends on the type of media used. In cases where the media are directly linked to performance measures (such as in direct marketing, personal selling, and online advertising), actual behavior can be used to evaluate the effectiveness of the communication campaign. Linking media to performance in this way, however, creates an *attribution bias*, whereby the communication formats that produce directly measurable results are exclusively credited for the outcome of the communication campaign.

Crediting media formats that produce an immediate and measurable impact often comes at the expense of other media formats such as public relations, social media, and event sponsorship, which create market value even though their impact cannot be measured directly. Thus, even though click-throughs and online searches lead to directly measurable outcomes, these outcomes often are a consequence of a company's coordinated efforts to create awareness, generate interest, and build preferences for its offerings. To accurately evaluate the effectiveness of a company's communication campaign, a manager must consider the way different components of the campaign interact with one another and use the appropriate measures to assess the unique contribution of each communication activity.

SUMMARY

Communication informs the relevant market entities — target customers, collaborators, and the company employees and stakeholders — about the specifics of the company's offering. Developments during the past decades have dramatically altered the way companies communicate with their current and potential customers. The key changes in communication management involve micro-targeting, inbound communication, peer-to-peer communication, geolocation, predictive analytics, occasion-based targeting, and measurability.

The development of a communication campaign is guided by the G-STIC framework, which involves five key decisions: setting the communication *goal*, articulating the communication *strategy* (identifying the target audience and developing the communication message), designing the communication *tactics* (selecting the media and developing the creative solution), *implementing* the communication campaign, and *controlling* (evaluating) the campaign results.

Setting *communication goals* involves identifying the focus of the company's actions and defining the performance benchmarks to be achieved. The *focus* of the communication campaign can involve creating awareness of the offering, building preference for the offering, and inciting an action such as purchasing the offering. *Performance benchmarks* outline the quantitative and temporal criteria for reaching the communication goal. A company's communication goals can be related to the customer decision journey, with different stages of the customer journey associated with different goals.

An important aspect of developing the communication campaign is determining the *budget* required to achieve the communication goals. The optimal level of communication expenditures is determined by three factors: available resources, communication goals, and the cost of achieving these goals.

The *target audience* encompasses the recipients of the company's communication. Identification of the target audience involves two aspects: strategic and tactical. Strategic targeting involves identifying the target audience based on the value that the company can create and capture from it. In contrast, tactical targeting involves identifying the specific ways in which the company can reach strategically important audiences with its message in the most effective and cost-efficient way.

The communication *message* can involve one or more of the attributes defining the company's offering: product, service, brand, price, incentives, and distribution. Thus, an important aspect of developing the communication message is deciding which and how many attributes to promote. The key principle in designing the communication message is that it should be aligned with the company's overarching communication and marketing goals.

The *media* defines the means used by the company to convey its message to the target audience. Based on the entity initiating the communication, there are two general types of media: outbound media, involving communication initiated by the company, and inbound media, involving communication initiated by the public. Outbound media can be further divided into three main types: paid, owned, and earned.

The *creative solution* involves translating the company's message into the language of the selected media format. Developing the creative solution to convey the communication message involves three key decisions: message source, message appeal, and message complexity.

A meaningful approach to *evaluating* communication effectiveness is to tie it to the communication goals. Accordingly, communication effectiveness must be assessed based on its ability to create awareness, build preference, and incite action.

MARKETING INSIGHT: KEY COMMUNICATION CONCEPTS

Above-the-Fold (ATF) Communication: Based on the specific location of an advertisement in the publication, there are two types of placements: above-the-fold, which refers to the upper half of the front page of a newspaper where the important news stories are often located, and below-the-fold (BTF), which refers to the lower half of the front page of a newspaper. In online communication, ATF refers to the viewable space on a webpage when it first loads, whereas BTF refers to the part of a webpage that cannot be seen without scrolling down.

Above-the-Line (ATL) Communication: Based on the type of media, communication is divided into two categories: Above-the-line (ATL) communication, which encompasses mass-media advertising such as television commercials, radio, and print advertisements; and below-the-line (BTL) communication, which includes public relations, event sponsorship, personal selling, and direct mail. Historically, the term ATL was used in reference to communication for which an advertising agency charged a commission to place in mass media, whereas the term BTL was used in reference to communication that involved a standard charge rather than a commission. Currently, the terms ATL and BTL are used loosely to indicate an emphasis on mass media (ATL) versus one-on-one communication and customer and trade incentives (BTL).

Advertising Awareness: The number of potential customers who are aware of the offering. Awareness is a function of the total volume of advertising delivered to the target audience and the number of exposures necessary for the target audience to become cognizant of the offering. In cases where a single exposure is sufficient to create awareness, the awareness level equals the advertising reach.

$$\text{Awareness} = \frac{\text{Reach} \cdot \text{Frequency}}{\text{Number of exposures needed to create awareness}}$$

Advertising Elasticity: The degree to which a change in advertising leads to a change in awareness, preferences, or behavior of the target audience. The higher the advertising elasticity, the more likely it is that increasing advertising expenditures can produce favorable results — increase awareness, strengthen preferences, and incite action.

Advertising Frequency: The number of times the target audience is exposed to an advertisement in a given period. Also used in reference to the number of times an advertisement is repeated in a specific medium during a specific period.

Advertising Reach: The size of the audience that has been exposed to a particular advertisement at least once in a given period (multiple viewings by the same audience do not increase reach). Reach can be stated either as an absolute number or as a fraction of a population. For example, if 40,000 of 100,000 different households are exposed to a given commercial at least once, the reach is 40%.

Affiliate Marketing: A communication strategy that involves revenue sharing between advertisers and online content providers. An affiliate is rewarded based on specific performance measures such as sales, click-throughs, and online traffic.

AIDA: Communication model outlining the key steps in the process of converting advertising to sales. The AIDA framework posits that the consumer decision process involves four key steps: attention, interest, desire, and action. According to the AIDA framework, before making a purchase decision consumers need to be made *aware* that the offering exists and be stimulated to take some *interest* in the offering. Then, a *desire* must be created among consumers to purchase the offering, which must be translated into *action* that leads to the actual purchase of the offering.[3]

Awareness Rate: The number of potential customers aware of the offering relative to the total number of potential customers.

Below-the-Fold (BTF) Communication: See *above-the-fold communication.*

Below-the-Line (BTL) Communication: See *above-the-line communication.*

Carryover Effect in Advertising: Impact of an advertising campaign that extends beyond the time frame of the campaign. To illustrate, an advertising effort made in a given period might generate sales in subsequent periods.

Comparative Advertising: Advertising that directly contrasts two or more offerings.

Competitive Parity Budgeting: Budget allocation method based on matching competitors' absolute level of spending or the proportion per point of market share.

Cooperative Advertising: Advertising in which a manufacturer and a retailer jointly advertise their offering to consumers. For example, a manufacturer can pay a portion of a retailer's advertising costs in return for the retailer featuring its products, services, and brands.

Cost Per Point (CPP): Measure used to represent the cost of a communication campaign. CPP is the media cost of reaching one percent (one rating point) of a particular demographic. See also *gross rating point (GRP).*

$$CPP = \frac{\text{Advertising cost}}{\text{GRP}}$$

Cost Per Thousand (CPM): Measure used to represent the cost of a communication campaign. CPM is the cost of reaching 1,000 individuals or households with an advertising message in a given medium (M is the Roman numeral for 1,000). For example, a television commercial that costs $200,000 to air and reaches 10M viewers has a CPM of $20. The popularity of CPM derives in part from its functioning as a good comparative measure of advertising efficiency across different media (e.g., television, print, and online).

$$CPM = \frac{\text{Advertising cost}}{\text{Total impressions}} \cdot 1{,}000$$

Creative Brief: An outline of the key aspects of the communication campaign designed to guide the creative development. The creative brief typically includes the communication goal, the target audience, the message to be communicated, and the choice of media.

Gross Rating Point (GRP): A measure of the total volume of advertising delivery to the target audience. GRP is equal to the percent of the population reached times the frequency of exposure. To illustrate, if a given advertisement reaches 60% of the households with an average frequency of three times, then the GRP of the media is equal to 180. GRP can also be calculated by dividing gross impressions by the size of the total audience. A single GRP represents 1% of the total audience in a given region.

$$GRP = \text{Reach} \cdot \text{Frequency}$$

Impression: A single exposure of an advertisement to one person.

Infomercial: A long-format commercial, typically five minutes or longer.

Institutional Advertising: Advertising strategy designed to build goodwill or an image for an organization (rather than to promote specific offerings).

Point-of-Purchase Advertising: Promotional materials displayed at the point of purchase (e.g., in a retail store).

Public Relations: A specific type of communication activity that aims to manage a company's relationship with society at large. There are three defining aspects of public relations as a form of communication. First, it is often directed not only to the company's customers, collaborators, and stakeholders but also to the general public. Second, it is a form of institutional communication that deals with issues concerning the reputation of the entire company rather than merely providing information about a particular offering. Third, it is most prominent at times of company crisis, a significant change in the company's business model, or a major shift in a company's internal and external policies. Public relations can involve the same types of media as other forms of communication, including advertising, event sponsorship, direct mail, press coverage, social media, and word of mouth.

Public Service Announcement (PSA): Nonprofit advertising that uses free space or time donated by the media.

Reminder Advertising: Advertising designed to maintain awareness and stimulate repurchase of an already established offering.

Search Engine Marketing (SEM): A process of promoting the company's offerings by increasing its ranking in the list of (paid) results returned by a search engine. Unlike the search engine optimization (SEO) approach, which aims to increase the website rank organically, SEM aims to attract more visitors using paid search such as pay-per-click listings and advertisements.

Search Engine Optimization (SEO): A process of optimizing a company's website to increase the number of visitors by ensuring that the site appears high on the list of results returned by a search engine. For example, a travel agency can optimize its website (e.g., by embedding the key search terms in the website, streamlining the website content, and linking it to external content) in a way that allows it to show up first when customers enter the word "travel" in their browsers.

Share of Voice: A company's communication expenditures relative to those of the entire product category.

$$\text{Share of voice} = \frac{\text{Advertising spend for an offering}}{\text{Advertising spend for the category}}$$

Target Rating Point (TRP): A measure of the total volume of advertising delivery to the target audience. TRP is similar to GRP, but its calculation uses only the target audience (rather than the total audience watching the program) as the base. Thus, a single TRP represents 1% of the targeted viewers in any particular region.

Teaser Advertising: Communication strategy designed to create interest in an offering while providing little or no information about it. Teaser advertising is often used to promote upcoming movies and events.

Top-of-Mind Awareness: The first brand identified by respondents when asked to list brands in a given product category.

Wearout: A decrease in the effectiveness of a communication campaign because of decreased consumer interest in the message, often resulting from repetition.

MARKETING INSIGHT: PROGRAMMATIC ADVERTISING

Programmatic advertising is the practice of managing the advertising process using software rather than the traditional approach of relying on managerial judgment. Simply put, programmatic advertising automates the decision-making processes of content creation, media buying, and matching the right customers with the right advertisements. Initially developed in the context of online communications, programmatic advertising is now used in most traditional advertising media, including television, radio, and print.

The rise of programmatic advertising can be attributed to several factors. Media have grown increasingly fragmented, resulting in a decline in mass-media outlets and a proliferation of media channels catering to relatively small audiences. The growth of online media has further contributed to the increased fragmentation of media channels, making it easier for companies to direct their communication to individual customers. The proliferation of smart mobile devices increased the importance of dynamically serving relevant and contextually current advertisements to target customers based on their location. This fragmentation of media and customers and the dynamic nature of content delivery have made the task of deciding where, what, and how much to advertise virtually impossible without relying on data analytics and automated processes. The growth of programmatic advertising has been further fueled by the advancement of data management systems, data analytics, and artificial intelligence, which have dramatically increased the effectiveness and cost efficiency of programmatic advertising.

Programmatic advertising encompasses two distinct processes: targeting and content customization. Programmatic targeting usually involves buying media (e.g., advertising space on a website) that is likely to be viewed by a company's target customers. Programmatic content customization, on the other hand, automatically tailors the advertisement to the needs of each individual target customer.

A distinct feature of programmatic advertising is that targeting and content customization can take place in real time. Traditionally, a company would develop one (or in some cases a few) advertisement targeting a relatively large customer segment and then seek to buy media to reach this particular segment. In contrast, with programmatic advertising, identifying the target audience and creating the advertisement for this audience can happen simultaneously. The company uses customer analytics to identify desirable customers based on their individual characteristics, followed by content-matching algorithms that dynamically create an advertisement most likely to evoke the desired customer reaction. The level of automatization can range from simply selecting the content that best fits the specific advertising context from a pool of already developed advertisements to creating the advertisements on the fly by using artificial intelligence to integrate text, images, and sound into a meaningful message for target customers.

One of the most common applications of programmatic advertising involves media-buying decisions. Programmatic media buying uses mathematical algorithms to match the available advertising inventory (e.g., media space and time available for advertising) with the advertisers seeking to promote their offerings. Programmatic media buying usually involves several intermediaries—demand-side platform, supply-side platform, and an advertising exchange—connecting media buyers (advertisers) and sellers (publishers). The key components of the process of programmatic media buying are illustrated in Figure 4 and outlined in more detail below.

Figure 4. Programmatic Media Buying

A *demand-side platform* (DSP) enables advertisers (companies seeking to provide information to their target audience) to manage their bids for the available advertising inventory, such as banner ads on websites, mobile ads on apps, and in-stream video.

A *supply-side platform* (SSP) enables publishers (the owners of the media where the advertisement appears) to manage their advertising space inventory, procure advertisements, and receive compensation. Unlike demand-side platforms, which serve advertisers, supply-side platforms provide services for publishers.

An *advertising exchange* is a digital marketplace that enables advertisers and publishers to buy and sell advertising space. Advertising exchanges give advertisers access to billions of daily impressions across a variety of devices and channels and at the same time give publishers access to scores of buyers of advertising media. Most advertising exchanges involve real-time buying by announcing the availability of each impression through supply-side platforms and using demand-side platforms to ask advertisers whether they are interested in buying this impression and at what price.

The programmatic media buying process depicted in Figure 4 works as follows. When a publisher detects a consumer browsing its online content, it sends the relevant information—such as the dimensions of the ad space available on the page displayed to the consumer and this consumer's information (e.g., user's behavior on the publisher's site and the cookie information contained in this user's browser)—to the supply-side platform. The supply-side platform relays this information to the advertising exchange, where it becomes available on the demand-side platforms of different advertisers. The demand-side platform then evaluates the available advertising opportunity and, if it matches the profile of the advertiser's target customers, submits a bid. The advertising exchange will then pick the winning bid, and the ad is ultimately sent to the consumer. Most exchanges involve real-time bidding, such that the entire process, from the moment a consumer lands on a publisher's site to the moment an advertisement is sent, typically takes milliseconds.

Automating the process of advertising enables companies to dramatically increase the effectiveness and cost efficiency of their communication efforts and enhances their ability to reach the right customer with the right message at the right time. At the same time, programmatic advertising is merely a tactical tool and cannot serve as a replacement for the strategic component of developing marketing communications. Without a clear understanding of who the target audience is and how the advertising campaign will create value for this audience as well as the company, programmatic advertising can prove to be counterproductive as it might end up targeting, with great precision, the wrong customers. Thus, to paraphrase famed British economist John Maynard Keynes, it is better to be vaguely right than precisely wrong.

MARKETING INSIGHT: DEVELOPING A COMMUNICATION PLAN

A company's communication activities can be delineated in a communication plan that follows a structure mirroring the organization of the marketing plan outlined in Chapter 3. Thus, the communication plan starts with an executive summary, followed by a situation overview; it then sets a goal, formulates a communication strategy, describes the tactical aspects of the company's communication, articulates a plan to implement the specific communication activities, defines a set of controls to monitor the progress of the communication campaign, and concludes with a set of relevant exhibits. The key components of the communication plan are illustrated in Figure 5 and summarized below.

Figure 5. The Communication Plan

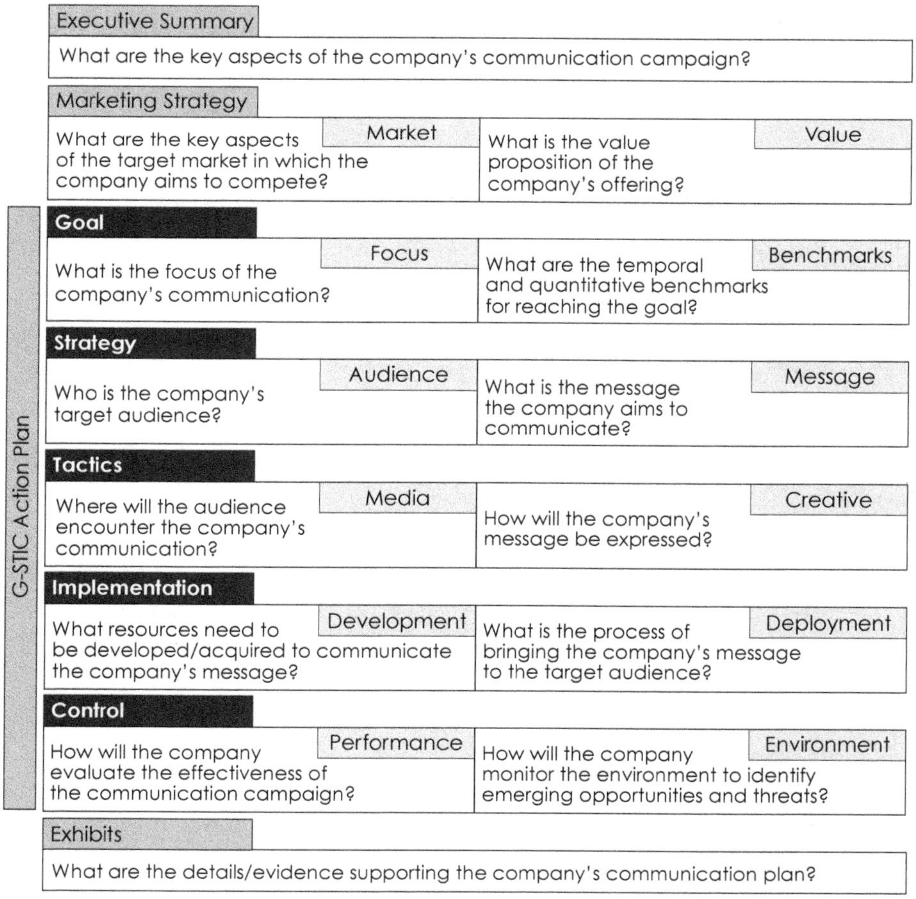

- The *executive summary* is the "elevator pitch" for the communication plan—a streamlined and succinct overview of the company's communication goal and the activities that will enable the company to reach this goal.

- The *marketing strategy* outlines the key aspects of the offering's strategy: the target market (defined by the Five Cs: target customers, competitors, collaborators, company, and context) and the company's value proposition in this market.

- The *G-STIC Action Plan* is the core of the communication plan. It involves five key components: setting the communication *goal*, which involves defining the focus of the company's communication activities and key benchmarks; articulating the communication *strategy*, which involves identifying the target audience and developing the communication message; designing the communication *tactics*, which involves selecting the media and developing the creative solution; *implementing* the communication campaign, which involves developing the key resources needed to carry out the campaign and the planned activities; and *controlling* the campaign results, which involves evaluating the achieved results and monitoring for changes in the environment in which the company operates.

- *Exhibits* help streamline the logic of the communication plan by separating the less important and/or more technical aspects of the plan into a distinct section in the form of tables, charts, and appendices.

The ultimate goal of the communication plan is to guide a company's actions. Accordingly, the core of the communication plan is defined by the G-STIC action plan delineating the company's goal and the proposed course of action. The other elements of the communication plan—the executive summary, situation overview, and exhibits—aim to facilitate an understanding of the logic underlying the plan and provide specifics for the proposed course of action.

CHAPTER FIFTEEN

PERSONAL SELLING

Salesmanship is limitless. Our very living is selling. We are all salespeople.
—James Cash Penney Jr., founder of J. C. Penney stores

Personal selling is a form of marketing communication that involves direct contact between the salesperson and the buyer. Personal selling uses this direct contact to inform customers about the company's offering, persuade them of the offering's benefits and, ultimately, generate sales. The role of personal selling in creating market value; the key considerations involved in designing, compensating, and managing a salesforce; and the process of managing the sale are the focus of this chapter. Specifically, we address the following topics:

- *Personal Selling as a Value-Creation Process* || Personal selling as a means of communication | Personal selling as a means of designing and delivering the offering
- *Designing, Compensating, and Managing the Salesforce* || Designing the salesforce | Compensating the salesforce | Managing the salesforce
- *Managing the Sale* || Understanding the buyer | Managing the selling process

The discussion of sales management and personal selling is complemented by an in-depth overview of two additional topics: the psychology of persuasion and the SPIN model of personal selling.

Personal Selling as a Value-Creation Process

Personal selling is a process in which one entity (the seller) aims to convince another entity (the buyer) to consider, purchase, and use a company's offering. Personal selling typically involves face-to-face interaction, although it is also used in reference to any one-on-one interaction that aims to generate a sale regardless of whether it is in person or remote (e.g., via phone, video, or online). Personal selling can encompass everything from sales of major equipment in a business-to-business context to sales of cosmetics in department stores.

Personal selling encompasses multiple aspects of the value-creation process. Although its primary function is to communicate the offering to potential buyers, personal selling can also help with the design and delivery of the offering. Thus, in addition to informing buyers about the offering, personal selling can create value by modifying the product, augmenting the service, defining the brand, negotiating the price, offering incentives, as well as delivering the actual product or service. The role of personal selling as a means of communicating, designing, and delivering the company's offerings is discussed in the following sections.

Personal Selling as a Means of Communication

The first and the foremost function of personal selling is to communicate the relevant information about the company's offering in a way that will increase buyers' preference for the offering and ultimately lead to a sale. In this context, personal selling can convey information about the features and benefits of the company's products and services, articulate the essence of the company's reputation captured in its brand(s), inform buyers about the offering's price and the relevant sales promotions, as well as delineate the logistics involved in delivering the company's offering.

As a form of communication, personal selling is similar to advertising in that it aims to provide information pertaining to the company's offering. The key difference between them is that whereas the primary function of advertising is to inform potential buyers about the company's products and services, personal selling goes beyond merely informing the buyer about the offering to actually transacting the sale of these products and services. Moreover, whereas advertising usually involves one-way transmission of information from the company to potential buyers, personal selling is interactive by nature, offering one-on-one communication that can address the concerns, questions, and needs of individual customers.

The ubiquity of personal selling stems from its multiple benefits over other forms of communication such as advertising, event sponsorship, and product placement. The social, face-to-face nature of personal selling helps make the shared information more relevant and credible, which, in turn, increases its impact on potential buyers. Furthermore, the interactive nature of the communication involved in personal selling enables the salesperson to gauge buyers' response to the communicated information and adjust the presentation accordingly to address potential concerns and underscore the key benefits of the offering. Another distinct feature of personal selling is that it enables the buyer and the seller to negotiate the conditions of the sale in order to close the deal. This is perhaps the most important benefit of personal selling because, unlike most other forms of communication, it has a direct and measurable impact on the company's bottom line.

The main disadvantage of personal selling, in comparison to other forms of communication, is its high cost. Indeed, over and above the ongoing costs associated with interacting with potential buyers, the development of a skilled salesforce familiar with the company's offerings typically involves a major long-term investment on the part of the company. Creating a dedicated salesforce also increases the size of the organization and requires additional layers of management. In addition to its high cost, personal selling involves human interaction, which makes the sales experience highly dependent on the idiosyncratic approach of the salesperson and the particular context of the selling situation. This variability of the selling experience is particularly relevant for companies that aim to convey a consistent brand image and/or control the flow of communication between the company and potential buyers for legal reasons.

Given its advantages and drawbacks, personal selling is typically used when a company has a limited number of buyers that are easy to reach, the buying decision process involves multiple entities with different needs and preferences, the company's products and services are complex and need detailed explanation, the profitability of each deal is high, and the after-sale service is important.

The overarching principle in deploying personal selling as a part of the company's communication activities is that it should be aligned with the other forms of communication to ensure consistency, increase cost efficiency, and maximize their joint impact. Marketing communication should support personal selling and, vice versa, personal selling should be coordinated with the company's communication efforts. For example, if an offering's unique selling proposition is centered around reliability and durability, this point should be the focus of the company's communication campaign. This focus ensures that buyers approached by a salesperson are already aware of the company's reputation, which, in turn, facilitates the sale.

The role of communication as a tool for supporting sales is well captured in the iconic advertisement that became known as the "Man in the Chair," run by McGraw-Hill Magazines in 1958. The ad featured a stern-faced, middle-aged executive wearing a bow tie and a conservative brown suit, sitting in an office chair, hands grasped together and looking intently at the reader. To promote the practical value of corporate advertising, the ad's body copy read: "I don't know who you are. I don't know your company. I don't know your product. I don't know what your company stands for. I don't know your company's customers. I don't know your company's record. I don't know your company's reputation. Now–what was it you wanted to sell me?" The ad concluded with, "Moral: Sales start *before* your salesman calls—with business publication advertising." Although over half a century old, the market insight shared by this advertisement is still relevant today: To ensure market success, sales and advertising should work together and complement each other.

Personal Selling as a Means of Designing and Delivering the Offering

Although its main function is to communicate the value of the company's offering, personal selling goes beyond merely communicating the company's offering to shape its different aspects—namely, its product, service, brand, price, incentives, and distribution.

Thus, the salesforce can customize a company's *product* and *service* to better fit the buyer's needs. For example, a dealer can customize the features of a car according to the buyer's preferences, an insurance agent can tailor a policy to best fit a buyer's particular situation, a travel agent can design a custom itinerary based on a traveler's preferences, and a sales representative can specify custom features for a piece of industrial equipment based on the client's needs. The salesforce can also provide after-sales service, such as familiarizing the buyer with the features of the purchased car, facilitating the filing of an insurance claim, providing assistance in resolving travel emergencies, and assisting with the installation of the purchased equipment.

Personal selling can further help the company build its *brand* by using the salesforce to project the company's values and demonstrate its commitment to serving its customers. Thus, the professional behavior of a company's salespeople, as well as their trustworthiness and expertise, can enhance and solidify the company's brand image. In fact, the reputation of companies such as Avon, Amway, and Mary Kay is created by their salesforce, which plays the role of brand ambassadors.

A company's salesforce can also be instrumental in setting, negotiating, and finalizing the offering's *price*. For example, real estate agents help sellers determine the optimal price for their property, facilitate negotiations with the buyers, and assist with finalizing a price that is acceptable to both the buyer and the seller. In addition to setting the price, a company's salesforce can also help determine the right *incentives* that can be instrumental in nudging the buyer toward closing the deal. For example, depending on buyers' needs and preferences, the salesperson can offer a variety of monetary and nonmonetary sales promotions ranging from price discounts to bonus products and services.

Another important aspect of personal selling is its ability to serve as a means of *distribution* and actually deliver the offering to the buyer. This function of personal selling is particularly relevant in consumer markets where the role of the salespeople is not only to inform and persuade the buyer to purchase the offering but also to physically deliver the offering. For example, companies like Avon, Mary Kay, Amway, Nu Skin, and Herbalife do not have traditional business-to-consumer distribution channels and instead use their salesforce as distributors.

Designing, Compensating, and Managing the Salesforce

The extent to which personal selling can create market value depends on the company's salesforce and the degree to which it has the skills and the motivation to persuade buyers to purchase the company's offerings. Designing, compensating, and managing the salesforce are the key ingredients to ensuring success of a company's personal selling activities. These three aspects of personal selling are discussed in more detail in the following sections.

Designing the Salesforce

Designing the salesforce involves defining the way in which a company organizes its salespeople and specifically, determining the *structure*, *size*, *territory allocation*, and *effort allocation* guiding its personal selling activities.

Defining Salesforce Structure

Salesforce structure defines the way in which salespeople are organized within the company and, specifically, the type of expertise and the degree of specialization implied by their activities. In this context, there are four common ways to organize the salesforce: *product focused*, *functional*, *geographic*, and *market focused*.

- The **product sales structure** involves assigning salespeople to a particular product or product line. Because their efforts are focused on a specific set of products, this type of sales structure implies a high degree of specialization and product expertise. The primary benefit of this approach is that the salesperson can gain product-specific expertise, which, in turn, would facilitate the selling process. Accordingly, the product-based sales organization is particularly suited for complex products and services that require specialized knowledge. The downsides of this approach include potential duplication of effort, customer confusion, and sales conflict when different salespeople interact with the same customer.

- The **functional sales structure** involves grouping salespeople based on the role they play in the organization and their area of specialization. This type of structure is often used when the sale involves a number of activities that could be greatly improved by having the members of the salesforce specialize in performing them. For example, some salespeople might specialize in generating leads, whereas others might have expertise in negotiating the terms and closing the sale. The primary benefit of this approach is the increased effectiveness and cost efficiency resulting from dividing the sales process into individual tasks and allocating these tasks to salespeople with expertise in a particular aspect of the sales process. On the downside, parsing out the sales process makes it more difficult for the salesperson to establish a meaningful relationship with customers and increases the risk of a breakdown in communication stemming from customers' interactions with different salespeople.

- The **geographic sales structure** involves assigning salespeople to a particular geographic area. This type of structure gives a broad set of responsibilities to salespeople, who usually end up being generalists without much expertise with particular products or markets. The primary benefits of the geographic structure are that it avoids duplication of effort and is relatively simple, meaning that it is easy to design and implement. On the downside, however, the geographic structure typically does not involve any kind of sales specialization (except by geographic area), which can make the selling of complex offerings more challenging. The geographic structure can also complicate sales to customers operating across different geographic areas because it might lead to internal conflicts between the salespeople assigned to these areas and complicate their relationship with the customer. As a result, the geographic sales structure is often used in cases of large assortments of relatively simple products sold to buyers whose operations are confined to a particular geographic region.

- The **market sales structure** involves assigning salespeople to specific customers rather than specific products or geographic areas. This approach recognizes that customers with similar needs and profiles are likely to face similar problems, make decisions in a similar fashion, and require similar levels of service. In this case, salespeople are likely to be generalists, performing all selling activities for all of the company's offerings for certain customers. The main benefit of the market sales structure is the ability for the salesperson to establish an ongoing relationship with the customer, be aware of this customer's current needs and preferences, and anticipate future ones. Because salespeople are assigned to specific accounts, this approach also helps eliminate a potential duplication of effort. On the downside, however, because they are responsible for all sales to a particular customer, salespeople are less likely to have in-depth expertise in all products and services they sell. As a result, the market sales structure is typically used for relatively simple, and sometimes even non-differentiated products, where the relationship with the seller is a key factor driving the purchase decision.

An important aspect of defining the market sales structure involves identifying the most important customers—commonly referred to as *key accounts*—who contribute a large portion of the company's sales and profits. These customers are usually assigned more experienced salespeople, who are given greater discretion over using the company resources. The primary function of key account managers is to manage the relationship with the customers they are assigned to in order to ensure that these valued customers receive a higher level of service. Thus, key account management includes not only sales but also planning and managing the entire relationship between a company and its most important customers.

Determining the Salesforce Size

Companies can improve salesforce performance by optimizing its size in a way that maximizes effectiveness while keeping costs at bay. Because the optimal salesforce size depends on a variety of factors such as the type of product being sold, the length of the selling cycle, and the competitive intensity of the market, there is no simple formula to determine the ideal number of salespeople for any given company. Instead, salesforce size is often determined on a case-by-case basis by examining the marginal benefits and costs associated with adding or discharging additional salespeople. In this context, companies typically consider two aspects of salesforce productivity: *monetary* and *strategic*.

The *monetary aspect* of the salesforce size decision aims to identify the optimal number of salespeople based on their productivity. The relationship between salesforce size and productivity is not linear: Adding more salespeople will not always be beneficial for the company. Indeed, the incremental benefits (e.g., marginal revenue) generated by the salesforce follows a concave function, such that after initial growth the marginal benefits created by adding more salespeople tends to decrease (for example, because the market has been saturated and salespeople start competing for the same accounts). At the same time, the costs associated with adding an extra salesperson do follow a linear function, meaning the costs associated with adding an extra salesperson (e.g., salary, commissions, and benefits) are constant and do not decrease with the increase in the salesforce size. As a result, there is a point at which the size of the salesforce is optimal and profits from the salesforce are maximized. There is also a break-even point after which adding more salespeople will have a negative impact on the company's financial performance, meaning that the cost of adding an extra salesperson will outweigh the revenues generated by that salesperson (Figure 1).

Figure 1. Sales Productivity as a Function of Salesforce Size

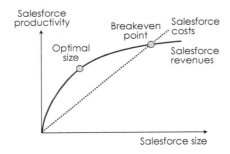

The *strategic aspect* of the salesforce size decision involves assessing the company's long-term goals and identifying the optimal salesforce strategy to achieve that goal. In this context, key considerations include overall market size, rate of growth, and the competitive intensity of the market. Another important consideration is the flexibility of the salesforce size and the ease with which a company can vary the size of its salesforce. Thus, companies with salaried full-time employees have many fewer degrees of freedom when it comes to modifying the size of their salesforces compared to companies that outsource their salesforces and hire external salespeople based on their current needs.

Because they focus on different implications, the strategic and monetary perspectives on salesforce size might not always be perfectly aligned. Thus, in rapidly growing markets, a company could invest in a salesforce that might operate at a loss when measured by its monthly or quarterly financial performance because its strategic goal is to gain a foothold with target customers and be ready to fulfill their increasing demand for its offering over time. Likewise, a company might increase its salesforce beyond the break-even point in order to crowd out the competition or to counter competitors' activities and prevent the loss of a strategically important account.

Allocating Sales Territories

A sales territory comprises the specific accounts assigned to a particular salesperson. Sales territories are often defined by a given geographic area or by markets representing a specific set of customers. The primary purpose of assigning salespeople to specific territories is to avoid duplication of effort and prevent potential conflicts if different salespeople end up approaching the same customer. Assigning sales territories has the additional benefit of delegating responsibilities for a specific set of accounts to a particular salesperson, which not only ensures that these customers receive the necessary sales support but also enables the company to more directly observe this salesperson's performance.

Allocating sales territories involves two key decisions: defining boundaries of each territory and deciding how many salespeople to allocate to each territory. Designing sales territories involves dividing target customers into markets, each of which are then assigned to specific salespersons. In the context of a market-based sales structure, defining individual territories is akin to a segmentation: The company aims to identify customers that are similar to one another so that their needs can be addressed by the same salesperson (or sales team) and yet distinct from other customers whose needs are best addressed by different salespeople.

Once sales territories have been identified, the next step involves deciding how many salespeople to allocate to each territory. A common approach to determine the number of salespeople per territory involves assessing the market potential in each territory and the amount of sales effort required to reach all target customers in that territory. Using an estimate of the average sales effort (e.g., time) invested by a single salesperson and taking into account the salesperson's cost, a company can then determine how many salespeople to allocate to a particular territory.

Managing the Effort Allocation

In addition to defining the structure and size of the salesforce and designing sales territories, a company must decide how much effort to allocate to different markets, territories, and customers. The term "effort" in this context is used in reference to the resources—time, energy, and money—that a company needs to expend to generate a sale. A common approach to determine the optimal effort allocation is to order different markets based on their attractiveness to the company and allocate effort proportionally.

In general, the attractiveness of a given market is a function of two types of factors: monetary and strategic. The monetary dimension of market attractiveness involves factors that have a direct impact on the company's bottom line, such as customers' revenue potential and the costs associated with reaching and serving these customers. The strategic dimension of market attractiveness, on the other hand, involves factors that ensure the company's ability to create superior market value in the long run, such as customers' growth potential and inherent loyalty. The greater the monetary and strategic value of a given market is to the company, the greater the effort a company should allocate to this market.

The amount of sales effort needed for a particular market also depends on whether this market is new or already developed. This is because developing new markets requires much greater effort, and hence, more salespeople, compared to markets with an established customer base. In addition to the differences in sales effort, new and established markets vary in the sales expertise they require. Thus, some salespeople (often referred to as "hunters") are much better at acquiring new customers, whereas others (often referred to as "farmers") perform much better at managing existing customer relationships. In this context, matching the right salesperson with the right type of market can further help the company increase salesforce productivity.

When allocating sales effort, a company must also consider not only the current market situation but also the dynamics of the market. In this context, a company might choose to allocate more salespeople and resources to markets that currently are not very attractive but are growing rapidly and are likely to present a viable sales opportunity in the future. In the same vein, a company might allocate more sales effort to strategically important markets in which its current competitive position is rather weak in an attempt to bolster its presence and steal share from the competition.

Compensating the Salesforce

Defining the compensation structure is of primary importance in managing the salesforce. Setting the right compensation and reward mechanism is crucial for a company's ability to attract and maintain a skilled salesforce. There are two general types of questions that need to be addressed when determining salesforce compensation: *pay structure* and *incentive design*.[1]

Setting the Pay Structure

Deciding on the *pay structure* involves determining the overall *pay level* and identifying the *pay mix*—that is, the relative percentage of fixed and performance-based compensation. The pay-level decision of how much the company should pay its salespeople determines a company's ability to recruit and retain a competent salesforce. Furthermore, to motivate salespeople to work harder and more accurately measure their performance, companies often vary the pay mix by splitting salesforce compensation into two components: fixed and variable.

Fixed compensation, which typically includes salary and benefits, provides salespeople with a stable income that does not depend on their performance. The advantages of fixed compensation include its simplicity, predictability, and transparency. In addition, because there is lower financial incentive to maximize sales, fixed compensation can promote a more collaborative work environment, facilitate building long-term customer relationships, and discourage the use of unethical sales techniques. Fixed compensation also ensures stability of income for the salesforce during economic downturns, thus helping the company decrease employee turnover. On the downside, fixed compensation does not incentivize salespeople to perform beyond the average level defined in their job description; it also requires a greater level of supervision on the part of the company and can create resentment among the more productive salespeople who are compensated at the same level as those who are less productive.

Variable compensation—which involves payouts such as commissions, bonuses, awards, and profit sharing—aims to encourage and reward the individual performances of salespeople. Variable compensation helps attract skilled salespeople and helps motivate them to achieve higher levels of performance, while at the same time creating a sense of fairness by relating compensation to work performance. Variable compensation also can be more cost efficient in industries with cyclical demand where salesforce compensation is typically a function of the generated sales volume. On the downside, however, variable compensation does not contribute to building the company culture and can create a less cooperative work environment as salespeople tend to focus on maximizing their own compensation. Furthermore, variable compensation might encourage salespeople to focus on maximizing short-term sales revenues (by nudging customers toward offerings that generate higher commissions) at the expense of building long-term relationships with customers.

To capitalize on the benefits of fixed and variable compensation structures and minimize their limitations, companies often use combined plans that involve both a salary component and a commission component. The specific ratio of fixed-to-variable compensation depends on a variety of factors such as the cyclicality of demand, the type of offering being sold, the length of the selling cycle, the number of salespeople typically involved in the sale, as well as whether the company employs a full-time, part-time, or external salesforce. The general principle when designing a salary-plus-incentives pay structure is to balance the advantages and drawbacks associated with fixed and variable compensation in a way that benefits both the salespeople and the company.

Designing the Incentives

In addition to deciding on the pay structure—the pay level and the pay mix—salesforce compensation involves determining the *incentives design*—that is, the specifics of the performance-based component of the variable compensation. Designing the incentives involves two types of decisions: defining the *performance metrics* and defining the *payout formula*.

Defining the performance metrics involves setting the criteria by which the performance of salespeople is evaluated. Common performance metrics include sales volume, sales revenues, and profit margin, with sales volume arguably being the most popular base for determining salesforce commissions. The metrics used to measure salesforce performance are also a function of the company's goals. When trying to gain market share, as is the case when entering new markets, a company might focus on sales volume rather than profits. In contrast, a company with an established position in a mature market might prioritize profit over sales volume.

Defining the performance metric serves a dual function: On the one hand, it aims to adequately measure performance and, on the other, it motivates salespeople to behave in a way that maximizes their performance on the set metric. As a result, a poorly thought-out performance metric will not only fail to accurately measure salespeople's performance but might also sway their behavior in a direction that is counterproductive to the company's goals. For example, salespeople whose performance is measured based on the number of units they sell in a given time frame might be willing to heavily discount the offering and sometimes even sell it at a loss to achieve higher sales volume. To better balance their own interests with those of the salesforce, some companies use composite metrics that involve several simple metrics.

Defining the *payout formula* reflects the relationship between a salesperson's performance on the selected metric(s) and the magnitude of the incentive received. Designing the payout formula involves three key decisions: *setting the commission rate*, *identifying the commission split*, and *determining the commission payout event*.

Setting the *commission rate* involves determining the way in which certain levels of performance translate to a salesperson's compensation. For example, a company might choose to pay its salespeople one percent of the gross sales revenues or a $100 flat fee on each unit sold. A company must also decide whether the commission rate should be constant, meaning that the payout is the same regardless of the level of performance; progressive, meaning that the payout increases with the level of performance; or regressive, meaning that the payout declines as the level of performance increases. Progressive rates are often used when the sales effort required to generate additional sales is greater than the effort involved in reaching buyers viewed as the "low-hanging fruit." In the same vein, regressive commission rates are often used in subscription-type offerings where the first sale is more difficult to achieve but the rest are nearly automatic and require little or no effort. The company can also designate a particular level of performance that needs to be achieved on the chosen performance metric in order to generate a commission. For example, the company can define a particular sales volume that must be reached for the salesperson to qualify for a commission.

Determining the *commission split* involves deciding how to allocate the commission between the different entities involved in the sale. For example, when multiple salespeople work as a team, the company must decide how much to reward each individual salesperson. In some cases, such as in real estate transactions, the commission can also be split between the salesperson and the company, which receives a share of the revenues in exchange for providing the infrastructure, reputation, and access to customers that are instrumental for generating the sale. Commission splits are particularly relevant in the case of multi-level marketing (also referred to as network marketing and pyramid marketing), where compensation is based not only on salespeople's own sales but also on the sales of those recruited by them. Because salespeople derive compensation from commissions based on the sales made by the salespeople they recruit, they are incentivized to attract others to join the company and become their down-line salespeople. Multi-level commission splits have been the key growth driver for companies like Avon, Tupperware, Mary Kay Cosmetics, and Herbalife.

Identifying the *commission payout* event involves defining when a commission is earned and when it is paid. Companies use different benchmarks to determine when a commission has been earned: when the sale is confirmed, when the customer is billed for the order, when the order has shipped, or upon receiving payment. The choice of a particular method depends on a variety of factors such as the type of merchandise being sold, payment terms, the grace period for canceling the sale, and the company's return policy. Earned commissions are usually paid on a monthly or even quarterly basis, which also enables the companies to adjust salespersons' earnings in the case of canceled sales or returns.

Managing the Salesforce

Managing salesforce performance focuses on seven key activities: recruiting, training, supporting, motivating, empowering, and controlling the salesforce as well as developing a sales culture to guide salespeople's behavior (Figure 2). These seven activities follow from the general principles of managing front-line employees in service industries (discussed in more detail in Chapter 10). We address these activities in more detail below in the context of optimizing salesforce performance.

Figure 2. Managing Salesforce Performance

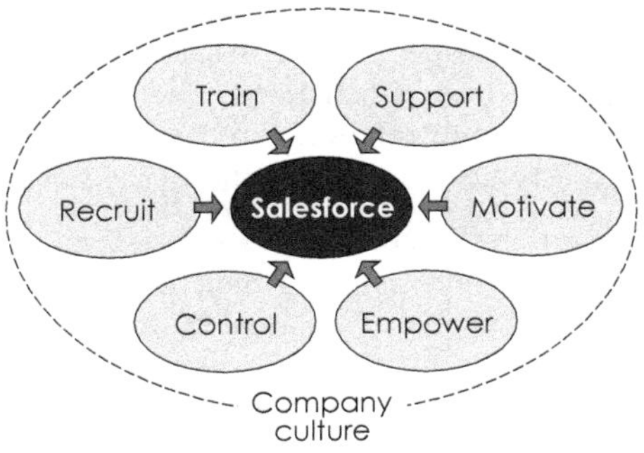

Recruiting the Right Salespeople

The importance of hiring the right people in personal selling cannot be overstated. The likelihood of a business interaction resulting in a sale depends to a large degree on the skills and personality of the salesperson. Accordingly, a key aspect of building a strong sales organization is the selection of capable and motivated salespeople. Although companies vary in the specific skills and knowledge they seek in the "ideal" candidate, there are several attributes that are common across different sales jobs. These attributes can be classified into three categories: core skills, company fit, and sales experience.

The set of *core skills* companies usually look for in a salesperson include communication skills, social skills, creativity, analytical abilities, ability to work in a team, capacity to learn, management skills, personal drive, and leadership skills. The *company fit* reflects the match between the aspirations, moral character, and personality of the individual and the company culture. Finally, *relevant experience* reflects the degree to which a particular individual already has sales experience in either the same or a related industry. Global companies and those serving specialized markets might also seek individuals with a specific background such as language skills and knowledge of the local culture, traditions, and behaviors.

Training the Salesforce

Even experienced salespeople benefit from training to inform them about the specifics of their job; familiarize them with their customers, competitors, and the products and services they will be selling; and immerse them in the company culture. To this end, many of the top sales organizations have formal training programs for new salesforce hires as well as ongoing training programs to improve the performance of their current salespeople. Sales training programs typically focus on five main topics: functional knowledge, company knowledge, customer knowledge, market knowledge, and selling skills.

Functional knowledge involves information about the company's products and services to enable salespeople to explain their benefits to customers, suggest the best offerings for their needs, and explain why the company's products and services are superior to competitors' offerings. *Company knowledge* involves information about the company's mission, vision, and corporate culture in order to ensure that the actions of the salesforce are aligned with the company's goals and values. *Customer knowledge* provides information about customers' needs, preferences, expectations, buying process, and personalities. *Market knowledge* involves information about the company's competitors and collaborators, as well as the sociocultural, technological, regulatory, economic, and physical context in which the company operates.

Selling skills involve a variety of practical abilities such as listening skills that aim to gain a better understanding of customers' needs, persuasion skills geared toward enhancing the salesperson's ability to effectively communicate the benefits of the company's offering, closing skills that bolster a salesperson's ability to bring the negotiation to a close and seal the deal, and relationship-building skills that focus on forging long-term relationships rather than churning one-time transactions.

Supporting the Sales Effort

An important aspect of managing the salesforce is providing salespeople with the necessary support and, specifically, ensuring that relevant product, customer, and market information is readily available. To this end, salespeople utilize salesforce management systems that help automate many of the supporting sales functions. The salesforce management system is a component of a company's customer relationship management system (discussed in more detail in Chapter 20), which is focused on streamlining the sales process.

The salesforce management system comprises a variety of components, including an *opportunity management* (lead generation) system that helps identify new viable prospects; a *sales process management* system that helps track all of the company's sales interactions with each individual prospect; a *pipeline optimization* system that helps streamline different sales activities; an *order management* system that tracks different aspects of customers' orders such as product specifications, purchasing, inventory, order processing, shipping, receiving, and billing; and a *salesforce compensation* system that monitors the performance and manages the compensation of the individual salespeople.

Motivating the Salesforce

Motivating salespeople to accomplish the company's goals is an important aspect of managing the salesforce as it can incentivize salespeople to invest extra effort and creativity in identifying, closing, and servicing new customers. A company can motivate its salesforce using two types of incentives: monetary and nonmonetary. Monetary incentives typically involve a fixed component such as salary and a variable component such as commissions and monetary bonuses (discussed earlier in this chapter).

Nonmonetary incentives are an important, yet often overlooked, tool for motivating the salesforce. These incentives include public recognition such as being acknowledged at the company's annual event, receiving a formal performance recognition (e.g., Road Warrior, Rising Star, and Rainmaker), and being named a member of an exclusive group of the best performing salespeople (e.g., Chairmen's Circle, President's Club, and Platinum Sales Club). Nonmonetary awards can also include performance bonuses such as free travel, bonus merchandise, and extra vacation days.

In addition to rewarding top performers, companies also seek to ensure that all employees achieve certain performance levels. To this end, many companies set sales quotas that need to be achieved within a certain time frame (a week, a month, or a year), with compensation tied to the degree of quota fulfillment. These sales quotas can involve a variety of criteria including sales revenues, sales volume, profit margins, selling effort, and customer satisfaction. Unlike awards and bonuses that are designed to enhance a salesperson's compensation package, setting sales quotas follows a carrot-and-stick approach: It can increase the compensation of those who exceed their quotas and lower the compensation of underachievers. Although in most cases having well-defined sales goals and quotas can motivate the salesforce, setting goals and quotas that are overly ambitious might have the opposite effect, demotivating salespeople and sometimes even leading to unethical behaviors that are inconsistent with the company's culture and core values.

Empowering Salespeople

The degree to which important decisions are made by salespeople rather than by the senior management is an important aspect of managing the salesforce. Determining the degree to which salespeople are empowered to make sales-related decisions calls for a fine balance between creating a top-down sales organization, in which the salesforce has to follow a set of rules defined by senior management without the freedom to adapt their behavior based on the specific situation, and a bottom-up organization in which individual salespeople act as free agents that can make the key sales-related decisions.

The top-down approach helps ensure that salespeople's actions are aligned with the goals of the company while at the same time facilitating consistent implementation of the company's sales policies across different accounts. At the same time, the top-down approach could suffocate individual initiative and limit salespeople's ability to effectively negotiate with customers and close deals in a timely fashion. Indeed, top-down sales management, particularly in larger organizations, cannot foresee all of the different situations that salespeople are likely to face and, hence, cannot create policies to guide salesforce behavior in atypical scenarios. In such cases, the top-down approach is likely to lead to inefficient and impractical outcomes that are not aligned with the company's ultimate goals.

Bottom-up salesforce management can help the company overcome the limitations of the top-down approach by allowing salespeople to adapt to the specific context in which they find themselves. Thus, the bottom-up approach gives salespeople greater discretion in negotiating deals, helping them establish trust and build long-term relationships with their customers. It also frees up management time and helps create a leaner sales structure that allows company executives to transition from managers to leaders who inspire and coordinate the efforts of the salesforce toward achieving the company goals. Despite its advantages, the bottom-up approach also has its limitations. Delegating too much power to individual salespeople might motivate them to focus on maximizing their own performance (e.g., focusing only on deals with the highest commission) even when it is detrimental to the other salespeople and the company. In this context, combining the top-down and the bottom-up approaches to empower salespeople can help balance their pros and cons, thus helping create an effective sales organization.

Controlling Salesforce Performance

Motivating and empowering salespeople goes hand in hand with controlling their performance to ensure that the actions of the salesforce are aligned with the company's goals. In this context, an important challenge that the sales organization faces in managing its salesforce involves the so-called *agency problem*, which refers to the disparity between interests of the company and those of the individual salespeople. For example, salespeople might be inclined to offer their customers a significant discount to close the deal and generate a commission rather than invest additional time and effort to sell the company's products and services on their benefits rather than on price. The conflict of interest here is that the price reductions typically have much greater impact on the profitability of the company (especially in cases when the fixed costs of its offering are high) than on the compensation of the salesperson (especially in cases when performance is measured on nonmonetary metrics such as sales volume). Having a well-designed incentive structure can help reduce the agency problem by better aligning the goals of the company with those of its salesforce.

In addition to monitoring salesforce productivity and profitability, most companies also monitor the degree to which the salesforce adheres to the relevant legal regulations and the company's ethical standards in conducting their business. Indeed, salespeople are often presented with moral hazards reflecting an opportunity to skirt certain ethical and legal rules in order to generate sales. For example, a salesperson might divulge privileged information about the company and its customers, promise customers a benefit that the company cannot deliver, charge customers for products and services they have not requested, and even misreport sales revenues and steal from the company.

Given the complexity of finding the right balance between motivating, empowering, and controlling the salesforce, companies tend to follow a multi-pronged approach to make certain that the behavior of its salespeople is aligned with the goals of the organization. One such approach involves creating a meaningful incentive structure and setting attainable goals for the salesforce. This approach also calls for the development of a dashboard that can track key performance metrics such as sales revenue, sales volume, profitability, and productivity for each salesperson. Another popular approach involves tracking customers' overall level of satisfaction and collecting specific feedback on a salesperson's performance. Another often overlooked approach for controlling salesforce performance involves building a strong company culture that helps facilitate monitoring and enforcing the company's values and policies.

Managing the Company Culture

The company culture defines the environment in which salespeople work and reflects their shared goals, values, and norms of behavior. It is a philosophy that permeates all aspects of the organization, from senior executives to the rank-and-file salesforce. The company culture captures the personality of the organization and determines the ethical norms that guide salesforce actions in situations not addressed by the company's policies. The company culture is often described as a reflection of salespeople's behavior when they know that management is not watching.

The first step to building a company culture is to articulate the company's mission, values, and the types of behavior endorsed by the organization and develop policies reflecting them. The development of a set of policies, although important, is not enough to ensure that these policies are internalized by the salesforce. The company must also train its salespeople and managers on these policies. Because a company's culture is a shared experience, it is essential that all salespeople and sales managers subscribe to a set of shared values and norms of behavior that, in turn, promote a spirit of teamwork and collaboration. In this context, it is particularly important that senior management lead by example and adhere to the norms and behaviors they expect of the salespeople in their organization. By uniting the salesforce behind a shared set of values, the company culture helps align individual goals with those of the organization.

Managing the Sale

The development of a skilled and motivated salesforce is a necessary but insufficient condition for a company to successfully promote and distribute its offerings. To maximize the impact of its personal selling activities, a company must be able to effectively manage the ways in which its salesforce interacts with potential buyers. The two main aspects of managing the sale—understanding the buyer and managing the selling process—are discussed in more detail in the following sections.

Understanding the Buyer

Any selling process starts with understanding the buyer. Without knowing who is making the buying decision, why they would purchase the company's offering, how they make the buying decision, and what factors influence their choice, it is virtually impossible to develop a meaningful selling strategy. The key aspects of understanding the buyer—*identifying the decision-making unit, understanding buyer needs and expectations, mapping the decision journey,* and *defining the buying context*—are outlined below.

Identifying the Decision-Making Unit

One of the first steps in managing the sale is to identify the *decision-making unit* comprising the entities involved in making the buying decision. The decision-making unit can be characterized by two main factors: the *entities* involved in the decision process and the *roles* they play in making the decision.

The decision-making unit can involve different *entities*, both in terms of their number and functions. In business-to-consumer markets, the decision-making unit can consist of an individual or a group of individuals, such as the members of a household. In business-to-business markets, it can also consist of representatives from different departments or functional areas within an organization, including senior management; product, service, and brand managers; as well as research and development, finance, accounting, legal, purchasing, marketing, salesforce, and information technology departments.

When making a purchase decision, the members of the decision-making unit can play several distinct *roles* (Figure 3).[2] *Initiators* originate the buying process by identifying an unmet need or a problem that needs solving. *Gatekeepers* influence the decision process by imposing certain restrictions with respect to the options being considered. *Influencers* have an impact on the decision process by expressing relevant preferences and recommendations. *Deciders* are in charge of making the ultimate selection of what, why, and when to buy. *Purchasers* negotiate the specifics of the purchase (e.g., price, delivery, guarantees) with the seller and execute the purchase transaction. Finally, *end users* are the ultimate consumers of the purchased product or service.

Figure 3. Decision-Making Unit: Key Roles

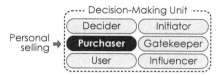

Note that the initiator, influencer, gatekeeper, decision maker, buyer, and end user are the decision roles assumed by individuals or groups of people. Thus, one role might involve the participation of multiple individuals, and one individual might play multiple decision roles. For example, a child, influenced by friends, might initiate the buying process by requesting a particular toy. The decision to buy the toy is then made by both parents, with one spouse taking on the role of gatekeeper to ensure that the purchase fits within the family budget and the other spouse making the actual purchase. The child then becomes the ultimate user of the toy.

In the same vein, the corporate buying process might be initiated by the research and development department, which could also be the end user of the offering; gatekeeping could be performed by the legal, accounting, and information technology departments; deciding could be done by senior management; and buying could be assigned to a purchasing manager. Finally, all of the above entities can play the role of an influencer in the decision process.

Understanding the composition of the decision-making unit and the role different entities play in the decision process enables the salesforce to develop relevant sales strategies for different decision entities based on their impact on the decision process. Understanding the decision process buyers use can also help the company better allocate its sales efforts and prevent it from overinvesting resources in entities that have only marginal impact on the buying decision. For example, even though a salesperson might interact with the individual making the purchase (the buyer), in reality this individual is not the decision maker but rather just the messenger of a decision that involves other parties. In this case, a more effective approach is to identify the key decision maker(s) and influencer(s) and interact with them directly.

Identifying Buyer Needs

To succeed in selling its products and services, a company must identify buyers' needs and the value buyers associate with the company's offerings. Without understanding the buyer, it is almost impossible to create a meaningful value exchange that benefits both the buyer and the seller.

The value created by a company's offering can be defined along three main dimensions: functional, psychological, and monetary (see Chapter 7 for more detail). The *functional value* is directly related to an offering's functionality and is represented by attributes such as performance, reliability, and durability. The *psychological value* is defined by the psychological benefits and costs associated with the offering and reflects the offering's ability to fulfill the needs of buyers seeking emotional and self-expressive benefits. Finally, the *monetary value* is defined by the monetary benefits and costs associated with the offering and is represented by attributes such as price, fees, discounts, rebates, and operation costs.

Because many purchase decisions are made by multiple entities, identifying the needs and preferences of all relevant entities in a buyer's decision-making unit is paramount for making a sale. Focusing only on the needs and preferences of the purchaser who will end up executing the sales transaction is not enough. The salesperson must also take into account the needs and preferences of all entities with input on the buying decision. More important, the salesperson must articulate how the company's offering will fulfill the needs and create value for each of these entities.

Because they play different roles in the buying process, individual members of the decision-making unit vary in the decision criteria they use and, specifically, the degree to which they focus on the functional, monetary, or psychological aspects of the value created by the offering. For example, in the case of a couple purchasing a vehicle, one spouse might give more weight to the functional and self-expressive aspects of the car, whereas the other might focus exclusively on its monetary aspects. In the same vein, in business purchase decisions, project managers and the research and development team might focus primarily on the functional benefits of the offering, including performance, reliability, and durability. In contrast, senior management—as well as the finance, accounting, and purchasing departments—might focus primarily on the monetary aspects of the offering. The members of the decision-making unit can also be driven by self-serving factors such as the desire to enhance their power and status within the organization, gain recognition, and satisfy their ego.

Understanding the needs and value drivers of the key entities involved in the buyer's decision-making unit can help the company improve its chances for making a sale, speed up the selling process, and result in greater customer satisfaction with the purchase. Unless salespeople understand the underlying motivation of the different parties in the decision process and the decision criteria likely to be used when making a purchase decision, any sales pitch they make amounts to a shot in the dark that might hit a target only by chance.

Mapping the Customer Decision Journey

Identifying the decision-making unit and the needs of the entities involved in the buying process, although important, does not paint a complete picture of the purchase decision. To fully understand the buyer, the salesperson must understand this buyer's decision journey, which captures the processes and experiences in selecting, buying, and using an offering to fulfill a particular need. In this context, the customer decision journey can be represented as consisting of seven components that denote different stages of the buying process (see Chapter 4 for a more detailed discussion of the decision journey in consumer markets). These seven stages are illustrated in Figure 4 and outlined in more detail below.

Figure 4. The Customer Decision Journey

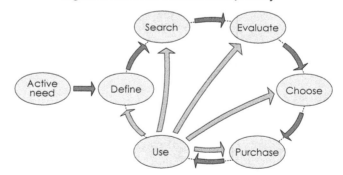

Need activation involves identifying an unmet need or a problem that must be solved. *Defining* the need involves identifying the specific features and benefits that the company seeks to receive from the offering it intends to purchase. *Search* involves gathering information about the available options from sources such as trade shows, catalogs, and advertisements as well as by soliciting proposals from interested entities. *Evaluation* involves an assessment of the relative attractiveness of the different options with respect to their ability to fulfill the active need. *Choice* involves selecting the offering that best matches the active need. *Purchase* involves finalizing the details and executing the transaction whereby the company receives the goods in exchange for an agreed-upon compensation. *Usage* involves the actual consumption of the product or service. Because customers are likely to have different information and varying needs during the different stages of their decision journey, identifying the customer's stage of the decision process and tailoring the sales approach to the customer's mindset at this stage can greatly facilitate the selling process.

Consider the following scenario. The CEO of a pharmaceutical firm learns that his competitor has recently invested in customer relationship management (CRM) software that promises to greatly reduce expenses and improve the efficiency of its marketing activities. Thinking that CRM software might prove beneficial for his firm, the CEO creates a task force comprising VPs of different departments to evaluate the viability of adopting CRM software. The task force comes back with an affirmative answer, and the decision is made to go ahead with the purchase of the CRM software (need activation). To determine the scope of the project and the specific functions that this software must perform, a new task force is formed, comprising both VPs and lower level managers who have hands-on experience with the current processes. The task force comes up with a list of features and functionality required by the company (need definition), and using this guidance the purchasing department develops a request for proposals (RFP) that is circulated among companies with expertise in developing CRM software (option search). As the deadline for the RFP passes, the company assesses the submitted bids (evaluation of the alternatives), examines their pros and cons, and ultimately selects one of the vendors (option choice). The purchasing department then finalizes the decision and makes the deal (option purchase). Finally, the company installs the software, integrates it with its existing software, and trains the IT personnel how to support the software and the marketing staff and salesforce how to use the software (offering usage).

Throughout the entire process, the company's decision is influenced by different entities, including consultants working for the company on various projects, vendors showcasing their own equipment, and industry experts providing detailed analysis of the pros and cons of different options. The company's chief marketing officer, whose focus is on enhancing customer experience and improving the company's interaction with its customers, champions the project by ensuring that each entity involved contributes to the decision in an effective and timely manner.

The above seven stages of the customer decision journey depict a sales scenario in which a customer considers an offering for the first time. On many occasions, however, customers make repeat purchases from the same product category. In such cases, customers can adopt a range of decision routes. On the one extreme, they might simply repurchase the same offering without considering other options. This, of course, is the most desirable scenario for the incumbent offering. On the other extreme, buyers might restart the decision process by redefining their needs, forming a new consideration set, making a new choice, and/or making different purchase arrangements. (The different routes to repurchase are depicted in light blue in Figure 4.)

Note also that, as with the consumer decision journey, the sequence of steps depicted in Figure 4 represents a typical journey that a company embarks on when making a purchase decision. These steps and their sequence are not absolute; rather, they hinge on the decision context, such that depending on the circumstances, the individual steps may occur together or in a different order. In addition, the decision process might go through several iterations until a final choice is made. In this context, the decision journey depicted in Figure 4 aims to illustrate the overall logic of the corporate buying process and its most common stages rather than defining a prescriptive model that companies must follow to make an optimal purchase decision.[3]

Mapping the buying process helps salespeople understand the criteria buyers use to make a purchase as well as identify the decision stage of the buyer when approached by a salesperson. Thus, the salesperson would adopt a different strategy when approaching buyers who do not yet realize they have a need that could be fulfilled by the company's offering than when approaching buyers who have either realized that they have a problem and are actively seeking a solution or have narrowed their choice to several alternatives and are deciding among them.

Adapting the Sales Approach to the Buying Context

To present the value proposition of the company's offering in a meaningful way and close the sale, sales teams need to monitor the context in which customers make the buying decision and adapt the selling strategy and tactics to the specifics of that context. The buying context reflects the aspects of the purchasing process that are particular to the specific point in time and the environment in which the buyer seeks to make a purchase. Thus, unlike buyers' needs and preferences, which are relatively stable over time, the buying context can rapidly change depending on a variety of situational factors both internal and external to the organization. This is particularly relevant for longer buying cycles when changes in the decision context are likely to occur even during the purchase process.

For example, a change in the context might involve a change in the financial situation of the buyer, a change in the composition of the decision-making unit (e.g., due to personnel being on leave, reassigned to a different project, or no longer with the company), and a change in the time frame and speed with which the buyer must make a decision. The buying process might also be influenced by a change in the company's strategies, priorities, and performance as well as by the dynamics of the internal organizational politics. Context changes might also involve pressure by a competitor who has introduced a better performing or lower priced product on the market that is superior to the company's offering.

Another context factor that can influence the buying process is the overall business environment in which the company operates. For example, new technological developments can stimulate customer demand and open new sales opportunities by changing the way customers think about the benefits and costs of the company's offerings and the ways the salesforce presents these offerings to buyers. The overall economic conditions may influence the company's decision to move forward with the purchase decision or hold off until the economy improves. New laws and regulations might have a significant impact on the buyer's business model and influence the manner in which purchase decisions are made.

All of the above changes in the business environment can influence whether buyers end up purchasing the company's offerings, which and how many products and services they will purchase, and how much they are willing to pay for them. Moreover, the changes in the context might influence not only whether and what the buyer purchases but also the ways in which they make decisions—how systematically they approach the decision process, how much time and effort they invest in considering different options, and the degree to which different entities are involved in the decision process. This fluidity of the buying context requires the sales team to closely monitor the market for changes and quickly adapt to the new selling context.

Managing the Selling Process

In addition to understanding the buyer, an important aspect of managing the sale is managing the specific activities involved in the process of selling the company's products and services. In this context, the selling process can be viewed as a sequence of six activities: identifying the key *prospects*, *customizing* the sales approach, *presenting* the offering, *negotiating* the deal, *closing* the sale, and *servicing* the account. These six activities are illustrated in Figure 5 and discussed in more detail below.

Figure 5. The Personal Selling Process

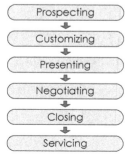

Prospecting

Prospecting is the process of identifying the potential buyers—the individuals (or companies) who may ultimately purchase the company's products and services. Prospecting can target the end users of the offering or buyers who purchase the offering on behalf of end users.

Prospecting is related to the process of strategic targeting, whereby the company identifies customers for whom it will tailor its offering. These processes are similar in that they focus a company's efforts on viable customers—those for whom the company can create value and who, in turn, can create value for the company. At the same time, targeting is focused on identifying the offering's end users, for whom the company will develop a meaningful value proposition. In contrast, prospecting is focused on identifying entities and individuals who will ultimately purchase the offering regardless of whether they will end up using the offering. For example, a jewelry retailer might create a necklace that will appeal to women, whereas a salesperson might identify men as potential buyers who will purchase the necklace as a gift. In the same vein, in a business-to-business environment, companies have dedicated purchasing managers who are responsible for making the buying decision.

Prospecting involves two key processes: (1) *identifying* potential buyers whose needs the company can fulfill with its offering and (2) *qualifying* these buyers based on the resources they have at their disposal. These two aspects of prospecting can be related to the two fundamental principles of targeting: The company should be able to create value for customers and, vice versa, customers should be able to create value for the company. Both identifying and qualifying prospects is important because it enables the salesforce to focus its efforts on buyers that are most likely to purchase the company's offering while creating value for the company.

In cases when the purchase decision involves multiple entities, such as in household or organizational buying, one important aspect of qualifying prospects is their decision power. Thus, even though one of the spouses has access to the resources needed to make a large household purchase, s/he might not be empowered to make this decision singlehandedly. In the same vein, in the case of organizational buying, the entity that needs the company's product or service might not have the authority to make the purchase. In this context, prospecting involves qualifying prospects based not just on their resources but also on their decision power to use these resources and authorize the purchase.

Customizing

Once the prospects have been identified, the next step is to customize the sales approach based on the specific circumstances of individual prospects. This step is also commonly referred to as *pre-approach* because it involves the homework the salesforce needs to do before approaching each prospect. The pre-approach aims to achieve two main goals: *gather information* about the prospect and use this information to *develop an effective sales approach*.

Gathering relevant background information about the prospect facilitates the sales process by enabling the salesperson to identify the best approach to present the relevant information and at the same time establish a personal connection with the buyer. To this end, the salesperson might gather information about the company while learning more about the professional responsibilities and personal interests of the individual(s) responsible for making the purchase decision. The speed, efficiency, and accuracy of the pre-approach can be facilitated by the use of specialized sales software and online sales-management platforms that can put this information at a salesperson's fingertips and make it available on the fly.

Following the collection of background information, a customized sales approach is developed that is tailored to the unique circumstances of the potential buyer. This stage in the process involves finding ways to establish initial contact with the prospect, selecting the features and benefits of the offering that are most likely to appeal to this prospect, as well as identifying the best approach to present these features and benefits. A popular approach to identifying a prospect's needs is the SPIN selling technique discussed in more detail at the end of this chapter.

Presenting

Presenting involves communicating the specifics of the company's offering to prospective buyers. Based on the specific context — the type of products and services being sold, the selling environment, and the personalities of the buyer and the seller — sales presentations vary on a variety of dimensions, including presentation style, focus, and format.

Based on their **style**, presentations can be narrative, where the salesperson delivers the sales pitch and then addresses the specific questions raised by the potential buyers, or interactive, where the sales presentation follows a more give-and-take format, with the salesperson both asking and answering questions. In general, narrative presentations are more common in formal setups and when the presentation involves larger groups, whereas interactive presentations are more common in informal setups and in one-on-one communication.

Based on their **focus**, presentations can emphasize the features, benefits, and advantages of the offering. *Features* are the technical specifications of the offering such as performance, reliability, and durability. Focusing on features is particularly useful when buyers have the necessary technical expertise and can translate these features into relevant benefits and costs. *Benefits* reflect the value that the offering can create for buyers. Benefits are subjective and are determined by the degree to which the features of the company's offering match the needs and expectations of the buyer. Focusing on benefits is particularly useful when dealing with lay buyers who lack the expertise to interpret the features of the company's offering in terms of the value that they can create for them. *Advantages* relate the features and benefits of the company's offering to a competitor's offering or the offering currently used by the buyer. Focusing on advantages involves framing the features and/or benefits of the company's offering in a way that clearly demonstrates their superiority over the alternative options. Focusing on advantages is particularly useful in cases when the buyer is actively considering competitive options or when the buyer is inclined to preserve the status quo and stay with the current offering.

Presentations vary in their **format** based on the type of products and services being sold, the selling context, and the individual experience of the seller. One popular presentation format involves starting by identifying a problem that the buyer faces, describing the company's product or service that can address this problem, defining the offering's benefits to the buyer and its advantage over the alternative solutions, substantiating the claims with credible evidence and/or demonstration, and concluding with a call for action on the part of the potential buyer. This approach is conceptually similar to the AIDA approach (awareness, interest, desire, and action), which is discussed at the end of Chapter 14.

Negotiating

In many cases buyers do not respond to sellers' presentations by immediately purchasing the company's products and services. Instead, buyers typically have questions, concerns, and objections to the arguments made in the sales presentation. These questions, concerns, and objections can involve a variety of issues, such as the features and benefits of the offering; its price, sales promotions, and distribution; as well as the ability of the offering to fulfill the buyer's needs better than the alternative options. In this context, negotiating aims to address these issues and come to a mutually beneficial, "win–win" agreement.

The first step in the negotiations is often to uncover and clarify buyers' concerns by going beyond the surface arguments and revealing the true nature of the objections to the company's offering. This process is important to avoid misunderstandings and starting negotiations on the wrong track. It is further helpful to identify the main objection(s) and prioritize these objections from the point of view of the buyer. This will help identify the key areas of contention. Next, it is important to identify areas of compromise. These are areas that are most important to the buyer and least important to the seller and vice versa. Zeroing in on these areas can help focus the negotiations on the key issues rather than on issues that are marginally important to both sides.

If a win–win solution cannot be reached, one option for the seller is to reconsider the importance of the deal in the context of the company's long-term business strategy. If this is an important deal and/or customer, the company might choose to accept a smaller profit margin. The company may even take a loss if the strategic importance of the deal outweighs the value derived from the individual transaction. On the other hand, if the deal is not crucially important for the company, walking away from the negotiations might be the better option in the long term. All things considered, if a mutually beneficial solution cannot be found, the negotiations will ultimately break down, and the company will move to the next prospect.

Closing

Closing the sale indicates that the seller and the buyer have reached an agreement to accept each other's terms and finalize the deal. Closing the sale is often viewed as the ultimate goal of the selling process. The importance of closing in personal selling is captured by the popular phrase often referred to as the ABC of selling: Always Be Closing.[4]

The closing can be contingent, meaning that a deal has been reached provided that the seller and/or the buyer meet certain conditions, or unconditional, meaning that the agreement is final. Common contingencies on a seller's part include the ability to demonstrate or document certain claims about the offering, to deliver the offering to a particular location on time, and to provide additional products and services. Common contingencies on the part of the buyer include the ability to obtain financing to purchase the offering, to acquire the necessary credentials to own/resell the offering, and to gain the necessary training and certification to operate the offering.

Closing the sale often involves concessions on the part of the seller, frequently in the form of additional incentives. These sales promotions can involve monetary incentives such as price discounts and special financing, as well as nonmonetary incentives, such as bonus products and services, prizes, and gifts. It is important to keep in mind that sales promotions, although useful to nudge the buyer toward accepting the terms of the deal, are rarely the key driver for the purchase. The purchase is driven mainly by the core features, benefits, and advantages of the offering; the sales promotions are the cherry on top that will move the needle toward purchase of the company's offering.

Servicing

Closing the deal is not the end of the sales process. Personal selling also involves value-added services that aim to enhance the benefits of the company's offering and maximize its value to the customer following the sale. The after-sale service includes providing additional information about the offering, technical assistance with using the offering, as well as delivery, installation, maintenance, and repair of the purchased goods.

There are several reasons for salespeople to offer services after the sale has closed. Even after the deal has been sealed, there are often contingencies that enable buyers to walk away from the deal. For example, consumers often return products and cancel services if they cannot figure out how to use them, realize that setting them up is much more complex than they anticipated, or experience buyer's remorse and fixate on the costs of the offering. In the same vein, commercial buyers cancel orders because the purchased products and services do not readily fit in their workflow without additional adjustments, because the employees using these products and services need special training, or because a competitor has offered them a better deal.

Servicing the buyer after the sale can help alleviate buyers' concerns by providing assistance with setting up the product and service, training customers how to use the purchased product and service, or validating their decision by pointing out benefits of the product and service. By providing such after-sale service, salespeople not only secure the individual transaction but also help change the nature of their interaction with buyers from one based on an individual transaction to a long-term relationship and, in some cases, even a strategic partnership. Moving away from transactions toward relationships and partnerships is particularly important in the case of frequently purchased products and services, as well as for companies with large portfolios of synergistic offerings that provide cross-selling opportunities. In this context, providing after-sale servicing can go a long way to grow the productivity of salespeople and the profitability of the company, in addition to increasing customer satisfaction.

SUMMARY

Personal selling is a process in which one entity (the seller) directly interacts with another entity (the buyer) in order to convince the latter to purchase a particular offering.

Although the primary function of personal selling is to communicate the offering to potential buyers, it can also help to design and deliver the offering. Thus, in addition to informing buyers about the offering, personal selling can create value by modifying the product, augmenting the service, defining the brand, negotiating the price, offering incentives, as well as delivering the actual product or service.

The extent to which personal selling can create market value depends on the company's salesforce and the degree to which it has the skills and the motivation to persuade buyers to purchase the company's offerings. The key ingredients to ensuring the success of a company's personal selling activities are: designing, compensating, and managing the salesforce.

Designing the salesforce defines the way in which a company organizes its salespeople and specifically, determines the structure, size, territory allocation, and effort allocation guiding its personal selling activities. *Defining the compensation structure* is paramount to ensure the company's ability to attract and maintain a skilled salesforce. The two main issues in determining salesforce compensation are defining the pay structure and designing the incentives. *Managing salesforce performance* focuses on recruiting, training, supporting, motivating, empowering, and controlling the salesforce as well as developing a sales culture to guide salespeople's behavior.

In addition to managing the salesforce, a company must *manage the selling process* by optimizing the ways in which its salesforce interacts with potential buyers. Managing the sale involves two main components: understanding the buyer and managing the selling process. The selling process starts with *understanding the buyer*, which involves identifying the decision-making unit, comprehending buyer needs and expectations, mapping the buyer decision journey, and defining the buying context. Building on its understanding of the buyer, a company must *manage the selling process*. This involves identifying the key prospects, customizing the sales approach, presenting the offering, negotiating the deal, closing the sale, and servicing the account.

MARKETING INSIGHT: THE PSYCHOLOGY OF PERSUASION

A key aspect of personal selling is the ability of the salesperson to persuade the buyer to purchase the company's offering. In this context, personal selling draws upon the research on social influence and persuasion in the domain of psychology. Building on this research, psychologist Robert Cialdini outlines six core principles that underlie persuasive communication.[5] These six "weapons of influence" are *reciprocity, consistency, consensus, liking, authority,* and *scarcity.*

- *Reciprocity.* The reciprocity principle suggests that people feel indebted when receiving a gift and are willing to reciprocate in kind. For example, one study shows that diners are likely to leave a greater tip if the waiter has brought them a small gift—a mint, candy, or a fortune cookie—around the same time as the bill. Moreover, the larger the gift, the greater the need to reciprocate; doubling the gift (two candies instead of one) more than doubled the amount of the tip. Accepting a gift makes the receiver feel obliged to reciprocate. The more personal and unexpected the gift, the greater the desire to reciprocate. The principle of reciprocity is one of the reasons why companies hand out free samples; in addition to experiencing the company's product, customers feel obliged to reciprocate by purchasing the offering. Another application of this principle involves asking for a particularly big favor and following its rejection asking for a much smaller favor (also referred to as the "door-in-the-face" approach). This is because the principle of reciprocity also applies to concessions, such that a concession by one of the parties (the downscaling of the request) is likely to be reciprocated with a concession by the other party (agreement to the modified request).

- *Consistency.* The consistency principle suggests that people have a strong desire to stand by commitments made and tend to behave in a consistent fashion. This principle stems from the overarching desire for consistency that has been argued by many psychologists to be a central motivator of human behavior. According to the principle of consistency, it is much easier to make people commit to a major action if they have previously committed to a related minor action. For example, in one study people who were asked to place a small postcard in the front window of their homes that indicated their support for a Drive Safely campaign in their neighborhood were four times more likely to subsequently agree to erect a large wooden board on their front lawn to support the Drive Safely campaign. One application of the consistency principle involves making people initially agree to a small request as a stepping stone for their subsequently agreeing to a larger request that is similar in nature to the original small request (also referred to as the "foot-in-the-door" approach).[6]

- *Consensus.* The consensus principle (also referred to as the social proof principle) suggests that when people face uncertainty and are unsure how to act, they tend to look to others to determine how to respond. Thus, the actions of others provide people with a shortcut decision rule on how to react in ambiguous situations, eliminating the need for a mentally taxing analysis of the situation. Notably, the social proof principle is most powerful when people observe the behavior of others who are very similar to themselves, meaning that people are more likely to follow the lead of a similar person than a dissimilar one. One application of the consensus principle involves advertising products as "best-selling," "most popular," and "highest in customer satisfaction" because this claim can serve as a social proof of the offering's attractiveness.

- *Liking.* The liking principle suggests that people tend to say "yes" to people they like. This liking can stem from three important factors: people tend to like those who are similar to them, those who pay them compliments, and those who share a mutual goal and cooperate with them. For example, in one study people who were asked to identify things that they had in common with one another were nearly twice as likely to come to an agreement in a negotiation task compared to those who were not asked to determine what they had in common. Studies have also shown that people are more likely to help people who look like them and even those who dress in a similar fashion. The principle of liking is related to the "halo" effect, whereby people tend to generalize one attribute of an individual to all attributes of this individual. For example, people tend to think that physically attractive people are more likely to possess favorable traits such as kindness, intelligence, and honesty. In the same vein, liking an individual because of a particular feature such as similarity, compliments, or cooperation, can create a "halo" effect that leads to a greater tendency to agree with this individual.

- *Authority.* The authority principle suggests that people trust credible experts and tend to act in an automated fashion to commands from figures of authority. Obedience to authority is ingrained in our minds as one of the core principles that enable society to function in an orderly fashion. For example, people are more likely to comply with a request from a person dressed in a uniform, or even a business suit, than from a person who is casually dressed. In the same vein, medical professionals are more likely to persuade their patients to comply with their advice if they display their diplomas on the walls of their offices. Even haute couture apparel, exotic cars, and expensive jewelry carry an aura of status and function as a more general form of authority that can exert a great degree of influence.

- *Scarcity.* The scarcity principle suggests that people have a stronger preference for things that are in short supply. Because the possibility of missing out on an opportunity increases the desire for an object, highlighting the unique aspects of an offering and its limited availability tends to increase its desirability. One application of the scarcity principle involves using the "limited-quantity" approach, which informs the buyer that a particular item is in short supply and might not be available in the near future. A similar approach to bolstering an offering's attractiveness is informing the buyer that the desired item just sold out but that the salesperson might be able to procure an additional item as long as the buyer commits to purchasing it.

MARKETING INSIGHT: SPIN MODEL OF PERSONAL SELLING

The SPIN model of personal selling introduced by Neil Rackham outlines a sequence of questions that aim to facilitate the selling process and provide the salesforce with a road map for managing buyer–seller interactions.[7] To this end, the SPIN model identifies four main types of questions that a salesperson might ask prior to articulating the benefits of the company's offering and trying to close the deal: *situation* questions, *problem* questions, *implication* questions, and *need–payoff* questions. These questions have a two-fold objective: They inform the salesperson about buyers' needs while framing these needs in a way that is aligned with the benefits provided by the company's offerings. The four questions defining the SPIN model and their purpose are illustrated in Figure 6 and outlined in more detail below.

Figure 6. The SPIN Model of Personal Selling

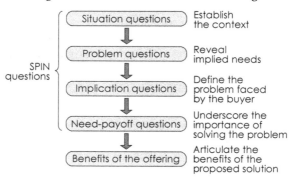

- *Situation questions* aim to establish background facts by collecting information about the customer's existing situation. They typically involve fact-finding questions about the type of equipment a company uses, the specific tasks for which this equipment is used, and the degree to which this equipment has been utilized. In cases when background information can be obtained by other means, such as conducting independent customer research, situation questions can be a relatively small part of the buyer–seller interaction.

- *Problem questions* aim to identify and explore problems, difficulties, and dissatisfactions that a customer faces. This type of question might focus on the degree to which customers are satisfied with their current equipment, the pros and cons customers experience in using the equipment, and whether this equipment meets customers' current and future needs. This step in the sales process also aims to prioritize problems based on their importance to the buyer and help the salesperson identify the focal problems. Asking problem questions is important because without knowing buyers' unmet needs and problems, the development of a meaningful value proposition is akin to a shot in the dark.

- *Implication questions* aim to make the buyer see the problem more clearly and feel it more acutely. This step in the sales process aims to identify the different dimensions of the problem and delineate the implications of not addressing it. Implication questions might focus on issues such as a decline in revenues, an increase in costs, and customer acquisition and retention. This type of question is particularly effective for tailoring the offering's value proposition to decision makers and top managers who might not be familiar with the specifics of the problem but might be concerned with its implications.

- *Need-payoff questions* aim to focus buyers' attention on the solution and its benefits. Unlike the implications questions, which focus on delineating the different aspects of the problem, need-payoff questions focus on the payoff from solving the problem. Need-payoff questions might focus on issues such as the importance of increasing revenues, lowering costs, and growing customer acquisition and retention. In this context, need-payoff questions aim to create a positive, constructive, and forward-focused decision environment that naturally lends itself to presenting the benefits of the company's offering.

A distinct characteristic of the SPIN model is that it focuses on identifying buyers' implicit needs and converting these implicit needs into explicit problems that buyers must address. Here, *implicit needs* reflect the motivation of a buyer who recognizes the existence of a problem and is unhappy with the status quo but has not yet made a decision to move forward and actively seek a solution to the problem. In contrast, *explicit needs* reflect the motivation of a buyer who not only recognizes the existence of a problem but has decided to abandon the status quo and move forward with searching for a solution to the identified problem. In this context, the SPIN model suggests that prior to describing the benefits of the offering, the salesperson should ensure that the buyer is in a problem-solving state of mind, meaning that the buyer has not only recognized the problem but also has realized its importance and is actively considering a solution.

Another important characteristic of the SPIN model is its focus on large sales. Such sales (often referred to as major sales) typically involve high-value goods, sophisticated buyers, purchase decisions made by multiple individuals, and an ongoing after-sale relationship between the buyer and the seller. In this context, the series of questions suggested by the SPIN model is particularly effective because of its focus on helping buyers identify unmet needs and realize the importance of fulfilling these needs while simultaneously providing them with the tools needed to persuade other members of the decision-making unit of the viability of purchasing the company's offering.

PART SIX

DELIVERING VALUE

INTRODUCTION

The new competition is not between what companies produce in their factories, but between what they add to their factory output in the form of packaging, services, advertising, customer advice, financing, delivery arrangements, warehousing, and other things that people value.

— Theodore Levitt, marketing educator

The value-delivery aspect of managing an offering defines the way in which the company's offering is delivered to target customers. The value-delivery process, commonly referred to as distribution, typically involves collaboration between a company and a set of channel partners — retailers, wholesalers, dealers, and distributors — for the purpose of delivering a company's offerings to its customers.

Managing distribution extends beyond simply identifying the places at which the company's offerings will be sold. It involves managing all aspects of the distribution process, including identifying distribution channel partners, managing the distribution logistics across all channel members, and developing an effective incentive system to ensure that the interests of all distribution channel members are aligned with the company goals.

Managing distribution can be viewed from two different perspectives — that of a producer of the goods being delivered to buyers and that of a retailer selling the producer's goods to customers. Despite their different roles in the value-creation process, manufacturers and retailers work together to create an effective and cost-efficient distribution channel that enables them to create customer value while capturing some of this value to achieve their own goals. The key aspects of the value-delivery process are discussed in Chapters 16 and 17. Specifically, the chapters included in this section address the following two topics: *managing distribution* and *retail management*.

- **Managing distribution channels** involves defining the ways in which a company delivers its offerings to target customers. The role of distribution in the value-creation process and the key aspects involved in managing distribution — designing distribution channels, managing channel relationships, and franchising — are discussed in Chapter 16.

- **Retail management** takes the perspective of a retailer and, in this context, outlines the ways in which a retailer can create value for its target market. The key trends in retail management and the main retail management decisions — developing the retail strategy and tactics; managing physical, online, and omnichannel retailing; and managing private labels — are discussed in Chapter 17.

The key to designing successful distribution channels is ensuring that they can deliver superior value to the relevant market entities — target customers, the company, and its collaborators. To this end, the activities of the different members of the distribution channel must be aligned in a way that optimizes the value created for these three entities. A systematic approach to developing and managing distribution is outlined in the following two chapters.

CHAPTER SIXTEEN

MANAGING DISTRIBUTION CHANNELS

*If you make a product good enough, even though you live in the depths of the forest,
the public will make a path to your door . . . But if you want the public
in sufficient numbers, you better construct a highway.*
— William Randolph Hearst, American newspaper publisher

Distribution channels deliver the company's offerings to its target customers. Managing distribution channels involves designing and streamlining the process of delivering a company's offering in a way that creates value for target customers, the company, and its collaborators. The key aspects of managing distribution channels are the focus of this chapter. Specifically, we address the following topics:

- *Distribution as a Value-Creation Process* || Distribution as a tool for creating market value | Distribution channel functions
- *Distribution Channel Design* || Defining the channel structure | Key considerations in channel design | Distribution coverage | Value added by the channel
- *Managing Channel Relationships* || Channel collaboration | Channel power | Channel conflicts | Channel dynamics
- *Franchising* || Franchising as a business model | The pros and cons of franchising

The discussion of distribution management is complemented by an overview of the relevant distribution concepts and just-in-time distribution.

Distribution as a Value-Creation Process

A company's distribution channel can involve three main types of entities: *merchants* such as retailers, wholesalers, dealers, and distributors that buy and resell the company's offering; *agents* such as brokers and sales representatives that help connect buyers and sellers; and *facilitators* such as transportation companies and banks that facilitate the exchange of goods and money between the company and its customers. Despite the differences in their functions, all three entities have a common purpose—to deliver manufacturers' offerings to their target customers in an effective and cost-efficient manner.

Creating market value by bringing manufacturers and customers together is at the heart of any distribution channel. The role of distribution channels as a tool for creating market value and the key channel functions are outlined in the following sections.

Distribution as a Tool for Creating Market Value

Distribution involves the channel(s) used to deliver an offering to a company's customers and collaborators. Working together with the other marketing tactics defining the offering—product, service, brand, price, incentives, and communication—distribution aims to create an optimal value proposition (OVP) for the relevant market entities: the company, its customers, and its collaborators (Figure 1). In this context, a manager's ultimate goal is to design distribution channels that create superior value for target customers in a way that benefits the company and its collaborators.

333

Figure 1. Distribution as a Tool for Creating Market Value

To effectively fulfill their value-delivery function, distribution channels must be aligned with the other attributes of the offering. Thus, an offering's distribution depends on its *product* and *service* attributes, such that novel, complex, and undifferentiated products often benefit from channels offering higher levels of sales support. Distribution must also be consistent with the offering's *brand*, such that lifestyle brands like Ralph Lauren, Lacoste, and Gucci benefit from using channels that enable them to exercise greater control to ensure a consistent brand image. Distribution also depends on *price*, with low-price, low-margin offerings typically associated with channels providing lower levels of service, and high-price, high-margin offerings typically associated with higher levels of service. The choice of a distribution channel also depends on the offering's *incentives*, such that incentive-rich offerings typically call for channels that offer frequent sales, whereas offerings that do not rely on incentives are a better fit with channels featuring everyday low pricing. Finally, the choice of a distribution channel depends on the channel's ability to effectively *communicate* the offering's benefits to target customers.

Because distribution is an integral aspect of the value-creation process, the choice of distribution channels depends on the market in which the company operates. Thus, distribution depends on the choice of target *customers*, with mass-market offerings more likely to involve multiple distributors across different geographic markets and niche offerings likely to involve a narrower distribution. The choice of a distribution channel also depends on the goals and resources of the *company*, such that a company seeking market dominance is likely to utilize diverse channels to achieve extensive coverage. An offering's distribution also reflects the balance of power between the company and its *collaborators*, whereby a company might select multiple distributors or open its own retail stores in order to minimize the power of any particular channel. The choice of a distribution channel is also a function of the *competition*, such that a company might seek channels in which its direct competitors are not present or, alternatively, seek channels in which it can compete head-to-head with similar offerings. Finally, distribution depends on the *context*; for example, customers in certain locations might favor smaller, individually operated retail outlets, whereas customers in other locations might favor consolidated superstore chains.

Distribution Channel Functions

The primary function of distribution channels is to deliver the company's offering to its target customers. This function involves delivering the company's product, service, brand, price, and incentives, as well as delivering information about different aspects of the offering. The role of distribution in the value-creation process and the different aspects of delivering the offering's value are outlined below.

- **Product delivery** involves transferring the physical possession and ownership rights of the product from the manufacturer to intermediaries (wholesalers, distributors, dealers, and retailers) and, ultimately, to end users. Functions such as transportation, inventorying, sorting, risk hedging, and handling returns can be allocated across different members of the distribution channel. For example, a manufacturer might choose to outsource most channel functions to a wholesaler and a retailer who can perform these tasks more effectively and cost efficiently. In the same vein, a retailer might choose to outsource some of the sorting and inventory functions to customers by selling in bulk and letting customers self-select the items they want to purchase.

- **Service delivery** involves customer-focused activities such as customization, repair, technical assistance, and warranty support, as well as collaborator-focused activities such as storage, inventory management, sorting, and repackaging. A company might choose to perform the service-related activities such as repairs, customization, and packaging, or, alternatively, it can delegate these functions to different members of the distribution channel.

- **Brand building** provides customers with an opportunity to experience the brand. For example, Apple, Disney, Hermès, and Harley-Davidson retail stores function as channels delivering these brands to their customers. Thus, a company can use its distribution channels as a means of communication to inform buyers about its brands while at the same time letting them experience the essence of these brands. To this end, many accessories, apparel, and cosmetics companies have allocated significant resources to build their brands at the point of purchase by setting up distinct "store-within-a-store" retail locations.

- **Collecting payments** involves collecting and processing payments from customers. Note that unlike other marketing tactics where the flow of items is from the company to its customers, in the case of pricing the flow is reversed: Payments are collected from customers and delivered to the company. In addition to collecting payments, channel members can set the prices at which the company's products and services are sold to customers.

- **Delivering incentives** involves distributing sales promotions such as coupons, rebates, and premiums to customers. A company has two basic options to deliver incentives: It can deliver them directly to target customers or delegate this function to channel members who are in direct contact with target customers. Thus, a manufacturer might adopt a pull strategy by creating and communicating the incentives directly to target customers to drive traffic to retailers that sell its products and services. Alternatively, the manufacturer can adopt a push strategy by offering promotional allowances to retailers who, in turn, develop sales promotions and "push" these promotions to target customers (see Chapter 13 for more detail).

- **Delivering information** involves keeping customers apprised of the different aspects of the company's offering by explaining the product and service benefits, communicating the meaning of its brand, and informing customers about the offering's price and incentives. The information-delivery function of distribution channels is an element of the company's overall communication activities, whereby distribution channels serve as a means of delivering the company's message to target customers.

Even though the primary function of the distribution channel is to deliver the company's offerings to target customers, its functions are not limited to delivering offerings that have already been designed by the company. Channel members also frequently participate in designing and communicating the offerings they deliver. For example, distribution channel members can help define the attributes of the offering, design financing and warranty services, craft the offering's brand, negotiate the sale price, develop point-of-purchase incentives, and shape the company's communication activities.

The flow of goods, services, and information is not always unidirectional. On some occasions the delivery process works in reverse. Thus, in addition to delivering the offering to target customers, distribution channels can process the return of unwanted goods, reusable materials (e.g., printer cartridges), and products and packages for recycling (e.g., beverage containers) and disposal (e.g., batteries). Distribution channels can also handle the reverse flow of payments as in the case of processing refunds, rebates, commissions, and rewards. In addition to managing the reverse flow of products and payments, distribution channels can also manage the information flow from customers to the company by soliciting and collecting customer feedback, suggestions, and complaints.

Distribution Channel Design

The process of designing and managing distribution channels involves several key decisions: *channel structure*, *distribution coverage*, and the *value added by the channel*. The main aspects of these decisions are outlined in the following sections.

Defining the Channel Structure

Channel structure defines the members of the distribution channel and the flow of goods and services from the manufacturer to customers. Based on their structure, channels can be *direct*, *indirect*, or *hybrid*. These three types of channels are depicted in Figure 2 and discussed in more detail below.

Figure 2. Distribution Channel Structure

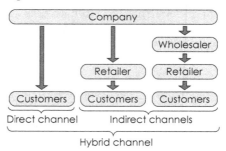

Direct Channels

Direct channels involve a distribution model in which the manufacturer and the end customer interact directly with each other without intermediaries. For example, Apple distributes many of its offerings directly to customers through its own online and brick-and-mortar retail outlets. In the same vein, many luxury brands such as Louis Vuitton, Gucci, Prada, and Hermès have established retail stores that they own and operate. Nestlé distributes its Nespresso coffee pods directly to consumers using its own online and physical retail stores.

When deciding whether to adopt a direct channel structure, a manager must keep in mind the different functions usually performed by the members of the distribution channel that the company would have to perform to create value for its target customers. Some managers erroneously believe that by moving from indirect to direct distribution channels—also referred to as disintermediation—a company can circumvent many of the functions traditionally performed by distribution channels.

Eliminating distribution channels does not eliminate the functions performed by these channels. For example, a manufacturer directly distributing its products has to assume all of the functions that are performed by the intermediaries in an indirect channel, including handling returns, managing service requests, offering financing, managing sales promotions, and informing customers about the specifics of its offerings. Failure to perform these functions can disrupt the company's ability to create market value. For example, eToys—one of the first online toy retailers—launched its operations without an established infrastructure for handling returns and was forced to store thousands of returned items in the hallways of its headquarters.

Thus, the question is not *whether* a particular channel function has to be performed, but *who* will perform this function. In this context, the decision to shift some of the channel functions upstream (to the manufacturer) or downstream (to the retailer and/or customers) is driven by determining who is best able to perform this function in an effective and cost-efficient manner.

Indirect Channels

Most companies do not sell their offerings directly to the public. Instead, they use intermediaries specialized in delivering the company's products and services to target customers.

Indirect channels involve a distribution model in which the manufacturer and the end customer interact with each other through intermediaries such as wholesalers, dealers, and retailers. For example, consumer goods companies like Procter & Gamble, Unilever, Coca-Cola, PepsiCo, Mondelēz, and Henkel use a variety of intermediaries ranging from small convenience stores to mega-retailers such as Walmart, Costco, Kroger, Tesco, and Carrefour.

An important decision in developing indirect distribution channels is deciding who should perform the different value-delivery functions. Allocating channel functions involves deciding on the ways in which the other key aspects of the company's offering—product, service, brand, price, incentives, and communication—will be delivered to target customers, and specifically, the roles that different entities—the company, intermediaries, and customers—will play in the value-delivery process.

Indirect channels can involve two types of coordination: contractual and implicit. *Contractual coordination* involves binding agreements among channel members, such as long-term distribution agreements, joint ventures, and franchise agreements. Distribution contracts specify the terms of the business interactions among the members of the distribution channel, including pricing, sales promotions, financing, returns, inventory levels, and delivery schedules. In contrast, *implicit coordination* is more informal and is based on established business practices rather than contractual agreements. The main benefit of implicit coordination is its flexibility. This flexibility, however, comes at the cost of the inability to predict the behavior of the channel members as well as their lower level of commitment, resulting in an unwillingness to invest resources to customize their operations to fit the needs of a particular manufacturer.

Hybrid Channels

Hybrid channels involve a distribution model in which the manufacturer and the end customer interact with each other through multiple channels, both directly and through intermediaries. In this case, a company distributes its offerings directly by taking and fulfilling customer orders while using a variety of indirect channels such as wholesalers, independent retailers, and retail chains. For example, in addition to directly interacting with customers, Apple relies on third-party distributors such as Best Buy, Walmart, and Target to bring its products to market.

Hybrid channels have numerous advantages that stem from combining the benefits of direct and indirect distribution. At the same time, hybrid channels are also subject to many of the disadvantages of both direct and indirect channels. An additional problem with using hybrid channels is the potential for channel conflict in cases when the direct and indirect channels compete for the same customers. Despite their disadvantages, hybrid channels are gaining popularity in markets where manufacturers can readily establish direct online distribution.

Key Considerations in Channel Design

One of the key decisions in defining the channel structure is whether to use intermediaries to reach target customers. The pros and cons of using intermediaries and the ways in which a company should decide on intermediaries are discussed in the following sections.

The Pros and Cons of Using Intermediaries

Collaborating with third parties to deliver a company's offerings to target customers has its advantages and drawbacks. Specifically, using indirect distribution channels offers several important *benefits* to manufacturers: *effectiveness, cost efficiency, flexibility, scale,* and *speed.*

- **Effectiveness.** Indirect distribution typically results in greater effectiveness of the value-delivery process because manufacturers benefit from the assets and competencies of intermediaries. Indeed, launching and managing a distribution channel requires resources that many manufacturers do not have. Because channel collaboration enables companies to take advantage of the expertise of others, it can provide channel members with a competitive advantage stemming from greater specialization.

- **Cost efficiency.** In addition to increasing the effectiveness of the value-delivery process, indirect distribution can also increase cost efficiency because each member of the distribution channel can achieve greater economies of scale and experience by specializing in a given function. Specialization might also encourage channel members to invest in new technologies that they would not invest in if they lacked a larger scale of operations.

- **Flexibility.** Relative to developing the necessary in-house distribution expertise, using intermediaries requires a lesser commitment of resources, thus offering much greater flexibility in terms of adopting new technologies, entering new markets, and exiting existing ones. For example, the development of a new distribution channel requires substantial resources and calls for a long-term commitment, whereas using an already existing distribution channel requires a smaller upfront investment and offers much greater flexibility.

- **Scale.** Compared to direct distribution, the use of intermediaries can ensure broad market coverage that enables a company to reach its target customers. Indeed, most companies lack the scale to develop a proprietary retail network to make its offerings available to all customers. As a result, by using intermediaries, a company can achieve greater market access than it could by using its own channels.

- **Speed.** Indirect distribution enables a company to achieve the desired results much faster than building in-house expertise. For example, a manufacturer can gain access to target markets virtually overnight using an existing distribution chain, whereas launching its own distribution channel, especially a brick-and-mortar one, would take considerably longer.

Despite their numerous benefits, indirect channels have several important *drawbacks* that include *loss of control, limited information, channel conflicts,* and *complex structure.*

- **Loss of control.** Delegating some of a company's activities to an intermediary often leads to loss of control over the selling environment. For example, relying on third parties to deliver its offering to customers greatly diminishes a company's ability to directly communicate with customers and present the offering in a way that draws customers' attention, underscores the offering's benefits, and nudges customers to buy the offering.

- **Limited information.** The use of indirect channels hinders a company's ability to monitor the performance of its offerings and optimize these offerings for the current market conditions. Thus, using intermediaries prevents manufacturers from having direct contact with customers and obtaining firsthand information about their needs and their reactions to the company's offerings.

- **Channel conflicts.** Indirect distribution brings the potential for vertical channel conflicts resulting from different strategic goals and profit-optimization strategies on the part of the company and its intermediaries. For example, a manufacturer might want the retailer to promote its offerings over those of the competition, whereas the retailer might find promoting competitors' offerings more beneficial. Different types of channel conflicts are discussed later in this chapter.

- **Complex structure.** Using multiple intermediaries can result in a complex channel structure that could complicate the management of these channels, leading to inefficiencies in the value-delivery process because of poor channel coordination. Furthermore, because manufacturers have to share the sales revenues with distribution channel partners, inefficiencies in the value-delivery process could lower manufacturers' profit margins.

As with most business decisions, deciding to use indirect distribution and enter into collaborative relationships with different channel members involves weighing the relevant benefits and costs. When the benefits from the collaboration outweigh the corresponding costs for both the producer and channel members, the collaboration is likely to be sustainable. In contrast, when the collaboration fails to create superior value for either party, the collaboration might be dissolved as the partners pursue alternative options such as finding new distribution partners or switching to direct distribution.

Defining the Optimal Channel Structure

Because different channel formats have their own pros and cons, the choice of a particular format ultimately depends on the strategic goals a company aims to achieve with its distribution channel. Thus, a company seeking to rapidly gain presence in diverse markets will be better served by using indirect channels, as these channels are likely to prove more effective and cost efficient. By doing so, however, a company should be willing to give up some of its ability to control the ways in which its offering is presented, sold, and delivered to its customers.

In contrast, a company that prioritizes the image of its offerings and the environment in which it is presented to customers is typically better served by establishing its own distribution channel, allowing the company to exercise greater control over the way in which customers interact with its offerings. As a result, many luxury, fashion, and lifestyle-brand companies end up developing their own retail outlets that they use not only to deliver the company's products to customers but also to build their brands. By choosing to dispense with intermediaries, these companies are willing to accept the higher upfront cost, narrower distribution coverage (in the case of physical stores), and lower levels of customer traffic (in the case of online stores) typically associated with manufacturer-operated retail outlets.

Distribution Coverage

In addition to determining the optimal channel structure, a company needs to decide on the number and type of outlets at which offerings are made available to target customers. In this context, there are three basic types of distribution coverage: *exclusive*, *selective*, and *intensive*.

- **Exclusive distribution** involves a limited number of intermediaries such that a company's offerings are available only in certain markets and only through a particular retailer or distributor. It is often used for specialized and high-end products and services requiring that the distributor have the relevant expertise to offer an experience consistent with customers' expectations and the image of the brand. Exclusive distribution often involves granting territorial rights for selling a company's offerings in exchange for distributors' commitment to these offerings. Exclusive distribution is common for automobiles, fashion, and high-end household appliances. For example, Ford, General Motors, and Chrysler have dedicated dealer networks authorized to sell and service their vehicles.

- **Selective distribution** involves a subset of all the available distribution channels. Selective distribution often uses channels that meet certain criteria such as geographic location, customer profile, level of service, product assortment (including the presence of competitive offerings), price tier, and reputation. For example, fashion companies such as Coach, Burberry, Dolce & Gabbana, and Michael Kors rely on selective distribution by working with high-end shopping malls located in upscale high-traffic areas that are frequented by their target customers.

- **Intensive distribution** involves a wide variety of outlets to ensure that an offering is readily accessible to a large proportion of customers in a given market. It is often used for offerings that target diverse customer segments across different purchase occasions. Intensive distribution is common for snacks, non-alcoholic beverages, and media products such as newspapers and magazines. For example, consumer goods companies such as Procter & Gamble, PepsiCo, Coca-Cola, and Kraft Heinz work with a wide variety of retailers across different geographic regions in order to bring their products to their diverse customer base.

A key advantage of exclusive distribution is the reliance on specialized channels that have the expertise and resources necessary to deliver superior customer value. In addition, exclusive distribution typically involves a relatively close collaboration between the different members of the distribution channel, which often results in a more effective and cost-efficient operation. These advantages, however, come at the cost of having relatively limited coverage and potentially limiting customers' access to the offering. As the distribution coverage increases, the company has to interact with a larger number of outlets that vary in resources and expertise, which, in turn, complicates channel coordination. Greater distribution coverage can also hinder the producer's ability to control channel members and ensure that their actions are aligned with the producer's goals. For example, the larger the coverage, the more difficult it is to ensure that retailers price and promote the offerings as intended by the company.

Value Added by the Channel

In addition to merely distributing a manufacturer's offerings, retailers can create customer value that extends beyond the value created by the products and services they deliver. Based on the incremental value they add, distribution channels comprise a spectrum of options, with value-added distribution channels at one end of the spectrum and streamlined distribution channels at the other.

Value-added distribution channels are defined by the relatively high marginal value they add to the company's offering. Value-added distribution channels can enhance the value of a company's offering by customizing the product to customer needs; offering additional services (e.g., delivery, installation, repair, and disposal); enhancing the offering's brand; informing buyers about the features and benefits of the offering; and providing greater convenience to customers by virtue of factors such as ease of shopping, hours of operation, location, and level of customer service within the store. Common examples of value-added channels are high-end department stores such as Neiman Marcus, Harrods, and Le Bon Marché.

Value-added channels tend to charge manufacturers higher margins for distributing their offerings to offset the cost of the resources required to provide the extra benefits to buyers. Because the value-added model is typically associated with higher retail prices, value-added distributors tend to generate lower sales volume compared to distributors offering fewer benefits at a lower price. As a result, most value-added distributors tend to operate using a high-margin/low-volume profit formula.

Note that the high margins that value-added distributors charge do not always mean that they also sell the company offerings at a higher price point. Indeed, rather than pass the costs of the value-added services to buyers, the company might choose to absorb these costs to keep prices uniform across different distribution channels. For example, Apple stores provide multiple value-added services without charging higher prices because in this case the cost of providing these services is partially built into the price of its products. In addition, Apple's stores serve as a means of informing customers about the company's offerings and creating a positive shopping experience, effectively directing some of the company's communication and brand-building budget into the distribution channel.

Streamlined distribution channels are characterized by the relatively low value they add to the company's offering. Streamlined retailers tend to perform only the most basic channel functions, making the company's products and services available to their target customers without investing extra effort to enhance the offering or to improve the overall shopping experience. Because streamlined channels do not require additional resources in order to provide a basic level of convenience and service to customers, these channels tend to charge manufacturers lower margins for distributing their offerings. Furthermore, because the streamlined model is typically associated with lower retail prices, streamlined retailers also tend to generate higher sales volume compared to value-added distributors. As a result, most streamlined distribution channels, such as Aldi, Carrefour, and Walmart, tend to operate using a low-margin/high-volume profit formula.

An extreme version of streamlined retailers are *fulfillment distributors* that do not perform any function other than distributing the company's offering. Fulfillment distributors act as a logistics arm of the manufacturer, helping the company deliver its offerings to its target customers without expending any effort to promote the offering or provide extensive customer service. Many wholesalers act as fulfillment distributors, providing a minimal level of service and charging a relatively low margin. Fulfillment distributors are somewhat similar in their operations to delivery service companies such as UPS, FedEx, and DHL. The key difference is that unlike shipping companies, which make money by charging delivery fees without being concerned about customer demand, fulfillment distributors are compensated based on sales and, hence, absorb the inventory risk of inaccurately estimating customer demand.

Most *mass-market channels* fall between the value-added and the streamlined distribution models, providing a moderate level of value-added services and collecting standard margins for providing these services. Many of these channels provide additional services—such as premier product placement, sales promotions, and communication campaigns—at an extra cost to the manufacturer, reflected in the various promotional allowances charged by the channel members. Because mass-market channels are able to offer both market reach and extended service options, they are commonly used by market leaders and companies that aim to expand their market reach by attracting new customer segments. For example, Procter & Gamble, Unilever, and Nestlé are working closely with Walmart, Costco, Tesco, Carrefour, and Kroger to ensure the availability of their offerings to their broad customer base.

Managing Channel Relationships

Because the company and members of its distribution channel often pursue different goals, their actions are often not perfectly aligned. As a result of this misalignment, channel relationships can spawn tensions arising from the different goals pursued by members of the distribution channel. Such tensions are often facilitated by the power imbalance of the channel members and frequently lead to explicit conflicts.

Channel Power

Channel power refers to the ability of one channel member to exert influence over another member of the same distribution channel. This influence often leads to an imbalance in the value exchange in favor of the more powerful entity. For example, a well-established manufacturer with a strong consumer brand is likely to receive preferential treatment from retailers, including premier shelf space, more favorable margins, discounts, allowances, and more flexible product-delivery schedules. In the same vein, large retailers often receive monetary and nonmonetary benefits from manufacturers, including preferential volume discounts, greater promotional allowances, and customized delivery schedules.

Channel power depends on a number of factors, including the *customer demand* for the offering, the *availability of alternative options*, and the *strategic importance* of the collaboration for each entity.

- **Customer demand.** Companies with differentiated offerings in high demand tend to have more channel power compared to companies with commoditized offerings. For example, manufacturers with strong brands such as Procter & Gamble, PepsiCo, Kraft Heinz, Unilever, and Nestlé have more power when dealing with their channel partners than companies with less powerful brands. In the same vein, high-traffic retailers such as Walmart, Carrefour, Amazon, and Aldi have more power when dealing with suppliers that have undifferentiated offerings.

- **Availability of alternative options.** A company is likely to have more power when there are fewer alternative options providing the same benefits. For example, companies like Walmart, Costco, Carrefour, and Tesco provide manufacturers with access to a broad customer base—a benefit that cannot be readily matched by many of their competitors.

- **Strategic importance.** A company tends to have more power when it accounts for a significant portion of a channel member's profits. As a result, larger entities—both manufacturers and retailers—tend to have more channel power than smaller ones.

For example, Walmart is in a position of power when negotiating with small manufacturers because their individual contribution to Walmart's net income is low, whereas Walmart accounts for a substantial part of their profits.

In the past several decades, power has been gradually shifting away from manufacturers that create the goods sold to distributors that control target customers' access to these goods. There are several reasons for this shift in channel power. First, the consolidation of retailers and the proliferation of smaller independent producers have significantly increased the role that channels play in a company's ability to create customer value. Furthermore, the increased availability of customer-generated product information such as product ratings and reviews, product popularity rankings, and the relative ease of identifying alternative options (e.g., similar products searched for or purchased by customers) have heightened the role of retailers as a key source of product-related information.

Heightened retailer power is further facilitated by retailers' increased ability to understand, engage, and maintain relationships with their customers. Because retailers typically are much closer to customers than manufacturers are, they are in a much better position to observe, interpret, predict, and influence buyers' behavior. The increased reliance on data analytics has enabled many retailers to link shoppers' profiles reflecting their prior activities to their in-store behavior, and use this information to direct them to offerings that are most likely to fit their current needs and preferences. The access to this information and the ability to influence buyers' behavior gives retailers the upper hand in negotiations with manufacturers, who might not be privy to the wealth of information collected by retailers and are often limited in their ability to independently influence target customers at the point of purchase.

Channel Conflicts

As with most business relationships, channel collaboration is not without conflicts. Channel conflicts are tensions among entities occupying different levels of the value-delivery chain. Tensions among channel partners are often caused by the differences in their strategic goals and profit-optimization strategies. Depending on the nature of the tension, there are two types of channel conflicts: *vertical* and *horizontal*.

- **Vertical channel conflict** involves tensions between entities within a given distribution channel. The most common type of vertical conflict is that between a manufacturer and a retailer. For example, vertical conflict might involve tensions regarding the size and composition of the manufacturer's product line carried by the retailer. The conflict here stems from the discrepancy between a manufacturer's desire that a retailer carry its entire product line and a retailer's desire to carry only the most profitable offerings from different manufacturers. Vertical conflict can also occur when one entity exercises its power to achieve its strategic goals to the detriment of its channel partner (e.g., the retailer raises product prices to maximize its own profits to the detriment of the manufacturer's profits).

- **Horizontal channel conflict** involves tensions among entities in multiple distribution channels (e.g., a manufacturer and two retailers). Horizontal conflicts occur when a manufacturer targets the same customers utilizing multiple distribution channels that operate with different cost structures and profit margins. For example, a manufacturer selling its products in high-margin, full-service stores and in high-volume, low-margin stores is likely to create channel conflict if the two retailers sell the same product at different prices to the same customers. Horizontal channel conflicts can also involve disagreements concerning the level of service and brand image provided by different outlets carrying offerings from the same producer. For example, a McDonald's franchisee that aims to delight its customers by offering superior service might be unhappy with a franchisee that tarnishes the image of all franchisees by offering inferior service. (This example might also involve a vertical conflict between the franchisee and the franchisor.)

Companies use diverse strategies for managing channel conflicts. A common approach for managing vertical channel conflict involves coordinating the assortment, pricing, and promotion of a company's offerings with the retailer in order to optimize the profitability of both the manufacturer and the retailer. In the same vein, a popular approach for managing horizontal channel conflict involves the development of channel-specific product variants that have minor differences in functionality and, therefore, cannot be directly compared. For example, Procter & Gamble might develop unique packaging for its laundry detergents for large retailers such as Walmart and Costco that is not available in other retail outlets. Mitigating the likelihood of vertical and horizontal channel conflicts is an essential aspect of developing a successful value-delivery strategy that benefits all members of the distribution channel.

Channel Dynamics

Once created, distribution channels do not stay static; they evolve over time. Changes in technology and market structure often lead to reallocation of the functions performed by the different channel members. For example, a manufacturer might decide to create its own direct distribution network, or a retailer might decide to start manufacturing the products it has been selling on behalf of a third party. To this end, a company might decide to insource the activities that were performed by collaborators by creating a new entity or by acquiring (or merging with) an existing entity.

Depending on the relative position of the entities in the value-delivery process, there are two types of channel integration: *vertical* and *horizontal*.

- **Vertical integration** typically involves the acquisition of an entity occupying a different level of the value-delivery chain. Depending on the relative position of the entities, there are two common types of vertical integration: forward and backward. Extending ownership upstream (toward suppliers) is referred to as backward integration, whereas extending ownership of activities downstream (toward buyers) is referred to as forward integration. For example, a retailer acquiring a manufacturer is a form of backward integration, whereas a manufacturer acquiring a retailer to establish its own distribution system is a form of forward integration.

  Vertical integration is favored by companies seeking to control the key aspects of the value-delivery process. For example, ExxonMobil engages in worldwide oil and gas exploration, production, supply, and transportation. Starbucks directly manages all aspects of its business, including sourcing, roasting, distributing, and overseeing how its coffee is served. American Express directly markets to customers, issues its cards, processes the payments through its own network, and directly acquires the merchant relationships. By consolidating the distinct aspects of the value-delivery process, these companies aim to create offerings that consistently deliver superior market value.

- **Horizontal integration** involves acquiring a business entity at the same level of the value-delivery chain. For example, a retailer acquiring another retailer or a manufacturer merging with another manufacturer constitutes horizontal integration. Horizontal integration might occur among entities with similar core competencies—a common scenario for companies seeking economies of scale through consolidation and for those seeking economies of scope through diversification.

  Horizontal integration is favored by companies for a variety of reasons, including gaining access to new markets, acquiring the rights to proprietary technology or research, reducing the competition in strategically important markets, and gaining power over the other entities in the value-delivery chain. For example, Amazon's acquisition of Whole Foods helped the online retailer establish a physical footprint in the grocery market as well as gather information about the food-buying patterns and preferences of many of its own customers.

Franchising

Rather than manage its own distribution channels, a company might decide to delegate distribution and some of its operations to third parties in order to rapidly scale up its customer base, revenues, and profits. The most common way in which a company can let others use its business model and distribute its offerings is through franchising. The key aspects of franchising as a business model and the pros and cons of franchising are discussed in more detail in the following sections.

Franchising as a Business Model

Franchising offers another party access to the resources needed to operate a business with an already established business model. The franchise grants an entity the right to produce, promote, and distribute a company's products, services, and brands within a certain territory. These franchises are separate entities that have their own goals, resources, and financials. Franchisees own the business they operate, benefit from the profits, and assume the losses generated by the business. In return for the rights to distribute the franchisor's offerings, use its intellectual property, and have access to additional resources, franchisees offer monetary compensation to the franchising company.

The franchising model is used by companies in a broad range of industries. For example, in the fast-food service industry popular franchises include McDonald's, Subway, Dunkin' Donuts, Arby's, Denny's, Pizza Hut, Taco Bell, and KFC. Popular hospitality franchises include Hilton, Howard Johnson, Accor, Choice Hotels, Crowne Plaza, Hyatt, Marriott, Westin, Sheraton, Wyndham, and Motel 6. The franchise model is also popular among retailers and includes names such as GAP, The Body Shop, Benetton, ACE Hardware, and GNC. Popular franchises in the service space include Jiffy Lube, H&R Block, uBreakiFix, FASTSIGNS, The UPS Store, RE/MAX, Great Clips, Supercuts, Planet Fitness, The Maids, Pearle Vision, and Two Men and a Truck.

Under the franchise model, franchisors specify the products, services, and brands to be offered; grant intellectual property rights to these products, services, and brands; and offer logistical, financial, and marketing support for the franchisee operations. The franchisee acquires the right to use the identity of the franchisor when interacting with its customers, who, in turn, believe that they are interacting with a subsidiary of the franchisor's company.

To become a franchisee, a company agrees to follow a set of rules laid out by the franchisor that aim to ensure consistent functionality, presentation, and delivery of the franchisor's goods. In addition, the franchisee agrees to pay an upfront one-time franchise fee as well as an ongoing royalty fee (often determined as a percentage of the sales revenues). Franchisees are also responsible for acquiring the equipment necessary to operate the business as well as for securing the financing (although buying into an established franchise might facilitate access to capital).

The franchisor provides the franchisee with information about the business model, an operating manual, employee training, administrative support, and general assistance in setting up the business. In addition, the franchisor can help franchisees procure raw materials and supplies at a lower cost, which in turn, helps franchisees offer their goods at competitive prices. The franchisor also invests in improving its products and services as well in building, enhancing, and protecting the brand. By doing so, the franchisor helps streamline the franchisee operations, reduce the risk of failure, and ensure consistency across the products, services, and the brand image created by different franchisees.

The success of a franchise depends on the viability of its business model, which, in turn, hinges on the franchisees' ability to ensure consistency of the offering across all locations. Indeed, because all franchisees use the franchisor's brand, customers — even if they are aware that different stores might be franchised — expect the same experience across all outlets. This, in fact, is the main purpose of using a single brand — to assure customers that the offerings associated with this brand conform to certain levels of performance.

When deciding to franchise its operations, a company might choose not to franchise all of its operations. Instead, it might have a dual-distribution system whereby some of the outlets are directly managed by the company while others are given to franchisees. For example, some of the largest franchisors such as McDonald's, Pizza Hut, and Papa John's also operate their own stores.

There are several reasons why a company might decide to diversify its distribution channel by having franchises while also maintaining its own locations. First, managing its own stores enables the company to fine-tune operations, taking into account the geographic location, specific customer preferences, and the competitive landscape. This fine-tuned model of operations—which can include factors such as product assortment, hours of operation, procurement, and inventory management—can be transferred to the franchises operating in similar business environments. Furthermore, the company stores can be used to test and introduce new products and services in a way that gives the company maximum flexibility and control of the different aspects of these products and the selling environment. Once perfected, these products and services are then implemented by franchisees. Finally, a company can use its own stores to enter a new market to prove a business opportunity exists in this market for potential franchisees, and at the same time introduce the franchise brand to customers in that market.

An important aspect of the franchise business model is territorial exclusivity that enables the franchisee to operate in a well-defined territory without having to compete for the same customers with other franchisees. In addition to minimizing the competition among franchisees, this territorial exclusivity allows the franchisor to control the density and the specific locations of the individual franchisees to achieve the optimal distribution coverage without cannibalizing its own sales. The same logic applies in cases when, in addition to franchising, the franchisor operates its own stores. In this case, the franchisor typically keeps some territories for itself to prevent channel conflict with its franchisees.

The franchising business model is similar to licensing in that in both cases one entity (the franchisor or the licensor) provides another entity (the franchisee or the licensee) with the right to use its intellectual property. At the same time, franchising often goes beyond licensing to provide the franchisee with a complete operating system that includes administrative and logistical support, training, and access to proprietary resources. In addition, unlike licensing, franchising typically involves a well-defined business model within a particular industry. For example, McDonald's franchises fast-food restaurants, Sheraton operates in the hospitality industry, and RE/MAX is focused on real estate. In contrast, licensing often involves arrangements across industries and business models. For example, Lacoste licenses its name (and its green crocodile logo) across the globe for use on a variety of products that include apparel, shoes, sunglasses, luggage, and cosmetics. In the same vein, the Walt Disney Company licenses its characters, including—Mickey Mouse, Snow White, and Cinderella—for use across a broad range of products and services.

The Pros and Cons of Franchising

Franchising offers multiple benefits to both franchisors and franchisees, a fact that explains the popularity of the franchising business model across a variety of industries. At the same time, not every business is suitable to be franchised. To determine whether to franchise its business, a company must understand the pros and cons of franchising and make a sound judgment based on the value franchising can create for the company and its franchisees.

Pros and Cons for Franchisors

Franchising offers several important *benefits* to franchisors. It generates incremental revenues for the company by scaling up its business model. Because granting a franchise involves minimal costs on the part of the company, the greater distribution coverage usually translates into incremental profits for the franchisor. Franchising can also strengthen the franchisor's brand by increasing its visibility across different purchase and usage occasions. For example, franchising helps McDonald's sustain top-of-mind awareness of its brands by increasing the instances when customers are confronted with the brand.

Another important benefit of franchising is that it enables the franchisor to focus its efforts on developing new offerings, streamlining operations, building the brand, and expanding the business without having to manage day-to-day operations of each individual location. The ability to scale up the business also enables the franchise to benefit from economies of scale in a number of areas such as sourcing raw materials, securing production and transportation logistics support, and advertising.

Despite its numerous benefits, franchising has a number of important *drawbacks* for franchisors. In fact, these drawbacks are one of the reasons why some companies like Starbucks, Chipotle Mexican Grill, and In-N-Out Burger have made the strategic decision not to franchise their operations. The most significant drawback of franchising is the loss of direct control over the operations of the individual locations. For example, franchisors are often unable to control the prices set by franchisees and, hence, cannot ensure consistent pricing and sales promotions across different locations.

Another drawback is the potential for damage to the franchise's brand image because the company has a decreased ability to ensure meaningful and consistent brand positioning. Indeed, franchising grants a third party the right to use a brand without the franchisor being able to ensure that the brand always will be displayed in a way that is consistent with the desired brand image. To address this concern and ensure brand integrity, many franchisors have developed strict guidelines regulating the use of their brands while at the same time monitoring that franchisees adhere to these guidelines. The franchisor's brand can also be damaged by the actions of its franchisees, which could provide subpar products, deliver inferior service, employ misleading advertising, and behave unethically with customers and business partners.

Another downside of franchising is the high cost of terminating franchise contracts if the company decides to exit a particular distribution channel, close certain locations, or insource its operations. In such scenarios, the company pays the franchisees termination fees or buys out their operations; both of these options can involve significant expense on the part of the company.

Pros and Cons for Franchisees

In addition to creating value for the franchisor, franchising offers important *benefits for franchisees*. Perhaps the most important benefit for franchisees is that they are buying into a proven business model rather than having to develop a new business by means of trial and error. The reliance on an established set of resources and processes enables franchisees to dramatically reduce the risk of failure compared to starting an independent business enterprise. Entering into a franchising agreement also enables a franchisee to obtain the benefits of the franchisor's brand without having to invest the time, money, and other resources needed to create its own brand. Thus, a franchisee can outsource the branding function by leveraging the franchisor's brand assets and brand-building competency.

In addition to gaining almost instant recognition through use of the franchisor's brand, franchisees can benefit from the efficiencies of scale associated with procuring supplies and raw materials required for operating the business. Entering into an agreement with an established franchisor with a proven business model can also increase the reputation and the credibility of the franchisee's company and facilitate interactions with its business partners— suppliers, distributors, and financial institutions. This, in turn, can help franchisees gain access to entities that might otherwise be unwilling to collaborate with them.

Despite the numerous benefits for franchisees, franchising also has a number of important *drawbacks*. The most obvious of these drawbacks are the fees that the franchisees must pay for the right to use the franchisor's business model. The franchising fees—which depend on the profitability of the operations, the scale of the business, and the strength of the brand— can be substantial for successful franchises. Another important drawback is the forgone opportunity for the franchisee to establish its own independent business, build its own brand, and develop competency in designing, launching, and sustaining a new business. By creating its own brand and operating procedures, a company can build a successful business that it could potentially franchise to others.

In addition, in some cases the goals and profit-optimization strategies of the franchisor and the franchisee might be misaligned, leading to conflicts about issues such as managing product quality, customer service, pricing, sales promotions, investing in renovations, and purchasing new equipment. For example, the franchisor might want franchisees to invest in new equipment to improve the customer experience and better align it with the brand promise, whereas the franchisee, who must bear the expenses associated with the installation of the new equipment, might be fully content with the current equipment.

SUMMARY

Distribution involves collaboration between a company and a set of channel partners—retailers, wholesalers, dealers, and distributors—for the purpose of delivering a company's offerings to target customers. When designing distribution channels, a manager's ultimate goal is to create value for target customers in a way that benefits the company and its collaborators. Channels create market value by delivering the different aspects of the company's offering to target customers: They deliver the company's products and services, enhance the offering's brand, collect payments, distribute and process incentives, and communicate the offerings' benefits to buyers.

Channel structure defines the members of the distribution channel and the flow of goods and services from the manufacturer to customers. Based on their structure, channels can be direct, indirect, or hybrid. *Channel format* defines the distribution coverage and the value added by distribution channels. Channel coverage reflects the number of outlets at which offerings are made available to target customers. Channel coverage can be exclusive, selective, and intensive. Channel value added reflects the marginal benefits created by the members of a company's distribution network. Based on the value they add, channels comprise a spectrum of options, with value-added distribution channels at one end of the spectrum and streamlined distribution channels at the other.

Like any collaboration, partnering with other entities for the purpose of distributing a company's offerings has both pros and cons. The key *benefits* of collaboration include greater effectiveness, cost efficiency, flexibility, and quicker time to market; the *drawbacks* include a loss of control, loss of competencies, and the possibility of strengthening the competition.

Channel power refers to the ability of one channel member to exert influence over another member of the same distribution channel. This influence often leads to an imbalance in the value exchange in favor of the more powerful entity, which frequently benefits from higher margins, discounts, and allowances; preferential access to scarce resources; premier shelf space; and more favorable product-delivery schedules.

Channel conflict describes tensions among channel members, often caused by differences in their goals. Distribution channels face two common types of channel conflicts: vertical conflicts, which involve different levels of the same channel (e.g., a manufacturer and a retailer), and horizontal conflicts, which involve entities within the same channel level (e.g., two retailers).

Once created, distribution channels evolve. A common form of *channel dynamics* is channel integration, whereby a company insources the activities that were performed by collaborators. Depending on the relative position of the entities in the value-delivery process, there are two types of channel integration: vertical integration, which involves the acquisition of an entity occupying a different level of the value-delivery chain, and horizontal integration, which involves acquiring a business entity at the same level of the value-delivery chain.

Franchising offers another party access to the resources needed to operate a business with an already established business model. The franchise grants an entity the right to produce, promote, and distribute a company's products, services, and brands within a certain territory. Franchisees own the business they operate, benefit from the profits, and assume the losses generated by the business.

Franchising offers multiple *benefits* to franchisors. It generates incremental revenues for the company by scaling up its business model. Franchising can also strengthen the brand of the franchise by increasing its visibility across different purchase and usage occasions. The ability to scale up the business also enables the franchise to benefit from economies of scale in a number of areas such as sourcing raw materials, securing production and transportation logistics support, and advertising.

Franchising also has important *drawbacks* for franchisors such as the loss of direct control over the operations of the individual locations, the potential damage to the franchise's brand image because of decreased ability to ensure meaningful and consistent brand positioning, and the high cost of terminating franchise contracts if the company decides to exit a particular distribution channel, close certain locations, or insource its operations.

MARKETING INSIGHT: RELEVANT DISTRIBUTION CONCEPTS

All-Commodity Volume (ACV): A measure of an offering's availability, typically calculated as the total annual volume of the company's offering in a given geographic area relative to the total sales volume of the retailers in that geographic area across all product categories.

$$ACV = \frac{\text{Total sales of stores carrying the company's offering}}{\text{Total sales of all stores}}$$

Broker: Business entity that serves the function of bringing buyers and sellers together by establishing initial contacts and facilitating negotiations. Brokers are typically specialists within a particular industry, such as real estate brokers, insurance brokers, and food brokers. Brokers are typically paid a commission (usually a percentage of the selling price) by the entity hiring them.

Channel Captain: A member of the distribution channel that, by virtue of its power, is able to coordinate the activities of the other channel members. A channel captain can be a manufacturer such as Procter & Gamble and Unilever, a wholesaler such as Alibaba and W. W. Grainger, or a retailer such as Amazon and Walmart.

Detailers: Indirect salesforce promoting pharmaceuticals to doctors and pharmacists so that they recommend the brand to the consumer.

Drop Shipping: Distribution method in which the product ordered in a store is shipped directly from the manufacturer to the customer (instead of the manufacturer shipping it to the retailer who then delivers it to the buyer).

Forward Buying: Increasing the channel inventory, usually to take advantage of a manufacturer's promotion or in anticipation of price increases.

Grey Market: A market in which products are sold through unauthorized channels.

Merchandisers: Indirect salesforce that offers support to retailers for in-store activities such as shelf location, pricing, and compliance with special programs.

Parallel Importing: The practice of importing products from a country in which the price is lower to a country in which the same product is priced higher. A hypothetical example of this practice is importing drugs from Canada to the United States. In most cases, parallel importing is illegal in the United States.

Reverse Logistics: The process of reclaiming recyclable and reusable materials and returns for repair, remanufacturing, or disposal.

Share of Shelf Space: Shelf space allocated to a given offering relative to the total shelf space in a given geographic area.

Supply Chain Management: The design, planning, execution, control, and monitoring of the supply-side aspect of the process of creating market value. Supply chain management includes procurement of the raw materials, managing inventory, and streamlining the flow of goods and services for the purpose of creating an effective and cost-efficient value exchange.

MARKETING INSIGHT: MANAGING JUST-IN-TIME DISTRIBUTION

Just-in-time distribution is a supply-chain management system that involves minimal inventory and aligns product orders from suppliers with customer demand. Thus, just-in-time distribution means carrying an inventory that includes only what is needed, when it is needed, and in the amount needed. It involves receiving goods from suppliers as they are required, rather than keeping a large inventory on hand. In this context, just-in-time distribution can be contrasted with "just-in-case" distribution, in which retailers maintain large inventories to ensure product availability in case of spikes in demand or a disruption in the supply system.

The just-in-time approach is not unique to distribution channels: It is also common in manufacturing. This approach to supply-chain management is a key component in the philosophy of lean manufacturing, which is focused on optimizing production efficiency. For example, to efficiently assemble automobiles, which can consist of approximately 30,000 parts, car manufacturers such as Toyota operate with very low inventories of parts. Instead, Toyota relies on its supply chain for timely delivery of the parts it needs to build cars, thereby reducing costs, eliminating inconsistencies, and increasing productivity.[1] The just-in-time approach in retailing is very similar, with the key difference that instead of optimizing the supply chain to meet the needs of the production process, the focus is on anticipating customer demand and only getting the product in front of buyers right when they need it.

The just-in-time approach has several advantages over the traditional approach to distribution, which involves carrying large inventories:

- *Smaller store footprint.* Just-in-time inventory management enables retailers to reduce the footprint of their outlets by reducing the amount of space devoted to storing products—a benefit particularly valuable in densely populated urban areas where retail real estate is limited and costly. For example, in Japan many urban retailers operate on the just-in-time principle, receiving inventory multiple times a day. This approach lets retailers use the entire store footprint by limiting the warehouse and storage space and reducing the shelf space assigned to each SKU, which in turn allows them to have greater product variety.

- *Reduced inventory costs.* Carrying less on-hand inventory decreases the investment necessary to acquire this inventory, freeing up company resources for other activities. In this context, lowering inventory costs can be particularly beneficial for small companies that might not have the resources to acquire and maintain large inventories. In addition, lower levels of inventory associated with the just-in-time approach involve less risk of inventory becoming obsolete due to a shift in customer tastes, being damaged from storage-related accidents, and deteriorating or becoming spoiled while in storage.

- *Agility.* Just-in-time distribution makes it easier to respond to emerging customer needs. This agility can give a retailer who has faster access to more varied inventory a significant advantage over competitors that carry much larger inventories and are unable to speedily adjust their assortments to customer needs. This agility not only allows the just-in-time approach to help reduce costs by minimizing the likelihood of inventory obsolescence but can also increase revenues by enhancing retailers' ability to provide buyers with offerings that best reflect their immediate needs. For example, the success of fast-fashion apparel retailer Zara is largely due to its agility. It needs just one week to develop a new product and place it in stores, compared to the industry average of three to six months.

Despite its popularity, the just-in-time approach has several important disadvantages, including:

- *Vulnerability to disruptions in the supply chain.* The just-in-time inventory approach requires a high degree of trust and coordination between the different members of the distribution channel. The leaner and more efficient the just-in-time inventory management, the greater the consequences from channel disruption. In addition to suppliers failing to fulfill their obligations to the other members of the channel, just-in-time distribution is vulnerable to disruptions such as natural disasters and disruptions in the transportation network (e.g., due to information system failures or labor disputes) that are beyond the control of channel members.

- *Vulnerability to fluctuations in demand.* A key assumption in just-in-time distribution is the ability of companies to forecast the demand for their offerings. While predictable spikes in demand, such as those occurring during seasonal sales, enable retailers to ensure they have a higher quantity of particular items on hand, unexpected spikes in customer demand put retailers at risk of running out of stock. For example, the demand for food staples tends to spike exponentially ahead of major natural disasters such as hurricanes, tsunami, and snowstorms, when store shelves can be emptied within hours. This issue is especially relevant for countries such as Japan, South Korea, and Singapore, where many urban retailers carry minimal inventory on hand.

- *Increased distribution costs.* Because retailers relying on just-in-time distribution purchase goods in smaller quantities, they often end up paying higher prices compared to retailers that purchase larger quantities and store the items in their own warehouses. In the same vein, just-in-time inventory management also leads to higher delivery costs compared to retailers able to carry larger inventories. Thus, some of the savings a retailer might receive from having a smaller store footprint and reduced inventory costs are offset by the higher costs of acquiring and delivering the goods it sells.

- *High level of channel coordination.* To be effective, just-in-time inventory management mandates a high degree of coordination among channel members, which often requires companies to make investments in technology that links the information systems of the retailer with its suppliers, reorganize operations and logistical support, and sometimes even redesign the manufacturing process so that they can ensure the seamless delivery of goods. In addition, because of its complexity, the implementation of just-in-time inventory management involves a steep learning curve for all entities involved in the process.

Many of the disadvantages of just-in-time distribution can be tempered by proactive management that aims to minimize the negative consequences of potential supply-system disruptions. Such proactive management focuses on three key components. The first component involves the use of data analytics to better forecast customer demand and streamline the flow of goods between manufacturers and members of the distribution channel. The second aspect of effective just-in-time management involves ensuring better coordination by aligning the incentives of the different channel members and implementing information systems that enable real-time monitoring of the supply levels across all channel members. Finally, just-in-time management can benefit from ensuring supply-chain redundancies — that is, distribution contingencies in case of disruptions in the main distribution network. These redundancies include sourcing from different vendors, using alternative modes of transportation, and even keeping limited inventories of best-selling items on site. Although built-in contingencies reduce the efficiency of day-to-day operations, they can increase the long-term efficiency of the just-in-time distribution approach by minimizing the negative impact of supply-chain disruptions.

CHAPTER SEVENTEEN

RETAIL MANAGEMENT

To open a shop is easy, to keep it open is an art.
—Chinese proverb

A retailer is a business enterprise engaged in the selling of products and services to consumers. Building on the discussion in the previous chapter, which took the perspective of the manufacturer aiming to design the optimal distribution channel for its offerings, this chapter takes the perspective of a retailer and examines the key decisions a retailer must make in order to successfully serve its target market. Specifically, this chapter addresses the following topics:

- *Key Trends in Retail Management*
- *Developing the Retail Strategy* || Selecting the target market | Developing the value proposition | Retailing as a value-creation process
- *Developing the Retail Tactics* || Defining the product policy | Outlining the service policy | Building the retailer's brand | Setting the price and incentives policy
- *Managing Physical, Online, and Omnichannel Retailing* || Managing physical retailers | Managing online retailers | Omnichannel retailing
- *Managing Private Labels* || The essence of private labels | Private labels as a means of creating retailer value | Managing private-label portfolios

The discussion of retail management is complemented by an in-depth overview of two additional topics: the popular retail formats and managing the price image of a retailer.

Key Trends in Retail Management

Over the past several decades, the retail industry has undergone a number of significant changes driven by changes in buyer preferences and shopping behavior, an intensified competitive environment, and developments in the domain of technology and information services. Some of the key changes involve the *consolidation* of distribution channels, the increase in *retailer power*, the growth of *private labels*, the ubiquity of *omnichannel retailing*, the emergence of *new retail formats*, the increased focus on *speed* and *convenience* among both shoppers and retailers, the growth of *mobile shopping*, the increased reliance on *customer insight* to deliver market value, and the growing sophistication of *retail logistics*. These changes are depicted in Figure 1 and outlined below.

Figure 1. Key Trends in Retail Management

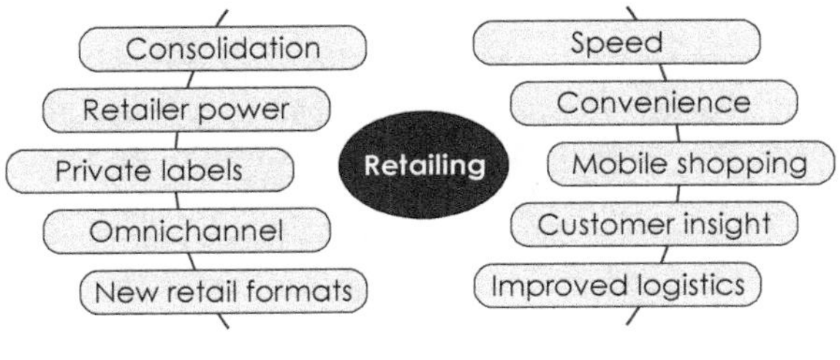

- **Consolidation.** One of the most important retail trends is the consolidation of fragmented retail outlets into powerful retail chains and superstores. In addition to creating large-scale mass merchandisers such as Amazon and Walmart, this consolidation has produced a number of specialized retailers concentrating on a single category such as home repairs (Home Depot), electronics (Best Buy), and pet supplies (PetSmart). By virtue of their massive buying power, superior market insights, and efficient and cost-effective logistics, these concentrated retailers crowd out smaller retailers that lack the scale to successfully compete for a share of customers' wallets.

- **Retailer power.** In addition to crowding out smaller merchants, retail consolidation contributes to the shift in the power balance between manufacturers and retailers. Historically, large manufacturers such as Procter & Gamble, General Mills, Nestlé, and Unilever were able to reap certain benefits from the imbalance of power when operating in a market comprised of small, unrelated retailers. Because these large manufacturers formed buyers' preferences and drove customer demand, retailers had little choice but to carry these products on manufacturers' terms. Retail consolidation has helped to dramatically change the nature of the relationship between manufacturers and retailers, giving much more power to retailers, many of whom have gained the upper hand in forming buyers' preferences and driving customer demand.

- **Private labels.** Another important trend in retailing involves the growth of private labels. As retailers become more concentrated and gain customer traffic, trust, and loyalty, they also become less dependent on carrying established brands. Not only do these brands tend to have lower profit margins for retailers, they also make it more difficult for retailers to meaningfully differentiate their offerings from one another. Indeed, if retailers carry the same set of brands, they are likely to end up competing on price. In this context, having their own store brands provides retailers with the option to differentiate their assortment while building customer loyalty.

- **Omnichannel retailing.** Another important trend is that online retailers have gained ground on traditional brick-and-mortar stores. In fact, in many markets online shopping has become the norm rather than the exception. As a result, a growing number of retailers have adopted a multi-channel approach, with brick-and-mortar stores adding online outlets to their operations. In addition, to better compete with brick-and-mortar stores, online retailers are seeking to add a physical footprint to their distribution network. This shift toward omnichannel selling has important implications for retailers not only in terms of establishing a physical and online presence but also ensuring seamless integration between these channels so that they complement rather than compete with each other.

- **New retail formats.** The consolidation and specialization of retailers and the growth of omnichannel retailing has resulted in the emergence of novel retail business models aimed at accommodating the complex and dynamic nature of the retail environment. For example, an increasing number of retailers focus on augmenting their core functionality with auxiliary offerings such as travel services, life insurance, and fitness club memberships to maximize the value they can create for and capture from their customers. Another popular format involves pop-up stores—temporary retail outlets typically located in high-traffic areas designed to promote the retailer and its offerings. In the same vein, many startup and established restaurants use food trucks to build and expand their business without having to invest in developing a permanent physical location.

- **Speed.** The development of new technologies and the availability of more effective and cost-efficient logistics solutions have introduced speed as another dimension on which retailers can compete with one another. Companies like Amazon have pushed the envelope by promising virtually instant delivery on frequently purchased items in many metropolitan areas. The availability of such rapid delivery has shifted customer expectations toward presuming almost instant gratification when making a purchase.

- **Convenience.** The growth of online retailing has helped change consumers' buying experience and reshape their expectations when shopping at brick-and-mortar stores. Indeed, the online environment enables retailers to make the process of locating specific items, placing the order, making a payment, providing delivery instructions, re-ordering routinely purchased items, and even processing returns much less effortful for the buyer. Accustomed to the convenience of online shopping exemplified by companies like Amazon, Zappos, and Jet.com, customers have begun to expect the same level of convenience from brick-and-mortar retailers, pushing them toward redesigning their business models to accommodate buyers' appetite for convenience.

- **Mobile shopping.** The ubiquity of online connectivity has fundamentally changed the nature of the shopping experience, with mobile devices playing a key role in shaping the decision of what, where, and when to buy. One consequence of this trend toward mobile shopping is that it enables a retailer to identify and geolocate potential buyers and custom-tailor offerings based on consumers' prior browsing and purchase history, as well as their proximity to its store or even their current location within the store. The relatively small screen of most mobile devices increases the importance of the assortment of options presented to shoppers, underscoring the role of the retailer as a curator of the item selection within the buyer consideration set.

- **Customer insight.** Advancements in information technology, data processing, and artificial intelligence have dramatically changed retailers' ability not only to understand but also to predict buyer needs, preferences, and behavior. Empowered by customer insights, retailers are in a much better position to identify their target customers, select promotional incentives for offerings that are most likely to appeal to these customers, and deliver these incentives at times when they are most effective.

- **Enhanced logistics.** The changes in the dynamics of the delivery logistics, often attributed to the "Amazon effect," have resulted in the development of dynamic, fast, and integrated logistics solutions across different channels and platforms. Both retailers and logistics companies are coordinating their efforts to orchestrate the supply chain's flexibility, efficiency, speed, service, and cost efficiency. The advancements in technology have facilitated the development of end-to-end supply chains that offer a high degree of synchronization and collaboration, enabling faster and more accurate order fulfillment at a significantly lower cost.

These profound changes underscore the growing importance of retailers in creating market value. As retailers become more concentrated, gain market power, attain better insights into shopper needs and behaviors, and become more effective and cost efficient in their operations, they are dramatically changing the nature of the competitive landscape. In this context, understanding the value-creation process from a retailer's viewpoint and developing viable business models that create a sustainable value exchange is of utmost importance for retail management.

The business model and daily operations of retailers are guided by two types of decisions: strategic decisions that focus on the value these retailers want to create and capture in the market in which they operate, and tactical decisions that articulate product, service, brand, price, communication, and incentives policies. The key aspects of these decisions are addressed in the following sections.

Developing the Retail Strategy

The general framework for strategic analysis and management outlined in Chapter 2 applies to retail companies as well. A retailer's strategy is defined by two key decisions: Identifying the target customers whose needs this retailer aims to fulfill and developing a value proposition that will fulfill these needs better than the competition. These two aspects of developing a retailer's strategy are outlined in the following sections.

Selecting the Target Market

Selecting the target market involves selecting customers for whom the company will tailor its offering, choosing the key collaborators that will help the retailer create value for these customers, identifying the competitors who aim to create value for the same customers, and assessing the retailer's resources that will enable it to succeed in the chosen market.

- **Selecting target customers.** The choice of target customers is a key strategic decision that any retailer must make. Until it defines the customer needs it aims to fulfill, a retailer cannot make consistent decisions about product assortment, service level, pricing, sales promotions, and store location and design. The choice of target customers is fundamental to the company's operations and to a large degree, defines a retailer's business model.

  As is the case with any company—be it a manufacturer or a retailer—the choice of target customers involves making a tradeoff between the decision to serve some customers while ignoring others. In this context, a retailer's success is determined by its ability to understand the underlying customer needs it aims to fulfill and center its efforts on fulfilling that need. For example, Neiman Marcus and Tiffany focus on serving customers interested in luxury products and experiences, Home Depot and Lowe's serve customers interested in home improvement, Whole Foods and Wegmans cater to customers interested in organic and natural foods, Petco and PetSmart cater to customers with pets, and Advanced Auto Parts and AutoZone serve do-it-yourself car enthusiasts and auto repair shops.

- **Identifying the main competitors.** A retailer's main competitors are the other sellers that aim to fulfill the same needs of the same target customers. The other entities that a retailer has to compete with is determined by the retailer's choice of target customers. Thus, the retailer does not directly choose its competitors. Instead, the choice of competitors directly follows from a retailer's selection of target customers. To ensure that it creates superior customer value relative to its competitors, a retailer must be able to clearly identify the other sellers with whom it will compete, assess their strengths and weaknesses, and determine the areas in which it can serve its customers better than the competition.

- **Choosing the key collaborators.** Because collaborators aim to facilitate the company's efforts to create customer value, the choice of target customers also narrows down the set of collaborators the retailer can work with to serve these customers. The most common type of collaborators in the retail space are the producers of the goods and services sold by the retailer; the upstream members of the distribution channels such as wholesalers, distributors, and logistics companies; and the companies providing various support functions such as market research companies, firms offering information technology solutions, and communication agencies that inform the public about the retailer's initiatives. The main principle in choosing partner entities is that their relationship with the retailer is mutually beneficial, enabling the retailer to create superior value for target customers in a way that benefits both the retailer and its collaborators.

- **Evaluating the retailer's resources.** To ensure market success, a retailer must have the resources—core competencies and strategic assets—that will enable this retailer and its collaborators to create greater value for target customers than the competition. For example, a retailer that aims to serve customers interested in luxury products and experiences can benefit from being able to procure high-quality offerings and provide exceptional customer service, having a strong brand associated with luxury and status, being in a prestige location, and providing lavish store ambiance. Because customer needs and competitive offerings tend to evolve over time, a company must constantly assess its competitive position and invest in building the resources needed to prevent its falling behind the competition.

Retailers' choice of a target market is reflected in the types of products and services they offer, the prices at which they sell these products and services, and the ways in which they promote their offerings. In the case of brick-and-mortar retailers, the choice of target customers is also reflected in the selection of the physical location of their stores, hours of operation, and store ambiance. Thus, the choice of target customers determines the retailer's value proposition for these customers, which, in turn, guides all tactical decisions involved in managing day-to-day operations.

Developing the Value Proposition

The value proposition defines the benefits and costs associated with a retailer's offerings. To succeed, a retailer's offerings must create superior value for the three key entities: target customers, the retailer (the company), and its collaborators.

Developing the Customer Value Proposition

The basic principles of developing a meaningful customer value proposition outlined in Chapter 7 apply to retailers as well. Thus, depending on the customer needs it aims to fulfill, a retailer can create value across three domains: functional, psychological, and monetary.

- **Functional value** reflects the benefits and costs directly related to a retailer's performance. Attributes that create functional value include the size of the retailer's assortment, hours of operation, the speed of processing and delivering orders, the overall convenience of the shopping process, the availability of product-related information and advice, the ease of processing returns, and the level of customer service. The functional value is particularly important for customers who prioritize utilitarian benefits such as the ability to locate and purchase the desired items with a minimal amount of time and effort.

- **Psychological value** reflects the psychological benefits and costs associated with the retailers' offerings. Psychological value goes beyond the functional benefits of the offering to create emotional, self-expressive, and societal benefits. For example, customers might value the emotional benefits associated with shopping such as the enjoyment derived from browsing new fashion styles; the self-expressive benefits and social status conveyed by shopping at a high-end retailer; and the societal benefits stemming from the retailer's environmentally friendly activities, community support, and charitable giving. The psychological value is particularly relevant for customers who prioritize emotional, self-expressive, and societal benefits provided by the shopping experience.

- **Monetary value** reflects the monetary benefits and costs associated with the retailers' offerings. Attributes that create monetary value include retailers' prices, discounts, and rebates, as well as the various fees associated with delivery and installation of the purchased items. Even though monetary value is typically associated with costs, a retailer can also provide monetary benefits such as cash-back offers, bonuses, cash prizes, and low-interest financing. Monetary value is particularly important for shoppers who face financial constraints as well as those who place relatively low value on the functional and psychological benefits provided by retailers.

Even though they represent different dimensions of customer value, these domains are not mutually exclusive. A retailer can strive to provide benefits along all three dimensions. The development of a meaningful value proposition often requires prioritizing some of these dimensions over others. For example, providing greater functional and psychological benefits can also lead to increased channel costs and higher retail prices. The recent developments in technology have enabled some retailers to increase the functionality and personalization of their services while offering competitive prices. To excel on all three dimensions of value, however, is not trivial. It requires a fairly large scale of operations and a significant investment in research and development and operational infrastructure that is beyond the reach of most small retailers.

Developing the Retailer Value Proposition

To ensure a sustainable value exchange, a retailer's business model should aim not only to create value for target customers but also to capture some of this value for its stakeholders.

As with most companies, the value captured by a retailer can be defined along two dimensions: monetary and strategic.

- **Monetary value** is the most common type of value sought by retailers. Monetary value reflects the impact of the retailer's activities on its financial performance. Retailers derive monetary value from the difference between the purchase and the selling price of the goods they carry. An additional source of monetary value are the allowances retailers receive from manufacturers in exchange for various services such as promoting their offerings, providing prime shelf space, and maintaining a larger inventory to prevent stock-outs.

- **Strategic value** involves nonmonetary benefits and costs that are of strategic importance to the retailer. For example, a retailer might place value on activities such as gaining market share, building a strong brand, creating a strong corporate culture, and engaging in socially responsible activities. Although these activities might eventually benefit the retailer's financial performance, they typically do not result in immediate monetary gain.

For most retailers, creating monetary value is of primary importance. Monetary value is typically assessed using metrics such as net income, profit margins, and sales revenue. In addition to the traditional means of measuring a company's overall financial performance, a popular metric for measuring retailers' performance is same-store sales. This metric focuses on sales in stores that have been open for a year or more and have historical data that allows comparison of the current year's sales to the previous year's sales. Same-store sales have become a commonly used metric because it takes store closings and chain expansions out of the mix, indicating the portion of new sales that resulted from sales growth and the portion that resulted from the opening or closing of stores.

Developing the Collaborator Value Proposition

In addition to creating value for target customers and its stakeholders, a retailer must create value for its collaborators, particularly its vendors. Indeed, given that a retailer's primary function is to sell and distribute goods produced by vendors, its ability to secure products and services that are sought by consumers is paramount. As is the case with the value proposition for the retailer, the value proposition for its collaborators comprises two components: monetary and strategic.

- **Monetary value** is the primary source of value sought by the producers of goods sold by retailers. Retailers create monetary value for these producers by sharing the revenues received from selling their goods to consumers. While receiving a portion of the sales revenues, producers typically have to share some of these revenues with the retailers as well as pay various fees and allowances for services rendered by retailers that aim to facilitate the sale of the producers' goods.

- **Strategic value** reflects the nonmonetary benefits and costs that are of strategic importance to the producer. For example, in addition to receiving a stream of revenues, a producer might derive value from increasing the visibility of its brand, growing its market share, and gaining access to strategically important customers. In addition to providing these benefits, retailers also perform a variety of services for producers such as inventory management, logistical support, and the gathering of consumer insights.

The collaboration between a retailer and the producer of the goods sold by this retailer is marked by the fact that they share the same ultimate customer—the shopper that will purchase the producer's good from the retailer. In this context, the retailer creates value for the producer in two ways—by sharing the sales revenues with the producer and by working with the producer to create value for their customers. For example, retailers might assume some of the customer management activities such as providing sales and service support, handling returns, and distributing and redeeming coupons and promotional offers.

Retailing as a Value-Creation Process

The ultimate goal of retailing is to create value for the retailer, its customers, and collaborators. To this end, the retailer must craft a value proposition that creates value for all three entities. This optimal value proposition represents a balance between the functional, psychological, and monetary value created by the retailer for its customers and the monetary and strategic value created by the retailer for its collaborators and stakeholders.

To become a reality, the retailer value proposition must be translated into a set of actionable decisions. To this end, a retailer's value proposition serves as a beacon that guides its tactical decisions, including defining its product and service policy, brand-building activities, pricing, sales promotions, communication, and distribution. These decisions and their relationship to the retailer's optimal value proposition (OVP) for its customers, collaborators, and stakeholders is illustrated in Figure 2.

Figure 2. Retailing as a Value-Creation Process

To successfully execute its strategy and create market value, a retailer must ensure that all of its tactical decisions are aligned with the value it aims to create for its customers, collaborators, and stakeholders. The specific approaches to managing the tactical aspects of a retailer's business model are discussed in more detail in the following sections.

Developing the Retail Tactics

Tactics translate the overarching retail strategy into a set of specific decisions the retailer can act upon to create market value. The key aspects of retail tactics—defining the product and service policies, building the retail brand, and setting the price and promotion policies—are detailed below. The issues pertaining to communication and distribution in physical, online, and omnichannel retailing are discussed in the following section.

Defining the Product Policy

One of the most important tactical decisions a retailer has to make involves the selection of merchandise that it will offer to its customers. This decision involves defining the breadth and the depth of the product assortment carried by the retailer as well as deciding how to organize this assortment and manage product inventory.

Defining the Product Assortment

Selecting the merchandise to carry is of utmost importance to any retailer. Indeed, a retailer's ability to generate traffic is to a large degree a function of the product assortment carried by this retailer. Specifically, the selection of merchandise involves defining the breadth and the depth of the product assortment that the retailer offers its customers.

The *breadth* of the assortment refers to the number of different product categories offered by a particular retailer. Based on the breadth of their assortments, channels can be classified into one of two types: specialized or broad. Specialized retailers such as Foot Locker, Office Depot, and CarMax tend to carry a narrow assortment focusing on relatively few product categories. In contrast, mass retailers such as Walmart, Costco, and Carrefour tend to carry much broader assortments.

The *depth* of an assortment refers to the number of items a retailer carries within a given product category. Based on the depth of the assortment, channels can be classified as limited or extensive. Limited-assortment retailers such as 7-Eleven and Circle K carry a relatively small number of items within each category, whereas extensive-assortment retailers such as Home Depot, Best Buy, Staples, and PetSmart carry a large number of items in each category.

When selecting the merchandise, a retailer's goal is to ensure that the product assortment adequately reflects the needs of target customers. Carrying larger assortments increases retailers' costs and can have a negative impact on profitability in the absence of customer demand. In the same vein, carrying a relatively small assortment runs the risk of not being able to meet customer needs and cover the fixed costs involved in operating the retail outlet. The assortment decision is also influenced by the retailer's overall positioning, such that higher end retailers often offer a narrower range of options that have been curated to fit the needs of their customers. Thus, a retailer's ultimate goal is to select an assortment that reflects customer needs while minimizing the chance of allocating shelf space to products for which there is little or no demand.

The selection of items within each category is typically done by a manager whose job is to ensure that the variety of different products, sizes, and brands carried by the retailer reflects customer demand. Having a single manager for the entire category (rather than having managers that deal with multiple product categories from the same vendor) helps optimize the retailers' assortment by minimizing the possibility of having multiple offerings from different brands compete for a relatively small customer segment while not providing enough variety to address the needs of a much larger customer segment.

Once chosen, the product assortment carried by a retailer is dynamic and evolves over time based on customer demand. This raises the question of how a company should decide which merchandise to support and which to discontinue. One approach to realigning a retailer's portfolio with customer demand involves ranking the SKUs[1] of all products by key performance measures such as sales, gross margin, inventory turnover, and the gross margin return on inventory investment.

By analyzing the performance of its assortment, a retailer can better understand the incremental value that each offering is likely to add to its bottom line and realign its assortment accordingly. Consequently, the retailer can place more emphasis on the best-selling and most profitable items by increasing their inventory levels, advertising, and sales promotions. By the same token, the merchandise unlikely to contribute in a meaningful way to the retailer's bottom line can be disposed of in several ways, including returning it to vendors, marking it down for quick sale, moving it to outlets and clearance centers, selling it to off-price retailers, auctioning it, donating it to charity, or inventorying it for the next season.

It is important to note, however, that performance-based ranking of individual SKUs do not take into account synergies between different items and the fact that an item generating low profits might be essential to support the demand for some of the top-selling and/or most profitable items. For example, a retailer might decide to sell a high-demand item at cost (or even at a loss) in order to generate store traffic. Such items, commonly referred to as loss-leaders, are not profitable in themselves but are part of a retailer's profit formula; hence, their overall impact on a retailer's performance must be considered when designing the optimal product assortment.

Organizing the Assortment

In addition to deciding on the breadth and depth of the assortment, a retailer must decide how to organize the individual products within the chosen assortment. The product organization decision has two basic levels: defining the product categories by grouping the individual products and arranging these products within each category.

Defining product categories. A retailer can organize offerings into different categories using one of two general principles: based on product similarity or based on the goals consumers are aiming to achieve with different offerings. For example, category-based organization would involve grouping dairy products, cereal, canned goods, spices, and produce in separate sections throughout a grocery store. In contrast, goal-based organization might group milk, cereal, and certain fruits (such as bananas, strawberries, and blueberries) under the goal-derived category of breakfast meals; and group pasta, pasta sauce, and parmesan cheese under the goal-derived category of "dinner." In the same vein, a mass-merchandise retailer catering to customers who are new parents might group infant-related products including apparel, toddler toys, and bedding rather than spread them out across different departments.

Category-based product organization is by far the more popular because it has universal customer appeal and takes into account the fact that customers might use the same products to fulfill different needs and achieve different goals. Furthermore, in some cases, product organization is driven by logistical consideration such as product size and storage requirements (e.g., fresh milk must be kept in a refrigerated storage unit). At the same time, because of its relevance to customer needs, goal-derived organization is often used in cases when most customers are likely to act in a similar fashion. For example, products typically located at checkout counters — chocolates, chewing gum, newspapers, and novelty items — are selected based on their ability to generate an impulse purchase. Goal-derived organization is gaining ground in online retailing as companies increasingly use customer insights and predictive analytics to construct the optimal assortment based on each customer's goals and preferences.

The organization of a retailer's assortment into product-based or goal-derived categories is important because it can influence whether, what, and how much consumers buy. Thus, retailers can influence consumer decisions through *choice architecture* — a process of arranging the available options in a way that is likely to simplify consumer choices and increase the likelihood that consumers will find and purchase the products they need. For example, IKEA creates an elaborate browsing experience with products organized around consumer lifestyles and displayed in a way that they are likely to be arranged in their customers' homes. Such a layout enables buyers to experience different products and lifestyles; identify the one that best matches their needs and personalities; and visualize the way the furniture will look in their own living rooms, bedrooms, and kitchens.

As the product assortment and store layout become increasingly complex, retailers invest more effort in planning the organization of the items throughout the store. To this end, many retailers develop *planograms* — charts that reflect the configuration of products on the store shelves. The ultimate goal of planograms is to optimize the organization of the retailer's assortment in a way that enhances customers' experience and helps the retailer to achieve its goals.

Arranging products within a category. In addition to deciding how to locate different types of products (product categories), retailers must decide how to organize items within each category. Retailers often arrange products around vendors, brands, and product benefits. As the depth of the assortments carried by a retailer increases, managers find it more difficult to organize these items in a way that will both simplify consumer decisions and maximize sales. To this end, some retailers appoint one vendor, known as the *category captain*, to manage a particular category. For example, a retailer might use Coca-Cola to manage the non-alcoholic beverage (soda) category, Kellogg to manage breakfast foods, Hershey to manage candy, Wrigley to manage confectionery goods, Kraft Heinz to manage cheese, Frito-Lay to manage salty snacks, and E. & J. Gallo Winery to manage wine.

The rationale for outsourcing category management to an external entity (rather than doing it internally) is that the category captain — usually the market leader — is intimately familiar with customer needs and, hence, is in a better position to organize the assortment in a way that is optimal from a customer's perspective. In fact, the category captain not only can help retailers make decisions on how to organize products within the particular category but can also make merchandising recommendations for the category, including assortments, inventory, store layout, pricing, sales promotions, and communication. The downside of designating a vendor to manage the entire category is that the vendor could take advantage of its position and manage the category in a way that maximizes its own sales and profits to the detriment of its competitors (e.g., preventing other companies from gaining shelf space) and the retailer (e.g., carrying and promoting offerings that are most profitable for the manufacturer rather than the retailer).

Managing Inventory

To maximize sales revenues, a company should carry a very large inventory so it never runs out of any items and can instantly fill all customer orders. This approach, however, is not cost efficient, meaning that the expenses incurred in carrying a large inventory might exceed the marginal revenues generated by selling a few extra items. Thus, there is an optimal range of inventory that helps maximize retailers' profitability by balancing the associated incremental sales revenues and costs.

An important inventory decision involves determining the proportion of merchandise that is readily available to customers (e.g., placed on a retailer's shelves) and the merchandise to which customers do not have instant access. For example, some retailers like Costco and Sam's Club use a warehouse approach with all inventory readily accessible to customers. Other retailers function primarily as showrooms, with most of their inventory warehoused at a different location. Thus, many brick-and-mortar furniture and appliance retailers as well as most online retailers have limited, if any, inventory that is readily accessible to buyers, with items being delivered to buyers directly from the warehouse.

When deciding how much inventory to stock, retailers should consider the following key factors:

- **Space productivity** reflects the revenues generated per unit of retail space, such as per square foot for free-standing merchandise and per linear foot for merchandise displayed on shelves. In general, greater space productivity calls for higher levels of inventory.

- The **product impact on store revenues** reflects the synergies that exist between the sales of a particular item and the other items sold by the retailer. Thus, even though certain products in themselves are not major sources of revenue, they may nevertheless be important because they help drive store traffic and facilitate the sales of complementary high-revenue offerings. For example, milk is a strategically important product for supermarkets because it drives repeat store traffic.

- **Inventory turnover** reflects the number of times that inventory is replenished, typically calculated as the ratio of annual revenues generated by a given offering to average inventory. Inventory turnover can further influence the space-allocation decision, with high-turnover items often allocated more space. This is because high-turnover merchandise helps provide a quicker return on the inventory investment and typically requires greater inventory space to ensure against stock-outs.

- **Space allocation** is a function of the type of merchandise, such that certain types of merchandise—fashion, cosmetics, appliances, and produce—tend to require more space and special displays than many consumer packaged goods.

- **Perishability** of the items can have a direct impact on inventory. Perishable items such as food and fashion that have shorter longevity are more likely to have lower levels of inventory and need to be replenished more frequently.

To better manage inventory levels and minimize carrying costs, some retailers are adopting a *zero-inventory (just-in-time)* model, in which a company keeps very little or no inventory at hand, ordering exactly what it needs to sell and receiving it in a timely fashion. For example, many furniture retailers have virtually eliminated in-stock inventory and instead place an order with the manufacturer only after the customer has already made a purchase. In the same vein, some bookstores avoid carrying a large inventory of rarely purchased books by using a *print-on-demand (sell one, make one)* model, printing individual copies of the book once an order for the book has already been placed. The just-in-time model was discussed in more detail in Chapter 16.

Outlining the Service Policy

Another important decision involves defining the level and type of services a retailer will offer to its customers. With many retailers carrying the same products, the service aspect of retailing is becoming a key source of creating customer value. This decision involves factors such as product purchase and delivery, returns, payment and financing, warranties, and installation and repairs.

- **Product purchase and delivery.** An important decision that retailers must make involves determining the level of assistance they will offer to help shoppers locate the desired products, make the purchase, and arrange delivery to the desired location. Retailers vary in the way they approach these decisions. Many high-end retailers offer extensive sales support to help shoppers make the purchase, along with a variety of delivery options that let customers decide how and when they would like orders to be delivered. In contrast, other retailers offer minimal in-store sales support, primarily relying on customer self-service when it comes to locating the products of interest, making the purchase, and arranging delivery.

- **Returns.** Regardless of the quality of the products carried by the retailer and the level of sales support, returns are unavoidable. Therefore, to effectively manage customer satisfaction and the reverse logistics associated with product returns, a retailer must develop a clear policy and establish a set of procedures that delineate whether, when, and how shoppers can return purchased items. Depending on its business model, a retailer can set a relatively strict return policy with significant limitations, or it can offer a fairly liberal policy with substantial flexibility in terms of the ease of processing returns and the time frame within which purchased items can be returned. For example, clothing and outdoor recreation equipment retailers L.L. Bean and REI have long been known for their generous return policies that enable shoppers to return virtually any item regardless of the date of purchase. In the same vein, many high-margin fashion retailers including Nordstrom and Zappos have set return policies that prioritize customer satisfaction over the financial costs and the logistical complications associated with processing a large number of returns.

- **Payments and financing.** Another important decision involves payment formats and the availability of financing. Retailers vary in their payment and financing policies. Full-service retailers typically make a wide range of payment methods available to give shoppers more flexibility when making purchases, extending credit and accepting different forms of payment such as credit cards, personal checks, cash, and even bitcoins. Many high-volume, low-margin retailers, on the other hand, have limited payment options (e.g., cash-and-carry retailers do not offer credit accounts and require customers to pay cash for the goods they purchase). Note that some retailers might limit payment methods for strategic reasons. For example, some retailers do not accept cash payments in order to streamline transactions and ensure equitable allocation of high-demand items. To illustrate, to prevent customers from reselling the newly launched iPad, Apple restricted payment methods to credit and debit cards (the policy was later reversed, enabling customers to make purchases with cash).

- **Warranties.** Retailers must make two important warranty-related decisions: whether to assist customers in using manufacturers' warranties to cover product failures, repairs, and replacements, and whether to offer an extended warranty above and beyond that offered by the manufacturer. To enhance customers' experience and build trust, some retailers offer an extended return policy that effectively transfers the effort involved in repairing or replacing the product from the customer to the retailer. To further reduce customer risk, many retailers offer protection plans and repair services that provide shoppers with product protection that enhances or extends the coverage offered by the manufacturer. Such extended warranties are typically offered to customers for an additional cost, thus contributing to retailers' bottom line.

- **Installation and repairs.** Certain types of products such as new technology, furniture, appliances, and fitness equipment require initial installation upon purchase and might need repair over their life span. Accordingly, a retailer must decide whether to offer its customers installation and repair services for such products. This is important because ease of installation and maintenance can be a key selling point for buyers who have limited experience and resources to deal with these issues. By offering these services, a retailer can grow sales, increase customer satisfaction, and encourage repeat business. To this end, a number of retailers such as Amazon, Home Depot, and Lowe's partner with local service providers to offer installation and repair services to their customers.

Building the Retailer's Brand

Creating a strong brand is of utmost importance for retailers: It not only helps drive traffic but also frames consumers' overall experience with the retailer. Retail branding is conceptually similar to designing a manufacturer's brand in that it involves two key components: defining the *brand positioning*, which reflects the meaning that the retailer aims to associate with its brand, and defining the key *brand attributes* that capture the brand's positioning.

Developing a Meaningful Brand Positioning

Brand positioning is the process of creating a meaningful and distinct image of a retailer's brand in shoppers' minds. To create such an image, a retailer might position its brand based on three types of benefits: functional, psychological, and monetary.

- Positioning on **functional benefits** involves focusing on the functional value created by the retailer. For example, Amazon emphasizes the convenience and speed of the shopping experience, Nordstrom and Zappos emphasize their customer service, and Whole Foods emphasizes the quality of the items it sells.

- Positioning on **psychological benefits** emphasizes the emotional, self-expressive, and societal value created by the retailer. For example, shopping mall operators often underscore the fun, excitement, and enjoyment associated with visiting their retail locations. In addition to creating emotional benefits, retail brands can create self-expressive benefits by enabling individuals to express their individuality and socioeconomic status. For example, located on Rodeo Drive in Beverly Hills, Bijan, often described as "the world's most expensive store," provides its elite clientele with access to some of the most exquisite haute couture apparel, enabling them to showcase their taste and wealth.

- Positioning on **monetary benefits** aims to signal the overall level of prices associated with the retailer's products and services. For example, the Walmart brand mottos *Always Low Prices. Always* and *Save Money. Live Better* foster the belief that Walmart's products and services have the lowest prices in the market. The price image conveyed by a brand is particularly important for retailers because many shoppers are unaware of the market prices and often rely on the store's reputation to infer price attractiveness. The concept of price image and its antecedents and consequences are discussed in more detail at the end of this chapter.

Although retailers can create value on all three dimensions, brand positioning often calls for singling out a specific dimension (or in some cases two dimensions) with which a retailer would like its brand to be associated in shoppers' minds. Indeed, in most cases it is difficult for a retailer to credibly establish its superiority on all three dimensions. For example, a brand associated with monetary benefits such as affordable prices might not be credible in signaling wealth and social status. Successful brand positioning requires a clear focus on benefits that are backed up by this retailer's resources and capabilities.

Designing Brand Attributes

To effectively convey its brand positioning to target customers, a retailer must decide on the specific attributes defining its brand. Brand attributes can be divided into two categories: brand identifiers and brand referents.

- **Brand identifiers** are the brand elements that are developed, managed, and owned by the retailer. The key brand identifiers are the name, logo, motto, character, soundmark, store design, and packaging. For example, McDonald's value proposition is captured in its brand motto: *I'm Lovin' It*, Best Buy's motto posits *Expert Service. Unbeatable Price*, and Home Depot's motto reflects the brand's promise: *You Can Do It. We Can Help*. In addition, many retailers have adopted a unique color scheme to differentiate their brands: IKEA features the yellow and blue colors of the Swedish flag, Home Depot has adopted orange as its primary color, and BP gas stations and convenience stores are painted green. Even the packaging used to wrap the purchase can be an important attribute of a retailer's brand, as evinced by Tiffany's signature blue box crowned with a white ribbon.

- **Brand referents** play a somewhat different role in defining a retailer's brand. Unlike brand identifiers, which are owned and managed by the company, brand referents exist independently of the company and aim to enhance the value of the brand by "borrowing" the meaning associated with the referents. Simply put, brand referents are the different associations—customer needs, benefits, experiences, occasions, activities, places, people, concepts, objects, products, services, and other brands—that the retailer can connect with its brand to build a meaningful image in shoppers' minds. For example, Walmart uses referents such as caring, authentic, innovative, straightforward, and optimistic to define its brand personality.

Both types of brand attributes—identifiers and referents—play an important role in helping the retailer build its brand and share the brand narrative with its customers. The better articulated this narrative is, the greater the likelihood that the brand message will register in a meaningful way in shoppers' minds.

Setting the Price and Incentives Policy

Another important decision made by retailers involves setting their price and sales promotion policies. The strategic importance of these decisions cannot be overstated because they can have a direct impact both on customer demand and on the retailers' revenues and profits.

Managing Price and Incentives

When setting the price for a particular product or service, a retailer might pursue different goals. First, it might aim to maximize the profitability of each individual item by setting a price at which this item will make the greatest contribution to the retailer's bottom line. Alternatively, the retailer might focus on managing the prices of individual items in a way that maximizes its overall profitability. For example, a retailer might price a particular high-demand item at or even below cost to drive customer traffic to the store and make up the lost profit with the other items purchased by these customers (loss-leader pricing). A retailer's pricing of the individual items might also be driven by the desire to create a certain price image that reflects shoppers' impression of the overall level of prices in the store.

In addition to managing the price, retailers can modify the value of their offering by using incentives. Compared to price changes, incentives are more agile and can be frequently modified depending on customer demand, the available inventory, and the competitive environment. This agility makes incentives one of the most frequently used tools to stimulate customer demand, sell excess inventory, and respond to competitors' pricing and sales promotion activities.

Retailers typically offer two types of incentives: *pass-through incentives* that retailers distribute on behalf of manufacturers and *direct incentives* that are initiated and subsidized by the retailer. As retailers become more concentrated and gain power over manufacturers, most sales promotions offered at the retail level—price discounts, coupons, and rebates—tend to be pass-through incentives sponsored by manufacturers.

The most popular form of direct incentives, in addition to sales promotions, are *loyalty programs* offered by retailers. The popularity of these programs stems from their ability to create value both for shoppers and retailers. For shoppers, loyalty programs create value by offering usage-based discounts and bonus offers. For retailers, loyalty programs offer valuable insight into the needs and behavior of each individual customer, thus enabling retailers to optimize their operations and customize their offerings to better fit the needs of their customers. Loyalty programs are a key tool for gathering market insights and channeling promotional offers for many retailers including Target, Costco, and Nordstrom.

Everyday Low Pricing and High-Low Pricing

An important decision when setting a price policy involves the degree to which a retailer relies on sales promotions in order to drive traffic. In this context, there are two popular pricing approaches: Every Day Low Pricing and High-Low pricing. *Every Day Low Pricing*, or EDLP, is a pricing approach in which a retailer maintains low prices without running frequent price promotions. The concept of everyday low pricing has been most prominently associated with Walmart, which frequently uses it in its communication campaigns (Walmart's "price rollbacks" are longer term price reductions that are considered changes in price rather than sales promotions). *High-Low pricing*, or HiLo pricing, is a pricing approach in which a retailer's prices fluctuate frequently, typically a result of heavy reliance on sales promotions. Department stores such as Macy's, JCPenney, and Kohl's tend to use high-low pricing, offering heavily advertised sales promotions around major holidays as well as seasonal sales promotions to drive store traffic.

The EDLP approach has the benefit of eliminating uncertainty on the part of the customer concerning the timing of the purchase. Maintaining constant prices also benefits customers who need a given product or service instantly and do not have the time to wait for a future sale. From a company's standpoint, EDLP is beneficial because it can help smooth customer demand and at the same time reduce the monetary costs and logistical complexity associated with running constant sales and promotions.

The HiLo approach, on the other hand, has the benefit of generating sales, especially from price-sensitive and promotion-sensitive customers. Indeed, the low end of the range of prices in the HiLo approach is often lower than the EDLP price, creating greater monetary value for customers who are aware of the promotion and can time their purchases to take advantage of the low prices. In addition to offering lower prices, the HiLo approach can create further value for customers who derive emotional gratification from being "smart shoppers" and taking advantage of retailers' price promotions. Thus, the mere fact that an item is on sale can provide customers with a reason to buy the offering and create psychological value from taking advantage of the promotion.

Because of their pros and cons, EDLP and HiLo methods represent the two ends of a spectrum along which various pricing methods are located. Thus, some retailers use a combination of EDLP and HiLo pricing across different items in their assortment so that certain product categories rarely go on sale while others offer frequent deep discounts. In addition, rather than offering several deep discounts throughout the year on most merchandise, some retailers offer everyday sales promotions on a relatively small number of items, frequently rotating the promoted merchandise.

Along with determining the degree to which prices will vary over time, retailers can use a variety of tools to manage prices. First, a retailer might employ dynamic pricing that varies as a function of customer demand and available inventory—an approach common in the transportation and hospitality industries. Furthermore, rather than setting the same price for all shoppers, retailers can use price segmentation, offering different prices to different customers. The advancement of online retailing with its ability to tailor the offering to each individual buyer can facilitate the use of price segmentation and custom pricing on a larger scale. Another popular pricing tool involves the use of permanent price reductions (markdowns) that enable retailers to clear inventory to free up space for new items, dispose of perishable or seasonal items such as produce and fashion apparel, promote items in high demand, as well as respond to competitive actions by matching or undercutting competitors' prices.

Managing Physical, Online, and Omnichannel Retailing

Depending on the manner in which they interact with shoppers, retailers can be divided into three categories: physical retailers, online retailers, and omnichannel retailers. The key decisions involved in managing these three types of retailers are discussed in the following sections.

Managing Physical Retailers

Brick-and-mortar stores are the oldest form of trading and involve a direct interaction between buyers and sellers who are located in the same physical location. Typically, the display of goods, warehousing, and sales are located under the same roof, and customers can physically observe and experience the products they are interested in. The key decisions involved in managing brick-and-mortar retailing include selecting the retail location, designing the store layout, managing in-store communication, managing loss prevention, and dealing with showrooming.

Selecting the Retail Location

The popular adage that the three most important rules in real estate are *location, location, location* also applies to brick-and-mortar retailing. The choice of location can significantly influence the business model, including the type of customers frequenting the retail stores, the volume of customer traffic, and the type of products customers tend to purchase. Based on their location, the most popular retail formats include the following:

- **Free-standing stores** are stand-alone retailers that are not a part of a retail center and are not connected directly to other stores.

- **Shopping malls** contain a relatively large number of stores often located in the same building or architectural space and sharing common public areas. Shopping malls are frequently anchored by one or more department stores such as Macy's, Bloomingdale's, and JCPenney.

- **Shopping centers** involve a group of stores located in close proximity to one another but not necessarily sharing common areas. Shopping centers are often anchored by one or more big-box stores such as Walmart, Target, and Meijer. Smaller shopping centers (shopping strips) involve a cluster of relatively small stores such as a grocery, dry cleaner, and hair salon serving the needs of the local community.

- **Urban retailers** are attached to other physical structures—residential, business, or retail—and usually are located in high-traffic areas such as the central business district, shopping areas, and airports.

- **Store-within-a-store** retailers are located within a larger retailer. This retail format is used by fast-food establishments such as McDonald's, Burger King, and Starbucks, whose outlets can be found in larger stores. The store-within-a-store format is also often used by fashion brands such as Calvin Klein, Nautica, and Burberry to create a unique selling environment and convey their brand identity in department stores.

When choosing a retail location, a company must take into account a variety of factors including the demographics of local shoppers, local competition, cannibalization, and operating costs. Customer demographics are important because they determine the type of merchandise that customers are likely to seek, customers' ability and willingness to pay, as well as the overall population growth in the area. Competition plays an important role in choosing a retail location as well. The higher the density of competitors serving the same customers, the more challenging it is for a retailer to differentiate its offerings from those of the competition.

The choice of a retail location can also influence the degree to which a retailer can cannibalize its own sales. Thus, oversaturating a particular location can lead to cannibalization, with sales from a new store coming at the expense of sales in established stores. In addition, location can influence the costs of operating a store, including the real estate lease, insurance, and labor costs. Retailers' costs can also be influenced by their proximity to shipping and distribution facilities of major rail, ground, and air carriers such as BNSF (railway), Knight-Swift (commercial trucking), UPS and FedEx.

In addition to assessing the viability of a particular geographic area, retailers also must assess the attractiveness of different sites within that area. This is a more nuanced decision that is influenced by factors such as traffic flow, accessibility, adjacent tenants, and local restrictions. A high-traffic location helps increase the number of customers likely to enter the store and eventually make a purchase. Accessibility — the ease with which customers can get in and out of the retail location, proximity to major roads and public transportation, and ease of parking — can further help generate store traffic.

Another important consideration in choosing a specific retail location involves the adjacent businesses. In the ideal scenario, the adjacent businesses can help build traffic to the retail location without having a negative impact on the retailer's brand. For example, a Walmart can help drive traffic to nearby fast-food restaurants such as Burger King and Subway, but it might hurt the image of a higher end retailer such as Nordstrom, Neiman Marcus, or Tiffany. When choosing a retail location, a company must also consider the local regulations and restrictions concerning factors such as hours of operation, commercial delivery routes, and outdoor advertising.

Designing the Store Layout

When designing the layout of its outlets, a retailer aims to achieve multiple goals: increase the revenue generated by each customer during each shopping trip, build long-term customer loyalty, minimize costs involved in running the store (energy costs, shrinkage costs, and logistic and inventory costs), pursue socially responsible goals (conserve energy and water, reduce waste, recycle, and minimize the carbon footprint), and comply with legal regulations (fire safety codes, occupational safety and health standards, and disability requirements).

Based on their design, there are three popular store layouts: grid layout, racetrack (loop) layout, and free-flow layout. The *grid layout* is one of the most common supermarket layouts, featuring parallel aisles with merchandise located on both sides of the aisles. The grid layout is easy to navigate, functional, and cost efficient. The downside is that the grid layout is generic, making it more difficult for a retailer to establish an emotional connection with customers and differentiate its store from the competition. The grid layout also is less likely to engage customers' imagination in a way that encourages impulsive purchases inspired by customers' experience in the retail outlet. In addition, the middle aisles tend to be less trafficked since shoppers often go along the periphery of the store, glance down the aisles, and from time to time walk down certain aisles to pick up desired items.

The *racetrack layout* is more common for department stores. It features a wide aisle that loops around the store, guiding customer traffic around different departments, often with minor loops around the main aisle. Items likely to be purchased impulsively, such as cosmetics and accessories as well as many of the promoted items, are often located on both sides of the main aisle. The racetrack layout typically has multiple entrances, with the merchandise organized in a way that appeals to customers regardless of their entry point. The racetrack layout offers ample options for product display and, thus, enhances the experiential aspects of the shopping trip and stimulates spontaneous purchases. It also produces a relatively predictable traffic pattern that facilitates the placement of product displays and promotional items. At the same time, the racetrack layout makes it more effortful for customers who know what they are looking for to locate a particular item. As a result, the racetrack design is not ideal for product categories in which consumers have established shopping habits and might not appreciate the opportunity to examine and experience the retailer's other offerings.

The *free-flow layout* allows maximum flexibility and is easily changed and updated. The free-flow format is most frequently used to promote browsing, create an experiential retail space that encourages shoppers to interact with the store offerings, and incite impulse purchases. Because of its open design, the free-flowing format is often used by boutiques and upscale retailers who focus on creating a unique store experience rather than on emphasizing the sheer number of items available. One of the most important drawbacks of the free-flow retail format is that it makes it more difficult for customers to find the items they are looking for. The free-flow format can also be more difficult to implement due to the lack of a specific template and a set of specific guidelines to follow.

Managing In-Store Communication

Another important component of managing physical stores involves in-store communication designed to inform shoppers about specific products, advertise sales promotions, and encourage spontaneous purchases. Popular in-store communication formats include signage, product displays, and in-store advertisements.

Signage aims to point out the location of the merchandise within the store, provide product information, and promote certain items. Signage can also help enhance the retailer's ambiance and reinforce its brand image. Signage can be static, as in the case of printed displays, or dynamic, as in the case of digital screens that can vary the display content based on the day of the week, time of day, weather, store traffic, and product inventory.

Product displays aim to promote specific merchandise by prominently featuring it, usually in high-traffic locations. Common types of product displays include store windows, freestanding displays located throughout the store, vertical displays mounted on store walls, and end caps located at the end of aisles in stores with grid layouts. Product displays can also include live demonstrations that allow customers to try or experience products.

In-store advertisements aim to introduce new products, nudge customers toward a particular product, encourage impulse purchases, as well as relay information about sales promotions and special events. Common in-store advertising formats include digital displays, radio programming, floor graphics, overhead messaging, and messages posted on shopping carts and checkout counter dividers. Another popular form of advertisements are in-store newsletters and flyers that feature sales promotions, new offerings, and store events. Some stores also use in-store beacons to connect with shoppers through their mobile devices and send product information and incentives to buyers based on their location.

Loss Prevention

In addition to selecting the retail location, designing the store layout, and managing in-store communication, a retailer must consider a loss prevention program to protect its merchandise. The term *shrinkage* is commonly used by retailers to describe inventory loss due to logistical errors, inaccurate recordkeeping, and theft of goods by customers and employees. Losses due to shrinkage can amount to billions of dollars, ranging from 2% of the total sales revenues for products such as office supplies to as high as 30% for specialty apparel.[2] Given the ubiquity and high costs of shrinkage, the development of a loss prevention program to reduce shrinkage can have a meaningful impact on the company's bottom line.

Shoplifting is one of the primary causes of shrinkage. Most frequently shoplifted merchandise includes small-size, high-value items such as shaving cartridges, cigarettes, cosmetics, and fashion items. Shrinkage is facilitated by the existence of secondary markets such as eBay, Alibaba, and Amazon at which the stolen merchandise can be sold. The ability to easily resell illegally acquired merchandise propels the growth of theft by both employees and professional shoplifters.

When managing loss prevention, retailers face a tradeoff between providing buyers with greater convenience, a more attractive store ambiance, and an overall more pleasant shopping experience, on the one hand, and protecting their merchandise, on the other. The advancement of technology has made it easier to observe shoppers' behavior in the store. One popular approach involves tracking the merchandise by embedding RFID (*radio-frequency identification*) tags that transmit identifying information and ensure the accuracy of the prices at which the merchandise is sold. Despite these advancements, however, some shrinkage is unavoidable, and retailers often view shrinkage as a cost of doing business and request a shrinkage allowance from manufacturers.

Dealing with Showrooming

The term *showrooming* refers to a pattern of behavior whereby shoppers visit physical stores primarily to learn more about products they are interested in and then end up buying these products from a different retailer, typically to obtain them at a lower price. Although often associated with customers of online retailers, showrooming is not limited to purchases made online rather than from a brick-and-mortar store. Showrooming is really about the arbitrage between high-service/high-price retailers and those offering lower levels of service at lower prices. Showrooming buyers are trying to get the best of both worlds: full-service experience and sales support at a low price.

In addition to allowing customers to take advantage of the available sales support, showrooming enables customers to physically examine the products they are interested in. Thus, showrooming helps buyers overcome one of the important disadvantages of online shopping—the uncertainty associated with the physical look and feel of the products. For example, a customer interested in purchasing a new television set might visit a store to compare the available options side by side, ask the salesperson for additional information and advice, then pull out a mobile device and buy the desired option online. Clearly, this pattern of behavior hurts the bottom lines of brick-and-mortar stores while benefiting online-only retailers that have the advantage of lower overhead, inventory, and salesforce costs.

To combat showrooming, some retailers such as Best Buy and Target have introduced a price-match guarantee, promising to match the prices of major online retailers. Other retailers have launched their own online stores featuring prices that are competitive with those of online retailers. Perhaps the most drastic response to the showrooming phenomenon is that of Best Buy, which revamped its entire business model in a way that encourages rather than dissuades showrooming. Specifically, Best Buy began charging companies for displaying their products at its physical stores, effectively turning their stores into showrooms. This approach was welcomed by companies such as Microsoft, Samsung, Apple, Dell, and HP, which sought to expand their physical footprint and saw the option to have a store-within-a-store presence in Best Buy as an effective and cost-efficient way to achieve this goal. In addition to offering distinct retail space, Best Buy also provides companies with dedicated employees trained to assist customers with questions particular to each company's products. Adjusting its business model to embrace showrooming enabled Best Buy to secure an additional stream of revenue to offset the loss of sales due to customers making purchases from lower priced online retailers.

Managing Online Retailers

Online retailing has seen remarkable growth in the past decade as consumers become more comfortable with online shopping and as the online buying experience and delivery have continued to improve. Online retailers cover a broad range of distribution outlets, from mass-merchandisers such as Amazon and Jet.com to boutiques such as purveyor of prescription eyeglasses and sunglasses Warby Parker and upscale fashion retailer Net-a-Porter.

The business model of online retailing is based on separating the display, inventory, and delivery functions that are typically combined in brick-and-mortar stores. Thus, the display and informational function is performed by the retailer's website; the inventory is typically managed in a separate warehouse located in areas with low rent, low labor costs, and easy access to means of transportation; and the delivery is outsourced to third parties such as shipping, commercial trucking, and logistics companies.

The ubiquity of online retailing can be attributed to its many advantages over brick-and-mortar retailing. Online retailers have a relatively *low-cost structure* because of lower overhead, labor, and inventory costs, as well as greater efficiency of operations due to scale and automation. The *scalability* of online retailing facilitates growth and expansion without the need to relocate physical operations. Because they are in a better position to track and capture shoppers' behavior, online retailers often have a better *understanding* of the purchasing habits of their individual customers. This customer insight also makes it easier for online retailers to *customize* the selection of goods offered to each individual customer based on that customer's personal preferences. Online retailers can facilitate shopper decisions by sharing the *ratings* and experiences provided by other shoppers. Finally, online retailers can greatly improve the *convenience* of shopping by streamlining the processes of ordering, reordering, delivery, and returns.

Despite its multiple advantages, online retailing has important drawbacks. The most obvious drawback is customers' limited ability to experience the products they intend to purchase. This limitation is more important for products such as apparel, accessories, and cosmetics, where preferences are defined by idiosyncratic tastes and shoppers are less likely to rely on the opinions of others. To combat this issue, some online retailers such as Amazon, Warby Parker, and Zappos have streamlined the process of returning purchased goods, absorbing most or all of the costs associated with handling returns and offering generous return policies. In addition, in most cases (with the exception of digital products and services) customers cannot immediately receive the purchased item as they can in a brick-and-mortar store.

Another drawback of online retailing involves the virtual nature of consumers' shopping experience which makes it more difficult for online retailers to differentiate themselves from their brick-and-mortar competitors. Indeed, some of the key factors used by brick-and-mortar retailers to differentiate their offerings — location, store ambiance, and customer service — are less prominent in an online environment. An additional challenge faced by online retailers involves privacy concerns as an increasing number of consumers are becoming apprehensive about the use of the data collected by online retailers.

Omnichannel Retailing

Omnichannel retailing aims to leverage the benefits of both online and offline channels by providing a convenient and engaging experience for shoppers. To this end, omnichannel retailers couple the broad selection, rich product information, and customer ratings and reviews offered by online stores with the personal service, the ability to see and experience products, and the on-hand product availability offered by physical stores. The ultimate goal of the omnichannel model is to provide a seamless shopping experience across different types of outlets in a way that creates superior customer value and helps retailers stay competitive while increasing their bottom line.

Most retailers adopt the omnichannel model by following one of two routes. The most common route involves already established brick-and-mortar retailers such as Walmart, Macy's, JCPenney, and Home Depot launching online stores and encouraging customers to move some of their shopping activities online. The alternative approach involves online retailers such as Amazon, Warby Parker, and Bonobos expanding their presence to include physical locations. These two routes — offline to online and online to offline — vary in terms of the goals retailers aim to achieve and the strategies they adopt to achieve these goals.

Brick-and-mortar retailers seek to establish an online footprint for a variety of reasons. The initial impetus for going online was to combat the competition from online-only retailers such as Amazon, whose low-cost structure and ability to offer a more convenient shopping experience were gaining ground on brick-and-mortar retailers. In this context, the initial omnichannel strategy was to encourage shopping across different types of retail outlets so that customers who shopped only in physical stores would begin also buying online. Over time, many of these retailers realized that, in addition to serving as a competitive defense tool, the omnichannel approach could improve the customer experience across both channels, thus helping retailers grow sales revenues and profits.

Online retailers seek to establish a physical presence for many of the same reasons brick-and-mortar retailers seek to move online: to enhance the shopping experience and gain ground on the competition. By going offline, online retailers aim to take advantage of some of the key benefits of physical stores such as personal service, the ability to touch and feel products, and the option to instantly obtain the desired products. In addition, unlike online shopping, which tends to be goal oriented and transactional, physical retailers are often able to offer a more meaningful in-store shopping experience. For example, Apple launched brick-and-mortar retail stores to augment its online operations in order to provide an optimal environment for shoppers to interact with its products, learn about new product features, as well as experience Apple's brand.

Omnichannel retailing goes beyond just having a physical and digital presence. It also reflects a retailer's ability to deliver a seamless, effortless, and consistent customer experience across all online and offline touch points in a way that creates superior value for both customers and the retailer. For example, a customer might gather information about the product from the retailer's website; visit the store to see, touch, and feel the actual product; gather additional information and ultimately purchase the product online; and, if needed, return the product to the physical store location. Optimizing the effectiveness and cost efficiency of different functions by shifting their emphasis either online or offline can further help increase customer loyalty while contributing to the retailer's bottom line.

Managing Private Labels

Even though retailers' primary function involves collaborating with manufacturers to deliver their products and services to customers, retailers can also compete directly with these manufacturers by introducing their own products and services targeting the same customers. Such competition occurs when retailers launch offerings—commonly referred to as private labels—using their own brand and position them as replacements for nationally advertised brands. Fueled by the consolidation in the retail space and the growing power of retailers, private labels have become a major factor in retail management. The essence of private labels and the key issues in managing private-label portfolios are discussed in the following sections.

The Essence of Private Labels

Private labels (or store brands) are brands owned and managed by a retailer. Most private labels are retailer specific and not available across multiple distribution channels. Furthermore, because of a retailer's ability to promote its own brands, private labels are usually not advertised outside of the specific retail channel. In addition, the lower brand-building and promotion costs mean that private labels are often (but not always) priced at parity with or lower than manufacturers' brands. To illustrate, Bayer aspirin, a manufacturer's brand, is available across a variety of distribution channels and promoted through diverse communication channels, whereas CVS aspirin, a private label, is available only through CVS and is not promoted outside of CVS.

Note that the term *private label* merely indicates that the branding function is performed by the retailer; it does not mean that the associated products are manufactured by the retailer. The store-branded product can be manufactured by an entity that also manufactures its own branded version of the same product, or it can be manufactured by a third party that specializes in manufacturing and does not deal with branding. For example, Whirlpool manufactures appliances that Sears distributes under its own Kenmore brand.

The growth of private labels is often attributed to the increased productivity of manufacturers' operations, which has resulted in production levels that exceed market demand. Rather than lowering prices and hurting their profit margins across the board, these manufacturers sell excess unbranded products to retailers at lower prices, who, in turn, resell them to their customers under their own store brand. By selling lower priced unbranded products to retailers and letting them do their own branding, manufacturers aim to increase production and gain economies of scale without diluting their own brands. Over time, however, the private-label strategy has proved to be a double-edged sword. Private labels have gained popularity among consumers and become a powerful tool that has helped retailers gain the upper hand in the manufacturer–retailer relationship and even directly compete with manufacturers. The ways in which private labels create value for retailers are discussed in the following sections.

Private Labels as a Means of Creating Retailer Value

Private labels offer multiple benefits to retailers, a fact that has fueled the rapid growth of private labels in recent decades. The benefits of private labels include *differentiation, targeting price-sensitive customers, greater channel power,* and *higher profit margins.*

- **Differentiation.** Private labels help retailers differentiate their offerings. Indeed, if rival retailers carry exactly the same products, they often end up competing on price to attract customers. Developing products that are sought by customers but are carried only by a particular retailer helps retailers build a loyal customer base rather than compete purely on price. For example, Target has more than 1,000 grocery items under its Archer Farms and Market Pantry private labels, many of which have a loyal customer following. Because these items are available only at Target, these private-label-loyal customers are likely to continue patronizing Target and are less likely to switch to a competitor that does not have their favorite brands.

- **Targeting price-sensitive customers.** Private labels enable the retailer to target price-conscious customers. Indeed, not only are private labels typically priced lower than the leading brand, but they also signal value to customers, who often attribute the low price to the lack of advertising rather than to inferior product quality.

- **Channel power.** Private labels create value for retailers by enhancing their power with respect to the manufacturers of branded products. Private labels can give retailers a greater degree of leverage when negotiating with the manufacturers of branded products because retailers now have a functionally similar yet less expensive product that can compete with those branded by the manufacturer.

- **Profit margins.** Because they cost less to procure, private labels can lead to higher profits compared to national brands. Indeed, nationally branded products typically have much higher wholesale prices (the prices at which retailers purchase the merchandise) because these prices also include producers' brand-building and promotion costs, some of which they ultimately pass on to the retailer. Rather than bearing the costs of brand building and promotion, as do the producers of branded products, the retailer leverages its relationship with customers to build and promote its private labels.

Despite the multiple benefits private labels create for retailers, they also have important drawbacks, including the *need for brand-building expertise, lack of manufacturer incentives*, and *limited scope*.

- **Need for brand-building expertise.** Creating and managing private labels require competency in brand building that many retailers lack. Because historically they have focused on distributing branded products created by other entities, most retailers do not have the brand-building expertise required to manage private labels.

- **Lack of manufacturer incentives.** Retailers must absorb the costs associated with managing private labels. Even though retailers typically can realize higher gross margins on their private labels than on manufacturer-branded products, they also receive various incentives (e.g., slotting, stocking, and display allowances) on manufacturer-branded products that they do not have when selling their own private labels. These forgone incentives can significantly decrease the profit margins of private labels.

- **Limited scope.** Because they are used to differentiate a retailer's offering from those of other retailers, private labels are typically available only within a particular distribution channel. As a result, their target market and growth potential are limited by the retailer's customer base.

The growing popularity of private labels stems from several factors. First, because customers have greater access to information that enables them to assess product performance, they rely much less on the brand when making a purchase—a trend that benefits private labels that are able to deliver similar functional performance at a lower price. In addition, once customers establish a relationship with a particular retailer, they are likely to trust this retailer and purchase products associated with this retailer's brands. Finally, the popularity of private labels has been facilitated by the weakening of national brands, associated with the increased product commoditization and the declining effectiveness of companies' brand-building activities.

Managing Private-Label Portfolios

Similar to companies managing traditional brands, retailers often face decisions concerning their private-label portfolios. The two general brand portfolio strategies—single-brand strategy and multi-brand strategy—are common among retailers as well. Specifically, the single-brand strategy is represented by two approaches depending on whether the retailer's private label bears the name of the retailer or has a distinct name. For example, IKEA, Carrefour, and

Trader Joe's use their own names to brand their private labels, whereas Costco and Loblaw use a single brand that is distinct from their own names (Costco uses Kirkland Signature and Loblaw uses President's Choice).

Retailers with multi-brand portfolios include Target, Sears, Walmart, and Whole Foods. Archer Farms, Market Pantry, Cherokee, Room Essentials, Up & Up, Xhilaration, Circo, Merona, Mossimo, Threshold, Gilligan & O'Malley, Project 62, Goodfellow & Co, JoyLab, and A New Day are private labels owned and managed by Target. George, Great Value, Equate, Faded Glory, No Boundaries (NOBO), Ol' Roy, Parent's Choice, Pay Day, Price First, Sam's Choice, Special Kitty, and White Stag are Walmart's private labels. Whole Foods Market, 365 Everyday Value, and Whole Paws are Whole Foods' private labels. Sears uses Kenmore for appliances, Craftsman for tools, and DieHard for batteries.

The two private-label strategies can be related to the more general house-of-brands and branded-house strategies (discussed in Chapter 11). The single-brand (branded-house) strategy has the main advantage of having lower brand-building costs since the retailer can channel its brand-building resources into creating a single store brand. The multi-brand (house-of-brands) strategy, on the other hand, enables the retailer to create unique brand identities for different types of goods, thus avoiding the potential dilution of the meaning of a brand that is associated with a variety of products that span diverse categories.

Even though the general principles for managing brand and private-label portfolios are the same, managing private-label portfolios has several distinct aspects:

- **Low cost.** The relatively lower cost of introducing private labels (compared to traditional brands) and the ability to directly communicate with customers enable retailers to be more effective and cost efficient in designing and managing private labels.

- **Channel cobranding.** Private labels are implicitly cobranded with the retailer's brand because customers are typically aware that certain brands are offered only by the retailer. For example, many customers are aware that 365 Everyday Value identifies Whole Foods' own products. As a result, private labels are rarely explicitly cobranded with the store brand (e.g., 365 Everyday Value brand is not directly associated with the Whole Foods brand).

- **Control.** Retailers often have greater flexibility regarding where in the store to place their private labels compared to the products branded by producers who often have to coordinate product location and their shelf space with the retailer (or with the category captain appointed by the retailer). Thus, the retailer can arrange its private labels by contrasting them to the leading brands and showcasing them in a way that emphasizes their advantages.

The multiple benefits private labels offer to retailers is one of the reasons for their proliferation in recent decades. More retailers have ventured into creating their own brands, and those with extant private labels are broadening the scope of their brands and extending their brand portfolios. As retailers continue to consolidate their market power, the impact of private labels is likely to increase, and managing private-label portfolios will become one of the key issues in the way retailers create market value.

SUMMARY

Retailing includes the activities involved in the sale of products and services to consumers. Over the past several decades, the retail industry has undergone a number of significant changes, including the consolidation of distribution channels, the increase in retailer power, the growth of private labels, the ubiquity of omnichannel retailing, the emergence of new retail formats, the heightened focus on speed and convenience among both shoppers and retailers, the surge in mobile shopping, the greater reliance on customer insight to deliver market value, and the growing sophistication of retail logistics.

A retailer's *strategy* is defined by two key decisions: Identifying the target customers whose needs this retailer aims to fulfill and developing a value proposition that will fulfill these needs better than the competition. Selecting the *target market* involves selecting customers for whom the company will tailor its offering, choosing the key collaborators that will help the retailer create value for these customers, identifying the competitors who aim to create value for the same customers, and assessing the retailer's resources that will enable it to succeed in the chosen market.

A retailer's *value proposition* defines the benefits and costs associated with its offerings. To succeed in the market, a retailer's offerings must create superior value for the three key entities: target customers, the company (retailer), and its collaborators. A retailer's value proposition for its target customers comprises three components: functional, psychological, and monetary. A retailer's value proposition for its stakeholders and collaborators involves monetary and strategic value.

A retailer's *tactics* translate the overarching retail strategy into a set of specific decisions the retailer can act upon to create market value. One of the most important tactical decisions is a retailer's *product policy*, which involves defining the breadth and the depth of the product assortment carried by the retailer, as well as deciding how to organize this assortment and manage product inventory. Another important decision involves defining this retailer's *service policy*, which reflects the level and type of services it will offer to its customers, including delivery, returns, payment and financing, warranties, and installation and repairs.

Retail *branding* aims to create a meaningful brand image in the minds of target customers. It involves two key components: defining the brand positioning, which reflects the meaning that the retailer aims to associate with its brand, and defining the key brand attributes that capture the brand's positioning. Another important retail decision involves setting the *price* and *incentives policy*. The two popular pricing/promotion approaches are Every Day Low Pricing (EDLP) in which a retailer maintains low prices without frequent price promotions, and High–Low pricing in which a retailer's prices fluctuate frequently, typically as a result of heavy reliance on sales promotions.

Physical retailing involves a direct interaction between buyers and sellers who are located in the same physical location. The key decisions involved in managing brick-and-mortar retailing include selecting the retail location, designing the store layout, managing in-store communication, managing loss prevention, and dealing with showrooming. *Online retailing* involves separating the display, inventory, and delivery functions. The display and informational function is performed on the retailer's website. The inventory is typically managed in a separate warehouse located in areas characterized by low rent, low labor costs, and easy access to means of transportation, and the delivery is often outsourced to third parties. *Omnichannel retailing* aims to leverage the benefits of both physical and online channels by providing a convenient and engaging experience for shoppers. The ultimate goal of the omnichannel model is to provide a seamless shopping experience across different types of outlets in a way that creates superior customer value, helps retailers stay competitive, and increases their bottom line.

Private labels (store brands) are brands owned and managed by a retailer. Most private labels are not available across multiple distribution channels, are not advertised outside of the specific retail channel, and are priced at parity with or lower than manufacturers' brands. Private labels offer multiple benefits to retailers, including the ability to differentiate their products, target price-sensitive customers, gain greater channel power, and achieve higher profit margins. On the downside, private labels have important drawbacks, including the need for brand-building expertise, lack of manufacturer incentives, and limited scope. Similar to traditional brands, private labels can follow the house-of-brands, branded-house, or hybrid product-line strategies.

MARKETING INSIGHT: POPULAR RETAIL FORMATS

Depending on the type of items sold, the purchase quantity, the price point, and the level of service, retailing can take many different formats. The most common retail formats are listed below:

- *Supermarkets* are large self-service retailers offering both food and nonfood household items. A typical supermarket such as Albertsons, Kroger, Carrefour, and Tesco might carry approximately 30,000 different items (SKUs). Extreme-value supermarkets like Aldi, are a particular type of supermarket that carries a much smaller assortment (usually less than 3,000 SKUs), which enables them to achieve greater efficiency of operations and offer lower prices to their customers than conventional supermarkets.

- *Mass-market retailers* are similar to supermarkets but much larger in size, carrying a much greater variety of items. Mass-market retailers can sell primarily household and food items as in the case of Meijer and Kroger, or they can carry a broader selection of items that include appliances, electronics, furniture, and sports equipment, as in the case of Target, Carrefour, and Metro. Some mass-market retailers like Amazon, Walmart, Alibaba, and eBay operate on a very large scale and play a dominant role in the market. Mass-market retailers can have both brick-and-mortar and online presence; however, it is usually the online component that enables them to truly scale up the business. Even Walmart, which built its retail empire with brick-and-mortar stores, has rapidly grown its online presence.

- *Category specialists*, also referred to as category killers, are large retailers with a focus on a single category and carry an extensive assortment within that category. This type of retail store includes Home Depot and Lowe's (home improvement), PetSmart and Petco (pet supplies), Staples (office supplies), Best Buy (electronics), and IKEA (furniture).

- *Club stores* offer a limited assortment of food and general merchandise in larger quantities and at lower prices. Unlike most other types of retailers, club stores require shoppers to have a membership in order to make a purchase. Large club store chains include Costco, Sam's Club (Walmart), and BJ's.

- *Discount stores* are retailers selling low-priced or discounted merchandise. One type of discount store includes extreme-value retailers such as Dollar General, Family Dollar, Aldi, and Lidl that sell a relatively small assortment of low-priced items targeting primarily low-income consumers. Discount stores also include *off-price retailers* such as TJ Maxx, Marshalls, Ross, Big Lots, and Overstock.com that offer branded merchandise at a significant discount. Off-price retailers usually purchase excess inventory from other retailers seeking to offload slow-moving merchandise in order to free up space for items in higher demand. Discount stores also include outlet stores, off-price stores owned by a manufacturer (Coach Outlet, Levi's Outlet Store, and Nike Factory Store) or a retailer (Nordstrom Rack, Saks OFF 5th, and Neiman Marcus Last Call).

- *Department stores* are retailers that carry a broad variety of merchandise organized by category in distinct departments. Department stores sell nonperishable goods such as apparel, home furnishings, cosmetics, and electronics. They can be stand-alone stores or the centerpiece of a shopping mall featuring a variety of smaller retailers that benefit from the traffic generated by the department store. Large department stores include Macy's, JCPenney, Kohl's, and Nordstrom (US); Selfridges and Harrods (UK); Au Bon Marché and Galeries Lafayette (France); and David Jones (Australia).

- *Convenience stores* are retailers that carry a narrow assortment of routinely purchased items and are located in high-traffic, easy-to-access locations. This type of store typically charges higher prices compared to supermarkets and in return offers greater convenience in terms of location and hours of operation. Large convenience store chains include 7-Eleven, Circle K, and Oxxo (Mexico). Many convenience stores such as Speedway, Sunoco, BP, and Chevron also sell gasoline and are designed to service consumer and commercial drivers.

- *Specialty stores* are retailers that carry a relatively narrow but deep assortment (few product categories with a large variety of items within these categories) and offer a high level of service. Manufacturer-owned specialty stores are designed to showcase a particular brand as in the case of Abercrombie & Fitch, Zara, Godiva, Samsonite, Disney, and Apple. Specialty stores also include independent retailers selling third-party merchandise as in the case of Sephora, Foot Locker, Crate & Barrel, and The Body Shop. Specialty retailers can be free-standing stores or can be set up as part of a larger store (store-within-a-store).

- *Drugstores* are retailers focusing on health and beauty care, with prescription pharmaceuticals typically a key source of revenues. Drugstores can exist as free-standing stores as are CVS, Walgreens, and Rite-Aid, or they can be located within supermarkets, supercenters, or club stores such as Albertsons, Walmart, Target, and Costco. Many online drugstores, such as Express Scripts, OptumRx, and CVS Pharmacy focus primarily on prescription pharmaceuticals.

- *Service retailers* are stores that sell primarily services rather than products. Service retailers include banks, investment centers, airlines, car rental agencies, hotels, health clubs, insurance agencies, hospitals, academic institutions, entertainment establishments, and restaurants. A key difference between retailers selling products and those selling services is that most services are produced and consumed at the same time and, hence, they cannot be inventoried for future consumption. For example, if the rooms in a hotel, seats on an airplane, or tables in a restaurant are not utilized at any given point in time, they have little or no future value. Another important difference is that the customer experience depends much more on the retail environment in the case of services than products. Indeed, because the quality of the service is intangible and to a large degree dependent on the service provider, employee selection, training, incentivizing, and monitoring play a particularly important role in service retailing.

MARKETING INSIGHT: MANAGING THE PRICE IMAGE OF A RETAILER

Price image reflects a shopper's general impression of the overall level of prices at a given retailer. For example, consumers might think of Walmart as being fairly inexpensive and consider Target to be more moderately priced. Unlike prices, which are expressed in numeric terms, price image is qualitative in nature, meaning that consumers think of a retailer's pricing in categorical terms, such as "expensive" or "inexpensive." Because price image resides in the minds of the buyers, it might not adequately reflect the actual level of prices at a given retailer; instead, it reflects buyers' perception of the overall level of prices at this retailer relative to the rest of the market.

Price image is important because it influences consumers' evaluations of the attractiveness of prices of the items offered by this retailer, meaning that the same item can be evaluated as either expensive or inexpensive depending on the price image of the retailer offering this item. The impact of price image is not limited to the evaluation of individual prices; it can influence consumers' every interaction with a retailer, including the decision of where to shop, the perceived fairness of the store's prices, the likelihood of purchasing the item rather than looking for a better price elsewhere, as well as the size of the basket of goods purchased.

A common belief among many managers is that price image is merely a summary judgment of the individual store prices and, as such, can be managed by optimizing the prices of individual items. Accordingly, the primary tool for lowering a retailer's price image has been lowering the prices of the items comprising its assortment. The popularity of this approach to managing price images stems in part from the intuition that if price image reflects consumer beliefs about the overall level of prices at a given retailer, then one should be able to lower price image by lowering prices.

The intuition that a retailer's price image can be managed solely by varying its prices, however, is not borne out in reality. Whereas low prices are an important factor in determining a retailer's price image, they are not the only factor that contributes to its formation. In addition to being influenced by individual prices, price image is also a function of a number of factors that go beyond the actual level of prices set by the retailer.[3] The key price image drivers and the related market outcomes are depicted in Figure 3 and discussed below.

Figure 3. Price Image Drivers and Market Outcomes

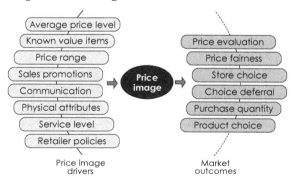

- *Average price level.* Actual prices of the items carried by a particular retailer have a direct impact on the formation of this retailer's price image. A store whose prices are substantially higher than those of its rivals will have a difficult time convincing customers it is a low-priced leader, regardless of what else it does to manage its price image. Despite its evident impact on price image, the average level of prices is only one of the factors that influence the formation of a retailer's price image. Indeed, because many shoppers are unaware of the actual prices of many of the products they buy and do not inspect the prices of all items available in the store, they often rely on other cues to infer the competitiveness of the prices of a particular retailer.

- *Known-value items.* Rather than examining all of the retailer's prices, consumers might focus on a few items whose prices they are familiar with. These items, commonly referred to as known-value items (or signpost items) have prices that shoppers are aware of and, consequently, use to determine whether a particular price is competitive or not. Although most shoppers are aware of and pay attention to prices of a relatively small subset of items from a retailer's assortment, the specific items they pay attention to might vary across shoppers. In general, known-value items tend to be frequently purchased items like milk, soda, and snacks, whose prices can readily be compared across different retailers.

- *Price range.* Price image is a function not just of the average price level, but also of the array of prices within the store. For example, a retailer that carries a few extremely high-priced items in addition to the most commonly purchased items is likely to have a higher price image than a retailer that carries a few extremely low-priced items in addition to the most commonly purchased items. Because shoppers tend to anchor on extreme prices when forming value judgments, a shift in a retailer's price image stemming from extending its price range might occur even if the average price level of its offerings remains the same.

- *Sales promotions.* Price image might also be influenced by how prices vary over time and, specifically, by the presence of sales promotions. At one extreme is everyday low pricing (EDLP), with prices that remain relatively stable (and low) over time. At the other extreme is high–low (HiLo) pricing, with prices that vary frequently because of temporary deep discounts on regularly high-priced items. Despite the conventional wisdom that EDLP conveys a lower price image than HiLo pricing, there is no consistent empirical evidence to support this argument. Thus, it is possible that for some shoppers HiLo pricing might lead to a lower price image compared to EDLP even when the average level of prices is the same.

- *Price communication.* Because most shoppers do not examine the prices of all items offered by all retailers, communicating these prices to consumers is of utmost importance for the formation of a price image. In general, price-focused communication tends to heighten buyers' price sensitivity by increasing their focus on price. Buyers' greater attention to prices, in turn, is likely to lead to more accurate price-image assessments as buyers tend to base their evaluations on price-related factors rather than on various nonprice cues. Furthermore, communication underscoring savings—for example, by providing reference prices or articulating the amount to be saved—tend to facilitate the formation of a low price image.

- *Physical attributes.* A store's physical features affect price image by conveying information about both store costs and sales volume. For example, a store in a prime location neighboring luxury retailers, featuring exquisite décor, and offering high-end amenities is likely to be associated with high costs, thus signaling a higher price image. In the same vein, large stores located in shopping malls and featuring expansive parking lots are likely to signal high sales volume and, hence, be associated with a low price image. A retailer's physical characteristics are especially important because shoppers often encounter these cues—and begin forming a price image—before they see the actual prices within the store.

- *Service level.* Service—good or bad—can be a very prominent signal that customers use to determine a retailer's price image. In general, higher levels of service tend to be associated with a higher price image, even in the absence of a difference in actual prices. This is because consumers tend to believe that a high level of service is likely to be associated with higher costs for the retailer, which, in turn, are likely to translate to higher retailer prices.

- *Store policies.* Customers can use the generosity of store policies to infer a retailer's price image. Certain policies, such as a price-match guarantee, signal a store's commitment to delivering customer value and confidence in the competitiveness of its prices across all product categories, and hence, are likely to lead to a lower price image. On the other hand, policies such as a generous return policy might be associated with higher costs for the retailer, and thus, result in a higher price image.

To effectively manage its price image, a retailer must consider all of the above factors and take advantage of those that are relevant to its specific situation. To this end, managers must look beyond the notion that price image is determined solely by the prices of the items carried by the retailer and that managing (lowering) its price image merely involves managing (lowering) retail prices across the board. Aligning the entire gamut of price-image drivers with the retailer's overall strategy and tactics can help build and sustain a meaningful price image that creates value for both the retailer and its customers.

PART SEVEN

MANAGING GROWTH

INTRODUCTION

You will either step forward into growth
or you will step back into safety.
— Abraham Maslow, American psychologist

Growth is at the heart of every business enterprise. Without a viable growth strategy, a company is in danger of losing its market position and being engulfed by competitors. Therefore, to sustain and enhance its market position, a company must constantly seek novel ways to grow its current markets and capture new ones. To this end, companies seek to foster growth by exploring new opportunities, identifying new markets, and uncovering new customer needs.

Managing growth is the primary focus for many organizations and the most common route to increasing profitability. Compared to cost-cutting — the alternative approach to profitability — ensuring top-line growth is the preferred strategy of most organizations because it can produce sustainable outcomes and enable these organizations to achieve their long-term goals. In addition to enhancing profits, focusing on growth adds vitality to organizations by providing challenges and fostering creativity.

Three aspects of managing growth merit attention: how to manage a company's market position, how to design and launch new offerings, and how to manage the company's relationship with its customers. These three aspects of managing growth are discussed in Chapters 18–20. Specifically, these chapters address the following topics: *gaining and defending market position*, *developing new offerings*, and *customer relationship management*.

- **Gaining and defending market position** focuses on creating and sustaining growth in a competitive environment. A key driver of an offering's market position is managing sales growth that stems from adoption of the offering by new customers as well as increased usage by the offering's existing customers. The key aspects of gaining and defending market position — pioneering new markets, managing sales growth, and managing product lines — are discussed in Chapter 18.

- **Developing new offerings** is the engine driving sustainable growth. The development of new products, services, and brands enables companies to strengthen their market position by capturing new opportunities to create market value. The key issues in developing new offerings — managing risk, the stage-gate approach, and understanding the adoption cycle of new products — are the focus of Chapter 19.

- **Customer relationship management** involves a set of activities aimed at managing a company's interactions with its customers in a way that creates value for both the company and customers. The key aspects of customer relationship management — managing customer loyalty, building customer equity, and designing a customer-centric organization — are the focus of Chapter 20.

The selection of a growth strategy is ultimately determined by the company's goals and strategic resources, as well as by the market in which it creates value. To successfully grow its business, a company must constantly seek new ways to create value for its customers, collaborators, and stakeholders. An integrative approach to managing growth that stems from the fundamental marketing principle of value creation is outlined in the following chapters.

CHAPTER EIGHTEEN

GAINING AND DEFENDING MARKET POSITION

Opportunities multiply as they are seized.
—Sun Tzu, Chinese military strategist

In today's competitive business environment, the pressure to grow is unrelenting. To stay relevant, a company must constantly seek new avenues for growth. If a company is not growing, it is inevitably declining by relinquishing its market position to the competition. The key aspects of managing growth—managing a company's market position, managing sales growth, and managing product lines—are the focus of this chapter. Specifically, we address the following topics:

- *Managing Market Position* ‖ Market position as a business concept | Gaining market position | Defending market position | Pioneering new markets | Building core competencies

- *Managing Sales Growth* ‖ Managing offering adoption | Managing offering usage

- *Managing Product Lines* ‖ Product lines as a means of creating market value | Managing product-line extensions | Managing product lines in a competitive context

The discussion of gaining and defending market position is complemented by an in-depth overview of three additional topics: managing disruptive innovation, identifying product–market growth strategies, and assessing the break-even rate of cannibalization.

Managing Market Position

Managing a company's market position is central to its ability to create and capture market value. The essence of market position as a business concept, common strategies for gaining and defending market position, the pros and cons of pioneering new markets, and the core competencies that substantiate a company's market position are discussed in the following sections.

Market Position as a Business Concept

Depending on the frame of reference, a company's market position can be defined in different ways: as a share of the market in which it competes, as a share of mind among its target customers, and as a share of target customers' hearts.

- **Share of market** reflects a company's share of the market in which it competes. Market share can be defined in terms of the number of units sold within a given period of time (usually annually) or in terms of the monetary value of these units. For offerings sold at similar price points, monetary and unit-based measures of market share are likely to coincide. For offerings sold at different price points, unit-based market share can be more informative because it reflects the sales volume independently of the price at which different offerings are sold. At the same time, focusing exclusively on unit share can be dangerous because without a corresponding increase in revenues, increase in sales volume might lead to profit erosion.

- **Share of mind** reflects the degree to which a company's target customers are aware of its offerings. Share of mind can be thought of as the extent to which a company's products, services, and brands are associated with a particular customer need or category. A high share of mind means that the names of the company's offerings are likely to be the first that comes to customers' minds when they think about a particular need or product category. For example, Kleenex is often the first facial tissue brand that comes to mind, Band-Aid has a leading share of mind in the adhesive bandage category, Rollerblade has top-of-mind awareness in inline skating, and Gillette enjoys the mindshare lead in shaving.

- **Share of heart** reflects the degree to which a company's target customers have a personal connection with the company and its offerings. A high share of heart means that customers have a deep emotional connection with the company's offerings. Brands that have established leadership in gaining a share of customers' hearts have managed to become lovemarks—a term coined by Kevin Roberts, former CEO Worldwide of the advertising company Saatchi & Saatchi. Brands like Harley-Davidson, Porsche, and Apple have developed a loyal following that includes many customers who have become company evangelists voluntarily advocating on behalf of these brands.

The above three measures of market position, although related, do not necessarily overlap. Thus, a company might have a high market share because of low prices and extensive distribution coverage without necessarily having a strong share of mind or heart. In the same vein, a company's high share of mind might not necessarily translate into a high market share if it is high priced and/or has weak distribution. For example, Twinkies snack cakes enjoyed a high share of mind even after the manufacturer Hostess Brands went bankrupt and stopped making them. Likewise, companies like Porsche, Tesla, and Ferrari enjoy a high share of consumers' hearts and minds while having a relatively small market share.

In general, companies that are able to increase their share of customers' hearts and minds are poised to gain share in the market in which they compete and achieve market leadership positions as have Amazon, Apple, Facebook, and McDonald's. Thus, even though market position is typically measured in terms of market share, a company's share of customers' hearts and minds is a precursor of its market share and, hence, is a key driver of this company's market position.

A company's market share depends on the way in which the market is defined. The broader the definition of the market, the more competitors it is likely to include and, hence, the smaller the company market share is likely to be. For example, the market share of Vitaminwater—a vitamin-enhanced mineral water—will vary depending on whether its sales are compared to those of other vitamin-enhanced mineral water brands, to sales of all energy drinks including Red Bull and Powerade, or to sales of all soft drinks including Coca-Cola, Pepsi, and Gatorade.

In competitive markets, companies are constantly jockeying to solidify their market position and gain competitive advantage. The constantly evolving nature of the competitive landscape calls for developing dynamic strategies to manage a company's market position. In this context, companies are presented with two perennial questions: how to gain market position and how to defend their current market position. We discuss these two questions in the following sections.

Gaining Market Position

From a competitive standpoint, a company can gain share by using four core strategies: stealing share from competitors already serving the market, growing the market by attracting new customers to the category, growing the market by increasing sales to current customers, and creating new markets. These four strategies are outlined in more detail below.

Steal-Share Strategy

The *steal-share strategy* refers to a company's activities aimed at attracting customers from its competitors rather than trying to attract customers who are new to the product category. Examples of the steal-share strategy include Apple targeting Windows users rather than targeting customers who have never had a computer, Dollar Shave Club targeting Gillette customers rather than those who are just starting to shave, and T-Mobile targeting Verizon and AT&T customers rather than those who are subscribing to a wireless service for the first time. A company's steal-share strategy can vary in breadth: It can narrowly target customers of a specific competitor (e.g., Pepsi targeting Coke customers), or it can broadly focus on the competitor's market as a whole (e.g., RC Cola trying to steal share from cola market leaders such as Coke and Pepsi).

The steal-share strategy is illustrated in Figure 1, in which the blue-shaded segment represents the company's current market share, and the yellow-shaded segment represents the share it aims to gain from the competition. Because of its focus on attracting only competitors' customers, the steal-share approach is also referred to as the *selective demand strategy*.

Figure 1. Steal-Share Strategy

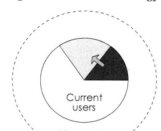

To succeed in attracting competitors' customers, a company needs to present these customers with a compelling value proposition. In this context, there are two main steal-share strategies: a *benefit-differentiation strategy* and a *cost-differentiation strategy*.

- **Benefit differentiation** aims to steal share from the competition by demonstrating the superiority of the company's offering on functional attributes such as performance, reliability, and durability and/or by its ability to create psychological value, such as conveying emotions and enabling customers to express their identity. Based on the offering's price point, there are three benefit-differentiation strategies: premium positioning (greater benefits at a higher price), price-parity positioning (greater benefits at the same price), and dominant positioning (greater benefits at a lower price).

- **Price differentiation** aims to steal share from competitors by virtue of the offering's price advantage. Based on the offering's benefits, there are two price-differentiation strategies: a "same-for-less" positioning (lower price for the same benefits) and a "less-for-less" positioning (lower price for lower benefits). A particular form of the "same-for-less" strategy is cloning, which involves emulating a competitor's offering, usually with slight variations to avoid patent, trademark, and copyright infringement liability.

In cases when a company is trying to gain share from established competitors, the steal-share strategy usually involves comparative positioning, whereby the company's offering is directly compared to those of its competitors. Comparative positioning is less likely to be utilized by the market leader because by comparing itself to a lesser known competitor the company ends up creating awareness of and sometimes even implicitly promoting the competitor's offering. For example, an underdog in the personal computer market, Apple directly compared its offerings to Microsoft-based personal computers, which comprised the vast majority of the market. By the same token, Samsung directly compared its Galaxy mobile phones to the market leader iPhone.

Market-Growth Strategy

Unlike the steal-share strategy, which targets competitors' customers, the market-growth strategy aims to attract customers who are new to the category (Figure 2). For example, an advertising campaign promoting the benefits of smart watches builds the entire category by encouraging first-time buyers to purchase a smart watch rather than to switch from another brand of smart watches. Because of its focus on increasing the overall category demand, the market-growth strategy is also referred to as *primary demand strategy*.

Figure 2. Market-Growth Strategy

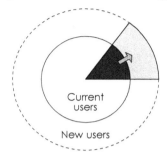

Since the market-growth strategy is aimed at growing the entire market, it typically benefits *all* companies competing in that market. Therefore, this strategy is usually adopted in the early stages of an offering's life cycle when the overall market growth is high and competition is not yet a primary issue. In addition, because offerings tend to gain share proportionately to their current market position, in the case of mature products the market-growth strategy is likely to benefit the market leader.

A notable exception to the scenario illustrated in Figure 2 is a company whose offering has a superior value proposition relative to the competition (because of a technological breakthrough, the addition of unique product benefits, or a price advantage), making it likely to gain a disproportionately large share (relative to its current market share) of new customers. In this case, both a small-share company and the market leader can benefit by using a market-growth strategy (Figure 3). For example, a pharmaceutical company that has developed a proprietary drug that is more effective than the competition might focus on generating primary demand in the belief that the majority of new customers will prefer its offering.

Figure 3. Market-Growth Strategy for a Superior Offering

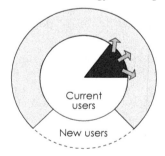

Because it aims to increase the size of the entire market, the market-growth strategy rarely involves comparative positioning. Instead, to grow the market, a company is likely to relate the benefits of its offering to customers' needs and underscore the ways in which the offering will fulfill these needs.

Market-Penetration Strategy

The market-penetration strategy aims to grow sales by increasing the quantity purchased by the company's own customers rather than explicitly trying to "steal" competitors' customers or attract new buyers to the product category (Figure 4). For example, Listerine encourages its customers to use its mouthwash twice a day rather than once, Starbucks' loyalty programs entice customers to visit its coffee shops more frequently, and Campbell urges its customers to eat soup in the summer.

Figure 4. Market-Penetration Strategy

The competitive impact of market penetration varies based on buyers' behavior and, specifically, whether the sales volume stems from substituting competitive offerings for the company's products and services or results from incremental demand that expands the overall category usage. When the market-penetration strategy leads to switching behavior, with customers buying larger quantities of the company's offerings instead of buying competitors' offerings, the net effect of this strategy is very similar to that of the steal-share strategy. The only difference is that instead of directly stealing competitors' customers, the company is stealing a share of purchases that its customers would have made from the competition. In contrast, a market-penetration strategy that leads to an increase in sales without necessarily stealing share from the competition—a common scenario in categories such as food, beverage, and apparel where the quantity purchased and consumed by customers can be influenced by marketers—is akin to growing primary demand that expands the overall category usage.

Market-Creation Strategy

The market-creation strategy is similar to the market-growth strategy in that a company gains market position by attracting customers who are not using any of the products and services offered in a given category (Figure 5). The key difference is that instead of attracting new customers to an existing market in which the company faces numerous rivals, the company defines an entirely new category in which direct competitors are absent. Companies that have created new markets include eBay (online peer-to-peer marketplace), Netflix (digital streaming), Facebook (social networking), Groupon (group-based discounts), Uber (ridesharing), and Airbnb (short-term lodging).

Figure 5. Market-Creation Strategy

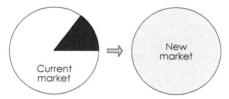

Because of its focus on uncontested markets, the market-creation strategy often leads to high profit margins and rapid growth—a scenario that inevitably attracts new market entrants. Therefore, to sustain its position in the newly created market, a company must begin to fashion a sustainable competitive advantage as soon as it starts creating the new market.

Defending Market Position

Because business success inevitably attracts competition, in addition to thinking about how to expand its offerings, a company must develop strategies to defend its market position. There are four basic ways in which a company can react to a competitor's actions aiming to erode its market position: *stay the course, enhance its offering* (increase its benefits or lower the price), *reposition its offering* (move upscale or downscale), and *launch new offerings*. These strategies are illustrated in Figure 6 and discussed in more detail in the following sections.

Figure 6. Defensive Market Strategies[1]

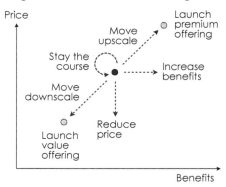

Stay the Course

Staying the course can be a viable response to changes in the market conditions. Thus, the decision to ignore a competitor's action(s) reflects a manager's belief that this action either will have no material impact on the company's market position or that the competitive threat is not sustainable and will dissipate by itself. For example, a manager might decide that its upscale offering will not be affected by the entry of a low-price, low-quality competitor and, therefore, not consider this action a direct threat. In the same vein, a manager might not react to a competitor's price reduction in the belief that this low-price position is not sustainable in the longer term.

Staying the course can also reflect a manager's belief that there is simply not enough information to decide whether and how to act, and that additional data must be gathered to identify the best course of action. Indeed, without having a clear understanding of the challenges facing the company and their root cause, any action can end up being counterproductive, complicating rather than improving the situation.

Enhance the Existing Offering

A popular strategy to defend a company's market position is to enhance the attractiveness of its current offerings. This can be achieved by one of two routes: *increasing the offering's benefits* or *lowering its price*.

- **Increasing an offering's benefits.** One approach to increase the attractiveness of an offering is to increase the customer benefits it creates. To this end, a company might enhance the functional benefits of the offering (by improving the offering's performance), increase the monetary benefits (by enhancing the financial value of the offering), and increase the psychological benefits (by strengthening the offering's image). For each of these strategies, the increase in the offering's benefits must be meaningful to lead to a change in customer behavior; adding attributes that are irrelevant to target customers is not likely to enhance the offering's customer value.

- **Lowering an offering's price.** Rather than increase an offering's benefits, a company might increase the offering's value by lowering its monetary costs. To this end, a company might outright reduce the price of its offering and offer monetary incentives such as price discounts, coupons, and rebates. Lowering an offering's costs using price incentives (rather than lowering the offering's price) is the prevalent strategy because it is easier to modify at a later point when market conditions have changed.

The choice of a particular strategy — increasing benefits or lowering costs — depends on the company's overarching strategy. Thus, targeting customers who prioritize performance over price calls for enhancing an offering's performance, whereas targeting price-sensitive customers is better aligned with lowering the offering's price. In the same vein, the choice of a particular strategy to enhance an offering's value is a function of the company's competencies and assets. A company with a strong research and development background might focus on augmenting the offering's benefits with innovative new features. In contrast, a company focused on operational logistics and mass production might choose to compete on price rather than offer a higher level of benefits.

Reposition the Existing Offering

Unlike enhancing the company's offering, which is usually associated with a relatively minor increase in its benefits or a decrease in price, repositioning involves a more dramatic change in the benefits and the price of the offering. There are two ways in which a company can reposition its offering: *move upscale* or *move downscale*.

- **Upscale repositioning** involves modifying the value proposition of an offering by moving it into a higher price tier. In this case, the company not only increases the benefits of an offering but also increases the offering's price. For example, in the late 1990s the German manufacturer of upscale writing instruments Montblanc repositioned its offerings in the United States by withdrawing from office supplies stores such as Office Depot and Staples; upgrading its product line to include luxury watches, jewelry, and leather goods; and investing in its own stores and luxury boutiques.

- **Downscale repositioning** involves modifying the value proposition of an offering by moving it into a lower price tier. Unlike enhancing an offering by lowering its price, in this case the company lowers the price of an offering while also decreasing its benefits. Because it typically leads to lower profit margins, downscale repositioning is rarely used as a strategy to defend a company's market position.

The decision to move upscale or downscale is usually determined by the company's strategic vision and, specifically, whether it is focused on margins, willing to sacrifice sales volume, or aims to compete on volume, albeit at lower profit margins. To be effective, repositioning must be aligned with the needs of the target customers, the competitive offerings, and the company's goals and resources.

Launch a New Offering

In addition to repositioning its existing offerings, a company can respond to competitive actions by adding new offerings to its product line. A product-line extension is similar to repositioning, with the key distinction that instead of modifying the value proposition of an existing offering, the company launches a new offering with a different value proposition. There are two common product-line extension strategies: *vertical* and *horizontal*.

- **Vertical extensions** are new offerings differentiated by both benefits and price, with higher priced offerings delivering a higher level of benefits. A popular strategy to fight low-priced rivals involves launching a *fighting brand*—a downscale offering introduced to shield the core offering from low-priced competitors. A slightly more complex approach to dealing with low-priced competitors is the *sandwich strategy*, which involves both the introduction of a downscale offering and upscale repositioning of the core brand. An alternative approach to deal with low-priced rivals is the *good–better–best strategy*, which involves introducing both an upscale and a downscale offering, resulting in a three-tier product line. These three strategies are discussed in more detail later in this chapter.

- **Horizontal extensions** are new offerings that are differentiated primarily by functionality and not necessarily by price (e.g., a sedan vs. a minivan). As product categories mature, their user base becomes more diverse, calling for specialized offerings tailored to the needs of different customer segments. Consequently, the pioneer might preempt the competition by extending its product line with offerings tailored to each strategically important customer segment.

A detailed discussion on managing product lines and the pros and cons of vertical and horizontal line extensions is offered later in this chapter.

Pioneering New Markets

Based on the domain in which the company becomes the first mover, there are several types of pioneers: *technology pioneer*—the company that first introduces a new technology, *product pioneer*—the company that is first to commercially introduce a new product, and *market pioneer*—the company that first introduces an offering to a particular market. Recognizing the importance of being a technology and product pioneer, the rest of the discussion focuses on market pioneering. In this context, the term *pioneer* or *first mover* refers to the first company to establish its presence in the market.

To be a market pioneer, a company does not need to be a technology pioneer or a product pioneer. In fact, it is often the case that the company first to develop a new technology or first to launch a new type of product is not the company that becomes the market pioneer. *To pioneer a market, a company must be the first to gain a leading share of customers' hearts, minds, and wallets.* For example, Apple's Newton was the product pioneer in the personal digital assistant category by being the first to feature handwriting recognition. Newton, however, never gained market traction; it was Palm, introduced several years later, that took the market by storm, becoming the de facto market pioneer. In the same vein, even though the first portable MP3 player was the MPMan introduced by South Korean company Saehan Information Systems, it was Apple's iPod that ultimately pioneered the portable digital player market.

The Benefits of Pioneering

Pioneering a market offers the incumbent a number of advantages that are not available to later entrants. These advantages include *shaping consumer preferences, creating switching costs, gaining access to scarce resources, creating technological barriers to entry,* and *taking advantage of the learning curve.*

- **Preference formation.** A pioneering company has a unique opportunity to shape customer preferences, creating a close association between its brand and the underlying customer need. For example, Jeep, Google, Amazon, eBay, Twitter, Uber, and Xerox not only helped shape customer preferences but also became synonymous with the entire category.

- **Switching costs.** As a pioneer, a company has the opportunity to build loyalty by creating switching costs for its customers. These switching costs can be functional (loss of the unique benefits created by the pioneer's offering), monetary (the cost of replacing current equipment or a penalty for breaking a contract), or psychological (the cost of learning the functionality of a competitor's offering). For example, iPhone users might find it difficult to switch because of the iPhone's compatibility with other Apple devices (functional cost), the cost involved in purchasing a replacement device and accessories (monetary cost), and the effort involved in learning how to operate a competitive device (psychological cost).

- **Resource advantage.** The pioneer can benefit from securing scarce resources such as raw materials, human resources, geographic locations, and collaborator networks. For example, the pioneer might be able to lock out the competition by securing exclusive access to strategically important mineral resources. Similarly, the pioneer might preempt competitors' access to particular human resources in short supply, such as engineers, designers, and managers. The pioneer may also preempt strategically important geographic locations in both real space (Starbucks, McDonald's, and Walmart) and online (flowers.com, drugstore.com, stamps.com, and cars.com). The pioneer can also preempt the competition by forging alliances with strategically important partners such as distributors or advertisers. For example, Nike offered exclusive long-term contracts to promising athletes early in their careers, thus precluding competitors from collaborating with these athletes when their careers took off.

- **Technological barriers.** The pioneer can create technological barriers to prevent competitors from entering the market. For example, the pioneer can establish a proprietary technological standard (e.g., operating system, communication protocol, or video compression algorithm) that can give it a leg up by forcing later entrants to make their offerings compatible with this standard. Apple's iOS and Google's Android operating systems created technological standards that gained wide adoption, thus erecting entry barriers for new competitors.

- **Learning curve.** The pioneer can also benefit from learning curve advantages, allowing it to heighten its technological know-how, productivity, and efficiency as it gains experience over time. The rate at which these advantages can be acquired by the competition is defined by the nature of the learning curve, such that a steeper slope means a quick increment of skill over time, making it easier for competitors to catch up with the pioneer. (Although in conversational language steep learning curve means a difficult learning process, a learning curve with a steep start actually represents rapid progress.)

Given the multiple benefits for the company that pioneers a given market, one might conclude that the company that is first to invent a new business model, debut a new technology, or launch a new offering will inevitably become the dominant market player. This, however, is not the case. While being a pioneer creates certain advantages, pioneers also face a number of disadvantages.

The Drawbacks of Being a Pioneer

It is far from a sure thing that the pioneer will succeed in becoming the market leader. This is because pioneers face a distinct set of challenges that might impede rather than facilitate their market success. The three most common challenges include *free riding*, *incumbent inertia*, and *market uncertainty*.

- **Free riding.** A later entrant might be able to benefit from the pioneer's resources, including its investments in technology, product design, customer education, regulatory approval, and infrastructure development at a fraction of the pioneer's cost and effort. To illustrate, after spending millions of dollars to develop the technology and educate the American audience about the advantages of a personal digital recorder, TiVo found itself in competition with cable and satellite operators selling similar services to its already educated customers. A later entrant might also reverse-engineer the pioneer's product and improve on it, while investing only a fraction of the resources required to develop the original product. For example, FedEx built on DHL's idea to start overnight deliveries in the United States, IBM launched its personal computer by building on the earlier product introductions from Apple and Atari, and Best Buy launched a rapid expansion of superstores based on the success of the business model introduced by Circuit City.

- **Incumbent inertia.** Being a market leader often leads to complacency, thus leaving technological and market opportunities open to competitors. To illustrate, IBM's reliance on mainframes, even when mainframes were being replaced by desktops and networked computers, enabled competitors such as Dell and Hewlett-Packard to gain a foothold in IBM's markets and steal some of its most valuable clients. Incumbent inertia might also be driven by a reluctance to cannibalize existing product lines by adopting a new technology or a new business model. For example, brick-and-mortar booksellers such as Barnes & Noble and Borders failed to recognize the importance of e-commerce, allowing Amazon to establish a dominant presence in online book retailing. Incumbent inertia might also result from a "sunk-cost mentality," whereby managers feel compelled to utilize their large investments in extant technology or markets even when technological advancements and market forces make these investments unfeasible. For example, one of the reasons Ford lost its leading market position to General Motors in the 1930s was its reluctance to make the necessary investments to modify existing manufacturing facilities to diversify its product line.

- **Market uncertainty.** Another potential disadvantage in being a pioneer is the uncertainty associated with the offering. Thus, the uncertainty associated with designing the offering and anticipating customers' reaction to this offering is one of the main factors responsible for the high degree of failure involved in pioneering a market. Whereas the pioneer has to deal with the uncertainty surrounding the technology and market demand, a follower can learn from the pioneer's successes and failures and design a superior offering. Because of the uncertainty associated with the introduction of a new offering, companies with strong brands and distribution capabilities might choose to be late-market entrants in order to learn from the pioneer's experience and develop a superior market-entry strategy. These companies use their brand and channel power to gain market share and successfully compete with market pioneers. For example, the first sugar-free soft drink was introduced in the United States by Cott in 1947, and the first sugar-free cola was introduced by Royal Crown in 1962, only to be overtaken by Coca-Cola and PepsiCo, which used their branding and distribution muscle to dominate the consumer soft drink market.

The numerous drawbacks of being a market pioneer suggest that when entering new markets, a company should strive not only to gain share but also to create a business model that cannot be easily copied by its current and future competitors. Because market success inevitably attracts competition, creating a *sustainable* competitive advantage is the key to a successful pioneering strategy.

Building Core Competencies

To gain and defend market position, a firm needs to develop core competencies that will give it a sustainable competitive advantage. A core competency involves expertise in an area essential to the company's business model, allowing the company to create superior market value. From a marketing standpoint, there are six key areas in which a company can develop a core competency: *business process management, operations management, technology development, product development, service management,* and *brand building.*

- **Business process management.** Competency in business management refers to a company's ability to build and manage a viable and sustainable business model that creates market value for the company, its customers, and its collaborators. This competency typically leads to the strategic benefit of *business model leadership*. Examples of companies with demonstrated competency in business innovation include Amazon, Uber, Netflix, Facebook, Google, and Airbnb.

- **Operations management.** Competency in managing operations refers to expertise in manufacturing and supply-chain management. Companies with this competency are proficient at optimizing the effectiveness and cost efficiency of their processes, which typically leads to two strategic benefits: *logistics leadership* and *cost leadership*. Logistics leadership involves proficiency in supply-chain management that enables a company to excel in sourcing, manufacturing, and distribution. For example, Foxconn—arguably the world's largest electronics contract manufacturer and a supplier for companies like Amazon, Apple, Dell, Google, Huawei, Intel, Microsoft, Nintendo, Toshiba, and Xiaomi—stands out for its dynamic, high-volume production of complex electronics products. Examples of companies with demonstrated competency in logistics include UPS, FedEx, and DHL. Cost leadership reflects the company's position as the lowest cost (although not necessarily the lowest price) producer in the market. For example, Walmart's competency in operations management is reflected in its dominant position as a low-cost retailer. Other examples of companies with demonstrated cost leadership include Costco, Carrefour, H&M, and Zara.

- **Technology development.** Competency in technology development refers to a company's ability to devise new technological solutions. This competency typically leads to the strategic benefit of *technological leadership*. Technological leadership involves proficiency in developing new technologies that enable the company to excel in establishing technological standards in markets in which it operates. Examples of companies that have demonstrated this competency include Motorola, BASF, Google, and Intel. Competency in developing new technologies does not necessarily imply competency in developing commercially successful products. To illustrate, Xerox and its Palo Alto Research Center (PARC) have invented numerous new technologies including photocopying, laser printing, graphical user interface, client-server architecture, and the Ethernet but have been slow in commercializing these technologies.

- **Product development.** Competency in product development describes a company's ability to develop products that deliver superior customer value. This competency typically leads to the strategic benefit of *product leadership*. Product leadership involves proficiency in creating new products that enable the company to excel in gaining and sustaining its market position. Examples of companies with demonstrated competency in this area include Apple, Microsoft, Tesla, Johnson & Johnson, and Merck. Note that competency in product development does not necessarily imply competency in technology development. Technologically inferior products delivering superior customer benefits are often more successful than technologically advanced products that fail to meet customer needs.

- **Service management.** Competency in service management reflects a company's ability to develop services that deliver superior customer value and typically leads to the strategic benefit of *service leadership*. Service leadership involves proficiency in initiating and growing customer relationships that enable the company to excel in gaining and sustaining a strong market position. Examples of companies with demonstrated competency in this area include The Ritz-Carlton, American Express, Amazon, Zappos, and Nordstrom.

- **Brand building.** Competency in brand building describes a company's ability to build strong brands that deliver superior customer value. This competency typically leads to the strategic benefit of *brand leadership*, which reflects a company's ability to build and sustain strong brands that capture customers' hearts and minds and engender customer loyalty. Examples of companies with demonstrated competency in this area include Harley-Davidson, Lacoste, Hermès, McDonald's, and Coca-Cola.

The above core competencies are not mutually exclusive; achieving excellence in one area does not prevent the company from excelling in another. To stay competitive, a company must develop competencies in multiple areas. For example, the success of Amazon, Google, and Facebook stems from building core competencies in all of the above domains — from business model development to brand building.

Managing Sales Growth

Sales growth is a key component of a company's efforts to gain and defend its market position and ensure long-term profit growth. Sales growth can be achieved organically by using existing resources, or it can be achieved by acquiring or merging with another company. Here, we focus on organic growth, which is the most common sales growth strategy. Organic sales growth can stem from two sources: an increase in the offering's sales volume and a change in the offering's price. In this section, we focus on strategies for growing sales by increasing sales volume (the impact of pricing on sales volume is discussed in Chapters 8 and 12).

Increasing sales volume can be achieved with two core strategies: increasing the rate of adoption of a company's offering by new customers and increasing the offering's sales to existing customers. These two strategies for increasing the sales volume of a company's offerings — *managing adoption* and *managing usage* — are discussed in more detail below.

Managing Offering Adoption

To identify the optimal strategy for increasing sales volume when introducing new market offerings, a company first needs to understand the process by which its target customers adopt new offerings, then identify the impediments to new product adoption in different stages of the process, and, finally, develop an action plan to remove these impediments. These aspects of managing the adoption of new offerings are discussed in more detail below.

Understanding the Adoption Process

From a customer's perspective, the adoption of a new offering can be viewed as a process comprising four main stages: awareness, attractiveness, affordability, and availability. Thus, for customers to adopt an offering, they must be *aware* of the offering, find its benefits *attractive*, perceive the offering to be *affordable*, and have access to the offering, meaning that the offering should be *available* for purchase and use.[2] Because the number of potential customers who ultimately purchase the offering tends to decrease with each progressive step, the adoption process is also referred to as an *adoption funnel*. The adoption funnel illustrates how potential buyers progress through the experience of purchasing a new offering. The key components of the adoption funnel—awareness, attractiveness, affordability, and availability—are illustrated in Figure 7 and outlined in more detail below.

Figure 7. The Adoption Funnel

- **Awareness** reflects customers' knowledge of the offering. Awareness can be generated by the company's direct communications with its target customers; by communication initiated by its collaborators; or by third-party communication such as press coverage, social media, and personal communication.

- **Attractiveness** reflects the benefits associated with a given offering, typically considered in a competitive context. Thus, an offering's attractiveness reflects its ability to satisfy a particular customer need better than the competition.[3]

- **Affordability** reflects customers' perceptions of the monetary costs associated with the offering and their ability to cover these costs. Considered together, attractiveness (benefits) and affordability (costs) determine the overall value (utility) of the offering for target customers.

- **Availability** reflects customers' ability to acquire the offering. An offering's availability is a function of the density of the distribution channels catering to a given customer segment and the in-stock availability of the offering in these channels on a day-to-day basis.

Note that the order in which potential buyers experience the different stages of the adoption process might vary. For example, an offering might be available to all potential buyers, but only a few might be aware of it before encountering it on the store shelves. Thus, the organization of the adoption funnel can vary depending on the specifics of the situation at hand.

Identifying and Closing Adoption Gaps

Managing product adoption calls for identifying and eliminating impediments at different stages of the adoption process. These impediments, referred to as *adoption gaps*, can be illustrated by mapping the dispersion of customers across different stages of the adoption funnel. The goal of this analysis is to provide a better understanding of the dynamics of the adoption process and identify problematic areas that must be addressed.

To visualize the adoption hurdles, the dispersion of customers across different stages of the adoption process can be represented by a series of bars, as shown in Figure 8. Here, the yellow part of each bar corresponds to the share of potential customers who have not transitioned to the next stage of the adoption process. The ratio of the yellow portion to the blue portion of the bar reflects the effectiveness of the company's actions at each step in acquiring new customers.

Figure 8. Identifying Adoption Gaps

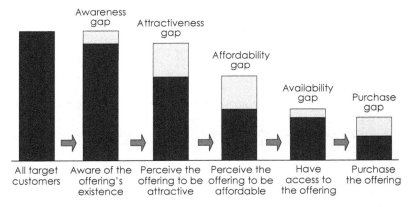

Evaluating the loss of potential customers at each step of the process offers a simple way to identify impediments to adoption. In this context, gap analysis can be used both to pinpoint the problem spots in product adoption and to identify specific solutions to close adoption gaps. The key performance gaps and the common solutions for closing these gaps at the different stages of the adoption process are outlined below.

- **Awareness gaps** call for increasing awareness of the offering among target customers. This type of gap requires improving company communication, which can involve increasing communication spending, streamlining the message, developing a better creative solution, or improving the effectiveness of reaching target customers. In addition to directly communicating the offering to target customers, the company can also partner with collaborators—for example, by engaging in joint (co-op) advertising with its channel partners and by fostering third-party communication such as facilitating publicity about the offering and encouraging media coverage.

- **Attractiveness gaps** call for improving the benefits of the offering. Typically, this is achieved by redesigning the benefit-related aspects of the offering—specifically, its product, service, and brand components. Attractiveness gaps do not always imply that the offering lacks the benefits desired by buyers; they can also stem from buyers' failure to comprehend the offering's benefits. Such gaps in customers' understanding of the offering's benefits can be closed by improving communication and providing target customers with an option to experience the offering via product samples and demonstrations.

- **Affordability gaps** call for lowering the costs of the offering. Lowering the monetary cost might involve lowering the offering's price and adding monetary incentives to decrease the offering's cost to customers. As is the case with attractiveness gaps, affordability gaps do not always imply that the actual cost of the offering is high; they might also result from customers' misperception of the offering's actual costs. Such misperceptions of the offering's cost can be surmounted by communication aimed at correcting customers' erroneous beliefs.

- **Availability gaps** indicate that target customers do not have access to the offering. For example, an offering might be in short supply because a company underestimated its appeal to target customers or because of inadequate distribution coverage. Depending on the cause of the availability gap, improving an offering's availability can involve ramping up production to meet demand, improving the geographic coverage of distribution channels to give target customers better access to the offering, and improving channel operations to reduce stock-outs.

- **Purchase gaps** indicate that even though customers are aware of the offering and find it attractive, affordable, and available, they have not yet purchased the offering—for example, because of time or budgetary constraints. Closing purchase gaps typically involves introducing time-sensitive incentives such as short-term price discounts, coupons, and financing options.

Following identification of the adoption gaps and the means of closing these gaps, a company must evaluate the magnitude of each gap and its impact on sales revenues and profits against the feasibility and the costs associated with closing each gap. This analysis can enable the company to prioritize the adoption gaps and develop an effective and cost-efficient approach to managing sales growth by attracting new customers.

Managing Offering Usage

The discussion so far has focused on growing sales volume by increasing product adoption by new customers. An alternative approach to growing an offering's sales volume involves increasing its usage by current customers and identifying and closing usage gaps.

Understanding Offering Usage

Many purchases are recurring in nature, whether they are products for daily usage such as food, apparel, and cosmetics, or durable goods such as cars, household appliances, and electronics. In this context, managing recurring consumption can have a significant impact on sales volume, especially in cases of frequently purchased high-ticket items.

The total quantity of offerings purchased over time by a given customer depends on several factors, including overall satisfaction with the offering, the frequency with which this customer uses the offering, the quantity used on each usage occasion, and the ease of repurchase. As in the case of customer adoption, these factors can be presented in the form of a funnel illustrating factors influencing repurchase frequency (Figure 9).

Figure 9. The Usage Funnel

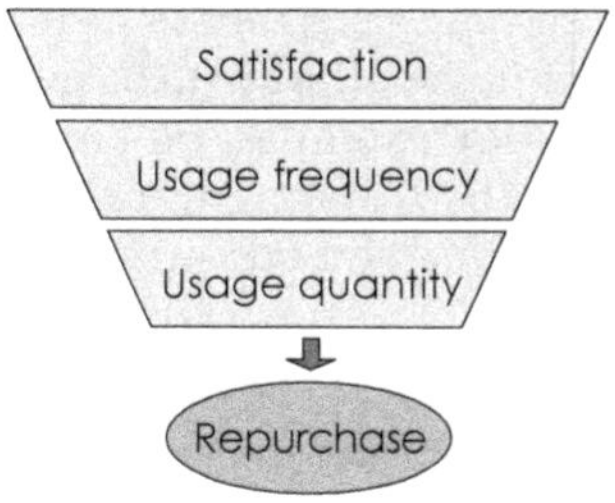

- **Satisfaction** reflects customers' experience with the offering. Unlike the attractiveness stage in product adoption, which is based on expectations of an offering's value, satisfaction reflects the post-consumption evaluation that takes into account customers' actual use of the offering.

- **Usage frequency** reflects the number of occasions on which the offering is used. For example, for cars, usage frequency refers to how often customers drive; for toothpaste, it refers to the number of times people brush their teeth; and for shaving, it indicates how frequently customers shave.

- **Usage quantity** reflects the amount customers use on each occasion. For example, usage quantity for toothpaste depends on the amount of toothpaste people use to brush their teeth. In the case of unit-based products such as printer cartridges, water filters, and razor blades, which customers determine when to replace, usage quantity is defined by the replacement frequency.

- **Ease of repurchase** reflects the ease with which customers can obtain a replacement for the company's offering once it has been consumed.

Identifying and Closing Usage Gaps

A practical approach to closing usage gaps calls for identifying and eliminating impediments at the different stages of product usage. The potential impediments to product usage can be visualized by a series of bars, as shown in Figure 10. Here, the yellow portion of each bar corresponds to the share of customers whose consumption behavior is off target, and the ratio of the yellow portion to the blue portion reflects the effectiveness of the company's actions at each step of the consumption process.

Figure 10. Identifying Usage Gaps

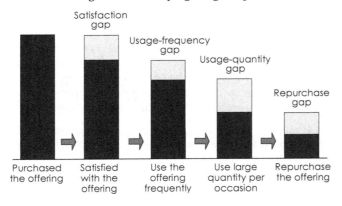

Evaluating the effectiveness of each stage of consumption offers a relatively simple way to identify usage gaps and develop solutions for closing such gaps.

- **Satisfaction gaps** call for improving customers' experience with the offering. Depending on the cause of the satisfaction gap, closing this gap might involve enhancing the benefits and reducing the costs of the offering to make it more competitive and to better align the offering's value proposition with customer preferences.

- **Usage-frequency gaps** call for increasing the rate at which customers use the offering. For example, sales of a laundry detergent can be increased if customers wash their clothes more often, sales of toothpaste can be increased if customers brush their teeth more frequently, and sales of razors can be increased if customers shave more frequently. Sales volume can also be increased by identifying new ways to use the offering. To illustrate, Campbell promotes the use of its soup (usually consumed in winter time) during the summer, and Arm & Hammer promotes baking soda not only for baking but also as a household cleaner and deodorizer.

- **Usage-quantity gaps** call for increasing the amount of product used on each occasion. Usage quantity can be increased by educating customers about the optimal usage quantity. A classic example of this approach is the "rinse and repeat" shampoo advertising campaign. Another approach involves increasing the size of the packaging in categories where bigger package size typically leads to consuming a larger quantity. Usage volume also can be increased by designing the product in a way that ensures dispensing of the optimal quantity per usage occasion. For example, Heinz introduced a plastic squeeze bottle, increased the size of the opening in the bottle neck, and designed the "upside-down bottle" so ketchup can be poured without having to wait for the contents to slide down to the opening of the bottle.

    In cases of unit-based products such as printer cartridges, razor blades, and water filters, usage-quantity gaps call for increasing the frequency with which customers replace the product. Replacement frequency can be managed by informing customers about the optimal usage duration and replacement frequency. For example, to encourage customers to replace their toothbrush, the Oral-B toothbrush features blue bristles that fade to alert users that they need a new brush.

- **Repurchase gaps** call for streamlining the ways in which the offering is replenished after it has been consumed. Closing repurchase gaps can involve enabling customers to monitor the current level of product performance and informing them in a timely manner that the offering needs to be replaced. For example, printers include toner-level indicators to alert users that the cartridge will soon need replacement. Likewise, Gillette cartridges feature colored strips that fade with use, letting the user know that it is time to replace the cartridge. A company might also invest in educating its customers about the optimal frequency of repurchasing its offering. For example, oil change chains such as Jiffy Lube have been successful in promoting the idea that a car's oil must be changed every 3,000 miles to prevent engine wear — a belief that persisted long after technological improvements have made changing oil that frequently unnecessary and wasteful.[4]

Another approach to closing purchase gaps involves offering incentives that encourage customers to buy the offering in advance of the need to replace it so that they never run out. Repurchase can also be facilitated by simplifying the process of reordering the offering, such as introducing subscription programs (e.g., Amazon Subscribe and Save) and one-step reordering devices (e.g., Amazon Dash).

Because they deal with recurring purchases, usage gaps often hold greater potential to increase sales volume than do adoption gaps. This is especially true for companies with a dominant position in the market because of the relatively large installed base of users. Optimizing the consumption experience in this case can have a significant impact on the company's ability to grow sales volume.

Managing Product Lines

An important aspect of gaining and defending a company's market position involves organizing and managing the individual offerings as part of a company's product line. In this context, product-line management aims to optimize the value delivered by the individual offerings that are contained in a company's portfolio. The key aspects of managing a company's product line — *managing vertical and horizontal extensions, managing product-line cannibalization,* and *using product lines to gain and defend market position* — are the focus of this section.

Product Lines as a Means of Creating Value

The core principle in designing and managing product lines is that the company's offerings — considered individually and as a whole — should create superior value for target customers, the company, and its collaborators. The ways in which product lines create value for these three market entities are outlined in more detail below.

Product Lines as a Means of Creating Customer Value

Product lines create value for customers by providing them with offerings that more closely match their needs. Indeed, the more extensive a company's product line, the greater the chance that individual customers will find their "ideal" option. Product lines can also create customer value by appealing to a customer's desire for variety with offerings that are differentiated on relatively minor attributes (e.g., flavor, scent, and color). Finally, an extensive product line can appeal to a customer's desire for freedom of choice and to the feeling that they are not forced to choose from a limited roster of options.

Despite the multiple benefits that product lines can create for target customers, increasing the number of available options is not without drawbacks. One such drawback is that a greater number of options can lead to customer confusion stemming from the inability to choose among the available alternatives. Indeed, although the premise for offering a greater variety of options is that it allows consumers to identify their "ideal" option, providing consumers who do not have well-defined preferences more options can backfire by complicating their decision. As a result, buyers might defer making a purchase decision or select a competitor's offering with a smaller variety of options that are easier to choose from.

Product Lines as a Means of Creating Collaborator Value

Product lines can benefit collaborators by enabling the company to customize its offering to match the specific needs of its collaborators. For example, product lines can help minimize conflicts that might occur among distribution channels with different cost structures, such as mass-market retailers and specialty stores that offer the same product at different price points to the same customers. Companies can address such conflicts by developing product lines comprising different versions of the same product that vary on minor attributes such as color, packaging, and optional features. For example, a toy manufacturer might develop two different versions of the same toy: a higher priced one for high-end toy stores and a lower priced one for mass-market stores. To ensure that shoppers do not feel overcharged by the high-end store, the toys sold in these two outlets feature different packaging and functionality, thus making it difficult for shoppers to compare offerings across retailers.

A downside of a large product line from a retailer's standpoint is that having to carry a greater number of options tends to increase costs while also taking valuable shelf space. Thus, while a manufacturer's preference is that retailers carry its entire product line (and none of the competitors' options), a retailer's profit-optimization strategy often involves carrying only the most profitable offerings from competing manufacturers rather than a single company's entire product line.

Product Lines as a Means of Creating Company Value

Product lines can benefit the company by creating additional sources of revenue and profits. Thus, the more comprehensive a company's product line, the greater the company's ability to create superior value for different customer segments. Product lines can also create value for the company by helping it deal with the competition. Having a product line that targets multiple customer segments can help a company deter market entry by new competitors, which are less likely to target customers whose needs are already fulfilled by an existing offering. In addition, product lines can "crowd out" existing competitors by taking up premier shelf space in distribution channels.

Despite their multiple benefits, product lines have several important drawbacks for companies. The most obvious drawback is the increase in product development, manufacturing, distribution, and management costs associated with developing multiple offerings. In addition, designing and managing a product line can pull resources from the offerings that drive a large part of the company's profits. There is also the potential danger that instead of attracting new customers, the new offerings might end up cannibalizing the sales of the company's existing offerings.

Managing Product-Line Extensions

A common approach to building product lines involves starting with a single offering and then adding related offerings, commonly referred to as product-line extensions. Depending on the relationship between the incumbent offering and the added offering(s), product-line extensions can be divided into two types: *vertical* and *horizontal*. These two types of extensions are discussed in more detail in the following sections.

Managing Vertical Product-Line Extensions

Vertical product-line extensions involve adding new offerings in different price tiers. Specifically, a company might add an offering that delivers a higher level of benefits at a higher price in the case of an *upscale vertical extension*, or an offering that delivers a lower level of benefits at a lower price in the case of a *downscale vertical extension*. The two types of vertical extensions—upscale and downscale—are illustrated in Figure 11 and discussed in more detail below.

Figure 11. Vertical Product-Line Extensions

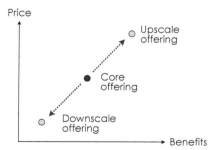

Upscale extensions involve extending the company's product line by adding an offering that delivers a higher level of benefits at a higher price compared with the core offering. One of the main reasons for introducing an upscale extension is to capture a more lucrative, higher margin market. For example, to gain a foothold in the growing market for professional tools, leading home improvement company Black & Decker introduced DeWalt—a line of professional, high-end power tools (discussed in detail in Appendices A and B in the last part of this book). Upscale extensions are often used to follow customers through different stages of their life cycle by creating offerings that fit their evolving needs and changing buying power. For example, building on the success of its low-priced cars, Volkswagen introduced the more upscale Jetta and Passat aimed at customers who seek larger, better performing vehicles.

In addition to providing access to higher end markets, upscale extensions can provide synergies with existing offerings. For example, adding an upscale offering can lift the image of the low-end offerings in the company's product line. Introducing a line of premium, award-winning Gallo-branded wines helped E. & J. Gallo Winery strengthen the image of its core offerings. Companies also introduce upscale extensions to gain a competitive advantage in developing advanced technologies. For example, car manufacturers often develop high-performance versions of their vehicles to strengthen their core competencies and further the advancement of technologies that can be used in their mass-produced lower end models.

Despite their multiple advantages, upscale extensions present numerous challenges. Developing upscale offerings usually requires specific resources that a company specializing in lower tier products and services might not readily possess. The lack of such resources might prevent a company from developing an offering that can successfully compete in the upscale market. For example, launching an upscale apparel brand requires a variety of specific resources such as knowledge of fashion trends, product development know-how, high-end manufacturing capabilities, a reputable brand, and access to specialized suppliers and upscale distribution channels that a lower end manufacturer might not have.

Because most companies do not readily have the resources necessary to introduce higher quality offerings, successful organic (internally developed by the company) upscale extensions usually take time to implement and are not very common. Instead, companies often gain access to upscale markets by acquiring existing high-end offerings. This acquisition strategy is illustrated by Fiat's entry into the racing car market with the acquisition of Ferrari; Volkswagen's acquisition of Bentley, Bugatti, and Lamborghini; and Marriott's acquisition of Ritz-Carlton.

Downscale extensions involve extending the company's product line by adding an offering that delivers a lower level of benefits at a lower price. Downscale extensions are driven by a company's desire to increase its customer base by attracting less affluent customers who are currently not served by its offerings. Examples of downscale extensions include Armani's launch of Armani Exchange, Mercedes' introduction of the A-Class, and Gap's introduction of Old Navy stores.

The main appeal of downscale extensions is the high volume of sales resulting from serving customers in lower socioeconomic tiers. Downscale extensions also enable companies to gain access to customers early in their life cycle by providing a lower entry point for a company's offerings. For example, Audi and BMW's "1" series cars provide access to younger customers, who despite current constrained resources are likely to evolve into a lucrative customer segment in the future.

Downscale extensions are especially beneficial to companies operating in industries requiring high fixed-cost investments—such as the airline, hotel, and automotive industries—in which economies of scale might be achieved. For example, many upscale car manufacturers—including Mercedes, BMW, and Porsche—have opted to use their design and manufacturing resources to develop downscale product offerings. Downscale extensions are quite popular among managers seeking to achieve quick results because they build on the company's existing resources and are often easier to implement than upscale extensions.

Despite their numerous advantages, downscale extensions have a number of significant drawbacks. A key concern is the threat of cannibalization of higher end offerings by the downscale extension (discussed in more detail later in this chapter). In cases when the extension carries the same brand as the upscale offering, the downscale offering can also weaken the brand by creating undesirable associations with a low-quality/low-priced offering. Another area of concern is that downscale extensions yield lower margins compared to higher end offerings and, as a result, they need to generate substantial sales volume to be profitable. Furthermore, serving price-conscious customers can be challenging because these customers tend to be less loyal and are more likely to switch to lower priced competitive offerings.

Managing Horizontal Product-Line Extensions

Offerings in a horizontally differentiated product line typically belong to the same price tier and differ primarily in the type of benefits they offer (Figure 12). Unlike vertical extensions, in which the different levels of offering benefits can be clearly ordered in terms of their attractiveness (for example, Ritz-Carlton is likely to be regarded as more attractive than Marriott, and a luxury car is likely to be viewed as more appealing than an economy car), horizontal extensions do not imply such universal preference ordering. Instead, horizontal extensions are differentiated on benefits that are idiosyncratic and are likely to vary in their attractiveness across customers. For example, different designs, styles, colors, and flavors are likely to appeal to different tastes without necessarily implying differential pricing. Thus, even though prices might vary across horizontally differentiated offerings, they are not the key differentiating factor.

Figure 12. Horizontal Product-Line Extensions

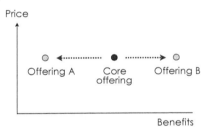

Horizontal extensions create value by providing customers with offerings that better match their preferences. Unlike vertical extensions, which provide a better preference match in a different price–quality tier, horizontal extensions aim to accommodate customers' tastes within the same price–quality tier. By providing an assortment of diverse options, horizontal extensions help companies fulfill the needs of customers with different tastes while satisfying the variety-seeking behavior of these customers. For example, Colgate-Palmolive, Procter & Gamble, and Unilever have introduced more than a hundred varieties of toothpaste to appeal to consumers' diverse tastes in order to provide individual customers with a greater variety of options to choose from.

Because they draw on a company's existing resources, horizontal extensions are often easier to implement than vertical extensions. Moreover, because they are sold at similar price points and have a similar cost structure, horizontal extensions have profit margins comparable to those of the existing offerings, thus attenuating cannibalization concerns—a key advantage over downscale extensions.

Despite their multiple benefits, horizontal extensions have several important drawbacks. Because customers vary in their tastes, horizontal extensions often call for expansive product lines, which in turn increase the complexity and the costs associated with developing and managing the offerings in these product lines. In addition to greater complexity and costs, extensive assortments of similar options can lead to customer confusion and choice deferral, especially in cases when customers are unable to readily ascertain which of the available options best matches their preferences.

Managing Product-Line Cannibalization

When extending its product line, a company's goal is to generate additional sales and profits by stealing share from the competition and/or bringing new users into the category. Ideally, all the sales generated by the new offering will come from competitors' offerings or from growing the overall category. In reality, however, this is rarely the case. A common consequence of launching a new offering is that in addition to stealing share from competitors it can cannibalize some of the company's current offerings.

Product-line cannibalization is illustrated in Figure 13. Figure 13A depicts the market prior to the introduction of the new offering; Figure 13B depicts the "ideal" scenario, in which the new offering steals share exclusively from competitive offerings; and Figure 13C depicts the more typical scenario, in which the new offering steals share from both the competitive offerings and the company's own offering.

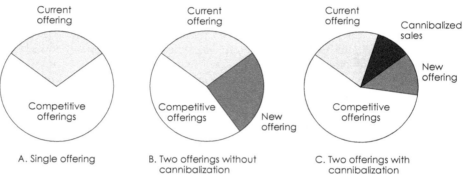

Figure 13. Product-Line Cannibalization

A. Single offering   B. Two offerings without cannibalization   C. Two offerings with cannibalization

Cannibalization describes a scenario in which the sales of one offering come at the expense of the sales of another offering from the same company. Cannibalization is not always problematic, and on certain occasions a company might actively seek to cannibalize the sales of some of its offerings. For example, by launching a newer version of its flagship offering, a market leader might aim to cannibalize its current flagship offering in order to provide customers with a better experience and gain higher profit margins.

Cannibalization is a primary concern in the case of downscale product-line extensions because they typically have lower profit margins than the offerings they end up cannibalizing. To minimize the possibility of cannibalization, a company needs to ensure that its downscale extension is substantially differentiated from its current offerings. This means that differentiation on price must also involve differentiation on benefits, such that lower price is associated with a lower level of benefits. Indeed, when the new offering provides the same benefits as the incumbent offering at a lower price, customers have no reason to prefer the higher priced offering and will ultimately gravitate toward the lower priced extension. Therefore, meaningful differentiation is key to sidestepping cannibalization.

When differentiating its downscale extension, a company walks a fine line between curbing potential cannibalization by ensuring that the downscale extension is not more attractive than the incumbent offering and building the market for the downscale extension by bolstering its appeal. In its desire to minimize cannibalization, a company can stretch its downscale extension so far that it becomes inferior to those of its direct competitors. For example, in an effort to avoid cannibalization, Intel overstretched its downscale extension, Celeron, making its performance subpar to its low-priced competitors. Over-differentiation can also involve overpricing the lower end offering. Gap Warehouse, the forerunner of Old Navy, failed because in an effort to avoid cannibalizing sales in Gap's core stores it set relatively high prices, which put it at a disadvantage relative to its direct competitors.

Poorly differentiated downscale (lower priced) vertical extensions are not the only cause of cannibalization; poorly differentiated horizontal extensions can result in cannibalization as well. Even when offerings in horizontal product-line extensions are priced at parity and have similar margins, a company's overall profitability might decrease when a larger number of company offerings ends up chasing the same number of customers. Thus, when the newly added offerings in a company's product line address the same need of the same target customer as the existing offerings, extending a product line can ultimately lead to substitution between offerings rather than stimulating new demand. In this case cannibalization is likely to hurt a company's bottom line because the increased costs of developing new offerings are not offset by a corresponding increase in sales volume.

Cannibalization is of primary concern when the margins of the new offering are lower than those of the offering being cannibalized, which means that every time a customer buys the new, lower margin offering instead of the higher margin one, the company generates lower profits. A key issue, therefore, is how much cannibalization a company can afford before the new offering produces a net loss. The maximum amount of cannibalization of an existing offering by a new one is given by the *break-even rate of cannibalization*. Assessing the break-even rate of cannibalization is discussed in more detail at the end of this chapter.

Managing Product Lines in a Competitive Context

In addition to creating value for customers, product-line extensions can help companies gain and sustain market position by optimizing a company's value proposition relative to its competitors. Three of the most popular competitive product-line strategies—the *fighting-brand strategy*, the *sandwich strategy*, and the *good–better–best strategy*—are outlined in more detail below.

The Fighting-Brand Strategy

A common strategy to compete with low-priced rivals involves launching a fighting brand—an offering that matches or undercuts the competitor's price (Figure 14). For example, to compete with low-price rivals while preserving the market position of its flagship Marlboro brand, Philip Morris aggressively priced its Basic cigarette label, making it a fighting brand. Similarly, Procter & Gamble launched Oxydol laundry detergent as a low-price alternative to its flagship brand, Tide.

Figure 14. The Fighting-Brand Strategy

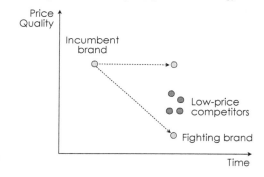

Fighting brands are created specifically to combat low-priced rivals that are encroaching on the company's incumbent offering. Rather than tackle the threat head-on and lower the price of its core offerings, the fighting-brand strategy involves introducing a lower priced, lower quality offering to address the needs of price-conscious consumers while leaving intact the value proposition of the original offering. In addition to protecting the company's premium offerings, fighting brands enable the company to reach a new market segment of price-conscious customers willing to accept a lower level of performance in order to receive a lower price.

Despite its popularity, the fighting-brand strategy has certain limitations. Thus, in some cases the introduction of a lower priced offering might lead to cannibalization, whereby customers who normally would have purchased the company's premium offering now purchase the lower priced, lower margin offering. Such cannibalization is particularly likely in cases when the premium and the low-priced offering carry the same brand name—an approach that, in addition to facilitating cannibalization, has the potential to dilute the image of the offering's brand. Moreover, the fighting-brand strategy assumes a two-tiered market in which some buyers care about quality more than price and others are willing to sacrifice quality for price. In reality, however, the market structure might be more complex and a different strategy, such as good–better–best (discussed later in this section), might be more appropriate.

The Sandwich Strategy

The sandwich strategy involves introducing a two-tiered product line comprising a high-quality offering and a low-priced offering, effectively sandwiching low-priced competitors. This strategy is typically achieved by launching a downscale extension while simultaneously moving the existing offering upscale (Figure 15). For example, in anticipation of an inflow of cut-price competitors following the patent expiration of its blockbuster prescription drug Prilosec, AstraZeneca introduced a low-priced, over-the-counter version (Prilosec OTC) and at the same time replaced Prilosec with Nexium—a premium-priced and slightly more effective version of the drug.

Figure 15. The Sandwich Strategy

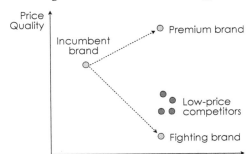

The sandwich strategy resembles the fighting-brand strategy because in both cases the incumbent brand introduces a low-priced offering. Where the sandwich strategy differs from the fighting-brand strategy is that in addition to introducing a downscale offering it also moves the core offering upscale. This upscale repositioning of the incumbent offering reflects the change in the target market following the introduction of low-price offerings by competitors. Indeed, after the incumbent offering loses some of its price-sensitive customers to lower priced rivals, the remaining customers are, on average, less price sensitive and more quality oriented. As a result, the incumbent offering is no longer optimally positioned for these customers (it is underpriced) and can benefit from moving upscale.

The sandwich strategy is an effective approach for dealing with lower priced competitors in cases when buyers have clearly articulated preferences for either quality or price. At the same time, this strategy might backfire in markets where buyers have uncertain preferences. In such markets, buyers often prefer options that offer a compromise among the extreme alternatives rather than either the high-quality or the low-price option. To illustrate, when choosing from a set composed of a high-priced/high-quality offering, a low-priced/low-quality offering, and an average-priced/average-quality offering, buyers often select the middle option because it allows them to avoid trading off price and quality. In this case, trying to "sandwich" the low-priced brand by simply launching a fighting brand and moving the core brand upscale without offering a mid-price/mid-quality option might be counter-productive because the "sandwiched" competitor might benefit from becoming the compromise option.

The Good–Better–Best Strategy

The good–better–best strategy involves introducing a downscale offering (fighting brand) as well as an upscale offering (premium brand) while preserving the core brand. The good–better–best strategy is similar to the sandwich strategy in that it involves the introduction of a low-priced offering. However, instead of a two-tiered product line that involves an upscale repositioning of the core brand, the good–better–best strategy calls for launching a new premium offering that yields a three-tiered product line (Figure 16).

Figure 16. The Good–Better–Best Strategy

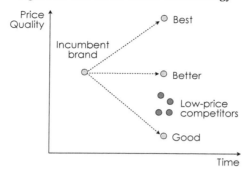

The good–better–best strategy can be illustrated by Apple's response to low-priced competitors of its iPod music player. Instead of directly competing with lower priced offerings, Apple extended its product line downscale by first introducing the iPod Shuffle and then the iPod Nano. The iPod's good–better–best product line reflects Apple's view of the market as comprising three key segments: a segment seeking a fully functional player (iPod), a segment seeking basic functionality (iPod Nano), and a segment seeking a low-priced offering with limited functionality (iPod Shuffle). The good–better–best strategy is also exemplified by Gap's three-tiered structuring of its retail stores: Old Navy, Gap, and Banana Republic.

The good–better–best strategy works well in tiered markets comprising three key segments: a quality-focused segment, a price-focused segment, and a segment seeking a compromise between high quality and low price. In such three-tiered markets, the two-pronged sandwich strategy would not work because moving the core offering upscale without having a mid-tier option leaves the company vulnerable to competitive offerings of mid-point quality and price. In addition to being an effective tool to fend off cut-price competitors in three-tiered markets, the good–better–best strategy could also be effective in markets in which buyers have uncertain preferences and are likely to select the middle option in order to avoid making a tradeoff between price and quality.

Despite its advantages, the good–better–best strategy also has important limitations. One such limitation is that this strategy requires that the company have the necessary resources to develop three different market offerings that vary in the level of benefits they provide to customers while ensuring that each offering delivers value to its target segment. The introduction of multiple offerings is also likely to result in additional product development and management costs that put additional pressure on the company to increase sales revenues. Finally, in the absence of clearly delineated differences in performance between the good, better, and best offerings, the lowest priced offering is likely to cannibalize the sales of the higher priced offerings, eroding the company's sales revenues and profits.

SUMMARY

A company's *market position* can be defined as a share of the market in which it competes, as a share of mind among its target customers, and as a share of target customers' hearts.

A company can *gain market position* by using four core strategies: stealing share from competitors serving this market (steal-share strategy), growing the market by attracting new customers to the category (market-growth strategy), growing the market by expanding sales to current customers (market-penetration strategy), and creating new markets (market-creation strategy). Because business success inevitably attracts competition, a company needs to develop strategies to *defend its market position*. Common approaches for reacting to a competitor's actions involves staying the course, enhancing or repositioning existing offerings, and adding new offerings.

A company can gain market position by *pioneering new markets*. The key benefits of market pioneering include the opportunity to shape customer preferences, create switching costs for collaborators and customers, preempt scarce resources, create technological barriers to entry, and reap learning curve benefits. The key drawbacks of being a pioneer include free riding by competitors, pioneer inertia, and uncertainty associated with the offering's technology and with customer demand.

To gain and defend market position, a company needs to develop *core competencies* that will give it an advantage over the competition. Core competencies involve expertise in one or more of six key areas: business innovation, operations management, technology development, product development, service management, and brand building.

Sales growth is a key component of a company's efforts to gain and defend its market position. The two core sales growth strategies are managing adoption and managing usage. *Managing adoption* deals with acquiring new customers. It focuses on four key factors: awareness, attractiveness, affordability, and availability. A practical approach to managing adoption involves identifying and eliminating impediments (adoption gaps) throughout the adoption process. *Managing usage* deals with the ways in which a company's customers use its offerings. It focuses on three key factors: satisfaction, usage frequency, and usage quantity. A practical approach to managing usage involves identifying and eliminating impediments (usage gaps) to repurchasing the offering.

Product-line management aims to optimize the market value created by a company's offerings. A key principle of managing product lines is that each offering should have its own unique value proposition that fits the needs of a particular customer segment without cannibalizing sales of other offerings.

There are two types of *product-line extensions*: vertical and horizontal. *Vertical extensions* involve adding new offerings that are in different price tiers. Depending on the price tier of the newly added offering, vertical extensions can be upscale (in a higher price tier) or downscale (in a lower price tier). *Horizontal extensions* aim to accommodate customers' tastes within a given price–quality tier. An important concern with downscale extensions is *cannibalization*, which describes a scenario in which the sales of the company's new downscale offering come at the expense of the sales of the incumbent offering.

In addition to optimizing the value for target customers, product-line management can help a company defend its market position against the competition. Popular competitive product-line management strategies include the *fighting-brand strategy*, the *sandwich strategy*, and the *good–better–best strategy*.

MARKETING INSIGHT: MANAGING DISRUPTIVE INNOVATION

Disruptive innovation, a term coined by Harvard professor Clayton Christensen, refers to technological developments that create a new market that eventually displaces an established market.[5] In his seminal book, *The Innovator's Dilemma*, Christensen argues that organizations do not always lose their market position because of bad management. Instead, they often fail because of what is traditionally considered good management: They listen to their customers, invest aggressively in new technologies to develop more and better products requested by these customers, diligently examine market trends, and invest resources in innovations that promise the best returns. Yet, because of their exclusive focus on current markets and customers, these companies fail to take advantage of new technologies and to invest in emerging markets fueled by these technologies. This tendency, in turn, makes these companies vulnerable to new market entrants that take advantage of disruptive technologies.

The essence of disruptive innovation can be better understood when contrasted with traditional innovation driven by sustaining technologies, which encompass most technologies in a given product category. Sustaining technologies foster improved performance of existing products on attributes that have been traditionally valued by customers. In contrast, disruptive technologies have a value proposition that differs from what is available in the market. Offerings built on disruptive technologies, while well received by members of smaller customer segments who value their benefits, tend to underperform established offerings in mainstream markets. Indeed, market leaders' largest and most profitable customer segments initially do not need and often cannot use offerings based on disruptive technologies.

There are several key reasons why established companies tend to ignore disruptive technologies.

- *Customers and investors rather than managers ultimately determine a company's strategic direction.* Contrary to the conventional wisdom that managers control the allocation of the company's resources—including the decision to invest in new technologies—it is the customers and investors who ultimately make these decisions. Because managers' decisions are driven by the desire to create value for their stakeholders, they are unlikely to allocate adequate resources to low-margin opportunities that exist in relatively small markets.

- *Small markets do not solve the growth needs of large companies.* As companies grow larger, they become less interested in focusing on small markets. To sustain their rate of growth, companies need to invest in markets that are progressively larger. Thus, to achieve 10 percent revenue growth, a company with revenues of $10 million needs to generate an additional $1 million, whereas a company with $10 billion in revenues needs to generate an additional $1 billion. Yet, disruptive technologies are rarely able to instantly create billion-dollar markets. As a result, large companies often choose to sit on the sidelines, waiting for emerging markets to become large enough to have a meaningful impact on their revenues and profits. The problem with this wait-and-see approach is that companies that enter these emerging markets early can benefit from significant pioneering advantages over later entrants.

- *Markets that do not exist cannot be analyzed.* Most established companies recognize the value of good market research: It enables them to assess market size, analyze the competition, and forecast demand. As a result, these companies have processes in place that require quantitative assessments of market size and financial returns before entering new markets. Yet, much of this information—which is typically available for offerings built on sustaining technologies—is not readily available in the case of disruptive technologies. Presented with a scenario in which market demand, revenues, and costs are unknown, established companies often resort to inaction, waiting for more detailed and conclusive data to emerge.

- *An organization's processes and values are resistant to change.* Merely acquiring the necessary resources (assets such as people, equipment, and capital that enable the company to succeed in creating market value) is not sufficient for a company to succeed in new markets. Unless they are aligned with the company's existing processes (the ways in which a company transforms resource inputs into offerings of value to its customers) and values (the criteria by which the company prioritizes its actions), the newly acquired resources will do little to ensure the company's market success. While resources can be acquired within a relatively short time frame, aligning a company's processes and values with the needs of the markets driven by disruptive innovation takes significant time and effort to accomplish.

- *Technological improvements often exceed market needs.* The pace of technological progress associated with sustaining innovation often exceeds the rate of performance improvement that is meaningful to customers. This directly follows the principle of diminishing marginal value (discussed in Chapter 4), which posits that improving an offering's performance produces marginally diminishing increases in the customer value created by this offering. As a result, in order to provide better products than their competitors, companies often overdevelop their offerings, giving customers more than they need and are willing to pay for. In doing so, these companies leave the rest of the market uncontested, enabling competitors leveraging disruptive technologies to launch offerings that create superior customer value.

To overcome the impediments associated with adopting disruptive innovation, companies must recognize the challenges and develop strategies that make it feasible for them to enter new markets. Some of these strategies include:

- *An autonomous organization.* To successfully harness the potential of disruptive technologies, managers must ensure the availability of adequate resources to pursue the development of truly innovative offerings that a company's current customers do not want and company stakeholders are unwilling to invest in. Making adequate resources available often means setting up a new, autonomous organization tasked with creating a new business around the disruptive technology, aimed at customers who are willing to embrace the products of disruptive innovation.

- *Discovery-based planning.* To overcome "analysis paralysis" associated with the lack of detailed market data, managers must approach the market opportunity created by disruptive innovation with the mindset that it is impossible to accurately identify the market in advance. Accordingly, rather than trying to develop well-articulated marketing plans for launching new offerings in an environment of high uncertainty, managers might engage in discovery-based planning, which involves developing plans focused on learning about new market opportunities instead of implementing an already developed business model.

- *Customer-focused product development.* To maintain the company's market position, managers must realize that the marginal value of the improvements delivered by sustaining innovation tend to decline over time and embrace alternative technologies that promise greater rates of return on the technological improvements. Embracing these ideas involves shifting the focus of a company's research and development efforts from improving product features to fulfilling customer needs and delivering superior customer value.

MARKETING INSIGHT: PRODUCT–MARKET GROWTH FRAMEWORK

The Product–Market Growth framework (also referred to as the Ansoff matrix) outlines four key sales-growth strategies by linking the customer segments served by the company to the company's product-development opportunities.[6] This framework is typically presented as a 2×2 matrix in which one of the factors represents the type of product (current or new) and the other factor represents the type of customers (current or new). The resulting four product–market strategies — *market penetration*, *market development*, *product development*, and *diversification* — are illustrated in Figure 17 and described in more detail below.

Figure 17. The Product–Market Growth Framework

- *Market penetration* aims to increase sales of an existing offering to a company's current customers. A common market-penetration strategy involves increasing the offering's usage rate. To illustrate, airlines stimulate demand from current customers by adopting frequent-flyer programs, cereal manufacturers enclose repurchase coupons in their offerings, and orange juice producers promote drinking orange juice throughout the day rather than only for breakfast. Companies following a market-penetration strategy employ a variety of tactics directed at current customers, such as increasing the value of the offering (e.g., by lowering the price and running sales promotions), increasing awareness of the offerings (e.g., by increasing advertising and personal selling), and improving the availability of the offering (e.g., by increasing the density of the distribution channels and making the process of acquiring the offering more convenient).

- *Market development* aims to grow sales by promoting existing offerings to new customers. To illustrate, a company that has its products and services available in a particular geographic area (e.g., a city, state, or a country) might choose to expand its operations by entering a new market. The market expansion need not be defined in geographic terms: It can be defined in terms of demographic characteristics such as age, gender, and ethnicity, among others. In business markets, a company can expand its operations by looking to acquire a different type of company based on factors such as size, industry, and growth potential. Tactics employed by companies following a market-development strategy are similar to those used by companies following a market-penetration strategy, with the key difference that instead of focusing on their current customers they focus their efforts on customers they do not currently serve.

- *Product development* aims to grow sales by developing new (to the company) offerings for existing customers. This strategy is similar to the market penetration strategy in that it aims to fulfill the needs of the company's current customers. Where these two strategies part ways is in how they fulfill customer needs: Rather than trying to sell more of its current offerings to current customers, companies following the product-development strategy focus their efforts on developing new offerings. Companies vary in the extent to which the offerings they develop are truly novel. Thus, some companies end up developing new offerings that are substantively different from those in their current product portfolio, whereas others extend their current product line by modifying existing offerings. Unlike companies following market-penetration and market-development strategies that focus their efforts on tactics such as pricing, incentives, communication, and distribution, companies following a product-development strategy typically focus their efforts on creating new products, services, and brands. The other tactics, although relevant, play a relatively less important role, aiming to support the introduction of the company's new offerings.

- *Diversification* aims to grow sales by introducing new offerings to new customers. This approach is similar to the market-development strategy in that it goes beyond a company's current market. It is also similar to the product-development strategy in that it extends a company's current product line. What differentiates this approach from the other three market-expansion strategies is that the company does not rely on two of its key resources—its customer base and its portfolio of offerings. Because both the offering and the customers are new to the company, this approach tends to be riskier than the other product–market growth strategies.

  There are a variety of reasons why a company might choose to diversify its market position. A common rationale for diversification is to take advantage of growth opportunities in areas in which the company has no presence. Alternatively, a company might be forced to diversify due to the emergence of a new technology that has eroded its customer base by making its products obsolete. In addition, some companies diversify in order to ensure a more consistent stream of revenues that can be achieved by fulfilling the distinct needs of diverse customer segments.

The four strategies defined by the product–market growth framework are not mutually exclusive: A company can pursue multiple market-expansion strategies to grow sales revenues and enhance its market position. However, a company using multiple growth strategies needs to prioritize these strategies and allocate resources based on the extent to which these strategies enable the company to achieve its strategic goals.

MARKETING INSIGHT: ASSESSING THE BREAK-EVEN RATE OF CANNIBALIZATION

The break-even rate (BER) of cannibalization indicates the maximum proportion of the new offering's sales volume that can come from the existing offering(s) without the company incurring a loss. The greater the break-even rate of cannibalization, the larger the percentage of an incumbent offering's sales a new offering can cannibalize while still having a positive impact on the company's bottom line (Figure 18).

Figure 18. Break-Even Rate of Cannibalization

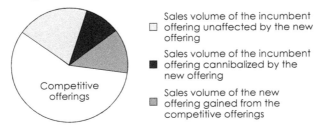

The break-even rate of cannibalization is derived as follows: To avoid loss of profit across all offerings, profit from the new product must be equal to or greater than the lost profits from cannibalization:

$$\text{Profit}_{\text{New offering}} \geq \text{Lost profit}_{\text{Old offering}}$$

Because profit is a function of unit volume and unit margin, the above equation can be modified as:

$$\text{Volume}_{\text{New offering}} \cdot \text{Margin}_{\text{New offering}} \geq \text{Lost volume}_{\text{Old offering}} \cdot \text{Margin}_{\text{Old offering}}$$

When the two sides of the equation are equal, the new offering is breaking even with respect to cannibalization of the old offering. In this case, the above equation can be represented as follows:

$$\frac{\text{Lost volume}_{\text{Old offering}}}{\text{Volume}_{\text{New offering}}} = \frac{\text{Margin}_{\text{New offering}}}{\text{Margin}_{\text{Old offering}}}$$

The left part of the equation is the ratio of sales volume of the old offering that was lost because of cannibalization by the new offering, which is the definition of the break-even rate of cannibalization (BER$_C$).[7] Hence:

$$\text{BER}_C = \frac{\text{Margin}_{\text{New offering}}}{\text{Margin}_{\text{Old offering}}}$$

For example, consider a company launching a new product priced at $70 with variable costs of $60, which cannibalizes the sales of an existing product priced at $100 that also has variable costs of $60. In this case, Margin$_{\text{New Offering}}$ = $70 – $60 = $10 and Margin$_{\text{Old Offering}}$ = $100 – $60 = $40. Therefore, the break-even rate of cannibalization can be calculated as follows:

$$\text{BER}_C = \frac{\$10}{\$40} = 0.25$$

The break-even rate of cannibalization in this case is 0.25 or 25%, which means that to be profitable for the company, no more than 25% of the sales volume of the new offering should come from the current offering, which in turn implies that at least 75% of the sales volume should come at the expense of competitors' offerings and/or from increasing the overall size of the market.

CHAPTER NINETEEN

DEVELOPING NEW MARKET OFFERINGS

In the middle of difficulty lies opportunity.
— Albert Einstein, theoretical physicist

The development of new offerings is the engine that fuels the growth of a business enterprise. New product success is often attributed to intuition. Indeed, some offerings that stem from intuition do make it big. Yet many others crash and burn. These failures occur because intuition is only one aspect of new product development. The other key ingredient of success is having a systematic approach to developing new market offerings. Such a systematic approach for developing new offerings that create market value is outlined in this chapter. Specifically, we address the following topics:

- *New Offering Development as a Value-Creation Process* || Managing risk in developing new offerings | The stage-gate framework for developing new offerings | The development of new offerings as an iterative process

- *Idea Generation* || Generating new ideas | Problem-solving and experience-enhancing ideas | Idea validation

- *Concept Development* || Prototyping | Concept validation

- *Business Model Design* || Designing the business model | Business model validation

- *Offering Development* || Developing the core resources | Developing the market offering

- *Commercial Deployment* || Selective market entry | Market expansion

- *Understanding the Adoption of New Offerings* || New product adoption | Rogers' model of adoption of innovations | Moore's model of adoption of new technologies

The discussion of the development of new offerings is complemented by an in-depth overview of two additional topics: the minimum viable offering and the key principles of prototype development.

New Offering Development as a Value-Creation Process

New offerings are the key to sustainable growth. The development of new products and services enables companies to gain and sustain their market position by taking advantage of the changes in the market to create superior customer value. Some of the key issues in developing new offerings—managing risk, using the stage-gate approach, and understanding the iterative nature of new product development—are discussed in the following sections.

Managing Risk in Developing New Offerings

Depending on the degree of novelty involved, there are two main types of new offerings: revolutionary offerings that deliver new-to-the-world benefits and evolutionary offerings that involve relatively minor modifications of existing offerings, such as different colors, flavors, tastes, sizes, designs, or packaging variations. Revolutionary offerings such as Netflix, Uber, and Airbnb can disrupt entire industries by providing a set of benefits that cannot be readily matched by their current competitors. In contrast, evolutionary offerings such as different generations of mobile phones, computers, and razors provide higher levels of performance on existing attributes without dramatically changing the competitive playing field.

While the concepts discussed in this chapter apply to both revolutionary and evolutionary offerings, the issue of managing risk is particularly relevant in the case of new-to-the-world offerings.

One of the key challenges in developing new offerings is managing the uncertainty associated with launching new products and services. Because uncertainty increases the risk of failure, managing risk is one of the key aspects of developing new offerings. Managing risk involves minimizing the chance that the new offerings will fail, thus wasting the resources expended on their development. There are two types of risk in developing new offerings: market risk and technological risk.

- **Market risk** reflects the uncertainty associated with the five factors (the Five Cs) defining the market in which the company aims to create value. Thus, the customer need that the new offering aims to fulfill might be transient or might exist only for a *customer* segment that is not large enough to justify the development, production, promotion, and distribution costs of the offering. The company's *collaborators* might not allocate the necessary support to ensure the success of the offering. The *company* might not be able to gather sufficient resources to develop and launch the offering. *Competitors* might emulate the company's technology to design a cheaper product or build on the company's technology to develop a functionally superior offering. Finally, the *context* in which the company operates might evolve due to the development of superior technologies; fluctuating sociocultural trends; the state of the economy; new regulatory restrictions; as well as new tariffs, taxes, and fees.

- **Technological risk** reflects the uncertainty associated with the technological viability of the new offering. For example, the desired product features might not be achievable with currently available technologies, product design might not be compatible with the functional requirements, and product reliability might be compromised by the use of new, unproven technologies. Technological risk might also extend the time frame for developing the new offering, which in turn can increase the market risk associated with interim changes in the market.

The high levels of uncertainty and risk associated with the development of new offerings mean that for every offering that succeeds in the market there are many more that fail to gain market traction. The high failure rate calls for using a systematic approach to channel the company's resources to projects that have a higher likelihood of gaining market success while screening out projects that are less likely to succeed.

The Stage-Gate Framework for Developing New Offerings

A popular approach to managing risk calls for breaking down the offering development process into separate components (stages) and introducing benchmarks (gates) that must be met in order for an idea, concept, or product to proceed to the next stage of development. Considered together, the individual steps in the development of a new offering and the corresponding benchmarks form the *stage-gate framework* for developing new offerings.

By outlining a process for designing and validating the business model, the stage-gate framework helps minimize risk and optimize allocation of the company's resources. In this context, the stage-gate framework enables a company to apply a systematic approach to the development of new offerings and ensure that the product development process results in an offering that will create value for target customers while enabling the company and its collaborators to reach their goals.

The stage-gate approach breaks down the process of developing new offerings into individual components and introduces checkpoints (gates) that aim to ensure that the offering is likely to create and capture market value. A streamlined version of the stage-gate framework for developing new offerings involves five key stages—*idea discovery, concept development, business model design, offering development,* and *commercial deployment*—separated by hurdles that aim to validate the actions taken in the previous step (Figure 1).

Figure 1. The Stage-Gate Framework for Developing New Offerings

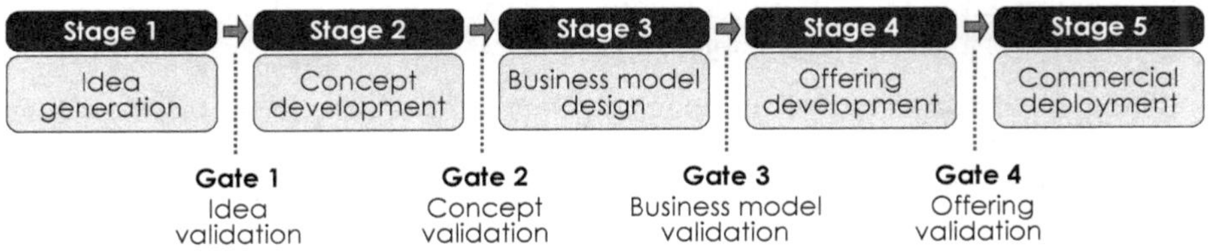

The key components of the stage-gate approach can be summarized as follows:

- **Idea generation.** The development of a new offering starts with the discovery of an unmet market need and the generation of an idea that addresses this need in a novel way. Ideas can be derived from different sources: They can stem from the company (e.g., by virtue of marketing research and employee suggestions), from customers (e.g., via customer feedback and crowdsourcing), and from collaborators (e.g., suppliers, distributors, and co-developers). The idea discovery is followed by a validation of the soundness and the key assumptions of the underlying idea.

- **Concept development.** The validated idea is further refined and fleshed out to create a detailed sketch of the initial concept that delineates the key technological and market aspects of the proposed offering. This step is followed by concept validation, which evaluates the technological feasibility and the desirability of the concept by target customers.

- **Business model design.** The validated concept evolves into a business model that articulates the company's target market, defines the value created and captured by the company in this market, and outlines the key aspects of the company's offering. This stage is followed by business model validation, which evaluates the offering's ability to fulfill the identified customer need in a way that creates value for the company and its collaborators.

- **Offering development.** The design of a viable business model is followed by the development of the resources needed to create the company's offering as well as the design and production of the actual offering. This stage is followed by the offering's validation in which its business viability is tested. Typically, validation involves testing the product by releasing it on a smaller scale. In cases when manufacturing the actual product is complex and/or costly, the company might develop and launch a scaled-down version of the offering in a test market. In addition to assessing customers' response to the offering, market testing can also be conducted to improve the design and functionality of the offering before commercializing it.

- **Commercial deployment** involves deploying the new product in the target market. To minimize risk and go-to-market expenditures, a company might initially deploy its offering in selected markets that are the least costly to reach and where customers are most likely to adopt it. Once the offering gains traction in these markets, a company can expand its reach and make the offering available to all target customers.

The ultimate goal of the stage-gate approach is to develop an offering that is *desirable* (target customers find it attractive), *feasible* (it is technologically possible), and *viable* (it can create value for the company). Thus, idea generation is usually focused on the desirability and viability of the offering, concept development combines desirability with feasibility, and business model design aims to ensure that all three criteria are met prior to developing and commercializing the offering.

The Development of New Offerings as an Iterative Process

The stage-gate framework presents a stylized version of the process of developing a new offering. In reality, the development of a new offering is not always a linear process in which the initial idea evolves into a successful market offering. Rather, it is an *iterative process* of discovering a novel idea and translating this idea into a viable market offering. In this context, the development of new offerings involves a series of iterations—*realignments* and *pivots*—aimed to create a desirable, feasible, and viable market offering.

- **Realignments** are relatively minor changes to an idea, concept, or offering that do not substantially alter its core attributes. Realignment typically involves making tactical changes and modifying certain aspects of the offering without changing its core value proposition.

- **Pivots** are major changes that involve going back to the drawing board and modifying some (or all) of the key aspects of the initial idea, concept, or core functionality. Pivots are *strategic inflection points* that change the fundamentals of the new offering's value proposition.

Because of the high uncertainty typically associated with the development of new offerings, realignments and pivots are the rule rather than the exception. It is not unusual for a project to pass the idea-generation stage and subsequently fail to convert into a desirable and feasible concept. In the same vein, a project might reach the implementation stage and be unable to secure the resources (e.g., intellectual property, raw materials, or capital) necessary to develop the offering. When this happens, the company must go back to the previous stage(s), reevaluate their validity, and, if necessary, restart the project until the offering can overcome the hurdles set to help ensure its market success.

A prominent example of pivoting involves *The Point*, a social media company designed to facilitate fundraising. The problem The Point was trying to solve was that people were reluctant to donate because of concerns about the social relevance of the cause involved and the reputation of the fundraising organization. To address these concerns, the company enabled the fundraising entity to set a tipping point—a certain amount of money or number of participants required for the program to be activated. The actual donations were not collected until the set goal was met, thus assuring potential donors that they were contributing to a socially relevant cause supported by many other donors.

Despite being a promising idea that addressed what appeared to be a valid customer concern, The Point did not gain much traction with its target audience. There was one bright spot though: A growing number of consumers used the website to find lower prices and sales, and the most successful campaigns were those that enabled consumers to combine their buying power to save money. Following this trend, The Point redefined its business model to focus on business owners rather than fundraisers and created an entirely new value proposition: enabling vendors to set a tipping point that would activate a promotional offer. Participating vendors could benefit from the new business generated by the promotional offer without having to pay anything if their offer did not generate sufficient customer demand. Pivoting to redefine its business model turned the struggling social media fundraising company The Point into *Groupon*, the multibillion-dollar deal-of-the-day company.

In the same vein, Glitch—a massive multiplayer online game developed by game developer Tiny Speck—realizing that it would most likely not attract a customer base large enough to sustain its business model, closed its doors only to reemerge as Slack, the widely successful team-collaboration platform. Building on its gaming expertise and using a unique messaging technology, the company created an intuitive interface that made it very simple for business users to adopt Slack. The pivot from an online game with an unsustainable business model to a largely scalable team-based workplace environment helped Slack reach a $1 billion valuation less than a year after its launch.

Idea Generation

The development of a new offering begins with the generation of an idea that identifies an unmet market need and a novel way to address this need. The idea can involve a new technology, a new approach to brand building, a new pricing mechanism, a new way of managing incentives, new channels of communication, or a novel distribution method. The different approaches to generating new ideas, the essence of problem-solving and experience-enhancing ideas, and the process of idea validation are discussed in the following sections.

Generating New Ideas

Companies use different strategies to come up with new ideas. Based on the specific way in which ideas are born, there are two basic ways in which business ideas are generated: *top down* and *bottom up*.

Top-Down Idea Generation

Top-down idea generation starts with identifying a market opportunity and is followed by an invention that addresses this opportunity (Figure 2). When exploring a market opportunity, the company seeks to identify an important customer problem that it can solve better than the available alternatives. Accordingly, top-down idea generation starts with a market analysis to identify an unmet need that the company can fulfill better than the competition.

Figure 2. Top-Down (Market-Driven) Idea Generation

Top-down idea generation has resulted in a number of successful products designed to seize an identified market opportunity. Apple's iPod addressed the need for a user-friendly device that enables people to carry their favorite music with them. Apple's iPhone addressed the need for a user-friendly device that combines the functionality of a mobile phone, a personal digital assistant, a music player, and a camera. Apple's iPad addressed the need for a portable, user-friendly mobile device that offers enhanced iPhone functionality with a larger display.

In the same vein, Procter & Gamble designed Swiffer to address the need for a cleaning tool that is more effective than a mop and cuts down on cleaning time. Herman Miller designed the Aeron chair to address the need for an office chair that is both comfortable and stylish. Tesla designed its Model S sedan to address the need for an environmentally friendly, fuel-efficient, premium car that is fast, spacious, and stylish. Dyson formulated its iconic vacuum cleaner to fulfill the need for a vacuum that retains its suction with usage. Uber offered a solution to customers who needed fast, convenient, and reliable transportation. Airbnb offered housing to travelers seeking less expensive and more personalized alternatives to traditional hotels.

The top-down approach is arguably the most common way of generating business ideas. Because it starts with identifying a market opportunity, it is more likely to result in an offering that fulfills a real market need and, thus, more likely to create market value. At the same time, the top-down approach does not guarantee that a meaningful solution to the unmet need can ultimately be identified: A company might end up spinning its wheels trying to address a problem that cannot be solved using current technologies.

Bottom-Up Idea Generation

Bottom-up idea generation starts with an invention, followed by identification of a market need that can be fulfilled by this invention (Figure 3). Unlike top-down idea generation, the invention here is not driven by an identified market need but by technological innovation. In this context, the bottom-up approach to idea generation is more often the province of scientists in research labs than managers in marketing research departments.

Figure 3. Bottom-Up (Invention-Driven) Idea Generation

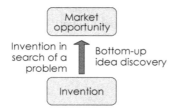

Bottom-up idea generation has resulted in a number of successful products that stem from technological innovation. Penicillin — an antibiotic used to combat bacterial infections — was discovered by Scottish biologist Alexander Fleming, who noticed that the fungus growing on contaminated Petri dishes had killed the staphylococci bacteria he was researching. Post-it Notes were invented by a 3M chemist who created a very weak pressure-sensitive adhesive while trying to come up with a super strong adhesive for use in the aerospace industry. The microwave was discovered by a Raytheon Corporation engineer who noticed that the chocolate bar in his pocket melted when he walked in front of a vacuum tube generating microwaves.

Likewise, velcro was discovered by a Swiss engineer who found during a hiking trip that the hooks in burrs clung to anything loop-shaped — in this particular case, his pants and his dog's fur. Rogaine (minoxidil) — the popular over-the-counter drug for treating hair loss — was originally used to treat high blood pressure; however, patients taking drugs containing minoxidil began to notice increased hair growth on their balding scalps, as well as on other parts of their bodies. Viagra, the multi-billion-dollar erectile dysfunction drug, resulted from a Pfizer Company drug that was not particularly effective in treating angina, a condition constricting the vessels that supply blood to the heart. Teflon, the widely used nonstick coating for cookware and other products, was the discovery of a DuPont engineer searching for a better refrigerant.

Even though bottom-up idea generation starts with an invention, to evolve into a successful market offering the invention must address a viable market opportunity. Novel technology per se is not a reason for a company to develop a new offering. While new technologies are often an important factor, the key driver of market success is the company's ability to apply this technology to address an unmet market need. Idea generation, whether top down or bottom up, should always be linked to the market value it creates.

To transform a technological invention into a viable business idea, the company must identify a problem that this invention can solve and the market value it can create. Therefore, even though successful products can be born serendipitously from a technological invention, the top-down approach is the preferred idea generation method in new product development. Because the success of an offering ultimately depends on its ability to deliver market value, by starting with identifying market opportunities a company can increase its chances of developing an invention that will enjoy market success.

Problem-Solving and Experience-Enhancing Ideas

To create value, an offering must increase customers' well-being by fulfilling an unmet need. Based on the degree to which a particular need has been activated, there are two types of ideas: *problem-solving ideas* designed to address a problem faced by customers and *experience-enhancing ideas* designed to improve on an existing solution to a given problem.

- **Problem-solving (must-have) ideas** provide a solution to an important unmet need that customers actively seek to fulfill. Because problem-solving ideas address an essential need that customers deem unresolved, offerings stemming from these ideas are typically easy to communicate and tend to be rapidly adopted by customers.

- **Experience-enhancing (nice-to-have) ideas** improve on an offering that fulfills a given need reasonably well in order to provide customers with an even greater level of satisfaction. Because experience-enhancing ideas address a need that is not considered a problem, the resulting offerings are adopted at a much slower rate than problem-solving offerings.

Problem-solving and experience-enhancing ideas can also be defined in terms of customer pain and gain. Problem-solving ideas can *alleviate customer pain* by eliminating an important source of dissatisfaction. Experience-enhancing ideas, on the other hand, can be perceived as a means of providing *customer gain* because they improve on an already satisfactory offering. Thus, problem-solving ideas typically lead to the development of *must-have* offerings—products and services that customers immediately see the value of. In contrast, experience-enhancing ideas result in *nice-to-have* offerings that customers view as discretionary.

The distinction between problem-solving and experience-enhancing offerings is important because customers more eagerly embrace offerings that provide a solution to a problem than offerings that aim to enhance an already satisfactory experience; as a result, problem-solving offerings enjoy faster adoption than experience-enhancing ideas. Because it takes much longer for customers to understand the benefits of experience-enhancing offerings and recognize their value, a company must expend greater resources to inform customers about the advantages of such offerings.

Identifying the likely speed of adoption of the innovation is important at the later stages of new product development when the company must build a business model around the idea. Indeed, many companies have failed to achieve their growth projections because of the erroneous belief that they could easily educate their customers and change their behavior to appreciate the benefits of offerings that did not address a pressing problem (pain point) faced by these customers. For example, many software companies, including Microsoft, Adobe, and Intuit, have had a difficult time inducing their customers to upgrade to the most recent versions of their offerings because the earlier versions are perfectly capable of fulfilling the needs of these customers. Facing the same predicament, the product-upgrade cycle of many consumer electronics manufacturers—including Apple, Samsung, and LG—is slowing down because consumers are satisfied with the performance of their current offerings.

Idea Validation

Idea validation assesses the soundness of the idea for the proposed offering and the validity of its assumptions. Typically, idea validation involves a preliminary assessment of the *desirability* and *viability* of the offering—namely, whether an offering based on this idea is likely to fulfill an unmet customer need and do so in a way that benefits the company. To validate an idea, a manager should ask the following questions:

Does the idea present a solution that will fulfill an unmet customer need?

Would an offering based on this idea create value for the company?

When evaluating ideas, a company can make two types of errors. The first error is failing to reject an idea that has no merit and is unlikely to result in a successful market offering. The second type of error involves making the opposite mistake—rejecting a good idea. Given the high rate of new product failures, one might conclude that failing to reject bad ideas is more common than rejecting good ones.[1] This, however, is not necessarily correct. In addition to stemming from poor ideas, new product failures can be caused by a high rejection rate of good ideas, as well as by the inherent technological and market risk associated with new product development.

In order to proceed to the next stage of concept development, the company must be able to answer the above questions. If these questions cannot be satisfactorily addressed, the idea must be redefined.

Concept Development

Concept development is a process that aims to minimize the risk inherent in product development by creating a simplified version of the offering that can be used to determine the offering's level of desirability and feasibility. Because bringing new offerings to market typically requires a large expenditure of time, money, and effort, a company can streamline the product development process by first creating and validating a concept that captures the essential features of the offering prior to developing the actual offering.

Developing a Concept Storyboard

Concept development can benefit from the development of a storyboard that outlines the key features and benefits of the new offering in an organized and logical manner. Storyboards help gather customers' opinions about this offering and facilitate presenting the offering's concept to the product development team and company management and stakeholders. Based on the means used to depict the offering, storyboards can be verbal, visual (drawing, picture, diagram), or both. Depending on the mode of presentation, storyboards can be purely descriptive, delineating the attributes of the offering, or narrative, telling a story about the offering (for example, showing how the offering can address a particular customer need). Storyboards can also be stand alone, presenting a single concept, or they can be comparative, presenting several concepts side by side.

A popular approach to developing a concept storyboard starts with identifying the customer problem that the company aims to solve. The problem identification is followed by an outline of the alternative means that customers currently use (and are likely to use in the future if the company does not introduce its offering) to solve the problem. Next, the storyboard might articulate the specifics of the proposed offering, focusing on its most important aspects. The offering's description is followed by an outline of the ways in which the company's offering will create value for target customers—specifically, how it will solve the identified problem better than the alternative options. A schematic illustration of these four aspects of developing a concept storyboard is shown below (Figure 4).

Figure 4. Concept Storyboard

(1) Customer Problem	(2) Alternative Options	(3) Company Offering	(4) Customer Value
What customer problem does the company aim to solve?	What are the alternative means to solve this problem?	What are the key aspects of the company's offering?	How does the offering solve customers' problem better than the alternative options?

Based on the creative approach used to present the information, storyboards can be substantive, presenting the specifics of the offering without any embellishment, or commercialized, presenting the offering in a way in which it will be promoted to customers. Typically, substantive storyboards are used to test the value proposition of the offering, whereas commercialized storyboards test different ways of communicating the offering to customers.

Prototyping

Concept development typically involves creating a scaled-down version, commonly referred to as a *prototype* (from the Greek πρωτότυπον, meaning *primitive form*). Prototyping aims to refine and flesh out a potentially viable idea and create an initial version of the company's offering with a minimum investment of time, money, and effort. Prototypes need not be functional products; they might merely be rough models of the offering created for the purpose of eliciting the reaction of potential customers. The ultimate goal of prototyping is to evaluate target customers' response to the core benefit of the offering and mold the offering in a way that maximizes its market potential. Illustrating the importance of prototyping is the MIT Media Lab credo, "Demo or Die," which stresses that ideas have little value to customers or the company unless they are expressed in tangible, practicable form.

Prototypes can vary in complexity. Some prototypes involve relatively simple representations of the underlying concept, such as a diagram illustrating the functionality of the offering, a drawing delineating the overall look and feel of the offering, or a rudimentary model that is limited to the key functionality of the offering and addresses the most important aspect of the proposed product or service. Other prototypes might involve more advanced versions of the offering both in terms of their design and functionality. Based on their level of complexity, different prototypes are employed at different stages of the new product development process. Simpler prototypes are more likely to be employed at the idea-generation and concept-development stages of the offering. In contrast, more complex prototypes tend to be employed at the more advanced stages of new product development, such as during the offering-development stage.

Prototyping is not a linear process in which the initial idea naturally evolves into a viable prototype. Rather, prototyping typically involves testing the key assumptions of the initial concept in order to improve it—a process referred to as *validated learning*. Validated learning begins even before the prototype is conceived. It starts with observing the market, identifying an unmet need, and generating an idea for an offering that addresses this need. This idea is then turned into a prototype that captures the core concept of the offering and is tested to ensure its desirability and feasibility. This process is repeated until a satisfactory outcome is achieved, and the company can proceed to design a business model before building and launching the actual offering (Figure 5).

Figure 5. The Validated-Learning Approach

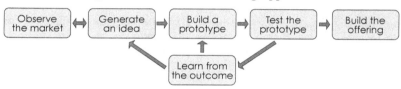

Validated learning is based on data, not gut feeling. It typically involves empirical tests aimed at optimizing the initial concept by varying different attributes of the offering and evaluating their impact on its feasibility and desirability. Stepwise product development, combined with experimentation aimed at verifying the key assumptions guiding the development process, is the hallmark of the validated-learning approach. Rather than conducting *all* market research prior to developing the offering—a legacy approach favored by many corporations—the validated-learning approach is an iterative process of designing, testing, and modifying different aspects of the offering.

To ensure that the new offering is well received in the market, companies rigorously test prototypes at different stages of their development. There are two types of prototype tests: *alpha testing*, which involves an evaluation of the product within the company, and *beta testing*, which tests the product with end users. The more novel and complex the offering, the greater amount of alpha and beta testing it is likely to undergo. Beta testing is particularly important for products and services that have multiple applications and are used by different customers in different contexts. For example, new software products and services typically go through extensive user testing to ensure their functionality across different platforms and applications.

Concept Validation

Concept validation assesses the soundness of the core concept underlying the proposed offering. Concept validation typically addresses two factors: the feasibility of the offering to determine if creating the offering is technologically possible, and its desirability to assess whether target customers find the offering attractive. Accordingly, to validate the concept behind the offering, a manager should ask the following questions:

Is the offering feasible? Can a functional prototype of the offering be built? Can a fully functional version of the offering be built?

Does the core concept of the offering appeal to its target customers? Does it address the identified customer need better than the alternative options? Are different attributes of the offering optimized to create customer value?

In order to proceed to the next stage of business model design, a company must validate the core concept underlying the company's offering. If the concept cannot be validated, the company must pivot and redefine the concept. If after multiple iterations the concept cannot be validated, the company must step back and reevaluate the underlying idea.

To illustrate, inventor Sir James Dyson—whose prior inventions include the eponymous transparent vacuum cleaner, the energy-efficient Airblade hand dryer for public restrooms, and the bladeless Air Multiplier fan—spent over four years developing his Supersonic hair dryer. The development of the hair dryer involved a rigorous validation process that included making in excess of 600 prototypes before reaching the final design. Over 100 engineers were involved and more than 250 patents were filed during the development of the new hair dryer. To create a perfect hair dryer, Dyson, who is often referred to as the "Steve Jobs of domestic appliances," conducted tests on 1,000-plus miles of human hair both in his labs and through more than 200 user tests. In pursuit of perfection, engineers also conducted over 7,000 acoustic tests to ensure that the dryer would be sufficiently quiet. The result: a hair dryer that is faster, quieter, lighter, and more aesthetically pleasing than any other product in its category.

Business Model Design

Development of a viable concept is followed by designing a business model that delineates the ways in which an offering will create and capture market value. Unlike concept development, which focuses on the feasibility and the desirability of the offering, business model design also focuses on the offering's viability—the ability of the offering to create value for the company.

Designing the Business Model

Designing the business model involves three key components (discussed in detail in Chapter 2): identifying the *target market*, articulating the offering's *value proposition* in that market, and delineating the key attributes of the *market offering* (Figure 6).

Figure 6. The Key Components of a Business Model of a New Offering

- The **target market** delineates the market in which a company's offering strives to create value. The target market comprises target customers, competitors, collaborators, the company, and the market context.

- The **value proposition** describes the value that the company plans to create for target customers and collaborators as well as the value that the company aims to capture for its stakeholders.

- The **market offering** defines the ways in which the company will create, communicate, and deliver value to its target customers, collaborators, and stakeholders. Specifically, this involves delineating the product, service, brand, price, incentives, communication, and distribution aspects of the offering.

The creation of market value is the ultimate goal of the business model. Accordingly, the success of an offering is determined by the degree to which it can create value for its target customers, collaborators, and the company. Thus, the design of a business model for a new offering is guided by three key questions:

How does the offering create value for target customers? How does it fulfill customer needs better than the alternative options?

How does the offering create value for the company's collaborators? How does it enable the company's collaborators to achieve their goals better than the alternative options?

How does the offering create value for the company? How does it enable the company to achieve its goals better than the alternative options?

The key principles involved in developing the value proposition and the process of creating customer, company, and collaborator value maps were discussed in detail in Chapter 2.

Business Model Validation

The ultimate goal of the business model is to create market value. To this end, the initial idea undergoes a number of pivots and realignments, resulting in a sustainable business model. Pivots and realignments in designing the company's offering are guided by three key principles: *desirability*, *feasibility*, and *viability*.

- **Desirability** reflects the degree to which target customers find the offering attractive. Because customer value is a function of benefits and costs, an offering's desirability might be hindered by its inability to deliver the benefits sought by customers and by the high costs—money, time, and effort—associated with the offering. For example, Crystal Pepsi, a clear, caffeine-free alternative to regular colas, failed despite a massive promotional campaign because consumers did not find the concept of a clear cola appealing. Lisa, a personal computer designed by Apple in the early 1980s, failed largely due to its $10,000 price tag that far exceeded customers' willingness to pay for the device.

- **Feasibility** reflects the degree to which the company has the ability to build an offering that has the functionality desired by customers. Feasibility is a function of current technologies and the company's ability to utilize these technologies. For example, until recently long-range electric cars were not feasible because of limited battery capacity. Ultimate examples of projects that are not considered feasible are a perpetual motion machine and a time machine.

- **Viability** reflects the degree to which an offering is capable of creating value for the company. The viability of an offering from a for-profit perspective is reflected in its ability to generate profits. Viability is typically a function of the expected revenue streams from an offering and its cost structure. The inability to align revenues and costs is often a precursor of market failure. For example, despite its high-profile promotional campaign and a widely recognized brand, online pet supply retailer Pets.com lost money on most of its sales and ultimately went out of business due to its weak fundamentals.

Because a company's success is driven by the desirability, feasibility, and viability of its offerings, the sustainability of the business model is determined by the answers to the following three questions:

Do target customers find the offering attractive?

Does the company have the resources to build the offering?

Can the offering create value for the company?

The desirability, feasibility, and viability aspects of the offering are typically related, such that failure to meet acceptable levels on one dimension is also likely to lead to failure on other dimensions. Thus, an offering that is undesirable to customers would likely not prove to be viable because it would not generate sufficient customer demand to create value for the company. In the same vein, an offering that is not technologically feasible would also fail the desirability test because the offering that can actually be built would not fulfill customer needs.

Offering Development

Offering development is the process of creating the actual offering that the company will introduce in the market. This process involves two main steps: *developing the resources* necessary for the business model to be put into action and *producing the market offering*.

Developing the Core Resources

To succeed, a company must have the necessary resources to implement its business model. It is common for a company not to have all of the resources necessary to create and launch the offering. Thus, after the business model has been designed, the logical next step is to develop the necessary resources by building, outsourcing, or acquiring them.

Resource development involves several activities that can be tied to the resources needed to ensure a company's ability to create market value (discussed in Chapter 6). These activities include:

- Establishing the **business infrastructure**, which includes activities such as procuring manufacturing equipment, developing sales and service call centers, and building the necessary information technology links.

- Developing **supply channels** to obtain the materials needed to create the offering.

- Recruiting, training, and retaining **skilled employees** who can contribute the required technological, operational, and business expertise.

- Gathering the relevant **knowledge** to enable the company to implement different aspects of the offering's business model.

- Developing ancillary **products** and **services** that act as an ecosystem for the new offering.

- Developing **communication channels** to educate target customers about the offering.

- Developing **distribution channels** through which the offering will be delivered to target customers.

- Providing **access to capital** to secure the financial resources needed to implement the business model.

To gain the resources needed to successfully launch the new offering, a company might adopt one of two different strategies. First, the company might create its own resources by internally developing its assets and capabilities or by acquiring the necessary resources from a third party. Alternatively, rather than building its own resources, a company might choose to collaborate with other entities that have the resources required to develop, manufacture, distribute, and promote the offering, and leverage these resources without assuming ownership of them.

As with most business decisions, entering into a collaborative relationship with other entities to gain the resources needed for offering development involves weighing the relevant benefits and costs. On the *benefit* side, collaboration enables each party to take advantage of the other's expertise, providing both entities with a competitive advantage stemming from greater specialization. Furthermore, collaboration can also increase cost efficiency because each collaborator can achieve greater economies of scale and experience by specializing in a given function. In addition, collaboration requires a lesser commitment of resources in comparison to developing the necessary in-house expertise, thus offering much greater flexibility in terms of switching technologies, entering new markets, and exiting existing ones. Finally, collaboration enables a company to achieve the desired results much faster than building in-house expertise.

Despite its numerous benefits, collaboration has several important *drawbacks*. First, delegating certain aspects of a company's activities to an external entity often leads to loss of control over the process of developing and managing the offering. Furthermore, outsourcing key activities tends to weaken a company's core competencies and its ability to drive innovation. Outsourcing also might enable collaborating entities to develop a set of strategic competencies, thus becoming a company's potential competitor. For a collaboration to be sustainable, its benefits must outweigh the potential drawbacks, such that the collaboration creates value for both the company and its collaborators.

Developing the Market Offering

Developing the market offering involves turning the offering concept (prototype) into the actual product and service that the company will introduce in the market. To this end, producing the offering involves deployment of the company's resources—its own as well as those of its collaborators—needed to implement the business model.

Developing the offering often involves advanced prototyping and market testing to ensure that the offering will succeed in creating market value. The amount of prototyping and testing done is influenced by a variety of factors such as product novelty, product complexity, and the investment required to modify the offering after it has been launched. New-to-the-world products warrant more market testing than products that involve slight modifications from what is already available in the market. More complex products are more likely to benefit from market testing compared to simpler products. Products that require high levels of investment to be modified after launch (e.g., retooling the manufacturing plant to modify the design of a car) are in greater need of advanced prototyping and market testing compared to products that can be modified relatively easily post launch.

An important decision in producing the new offering is whether to start by developing the ultimate, fully functional version of the offering or to initially develop a simplified version that features only the key functionality of the offering. In this context, a company may consider developing a *minimum viable offering*—the simplest version of the offering that is able to deliver the primary benefit(s) sought by target customers. The alternative to developing a minimum viable offering—developing a fully functional, full-scale offering without previously testing a simplified version—requires substantial investment at a time when market and technological uncertainty are relatively high. As a result, a company risks losing significant resources should some of its assumptions about the market and the technological feasibility of the offering prove to be incorrect. Rather than taking the risk of building a full-scale product or service, starting with a relatively simple version of the offering and validating this version prior to developing the final version reduces the uncertainty associated with bringing new products to market. The concept of the minimum viable offering is discussed in greater detail at the end of this chapter.

Commercial Deployment

Commercial deployment involves informing target customers about the company's offering and making the offering available to these customers. Because large-scale rollouts are associated with greater uncertainty and higher costs, companies often test the offering by initially launching it in a few selected markets prior to introducing it to all target customers. Thus, commercial deployment often includes two steps: *selective market entry*, which involves deploying the offering in selected markets, and *market expansion*, which involves making the offering available to the entire target market.

Selective Market Entry

Market entry via selective deployment aims to test the offering in a natural environment and observe how target customers, competitors, and company collaborators react to the offering. Because of its smaller scale, selective market deployment enables the company to be more agile in adjusting different aspects of the offering in order to maximize its market impact.

The subset of target customers that is the focus of the offering's initial deployment is also referred to as the *primary target*. The primary target is typically the low-hanging fruit that the company initially targets to prove the viability of its business model, fine-tune the offering, and generate a stream of revenue. The choice of the primary target is driven by three key factors: *target attractiveness*, *resource efficiency*, and *scale sufficiency*.

- **Target attractiveness** reflects the degree to which customers in a given market are likely to adopt the company's offering. Prioritizing customers based on the likelihood that they will adopt the offering typically follows *the path of least resistance*. Thus, the likelihood that customers will be among the first to adopt a company's offering depends on whether they (1) have the need that the offering aims to solve, (2) view this need as a problem that needs solving, and (3) actively seek a way to address this problem. Customers for whom all three conditions hold are the most likely to adopt the company's offering and, hence, also the most likely to be chosen as the primary target. Customers for whom only the first condition holds — those who can benefit from the company's offering but are reasonably satisfied with the status quo — are the least likely to be selected as primary targets (Figure 7).

Figure 7. The Path of Least Resistance

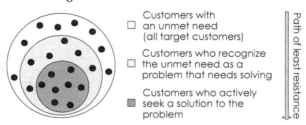

- **Resource efficiency** reflects the company resources needed to communicate and deliver the offering to target customers. In choosing its primary target, companies often follow *the path of least resources*, determined by the company's ability to effectively and cost efficiently communicate and deliver the offering to these customers. For example, a company might choose its primary target because these customers are already aware of the company's brand and the company has the distribution channels in place to reach these customers (Figure 8). Note that the identification of customers based on the costs of informing them about the offering and delivering the offering often takes place simultaneously, as the company seeks to identify segments that are characterized by relatively low communication *and* distribution costs.

Figure 8. The Path of Least Resources

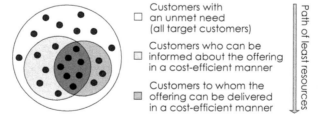

- **Scale sufficiency** reflects the minimum size of the primary market needed to ensure that this market is viable from the company's standpoint. The choice of the primary market can be facilitated by the assessment of the *minimum viable target* — the smallest subset of target customers that is of adequate size to generate the revenue needed to sufficiently offset the company's costs of producing, promoting, and distributing the offering.

The primary target is defined by the convergence of the path of least resistance, the path of least resources, and the minimum viable scale. Therefore, when choosing a primary target for a new offering, a company should focus on markets (1) in which customers have a burning unresolved problem that they are actively seeking to address, (2) that can be easily reached by the company, and (3) that are large enough to enable the company to achieve its goals.

Market Expansion

Market expansion involves going beyond the primary target to include all customers for whom the company's offering aims to create value. Market expansion is the next logical step following successful deployment of the company's offering in its primary target market.

To expand beyond the primary target market, a company needs to (1) scale up the operations involved in the production of the offering, (2) promote the offering to all target customers, and (3) ensure that the offering is available across the entire target market. During market expansion, a company is typically moving into more challenging markets in which customers are less likely to immediately recognize the value of its offering and are more difficult to reach. As a result, the time, effort, and resources involved in market expansion are likely to exceed those involved in initial market deployment.

Because broader markets tend to involve customers with more diverse needs and preferences, market expansion often involves a shift from a single offering to a product line comprising offerings tailored to the different needs and preferences of its customers. Thus, a company might start with a single offering targeting its most likely adopters, and, as it expands to the broader market over time, introduce variations of this offering that are likely to appeal to different customers within the target market. The increased assortment of company offerings associated with market expansion, in turn, calls for additional resources to ensure the success of these offerings in the broader market. The issue of managing product lines is discussed in more detail in Chapter 17.

Understanding the Adoption of New Offerings

A thorough understanding of how buyers make their purchase decisions and how quickly they adopt products is essential to managing new offerings. The process by which a good, service, or idea spreads from its source to its ultimate users or recipients is often referred to as diffusion of innovation. Three popular frameworks that examine customers' reaction to new offerings are *the S-Curve model of new product adoptions, Rogers' model of adoption of innovations,* and *Moore's model of adoption of new technologies.*

New Product Adoption

New product adoption is often depicted by an S-shaped curve that indicates the total number of adoptions for an offering at a given point in time. The S-shape of the curve reflects the fact that adoptions tend to grow slowly at first, then accelerate before eventually beginning to slow down until the offering reaches its full market potential.

The S-Curve model of new product adoptions is defined by two key factors: the *market potential*, which reflects the total number of customers that are likely to adopt the offering, and the *speed of diffusion*, which reflects the time frame when the inflection point (where the rate of total adoptions begins to slow down) will be reached. The speed of diffusion is often defined based on how fast adoption of the offering can reach the inflection point, which is when the growth rate starts declining and the shape of the S-curve turns from convex to concave (Figure 9).

Figure 9. The S-Curve of the Total Number of Adoptions of an Innovation

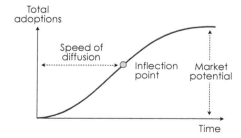

An alternative way to represent new product adoption is by using the rate of new adoptions, instead of total adoptions, at a given point in time. The pattern of adoption of innovation in this case is depicted by a bell-shaped curve indicating that the relatively small number of customers who adopt the product initially is followed by an increase in the number of adoptees, which again declines after reaching a peak (Figure 10). Note that the peak of adoptions in Figure 10 corresponds to the inflection point in Figure 9, which represents the beginning of the decline in the growth rate of adoptions.

Figure 10. The Bell-Shaped Curve of New Adoptions of an Innovation

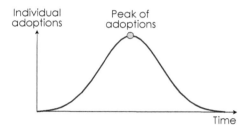

New product adoption does not always occur in a manner that produces a symmetric bell-shaped curve. For example, adoption might start very slowly and not reach the point at which the majority of target customers have adopted the offering until quite late in the adoption process. Alternatively, a large number of customers might adopt a new offering immediately after its launch, with sales tapering off slowly until the product is adopted by all target customers (Figure 11).

Figure 11. Alternative Patterns of Adoption of Innovation

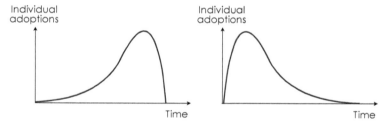

The pattern of the adoption curve and the speed of adoption depend on several factors:

- **Prominence of the underlying need.** Offerings that address an important need that has been recognized by customers as a problem (need-to-have offerings) are more likely to enjoy faster adoption. Conversely, offerings that address a need that customers do not view as an important problem that must be solved (nice-to-have offerings) are typically adopted much more slowly. For example, Dollar Shave Club gained rapid acceptance among men who were dissatisfied with the price of Gillette's razors and were ready to switch to a lower price option as soon as it became available.

- **Inherent value of the offering.** The inherent value of a new offering reflects the benefits and costs it creates for target customers. The speed with which a new offering is adopted is directly related to its inherent value: Offerings that fully address a particular customer need (or a set of needs) are likely to be adopted faster than offerings that only partially meet customer needs. For example, one of the reasons for the iPhone's rapid success was that it performed multiple functions—a communication device, an address/phone book, a portable music player, a camera and a camcorder, and a gaming device—thus addressing multiple customer needs.

- **Relative advantage.** An offering that has a larger edge over competitive options is more likely to be adopted than an offering with a smaller competitive edge or an offering whose value is at parity with the competition. For example, the popularity of Netflix was in part due to the fact that it offered numerous advantages—including convenience, variety, and price—over the traditional video rental stores such as Blockbuster.

- **Transparency of benefits.** Customers are more likely to adopt offerings with benefits that can be readily observed and experienced compared to offerings with benefits that cannot be readily observed. For example, many consumers were reluctant to purchase TiVo, the first digital video recorder, because most of its benefits were not observable at the time of purchase and buyers had to experience the product in order to truly appreciate the improvement it could make to their television-viewing experience.

- **Compatibility.** An offering that is compatible with existing systems and processes used by customers and does not require these customers to change their behavior is more likely to be adopted by customers. For example, customers are more likely to adopt offerings from companies like Microsoft, Apple, and Adobe, which have established product platforms and ecosystems, than offerings whose compatibility is uncertain.

- **Perceived risk.** Customers are more likely to adopt an offering when the risk associated with acquiring it is low. The greater the consumer uncertainty about how a new offering will perform and whether it will meet their particular needs, the lower the likelihood that customers will rush to adopt the new offering. For example, Warby Parker reduced the uncertainty associated with buying designer eyewear online by enabling customers to upload a photo and try on frames virtually, as well as by offering a program that allows shoppers to try on up to five frames at home free of charge.

- **Promotional activities.** Greater promotional activity—including advertising, social media, and promotional incentives—tends to increase the likelihood that the new offering will be adopted by customers. For example, using an aggressive promotional campaign, Casper, an online retailer of sleep products, managed to generate over $1 million in sales revenues in less than a month after the launch of the company.

- **Availability.** The speed of adoption and the market potential is also a function of customers' ability to acquire the company's offering. The greater the availability of the offering, such as the density of the distribution channels that carry the offering and the offering's in-stock supply, the greater the likelihood that customers will adopt the offering. For example, Dasani—bottled water distributed by Coca-Cola Company—owes its popularity to a large degree to the company's strong presence in distribution channels, which helped make the brand available to shoppers.

- **Purchase frequency.** The adoption pattern of new offerings is also a function of the length of the repurchase cycle. Thus, customers are more likely to adopt a new offering in frequently purchased categories than in categories in which purchases are infrequent. For example, consumer packaged goods such as snacks, beverages, and cosmetics are likely to enjoy a faster adoption cycle compared to durable goods such as automobiles, appliances, and furniture.

Rogers' Model of Adoption of Innovations

Rogers' model, named after American sociologist Everett Rogers, is arguably the most common classification of customers according to the speed with which they adopt new offerings.[2] A key premise underlying Rogers' model is that some individuals are inherently more open to innovation than others. This model further assumes that the adoption of innovation follows a bell-shaped curve and that individuals are located along this curve depending on the time frame in which the innovation is adopted (Figure 12). In this context, Rogers' model distinguishes five categories of customers: innovators (the first 2.5% of the adopters), early adopters (the 13.5% of adopters following the innovators), early majority (the next 34% of adopters), late majority (the next 34%), and laggards (the remaining 16%).[3]

Figure 12. Rogers' Categorization of Customers Based on the Timing of Adoption of Innovation

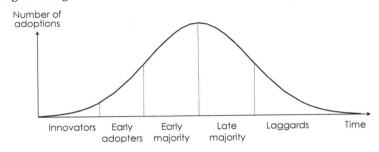

The percentages associated with each customer category are based on the assumption that the process of adoption of innovations is characterized by a normal (in statistical terms) distribution pattern that is defined by its mean and its standard deviation (the variation from the mean). In this context, Rogers' model defines the early and late majorities as one standard deviation from the mean and early adopters as two standard deviations from the mean. The classification of customers across the adoption curve is non-symmetric, with three categories to the left of the mean and two categories to the right. This occurs because the segment on the far left of the mean is divided into two categories, innovators and early adopters, that together are the same size as the laggards segment on the right. Rogers' reasoning for this division is that innovators and early adopters show a distinctive adoption behavior that needs to be considered separately.

Despite its popularity, Rogers' model has a number of limitations. One limitation is that it is solely a descriptive model. Although it identifies five different categories of adopters, it does not offer a decision rule to help determine whether a particular customer will become an early adopter or a laggard. Rogers' model is also limited by the (often unrealistic) assumption that adoption of innovations always follows the symmetrical bell-like pattern of a normal distribution, whereby the percentage of individuals falling into each of the five categories is based on the degree of standard deviation from the midpoint of the adoption curve. Furthermore, individuals are assigned to one of the five categories based on relatively stable personality traits, even though in reality a customer who is an innovator in one domain might be a laggard in another. The above limitations restrict the applicability of Rogers' model to a descriptive classification of five common types of innovation adopters.

Moore's Model of Adoption of New Technologies

Moore's model, named after organizational theorist Geoffrey Moore, adapts Rogers' model to technology products.[4] Moore's model views the adoption of technology-based innovations as discontinuous, with different consumer groups displaying different adoption patterns that require disparate marketing strategies. Based on how they view technology, Moore's model allocates customers into five distinct categories that roughly correspond to the five categories defined by the Rogers model. Specifically, Moore labels innovators as *technology enthusiasts*, early adopters as *visionaries*, early majority as *pragmatists*, late majority as *conservatives*, and laggards as *skeptics*. These five categories of adopters of technology innovation are delineated below:

- **Technology enthusiasts** (innovators) are fundamentally committed to new technology and derive utility from being the first to experience new high-tech offerings.

- **Visionaries** (early adopters) are among the first to apply new technologies to solve problems and exploit opportunities in the marketplace.

- **Pragmatists** (early majority) view technological innovation as a productivity tool. Unlike enthusiasts, they do not appreciate technology for its own sake. Unlike visionaries, they do not use technological innovations to discover new opportunities but rather to optimize the efficiency and effectiveness of activities in their daily life.

- **Conservatives** (late majority) are generally pessimistic about their ability to significantly benefit from new technological innovations and are reluctant to adopt them.

- **Skeptics** (laggards) are critics of any innovative technology and are not likely to adopt such technologies even when they offer distinct benefits.

Unlike Rogers' model, which implies a smooth and continuous progression across segments during the life of an offering, Moore's model asserts that the adoption of technology-based innovations follows a discontinuous pattern. This discontinuity in the adoption process stems from the fact that different customers have different needs and, therefore, require different market strategies. Thus, once a technology has reached its market potential within a given customer segment, it might not naturally roll over to the next segment.

According to Moore, the largest gap in the adoption process is the one between the early adopters — a segment comprising enthusiasts and visionaries — and the mainstream market — a segment encompassing pragmatists, conservatives, and skeptics. Crossing this gap, referred to by Moore as the "chasm," is the biggest challenge in developing technological innovations and is the key hurdle that prevents technology pioneers from gaining widespread acceptance of their offerings (Figure 13).

Figure 13. Moore's Application of Rogers' Model to Technology Markets

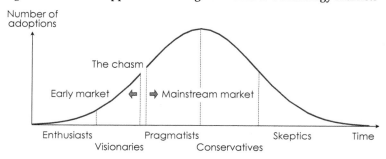

Moore argues that promoting technological innovations first to technology enthusiasts can help educate visionaries and mitigate some of the problems caused by discontinuity. Visionaries then can pave the way for pragmatists, who compose one of the two largest market segments. Experience with pragmatists should allow the company to gain valuable knowledge that leads to a more effective and cost-efficient product that will attract conservatives, the other large market segment. Moore's recommendation with respect to skeptics, referred to as the gadflies of technology, is not to pursue them at all.

Similar to the Rogers model, Moore's model has several limitations, including the assumption that the adoption process always follows a perfect bell-shaped curve, with a preset percentage of individuals allocated to each of the five categories. Furthermore, because individuals' adoption patterns tend to vary based on the type of innovations involved, a given individual might be very likely to adopt innovations in one domain and be unwilling to change their behavior in another. This is important because the gaps between segments — and in particular the gap between the visionaries and pragmatists — are an essential component of Moore's model, making the identification and size of each segment crucial. Thus, even though the idea behind Moore's model — that customers adopt new technology at a varying pace — is viable, it contains a number of important assumptions that limit its predictive validity. As a result, the primary applicability of Moore's model is as a conceptual model outlining some of the factors and processes guiding the adoption of technological innovations.

SUMMARY

New product development is an iterative process of discovering a novel idea and translating this idea into a viable, successful market offering through a series of realignments and pivots. New product development is commonly represented as a sequence of actions (stages) separated by hurdles (gates) that the new offering must overcome. This stage-gate approach divides the innovation process into five key stages — idea generation, concept development, business model design, offering development, and commercial deployment — separated by gates that aim to validate the actions taken in the previous step.

Innovation begins with *generating an idea* that pinpoints an unmet market need and suggests a novel way to address this need. Ideas can be generated top down, by starting with identifying a market opportunity, or bottom up, by starting with an invention and then seeking a market need it can fulfill. The top-down approach is the preferred idea generation method.

Concept development embodies a potentially viable idea by creating an initial version of the offering. It aims to reduce market and implementation risk by designing the offering in an effective and resource-efficient way and typically evolves from a description of the product's core benefits to a prototype that features the offering's core functionality. Prototype testing can involve an evaluation of the product within the company (alpha testing) and testing the product with customers (beta testing).

Business model design involves identifying the target market, articulating the offering's value proposition in that market, and delineating the key attributes of the market offering. Business model validation assesses the ability of an offering to create market value on three key dimensions: desirability (does the offering create value for target customers), feasibility (can the offering actually be built as conceived), and viability (does the offering create value for the company and its collaborators).

Offering development turns the conceptualized offering into an actual offering that is ready for market launch. Offering development involves two components: gathering the necessary resources to put the business model into action and producing the actual offering.

Commercial deployment informs target customers about the company's offering and makes the offering available to these customers. To minimize risk and resources, companies often deploy the offering in selected (primary) markets to test its viability before making the offering available to the entire target market. Identifying the primary market is guided by three key factors: target attractiveness, resource efficiency, and scale sufficiency. Market expansion involves ramping up the facilities involved in the offering's production, promoting the offering to all target customers, and ensuring that the offering is available to the entire target market.

Three popular frameworks examine how individuals adopt new offerings. *The S-Curve model* depicts the cumulative number of adoptions for an offering at a given point in time. *Rogers' model* depicts the number of new adoptions, rather than total adoptions, at a given point in time, and divides customers into five categories—innovators, early adopters, early majority, late majority, and laggards—based on the timing of new product adoption. Building on Rogers' model, *Moore's model* argues that in the case of technology products, the adoption of innovations is a discontinuous process marked by distinct adoption gaps, the largest of which is the gap between early adopters (enthusiasts and visionaries) and the mainstream market.

MARKETING INSIGHT: THE MINIMUM VIABLE OFFERING

The minimum viable offering (MVO) is a streamlined version of the offering that incorporates only features that are essential for fulfilling the customer need.[5] It is the simplest version of the offering that is able to deliver the primary benefit(s) sought by target customers.

The minimum viable offering is an alternative to developing a fully functional, full-scale offering. The primary goal of developing a minimum viable offering is to reduce the risk associated with making substantial investments in money, time, and effort during the early stages of the project, when both market and technological uncertainty are high and company assumptions about the market and the technological feasibility of the offering may later prove to be erroneous. The development of a minimum viable offering allows the company to ramp up investment in the offering as uncertainty and the corresponding risk of failure decrease. Thus, starting with a relatively simple version of the offering and seeking market validation before proceeding to the final version reduces the uncertainty associated with bringing new products to market.

Designing the minimum viable offering calls for balancing the key benefits sought by target customers with the resources needed to create these benefits. In this context, the aim of the minimum viable offering is to balance desirability (customer appeal), feasibility (achievability), and viability (company value) in order to optimize its market value. Thus, from a desirability standpoint, the minimum viable offering builds on the diminishing marginal value principle, whereby the majority of the customer benefits are created by relatively few attributes and the incremental value created by additional attributes tends to decrease as the overall attractiveness of the offering increases. From a feasibility standpoint, a greater number of features is often associated with greater technological complexity, which potentially could decrease the offering's feasibility. Finally, from a viability standpoint, complicating the offering by adding new features often leads to an exponential increase in the costs associated with the offering. In this context, the minimum viable offering aims to find the "sweet spot" that allows delivery of the key benefits to target customers at the lowest possible level of technological complexity and company costs (Figure 14).

**Figure 14. The Minimum Viable Offering as a Function of
the Offering's Desirability, Feasibility, and Viability**

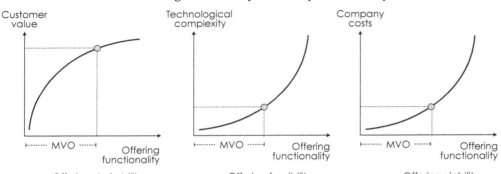

In addition to reducing the risk associated with the company's investment in the development of new products and services, the minimum-viable-offering approach allows the company to observe customers' reaction to the offering and, thus, get a better feel for the ways in which the offering can be modified to increase its desirability. Another important benefit of developing a minimum viable offering is that it can create a stream of revenue well before the final offering is launched. As such, the minimum viable offering can be viewed as a revenue-generating core module of the final offering that can offer a lifeline to cash-strapped startups and provide greater latitude to teams developing the offering in larger organizations.

It is important to note that despite its popularity, the minimum-viable-offering approach is not universal and is most relevant when developing relatively simple products and services whose core benefits can be captured by a streamlined version of the offering. This approach is particularly relevant for online services that can be easily scaled up by adding functionality and improving customers' overall experience. In the case of relatively complex offerings such as airplanes, automobiles, and household appliances, the minimum-viable-offering approach might not prove to be relevant, and the development of new offerings is better served by systematic planning and testing of the offering at the different stages of its development.

MARKETING INSIGHT: THE FIVE PRINCIPLES OF PROTOTYPE DEVELOPMENT

When developing new offerings, a company must determine the right balance between the resources invested in the project and the market and technological risks associated with the project. A common mistake made by companies, especially larger ones, involves overinvesting in the early stages of the development of a new product.

To ensure the right risk–reward balance, a company can benefit from following five basic principles: *start small, stay focused, keep it simple, fail fast,* and *fail forward.*

- *Start small.* Companies often start out by trying to prototype a complex idea that attempts to address multiple customer needs. The problem is that complex prototypes typically take time to develop and require considerable resources, which, in turn, can defeat the purpose of prototyping. Therefore, regardless of the complexity of the underlying idea, the initial prototype should focus on the most important aspect of the customer need rather than trying to implement all facets of the idea behind the offering.

- *Stay focused.* Prototyping typically offers a variety of ways in which an idea can be implemented. When presented with many possibilities, a manager can easily lose focus and end up pursuing a variety of different, sometimes mutually exclusive, ideas. This lack of focus results in a relatively simple idea branching out into multiple marginally related projects. Successful concept development calls for prototyping one idea at a time.

- *Keep it simple.* Remaining focused on a simple idea can still result in an overcomplicated prototype when the desire for perfection outweighs the primary purpose of a prototype — to develop a scaled-down version of the company's offering in order to minimize market risk. Overcomplicating an idea encumbers the prototype with a variety of bells and whistles that often end up being counterproductive to optimizing the core functionality of the offering.

- *Fail fast.* The ultimate goal of most companies is achieving market success. Yet, when developing a prototype, failing is not necessarily a negative outcome. The purpose of prototyping is not to avoid failing entirely but to fail fast — in other words, to fail early in the process before the company has committed significant resources to developing the offering. Failures allow the company to identify which aspects of the offering do not work and to improve them. In fact, failures — especially those that happen early in the process — can sometimes bring more information to light than successes. After the core concept of the offering is confirmed, a company can test the boundaries of the offering's success by identifying scenarios in which the offering does not do well in the market. Failing early in the process is important so that the company can use the insight gained from failure to develop a better version of the offering.

- *Fail forward.* Failure is inevitable when developing new products. The key to overcoming failure is to fail forward by turning the failure into a learning experience that can help improve the offering. As Thomas Edison noted, *Just because something doesn't do what you planned it to do doesn't mean it's useless.* Failing forward allows for analyzing the causes of failure and capitalizing on mistakes in order to succeed in the future. The key to successful prototyping is not avoiding failures but using them to learn and move forward.

CHAPTER TWENTY

CUSTOMER RELATIONSHIP MANAGEMENT

A manufacturer is not through with his customer when a sale is completed.
He has then only started with his customer.

— Henry Ford, founder of the Ford Motor Company

Customer relationship management comprises a set of activities for managing a company's interactions with its current and potential customers in a way that creates value for both the company and these customers. The key aspects of customer relationship management—managing customer loyalty, building customer equity, and designing a customer-centric organization—are the focus of this chapter. Specifically, we address the following topics:

- *Managing Customer Loyalty* || Understanding customer loyalty | Building customer loyalty | Managing dissatisfied customers
- *Building Customer Equity* || Customer equity as a marketing concept | Managing customer equity to drive profits
- *Designing a Customer-Centric Organization* || Customer centricity as a business philosophy | Developing a customer relationship management system

The discussion of customer relationship management is complemented by an overview of the key customer management metrics and a discussion of models for calculating lifetime customer value.

Managing Customer Loyalty

Marketing management is not just about developing products, services, and brands. It is also an ongoing process of building relationships with customers. A company's products and services change over time. What has the potential to remain unchanged is a company's relationship with its customers. The customer loyalty created over the course of this relationship, can serve as a platform for developing new offerings. The key aspects of managing customer loyalty are outlined in the following sections.

Understanding Customer Loyalty

Successful companies carefully cultivate the relationship with their customers to create long-term customer loyalty. Customer loyalty can help the company strengthen its market position by enhancing the value it creates and captures from its customers. The essence of customer loyalty, the value that it creates for companies, and the role of customer satisfaction as a key building block of customer loyalty are addressed in the following sections.

Customer Loyalty as a Marketing Concept

The term *customer loyalty* can have different meanings depending on the context in which it is used. Loyalty might be used in reference to a customer's positive attitude toward the company's offerings and the intent to repatronize the company's products, services, and brands. This type of loyalty is often referred to as *affective* or *share-of-heart loyalty*. Alternatively, loyalty might be used to refer to a pattern of behavior whereby a customer continues to purchase the company's offerings over time—a type of loyalty commonly referred to as *behavioral* or *share-of-wallet loyalty.*

To illustrate the difference between these types of loyalty, compare a customer who will only buy a Harley-Davidson motorcycle because of a deep emotional attachment to the brand with a customer who repeatedly flies with a particular airline out of habit or the lack of viable competitive offerings and who is ready to switch as soon as a viable option comes along. Both customers are loyal in the sense that they repatronize the company's offerings. However, they vary in the motivation that determines their behavior and, as a result, are likely to respond in a different manner to changes in the market environment (such as the emergence of a viable competitor).

True customer loyalty involves both affective and behavioral commitment. Affective loyalty is important because unless customers feel emotionally attached to the company's offering, their behavior might readily change when a more attractive option appears or repeated purchase becomes more difficult because of situational factors such as stock-outs or a temporary price increase. In the same vein, behavioral loyalty is important because in order for affective loyalty to create value for the company, customers need to take an action that reflects their attitudes by buying (or convincing others to buy) the company's offering.

The Value of Customer Loyalty

Cultivating customer loyalty is a key component in creating company value. Fostering a loyal customer base translates into value for the company. The benefits of having loyal customers, although not always directly observable, are nevertheless real.[1] In particular, customer loyalty is associated with the following company benefits:

- **Lower customer service costs.** Loyal customers are more familiar with the company's offerings, policies, and procedures. They know more about the products and services, tend to be more forgiving of trivial product discrepancies and minor service disruptions, and are often more efficient in their interactions with the company. As a result, a company's costs of serving loyal customers tends to be lower compared to serving newly acquired customers, who are using the company's products and services for the first time.

- **Greater effectiveness and cost efficiency of marketing activities.** Loyal customers are more likely to respond positively to a company's communication campaign, which, in turn, leads to a higher return on advertising expenses. Moreover, loyal customers are also less sensitive to price increases initiated by the company and less likely to respond favorably to competitors' price promotions. They are also less likely to respond to competitors' communication and less likely to try competitors' offerings.

- **Product, service, and brand advocacy.** Many loyal customers become vocal advocates of the company's offerings, promoting the benefits of these offerings to their acquaintances, friends, and family. As a result, loyal customers can become a major source of referral, driving the inflow of new customers to the company. For example, customer referrals were the key source of customer growth for companies such as Google, Amazon, Netflix, Instagram, eBay, and YouTube, enabling them to become market leaders in their industries.

- **Lack of acquisition costs.** Another important, yet often overlooked benefit of customer loyalty is that the company does not need to reacquire these customers every time they make a purchase. This benefit is particularly important in the face of rapidly growing customer acquisition costs in many product categories. Thus, rather than focusing on customer acquisition without paying much attention to retaining these customers, a company can significantly improve its market position and financial performance by channeling some of its efforts toward the retention of current customers.

The above benefits of customer loyalty can create significant value for the company and serve as a source of sustainable competitive advantage. Indeed, unlike the attributes of a company's products and services, which in many cases can be easily copied by competitors, customer loyalty cannot be easily replicated. Rather, customer loyalty must be earned—a process that takes time and focused effort on the part of a company.

Customer Satisfaction: The Key to Building Customer Loyalty

Customer satisfaction reflects how a company's products and services match a customer's needs and expectations. Delivering customer satisfaction is the key to cultivating a loyal customer base. Highly satisfied customers tend to have a longer tenure with the company, buy more of the company's current offerings, be more willing to endorse the company's offerings to others, and ultimately create greater value for the company.

To deliver customer satisfaction, the company needs to recognize that customers vary in their needs; thus, the same product or service might create different levels of satisfaction for different customers. Some customers might care about performance, others might emphasize reliability, and still others might deem convenience to be of utmost importance. Therefore, to create customer satisfaction, a company must tailor its offerings in a way that creates value for each and every customer. For example, for companies such as FedEx and DHL which provide mail courier services, speed is often the key attribute on which they need to deliver in order to stay competitive. In contrast, for container shipping companies such as Maersk and MSC, on-time delivery is often more important than speed because their customers need to coordinate the logistics needed for a ship's arrival (e.g., procuring the off-loading equipment, arranging trucking, and securing storage) to ensure cost-efficient processing of the shipped goods.

To ensure customer satisfaction, a company must constantly monitor the degree to which it has been able to fulfill the needs of its target customers. Although there are many ways to measure customer satisfaction, two particular methods have gained popularity among managers. Both methods are relatively simple to administer (they involve a single question), and their results are easy to interpret—a fact that has contributed to their popularity. The first approach directly asks customers to indicate the degree to which they are satisfied with the company's offering. The second approach commonly used to measure customer satisfaction is the Net Promoter Score, a metric designed to assess the likelihood that customers will spread positive word of mouth about a company and its offerings. This approach is based on the assumption that satisfied customers are likely to endorse the offering and recommend it to their acquaintances, friends, and family (see Chapter 5 for a discussion of the Net Promoter Score).

Building Customer Loyalty

Customer loyalty does not just happen. It requires a systematic effort on the part of the company. Several popular approaches for building customer loyalty—acquiring loyal customers, initiating reward programs, creating switching costs, and fostering user groups and brand communities—are outlined in more detail below.

Acquiring Loyal Customers

The profound changes in today's markets call for a new mindset in managing customer acquisition. Instead of acting as hunters seeking out target customers for the company's offerings, marketers should focus on building relationships. Just as gardeners work to promote growth, marketers must focus on creating and sustaining relationships with customers.

Cultivating loyal customers is the foundation of building successful offerings and brands. Yet, many companies think about retaining customers and cultivating customer loyalty only after customer attrition becomes an issue. This short-sighted approach to identifying target customers is counterproductive because the company's efforts to grow its market position end up focusing on deal-seeking buyers who are unlikely to become loyal customers.

Consider the case of a startup company launching a new subscription-based service. The company started by segmenting the market and identifying customers likely to respond favorably to the offering. Next, the company developed a strategy to attract these target customers. The initial customer response was great, and the new service was considered a success. A year later the company failed to meet its profit goals. A customer loyalty audit revealed high attrition rates. In response, the company launched a sales promotion program to improve customer retention rates (Figure 1).

Figure 1. Promotion-Driven Customer Acquisition

The above approach to customer management—considering a retention strategy only *after* realizing that the company is losing its customers—is not uncommon in today's market. Yet, to effectively cultivate a loyal customer base, a company should consider customer retention *before* designing its acquisition strategy. Because a company's ultimate goal is not just to acquire new customers but to create a loyal customer base, thinking about customer retention should precede thinking about acquisition.

Loyalty-driven strategic planning starts with understanding the sources of long-term customer value. The key question here is: "What value does the company's offering create for the customer in the long run?" Next, the company needs to develop a retention strategy that delineates how it would ensure customer loyalty in a competitive market. The question to ask here is: "How can the company ensure that customers stay loyal to its offerings?" The next step is to identify customers who are likely to create value for the company in the long run. The question here is: "Who are the customers that are likely to find the company's offerings desirable and stay loyal to its products, services, and brands?" The final step is to develop a strategy to attract customers with high lifetime-value potential. The question here is: "What is the most effective and cost-efficient approach to acquire high-value customers?" (Figure 2).

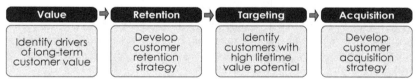

Figure 2. Loyalty-Driven Customer Acquisition

Unlike the acquisition-driven approach, a loyalty-driven customer acquisition strategy does not make customer retention the last step. Loyalty-driven strategic planning makes customer retention rather than customer acquisition the focal point of customer management—an approach that helps the company attract customers who hold the potential to stay loyal to the company's offerings. Because having a loyal customer base is one of the key drivers of profitable long-term growth, before launching a campaign to acquire new customers, a company should have a well-articulated strategy of how it plans to keep these customers. Building customer loyalty must begin with the development of a strategy focused on customer retention rather than on customer acquisition.

Developing Reward Programs

Reward programs (also referred to as loyalty programs) aim to reward customers who repatronize the company's offerings and buy these offerings frequently and/or in large quantities. Popular loyalty programs include frequent flyer programs offered by airlines, frequent-stay programs offered by hotels, and spending-based rewards programs offered by credit card companies.

By offering an attractive set of benefits, reward programs can help nudge customers to choose the company's offerings over those of the competition, as well as purchase these offerings more frequently and in larger quantities. Reward programs can also create psychological benefits for customers by demonstrating the company's appreciation for their patronage and making them feel special by offering extra benefits not available to other buyers.

In addition to engendering customer loyalty, reward programs can be used to collect customer data. These data can shed light on customer spending and help the company stratify customers based on their value to the company. This, in turn, enables the company to offer extra perks to its most valuable customers, cultivate customers who are likely to increase their business with the company, as well as reevaluate the viability of serving those who create marginal or even negative company value.

Creating Switching Costs

Another tool a company can use to promote customer loyalty is creating switching costs. These costs can involve negative financial consequences such as monetary penalties for switching companies or forfeiting the monetary benefits accumulated during the tenure with the company. Alternatively, the switching costs might be functional in nature, requiring customers to expend substantial time and effort to switch companies. Finally, the switching costs can be psychological, as is the case when customers who are already familiar with the particulars of the company's offering have to expend extra mental effort to learn the specifics of a competitor's offering.

Creating switching costs can be thought of as the opposite of launching a reward program. In fact, a reward program and switching costs are not unlike a carrot-and-stick approach. The reward program is the carrot luring customers to the company's offerings, and the switching costs function as the stick, punishing them for their lack of loyalty to the company. Thus, some reward programs aim to ensure customer loyalty with switching costs such as restricting the transferability of the benefits earned by customers. Although this strategy can increase behavioral loyalty, it might have the opposite effect on attitudinal loyalty if customers feel manipulated and resent the company for trying to prevent them from leaving.

Because many customers view switching costs as a company-imposed restriction of their ability to freely choose an offering that best matches their needs, a company must exercise extra effort when imposing such restrictions. Indeed, creating switching costs that seem unnecessary, unreasonable, or unfair can have the opposite of their intended effect on customers' attitude toward the company, creating the perception that the company is trying to take advantage of customer loyalty and goodwill. This negative reaction is particularly relevant in the case of switching costs that are associated with a monetary loss or substantial effort on the part of the customer.

Fostering User Groups and Brand Communities

A user group is a community of individuals that use a company's products or services and share relevant information and experiences. A brand community, on the other hand, is a community of individuals—customers as well as company employees—who have a sense of connection with the brand, identify with the brand, and share rituals and traditions that enhance and perpetuate the meaning of the brand.

User and brand communities can arise organically among product users and brand loyalists who want to share product-related information and their connection with the brand. Alternatively, they can be organized, sponsored, and facilitated by the company. For example, in 1983 Harley-Davidson created a passionate brand community called the Harley Owners Group (H.O.G.) as a way to strengthen the relationship between customers and the company and its employees. Sponsored by local Harley-Davidson dealers, Harley Owners Groups organize various community events including bike rallies and charity rides for its more than one million members worldwide.

User groups and brand communities benefit not only customers but also the company. They help the company by supporting other users and inspiring their passion for the brand while providing the company with valuable feedback regarding ways to improve its products and services. Moreover, user groups and brand communities can help to promote the company's offering among non-users, communicate the meaning of the company's brand, and create and enhance brand loyalty.

Managing Dissatisfied Customers

Despite a company's efforts to create value for all customers at all times, in reality this is not always possible. Indeed, because customers vary in their needs and preferences, customizing the offering in a way that perfectly fits the needs of each and every customer might not be economically and logistically viable. Moreover, even when the company can tailor its offering to a customer's needs, it might not be able to provide a flawless product and service in every instance because of inevitable manufacturing defects and service delivery inconsistencies. As a result, even when a company is able to deliver a high level of customer satisfaction, not all customers are satisfied all the time. The unavoidable presence of dissatisfaction raises the question of how to manage customers who for one reason or another are unhappy with the company's offerings.

Managing dissatisfied customers is important for several reasons. First, the negative impact of failing to meet customer expectations is disproportionate to the positive effect of exceeding their expectations. In other words, the degree to which customers are dissatisfied with an underperforming offering is significantly greater than the degree to which they are delighted by an offering that performs better than expected. As a result of this asymmetry, customers are likely to pay greater attention and experience a stronger emotional reaction to underperforming offerings than to offerings that meet or exceed their expectations.

Second, dissatisfied customers are more likely to share their negative experience with others compared to those who have been satisfied and even delighted by the company's offerings. Some estimates suggest that unhappy customers are three to four times more likely to share their dissatisfaction than those who had a satisfactory experience with the company. Because customers are more likely to share their dissatisfaction with underperforming offerings than their delight with offerings that meet or exceed their expectations, negative publicity about a company's offering is likely to spread much faster than positive publicity.

Finally, resolving a customer's issue in a prompt and effective manner can actually *increase* rather than simply restore customer loyalty. Indeed, on many occasions customers understand that despite the company's best efforts to fulfill the needs of its target customers, mistakes can happen. The fact that the company has taken an action to quickly rectify the error signals to customers that the company really cares about its customers. Thus, by effectively managing customer dissatisfaction, a company can turn expressions of discontent into an opportunity to increase loyalty.

Managing dissatisfied customers requires companies to walk a fine line between creating value for its customers and creating value for the company's stakeholders. Not all complaints can be solved to a customer's satisfaction.[2] Solving some complaints might call for investing resources that the company simply does not have. Other complaints might not be legitimate either because customers have unrealistic expectations of the company's offering or because customers are trying to take advantage of relatively minor transgressions to extract some form of compensation from the company.

When dealing with dissatisfied customers, a company should guard against making two types of errors: granting a disingenuous request from a customer who is trying to take advantage of the company or, alternatively, failing to honor a legitimate complaint by a customer who has been wronged by the company. The type of error a company is willing to accept depends on its business model. High-margin companies are often willing to accept the first type of error, whereas the low-margin companies tend to prefer the second type of error.

Building Customer Equity

Despite being a crucial component of a company's marketing strategy, cultivating a loyal customer base is not the company's ultimate goal. At the most general level, the company's goal is to create value for its stakeholders. Building and sustaining customer loyalty is just one aspect of achieving this goal. As a result, when delivering customer satisfaction and cultivating customer loyalty, a company must be cognizant of the value that these customers create for the company. Understanding the value customers are likely to create during their tenure with the company—also referred to as customer equity—is paramount for the company's market success.

Customer Equity as a Marketing Concept

To build customer equity, a company must have a clear understanding of the value customers are likely to create for the company, identify the key drivers of customer equity, and delineate how these drivers work together to create company value. These issues are discussed in more detail in the following sections.

The Essence of Customer Equity

Customer equity is the monetary equivalent of the lifetime value of a company's customers. The term *customer equity* is used in two different contexts: in reference to the lifetime value created by a *particular* customer as well as in reference to the combined lifetime value of *all* the company's customers.[3] Here we use the term customer equity in its latter meaning as the monetary expression of the total value that a company's customers are likely to create during their tenure with the company. We use the term customer lifetime value (CLV) in reference to the monetary equivalent of the lifetime value of a particular customer.

The concept of customer equity can be related to that of *brand equity*. Brand equity reflects the monetary equivalent of the value that a brand creates above and beyond the value created by the company's products and services. In this context, the more likely customers are to purchase the company's offering and pay a higher price because of the brand, the higher the brand's equity. Customer equity, on the other hand, reflects the monetary value generated by the company's customers over their tenure with the company. In this context, customer equity is broader than brand equity in that it is not limited to the impact of the company's brand but also takes into account the impact of the company's products and services. A practical way to look at brand equity and customer equity is as a cause and effect. The brand is one of the tools that a business can use—along with the other marketing tactics—to acquire and retain its customers. Thus, brand equity reflects the power of the brand, which is one of the drivers behind customer equity. In this context, the brand is the cause and customer equity is the effect.

Although expressed in monetary terms, customer equity is not limited to the sales revenues and profits directly generated by customers during their tenure with the company. In addition to the direct monetary benefits, customer equity also captures the strategic value created by the company's customers. The strategic aspect of customer equity reflects benefits that do not have direct monetary impact on the company, such as customers' endorsement of the company's products in their communication with others as well as the information that these customers might provide that helps the company increase the effectiveness and efficiency of its operations. The two aspects of customer equity—monetary and strategic—are illustrated in Figure 3 and delineated in more detail below.

Figure 3. The Customer Equity Framework

Monetary Value

Monetary value reflects the monetary benefits directly derived from a particular customer. This is the component of customer equity that is readily observable by the company. A customer's direct value is calculated as the difference between the sales revenues and costs during a customer's lifetime, discounted for the time value of money. In this context, the monetary aspect of customer equity can be viewed as a function of three customer-specific factors: *sales revenues, operational costs,* and *marketing costs.*

- **Sales revenues** can be calculated as a function of the average revenues per purchase occasion and the number of such occasions over a customer's lifetime. Calculating the number of purchase occasions entails predicting a customer's tenure with the company (e.g., the number of years a customer will use the company's offerings) and the customer's level of consumption per usage period (e.g., per year).

- **Operational costs** include costs incurred in the process of providing the company's products and services. The direct cost of an airline, for example, includes expenses associated with transporting a given passenger from point A to point B within a given timeframe and at a given level of service. Operational costs also include the expenses incurred in the process of servicing a company's existing customer base. This cost may include the cost of providing post-purchase product support and handling customer service inquiries and requests

- **Marketing costs** involve the costs of acquiring and retaining customers. Acquisition costs reflect expenses incurred in building a company's user base, including the cost of communicating with customers and the cost of the promotional incentives used to attract these customers. Retention costs reflect the cost of a company's activities aimed at increasing customer loyalty and retaining customers, such as the cost of customer loyalty programs and the incentives given to prevent customers from leaving the company.

The monetary aspect of customer equity is expressed as the net present value of the profits (sales revenues less operational and marketing costs) expected over the customer's tenure with the company. A specific approach to calculating the monetary aspect of customer equity is outlined at the end of this chapter.

Strategic Value

In addition to directly contributing to a company's bottom line, customers often create strategic value for the company. The two common ways in which customers can create company value that goes beyond direct monetary revenues and profits are to provide *advocacy* for the company's offerings and *insight* into their needs and the offering's ability to fulfill these needs.

- **Customer advocacy** reflects a customer's ability to promote the company's offering to acquaintances, friends, and family. Thus, the value of consumer advocacy typically reflects the positive referrals generated by satisfied customers who endorse the company's offerings and who, by sharing their experience with their peers and the company, influence other customers to buy the company's offerings.

- **Customer insight** involves information that enables the company to better serve its customers. The value of customer insights can be measured by the degree to which they improve the effectiveness and cost efficiency of a company's operations. In addition to providing information about customer needs, customer insights can also provide feedback about a company's ability to fulfill these needs. Vocal (satisfied as well as dissatisfied) customers add value to the company by pointing out new paths the company might pursue or identifying operational problems that the company can address in a timely fashion before they spread to the company's entire customer base.

Note that even though strategic value does not have a direct impact on a company's bottom line, it can indirectly create monetary value for the company. Indeed, promoting the company's offerings and providing information that will increase the effectiveness and cost efficiency of the company's activities can help the company grow its revenues and profits. The key difference here is that whereas direct monetary value is already in monetary units and can be readily observed, the impact of strategic value on the company's bottom line is indirect and is not readily visible.

Despite the fact that it is not readily observable, the indirect impact of customer advocacy and insight can be significant. Indeed, the value of customer advocacy and insight can extend beyond a particular customer to influence the revenues generated by many others. Therefore, when calculating customer equity, the strategic value of the company's customers must be diligently considered and accounted for. As Albert Einstein put it, *Not everything that counts can be counted, and not everything that can be counted counts*.

Managing Customer Equity to Drive Profits

To build customer equity, a company must have a clearly defined strategy articulating the specific ways in which it will capture the value created by its customers. In this context, two issues merit attention: balancing a company's acquisition and retention efforts, and aligning the company's efforts aimed at building customer equity with those aimed at creating customer value.

Using Customer Equity to Manage Acquisition and Retention

An important decision a company must make is allocating marketing resources between acquiring new customers and satisfying its existing ones. For most companies, resource allocation involves tradeoffs: Allocating more resources to customer acquisition often means fewer resources for retaining the company's current customers, and vice versa. These tradeoffs imply that companies need to find the optimal balance between investing in new customers and building long-term relationships with existing customers.

Most companies tend to spend much of their marketing budget on acquiring new customers. This exaggerated emphasis on acquisition is often counterproductive because most effort is spent on non-customers instead of on the returning customers who generate the majority of a company's revenues. Furthermore, profits are typically generated by existing customers as companies often lose money on new customers in the short term. Thus, by focusing on acquiring new customers and ignoring existing customers, companies might end up spending time, effort, and money to replace profitable customers with unprofitable ones.

The problem with focusing exclusively on customer acquisition is not that a company is investing in acquiring new customers but that the opportunity cost associated with not investing enough in its current customers can be very high. In a competitive market, companies that do not invest in their current customers become vulnerable to competitors' attempts to lure away these customers. Yet, some companies view customers as inventory that, once acquired, belongs to the company in perpetuity. What these companies do not realize is that just as they try to steal customers from other companies, their own neglected customers become the target of competitors' acquisition efforts. Ultimately, spending money on customer acquisition without a viable retention strategy for both new and current customers is like pouring water into a leaking bucket.

A company's ability to foster customer loyalty is a key driver of profitability and market strength. Because a company's market share does not take into account customer loyalty, it is an imperfect indicator of the health of a company. To illustrate, consider two companies with equal market shares. The first company has a low inflow of new customers and a low customer attrition rate. The second company is very successful in its acquisition efforts, yet the rate at which this company is losing customers is also very high. Despite the fact that both companies have equal market shares, the first company is likely to be more profitable than the second one. Indeed, because acquisition costs typically exceed retention costs, the first company is likely to have much lower promotional expenses and, hence, greater profits compared to the second one. The higher the customer attrition rates, the more difficult it is for a company to ensure sustainable profit growth.

To effectively manage its customer base, a company must compare the costs of acquiring new customers with the costs of retaining existing ones. All else being equal, a company can benefit from focusing on retaining its existing customers and minimizing customer attrition before venturing into a large customer acquisition endeavor. In this context, the customer lifetime value can serve as the metric for determining whether and how much a company should spend on customer retention. Thus, as long as a customer's lifetime value is greater than the cost of retaining this customer, a company should consider investing resources to keep this customer.

Aligning Customer Equity and Customer Value

Aligning customer value (the value that customers derive from a company's offering) and customer equity (the value that customers create for the company) is essential to ensure a company's market success. Without such alignment, a company is unable to create a sustainable value exchange that benefits both the company and its customers. Thus, the success of a company's offerings is predicated on the ability to create value for target customers while capturing some of this value for the company stakeholders.

To align customer value and customer equity, many companies track revenues and costs associated with serving individual customers, enabling more accurate estimates of the value of each customer. Knowing the lifetime value of their customers in turn allows companies to create customized offerings for different customers based on their value to the company. For example, airlines offer different levels of service to customers based on their spending and travel patterns. The most valuable customers get the highest level of service, including a dedicated customer service center staffed with trained representatives, priority check-in, waived fees, exclusive flight bonuses, and expanded seat availability. Likewise, hotels offer superior service to customers who stay frequently and spend the most at their properties.

The rationale for value-based customer stratification stems from the observation that in many industries the top 20 percent of the customers generate 80 percent of the revenues.[4] The 80/20 relationship was originally discovered in the late 1800s by economist Vilfredo Pareto, who formulated what later became known as the Pareto Principle: 80% of the outcomes can be attributed to 20% of the causes.[5] If 80% of revenues are indeed generated by 20% of customers, this also means that these customers are responsible for nearly all of the company's profits. In other words, a company might break even or lose money on the majority of its customers. In this context, one way to maximize a company's bottom line is to identify customers with the highest equity and focus a company's efforts on creating value for these customers.

A practical approach to ensure such alignment involves dividing customers into four categories based on the value they create for and receive from the company. A company's ideal customers are those with the highest equity, meaning that they create the greatest value for the company. Not all high-equity customers, however, derive the same value from the company's products and services. Some high-equity customers might derive relatively little value from the company's offerings and, hence, be vulnerable to competitive efforts to attract them. There also are customers who derive significant value from the company's offerings but create little value for the company, enjoying a free ride created by the inefficiency of a company's targeting activities. For example, an airline might offer special perks such as free upgrades, access to airport lounges, and complimentary tickets to customers who are not frequent flyers and typically buy the lowest fare tickets. Finally, there are those who create little value for a company and derive little value from the company's offerings. These four types of customers are depicted in Figure 4.

Figure 4. Aligning Customer Equity and Customer Value

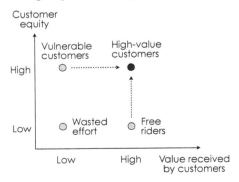

The above stratification of customers based on the value they create for and derive from the company implies that to align customer equity and customer value, a company must use different strategies to manage different types of customers. Thus, it must stay the course with its high-equity, high-value customers; enhance the value it creates for high-equity, vulnerable customers; increase the value it captures from low-equity, free-riding customers; and minimize the resources allocated to low-value, low-equity customers.

An important assumption of this value-based allocation of company resources is that the assessment of customers' equity should capture not only the current value of these customers to the company but also take into account the value that these customers could create for the company in the future. To illustrate, consider customers with $10,000 brokerage firm portfolios who follow a buy-and-hold strategy and do not make many trades. Based on their current profitability, they might be considered low-value customers, not worthy of the company's efforts. Yet, despite their current low equity, some of these customers are likely to have high-value potential. As their income grows, some will expand the size of their portfolios, and as they become more sophisticated might also increase their trading activity. Others might already have significant assets managed elsewhere, such that a $10,000 account might belong to a $10 million client.

When identifying a company's most valuable customers, it is important to keep in mind that evaluating customers based exclusively on their current value for the company does not necessarily reveal their growth potential and may result in an inadequate allocation of a company's customer management efforts. When assessing customer value, companies should take a long-term perspective and assess customers' lifetime value based not only on their current consumption pattern but also on the ways in which their consumption is likely to evolve in the future. Successful customer management is a marathon, not a sprint. It must focus on building long-term relationships rather than trying to maximize the value of a single transaction.

Designing a Customer-Centric Organization

Customer centricity is the cornerstone to customer relationship management. It is an overarching strategy that focuses a company's efforts on creating a loyal customer base and building customer equity. Customer centricity is both a business philosophy that encompasses all company activities and a system for managing a company's relationship with its customers. These two aspects of customer centricity are discussed in more detail in the following sections.

Customer Centricity as a Business Philosophy

Most businesses have formalized procedures to measure the profitability of their offerings. Typically, a profit-and-loss statement shows the contribution of each product and service to the company's bottom line and is used in conjunction with other strategic considerations, to determine whether an offering is a success or failure. Profitable offerings are expanded and unprofitable ones are discontinued, and the management teams responsible for these offerings are rewarded accordingly.

This emphasis on product, service, and brand management often conceals the fact that customers, not offerings, are the drivers of the profits that ultimately show up on the company's balance sheet. Yet, although companies might have well-defined processes for managing their offerings, they may lack corresponding procedures for managing customer relationships. This *customer management myopia* often stems from managers' failure to realize that the company's offerings are just tools for building customer equity. Because loyal customers are among a company's most valuable assets, managing customer relationships — rather than just managing products, services, and brands — is the key driver of the company's long-term success.

Among the reasons why many companies tend to focus on their offerings rather than on their customers are control and accountability. Companies can control their offerings by adding features, modifying packaging, adjusting price, changing the distribution strategy, and strengthening promotional activity. Not only can companies control the key aspects of their offerings, but in many cases they also can directly observe the tangible outcomes of their actions. For example, activities such as price changes and sales promotions tend to have an immediate and measurable impact, which provides managers with a sense of control and accountability. Yet, while control and accountability are definitely important, they are not the only determinants of the success of a company's activities. Indeed, although their impact is readily observable, excessive use of price discounts and sales promotions can erode customer loyalty and have a detrimental impact on customer equity.

To ensure sustainable market success, a company must embrace customer centricity as a core business philosophy. Customer centricity calls for aligning the design, communication, and distribution of the company's products and services with the evolving needs of its target customers in a way that creates value for both the company and its customers. A hallmark of a customer-centric organization is its ability to develop a system for managing customer relationships and building customer equity and incorporate this system into the company's management practices and organizational structure.

As a company's strategic focus evolves from managing offerings to managing customers, relationships replace transactions as the key performance benchmark, and customers replace products, services, and brands as the center of a company's profit equation. Customer equity augments brand equity as the key metric for valuing the intangible assets of service-based companies. When customer retention, rather than acquisition, becomes the primary goal of customer relationship management, the focus of the company's strategic planning expands from managing the product life cycle to also managing the customer life cycle.

Developing a Customer Relationship Management System

At the heart of the customer-centric organization is a customer relationship management system—a set of processes and corresponding tools designed to manage the company's relationship with its customers in an effective and cost-efficient manner. The customer relationship management system is often confused with customer relationship management (CRM) software. A customer relationship management system encompasses a set of strategic and tactical activities designed to enhance a company's ability to create and capture customer value. In contrast, CRM software is a tactical tool that a company can use to implement an already developed customer relationship management system and create customer value in a way that is both effective and cost efficient for the company.

An effective customer relationship management system requires that a company develop a comprehensive *incentive policy* that goes beyond rewarding loyal customers and includes motivating company employees to help cultivate customer loyalty. Despite the importance of cultivating a loyal customer base, many companies have incentive systems set up to reward customer acquisition but not customer retention. As a result, these companies end up focusing their efforts on acquiring new customers while neglecting their current customers. This excessive focus on acquisition often proves to be counterproductive if acquiring new customers comes at the expense of retaining existing customers. Shifting efforts to retaining current customers is often more beneficial for the company because these customers often are more valuable than the newly acquired customers. In this context, creating an internal reward system focused on customer retention in addition to acquisition is an important component of building a customer relationship management system.

Another important component of developing a viable customer relationship management system involves devising a streamlined approach to manage different aspects of the company's interaction with its customers. Many companies lack a cohesive approach to building and sustaining customer relationships and a comprehensive customer management system. It is not that these companies fail to care about their customers. On the contrary, most have numerous departments—marketing, customer service, sales, technical support, and billing—designed to provide adequate customer support. The problem is that these departments are often not coordinated in a way that enables them to effectively manage customer relationships.

This type of inefficiency occurs because in many organizations customer information is decentralized and stored in different "silos." In some cases, this lack of customer data integration results from technological issues such as database incompatibility. Most often, however, the cause of this "silo effect" lies in the way the company operates and the fact that different departments are not incentivized to share customer data. In such cases, a technological solution, such as implementing customer relationship management software, would not necessarily address the issue. Instead, the company needs to reevaluate and ultimately redesign its entire organizational structure in a way that prioritizes the needs of the customer over inter-departmental politics.

In establishing an effective customer relationship management system, it is also important to formalize the company's view of customer equity into a document—a *customer equity charter*—that becomes an integral component of the company's marketing plan. This charter provides guidelines for measuring and managing the lifetime value of the customer and articulates the company's view of customer equity as a key performance benchmark. It further describes the main factors that contribute to customer equity and delineates how customer equity is measured. In addition, the customer equity charter outlines a set of strategic and tactical guidelines for managing customer equity, including allocation of company resources between customer acquisition and retention, the development of customer loyalty programs, and the development of employee incentive programs directed at enhancing customer equity.

The main purpose of the customer equity charter is to establish customer equity as a key strategic benchmark of the company's performance. Developing a customer equity charter forces the company to clearly state its views on customer management and develop a meaningful approach for measuring and managing customer value. By highlighting the importance of customer equity and outlining a uniform measurement system, the customer equity charter fosters the view that costs associated with managing customer relationships are an investment rather than an expense. Regarding customer-related expenditures as an investment in customer equity can help shift a company's focus from short-term quarterly performance to long-term strategic planning.

SUMMARY

Customer relationship management comprises a set of activities for managing a company's interactions with its current and potential customers in a way that enables the company to create value for and capture value from these customers.

Fostering *customer loyalty* is a key component of customer relationship management. Fostering customer loyalty creates value for the company on several dimensions, resulting in lower customer service costs, greater effectiveness and cost efficiency of marketing activities, greater customer advocacy, and lack of acquisition costs. Delivering *customer satisfaction* is the key to cultivating a loyal customer base. Highly satisfied customers tend to have a longer tenure with the company, buy more of the company's current offerings, be more willing to try the company's new offerings, and be more likely to endorse the company's offerings to others.

Common approaches for *building customer loyalty* include acquiring inherently loyal customers, initiating reward programs, creating switching costs, and fostering user groups and brand communities. Loyalty-driven strategic planning makes customer retention rather than customer acquisition the focal point of customer management.

Customer equity is the lifetime value of a company's customers. Customer equity has two aspects: monetary and strategic. The monetary aspect of customer equity reflects the monetary benefits directly derived from a company's customers. A customer's direct monetary value is calculated as the difference between the sales revenues received and costs incurred during a customer's lifetime, discounted for the time value of money. The strategic aspect of customer equity reflects benefits that do not have direct monetary impact on the company, such as customers' endorsement of the company's products in their communication with others as well as the information that these customers might provide that helps the company optimize its operations.

To *build customer equity*, a company must have a clearly defined strategy and tactics articulating the specific ways in which it will create and capture customer value. To this end, a company must focus on two core issues: balancing its acquisition and retention efforts, and aligning its efforts aimed at building customer equity with those aimed at creating customer value.

Customer centricity is the cornerstone of customer relationship management. It is both a business philosophy that encompasses all company activities and a system for managing a company's relationship with its customers. As a business philosophy, customer centricity builds on the notion that managing customer relationships—rather than just managing products, services, and brands—is the key driver of the company's long-term success. As a customer relationship management system, customer centricity encompasses a set of strategic and tactical activities designed to optimize the ways in which the company creates and captures customer value.

The development of a customer-centric organization can be fostered by the development of a *customer equity charter*—a strategic document that provides guidelines for measuring and managing the lifetime value of customers. A key purpose of the customer equity charter is to establish customer equity as a key strategic benchmark of the company's performance.

MARKETING INSIGHT: KEY CUSTOMER MANAGEMENT METRICS

A key aspect of customer management involves tracking customer acquisition and retention. To this end, there are several metrics commonly used to monitor a company's customer base: awareness rate, conversion rate, penetration rate, retention rate, and attrition rate. These metrics are depicted in Figure 5 and described in more detail below.

Figure 5. Key Customer Management Metrics

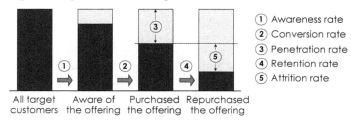

1. Awareness rate
2. Conversion rate
3. Penetration rate
4. Retention rate
5. Attrition rate

All target customers   Aware of the offering   Purchased the offering   Repurchased the offering

Awareness Rate: The number of potential customers who are aware of the company's offering.

Conversion Rate: The number of potential customers who have tried the offering relative to the total number of customers aware of the offering.

$$\text{Conversion rate} = \frac{\text{Current and former customers}}{\text{Potential customers aware of the offering}}$$

Penetration Rate: The number of customers who have tried the offering at least once relative to the total number of potential customers.

$$\text{Penetration rate} = \frac{\text{Current and former customers}}{\text{Potential customers}}$$

Retention Rate: The number of customers who have purchased the offering during the current buying cycle (month, quarter, or year) relative to the number of customers who purchased the offering during the last cycle. Also used in reference to the number of customers who have repurchased the offering relative to the total number of customers who have tried the product at least once.

$$\text{Retention rate} = \frac{\text{Active customers during the current period}}{\text{Active customers during the last period}}$$

Attrition Rate (Churn Rate): The number of customers who discontinue using a company's offering during a specified period relative to the average total number of customers during that same period.

$$\text{Attrition rate} = \frac{\text{Number of customers who disadopt an offering}}{\text{Total number of customers}}$$

MARKETING INSIGHT: MEASURING CUSTOMER LIFETIME VALUE

Customer lifetime value (CLV) is the present monetary value of the future cash flows attributed to a customer's relationship with the company. Knowing the lifetime of a company's customers can help managers develop effective customer acquisition and retention strategies that take into account the value that individual customers can create for the company. From a conceptual standpoint, the lifetime value of all of the company's customers can be quantified as follows:

$$CLV = \sum_{t=1}^{n} \frac{m_t}{(1 + i)^t}$$

where m_t is the margin (i.e., contribution) for each customer in a given time period t, i is the discount rate, and n is the period over which the customer was active (i.e., has purchased the company's offerings).

The above equation can be simplified by several assumptions. First, one can assume that the contribution received from a customer stays constant and does not vary significantly over time (this allows for m_t to be replaced with the constant m). Furthermore, one can assume that customers have only two states: active (meaning that they have purchased the company's offerings in a given period) and inactive (meaning that they have not made such a purchase). In this context, the probability that a customer is active within a given period of time can be expressed as a function of the retention rate r, which reflects the number of customers who have purchased the offering during the current period relative to the number of customers who purchased the offering during the last period. Assuming that across all customers the retention rate remains constant over time, the lifetime value of a given customer can be expressed as follows:[6]

$$CLV = m \cdot \left(\frac{r}{1 + i - r} \right)$$

For example, if a customer generates an annual margin m (i.e., revenues minus cost of goods sold and the cost of serving this customer) of \$100, the average retention rate r is 80% (i.e., the company retains 80% of its customers every year), and the discount rate i (i.e., the time value of money) is 10%, then the customer's lifetime value can be calculated as follows:

$$CLV = \$100 \cdot \left(\frac{.80}{1 + .12 - .80} \right) = \$250$$

The above calculations reflect a scenario in which customer margins do not change over time. On many occasions, however, a company might have sound reasons to expect the per-customer margin to increase over time (i.e., because of increased customer consumption, lower costs of goods sold, or reduced customer service costs). Assuming that the customer margin will grow at a constant rate during a period, the customer lifetime value formula can be augmented as follows:

$$CLV = m \cdot \left(\frac{r}{1 + i - r \cdot (1 + g)} \right)$$

where g is the rate of growth of the customer margin. For example, if in the above example the rate of margin growth is 4% (i.e., each year the \$100 margin would grow at a 4% rate compounded year over year), the customer lifetime value in this case can be calculated as follows:

$$CLV = \$100 \cdot \left(\frac{.80}{1 + .12 - .80 \cdot (1 + .04)} \right) = \$278$$

It is important to note that the above approach to calculating customer lifetime value is subject to several important limitations that stem from the assumptions made as well as the difficulty of assessing some of the components of the model. Thus, the customer lifetime value model does not take into account the dynamic nature of the market and the impact that changes in the market can have on customers' relationship with the company. For example, customer retention rates can be lowered by competitors' actions such as developing a superior offering, launching aggressive price discounts and promotions, and running an effective communication campaign.

Another limitation stems from the assumption that the retention rate is the same across all customers. The problem with this assumption is that it equates the probability of retaining a customer who has been loyal for many years with that of a customer who has made a single purchase from a company. As a result, when customers vary in their needs and behaviors, the above model is more appropriate for assessing the value of a company's entire customer base (i.e., for measuring customer equity) rather than the lifetime value of individual customers. In addition, by assuming that the margins customers are likely to generate over their tenure with the company are constant, the model does not account for changes in consumption patterns. As customers' needs evolve over time, their consumption patterns are likely to change, thus having a direct impact on the value created by these customers.

Despite its limitations, the customer lifetime value model has important practical implications. First, it can serve as an overall guideline and a rule of thumb for determining the monetary value of a company's customers. It can also serve as a basis for developing more complex models that enable a company to more accurately assess the value of its individual customers by taking into account differences in their needs and behaviors while simultaneously incorporating the dynamics of the market in which the company operates. The development of a more comprehensive model to calculate the monetary value of a company's customers can help set an upper limit on spending to acquire new customers and retain existing ones while providing a key input in the valuation of the company itself.

PART EIGHT

MARKETING TOOLBOX

INTRODUCTION

When the only tool you own is a hammer,
every problem begins to resemble a nail.
— Abraham Maslow, American psychologist

The first seven parts of this book presented a theory of marketing and outlined a framework for marketing management. The practical application of this theory and framework is facilitated by a set of tools that help managers accomplish common business tasks, which include identifying target markets, designing a business model, and writing a marketing plan. These three tasks are briefly outlined below, and the application of the marketing theory and framework to these tasks is discussed in more detail in the following chapters.

- **Identifying target markets** focuses on deciding which customers the company should tailor its offering to and which customers it should ignore. A systematic approach to identifying target customers, which builds on the theory presented in Chapter 6, is outlined in Appendix A.

- **Generating a business model** involves developing the key aspects of an offering's strategy and tactics. A systematic approach to generating a business model, which builds on the theory presented in Chapter 2, is outlined in Appendix B.

- **Writing a market plan** involves setting a goal and developing a course of action to achieve that goal. Two sample marketing plans, which build on the theory presented in Chapter 3, are outlined in Appendix C.

The generalized knowledge reflected in the key marketing concepts, principles, and frameworks can help managers circumvent common errors stemming from over-dependence on intuition and gut feel. By bridging marketing theory with managerial practice, the tools outlined here aim to facilitate the use of a systematic approach to identifying market opportunities, solving business problems, and creating market value.

SEGMENTATION AND TARGETING WORKBOOK

*There is nothing so useless as doing efficiently
something that should not be done at all.*
— Peter Drucker, founder of
modern management theory

D eciding which customers to serve is a defining aspect of a company's strategy. It influences all other aspects of the target market — competitors, collaborators, the company's
resources necessary to serve these customers, and the context in which the company operates. The fundamental role that identifying target customers plays in defining a company's
business model highlights the importance of applying a systematic approach to targeting.
Accordingly, this chapter presents an application of the targeting framework outlined in
Chapter 6. Specifically, it outlines the key steps of the process of identifying target customers
and illustrates the process of segmentation and targeting with a concrete example.

The Process of Identifying Target Customers

Identifying target customers can be represented as a sequence of steps a company should
take to decide which customers to target. Specifically, a company's targeting decision is represented by three key processes: *strategic targeting analysis*, *tactical targeting analysis*, and *target
selection*. These processes and the corresponding decisions are summarized in Figure 1 and
outlined in more detail below.

Figure 1. Identifying Target Customers

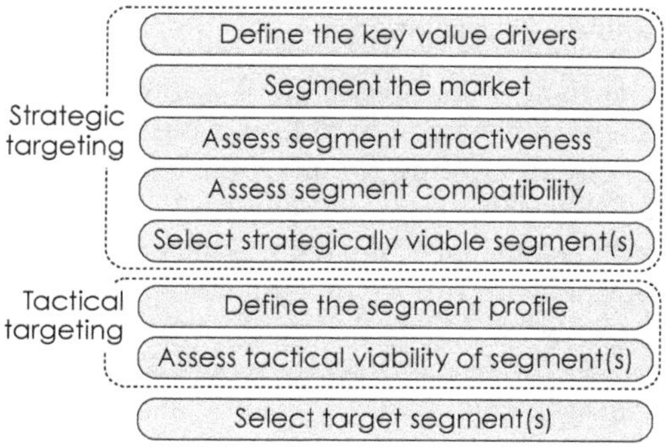

- **Strategic targeting** aims to identify which customers the company will target and
  which it will ignore — a decision based on the needs of these customers and the company's ability to fulfill these needs. Accordingly, the first step of analysis involves defining the key attributes (value drivers) that create customer value. This step is followed
  by segmenting the market into groups of customers with similar preferences based on
  the value they expect to receive from and can create for the company. The purpose of
  this segmentation is to select strategically viable segments that are compatible with the
  company's resources and at the same time can create value for the company.

- **Tactical targeting** aims to find effective and cost-efficient ways to reach the strategically viable segments. To this end, the company must identify the readily observable

characteristics (profile) of the strategically viable target customers and evaluate the tactical viability of pursuing this segment.

- **Target selection** follows analysis of the strategic and tactical viability of targeting different segments and involves the ultimate decision of which segment(s) the company will pursue. Depending on its strategic goals and resources, a company might choose to target a single segment or multiple segments. In cases when a company decides to pursue multiple segments, it must develop a separate business model for each target segment.

The different steps in identifying target customers are outlined in more detail in the following sections and are supplemented with a practical example that illustrates the process of identifying target customers in the context of a particular company.

Step 1: Define the Value Drivers for the Category

A common approach to segmentation is to start by identifying the *value drivers*—the relevant attributes that buyers consider when making a choice. The identified customer value drivers become the criteria that will guide the process of defining market segments and identifying target customers.

When identifying the value drivers, it is important to ensure that they are indeed *relevant*, meaning that buyers consider them when making a choice, as well as *comprehensive*, meaning that all relevant attributes are identified and included in the analysis. In addition, the attributes identified as value drivers should be *specific*. For example, "reliability" is a relatively specific attribute, whereas "quality" is not because it typically refers to the combination of all nonprice attributes. Finally, the value drivers should be relatively *independent* from one another in order to streamline the analysis. For example, "precision" and "accuracy" are likely to overlap in meaning and, hence, produce similar evaluations.

Step 2: Segment the Market

The next step involves identifying tentative customer segments based on the value that customers within these segments are likely to seek from a given product category. A good starting point is to ask the following value-related questions: *What motivates customers' purchases? On what occasions do customers purchase from this product category? What needs are customers trying to fulfill?* The goal of these questions is to identify the key customer segments—that is, groups of customers who are very similar in their buying behavior within each segment and at the same time are very different across segments.

Once the tentative segments have been identified, the next step is to define the value sought by each segment. A practical approach to defining the needs of a segment is to rate the importance of each attribute of an offering for all of the tentatively identified segments. For example, one might use a three-point rating scale with levels "high," "moderate," and "low," where "high" indicates that a particular attribute is very important to a given segment and "low" indicates that it is relatively unimportant. Note that the three-point scale described here is for illustration purposes only; any scale that rank-orders the importance of different attributes can work. In general, the more nuanced the scale, the greater its ability to detect relatively minor differences among segments.

Not all of the identified value drivers necessarily differentiate the segments: Some attributes might be equally important to all segments. For example, durability might be considered an important factor by all segments, whereas color might be viewed as relatively unimportant by all. This is not a problem; it merely indicates that these attributes are non-diagnostic with respect to the ability to differentiate among the tentatively identified segments.

Defining potential target segments is often a trial-and-error process that stems from a manager's intuition about the different types of buyers in a given market. Accordingly, it is important to ensure that the intuitively defined segments represent different groups of customers. It is quite possible that the first attempt at identifying viable market segments does not produce a viable segmentation. In such cases, one must go back to the "drawing board" and revise the initial segmentation. The number of iterations to achieve a valid segmentation depends largely on a manager's experience and knowledge of the particular market. Some managers might derive the "right" segmentation from the beginning, whereas others might go through several iterations to arrive at a valid customer segmentation.

Step 3: Assess Segment Attractiveness

Segment attractiveness reflects the ability of the customers in this segment to create value for the company. Evaluating segment attractiveness aims to answer the question of whether the members of a particular segment have the resources to create value for the company and whether they can create greater value than those in non-chosen segments. The evaluation of segment attractiveness is based on the assessment of two types of value: monetary value, which reflects a segment's ability to generate profits for the company, and strategic value, which reflects a segment's ability to create nonmonetary benefits that are of strategic importance for the company.

A practical approach to assessing segment attractiveness involves evaluating each segment with respect to its ability to create monetary and strategic value for the company. For example, one might use a three-point rating scale with levels "high," "moderate," and "low," where "high" indicates that a particular segment is extremely attractive and "low" indicates that it is relatively unattractive to the company (a more nuanced scale can offer greater accuracy).

Step 4: Assess Segment Compatibility

Following the analysis of segment attractiveness is the analysis of segment compatibility — that is, the degree to which the company can create superior value for this segment. In order to provide this assessment, the manager needs to know the competitive context in which customers will evaluate the company's offering. Therefore, evaluating segment compatibility begins with identifying the competitors for each of the identified customer segments.

Once relevant competitors have been identified, the next step is to evaluate the company's ability to fulfill the needs of each target segment better than the competition. Segment compatibility can be assessed by evaluating the benefits of the company's offering relative to the competition on each of the relevant attributes (identified in Step 1). For example, one might use a three-point rating scale with levels "high," "moderate," and "low," where "high" indicates that a particular offering performs very well on a given attribute and "low" indicates that it performs rather poorly on that attribute (a more nuanced scale can offer greater accuracy).

Step 5: Select the Strategically Viable Segment(s)

Following analysis of the attractiveness and compatibility of the identified segments is the selection of the strategically viable segment(s). This involves selecting the target segment that best meets the attractiveness and compatibility criteria.

Deciding on the viability of each segment typically involves a binary (yes/no) decision indicating whether pursuing a particular set of customers is a strategically viable option for the company. Note that in some cases a company might decide to pursue a strategically important segment even though it does not readily have the resources necessary to create superior value for these customers. In such cases, the company's decision to target this segment is predicated on its ability to build the deficient resources — a strategy that typically involves the investment of significant resources and/or a longer time horizon.

Step 6: Define the Profile(s) of the Strategically Viable Target Segment(s)

The goal of this step is to identify the readily observable characteristics (profile) of the strategically chosen segment(s) that can be used to communicate and deliver the offering in an effective and cost-efficient manner. This is important because without knowing the profile of its target segment(s) a company faces the risk of not reaching all target customers and/or not reaching them in a cost-efficient manner.

To identify the profile of the strategically viable segment(s), a company can rely on four types of factors: demographic factors (e.g., age, gender, and income), geographic factors (e.g., state, city, and current location), psychographic factors (e.g., values, interests, and hobbies), and behavioral factors (e.g., type of media viewed and distribution channels used). These factors are then used to identify the touch points at which the company can communicate and deliver the offering to its customers.

Step 7: Assess the Tactical Viability of the Strategically Viable Segment(s)

Assessing the tactical viability of serving the identified segment(s) involves an assessment of the company's ability to reach this segment in a cost-efficient manner. This step takes into account the company's access to communication and distribution channels to reach this segment as well as the cost of gaining access to such channels. Note that for tactical purposes each segment can be divided into sub-segments reflecting different channels through which the company can reach these customers to communicate and deliver the offering. The rationale for creating sub-segments is that although customers in the strategically identified segment(s) are similar with respect to their needs, they still could vary with respect to ways the company can best communicate with them and deliver its offering.

Step 8: Select Target Customer Segment(s)

Selecting the optimal target segment yields the ultimate *go* or *no-go* decision with respect to the identified customer segments. Because the strategic segments are defined by the varying needs of customers across segments, in most cases a company can target only one segment with a particular offering. Should a company find multiple customer segments viable, it should develop a unique value proposition and market offering for each target segment.

The Targeting Workbook

The process of identifying target customers can be presented as a matrix that encompasses the key aspects of the targeting decision (Figure 2). By imposing logical structure on the process of market segmentation and targeting, this matrix can also serve as a worksheet guiding the identification of a company's target customers.

Figure 2. The Targeting Workbook

		Step 2 ⇨ **Customer value analysis**			Step 4 ⇨ **Compatibility analysis**			
	Step 1 ⇩ **Value drivers**	Customer segments			Company offering	Competitive offerings		
		Segment A	Segment B	Segment C		Offering X	Offering Y	Offering Z
Strategic targeting	Attribute 1							
	Attribute 2							
	Attribute 3							
	Attribute 4							
	Attribute 5							
	Segment attractiveness				⇦ Step 3			
	Segment compatibility				⇦ Step 4 ←			
	Strategic viability				⇦ Step 5			
Tactical targeting	Segment profile				⇦ Step 6			
	Tactical viability				⇦ Step 7			
	Target selection				⇦ Step 8			

Because articulating the key drivers of customer value is an integral aspect of targeting, the analysis underlying the selection of target customers is also the basis for defining the offering's value proposition. Thus, the development of a value proposition directly follows from the targeting analysis and is an integral aspect of the development of a sound market strategy. The ultimate success of an offering is determined by the degree to which its value proposition is aligned with the needs and resources of its target customers. In this context, identifying target customers and designing a value proposition for these customers are the two aspects of an iterative process that culminates in the development of an internally consistent and viable marketing strategy. The process of developing a value proposition and a business model for the identified target markets is discussed in detail in Appendix B.

Segmentation and Targeting Workbook Example: Black & Decker

The process of identifying target customers can be better understood when illustrated with a specific example that highlights the decisions involved at each step of the targeting analysis. Accordingly, the following example focuses on Black & Decker, a large U.S. manufacturer of power tools and accessories, and the process by which it identified an underserved customer segment.[1]

Step 1: Defining the Value Drivers for the Category

Black & Decker's market analysis reveals five key attributes—power, reliability, service, brand image, and price—as the main factors that buyers of power tools consider when making a choice. These are the attributes on which Black & Decker needs to create superior value (relative to the other power tool manufacturers) for its target customers.

Step 2: Segmenting the Market

Based on the occasions on which power tools are used, initial market analysis suggests two segments: a *consumer segment*—buyers who use power tools around the house, and a *commercial segment*—buyers who purchase power tools for business use. Next, these segments need to be validated to ensure that (1) buyers in these two segments are different from one another in the value they derive from power tools and (2) that buyers within each of these two segments are very similar in their needs and preferences.

In Black & Decker's case, power and reliability are very important for commercial buyers but are of much lower importance to consumers, who care most about price and are moderately concerned with the brand of power tools they buy (Figure 3). The importance of service, brand, and price for commercial users, however, is much more difficult to pinpoint. There are reasons to argue that these three attributes are relatively unimportant to some of these buyers and reasons to argue that they are extremely important to others.

Figure 3. Customer Value Analysis Workbook (Two Segments)

	Customer segments	
Attributes	Consumer	Commercial
Power	Low	High
Reliability	Low	High
Service	Low	Medium – High
Brand	Medium	Low – High
Price	High	Low – Medium

The consumer–commercial segmentation is not effective because customers in the commercial segment exhibit significant variation in the importance they assign to service, brand image, and price. This variation means that this segment is heterogeneous and has to be segmented further to produce homogeneous (uniform) segments that have minimal within-segment variance in customer needs.

Subsequent analysis reveals that the commercial segment comprises two sub-segments: *tradesmen* — small businesses and independent contractors such as carpenters, plumbers, and electricians working in residential construction — that use power tools on the job; and *industrial buyers*, such as companies that purchase power tools for employee use. Once these sub-segments are taken into account, the resulting segments are fairly uniform with respect to customer preferences within each segment and yet reflect significant differences in customer preferences across segments (Figure 4).

Figure 4. Customer Value Analysis Workbook (Three Segments)

	Customer segments		
Attributes	Consumer	Tradesman	Industrial
Power	Low	High	High
Reliability	Low	High	High
Service	Low	High	Medium
Brand	Medium	High	Low
Price	High	Low	Medium

The customer value analysis shows that whereas customers in the two commercial segments — tradesmen and industrial buyers — share the belief that power and reliability are paramount, tradesmen place much greater importance on brand image and service. In other words, having fast repair service is more important for tradesmen than for industrial buyers, many of whom have their own service support. Furthermore, having tools that carry a professional brand can help enhance the professional image of tradesmen and is more important to them than to industrial buyers, who are purchasing the power tools for use by employees on commercial projects. Finally, the larger volume purchased by industrial buyers makes many of them more price sensitive than the tradesmen, who often buy a single tool.

Step 3: Assessing Segment Attractiveness

Analysis of the attractiveness of the identified customer segments reveals that all three segments — consumer, tradesman, and industrial — are attractive with respect to their ability to create value for Black & Decker. At the same time, even though the tradesman segment is the fastest growing of the three segments, Black & Decker's share of that segment is much lower compared to that of the other two segments. Accordingly, the tradesman segment presents the greatest market opportunity and is rated as a priority for Black & Decker.

Step 4: Assessing Segment Compatibility

Black & Decker's top competitors for the tradesman segment include Makita (the market leader, with nearly a 50% share), Milwaukee Tools, and Ryobi. In this context, analysis of the compatibility of the tradesman segment involves evaluating the performance of Black & Decker's offerings vis-à-vis its key competitors — Makita, Milwaukee Tools, and Ryobi — on each of the attributes identified in Step 1. The resulting attribute performance matrix is shown in Figure 5. The customer analysis ratings depicted in Figure 5 reflect the importance of each attribute for the tradesman segment, and competitive analysis ratings reflect the performance of each competitor on these attributes.

Figure 5. Compatibility Analysis Workbook (Tradesman Segment)

Attributes	Attribute importance	Market offerings			
		B&D	Makita	Milwaukee	Ryobi
Power	High	Medium	High	High	Medium
Reliability	High	High	High	High	High
Service	High	Medium	Medium	Medium	Low
Brand	High	Low	High	High	Low
Price	Low	Medium	High	High	Medium

The analysis depicted in Figure 5 indicates that Black & Decker is at parity with its key competitors in terms of reliability and service, and lags behind Makita and Milwaukee Tools in terms of power and brand image. With respect to price—an attribute that is of relatively low importance for tradesmen—Black & Decker is superior to Makita and Milwaukee Tools and on a par with Ryobi. This analysis suggests that to be at parity with the competition in the tradesman segment, Black & Decker must increase the power of its offerings and dramatically improve its brand image. Furthermore, Black & Decker could create a competitive advantage in terms of service, which would put it ahead of the competition. Finally, given the relatively low importance of price to the tradesman segment and Black & Decker's price advantage over Makita and Milwaukee Tools, there is room for Black & Decker to raise prices, provided that it can create superior value on the other attributes.

Step 5: Selecting the Strategically Viable Segment

Based on the value they can create for the company, tradesmen present the most attractive segment for Black & Decker. However, to successfully target the tradesman segment, Black & Decker must improve its offerings on two key dimensions—power and brand image. Improving the brand image is crucial because it is one of the attributes that target customers care most about and an attribute on which Black & Decker's brand is viewed to be vastly inferior to its top two competitors. Improving the power of its tools is also imperative for Black & Decker given its primary importance to target customers and competitors' advantage on that dimension. Furthermore, because tradesmen view service as a top priority, Black & Decker might also consider improving its service even though it is at parity with the competition. In this context, although its current offering is not optimal for the tradesman segment, Black & Decker can pursue this segment provided that it allocates resources to improve the power, service, and brand image of its offerings.

Step 6: Defining the Profile of the Strategically Viable Segment

Black & Decker's goal now is to identify effective and cost-efficient ways to reach tradesmen to communicate and deliver its offerings. The behavioral profile of tradesmen indicates that they read industry magazines such as *Builder* and *Electrical Contractor*, visit builder trade shows, and frequent home improvement stores.

Step 7: Assessing the Tactical Viability of the Strategically Viable Segment

To reach tradesmen, Black & Decker might advertise in industry magazines, such as *Builder* and *Electrical Contractor*, that are favored by the tradesman, promote the product at trade shows, as well as use point-of-purchase displays at home improvement retailers. To make its products readily available to tradesmen, Black & Decker might further focus its distribution efforts on retail outlets catering to these customers, including large home improvement centers such as Home Depot and Lowe's, smaller hardware chains such as Ace Hardware, and independently owned hardware stores. The above analysis suggests that the tradesman segment can be readily accessed via established communication and distribution channels and, hence, is viable from a tactical perspective.

Step 8: Selecting a Customer Target

Given the market opportunity associated with the tradesman segment, Black & Decker's ability to develop a value proposition compatible with the needs of this segment, and its ability to reach this segment in an effective and cost-efficient manner, Black & Decker can decide to go ahead with developing an offering for this segment.

To create value for the tradesman, Black & Decker must offer powerful and reliable tools from a trusted brand backed by dependable service (see Figure 4). To this end, Black & Decker must allocate resources to develop an offering that is superior to (or at least at parity with) the competition in terms of power, brand image, and service. Given the relatively low importance of price and the relatively high prices of its key competitors, Black & Decker might consider raising its prices—a strategy that not only can contribute to its bottom line but also can help build its brand reputation as a high-quality power tool. The specifics of Black & Decker's business model for creating value for the tradesman segment are outlined in Appendix B.

The Targeting Workbook

Black & Decker's segmentation and targeting analysis can be summarized in a targeting matrix, which outlines the key aspects of the process of identifying target customers (Figure 6). Note that Black & Decker's focus on the tradesman segment does not mean that other segments are not viable for the company. Rather, the segmentation and targeting analysis aims to identify market opportunities—segments in which Black & Decker is underperforming and has viable potential for growth.

Figure 6. The Targeting Workbook: Black & Decker

		Customer value analysis			Compatibility analysis			
		Customer segments			Black & Decker	Competitive offerings		
	Value drivers	Consumer	Tradesman	Industrial		Makita	Milwaukee	Ryobi
Strategic analysis	Power	Low	High	High	Medium	High	High	Medium
Strategic analysis	Reliability	Low	High	High	High	High	High	High
Strategic analysis	Service	Low	High	Medium	Medium	Medium	Medium	Low
Strategic analysis	Brand image	Medium	High	Low	Low	High	High	Low
Strategic analysis	Price	High	Low	Medium	Medium	High	High	Medium
Strategic analysis	Segment attractiveness	Medium	High	Medium				
Strategic analysis	Segment compatibility	Low	High	Low	← Improve on power, brand, and service			
Strategic analysis	Strategic viability	Low	High	Low				
Tactical analysis	Segment profile	–	Behavioral profile	–				
Tactical analysis	Tactical viability	–	High	–				
	Target selection	–	Yes	–				

For brevity, segment compatibility and the subsequent analyses shown in Figure 6 focus only on the most attractive segment (the tradesman). Assessments of the attractiveness and the strategic viability of the tradesman segment are based on the assumption that Black & Decker can develop the resources necessary to target this segment (power, brand, and service). The behavioral profile of the tradesman segment is defined by a set of characteristics, including reading industry magazines such as *Builder* and *Electrical Contractor*, attending homebuilder trade shows, and frequenting home improvement and hardware stores.

THE BUSINESS MODEL WORKBOOK

Innovation is not the product of logical thought,
although the result is tied to logical structure.
— Albert Einstein, theoretical physicist

An offering's business model delineates the ways in which a company creates value in a particular market. The ultimate goal of the business model is to design an offering that will create superior value for target customers in a way that benefits the company and its collaborators. Building on the theory presented in Chapter 2, here we illustrate the key aspects of the process of generating a business model.

Developing a Market Value Map

The business model is the master plan that charts the way in which a company can reach its goals. It streamlines the process by which a company identifies its target market, defines its value proposition in this market, and develops an offering that creates value for its target customers, its collaborators, and stakeholders. Having a clearly articulated, logical, and sustainable business model is a prerequisite for any business enterprise.

Each business model is unique. It outlines how a particular enterprise will address a specific customer need in a given market at a certain point in time. Despite their uniqueness, successful business models are all built on the same core principles. These principles apply to both startups and established companies, to companies that are privately owned as well as those that are publicly traded, to high-tech and low-tech companies, to companies involved in manufacturing as well as to companies providing services.

The business model comprises two key components: strategy and tactics. The strategy identifies the market in which the company operates and outlines the ways in which an offering will create value for the relevant market participants. Tactics, on the other hand, describe the actual offering that will create value in the target market. The strategy and tactics are intricately related: The strategy defines an offering's tactics, and tactics embody the offering's strategy.

The key aspects of a company's business model are captured in a market value map that outlines the specific ways in which an offering creates value for its target customers, collaborators, and the company. The primary purpose of a value map is to outline the key aspects of the business model and serve as a workbook that lays out the company's strategy and tactics. The market value map presents the business model in a schematic way, enabling managers to clearly articulate the key aspects of the company's business model.

The market value map follows the structure of the business model and delineates the three key components — *the target market, the value proposition,* and *the market offering* — that define the offering's strategy and tactics. Accordingly, the market value map is represented as a matrix: The left side outlines the key elements of the business model strategy — the target market (customers, collaborators, company, competitors, and context) and the value proposition (customer value, collaborator value, and company value). The right side outlines the market offering defined by its seven key attributes (product, service, brand, price, incentives, communication, and distribution). The key components of a market value map are shown in Figure 1.

Figure 1. The Market Value Map

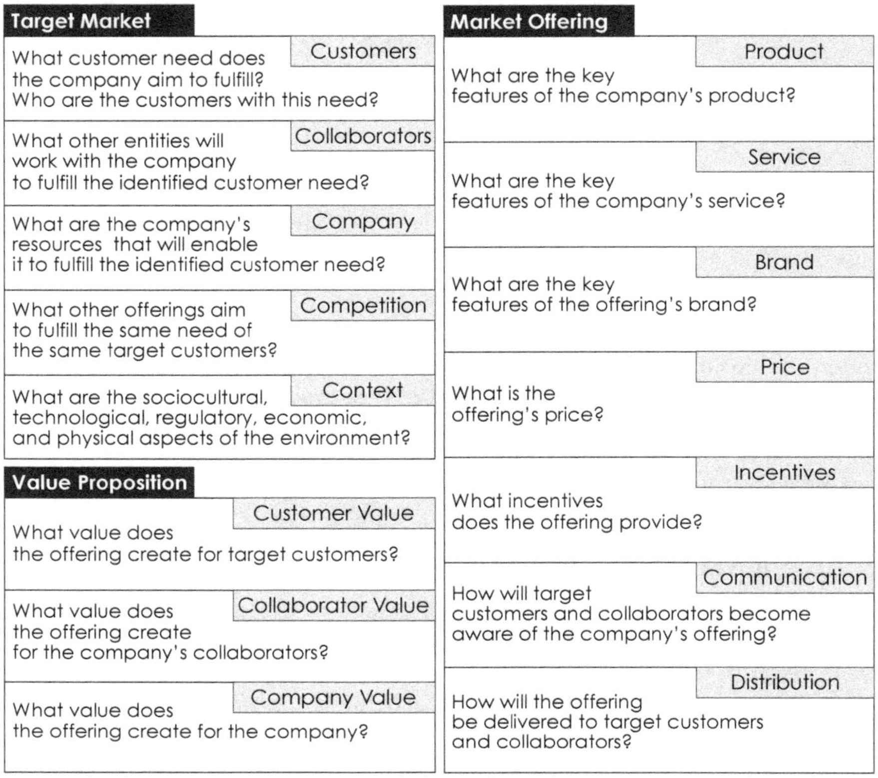

Target Market	
Customers — What customer need does the company aim to fulfill? Who are the customers with this need?	
Collaborators — What other entities will work with the company to fulfill the identified customer need?	
Company — What are the company's resources that will enable it to fulfill the identified customer need?	
Competition — What other offerings aim to fulfill the same need of the same target customers?	
Context — What are the sociocultural, technological, regulatory, economic, and physical aspects of the environment?	

Market Offering	
Product — What are the key features of the company's product?	
Service — What are the key features of the company's service?	
Brand — What are the key features of the offering's brand?	
Price — What is the offering's price?	
Incentives — What incentives does the offering provide?	
Communication — How will target customers and collaborators become aware of the company's offering?	
Distribution — How will the offering be delivered to target customers and collaborators?	

Value Proposition	
Customer Value — What value does the offering create for target customers?	
Collaborator Value — What value does the offering create for the company's collaborators?	
Company Value — What value does the offering create for the company?	

The market value map offers an overview of the ways in which an offering creates value for the three relevant market entities — customers, collaborators, and the company. Because each of these entities requires its own value proposition and employs different tools to create value, the market value map can be represented as three separate maps: the *customer value map*, the *collaborator value map*, and the *company value map*.

- The **customer value map** outlines the key aspects of the company's offering for target customers and the way in which this offering will create value for these customers.

- The **collaborator value map** outlines the key aspects of the company's offering for its collaborators and the way in which it will create value for these collaborators.

- The **company value map** outlines the key aspects of the company's offering and the way in which this offering will create value for the company.

These three value maps define a company's business model from the viewpoint of each of the three market entities involved in the value-creation process. Because the market success of the company's offering depends on the degree to which it can create value for its customers, collaborators, and the company, the three value maps must clearly identify the ways in which the company offering will create superior value for each of these entities. The key aspects of developing customer, collaborator, and company value maps are outlined in the following sections.

Developing a Customer Value Map

The customer value map outlines the way in which a company's offering can fulfill the needs of its target customers better than the competition. The customer value map consists of four building blocks: target customers, the competition, the customer value proposition, and the customer offering. The core components of the customer value map are shown in Figure 2 and are outlined in more detail in the following sections.

Figure 2. The Customer Value Map

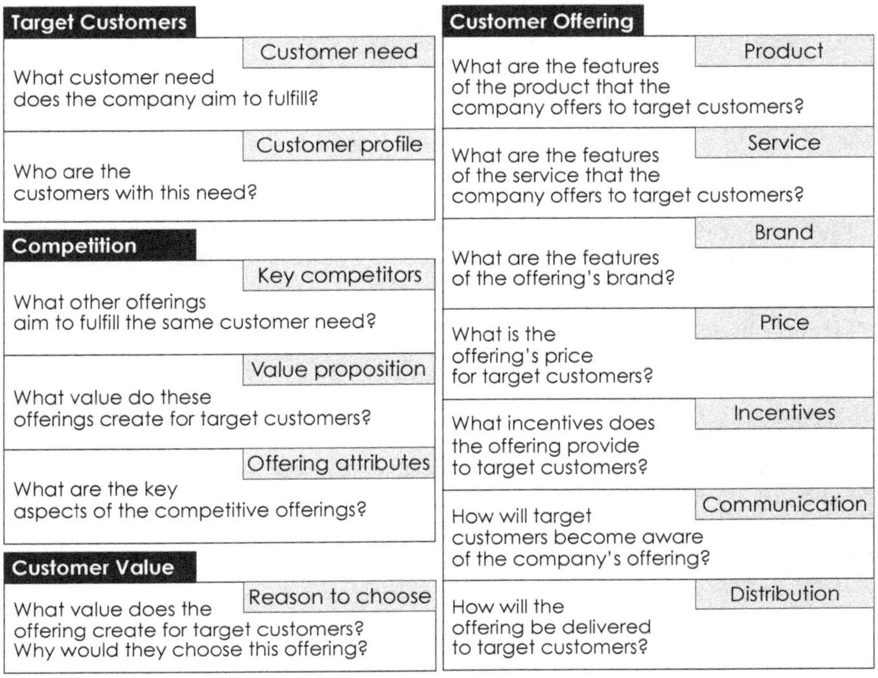

Target Customers		**Customer Offering**	
Customer need — What customer need does the company aim to fulfill?		Product — What are the features of the product that the company offers to target customers?	
Customer profile — Who are the customers with this need?		Service — What are the features of the service that the company offers to target customers?	
Competition		Brand — What are the features of the offering's brand?	
Key competitors — What other offerings aim to fulfill the same customer need?			
Value proposition — What value do these offerings create for target customers?		Price — What is the offering's price for target customers?	
Offering attributes — What are the key aspects of the competitive offerings?		Incentives — What incentives does the offering provide to target customers?	
Customer Value		Communication — How will target customers become aware of the company's offering?	
Reason to choose — What value does the offering create for target customers? Why would they choose this offering?		Distribution — How will the offering be delivered to target customers?	

Target Customers

Target customers are the buyers for whom the company is developing its offering. Identifying target customers involves identifying an unmet customer need that the company intends to fulfill and defining the profile of customers with this need.

- The **customer need** identifies a problem faced by customers that the company aims to address with its offering. The key questions that a manager should ask are: *What customer need does the offering aim to fulfill? How common is this need? Do customers view this need as a problem that has to be solved and actively seek alternative means to fulfill this need?*

- The **customer profile** identifies the observable characteristics of target customers that the company can use to communicate and deliver its offering to these customers. The key questions are: *Who are the customers that have the need the company aims to fulfill? What demographic characteristics of these customers can the company use to reach them? What behaviors of these customers can the company use to reach them?*

Competition

The competition consists of the alternative offerings that fulfill the same need of the same customers as the company's offering. Competitors are identified by their value proposition for target customers and the attributes defining the competitive offerings.

- **Key competitors** are the alternative offerings that target customers can use to achieve their goals. The key questions here are: *What means are target customers currently using to fulfill the identified need? If the company does not introduce its offering, what would these customers do? What product, service, or behavior does the company's offering aim to replace? What would target customers <u>not</u> choose if they were to choose the company's offering?*

- The **competitive value proposition** outlines the benefits and costs that competitive offerings create for target customers and the reasons why customers might prefer competitive offerings to those created by the company. The key questions here are:

What benefits do the competitive offerings create for target customers? What customer costs are associated with the competitive offerings? Why would customers choose a competitor's offerings?

- The **attributes of the competitive offerings** involve their product, service, brand, price, incentives, communication, and distribution components. The key questions here are: *What are the product, service, brand, price, incentives, communication, and distribution aspects of the competitive offering? How does each of the attributes of the competitive offering create customer value?*

The Customer Value Proposition

The customer value proposition defines the worth of a company's offering to target customers. It is identified by the customer benefits, the competitive advantage of the company's offering, and the reason why customers would choose the company's offering.

- **Customer benefits** identify the value created by the offering on each of the three dimensions of customer value: functional, psychological, and monetary. The key question here is: *What functional, psychological, and monetary benefits does the offering create for its target customers?*

- The **competitive advantage** is the ability of an offering to fulfill a particular customer need better than the alternative options. The key questions here are: *Why should target customers choose the company's offering instead of using alternative means of fulfilling the identified need? What are the points of dominance, points of parity, and points of compromise of the company's offering relative to the competitive offerings?*

- The **reason to choose** is the key factor that will motivate customers to buy and use the company's offering. The key questions here are: *What is the primary reason for customers to choose the company offering? How would customers justify choosing the company's offering?*

Customer Offering

The customer offering is defined by the seven attributes—product, service, brand, price, incentives, communication, and distribution—that delineate the company's offering and the value that these attributes create for target customers. The key questions here are: *What are the key features of the product, service, brand, price, and incentives the company offers to its customers? How will target customers become aware of the offering? How will the offering be delivered to target customers? How will different attributes of the offering create customer value?*

Developing a Collaborator Value Map

The collaborator value map outlines the ways in which an offering can help the company's collaborators achieve their goals better than the competitive offerings. Similar to the customer value map, the collaborator value map consists of four building blocks: collaborators, the competition, the collaborator value proposition, and the collaborator offering. The core components of the collaborator value map are shown in Figure 3 and are outlined in more detail in the following sections.

Key Collaborators

Collaborators are entities working with the company to create value for target customers. Identifying collaborators has two aspects: defining the profile of the partnering entities and their resources, and identifying the goals that these entities aim to achieve by partnering with the company.

- The **collaborator profile** reflects the key aspects of the partnering entity, such as resources, location, size, and industry. The key questions here are: *What resources needed to create superior value for target customers is the company looking to outsource? Which entities have the resources the company lacks and is looking to outsource? What are the key characteristics of these entities?*

- **Collaborator goals** are the outcomes that collaborators want to achieve through collaboration. The key question here is: *What monetary and strategic goals do collaborators aim to achieve by partnering with the company?*

Figure 3. The Collaborator Value Map

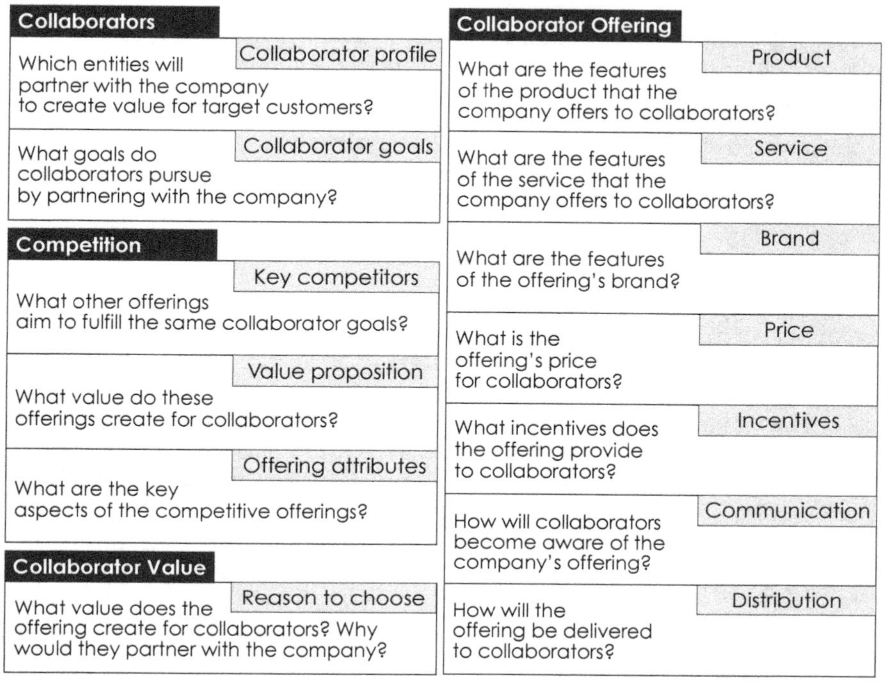

Competition

The competition consists of the alternative offerings that target the same goals of the same collaborators that the company does. The competition is defined by the key competitors, their value proposition for collaborators, and the attributes of the competitive offerings.

- **Key competitors** are the alternative means that company collaborators can use to achieve their goals. The key questions here are: *What are potential collaborators currently doing to achieve their goals? If they do not partner with the company, what will these collaborators do? What offering does the company aim to replace with its offering?*

- The **competitive value proposition** reflects the benefits and costs created by the competitive offerings for collaborators and the reasons why collaborators might prefer competitive offerings to those created by the company. The key questions here are: *What benefits and costs do the competitive offerings create for collaborators? What is the primary reason why collaborators might prefer a competitive offering to the company offering?*

- The **attributes of the competitive offerings** involve their product, service, brand, price, incentives, communication, and distribution components. The key questions here are: *What are the product, service, brand, price, incentives, communication, and distribution aspects of the competitive offerings? How does each attribute of the competitive offerings create collaborator value?*

The Collaborator Value Proposition

The collaborator value proposition defines the worth of an offering to the company's collaborators. The collaborator value proposition is identified by the collaborator benefits, the competitive advantage of the company's offering, and the reason why collaborators would choose the company's offering.

- The **collaborator benefits** identify the value created by the offering on two value dimensions: monetary and strategic. The key question here is: *What monetary and strategic benefits does the offering create for collaborators?*

- The **competitive advantage** reflects the ability of the company's offering to address collaborators' goals better than the alternative options. The key questions here are: *Why should collaborators choose to partner with the company instead of using alternative means to achieve their goals? What are the points of dominance, points of parity, and points of compromise of the company's offering relative to the competitive offerings?*

- The **reason to choose** identifies the key factor(s) that would motivate collaborators to partner with the company. The key questions here are: *What is the primary reason for collaborators to partner with the company? How would collaborators justify choosing the company's offering?*

Collaborator Offering

The collaborator offering represents the collaborator aspect of the market offering. It is defined by the seven attributes—product, service, brand, price, incentives, communication, and distribution—that delineate the company's offering and the value that each of these attributes creates for collaborators. The key questions here are: *What are the key features of the product, service, brand, price, and incentives the company offers to its collaborators? How will the offering be communicated to collaborators? How will the offering be delivered to collaborators? How will different attributes of the offering create collaborator value?*

Developing a Company Value Map

The company value map outlines the ways in which the offering can enable the company to achieve its goals better than it can with alternative options. The company value map has a structure similar to the customer and collaborator value maps and consists of four building blocks: the company, the alternative options, the company value proposition, and the company offering. The core components of the company value map are shown in Figure 4 and are outlined in more detail in the following sections.

Figure 4. The Company Value Map

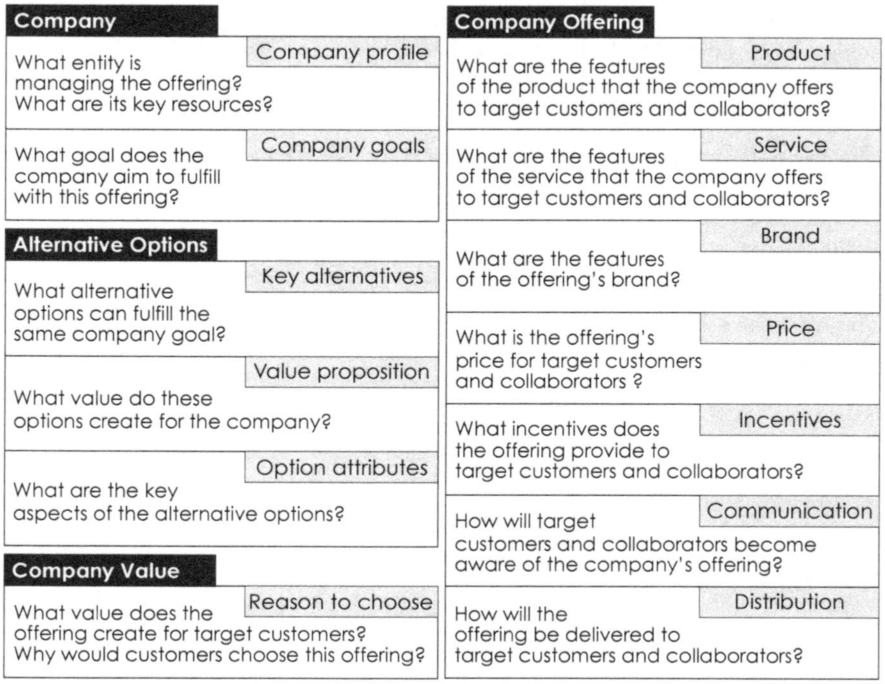

The Company

The company is the entity in charge of the offering. The company is defined by two factors: the company profile and the goals that the company aims to achieve with the offering.

- The **company profile** outlines the key aspects of the entity (e.g., a specific business unit of the company) in charge of the offering. The key questions here are: *What entity is in charge of the offering? What resources does the company have to fulfill the identified need of the target customers?*

- **Company goals** are the strategic and monetary outcomes that the company aims to achieve with the offering. The key question here is: *What monetary and strategic goals is the company pursuing by creating the offering?*

Alternative Options

From a company's perspective, alternative options are the different means that could enable the company to achieve its goals. The alternative options are identified by their value proposition for the company and by the specific attributes defining these options.

- **Key alternatives** are the other options that compete with the focal offering for the company's resources. The key questions here are: *What is the company currently doing to achieve its goals? What alternative offerings could enable the company to achieve its goals? What would the company give up if it chooses to invest in this offering?*

- The **value proposition of the alternative options** reflects the benefits and costs created by the options the company could pursue instead of investing in the focal offering. The key questions here are: *What benefits and costs do the alternative options create for the company? What is the primary reason why the company would choose to invest resources in the alternative options?*

- The **attributes of the alternative options** are the characteristics of the options that the company could pursue instead of investing in the focal offering. The key questions here are: *What are the product, service, brand, price, incentives, communication, and distribution aspects of the alternative options? How do the attributes of the alternative options create company value?*

The Company Value Proposition

The company value proposition defines the worth of an offering for the company stakeholders. The company value proposition is identified by the offering's benefits for the company, the relative advantage of the offering for the company over the alternative options, and the reason why the company would choose to invest in this offering.

- The **company benefits** reflect the value created by the offering on the two dimensions of company value: monetary and strategic. The key questions here are: *What monetary and strategic benefits and costs does the offering create for the company? What is this offering's profit formula?*

- The **relative advantage** reflects the focal offering's ability to address the company's goals better than the alternative options. The key questions here are: *Why should the company choose to invest resources in the focal offering instead of using alternative means to achieve its goals? What are the points of dominance, points of parity, and points of compromise of the focal offering relative to the alternative options?*

- The **reason to choose** is the key factor(s) that would motivate the company to invest in this offering. The key questions here are: *What is the primary reason for the company to pursue this offering? How would the company management justify choosing this offering?*

The Company Offering

The company offering represents the company aspect of the market offering. It is defined by the seven attributes — product, service, brand, price, incentives, communication, and distribution — that delineate the offering and the value that each of these attributes creates for the company. The key questions here are: *What are the key features of the product, service, brand, price, and incentives the company offers to its customers and collaborators? How will the offering be communicated to target customers and collaborators? How will the offering be delivered to target customers and collaborators? How will different attributes of the offering create company value?*

Business Model Workbook Example: Black & Decker (DeWalt)

The key components of a company's business model and the corresponding value maps can be illustrated with a company-specific example, which builds on the Black & Decker example introduced in Appendix A. In this context, the business model of the newly formed division of Black & Decker—DeWalt Industrial Tool Company—is outlined in the DeWalt market value map and detailed in the customer, collaborator, and company value maps.[1]

The Market Value Map (DeWalt)

DeWalt's business model and market value map are defined by three key components: the *target market* (the Five Cs), the *value proposition* for the relevant market entities—customers, the company, and its collaborators—and the key attributes of the *market offering*—product, service, brand, price, incentives, communication, and distribution. The specifics of DeWalt's business model are outlined in the market value map presented in Figure 5.

Figure 5. The Market Value Map (DeWalt)

TARGET MARKET	DESCRIPTION
Customers	Tradesmen—small businesses and independent contractors working in residential construction and using power tools on the job
Collaborators	Distribution channel partners: Wholesale distributors (serving smaller retailers), large home improvement centers (Home Depot, Lowe's), smaller hardware chains (Ace Hardware, ServiStar), and independently owned hardware stores
Company	DeWalt Industrial Tool Company (a business unit of Black & Decker, launched in 1992 to serve the tradesman segment)
Competition	Makita Electric (50% market share), Milwaukee Tools (10% market share), Ryobi (9% market share)
Context	*Economic context:* Recession, resulting in high unemployment, limited money supply (credit), and increased inflation *Business context:* Rapid growth of new home construction and remodeling prior to the recession, consolidation of home improvement retailers, and rise of big-box home improvement centers Home Depot and Lowe's *Regulatory context:* Price dumping allegations against some of the Japanese manufacturers, including Makita, raising the possibility of imposing import duties on certain tools imported from Japan

VALUE PROPOSITION	DESCRIPTION
Customer value	High-performance, reliable tools backed by a national service and quality commitment unparalleled in the power tool industry
Collaborator value	High-performance, reliable tools backed by a national service and quality commitment; large promotional budget to generate traffic; superior trade profits
Company value	Potential to increase market share from 8% to 50%, increase margins from 5% to 10%, increase the valuation of the company by creating a new brand, ensure a leadership position in the growing tradesman segment, and solidify Black & Decker's relationship with retailers by becoming a single-source supplier for both consumer and professional segments

Offering	Description	Customer Value
Product	Thirty-three high-performing power tools (drills, saws, sanders, and plate joiners) and 323 accessories designed to maximize power, precision, ergonomics, durability, and reliability	*Benefits:* Performance (power, precision, and ergonomics), durability, and reliability
Service	*Loaner Tool Policy:* DeWalt will lend a tool during the repair period *48-Hour Service Policy:* If a repair is not completed in 48 hours, DeWalt will provide a new tool for free *Technical Support:* Experts are available by phone at 1-800-4DEWALT to assist with DeWalt products, service, repair, or replacement *Free Service:* DeWalt will maintain the tool and replace parts free during the first year of ownership *Warranty:* DeWalt will warranty materials and workmanship for one year *Diagnostics:* DeWalt Certified Service Centers will diagnose problems quickly and accurately	*Benefits:* Minimized downtime (fast service and loaner availability), professional training, technical support, accurate diagnostics
Brand	*Brand name:* DeWalt® (replaces the Black & Decker Professional brand) *Brand logo:* **DeWALT.** *Brand color:* Yellow *Brand associations:* High-performance industrial tools; "no downtime" company *Related brands:* Black & Decker (service centers)	*Benefits:* Brand designed for professional (not consumer) use *Costs:* New brand with unknown reliability
Price	*List price:* Premium price tier (10% higher than Makita)	*Costs:* Price paid
Incentives	*Loyalty programs:* Preferred Contractor Program	*Benefits:* Price discounts
Communication	*Message:* Create awareness of the new offering; build the DeWalt brand to create customer brand loyalty. Taglines: *DeWalt. Guaranteed Tough* and *High Performance Industrial Tools** *Media:* Industry magazines (*Builder* and *Electrical Contractor;* $1M budget); trade shows; direct-mail catalogs ($300K budget); point-of-sale displays at home improvement retailers; ten vans visiting job sites promoting DeWalt products ($1M budget)	*Benefits:* Awareness of the offering and its specifics
Distribution	*Product:* Large home improvement centers (Home Depot, Lowe's), smaller hardware chains (Ace Hardware, ServiStar), and independently owned hardware stores *Service:* 117 Black & Decker authorized service centers with a dedicated DeWalt counter *Returns:* DeWalt will accept returns for any reason within 30 days from the date of purchase	*Benefits:* Product accessibility (wide distribution network), service accessibility (wide service network), peace of mind (30-day return policy)

The market value map shown in Figure 5 outlines DeWalt's business model. The ways in which DeWalt offerings create value for its target customers, collaborators, and the company are further detailed in its customer, collaborator, and company value maps, which are presented in the following sections.

The Customer Value Map (DeWalt)

The ways in which DeWalt creates value for its target customers is centered around four main components: *target customers*, the *competition*, the *customer value proposition*, and *customer offering* (Figure 6).

Figure 6. The Customer Value Map (DeWalt)[2]

STRATEGY	DESCRIPTION	
Customers	*Overview:* Tradesmen—small businesses and independent contractors working in residential construction and using power tools on the job *Customer needs:* Performance (power, precision, and ergonomics), reliability, service, and professional image *Customer demographics:* Small businesses and independent contractors (carpenters, plumbers, and electricians) working in residential construction. Tradesmen represent 28% ($420M) of the US power tools market and are the fastest growing segment (9%) of this market *Customer behavior:* Use power tools on the job; read trade press (*Builder* and *Electrical Contractor*); visit trade shows and home improvement stores including large home improvement centers such as Home Depot and Lowe's, smaller hardware chains such as Ace Hardware and ServiStar, and independently owned hardware stores	
Competition	*Key competitors:* Makita Electric (50% market share), Milwaukee Tools (10% market share), Ryobi (9% market share) *Competitive value proposition:* Reliable power tools; used by most contractors (Makita) *Offering attributes:* Wide variety of competitively priced power tools	
Value proposition	*Benefits:* High-performance, reliable tools backed by a national service and quality commitment unparalleled in the power tool industry *Competitive advantage:* More reliable than the competition *Positioning:* "No downtime" performance (reliability/service commitment)	

TACTICS	DESCRIPTION	VALUE
Product	Thirty-three high-performing power tools (drills, saws, sanders, and plate joiners) and 323 accessories designed to maximize power, precision, ergonomics, and reliability	*Benefits:* Performance (power, precision, and ergonomics) and reliability
Service	*Loaner Tool Policy:* DeWalt will lend a tool during the repair period *48-Hour Service policy:* If a repair is not completed within 48 hours, DeWalt will provide a new tool free of charge *Technical Support*: Experts are available by phone at 1-800-4DEWALT to offer assistance regarding DeWalt products, service, repair, or replacement *Free One-Year Service Contract*: DeWalt will maintain the tool and replace worn parts free any time during the first year of ownership *One-Year Warranty:* DeWalt will warranty materials and workmanship for one year *Superior Diagnostics:* DeWalt Certified Service Centers use state-of-the-art testing equipment to diagnose problems quickly and accurately	*Benefits:* Minimized downtime (fast service and loaner availability), professional training, technical support, accurate diagnostics
Brand	*Brand name:* DeWalt® (replaces the Black & Decker Professional brand) *Brand logo:* **DeWALT** *Brand color:* Yellow *Brand referents:* High-performance industrial tools; "no downtime" company; guaranteed tough	*Benefits:* Brand designed for professional (not consumer) use *Costs:* New brand with unknown reliability

Price	List Price: Premium price tier (10% higher than Makita)	Costs: Price paid
Incentives	Loyalty programs: Preferred Contractor Program	Benefits: Price discounts
Communication	Message: Create awareness of the new product line and service program; build the DeWalt brand to create customer brand loyalty. Taglines: DeWalt. Guaranteed Tough and High Performance Industrial Tools* Media: Industry magazines (Builder and Electrical Contractor; $1M budget); trade shows; direct-mail catalogs ($300K budget), point-of-sale displays at home improvement retailers; ten vans visiting job sites promoting DeWalt products ($1M budget)	Benefits: Awareness of the offering and its specifics
Distribution	Product: Large home improvement centers (Home Depot / Lowe's), smaller hardware chains (Ace Hardware / ServiStar), and independently owned hardware stores Service: 117 Black & Decker authorized service centers with a dedicated DeWalt counter Returns: DeWalt will accept returns for any reason within 30 days from the date of purchase	Benefits: Product accessibility (wide distribution network), service accessibility (wide service network), peace of mind (30-day return policy)

*A specific example of customer communication in the print media features a plate joiner (a woodworking tool used to join two pieces of wood together) following the headline: "The Joint Chief." The advertising copy reads: "The key to a plate joiner's performance is its fence. And that's what makes the DeWalt plate joiner a real stand-out in its field. Because the DeWalt fence lets you make a great variety of joints and move with speed and precision from one kind to another. And the angles are covered with an integral fence which tilts 0-90 degrees. The fence is calibrated from 0-90 degrees so you can make the cut at exactly the proper angle. The fence can also be located on the inside or outside of a mitered joint, according to your preference. In addition, flush cuts can be made at 0 degrees without having to remove the fence. Rack and pinion control provides easy, accurate height adjustment and keeps the fence parallel to the blade. With this feature, the risk of making an inaccurate cut is virtually eliminated. And this rack and pinion control is a feature unique to DeWalt. So, if you haven't decided which plate joiner to get, you don't have to guess anymore. All you have to do is try DeWalt. You'll add it to your staff immediately."[3]

The Collaborator Value Map (DeWalt)

The ways in which DeWalt creates value for its collaborators is defined by four main components: *collaborators*, the *competition*, the *collaborator value proposition*, and the *collaborator offering* (Figure 7).

Figure 7. The Collaborator Value Map (DeWalt)

STRATEGY	DESCRIPTION
Collaborators	Overview: Distribution channel partners Collaborator profile: Wholesale distributors (serving smaller retailers), large home improvement centers (Home Depot, Lowe's), smaller hardware chains (Ace Hardware, ServiStar), independently owned hardware stores Collaborator goals: Increase profits; generate traffic; enhance brand image
Competition	Key competitors: Makita Electric (50% market share), Milwaukee Tools (10% market share), Ryobi (9% market share) Competitor value proposition: Established brand with 50% market share (Makita) that brings traffic, revenues, and profits Offering attributes: Variety of power tools with standard trade margins
Value proposition	Value proposition: High-performance, reliable tools backed by a national service and quality commitment unparalleled in the power tool industry; supported by a large promotional budget to generate customer traffic; backed by Black & Decker; offering superior trade profits Positioning: More profitable for the retailer than the competition

TACTICS	DESCRIPTION	VALUE
Product	Thirty-three high-performing power tools (drills, saws, sanders, and plate joiners) and 323 accessories designed to maximize power, precision, ergonomics, and reliability; aimed to replace the Black & Decker Professional product line	*Benefits:* Superior product line better fitting the needs of tradesmen than the Black & Decker Professional line it replaces *Costs:* Discontinuing Black & Decker Professional products; introducing DeWalt products
Service	Trade support provided by Black & Decker (ordering, inventory management, returns)	*Benefits:* Superior trade support compared to that for the Black & Decker Professional line
Brand	*Brand name:* DeWalt® (replaces the Black & Decker Professional brand) *Brand logo:* **DeWALT.** *Brand color:* Yellow *Brand referents:* Profitable	*Benefits:* Adding the DeWalt brand to a retailer's brand portfolio helps solidify Black & Decker's image as a go-to shop for tradesmen
Price	*Price:* Trade margins 5% higher than Makita *Price protection:* Price protection from discounters (e.g., halting supplies to price-cutting retailers) to prevent horizontal channel conflict	*Benefits:* Superior margins relative to Black & Decker Professional; price protection from discounters *Cost:* Price paid
Incentives	*Point-of-sale promotions:* Trade incentives to ensure retailer "push"	*Benefits:* Trade incentives provide additional source of revenue
Communication	*Message:* Create awareness of the new product line and service program; build the DeWalt brand to create retailer loyalty. Tagline: *There's only one thing about DeWalt that's not tough: Making a profit** *Media:* Trade shows (National Association of Home Builders trade show); Black & Decker salesforce	*Benefits:* Increased store traffic from DeWalt customer communication
Distribution	*Product:* Distributed through the existing Black & Decker channels; direct distribution to home improvement stores, and indirect (wholesaler) distribution to hardware stores. $20M inventory buildup at launch to ensure product availability and avoid stock-outs *Returns:* DeWalt will accept returns for any reason within 30 days from the date of purchase	*Benefits:* Distributed by the same company (Black & Decker); sufficient inventory available at the time of launch; peace of mind (30-day return policy) *Costs:* Ordering and inventorying DeWalt products; reverse logistics for the remaining Black & Decker Professional products

*A specific example of collaborator communication for print media features a plate joiner (a woodworking tool used to join two pieces of wood together) following the headline: "There's only one thing about DeWalt that's not tough: Making a profit." The advertising copy reads: "In developing the complete line of DeWalt high-performance industrial tools and accessories, we've kept you in mind. By doing everything possible to make them profitable for you to sell. And this is what we've done. We've put together easy-to-understand pricing programs tailored to your specific needs. We've got a salesforce dedicated to helping the tools sell through. They'll be out on job sites putting tools in your customers' hands, creating demand and sales for you. All tools come with a 30-Day No Risk Satisfaction Guarantee plus a full 1-year warranty. And with our quick-return repair service, which includes a free loaner program, your customers will never have a problem with down time. Why are we doing all this? Because at DeWalt, we believe selling tools that work hard shouldn't have to be hard work. And, above all, it should make you a solid profit."[4]

The Company Value Map (DeWalt)

The ways in which DeWalt offerings create value for the company is defined by four main components: the *company*, the *alternative options*, the *company value proposition*, and the *company offering* (Figure 8).

Figure 8. The Company Value Map (DeWalt)

STRATEGY	DESCRIPTION	
Company	*Company profile:* DeWalt Industrial Tool Company (a business unit of Black & Decker, launched in 1992 to serve the tradesman segment) *Company goals:* Increase revenues and profits; gain leadership in the growing and profitable tradesman market	
Alternative options	*Key alternatives:* Promote the existing Black & Decker tools to tradesmen instead of launching the DeWalt line of tools *Value proposition:* Lower cost (compared to developing new products and building a new brand) *Offering attributes:* Existing product line branded as Black & Decker, promoted in trade magazines, and offered through current channels	
Value proposition	*Monetary value:* Potential to increase market share from 8% to 50%, increase margins from 5% to 10%, and increase the valuation of the company by creating a new brand *Strategic value:* Ensures leadership positioning in the growing tradesman segment. Solidifies Black & Decker's relationship with retailers by enabling retailers to have a single-source supplier for consumer and professional segments *Positioning:* "No downtime" performance (reliability and service commitment)	

TACTICS	DESCRIPTION	VALUE
Product	Thirty-three high-performing power tools (drills, saws, sanders, and plate joiners) and 323 accessories designed to maximize power, precision, ergonomics, and reliability ("the banner of quality")	*Benefits (strategic):* R&D innovation can benefit other product lines; the new product line establishes a quality benchmark for Black & Decker *Costs (monetary):* Product development and production costs
Service	*Customer service:* Loaner tool policy, 48-hour service policy, technical support, free one-year service contract, one-year warranty, superior diagnostics *Trade service:* Retailer support (ordering, inventory management, returns)	*Benefits (strategic):* Builds customer loyalty; offers sustainable competitive advantage over Makita *Costs (monetary):* Service implementation costs
Brand	*Brand name:* DeWalt® (replaces the Black & Decker Professional brand) *Brand logo:* **DEWALT** *Brand color:* Yellow *Brand referents:* High-performance industrial tools; "no downtime" company; guaranteed tough; profitable for retailers and Black & Decker	*Benefits (strategic):* Identifies the offering to create customer loyalty; builds brand (DeWalt) equity *Costs (monetary):* Brand-building expense
Price	*Price:* Premium price tier (10% higher than Makita and Black & Decker Professional)	*Benefits (monetary):* Captures customer value in the form of revenues *Benefits (strategic):* Premium price enables Black & Decker to invest in product development, service, brand building, and promotion

Incentives	*Loyalty programs:* Preferred Contractor Program *Point-of-sale promotions:* Trade incentives to ensure retailer "push"	*Benefits (strategic):* Stimulates customer demand *Costs (monetary):* Incentives-related expenses *Costs (strategic):* Monetary customer incentives could have detrimental impact on the DeWalt brand
Communication	*Customer communication:* $1M advertising in industry magazines (*Builder* and *Electrical Contractor*); $300K direct mail catalogs; $1M van promotion program; $200K point-of-sale displays; trade shows *Trade communication:* Black & Decker salesforce; trade shows	*Benefits (strategic):* Creates awareness of the offering; builds the DeWalt brand *Costs (monetary):* Communication expenses
Distribution	*Product:* Distributed through the existing Black & Decker channels offering direct distribution to large home improvement centers (Home Depot, Lowe's) and indirect (wholesaler) distribution to smaller hardware chains (Ace Hardware, ServiStar) and independent hardware stores. $20M inventory buildup at launch to ensure product availability and avoid stock-outs *Service:* 117 Black & Decker authorized service centers with a dedicated DeWalt counter *Returns:* 30-day return policy	*Benefits (strategic):* Solidifies Black & Decker's relationship with retailers by offering a comprehensive product portfolio *Costs (monetary):* Cost of making DeWalt available to the trade, cost of discontinuing Black & Decker Professional, cost of processing returns

Sample Marketing Plans

Chance favors only the prepared mind.
— Louis Pasteur, French microbiologist and chemist

This section presents two stylized examples to illustrate the process of writing a marketing plan. The marketing plans presented here follow the structure outlined in Chapter 3: They begin with an *executive summary*, followed by a *situation overview* and an *action plan*, and conclude with a set of relevant *exhibits*.

The crux of the marketing plan is the action plan, which follows the G-STIC framework. It includes an outline of the *goal(s)* that the company aims to achieve with its offering; an outline of the offering's *strategy*, which involves identifying the target market(s) — customers, the company, collaborators, competitors, and the context in which they operate — as well as the offering's value proposition for target customers, the company, and collaborators; a description of the marketing *tactics* (product, service, brand, price, incentives, communication, and distribution); an *implementation* plan that identifies the processes by which the company will develop the offering and deploy it in the market; and the *control* measures that provide the metrics for evaluating the company's performance and monitoring the external environment.

The marketing plans outlined here depict Align Technology Inc. — a startup with a proprietary method for treating the misalignment of teeth. Launched in 1997 by two MBA students with no professional experience in the field of orthodontics or dentistry, the company raised more than $140 million in private capital prior to going public in January 2001. The first round of financing was led by the Menlo Park, California-based venture capital firm Kleiner Perkins Caufield & Byers, an early investor in more than 300 technology startups, including Amazon, Compaq, Google, Netscape, and Sun Microsystems. Twenty years later, the company reached $1 billion in sales revenue and a market capitalization of more than $30 billion.

Align Technology's marketing plans demonstrate the importance of understanding and managing value for each of the three key players in the market: the company, its customers, and collaborators. In addition, this marketing plan illustrates a business model that combines both business-to-business and business-to-consumer components. Another factor that makes these marketing plans particularly relevant is that they not only illustrate decisions concerning all of the key marketing mix attributes (product, service, brand, price, incentives, communication, and distribution) but also highlight the relationship among them. Finally, Align's marketing plans illustrate the launch and the management of a new-to-the-world offering.

The two marketing plans laid out here illustrate the two most commonly used types of marketing plans: a *plan to launch a new offering* and a *plan to manage an existing offering*. Both types of plans follow the same structure; the key difference is in their focus. The plan for launching a new offering aims to identify a market opportunity and design an action plan to take advantage of this opportunity. The plan for managing an existing offering, in addition to identifying market opportunities, explicitly focuses on the changes in the marketing environment (opportunities and threats) to identify the corresponding modifications to be made to the course of action outlined in the current marketing plan.

Because their primary goal is to illustrate the organization of the marketing plan, the sample plans presented in this section are not comprehensive and do not cover all aspects of the offering in detail. Rather, they aim to illustrate the overall structure of the plan and highlight its key components. To better illustrate the relationship among the different elements of the marketing plan, the purpose of each section and the links between different sections of the marketing plan are highlighted in the sidebar.[1]

Product Launch Plan | Align Technology Inc.

Align Technology's product launch plan depicts the company's goals, strategy, tactics, implementation, and controls set to guide the development and the commercialization of its new offering.

1. Executive Summary

Align Technology Inc. designs, manufactures, and markets the Invisalign system, a new proprietary method for treating malocclusion, or the misalignment of teeth. The Invisalign system corrects malocclusion using a series of clear, removable appliances that gently move teeth to a desired final position.

Our target customers are adults and adolescents with mature dentition who suffer from mild forms of malocclusion. This target group consists of approximately 65 million potential customers.

For customers, the Invisalign system offers superior aesthetics, improved dental health, and greater overall convenience relative to conventional braces. For orthodontists, the Invisalign system offers increased patient volume, higher margins, and reduced chair time compared to conventional braces. Because it offers a unique set of benefits, we believe that the Invisalign system will be well received by both orthodontists and consumers and will rapidly gain acceptance as the preferred method for treating malocclusion.

Our *primary goal* is to create value for our stakeholders by establishing the Invisalign system as the standard method for treating malocclusion. We plan to turn a profit within three years of launching the Invisalign system.

This plan outlines our key marketing activities for the period January 1999 – December 2000. Following successful implementation of this plan, we intend to take the company public in early 2001.

> The executive summary in Section 1 offers a succinct overview of the key aspects of the offering.

2. Situation Overview

Malocclusion (misalignment of teeth) is one of the most prevalent clinical conditions in the United States, affecting more than 200 million individuals, or approximately 75% of the population. Of those, approximately two million annually elect orthodontic treatment. Only a relatively small proportion of people with malocclusion seek treatment because of the compromised aesthetics, discomfort, and other drawbacks associated with conventional orthodontic treatments.

Individuals who elect to be treated for malocclusion are interacting with two entities: (1) general-practice dentists, who typically diagnose the problem and provide a referral to a specialist; and (2) orthodontists who specialize in treating malocclusion.

- *General-practice dentists* are certified to perform all oral health procedures, including orthodontics. Many general dentists, however, choose not to perform orthodontic procedures be-

> Section 2 offers the background information on the market in which Align Technology operates. The situation overview offered in Section 2 is broader in scope than the description of the target market offered in Section 4.1, as it includes an overview of the entire market (including markets that are not targeted by the company).

cause of their complexity and the added risk of malpractice liability. There are more than 100,000 general-practice dentists in the United States.

- *Orthodontists* specialize in treating malocclusion. Only board-certified orthodontists can refer to themselves as orthodontists. This certification typically involves a two-year residency after dental school. There are approximately 8,500 orthodontists in the United States.

The providers of orthodontic services apply traditional techniques and principles of treatment developed in the early 20th century, which involves metal archwires and brackets, commonly referred to as braces.

The average treatment takes approximately two years to complete and requires several hours of direct orthodontist involvement, or chair time. To initiate treatment, an orthodontist will diagnose a patient's condition and create an appropriate treatment plan. In a subsequent visit, the orthodontist will bond brackets to the patient's teeth with cement and attach an archwire to the brackets. Thereafter, by tightening or otherwise adjusting the braces approximately every six weeks, the orthodontist is able to exert sufficient force on the patient's teeth to achieve desired tooth movement. Because of the length of time between visits, the orthodontist must tighten the braces to a degree sufficient to achieve sustained tooth movement during the interval. In a final visit, the orthodontist removes each bracket and residual cement from the patient's teeth.

Although braces are generally effective in correcting a wide range of malocclusion, they have many drawbacks, such as:

- *Unattractive appearance.* Braces are not visually appealing and often trap food, which further compromises appearance. Braces can also result in permanent markings and discoloration of teeth. In addition, many adults associate braces with adolescence.

- *Oral discomfort.* Braces are sharp and bulky. They can abrade and irritate the interior surfaces of the mouth. The tightening of braces during treatment results in root and gum soreness and discomfort.

- *Poor oral hygiene.* Braces compromise oral hygiene by making it more difficult to brush and floss, often resulting in tooth decay and periodontal damage.

- *Root resorption.* The sustained high levels of force associated with conventional treatment can result in root resorption, a shortening of tooth roots. This shortening can have substantial adverse periodontal consequences for the patient.

- *Emergencies.* At times, braces need to be repaired or replaced on an emergency basis. Such emergencies cause significant inconvenience to both the patient and the orthodontist.

- *Inability to project treatment.* The lack of a means to model the movement of teeth over the course of treatment limits the orthodontist's ability to estimate the duration of the treatment. Because most orthodontic treatment is performed on a fixed-price basis, extended treatment duration reduces profitability for the orthodontist.

- *Physical demands on orthodontists.* The manipulation of wires and brackets requires sustained manual dexterity and visual acuity from the orthodontist.

Fees for orthodontic treatment typically range between $3,000 and $5,000. Orthodontists also commonly charge a premium for the

The shortcomings of the traditional methods for treating malocclusion are later used to develop Invisalign's value proposition for target customers and collaborators (orthodontists).

more aesthetically appealing lingual or ceramic alternatives. Fees are based on the difficulty of the particular case and on the orthodontist's estimate of chair time and are generally negotiated in advance. Treatment that exceeds the orthodontist's estimate of chair time is typically covered by the orthodontist at no additional charge. Most insurance plans do not cover orthodontic treatments for adults and offer limited coverage for children and adolescents.

3. Goal

Our *primary goal* is to create value for our shareholders by establishing the Invisalign system as the standard method for treating malocclusion. We plan to turn a profit within three years of launching Invisalign.

To achieve our primary goal, we have set the following objectives:

- *Customer objectives.* Our key customer objectives are to create awareness of the benefits of the Invisalign system among 20% of our target customers, stimulate their interest, and incite action leading to treatment using the Invisalign system. Our goal is to have 50,000 patients initiate treatment with the Invisalign system by the end of 2001.

- *Collaborator objectives.* We aim to create awareness of the benefits of the Invisalign system among orthodontists, train them to use the system, and motivate them to promote it to patients as the standard method for treating malocclusion. Our goal is to create awareness among 90% of orthodontists and train 2,000 of them to use the Invisalign system by the end of 2001.

- *Internal objectives.* We strive to constantly improve the proprietary technology that underlies our supply-chain management processes to enhance product quality, increase production capacity, and reduce both unit costs and production times.

- *Competitive objectives.* Our primary competitive objective is to create barriers to entry for competitors. We will pursue further intellectual property protection through patent applications and nondisclosure agreements. We also seek to protect our proprietary technology under trade secret and copyright laws.

4. Strategy

4.1. Target Market

Customers

Based on the degree to which individuals suffering from malocclusion have developed dentition, they can be divided into two groups: (1) children/adolescents whose teeth/jaws are still developing and (2) adolescents/adults with mature dentition.

Our target customers are adults and adolescents with mature dentition who suffer from malocclusion and are otherwise suitable for treatment using the Invisalign system. This group represents approximately 65 million potential customers. Although we have clearance from the FDA to market the Invisalign system to treat patients with any type of malocclusion, we voluntarily restrict the use of the Invisalign system to adults and adolescents with mature dentition who are otherwise suitable for treatment. Accordingly, we will not treat children whose teeth and jaws are still developing, as the effectiveness of the Invisalign system relies on our ability to accurately predict the movement of teeth over the course of treatment.

Section 3 outlines the company's primary goal as well as a series of objectives focusing on customers, collaborators, the company, and competitors.

Section 4.1 follows the 5-C framework.

This section identifies the offering's target customers.

Note that the targeting decision involves not only target customers, but also those who are *not* targeted.

This section further identifies two different target segments that are likely to vary in their response to the Invisalign system. Dividing customers into appearance-conscious and

Our research indicates that, based on the primary reason for treatment, there are two groups of customers: *health conscious* and *appearance conscious*. Health-conscious consumers are primarily concerned with strengthening their teeth for health reasons and are less concerned about their appearance during treatment. In contrast, appearance-conscious consumers are concerned about their appearance and might not elect to undergo orthodontic treatment if it will affect their appearance during treatment.

These two segments are likely to differ in their preference for a treatment method. Because their primary concern is the health of their teeth, health-conscious consumers tend to rely on orthodontists' recommendations for choosing the treatment method (traditional braces vs. Invisalign). In contrast, appearance-conscious consumers are likely to approach orthodontists with a specific request for Invisalign treatment. Health-conscious and appearance-conscious consumers are also likely to differ in their decision-making process. Health-conscious consumers first visit an orthodontist and only then select a treatment, usually following the orthodontist's recommendation. In contrast, appearance-conscious consumers are likely to choose Invisalign as their treatment method of choice based on Invisalign advertisements prior to visiting an orthodontist. Exhibit 1 provides detailed information on the customer survey.

Collaborators

Our primary collaborators are US-based licensed orthodontists. We expect orthodontists to contribute to the success of the Invisalign system by (1) informing patients about the availability and benefits of the Invisalign system, (2) implementing the Invisalign treatment, and (3) providing performance feedback that will enable us to improve the Invisalign system.

The Invisalign system will be available only to orthodontists. Although dentists play an important role in informing patients about orthodontics and are a key source of referrals to orthodontists, the Invisalign system will not be available to general dentists.

Competitors

As a new technique for treating malocclusion, Align Technology does not have direct competitors and currently competes with the traditional techniques to treat malocclusion, the most common of which are metal braces. In the broader market for orthodontic products that treat malocclusion, we are indirectly competing with 3M Company, Sybron International Corporation, and Dentsply International, Inc.

We are not aware of any company that has developed or is marketing a system comparable to the Invisalign system. Because the availability of the Invisalign system is likely to generate new demand by attracting appearance-conscious consumers who would not otherwise choose an orthodontic treatment, we do not expect an immediate response from the manufacturers of traditional orthodontic products for malocclusion. However, over time we expect the competition in this segment to increase with the emergence of new competitors with similar products.

Company

Align Technology Inc. was incorporated in Delaware in 1997. The corporate headquarters are located in Santa Clara, California, where we house our manufacturing, customer support, software

---

health-conscious segments is later used to develop a segment-specific marketing mix, using a pull strategy for appearance-conscious consumers and a push strategy for health-conscious consumers.

This section identifies the key collaborators that will facilitate the success of the Invisalign system.

The positioning statement identifies the key competitors and evaluates the current and future competitive intensity of the marketplace.

This section provides general information about the company.

engineering, and administrative personnel. We also operate two facilities in the city of Lahore in Pakistan.

We currently have 320 employees, of whom 120 are employed in the United States, with the balance employed in Pakistan. Our organizational structure is outlined in Exhibit 2. Our management consists of (1) executive officers, (2) a scientific advisory board, and (3) a board of directors (listed in Exhibits 3–5). We are currently building specialized production facilities, creating a network of orthodontists trained to use the Invisalign system, building brand recognition, and creating an initial customer base.

Our core competency is producing highly customized, close tolerance, medical-quality products in volume. Our strategic assets include intellectual property (proprietary technology with pending patent application), manufacturing infrastructure, and the Invisalign and ClinCheck brands.

Context

Economic context: Continuous economic growth for seven consecutive years, low unemployment, high consumer confidence, low interest rates, and low inflation. Stock market powered by gains in technology stocks and a record number of technology-based IPOs.

This section outlines the context in which Align Technology operates.

Regulatory context: Laws regulating medical device manufacturers and healthcare providers cover a broad array of subjects, including:

- The confidentiality of patient medical information and the circumstances under which such information may be released for inclusion in our databases, or released by us to third parties, are subject to substantial regulation by state governments.

- Federal and state regulations prohibit paying any remuneration in exchange for the referral of patients to a person participating in federal or state healthcare programs, such as Medicare and Medicaid.

- Various states regulate the operation of an advertising and referral service for dentists and may require compliance with various requirements on how they structure their relationships with participating dentists.

- According to the FDA classification of medical devices, the Invisalign system is a Class I device, the least stringent class, that does not require a premarket approval, which includes, among other things, extensive preclinical and clinical trials.

4.2. Customer Value Proposition

Value Proposition

There is an unmet need among our target customers for a malocclusion treatment that eliminates many of the limitations of conventional braces. Test market data presented in Exhibit 6 show that the Invisalign system offers a number of unique benefits to our target customers:

This section outlines the key benefits of the Invisalign system for target customers. It answers the question: Why would target customers opt to straighten their teeth using the Invisalign system?

- *Excellent aesthetics.* Aligners are nearly invisible when worn, eliminating the aesthetic concerns associated with conventional braces.

- *Improved oral hygiene.* Patients can remove Aligners when eating, brushing, and flossing, a feature that can reduce tooth decay and periodontal damage during treatment.

- *Greater safety.* By replacing the six-week adjustment cycle of traditional braces with two-week stages, the Invisalign system moves teeth more gently, decreasing the likelihood of root resorption (shortening of tooth roots).

- *Increased comfort.* The Invisalign system is substantially more comfortable and less abrasive than conventional braces.

- *Reduced overall treatment time.* The Invisalign system controls force by distributing it broadly over the exposed surfaces of the teeth while reducing the likelihood of unintended tooth movements. This could significantly reduce overall treatment time relative to conventional braces.

- *Reduced incidence of emergencies.* Lost or broken Aligners could be simply replaced with the next Aligner in the series, minimizing inconvenience to both patient and orthodontist.

Positioning Statement

For adults and adolescents with mild forms of malocclusion, Invisalign is a better treatment than conventional braces because it offers superior aesthetics, improved dental health, and greater overall convenience.

> This section identifies target customers and the key benefits of the Invisalign system.

4.3. Collaborator Value Proposition

Value Proposition

The Invisalign system offers the following benefits to orthodontists:

> This section outlines the key benefits of the Invisalign system for orthodontists. It answers the question: *Why would orthodontists opt to use the Invisalign system instead of conventional braces?*

- *Ability to visualize treatment and likely outcomes.* The Invisalign system enables orthodontists to preview a course of treatment and the likely final outcome of treatment in an interactive three-dimensional computer model. This allows orthodontists to analyze multiple treatment alternatives before selecting the one most appropriate for the patient.

- *Ability to predict treatment time.* Because patient fees are based on the orthodontist's estimate of chair time and are generally negotiated in advance, treatment that exceeds the orthodontist's estimate of chair time is typically covered by the orthodontist at no additional charge. By improving the accuracy of the estimate of treatment time, Invisalign can help orthodontists better manage resources and optimize profits.

- *Ease of use.* Because the Invisalign system relies on the same biomechanical principles that underlie traditional orthodontic treatment, it is straightforward for orthodontists to learn and to use. The initial certification training can be completed in a one-day workshop, and orthodontists can be equipped to submit cases immediately thereafter with minimal financial outlay.

- *Increased patient base.* Currently, less than one percent of the more than 200 million people with malocclusion in the United States enter treatment each year. The Invisalign system allows orthodontists to broaden their patient base by offering a new, attractive treatment alternative to people who would not otherwise elect treatment.

- *Higher margins.* The Invisalign system enables orthodontists to more accurately estimate the duration of the treatment, thus decreasing the likelihood of underestimating the treatment length and increasing the overall profit margins per patient. Due to the substantial benefits to customers, orthodontists can also charge a premium for the Invisalign system comparable to other more aesthetically pleasing alternatives to conventional braces, such as ceramic and lingual braces.

- *Decreased orthodontist and staff time.* The Invisalign system reduces both the frequency and length of patient visits. It eliminates the need for time-intensive processes, such as bonding appliances to the patient's teeth, adjusting archwires during the course of treatment, and removing the appliances at the conclusion of treatment. As a result, use of the Invisalign system significantly reduces orthodontist and staff chair time and can increase practice throughput.

Positioning Statement

For orthodontists, the Invisalign system is a better method for treating most cases of malocclusion than conventional braces because it offers increased patient volume, higher margins, and reduced chair time.

4.4. Company Value Proposition

Value Proposition

Align Technology earns revenue primarily from the sale of our Invisalign system, which consists of the ClinCheck fee and a per-Aligner fee. Our per-customer revenue is $1,180 and our per-customer gross profit is $875. With a market potential of 65 million customers, this implies potential sales revenues as high as $75 billion.

Currently, we are the only company with a commercially available alternative to conventional braces. As our business grows, new competitors are likely to enter the market. The inherent complexity of producing highly customized, high-precision orthodontic devices in volume is a barrier to potential competitors. We further believe that our patents and other intellectual property provide a substantial lead over potential competitors. Therefore, we believe that our business model is sustainable and can offer long-term value to shareholders.

Due to our national advertising campaign, the expansion of manufacturing capacity, and continued research-and-development efforts, we expect to incur net losses for the next several years. We plan to turn a profit within three years of launching Invisalign sales. Detailed financial information and the key assumptions are provided in Exhibits 7–8.

Positioning Statement

To investors who are interested in investing in a startup company with a high growth potential, Align Technology offers an opportunity to pioneer a $75 billion market for orthodontic devices with a patented system that offers unique benefits to both patients and orthodontists.

Executive Compensation

Compensation schedules for our executive officers, scientific advisory board, and board of directors, as well as the composition of the executive compensation committee are disclosed in Exhibit 9.

Employee Compensation

Our full-time employees (excluding the salesforce) are compensated in two ways: salary and stock options. Salaries are competitive with the high end of comparable positions within the industry. The stock options are based on seniority with the company. We

---

Margin notes:

This section identifies the company's collaborators and the key benefits of the Invisalign system.

This section outlines the value of the offering to the company. Because the key aspects of company value are reflected in the company's goal, this section restates the goal outlined in Section 3.

This section further delineates the key benefits of the Invisalign system for stakeholders. It answers the question: *Why should stakeholders invest in Invisalign instead of pursuing other investment options?*

This section identifies the key stakeholders and the key benefits of the Invisalign system.

Employee satisfaction has a direct impact on performance and is an important component in defining an offering's value proposition.

also offer health insurance benefits to all full-time employees, effective the day they begin work.

Salesforce Compensation

Our salesforce is divided regionally and compensated on a 60 percent salary, 15 percent commission, and 25 percent bonus structure. Salaries are competitive with the high end of comparable positions within the industry. Commission is a function of the number of cases submitted, and bonuses are based on nonsales objectives, such as the number of workshops conducted for orthodontists. The compensation structure also includes a company car, stock options based on seniority, and full insurance benefits.

Because salesforce compensation constitutes a substantial part of the overall employee expenditures and has a distinct compensation structure, it is discussed in a separate section.

5. Tactics

5.1. Product

The Invisalign system is a proprietary new method for treating malocclusion. It consists of two components: ClinCheck and Aligners.

Section 5.1 outlines the product aspect of the Invisalign system.

- *ClinCheck* is an interactive Internet application that allows orthodontists to diagnose and plan treatment for their patients. ClinCheck uses a dental impression and a treatment prescription submitted by an orthodontist to develop a customized, three-dimensional treatment plan that simulates appropriate tooth movement in a series of two-week increments. ClinCheck allows the orthodontist to view this three-dimensional simulation with a high degree of magnification and from any angle.

- *Aligners* are custom-manufactured, clear, removable dental appliances that, when worn in the prescribed series, provide orthodontic treatment. Each Aligner covers a patient's teeth and is nearly invisible when worn. Aligners are commonly worn in pairs (over the upper and lower dental arches) for consecutive two-week periods that correspond to the approved ClinCheck treatment simulation. After two weeks of use, the patient discards the Aligners and replaces them with the next pair in the series. This process is repeated until the final Aligners are used and treatment is complete. The typical Invisalign system patient uses 22 sets of Aligners over 44 weeks of treatment. Detailed product specifications are provided in Exhibit 10.

The ClinCheck application can also be viewed as part of the service aspect of the Invisalign system (orthodontists do not acquire the rights to the software application but merely gain the right to use it on a limited basis); however, because it is an essential component of creating the product (Aligners), it is presented as a component of the product aspect of the offering.

5.2. Service

We offer support services to orthodontists who elect to use the Invisalign system. These services include initial training, assistance with current cases, and practice-building assistance.

Section 5.2 outlines the service aspect of the Invisalign system, focusing on the service provided to orthodontists using the Invisalign system.

- *Initial training* is conducted in a workshop format by our sales and orthodontic teams. The key topics covered in training include case selection criteria, instructions on filling out the Invisalign prescription form, guidance on pricing, and instructions on interacting with the ClinCheck software and using the Invisalign website.

- *Current-case support* may include assisting orthodontists with the applicability and use of the Invisalign system for specific patients.

- *Practice-building assistance* helps orthodontists promote their services to local general-practice dentists and to prospective patients through direct mail or other media.

5.3. Brand

We use two brands to differentiate our offering: ClinCheck and Invisalign.

- *ClinCheck.* We use the brand ClinCheck in reference to the interactive Internet application that allows orthodontists to diagnose and plan treatment for their patients. We use the ClinCheck brand in our communication to orthodontists and general-practice dentists; it is not used in consumer communication. The ClinCheck name is our registered trademark.

- *Invisalign.* We use the brand Invisalign in reference to the process of straightening teeth using a series of invisible Aligners. We use the Invisalign brand in our communication to consumers, orthodontists, and general-practice dentists. We have filed applications for several relevant trademarks with the US Patent and Trademark Office, including Invisalign and Invisalign system, as well as the Invisalign system logo. Our brand identity marks are illustrated in Exhibit 11.

Section 5.3 outlines the brands used by Align Technology to create a unique identity for its offering.

Note that while both brands—ClinCheck and Invisalign—are promoted to orthodontists, only the latter is used in consumer communication.

5.4. Pricing

The price for the orthodontic treatment is negotiated by the orthodontist and the patient. We expect the average retail price for the orthodontists' services (including Aligners) to be around $5,000 to $7,000 depending on the severity of the case.

Align Technology charges orthodontists $300 for the setup fee and $20 for each Aligner. The ClinCheck fee is invoiced when the orthodontist orders ClinCheck prior to the production of Aligners. The fee for Aligners is invoiced when we ship them. The average cost of the Aligners to orthodontists is about $1,180 per patient (assuming a course of treatment consisting of 22 pairs of Aligners at $20 each and a setup fee of $300).

Section 5.4 outlines the price of the Invisalign system for both patients and orthodontists.

Note that Align Technology does not determine the retail price of the treatment, but only the price of Invisalign for orthodontists.

5.5. Incentives

We offer incentives to both our target customers and collaborators.

- *Incentives for customers.* Because the specifics and cost of the treatment are negotiated directly between the orthodontist and the patient, we are not offering direct incentives to consumers.

- *Incentives for orthodontists.* We use a system of tiering orthodontists that encourages our salesforce to devote more time to those orthodontists most proficient in the use of the Invisalign system. We use objective criteria, primarily the number of cases initiated with the Invisalign system, to tier orthodontists. Inquiries from prospective patients through our customer call center and our website are directed to higher tier orthodontists. This tiering process should incentivize the selected orthodontists, rapidly increasing the use of the Invisalign system by their offices.

- *Incentives for general-practice dentists.* We have no immediate plans to offer incentives to dentists for referring potential Invisalign patients to orthodontists.

Section 5.5 outlines the incentives provided to target customers and collaborators.

5.6. Communication

Consumer Communication

Consumers can learn about the benefits of the Invisalign system in one of three ways: (1) directly from Align Technology, (2) from orthodontists, and/or (3) from general-practice dentists. Accordingly, we

This section outlines the communication to target customers.

use two basic strategies to reach our target customers. We use a *pull strategy* (direct-to-consumer communication) to target appearance-conscious consumers who might not consider orthodontic treatment unless they are made aware of the existence of an aesthetically appealing malocclusion treatment. In addition, we use a *push strategy* (informing and incentivizing orthodontists) to target health-conscious consumers who rely on orthodontists' advice for the choice of treatment.

Note that the use of pull vs. push strategy in the case of direct vs. indirect communication directly follows from the analysis of the target market in Section 4.1.

- *Direct-to-consumer (pull) communication*

  - *Media.* We promote the Invisalign system by communicating its benefits directly to consumers with a nationwide television and radio advertising campaign. We also provide consumers with information about the Invisalign system through our toll-free phone line (1-800-INVISIBLE) and our website (invisalign.com).

  - *Message.* Because the direct-to-consumer campaign targets appearance-conscious consumers, our message will focus on the aesthetic benefits and the overall convenience of using the Invisalign system.

  - *Slogan.* Our slogan is "Clear alternative to braces."

The content of the message to target customers follows directly from the value proposition and the positioning statement outlined in Section 4.2.

- *Indirect (push) consumer communication.* To facilitate recommendations of the Invisalign system, we provide orthodontists and general-practice dentists with promotional materials that include brochures, calendars, and posters to be displayed in their offices and/or given to patients who express interest.

Additional information on our consumer communication is provided in Exhibit 12.

Collaborator Communication

Orthodontists can learn about the Invisalign system from our mass-media consumer advertising as well as from our communication targeting orthodontists.

This section outlines the communication to the company's collaborators.

- *Media.* We use print advertisements in professional press targeting orthodontists, event sponsorship for orthodontic conventions and conferences, as well as direct mail and telemarketing targeting individual orthodontic practices. In addition, we have a sales team comprising approximately 30 salespeople experienced in orthodontic product sales.

- *Message.* Our message focuses on the potential to substantially improve orthodontic practice profitability through increased patient volume, higher margins, and reduced chair time.

The content of the message to orthodontists follows directly from the value proposition outlined in Section 4.3.

Additional information on our communication to orthodontists is provided in Exhibit 13.

5.7. Distribution

The Invisalign system is distributed exclusively through orthodontists and is not available for retail purchase by consumers directly from Align Technology. Only orthodontists are authorized to use the Invisalign system; it is not available to general-practice dentists. Orders are processed through headquarters and shipped in batches directly to orthodontist offices from the manufacturing facilities in Mexico. The first batch includes the first several months of treatment and is manufactured once the prescribing orthodontist approves ClinCheck. Thereafter, Aligners are sent at approximately six-month intervals until treatment is complete.

Section 5.7 outlines the distribution channel for the Invisalign system.

6. Implementation

6.1. Resource Development

We plan to expand our operations to two facilities in Santa Clara, California, which will serve as our manufacturing headquarters. These facilities are designed to produce highly customized, medical-quality products in high volume using a number of proprietary processes and technologies. These technologies include complex software solutions, laser, destructive and white light scanning techniques and stereolithography, wax modeling, and other rapid prototyping methods.

The fabrication and packaging of Aligners is outsourced to a contract manufacturer based in Juarez, Mexico. The creation of treatment simulations is done in our facilities in Lahore, Pakistan. The telephone support to handle information requests and orthodontist referrals is outsourced to a large national call center operator.

Additional information on the development of our business facilities, service infrastructure, supply channels, and salesforce is provided in Exhibit 14.

Section 6.1 outlines the resources necessary for implementing the marketing plan.

6.2. Developing the Invisalign System

To implement the Invisalign system we developed and tested the following five-stage process:

Section 6.2 outlines the process of developing the Invisalign system.

- *Orthodontic diagnosis and transmission of treatment data to Align Technology.* In an initial patient visit, the orthodontist determines whether the Invisalign system is an appropriate treatment. The orthodontist then prepares treatment data that consist of an impression of the dental arches, X-rays of the patient's dentition, photographs of the patient, and an Invisalign system treatment planning form, or prescription. The prescription describes the desired positions and movement of the patient's teeth. The orthodontist sends the treatment data to our Santa Clara facility.

- *Preparation of three-dimensional computer models of the patient's initial malocclusion.* On receipt, we use the treatment data to construct plaster models of the patient's dentition. We scan the plaster models to develop a digital, three-dimensional computer model of the patient's current dentition. We then transmit this initial computer model together with the orthodontist's prescription to our facilities in Lahore, Pakistan.

- *Preparation of computer-simulated treatment and viewing of treatment using ClinCheck.* In Pakistan, we transform the initial model into a customized, three-dimensional treatment plan that simulates appropriate tooth movement in a series of two-week increments. This simulation is then transmitted back to our Santa Clara facility for review. After passing review, the simulation is then delivered to the prescribing orthodontist via ClinCheck on our website. The orthodontist then reviews the ClinCheck simulation and, when necessary, asks us to make adjustments. The orthodontist then approves the proposed treatment and, in doing so, engages us for the manufacture of corresponding Aligners.

- *Construction of molds corresponding to each step of treatment.* We use the approved ClinCheck simulation to construct a series of molds of the patient's teeth. Each mold is a replica of the patient's teeth at each two-week stage of the simulated course of treatment. These molds are fabricated at our Santa Clara facility using custom manufacturing techniques that we have adapted for use in orthodontic applications.

- *Manufacturing of Aligners and shipment to orthodontist.* We ship these molds to Juarez, Mexico, where our contract manufacturer fabricates Aligners by pressure-forming polymeric sheets over each mold. The Aligners are then trimmed, polished, cleaned, packaged, and, following final inspection, shipped directly to the prescribing orthodontist.

We are currently conducting clinical trials to validate and optimize this process. We expect to exit the development stage in July 2000. Additional information on developing the Invisalign offering is provided in Exhibit 15.

6.3. Commercial Deployment

Commercial sales are planned to commence in July 1999 with a national direct-to-consumer advertising campaign. During the first year, the Invisalign system would be available through a limited number of orthodontists who will help us optimize our offering to better serve the needs of the patients and orthodontists. Our commercial deployment schedule is outlined in more detail in Exhibit 16.

Section 6.3 outlines the key aspects of the commercial deployment of the Invisalign system.

7. Control

7.1. Performance Evaluation

We are constantly monitoring our financial performance to ensure that we are on track toward achieving our goals. In addition to net revenues and sales revenues reported in our financial statements, we use the following metrics to monitor our performance:

- Number of new patients initiating treatment using Invisalign products

- Number of dental professionals trained to use the Invisalign system

- Penetration rate (number of dental professionals who have adopted the Invisalign system)

We also actively solicit product-related feedback from orthodontists and general-practice dentists to improve the technology underlying the Invisalign system.

Section 7.1 outlines the key metrics used to measure the progress toward the goal defined in Section 3.

7.2. Analysis of the Environment

We are constantly monitoring for changes in the environment, including the following:

- Changes in customer preferences

- Changes in our internal resources and competencies

- Changes in the value the Invisalign system delivers to our collaborators (orthodontists and general-practice dentists)

- Changes in the competitive landscape (e.g., entrance of new competitors)

- Changes in the economic, business, sociocultural, technological, regulatory, and physical context in which the company operates

To ensure that we are aware of the potential changes in the environment, we engage in the following activities:

Section 7.2 outlines the process of monitoring for changes in the environment in which the company operates.

- Monitor the USPTO database for new patent and trademark applications
- Participate in professional conferences and trade shows
- Examine professional publications
- Conduct proprietary research to examine consumer and dental professionals' experience with our offerings
- Review secondary research dealing with new developments in orthodontic technology and marketing practices

A detailed description of the performance metrics is offered in Exhibit 17.

8. Exhibits

Exhibit 1: Consumer survey

Exhibit 2: Organizational structure

Exhibit 3: Senior management

Exhibit 4: Board of directors

Exhibit 5: Scientific advisory board

Exhibit 6: Test market data

Exhibit 7: Financial statements and projections

Exhibit 8: Key assumptions

Exhibit 9: Executive compensation

Exhibit 10: Product specifications

Exhibit 11: Brand identity

Exhibit 12: Consumer communication

Exhibit 13: Communication to orthodontists

Exhibit 14: Infrastructure development

Exhibit 15: Developing the Invisalign system

Exhibit 16: Commercial deployment

Exhibit 17: Performance metrics

Section 8 outlines documentation supporting the marketing plan (for brevity, the actual exhibits are not included in this plan).

Annual Marketing Plan | Align Technology Inc.

Align's annual marketing plan, written ten years later, depicts the action plan guiding the company's activities aimed at gaining and defending its market position. Both the annual plan and the new product launch plan follow the same structure (derived from the G-STIC framework). The key difference between the two plans is that the new product launch plan is focused on defining the key aspects of the company's soon-to-be-launched offering, whereas the plan for managing an existing offering explicitly focuses on the changes that need to be made to the company's current action plan.

1. Executive Summary

Align Technology Inc. designs, manufactures, and markets the Invisalign system, a proprietary method for treating malocclusion, or the misalignment of teeth. The Invisalign system corrects malocclusion using a series of clear, removable appliances that gently move teeth to a desired position. For patients, the Invisalign system offers superior aesthetics, improved dental health, and greater overall convenience relative to conventional braces. For dental professionals, the Invisalign system offers increased patient volume and higher margins compared to conventional orthodontic procedures.

The executive summary in Section 1 offers a succinct overview of the key aspects of the offering, its goal, and key strategic initiatives.

Our *primary goal* is to create value for our stakeholders by establishing the Invisalign system as the standard method for treating malocclusion.

Our key *strategic initiatives* for the current planning period are:

- Continue growing our current target markets (adult consumers) in the United States and abroad.

- Expand our target market to include teenagers (age 12 and older) whose teeth are still growing.

- Increase adoption and utilization rate of Invisalign among dental professionals.

- Accelerate product and technology innovation to enhance clinical efficacy.

This plan outlines our key marketing activities for the period January 2008 – December 2008.

2. Situation Overview

Malocclusion (misalignment of teeth) is one of the most prevalent clinical conditions in the United States, affecting more than 195 million individuals, or about 65% of the population. Approximately 2.3 million people annually elect treatment by orthodontists in the United States; approximately 40% of these patients, or approximately 900,000, have mature dentition, with substantially completed teeth and jaw growth with mild to moderate malocclusion. Only a small proportion of people with malocclusion seek treatment because of the compromised aesthetics, discomfort, and other drawbacks associated with conventional orthodontic treatments.

Consumers who elect to be treated for malocclusion are interacting with two entities: (1) general-practice dentists, who typically diagnose the problem and provide a referral to a specialist; and (2) orthodontists who specialize in treating malocclusion.

- *Dentists.* General dentists are certified to perform all oral health procedures, including orthodontics. Many general dentists, however, choose not to perform specialized procedures, such as periodontics, prosthodontics, and orthodontics, because of their complexity and the added risk of malpractice liability. There are more than 100,000 general-practice dentists in the United States.

- *Orthodontists.* Orthodontists specialize in treating malocclusion. Only board-certified orthodontists can refer to themselves as orthodontists. This certification typically involves a two-year residency after dental school. There are approximately 10,500 orthodontists in the United States.

Malocclusion is traditionally treated with metal archwires and brackets, commonly referred to as braces. To improve treatment aesthetics, orthodontists occasionally use ceramic, tooth-colored brackets, or bond brackets on the inside, or lingual surfaces, of the patient's teeth.

The average treatment takes approximately two years to complete and requires several hours of direct orthodontist involvement, or chair time. To initiate treatment, an orthodontist will diagnose a patient's condition and create an appropriate treatment plan. In a subsequent visit, the orthodontist will bond brackets to the patient's teeth with cement and attach an archwire to the brackets. Thereafter, by tightening or otherwise adjusting the braces approximately every six weeks, the orthodontist is able to exert sufficient force on the patient's teeth to achieve desired tooth movement. Because of the length of time between visits, the orthodontist must

Section 2 offers the background information on the market in which Align Technology operates. The market overview offered here is broader in scope than the description of the target market offered in Section 4.1 as it includes an overview of the entire market (including markets that are not targeted by the company).

The market overview section also delineates the key changes in the market and outlines the progress achieved by Align Technology.

tighten the braces to a degree sufficient to achieve sustained tooth movement during the interval. In a final visit, the orthodontist removes each bracket and residual cement from the patient's teeth.

Although braces are generally effective in correcting a wide range of malocclusion, they have many drawbacks, such as:

- *Unattractive appearance.* Braces are visually unattractive and often trap food, which further compromises appearance. Braces can also result in permanent marks and discoloration of teeth. In addition, many adults associate braces with adolescence.

- *Oral discomfort.* Braces are sharp and bulky. They can abrade and irritate the interior surfaces of the mouth. The tightening of braces during treatment results in root and gum soreness and discomfort.

- *Poor oral hygiene.* Braces compromise oral hygiene by making it more difficult to brush and floss, often resulting in tooth decay and periodontal damage.

- *Root resorption.* The sustained high levels of force associated with conventional treatment can result in root resorption, a shortening of tooth roots. This shortening can have substantial adverse periodontal consequences for the patient.

- *Emergencies.* At times, braces need to be repaired or replaced on an emergency basis. Such emergencies cause significant inconvenience to both the patient and the orthodontist.

- *Inability to project treatment.* The lack of a means to model the movement of teeth over a course of treatment limits the orthodontist's ability to estimate its duration. Because most orthodontic treatment is performed on a fixed-price basis, extended treatment duration reduces profitability for the orthodontist.

- *Physical demands on orthodontists.* The manipulation of wires and brackets requires sustained manual dexterity and visual acuity from the orthodontist.

Fees for orthodontic treatment typically range between $3,500 and $7,000, with a median fee of approximately $5,000. Orthodontists also commonly charge a premium for the more aesthetically appealing lingual or ceramic alternatives. Fees are generally negotiated in advance based on the difficulty of the particular case and on the orthodontist's estimate of chair time. Treatment that exceeds the orthodontist's estimate of chair time is typically covered by the orthodontist at no additional charge. Most insurance plans do not cover orthodontic treatments for adults and offer limited coverage for children and adolescents.

So far, approximately 732,000 patients worldwide have started treatment using Invisalign. The Invisalign system is sold in North America, Europe, Asia-Pacific, Latin America, and Japan. We have trained over 48,000 dental professionals worldwide. The Invisalign technique has been incorporated into the curriculum of 63 university programs worldwide. In 2002, Invisalign was made available to general-practice dentists and in mid-2003, leading dental schools began adding Invisalign to their curriculum.

In 2005, Align introduced Invisalign Express (now Invisalign Express 10), a lower priced solution for less complex orthodontic cases, launched Invisalign in Japan, and achieved a manufacturing milestone of 15 million unique clear Aligners. In 2007, Align added distribution partners in Asia-Pacific and Latin America.

At the beginning of 2008, our product line includes two offerings: Invisalign Full, our flagship product, and Invisalign Express, a shorter duration solution for minor cases. Approximately 88% of our net revenues are generated by the sale of Invisalign Full and 8% are generated by the sale of Invisalign Express.

3. Goal

Our *primary goal* is to create value for our stakeholders by establishing the Invisalign system as the standard method for treating malocclusion. In particular, we aim to increase our revenue by 10% to $300 million, our gross margins from 73.6% to 75%, and our operating margins from 12.5% to 14%. To achieve this goal, we have set the following objectives:

- *Customer objectives.* Our key customer objectives are to create awareness of the benefits of the Invisalign system among 90% of our target customers, stimulate their interest, and generate new demand for our Invisalign offerings. We aim to have 200,000 patients initiate treatment with the Invisalign system in 2008.

- *Collaborator objectives.* We aim to create awareness of the benefits of the Invisalign system among dental professionals, train them to use the system, and motivate them to promote it to patients as the standard method for treating malocclusion. Our goal is to train 500 new orthodontists and 5,000 new general-practice dentists in the United States, and 2,000 dental professionals in Europe, our primary international market. In addition, we aim to increase the frequency of using the Invisalign system (utilization rate) per participating dental professional by 10%.

- *Internal objectives.* Accelerate product and technology innovation, while at the same time extend clinical efficacy. Streamline our supply-chain management processes to enhance product quality, increase production capacity, and reduce both unit costs and production times.

- *Competitive objectives.* Our primary competitive objective is to further differentiate our offerings from those offered by our competitors, while continuing to create barriers to entry for competitors. We will pursue further intellectual property protection through patent applications and nondisclosure agreements under trade secret and copyright laws.

4. Strategy

4.1. Target Market

Customers

Our current target market are *adults and adolescents with mature dentition* who are otherwise suitable for treatment. Our share is approximately 8% of the 900,000 patients with mature dentition who annually elect to seek orthodontic treatment. So far, we have elected not to treat children whose teeth and jaws are still developing because of our limited ability to accurately predict the movement of teeth during the course of treatment.

In 2008 we plan to expand our target market to include teenagers (age 12 and older) whose teeth are still growing, a move facilitated by the advances in technology that enable us to accurately control the movement of teeth over the course of treatment even for patients whose teeth are still growing.

Geographically, our target markets include the United States, Europe, Canada, Mexico, Brazil, Australia, Hong Kong, and Japan. We are not planning to expand into new markets in 2008.

Section 3 outlines the company's primary goal, as well as the specific customer, collaborator, company, and competitor objectives.

Section 4.1 follows the 5-C framework.

This section identifies the offering's target customers. It summarizes the key aspects of the target segment outlined in Section 3.3, providing a more detailed analysis of target customers.

Collaborators

Our primary collaborators are dental professionals: orthodontists and general-practice dentists. Dental professionals' choice of a treatment method is determined by the following key considerations: the aesthetic appeal of the treatment method, the effectiveness of treatment, comfort associated with the treatment method, oral hygiene, ease of use, predictability of the treatment outcome, the level of customer support, dental professionals' chair time, and price.

We expect dental professionals to contribute to the success of the Invisalign system by (1) informing patients about the availability and benefits of the Invisalign system, (2) implementing the Invisalign treatment, and (3) providing performance feedback that will enable us to improve the Invisalign system. We expect general-practice dentists to treat primarily mild cases of malocclusion and refer more complex cases to licensed orthodontists.

We have trained 8,310 orthodontists and 27,480 general-practice dentists in the United States and 12,340 dental professionals, predominantly orthodontists, internationally. The quarterly utilization rate of Invisalign among dental professionals is 4.9 cases per participating orthodontist, 2.3 cases per participating general-practice dentist, and 3.1 cases per non-US dental professional.

This section identifies the key collaborators that will facilitate the success of the Invisalign system.

Competitors

Our competitors include the manufacturers of traditional orthodontic products that treat malocclusion, such as 3M Company, Sybron International Corporation, and Dentsply International, Inc. In addition, in the past few years a number of direct competitors emerged, including *Clear Guide, Simpli5,* and *Red, White, and Blue System* by Allesee Orthodontic Appliances (AOA), a subsidiary of Sybron Dental Specialties, Inc.; *Incognito* braces by 3M; *Clearguide Express* by Insignia; MTM aligners by Dentsply International; *Damon Clear* and *Inspire ICE* by Ormco; *SureSmile* by OraMetrix; and *ClearCorrect.*

This section identifies the key competitors for the Invisalign system and evaluates the current and future competitive intensity of the marketplace.

Company

Align Technology Inc. was incorporated in Delaware in 1997. The corporate headquarters are located in Santa Clara, California, where we house our manufacturing, customer support, software engineering, and administrative personnel. In addition, we operate facilities in Mexico, Costa Rica, Europe, and Japan.

We currently have 1,307 employees, including 641 in manufacturing and operations, 340 in sales and marketing, 154 in research and development, and 172 in general and administrative functions. Geographically, our employees are located as follows: 576 in North America, 586 in Costa Rica, 134 in Europe, and 11 in Japan.

Our primary goal is to establish the Invisalign system as the standard method for treating orthodontic malocclusion. Our core competency is producing highly customized, close tolerance, medical-quality products in volume. Our strategic assets include intellectual property (proprietary patented technology), specialized production facilities, our network of dental professionals trained to use the Invisalign system, the Invisalign and ClinCheck brands, and our existing customer base.

This section provides general information about the company and its current offerings.

Context

Economic context: Economic crisis, increasing stock market volatility, mortgage crisis, plummeting housing market, credit crunch

This section outlines the specifics of the context in which Align Technology

threatening the solvency of the banking system, and declining consumer confidence and spending.

Regulatory context: Laws regulating medical device manufacturers and healthcare providers cover a broad array of subjects, including:

- The confidentiality of patient medical information and the circumstances under which such information may be released for inclusion in our databases, or released by us to third parties, are subject to substantial regulation by state governments.

- Federal and state regulations prohibit paying any remuneration in exchange for the referral of patients to a person participating in federal or state healthcare programs, such as Medicare and Medicaid.

- Various states regulate the operation of an advertising and referral service for dentists and may require compliance with various requirements on how they structure their relationships with participating dentists.

- According to the FDA classification of medical devices, the Invisalign system is a Class I device, the least stringent class, that does not require a premarket approval, which includes, among other things, extensive preclinical and clinical trials.

- Our global operations are subject to a variety of local regulations that define the relationships between Align Technology, dental professionals, and patients.

4.2. Customer Value Proposition

Value Proposition

The Invisalign system offers a number of unique benefits to our target customers:

- *Excellent aesthetics.* Aligners are nearly invisible when worn, eliminating the aesthetic concerns associated with conventional braces.

- *Improved oral hygiene.* Patients can remove Aligners when eating, brushing, and flossing—a feature that can reduce tooth decay and periodontal damage during treatment.

- *Greater safety.* By replacing the six-week adjustment cycle of traditional braces with two-week stages, the Invisalign system moves teeth more gently, decreasing the likelihood of root resorption (shortening of tooth roots).

- *Increased comfort.* The Invisalign system is substantially more comfortable and less abrasive than conventional braces.

- *Reduced overall treatment time.* The Invisalign system controls force by distributing it broadly over the exposed surfaces of the teeth while reducing the likelihood of unintended tooth movements. This could significantly reduce overall treatment time relative to conventional braces.

- *Reduced incidence of emergencies.* Lost or broken Aligners could be simply replaced with the next Aligner in the series, minimizing inconvenience to both patient and orthodontist.

Positioning Statement

For adults and teens with mild forms of malocclusion, Invisalign offers a convenient and unobtrusive solution to straighten their teeth.

---

will fulfill the needs of its target customers.

Section 4.2 follows the 3-V framework

This section outlines the key benefits of the Invisalign system for target customers. It answers the question: *Why would target customers opt to straighten their teeth using the Invisalign system?*

This section identifies target customers and Invisalign's main benefit for these customers.

4.3. Collaborator Value Proposition

Value Proposition

The Invisalign system offers the following benefits to dental professionals:

- *Ability to visualize treatment and likely outcomes.* The Invisalign system enables dental professionals to preview a course of treatment and the likely final outcome of treatment in an interactive three-dimensional computer model. This allows dental professionals to analyze multiple treatment alternatives before selecting the one most appropriate for the patient.

- *Ease of use.* Because the Invisalign system relies on the same biomechanical principles that underlie traditional orthodontic treatment, it is straightforward for dental professionals to learn and to use. The initial certification training can be completed in a one-day workshop, and dental professionals can be equipped to submit cases immediately thereafter with minimal financial outlay.

- *Increased patient base.* Currently, only one percent of the more than 200 million people with malocclusion in the United States enter treatment each year. The Invisalign system allows dental professionals to broaden their patient base by offering a new, attractive treatment alternative to people who would not otherwise elect treatment.

- *Higher margins.* The Invisalign system enables dental professionals to more accurately estimate the duration of the treatment, thus decreasing the likelihood of underestimating the treatment length and increasing the overall profit margins per patient. Due to the substantial benefits for customers, orthodontists can also charge a premium for the Invisalign system comparable to other more aesthetically pleasing alternatives to conventional braces, such as ceramic and lingual braces.

- *Decreased orthodontist and staff time.* The Invisalign system reduces both the frequency and length of patient visits. It eliminates the need for time-intensive processes, such as bonding appliances to the patient's teeth, adjusting archwires during the course of treatment, and removing the appliances at the conclusion of treatment. As a result, use of the Invisalign system significantly reduces orthodontist and staff chair time and can increase practice throughput.

Positioning Statement

For dental professionals, the Invisalign system is the best method for treating most cases of malocclusion because it offers increased patient volume and higher margins.

4.4. Company Value Proposition

Value Proposition

In 2007, our total revenues were $271 million; our gross margin was 73.6%, and our operating margin was 12.5%. In 2008, we intend to improve our financial performance by increasing our revenues by 10%, our gross margin to 75%, and our operating margin to 14%. Detailed financial information and the key assumptions are provided in Exhibits 1–2.

This section outlines the key benefits of the Invisalign system for dental professionals. It answers the question: Why would dental professionals opt to use the Invisalign system instead of conventional braces?

This section identifies the company's collaborators and the key benefit of the offering for these collaborators.

This section outlines the key benefits for shareholders. It answers the question: Why should stakeholders invest in Invisalign?

Positioning Statement

For investors who are interested in investing in a company with a high growth potential, Align Technology offers an opportunity to participate in a $75 billion market for orthodontic devices with a patented system that offers unique benefits for both patients and dental professionals.

5. Tactics

5.1. Product

The Invisalign system consists of two components: ClinCheck and Aligners.

- *ClinCheck* is an interactive Internet application that allows dental professionals to diagnose and plan treatment for their patients. ClinCheck uses a dental impression and a treatment prescription submitted by the dental professional to develop a customized, three-dimensional treatment plan that simulates appropriate tooth movement in a series of two-week increments. ClinCheck allows dental professionals to view this three-dimensional simulation with a high degree of magnification and from any angle.

- *Aligners* are custom-manufactured, clear, removable dental appliances that, when worn in the prescribed series, provide orthodontic treatment. Each Aligner covers a patient's teeth and is nearly invisible when worn. Aligners are commonly worn in pairs (over the upper and lower dental arches) for consecutive two-week periods that correspond to the approved ClinCheck treatment simulation. After two weeks of use, the patient discards the Aligners and replaces them with the next pair in the series. This process is repeated until the final Aligners are used and treatment is complete.

At present, we offer two treatment programs: Invisalign Full and Invisalign Express (introduced in 2005).

- *Invisalign Full* treatment consists of as many Aligners as indicated by ClinCheck in order to achieve treatment goals. The typical Invisalign Full patient uses 22 sets of Aligners over 44 weeks of treatment.

- *Invisalign Express* is intended to assist dental professionals in treating a broader range of patients by providing a lower cost option for adult relapse cases, minor crowding and spacing, or as a precursor to restorative or cosmetic treatment, such as veneers. Invisalign Express consists of up to 10 Aligners.

In 2008, we plan to launch two new treatment programs: Invisalign Teen and Vivera retainers.

- *Invisalign Teen* is designed to treat teenagers (age 12 and up) whose teeth are still growing. It includes features such as an Aligner-wear indicator to help gauge patient compliance and specially engineered Aligner features to address lingual root control issues and the natural eruption of key teeth common in teen patients. Invisalign Teen will also include up to six free individual replacement Aligners during active treatment to cover potential Aligner loss. We plan to introduce Invisalign Teen in the second quarter of 2008.

- *Vivera* is a retainer replacement program that delivers a new retainer to orthodontic patients every three months for one year. Vivera retainers are produced using the same proprietary technology and material as the Invisalign Aligners and

This section identifies the key stakeholders and the key benefit of the Invisalign system for them.

Section 5.1 outlines the product aspect of the Invisalign system and the proposed product changes.

The ClinCheck application can also be viewed as part of the service aspect of the Invisalign system (dental professionals do not acquire the rights to the software application but merely gain the right to use it on a limited basis); however, because it is an essential element of creating the product (Aligners), it is presented as a component of the product aspect of the offering.

offer an effective, aesthetic retention solution for both Invisalign and non-Invisalign patients. We plan to introduce Vivera retainers in the first quarter of 2008.

A detailed description of product specifications is offered in Exhibit 3.

5.2. Service

We offer support services to orthodontists who elect to use the Invisalign system. These services include initial training, case support, and practice-building assistance.

- *Initial training* is conducted in a workshop format by our sales
  and orthodontic teams. The key topics covered in training include case selection criteria, instructions on filling out the Invisalign prescription form, guidance on pricing, and instructions on interacting with the ClinCheck software and using
  the Invisalign website.

- *Current-case support* includes assisting orthodontists with the
  applicability and use of the Invisalign system for specific patients.

- *Practice-building assistance* helps orthodontists promote their
  services to local general-practice dentists and to prospective
  patients through direct mail or other media.

In 2008, we plan to introduce two new services: *Invisalign Assist*
and *Aligntech Institute.*

- *Invisalign Assist* is designed specifically for general-practice
  dentists who prefer an integrated approach to selecting, monitoring, and finishing Invisalign cases. Intended to help newly
  trained and low-volume general-practice dentists accelerate
  the adoption and frequency of use of Invisalign in their practice, Invisalign Assist is intended to make it easier for general-
  practice dentists to select appropriate cases for their experience level or treatment approach, submit cases more efficiently, and manage appointments with suggested tasks. New
  progress-tracking features allow dentists to submit new impressions every nine stages and receive Aligners modified according to the patient's progress.

- The *Aligntech Institute* program consolidates our extensive
  clinical education programs within a new interactive website
  (www.aligntechinstitute.com) that will provide clinical education and practice development training opportunities for our
  Invisalign-trained dental professionals on demand. These
  practice-development training opportunities will include in-
  structor-led training classes, seminars and workshops, confer-
  ence calls, online videos, case studies, and other clinical resources.

A detailed description of Invisalign Assist and Aligntech Institute
is offered in Exhibit 4.

5.3. Brand

We use two brands to identify our offering: Invisalign and
ClinCheck.

- *Invisalign.* We use the brand Invisalign in reference to the process of straightening teeth using a series of invisible Aligners.
  We use the Invisalign brand in our communication to consumers, orthodontists, and general-practice dentists. The Invisalign name is our registered trademark. The Invisalign

Section 5.2 outlines the service aspect of the In-visalign system, focusing on the service provided to dental professionals using the Invisalign sys-tem. This section also out-lines the proposed changes in the service provided to dental pro-fessionals.

Section 5.3 outlines the brands used by Align Technology to create a unique identity for its of-fering.

Note that while both brands—ClinCheck and Invisalign—are promoted brand is also used as an umbrella brand for two sub-brands: Invisalign Full and Invisalign Express.

- *ClinCheck.* We use the brand ClinCheck in reference to the interactive Internet application that allows dental professionals to diagnose and plan treatment for their patients. We use the ClinCheck brand in our communication to dental professionals; it is not used in consumer communication. The ClinCheck name is our registered trademark.

In 2008, we plan to reposition the Invisalign brand and extend our brand portfolio.

- *Repositioning the Invisalign brand.* We plan to reposition our brand to strengthen our brand recognition and better align it with our strategic initiatives. The new look and feel of Invisalign is dynamic, modern, and approachable, and communicates our vision of "healthy, beautiful smiles" in a way that is distinct and memorable. Our brand-repositioning strategy is based on the findings of our proprietary research and aims to increase Invisalign awareness and demand among consumers, and Invisalign adoption and utilization by dental professionals.

- *Extending our brand portfolio.* We plan to add two new Invisalign sub-brands: *Invisalign Teen* and *Invisalign Assist.* We will also introduce two new brands: *Vivera,* used with retainers, and the *Aligntech Institute* brand, which consolidates our educational programs. We have filed applications for these trademarks with the US Patent and Trademarks Office.

A detailed description of the Invisalign, Aligntech, and Vivera logos is offered in Exhibit 5.

5.4. Pricing

The price for the orthodontic treatment is negotiated by the dental professional and the patient. The average retail price for the orthodontists' services (including Aligners) is around $5,000 to $7,000 depending on the severity of the case.

Align Technology's products are offered to dental professionals on a fixed-price (rather than per-Aligner) basis. The average price for dental professionals is $1,500 per patient for Invisalign Full; $1,000 for Invisalign Express; $1,700 for Invisalign Teen; $1,900 for Invisalign Assist; and $200 for Vivera retainers. Detailed pricing information is shown in Exhibit 6.

5.5. Incentives

We offer incentives to both our target customers and collaborators.

- *Incentives for customers.* Because the specifics and the cost of the treatment are negotiated directly between the dental professional and the patient, we are not offering direct incentives to consumers. We expect dental professionals to offer their own discounts to customers to manage demand.

- *Incentives for collaborators.* We use a system of tiering dental professionals that encourages our salesforce to devote more time to those dental professionals most proficient in the use of the Invisalign system. We use objective criteria, primarily the number of cases initiated with the Invisalign system, to tier dental professionals. Inquiries from prospective patients through our customer call center and our website are directed to higher tier dental professionals. This tiering process should incentivize the selected dental professionals and increase the

---

to dental professionals, only the latter is used in consumer communication.

This section also outlines the proposed changes to the Invisalign brand.

Section 5.4 outlines the price of the Invisalign system for both patients and dental professionals.

Note that the Invisalign system is only one component of the treatment and that the dental professionals determine the customer price.

Section 5.5 outlines the incentives provided to target customers and collaborators.

use of the Invisalign system by their offices. A detailed description of collaborator incentives is offered in Exhibit 7.

5.6. Communication

Consumer Communication

Consumers can learn about the benefits of the Invisalign system in one of two ways: directly from us and/or from dental professionals. Accordingly, we use two basic strategies to reach our target customers. We use a *pull strategy* (direct-to-consumer communication) to target appearance-conscious consumers who might not consider orthodontic treatment unless they are made aware of the existence of an aesthetically appealing malocclusion treatment. In addition, we use a *push strategy* (incentivizing dental professionals) to target health-conscious individuals who rely on dental professionals' advice for the choice of treatment.

- *Direct-to-consumer (pull) communication.*

  Media. We promote the Invisalign system by communicating its benefits directly to consumers with a nationwide television and radio advertising campaign. We also provide consumers with information through our toll-free phone line (1-800-INVISIBLE) and our website (invisalign.com).

  Message. Because the direct-to-consumer campaign targets appearance-conscious consumers, our message will focus on the aesthetic benefits and the overall convenience of using the Invisalign system.

  Slogan. Our slogan is "Learn how to smile again."

- *Indirect (push) consumer communication.* To facilitate recommendations of the Invisalign system, we provide orthodontists and general-practice dentists with promotional materials—brochures, calendars, and posters—to be displayed in their offices and/or given to patients who express interest.

Our consumer communication is outlined in Exhibit 8.

Collaborator Communication

Dental professionals can learn about the Invisalign system from our mass-media consumer advertising as well as from our communication that targets dental professionals.

- *Media.* We use print advertisements in the professional press targeting dental professionals, event sponsorship for orthodontic and dental conventions and conferences, as well as direct mail and telemarketing targeting individual orthodontic and dental practices. In addition, we have a sales team comprising 136 direct sales representatives in North America and over 30 people engaged in sales and sales support internationally.

- *Message.* Our message focuses on the potential to substantially improve dental-practice profitability through increased patient volume and higher margins.

Additional information on our communication to dental professionals is provided in Exhibit 9.

5.7. Distribution

The Invisalign system is distributed exclusively through orthodontists and general-practice dentists; it is not available for retail purchase by consumers directly from Align Technology. Orders are processed through headquarters and shipped in batches directly to dental offices from the manufacturing facilities in Mexico as follows:

Margin notes:

This section outlines the communication to target customers and the proposed changes in this communication.

Note that the use of a pull vs. push strategy in the case of direct vs. indirect communication follows directly from the analysis of the target market in Section 4.1.

The content of the message to target customers follows directly from the value proposition and the positioning statement outlined in Section 4.2.

This section outlines the communication to dental professionals and the proposed changes in this communication.

The content of the message to dental professionals follows directly from the value proposition and the positioning statement outlined in Section 4.3.

Section 5.7 outlines the distribution channel for the Invisalign system and the proposed changes in the distribution system.

- *Invisalign Full* and *Invisalign Express* Aligners are delivered to orthodontists and general-practice dentists in a single shipment.

- *Invisalign Teen* Aligners (other than the replacement aligners) will be available only to orthodontists and will be delivered in a single shipment.

- *Invisalign Assist* Aligners will be shipped to dentists using progress tracking after every nine stages.

- *Vivera* retainers will be shipped to orthodontists and general-practice dentists every three months over a one-year period.

6. Implementation

6.1. Resource Development

At present, we have the essential resources to implement our business plan. We are continuing the development of automated systems for the fabrication and packaging of Aligners manufactured in Mexico. We also plan to increase the efficiency of our manufacturing processes by focusing our efforts on software development and improving the efficiency of operations in Costa Rica. A detailed outline of the proposed changes is provided in Exhibit 10.

6.2. Developing the Market Offering

We are currently engaged in the design, manufacture, promotion, and distribution of Invisalign Full and Invisalign Express. A detailed description of the implementation processes for managing Align Technology offerings is provided in Exhibit 11.

6.3. Commercial Deployment

We plan to launch Vivera retainers in the first quarter of 2008, Invisalign Teen in the second quarter of 2008, and Invisalign Assist in the third quarter of 2008. The detailed schedule for the commercial deployment of these offerings is outlined in Exhibit 12.

7. Control

7.1. Performance Evaluation

We are constantly monitoring our financial performance to ensure that we are on track toward achieving our goals. In addition to the standard financial metrics reported in our financial statements, we use the following metrics to monitor our performance:

- Number of patients initiating treatment using our products

- Number of dental professionals trained to use the Invisalign system

- Penetration rate (number of dental professionals who have used the Invisalign system during the past 12 months)

- Utilization rate (number of cases ordered per dental professional during each quarter)

We actively solicit feedback from orthodontists and general-practice dentists to improve the technology underlying the Invisalign system.

7.2. Analysis of the Environment

We constantly monitor for changes in the environment, including:

- Changes in customer preferences

- Changes in our internal resources and competencies

Section 6 outlines the processes involved in implementing the marketing plan.

Section 7.1 outlines the metrics used to measure the progress toward the goal defined in Section 3.

Section 7.2 outlines the process of monitoring for

- Changes in the value the Invisalign system delivers to our collaborators (orthodontists and general-practice dentists)
- Changes in the competitive landscape
- Changes in the economic, business, sociocultural, technological, and regulatory context in which the company operates

To monitor the environment, we engage in the following activities:

- Monitor the USPTO database for new patent and trademark applications
- Participate in professional conferences and trade shows
- Examine professional publications
- Conduct proprietary research to examine consumer and dental professionals' experience with our offerings
- Review secondary research dealing with new developments in orthodontic technology and marketing practices

Performance metrics are outlined in detail in Exhibit 13.

8. Exhibits

Exhibit 1: Financial information

Exhibit 2: Key assumptions

Exhibit 3: Product specifications

Exhibit 4: Invisalign Assist and Aligntech Institute

Exhibit 5: Invisalign, Aligntech, and Vivera logos

Exhibit 6: Pricing

Exhibit 7: Collaborator incentives

Exhibit 8: Consumer communication

Exhibit 9: Communication to orthodontists

Exhibit 10: Infrastructure development

Exhibit 11: Developing the Invisalign system

Exhibit 12: Commercial deployment

Exhibit 13: Performance metrics

changes in the environment in which the company operates.

Section 8 outlines documentation supporting the marketing plan (for brevity, the actual exhibits are not included in this plan).

References

Chapter 1

Thomas Davenport and Rajeev Ronanki, "Artificial Intelligence for the Real World," *Harvard Business Review* 96 (January–February 2018), pp. 108–116.

Peter Drucker, *The Practice of Management* (New York, NY: Routledge, 2017).

Philip Kotler, *Kotler on Marketing: How to Create, Win, and Dominate Markets* (New York, NY: Free Press, 1999).

Philip Kotler and Kevin Lane Keller, *Marketing Management,* 15th ed. (Upper Saddle River, NJ: Prentice Hall, 2016).

Nirmalya Kumar, *Marketing as Strategy: Understanding the CEO's Agenda for Driving Growth and Innovation* (Boston, MA: Harvard Business School Press, 2004).

Michael Porter, *Competitive Advantage: Creating and Sustaining Superior Performance* (New York, NY: Free Press, 1985).

Michael Porter and James Heppelmann, "Why Every Organization Needs an Augmented Reality Strategy," *Harvard Business Review* 95 (November–December 2017), pp. 46–57.

Alice Tybout and Bobby Calder, *Kellogg on Marketing* (New York, NY: John Wiley & Sons, 2010).

Frederick Webster Jr., "The Role of Marketing and the Firm," Barton Weitz and Robin Wensley, eds., *Handbook of Marketing* (London: Sage, 2002), pp. 39–65.

Chapter 2

David Aaker, *Strategic Market Management,* 10th ed. (New York, NY: John Wiley & Sons, 2013).

Alexander Chernev, *The Business Model: How to Develop New Products, Create Market Value and Make the Competition Irrelevant* (Chicago, IL: Cerebellum Press, 2017).

Robert Grant, *Contemporary Strategy Analysis,* 8th ed. (New York, NY: John Wiley & Sons, 2013).

Mark Johnson, Clayton Christensen, and Henning Kagermann, "Reinventing Your Business Model," *Harvard Business Review* 86 (December 2008).

Stelios Kavadias, Kostas Ladas, and Christoph Loch, "The Transformative Business Model," *Harvard Business Review* 94 (October 2016), pp. 90–98.

Michael Porter, "What Is Strategy?" *Harvard Business Review* 74 (November–December 1996), pp. 61–78.

Jagdish Sheth and Rajendra Sisodia, *The 4 A's of Marketing: Creating Value for Customer, Company and Society* (New York, NY: Routledge, 2012).

Orville Walker and John Mullins, *Marketing Strategy: A Decision-Focused Approach,* 8th ed. (New York, NY: McGraw-Hill Education, 2013).

Chapter 3

Tim Calkins, *Breakthrough Marketing Plans: How to Stop Wasting Time and Start Driving Growth,* 2nd ed. (New York, NY: Palgrave Macmillan, 2012).

Alexander Chernev, *The Marketing Plan Handbook,* 5th ed. (Chicago, IL: Cerebellum Press, 2018).

James Collins and Jerry Porras, "Building Your Company's Vision." *Harvard Business Review* 74, (September–October 1996), pp. 65–77.

Peter Drucker, *Management: Tasks, Responsibilities and Practices* (New York, NY: Harper and Row, 1973).

Eliyahu Goldratt and Jeff Cox, *The Goal: A Process of Ongoing Improvement,* 20th Anniversary Edition (New York, NY: Routledge, 2016).

Philip Kotler and Kevin Lane Keller, *Marketing Management,* 15th ed. (Upper Saddle River, NJ: Prentice Hall, 2016).

Simon Sinek, *Start With Why: How Great Leaders Inspire Everyone to Take Action* (New York, NY: Penguin Group, 2011).

Robert Quinn and Anjan Thakor, "Creating a Purpose-Driven Organization," *Harvard Business Review* 96 (July–August 2018), pp. 78–85.

Chapter 4

Dan Ariely, *Predictably Irrational* (New York, NY: HarperCollins Publishers, 2008).

James Engel, Roger Blackwell, and Paul Minard, *Consumer Behavior,* 9th ed. (Fort Worth, TX: Dryden, 2001).

John Howard and Jagdish Sheth, *The Theory of Buyer Behavior* (New York, NY: John Wiley & Sons, 1969).

Daniel Kahneman, *Thinking, Fast and Slow* (New York, NY: Farrar, Straus and Giroux, 2011).

Daniel Kahneman, Paul Slovic, and Amos Tversky, eds., *Judgment Under Uncertainty: Heuristics and Biases* (Cambridge, UK: Cambridge University Press, 1982).

Daniel Kahneman, Andrew Rosenfield, Linnea Gandhi, and Tom Blaser, "Noise: How to Overcome the High, Hidden Cost of Inconsistent Decision Making," *Harvard Business Review* 94 (October 2016), pp. 38–46.

Itamar Simonson, "Getting Closer to Your Customers by Understanding How They Make Choices," *California Management Review* 35 (Summer 1993), pp. 68–84.

Michael Solomon, *Consumer Behavior: Buying, Having, and Being,* 10th ed. (Upper Saddle River, NJ: Prentice Hall, 2013).

Richard Thaler and Cass Sunstein, *Nudge: Improving Decisions about Health, Wealth, and Happiness* (New York, NY: Penguin, 2009).

Chapter 5

David Aaker, V. Kumar, Robert Leone, and George Day, *Marketing Research,* 12th ed. (New York, NY: John Wiley & Sons, 2015).

Leandro Dallemule and Thomas Davenport, "What's Your Data Strategy?" *Harvard Business Review* 95 (May–June 2017), pp. 112–121.

Thomas Davenport and Jeanne Harris, *Competing on Analytics: The New Science of Winning* (Boston, MA: Harvard Business School Press, 2007).

Naresh Malhotra, *Marketing Research: An Applied Orientation,* 7th ed. (Upper Saddle River, NJ: Pearson, 2018).

Catherine Marshall and Gretchen Rossman, *Designing Qualitative Research,* 4th ed. (Thousand Oaks, CA: Sage Publications, 2006).

Roger Martin and Tony Golsby-Smith, "Management Is Much More than a Science: The Limits of Data-Driven Decision Making," *Harvard Business Review* 95 (September–October 2017), pp. 128–135.

Robert Palmatier and Shrihari Sridhar, *Marketing Strategy: Based on First Principles and Data Analytics* (New York, NY: Red Globe Press, 2017).

Foster Provost and Tom Fawcett, *Data Science for Business: What You Need to Know about Data Mining and Data-Analytic Thinking* (Sebastopol, CA: O'Reilly Media, 2013).

Chapter 6

David Aaker, *Strategic Market Management,* 10th ed. (New York, NY: John Wiley & Sons, 2013).

W. Chan Kim and Renée Mauborgne, *Blue Ocean Strategy: How to Create Uncontested Market Space and Make the Competition Irrelevant* (Boston, MA: Harvard Business School Press, 2005).

Clayton Christensen, Taddy Hall, Karen Dillon, and David Duncan, "Know Your Customers' 'Jobs to Be Done,'" *Harvard Business Review* 94 (September 2016), pp. 54–60.

Malcolm McDonald, *Market Segmentation: How to Do It and How to Profit from It,* 4th ed. (New York, NY: John Wiley & Sons, 2012).

Benson Shapiro and Thomas Bonoma, "How to Segment Industrial Markets," *Harvard Business Review* 3 (May–June 1984), pp. 104–110.

Colin Shaw and Ryan Hamilton, *The Intuitive Customer: 7 Imperatives for Moving Your Customer Experience to the Next Level* (New York, NY: Springer, 2016).

Alice Tybout and Bobby Calder, *Kellogg on Marketing,* 2nd ed. (New York, NY: John Wiley & Sons, 2010).

Art Weinstein, *Handbook of Market Segmentation: Strategic Targeting for Business and Technology Firms,* 3rd ed. (New York, NY: Haworth Press, 2013).

Chapter 7

Eric Almquist, John Senior, and Nicolas Bloch, "The Elements of Value," *Harvard Business Review* 94 (September 2016), pp. 46–92.

James Anderson, James Narus, and Wouter van Rossum, "Customer Value Proposition in Business Markets," *Harvard Business Review* 84 (March 2006), pp. 90–99.

Patrick Barwise and Sean Meehan, *Simply Better: Winning and Keeping Customers by Delivering What Matters Most* (Boston, MA: Harvard Business School Press, 2004).

Roger Best, *Market-Based Management: Strategies for Growing Customer Value and Profitability,* 6th ed. (Upper Saddle River, NJ: Prentice Hall, 2012).

Matthew Dixon, Karen Freeman, and Nicholas Toman, "Stop Trying to Delight Your Customers," *Harvard Business Review* 88 (July–August 2010), pp. 116–22.

W. Chan Kim and Renée Mauborgne, *Blue Ocean Strategy: How to Create Uncontested Market Space and Make the Competition Irrelevant* (Boston, MA: Harvard Business School Press, 2005).

Theodore Levitt, "Marketing Success through Differentiation—of Anything," *Harvard Business Review* 58 (January–February 1980), pp. 83–91.

Al Ries and Jack Trout, *Positioning: The Battle for Your Mind*, 20th Anniversary Edition (New York, NY: McGraw-Hill, 2000).

Alice Tybout and Bobby Calder, *Kellogg on Marketing* (New York, NY: John Wiley & Sons, 2010).

Chapter 8

Tim Ambler, *Marketing and the Bottom Line: The New Methods of Corporate Wealth*, 2nd ed. (London: Pearson Education, 2003).

Jim Collins, *Good to Great: Why Some Companies Make the Leap and Others Don't* (New York, NY: Harper-Collins Publishers, 2001).

Paul Farris, Neil Bendle, Phillip Pfeifer, and David Reibstein, *Key Marketing Metrics: The 50+ metrics every manager needs to know* (Harlow, UK: FT Publishing International, 2017).

James Anderson and James Narus, *Business Market Management: Understanding, Creating, and Delivering Value*, 3rd ed. (Upper Saddle River, NJ: Prentice Hall, 2009).

Bruce Henderson, "The Experience Curve Reviewed: Why Does It Work?," Carl W. Stern and George Stalk Jr., eds., *Perspectives on Strategy: From the Boston Consulting Group* (New York, NY: John Wiley & Sons, 1988).

Thomas Peters and Robert Waterman, *In Search of Excellence: Lessons from America's Best-Run Companies* (New York, NY: HarperCollins Publishers, 2006).

Hermann Simon, *Confessions of the Pricing Man: How Price Affects Everything,* (New York, NY: Springer, 2015).

S. David Young and Stephen O'Byrne, *EVA and Value-Based Management: A Practical Guide to Implementation* (New York, NY: McGraw-Hill, 2000).

Chapter 9

Tim Brown, *Change by Design: How Design Thinking Transforms Organizations and Inspires Innovation* (New York, NY: HarperCollins Publishers, 2009).

Clayton Christensen, *The Innovator's Dilemma: When New Technologies Cause Great Firms to Fail* (Boston, MA: Harvard Business School Press, 1997).

David Garvin, "Competing on the Eight Dimensions of Quality," *Harvard Business Review* 65 (November–December 1987), pp. 101–119.

Andrei Hagiu and Elizabeth Altman, "Finding the Platform in Your Product: Four Strategies That Can Reveal Hidden Value," *Harvard Business Review* 95 (July–August 2017), pp. 94–100.

Donald Lehmann and Russell Winer, *Product Management*, 4th ed. (Boston, MA: McGraw-Hill/Irwin, 2006).

Theodore Levitt, "Exploit the Product Life Cycle," *Harvard Business Review* 43 (November–December 1965), pp. 81–94.

Theodore Levitt, "Marketing Intangible Products and Product Intangibles," *Harvard Business Review* 59 (May–June 1981), pp. 94–102.

Youngme Moon, "Break Free from the Product Life Cycle," *Harvard Business Review* 83 (May 2005), pp. 87–94.

Chapter 10

Leonard Berry, *On Great Service: A Framework for Action* (New York, NY: Free Press, 2006).

Leonard Berry and A. Parasuraman, *Marketing Services: Competing Through Quality* (New York, NY: Free Press, 2004).

Leonard Berry, Venkatesh Shankar, Janet Turner Parish, Susan Cadwallader, and Thomas Dotzel, "Creating New Markets through Service Innovation," *Sloan Management Review* 47 (Winter 2006), pp. 56–63.

Dwayne Gremler, Mary Jo Bitner, and Valarie Zeithaml, *Services Marketing: Integrating Customer Focus Across the Firm*, 6th ed. (Boston, MA: McGraw-Hill/Irwin, 2012).

Vikas Mittal and Carly Frennea, "Customer Satisfaction: A Strategic Review and Guidelines for Managers," *Fast Forward Series* (Cambridge, MA: Marketing Science Institute, 2010).

Jeffrey Rayport and Bernard Jaworski, *Best Face Forward* (Boston: MA: Harvard Business School Press, 2005).

Mohanbir Sawhney, "Putting Products into Services," *Harvard Business Review* 94 (September 2016), pp. 82–89.

Bernd Schmitt, *Customer Experience Management* (New York, NY: John Wiley & Sons, 2003).

Venkatesh Shankar, Leonard Berry, and Thomas Dotzel, "A Practical Guide to Combining Products and Services," *Harvard Business Review* 87 (November 2009), pp. 94–99.

Chapter 11

David Aaker, *Brand Relevance: Making Competitors Irrelevant* (New York, NY: Jossey-Bass, 2011).

David Aaker and Erich Joachimsthaler, *Brand Leadership* (New York, NY: Simon and Schuster, 2012).

Alexander Chernev, *Strategic Brand Management*, 2nd ed. (Chicago, IL: Cerebellum Press, 2017).

Nigel Hollis, *The Meaningful Brand: How Strong Brands Make More Money* (New York, NY: Palgrave Macmillan, 2013).

Jean-Noël Kapferer, *The New Strategic Brand Management: Advanced Insights and Strategic Thinking*, 5th ed. (London, UK: Kogan Page Publishers, 2012).

Kevin Lane Keller, *Strategic Brand Management: Building, Measuring, and Managing Brand Equity*, 4th ed. (Upper Saddle River, NJ: Prentice Hall, 2012).

Bernd Schmitt and Alex Simonson, *Marketing Aesthetics: The Strategic Management of Brand, Identity, and Image* (New York, NY: Free Press, 1997).

Alice Tybout and Tim Calkins, *Kellogg on Branding* (Hoboken, NJ: John Wiley & Sons, 2005).

Chapter 12

Eric Anderson and Duncan Simester, "Mind Your Pricing Cues," *Harvard Business Review* 81 (September 2003), pp. 96–103.

Ronald Baker, *Implementing Value Pricing: A Radical Business Model for Professional Firms* (Hoboken, NJ: John Wiley & Sons, 2010).

Walter Baker, Michael Marn, and Craig Zawada, *The Price Advantage*, 2nd ed. (Hoboken, NJ: John Wiley & Sons, 2010).

Marco Bertini and Luc Wathieu, "How to Stop Customers from Fixating on Price," *Harvard Business Review* 88 (May 2010), pp. 85–91.

Thomas Nagle, John Hogan, and Joseph Zale, *The Strategy and Tactics of Pricing: A Guide to Growing More Profitably*, 5th ed. (Upper Saddle River, NJ: Pearson/Prentice Hall, 2010).

Omar Rodríguez and Sundar Bharadwaj, "Competing on Social Purpose: Brands That Win by Tying Mission to Growth," *Harvard Business Review* 95 (September–October 2017), pp. 94–101.

Adrian Ryans, *Beating Low Cost Competition: How Premium Brands Can Respond to Cut-Price Rivals* (West Sussex, England: John Wiley & Sons, 2008).

Hermann Simon, *Confessions of the Pricing Man: How Price Affects Everything* (New York, NY: Springer, 2015).

Jan-Benedict Steenkamp and Nirmalya Kumar, "Don't Be Undersold," *Harvard Business Review* 87 (December 2009), pp. 90–95.

Chapter 13

George Belch and Michael Belch, *Advertising and Promotion: An Integrated Marketing Communications Perspective*, 10th ed. (Boston, MA: McGraw-Hill/Irwin, 2014).

Robert Cialdini, *Pre-Suasion: A Revolutionary Way to Influence and Persuade* (New York, NY: Simon & Schuster, 2018).

John Philip Jones, "The Double Jeopardy of Sales Promotions," *Harvard Business Review* 68 (September–October 1990), pp. 145–152.

Roddy Mullin, *Sales Promotions: How to Create, Implement, and Integrate Campaigns that Really Work*, 5th ed. (Philadelphia, PA: Kogan Page Publishers, 2010).

Thomas Nagle, John Hogan, and Joseph Zale, *The Strategy and Tactics of Pricing: A Guide to Growing More Profitably*, 5th ed. (Upper Saddle River, NJ: Pearson/Prentice Hall, 2010).

Scott Neslin, *Sales Promotion* (Cambridge, MA: Marketing Science Institute, 2002).

Thomas O'Guinn, Chris Allen, Angeline Scheinbaum, and Richard Semenik, *Advertising and Integrated Brand Promotion*, 7th ed. (Boston, MA: Cengage, 2018).

Denish Shah and V. Kumar, "The Dark Side of Cross-Selling," *Harvard Business Review* 90 (December 2012), pp. 21–23.

Chapter 14

George Belch and Michael Belch, *Advertising and Promotion: An Integrated Marketing Communications Perspective*, 10th ed. (Boston, MA: McGraw-Hill/Irwin, 2014).

Jonah Berger, *Contagious: Why Things Catch On* (New York, NY: Simon & Schuster, 2016).

Tom Duncan, *Principles of Advertising and IMC*, 2nd ed. (New York, NY: McGraw-Hill/Irwin, 2005).

Douglas Holt, "Branding in the Age of Social Media," *Harvard Business Review* 94 (March 2016), pp. 40–50.

David Ogilvy, *Ogilvy on Advertising* (New York, NY: Crown, 1983).

Richard Petty and John Cacioppo, "The Elaboration Likelihood Model of Persuasion," *Communication and Persuasion* (New York, NY: Springer, 1986), pp. 1–24.

Dennis Wilcox, Glen Cameron, and Bryan Reber, *Public Relations: Strategies and Tactics*, 11th ed. (London, UK: Pearson, 2014).

Yoram Wind and Catharine Findiesen Hays, *Beyond Advertising: Creating Value Through All Customer Touchpoints* (New York, NY: Wiley, 2016).

Chapter 15

Thomas Bonoma, "Major Sales: Who Really Does the Buying?" *Harvard Business Review* 60 (May–June 1982), pp. 111–119.

Gilbert Churchill Jr., Neil Ford, Orville Walker Jr., Mark Johnston, and Greg Marshall, *Salesforce Management*, 9th ed. (New York, NY: McGraw-Hill/Irwin, 2009).

Robert Cialdini, *Influence: Science and Practice*, 5th ed. (New York, NY: Pearson, 2008).

Philip Kotler, Neil Rackham, and Suj Krishnaswamy, "Ending the War Between Sales & Marketing," *Harvard Business Review* 84 (July–August 2006), pp. 68–78.

Daniel Pink, "A Radical Prescription for Sales," *Harvard Business Review* (July–August 2012), pp. 76–77.

Neil Rackham, *SPIN Selling* (New York, NY: McGraw-Hill, 1988).

Thomas Steenburgh and Michael Ahearne, "Motivating Salespeople: What Really Works," *Harvard Business Review* 90 (July–August 2012), pp. 70–75.

Nicholas Toman, Brent Adamson, and Cristina Gomez, "The New Sales Imperative," *Harvard Business Review* 95 (March–April 2017), pp. 118–125.

Andris Zoltners, Prabhakant Sinha, Chad Albrecht, Steve Marley, and Sally Lorimer, *Sales Compensation Solutions* (Evanston, IL: ZS Associates, 2017).

Chapter 16

Sunil Chopra and Peter Meindl, *Supply Chain Management: Strategy, Planning, and Operation*, 6th ed. (New York, NY: Pearson, 2016).

Anne Coughlan, Dr. Sandy Jap, *A Field Guide to Channel Strategy: Building Routes to Market* (Scotts Valley, CA: CreateSpace 2016).

Thomas Davenport, Leandro Dalle Mule, and John Lucker, "Know What Your Customers Want Before They Do," *Harvard Business Review* (December 2011), pp. 84–92.

Niraj Dawar and Jason Stornelli, "Rebuilding the Relationship Between Manufacturers and Retailers," *MIT Sloan Management Review* (Winter 2013), pp. 83–90.

Julian Dent, *Distribution Channels: Understanding and Managing Channels to Market* (London, UK: Kogan Page Publishers, 2011).

Ray Kroc and Robert Anderson, *Grinding It Out: The Making of McDonald's* (New York, NY: St. Martin's Press, 1987).

Robert Palmatier, Louis Stern, and Adel El-Ansary, *Marketing Channel Strategy*, 8th ed. (New York, NY: Routledge, 2017).

V. Kasturi Rangan and Marie Bell. *Transforming Your Go-to-Market Strategy: The Three Disciplines of Channel Management.* (Boston, MA: Harvard Business Press, 2006).

Chapter 17

K. Gielens and E. Gijsbrechts, eds., *Handbook of Research on Retailing*, (Northampton, MA: Edward-Elgar Publishing, 2018).

Tony Hsieh, *Delivering Happiness: A Path to Profits, Passion, and Purpose* (New York, NY: Business Plus, 2012).

Nirmalya Kumar and Jan-Benedict Steenkamp, *Private Label Strategy: How to Meet the Store Brand Challenge* (Boston, MA: Harvard Business School Press, 2007).

Michael Levy, Barton Weitz, and Dhruv Grewal, *Retailing Management* (New York, NY: McGraw-Hill Education, 2018).

Robert Lewis and Michael Dart, *The New Rules of Retail: Competing in the World's Toughest Marketplace* 2nd ed. (New York, NY: St. Martin's Press, 2014).

Doug Stephens, *Reengineering Retail: The Future of Selling in a Post-Digital World* (Vancouver, BC, Canada: Figure 1 Publishing, 2017).

Brad Stone, *The Everything Store: Jeff Bezos and the Age of Amazon* (New York, NY: Little, Brown & Company, 2013).

Sam Walton, *Made in America* (New York, NY: Bantam Books, 1992).

Chapter 18

Robert Buzzell and Frederick Wiersema, "Successful Share-Building Strategies," *Harvard Business Review* 59 (January–February 1981), pp. 135–44.

Clayton Christensen, *The Innovator's Dilemma: The Revolutionary Book That Will Change the Way You Do Business* (New York, NY: HarperCollins Publishers, 2011).

Clayton Christensen and Michael Raynor, *The Innovator's Solution: Creating and Sustaining Successful Growth*, (Boston, MA: Harvard Business Review Press, 2013).

George Day, David Reibstein, and Robert Gunther, *Wharton on Dynamic Competitive Strategy* (New York, NY: John Wiley & Sons, 2004).

Nirmalya Kumar, "Strategies to Fight Low-Cost Rivals," *Harvard Business Review* 84 (December 2006), pp. 104–112.

A. G. Lafley and Roger Martin, *Playing to Win: How Strategy Really Works* (Boston, MA: Harvard Business School Press, 2016).

Youngme Moon, *Different: Escaping the Competitive Herd* (New York, NY: Crown Business, 2016).

Mark Ritson, "Should You Launch a Fighter Brand?," *Harvard Business Review* 87 (October 2009), pp. 87–94.

Chapter 19

Jonah Berger, *Contagious: Why Things Catch On* (New York, NY: Simon and Schuster, 2016).

Alexander Chernev, *The Business Model: How to Develop New Products, Create Market Value and Make the Competition Irrelevant* (Chicago, IL: Cerebellum Press, 2017).

Merle Crawford and Anthony Di Benedetto, *New Products Management,* 10th ed. (New York, NY: McGraw-Hill, 2011).

Bart De Langhe, Stefano Puntoni, and Richard Larrick, "Linear Thinking in a Nonlinear World," *Harvard Business Review* 95 (May–June 2017), pp. 130–139.

Nir Eyal, *Hooked: How to Build Habit-Forming Products* (London, UK: Penguin, 2014).

Joshua Gans, Erin Scott, and Scott Stern, "Strategy for Start-Ups," *Harvard Business Review*, 96 (May–June 2018), pp. 44–51.

Geoffrey Moore, *Crossing the Chasm: Marketing and Selling High-Tech Products to Mainstream Customers* (New York, NY: Harper Business, 1991).

Eric Ries, *The Lean Startup* (New York, NY: Crown Business, 2011).

Everett Rogers, *Diffusion of Innovations* (New York, NY: Free Press, 1962).

Chapter 20

Robert Blattberg, Gary Getz, and Jacquelyn Thomas, *Customer Equity: Building and Managing Relationships as Valuable Assets* (Boston, MA: Harvard Business School Press, 2001).

Peter Fader, *Customer Centricity: Focus on the Right Customers for Strategic Advantage* (Philadelphia, PA: Wharton Digital Press, 2012).

Sunil Gupta and Donald R. Lehmann, *Managing Customers as Investments* (Upper Saddle River, NJ: Wharton School Publishing, 2005).

Nirmalya Kumar, "Kill a Brand, Keep a Customer," *Harvard Business Review* 81 (December 2003), pp. 86–95.

Das Narayandas, "Building Loyalty in Business Markets," *Harvard Business Review* 83 (September 2005), pp. 131–39.

Richard Oliver, "Customer Satisfaction Research," Rajiv Grover and Marco Vriens, eds., *The Handbook of Marketing Research* (Thousand Oaks, CA: Sage Publications, 2006), pp. 569–87.

Frederick Reichheld, *Loyalty Rules* (Boston, MA: Harvard Business School Press, 2001).

Werner Reinartz and V. Kumar, "The Mismanagement of Customer Loyalty," *Harvard Business Review* 80 (July 2002), pp. 86–94.

INDEX

Terms listed in this index are grouped into four categories: marketing concepts; marketing frameworks; and companies, products, and brands.

COMPANIES, PRODUCTS, AND BRANDS

NOTES

Chapter 1

[1] Peter Drucker, *The Practice of Management* (New York, NY: HarperCollins, 1954).

[2] Ibid.

[3] Ibid.

[4] Theodore Levitt, "Marketing Myopia," *Harvard Business Review* 53 (September–October 1975), pp. 1–14.

Chapter 2

[1] The view of customer value creation as a process of managing attractiveness, awareness, and availability is a streamlined version of the 4-A framework that delineates *acceptability, affordability, accessibility,* and *awareness* as the key sources of customer value. Because acceptability and affordability can be related to the benefit and cost aspects of the value created by the company's offering, here we use a single term—attractiveness—that captures both the benefit and cost aspects of the offering. See Jagdish Sheth and Rajendra Sisodia, *The 4 A's of Marketing: Creating Value for Customer, Company and Society* (New York, NY: Routledge, 2012).

[2] Kenichi Ohmae, *The Mind of the Strategist: The Art of Japanese Business* (New York, NY: McGraw-Hill, 1982).

[3] E. Jerome McCarthy and William Perreault, *Basic Marketing: A Managerial Approach*, 12th ed. (Homewood, IL: Irwin, 1996).

[4] Michael Porter, "How Competitive Forces Shape Strategy," *Harvard Business Review* 57 (March–April 1979), pp. 137–145.

[5] www.inc.com/geoffrey-james/the-20-worst-brand-translations-of-all-time.html

Chapter 3

[1] Frances Frei and Anne Morriss, "Culture Takes Over When the CEO Leaves the Room," *Harvard Business Review* (May 10, 2012).

[2] James Collins and Jerry Porras, "Building Your Company's Vision," *Harvard Business Review* 74, no. 5 (September–October 1996), pp. 65–77.

[3] "LUV-ing" refers to "LUV"—Southwest Airlines' ticker symbol on the New York Stock Exchange.

[4] http://investors.southwest.com/our-company/purpose-vision-values-and-mission

[5] https://corporate.mcdonalds.com/content/corpmcd/about-us/our-values.html

[6] www.google.com/about/philosophy.html

[7] http://fortune.com/2012/01/19/larry-page-google-should-be-like-a-family/

[8] Peter Drucker, *Management: Tasks, Responsibilities and Practices,* (New York: Harper and Row, 1973).

[9] www.amazon.jobs/en/working/working-amazon

[10] John Doerr, *Measure What Matters: OKRs: The Simple Idea that Drives 10x Growth.* (New York: Penguin, 2018).

[11] www.patagonia.com/company-info.html

[12] https://about.nike.com/

[13] www.ikea.com/ms/en_US/this-is-ikea/company-information/index.html

[14] www.starbucks.com/about-us/company-information/mission-statement

[15] *Starbucks Annual Report 2003.*

[16] www.mcdonalds.com.my/company/mission-vision

[17] https://corporate.mcdonalds.com/mcd/our_company-old/mission_and_values.html

[18] http://investors.southwest.com/our-company/purpose-vision-values-and-mission

[19] James Collins and Jerry Porras, "Building Your Company's Vision," *Harvard Business Review* 74, no. 5 (September–October 1996), pp. 65–77.

[20] Note that there are cases when a company can increase its market share while lowering its promotional costs. Such instances, however, are not very common as they require a dramatic improvement in the efficiency of the company's marketing activities.

Chapter 4

[1] David Court, Dave Elzinga, Susan Mulder, and Ole Jorgen Vetvik, "The Consumer Decision Journey," *McKinsey Quarterly* 3 (2009), pp. 96–107.

[2] Alice Eagly and Shelly Chaiken. "Cognitive Theories of Persuasion," *Advances in Experimental Social Psychology, Vol. 17* (Academic Press, 1984), pp. 267–359; Amos Tversky and Daniel Kahneman, "Judgment Under Uncertainty: Heuristics and Biases," *Science* 185 (1974), pp. 1124–31; Daniel Kahneman, Paul Slovic, and Amos Tversky, eds., *Judgment Under Uncertainty: Heuristics and Biases* (Cambridge, UK: Cambridge University Press, 1982).

[3] Daniel Kahneman, *Thinking, Fast and Slow* (New York, NY: Farrar, Straus and Giroux, 2011).

[4] Adapted from Daniel Kahneman and Amos Tversky, "Prospect Theory: An Analysis of Decision under Risk," *Econometrica*, 47 (March, 1979), pp. 263–91.

[5] Daniel Kahneman, *Thinking, Fast and Slow* (New York, NY: Farrar, Straus and Giroux, 2011).

[6] Itamar Simonson, Ziv Carmon, and Suzanne O'Curry, "Experimental Evidence on the Negative Effect of Product Features and Sales Promotions on Brand Choice," *Marketing Science* 13, no. 1 (1994): pp. 23–40; Daniel Kahneman, *Thinking, Fast and Slow* (New York, NY: Farrar, Straus and Giroux, 2011).

[7] On average, for every 1,000 products tested, (a) 1 product is defective, and it is 100% certain there is a *true* positive test result for that product, so there is 1 *true* positive test result, and (b) among the 999 products that are not defective there are 5% *false* positive test results, so there are 49.95 *false* positive test results. Therefore, the probability that one of the products among the 50.95 (1 + 49.95) positive test results really is defective is $1/50.95 \approx 0.019627$.

[8] William Samuelson and Richard Zeckhauser, "Status Quo Bias in Decision Making," *Journal of Risk and Uncertainty* 1, no.1, (1988), pp. 7–59.

[9] Eric Johnson and Daniel Goldstein, "Do Defaults Save Lives?" *Science* 302, no. 5649 (2003), pp. 1338–1339.

[10] Itamar Simonson, "The Effect of Product Assortment on Buyer Preferences," *Journal of Retailing* 75 (Autumn 1999), pp. 347–370.

[11] Itamar Simonson, "Choice Based on Reasons: The Case of Attraction and Compromise Effects," *Journal of Consumer Research* 16 (September 1989), pp. 158–174.

Chapter 5

[1] Bradley Agle, Nandu Nagarajan, Jeffrey Sonnenfeld, and Dhinu Srinivasan, "Does CEO Charisma Matter? An Empirical Analysis of the Relationships Among Organizational Performance, Environmental Uncertainty, and Top Management Team Perceptions of CEO Charisma," *Academy of Management Journal* 49, no. 1 (2006), pp. 161–74.

[2] Fred Reichheld, "The One Number You Need to Grow," *Harvard Business Review* (December 2003), pp. 1–11.

Chapter 6

[1] Theodore Levitt, "Marketing Myopia," *Harvard Business Review* 53 (September–October 1975), pp. 1–14.

[2] The degrees-of-freedom approach was suggested by professor Eyal Maoz.

[3] Chris Anderson, *The Long Tail* (New York: Hyperion, 2006).

Chapter 7

[1] 27 CFR 5.22—The Standards of Identity, Alcohol and Tobacco Tax and Trade Bureau; U.S. Department of Treasury.

[2] Al Ries and Jack Trout, *Positioning: The Battle for Your Mind*, 20th Anniversary Edition (New York, NY: McGraw-Hill, 2000).

[3] Alexander Chernev, "Jack of All Trades or Master of One? Product Differentiation and Compensatory Reasoning in Consumer Choice," *Journal of Consumer Research* 33, no. 4 (2007), pp. 430–44.

[4] www.inc.com/laura-montini/a-lesson-from-harley-davidson-on-perfecting-product-positioning.html

[5] The examples used in this chapter are for illustration purposes only and might not adequately reflect the companies' actual positioning strategies.

[6] W. Chan Kim and Renée Mauborgne, *Blue Ocean Strategy: How to Create Uncontested Market Space and Make the Competition Irrelevant* (Boston, MA: Harvard Business School Press, 2015).

Chapter 8

[1] Note that the salesforce might serve a dual function—communicating and distributing the offering.

[2] To have a neutral or positive impact on the company's bottom line, the additional profits generated by the incremental volume resulting from a lower price must be equal to or greater than the lost profits that result from a lower margin.

$$\text{Profit}_{\text{New price}} \geq \text{Profit}_{\text{Old price}}$$

Given that profit is a function of unit volume and unit margin, the above equation can be modified as follows:

$$\text{Volume}_{\text{New price}} \cdot \text{Margin}_{\text{New price}} \geq \text{Volume}_{\text{Old price}} \cdot \text{Margin}_{\text{Old price}}$$

Hence, the increase in sales volume that needs to be achieved for a price cut to break even is:

$$\text{BER}_{\text{Price cut}} = \frac{\text{Volume}_{\text{New price}}}{\text{Volume}_{\text{Old price}}} = \frac{\text{Margin}_{\text{Old price}}}{\text{Margin}_{\text{New price}}}$$

Chapter 9

[1] Sigma refers to the Greek letter σ, commonly used in statistics as a measure of the degree of variance in a given population.

[2] Stock Keeping Unit (SKU) is a unique identifier assigned to each distinct product.

[3] Scott Young and Vincenzo Ciummo, "Managing Risk in a Package Redesign: What Can We Learn From Tropicana?" *Brand Packaging* (2009), pp. 18–21.

[4] A notable exception are product lines designed to address customers' variety-seeking needs. For example, a company might create different flavors of yogurt, snacks, and sodas to ensure that customers can fulfill their need for variety without switching to products from another company.

[5] Theodore Levitt, "Exploit the Product Life Cycle," *Harvard Business Review* 43 (November–December 1965), pp. 81–94.

[6] Adapted from Theodore Levitt, "Exploit the Product Life Cycle," *Harvard Business Review* 43 (November–December 1965), pp. 81–94.

[7] Adapted from Clayton Christensen, *The Innovator's Dilemma: When New Technologies Cause Great Firms to Fail* (Boston, MA: Harvard Business School Press, 1997).

[8] Tim Brown, "Design Thinking," *Harvard Business Review* 86, no. 6 (June 1, 2008); Tim Brown, *Change by Design: How Design Thinking Transforms Organizations and Inspires Innovation* (New York, NY: HarperCollins Publishers, 2009).

[9] Phillip Nelson, "Information and Consumer Behavior," *Journal of Political Economy* 78 (March–April, 1970), pp. 311–329.

[10] 35 U. S. C. § 154.

[11] In the United States, there is an exception to these requirements for disclosures made by the inventor less than one year before the patent application was filed. Thus, inventors can file a patent application within a year of their public disclosure of the invention. An invention cannot be patented if it has been for sale for over one year prior to the patent filing.

Chapter 10

[1] *Two Pesos, Inc. v. Taco Cabana, Inc.*, 505 U.S. 769, (1992) and *Wal-Mart Stores, Inc. v. Samara Brothers, Inc.*, 529 U.S. 205, 215 (2000).

[2] http://ritzcarltonleadershipcenter.com/2013/08/440/

[3] www.thebalance.com/zappos-company-culture-1918813 and www.entrepreneur.com/article/249174

[4] A. Parasuraman, Valarie Zeithaml, and Leonard Berry, "A Conceptual Model of Service Quality and Its Implications for Future Research," *Journal of Marketing* 49, no. 4 (1985), pp. 41–50.

[5] Adapted from A. Parasuraman, Valarie Zeithaml, and Leonard Berry, "A Conceptual Model of Service Quality and Its Implications for Future Research," *Journal of Marketing* 49, no. 4 (1985), pp. 41–50.

[6] Piyush Sharma, Roger Marshall, Peter Alan Reday, and WoonBong Na, "Complainers vs. Non-Complainers: A Multi-National Investigation of Individual and Situational Influences on Customer Complaint Behaviour," *Journal of Marketing Management* 26 (February 2010), pp. 163–80.

Chapter 11

[1] Nader Tavassoli, Alina Sorescu, and Rajesh Chandy, "Employee-Based Brand Equity: Why Firms with Strong Brands Pay Their Executives Less," *Journal of Marketing Research* 51, no. 6 (2014), pp. 676–690; C. B. Bhattacharya, Sankar Sen, and Daniel Korschun, "Using Corporate Social Responsibility to Win the War for Talent," *MIT Sloan Management Review* 49 (January 2008), pp. 37–44.

[2] United States Supreme Court, *Wal-Mart Stores, Inc. v. Samara Brothers, Inc.*, 529 U.S. 205, 120 S. Ct. 1339, 146 L. Ed. 2d 182 (2000). See also *Abercrombie & Fitch Co. v. Hunting World, Inc.*, 537 F.2d 4 (2d Cir. 1976).

[3] A company might prefer to use the phonetic spelling rather than the grammatically correct one in order to protect the brand. For example, because *zapatos* is the common word for shoes in Spanish, it cannot be legally protected, whereas Zappos affords a greater degree of legal protection.

[4] www.nestle-nespresso.com

[5] Note that, even though associating the brand with new products and services might also change (typically broaden) the brand's meaning, this change is not the goal but rather a consequence of extending the brand.

[6] The accounting rules regarding the inclusion of brand equity on the balance sheets of a company vary across countries. Thus, in the United States, companies do not list brand equity on their balance sheets, whereas in the United Kingdom and Australia balance sheets include the value of the company's brands.

[7] IFRS (2012) *IAS 38. Intangible Assets*, London, UK: International Financial Reporting Standards.

[8] Kevin Lane Keller, *Strategic Brand Management: Building, Measuring, and Managing Brand Equity,* 4th ed. (Upper Saddle River, NJ: Prentice Hall, 2012).

[9] Interbrand, *Interbrand Best Global Brands* (2015), www.bestglobalbrands.com

Chapter 12

[1] www.bloomberg.com/news/articles/2016-12-02/hastens-vividus-mattress-review-price

[2] Eric Anderson and Duncan Simester, "Effects of $9 Price Endings on Retail Sales: Evidence from Field Experiments," *Quantitative Marketing and Economics* 1 (March 2003), pp. 93–110.

[3] Henry Ford, *My Life and Work* (New York, NY: Doubleday, Page & Company, 1923), pp. 146–147.

[4] Margaret Campbell, "Perceptions of Price Unfairness: Antecedents and Consequences," *Journal of Marketing Research* 36, no. 2 (1999), pp. 187–199.

Chapter 13

[1] www.theguardian.com/sustainable-business/financial-incentives-bonus-schemes-lloyds-fine

[2] Ibid.

[3] www.theguardian.com/business/us-money-blog/2016/sep/22/wells-fargo-scandal-john-stumpf-elizabeth-warren-senate

Chapter 14

[1] Direct mail is considered owned (rather than paid) media because in most cases the company does not pay for the cost of the actual media as with television, print, and radio advertisements. In cases when a company has to pay for access to recipients, direct mail is considered paid media.

[2] Note that while social media is considered earned media, advertisements embedded in social media (e.g., Facebook, Instagram, and YouTube ads) are a form of paid media.

[3] Walter Scott, *The Psychology of Advertising* (Boston, MA: Small Maynard, 1913); Robert Lavidge and Gary Steiner, "A Model for Predictive Measurements of Advertising Effectiveness," *Journal of Marketing* 25, no. 6 (1961), pp. 59–62.

Chapter 15

[1] Andris Zoltners, Prabhakant Sinha, Chad Albrecht, Steve Marley, and Sally Lorimer, *Sales Compensation Solutions* (Evanston, IL: ZS Associates, 2017).

[2] These roles were originally proposed by marketing professors Frederick Webster and Yoram Wind to describe the ways in which organizations make purchase decisions. The original list of five roles was later expanded by Thomas Bonoma to include the role of initiator. See Yoram Wind and Frederick Webster, *Organizational Buying Behavior* (Upper Saddle River, NJ: Prentice Hall, 1972); Thomas Bonoma, "Major Sales: Who Really Does the Buying?," *Harvard Business Review* 60 (May–June, 1982), pp. 111–119.

[3] The customer decision journey map discussed here is a more general version of the decision journey map discussed in Chapter 4 and applies to both consumer and business decision making. The decision journey map presented in this chapter distinguishes need definition as a separate stage in the decision process. This distinction reflects the fact that in business decisions the definition of a company's needs and the search for options to fulfill these needs are often made by different entities within the company and, hence, merit special consideration in analyzing the corporate decision-making process.

[4] The ABC (Always Be Closing) principle was most prominently introduced and popularized by Alec Baldwin's character in the classic movie Glengarry Glen Ross.

[5] Robert Cialdini, *Influence: The Psychology of Persuasion* (New York, NY: HarperCollins Publishers, 2007).

[6] Jonathan Freedman and Scott Fraser, "Compliance without Pressure: The Foot-in-the-door Technique," *Journal of Personality and Social Psychology* 4, no. 2 (1966), pp. 195–202.

[7] Neil Rackham, *SPIN Selling* (MGraw-Hill, 1988).

Chapter 16

[1] www.toyota-global.com/company/vision_philosophy/toyota_production_system/just-in-time.html

Chapter 17

[1] SKU (Stock Keeping Unit) is the unique identifier assigned to each distinct product.

[2] *National Retail Security Survey* (National Retail Federation, 2017).

[3] Alexander Chernev and Ryan Hamilton, "Price Image in Retail Management," Katrijn Gielens and Els Gijsbrechts, eds., *Handbook of Research on Retailing*, (Northampton: Edward-Elgar Publishing, 2018), pp.132–152. Ryan Hamilton and Alexander Chernev, "Low Prices are Just the Beginning: Price Image in Retail Management," *Journal of Marketing* 77, no. 6 (2013), pp. 1–20.

Chapter 18

[1] Adapted from Stephen Hoch, "How Should National Brands Think about Private Labels?" *Sloan Management Review*, 37 no. 2 (1996), pp. 89–102.

[2] Jagdish Sheth and Rajendra Sisodia, *The 4 A's of Marketing: Creating Value for Customer, Company, and Society* (New York, NY: Routledge, 2012).

[3] Attractiveness can also be defined as the combination of both benefits and costs (as in Chapters 2, 12, and 13). For the purposes of understanding the adoption process, this chapter uses a narrower view of attractiveness that focuses only on the benefits of a company's offering.

[4] www.scientificamerican.com/article/oil-change-truths/

[5] This section is based on Clayton Christensen's book, *The Innovator's Dilemma: The Revolutionary Book That Will Change the Way You Do Business* (New York, NY: HarperCollins Publishers, 2011).

[6] Igor Ansoff, *Strategic Management* (New York, NY: John Wiley & Sons, 1979).

[7] Note that the above equation assumes that the launch of the new offering is not associated with an increase in the fixed costs and that such costs—if they do exist—are included in the margins of the old and the new offerings.

Chapter 19

[1] A more detailed discussion of type I and type II errors is offered in Chapter 5.

[2] Everett Rogers, *Diffusion of Innovations* (New York, NY: Free Press, 1962).

[3] Ibid.

[4] Geoffrey Moore, *Crossing the Chasm: Marketing and Selling High-Tech Products to Mainstream Customers* (New York, NY: Harper Business, 1991).

[5] Eric Ries, *The Lean Startup* (New York, NY: Crown Business, 2011).

Chapter 20

[1] Frederick Reichheld and Thomas Teal, *The Loyalty Effect* (Boston MA: Harvard Business School Press, 1996).

[2] Lea Dunn and Darren Dahl, "Self-Threat and Product Failure: How Internal Attributions of Blame Impact Consumer Complaining Behavior," *Journal of Marketing Research* 49 (October 2012), pp. 670–81.

[3] Peter Fader, *Customer Centricity: Focus on the Right Customers for Strategic Advantage* (Wharton Digital Press, 2012). See also Roland Rust, Katherine Lemon, and Valarie Zeithaml, "Return on Marketing: Using Customer Equity to Focus Marketing Strategy, *Journal of Marketing* 68, no. 1 (2004), pp. 109–127.

[4] Jay Curry and Adam Curry, *The Customer Marketing Method: How to Implement and Profit from Customer Relationship Management* (New York, NY: Free Press, 2000).

[5] Richard Koch, *The 80/20 Principle: The Secret to Success by Achieving More with Less* (New York, NY: Doubleday, 1998).

[6] For a more detailed explanation of this approach, see Sunil Gupta and Donald Lehmann, "Customers as Assets," *Journal of Interactive Marketing* 17, no. 1 (2003), pp. 9–24.

Appendix A

[1] This example illustrates the main steps and the key considerations in the process of selecting target customers; it should not be used as a source of primary data about the company, customer segments, and/or market conditions. The reported data are based on "The Black & Decker Corporation (A): Power Tools Division" (595-057), "The Black & Decker Corporation (B): 'Operation Sudden Impact'" (595-060), "The Black & Decker Corporation (B): 'Operation Sudden Impact'" (596-510), and "The Black & Decker Corporation (C): 'Operation Sudden Impact' Results, 1992–1994" (595-061), Harvard Business School Publishing, Boston, MA.

Appendix B

[1] This example illustrates the main steps and the key considerations in articulating a company's business model; it should not be used as a source of primary data about the company, customer segments, and/or market conditions. The reported data are based on "The Black & Decker Corporation (A): Power Tools Division" (595-057), "The Black & Decker Corporation (B): 'Operation Sudden Impact'" (595-060), "The Black & Decker Corporation (B): 'Operation Sudden Impact'" (596-510), and "The Black & Decker Corporation (C): 'Operation Sudden Impact' Results, 1992-1994" (595-061), Harvard Business School Publishing, Boston, MA.

[2] "The Black & Decker Corporation (B): 'Operation Sudden Impact,'" (595-060), Harvard Business School Publishing, Boston, MA.

[3] Ibid.

[4] Ibid.

Appendix C

[1] This sample marketing plan was developed solely for the purposes of this book. Some of the information contained in this document has been modified to better illustrate specific aspects of writing a marketing plan. This document should not be used as a primary source of information either for Align Technology or for its offerings. This marketing plan is based on the S-1 registration statement for the initial public offering of Align Technology Inc., as filed with the Securities and Exchange Commission on November 14, 2000, and the 10-K reports (annual reports) filed by Align Technology Inc. with the Securities and Exchange Commission in 2008, 2009, and 2010. Some of the information in Section 2.2 is based on *Invisalign: Orthodontics Unwired* (2004) by Anne Coughlan and Julie Hennessy, Kellogg School of Management, Northwestern University.